# About Pearson

*Pearson is the world's learning company, with presence across 70 countries worldwide. Our unique insights and world-class expertise comes from a long history of working closely with renowned teachers, authors and thought leaders, as a result of which, we have emerged as the preferred choice for millions of teachers and learners across the world.*

*We believe learning opens up opportunities, creates fulfilling careers and hence better lives. We hence collaborate with the best of minds to deliver you class-leading products, spread across the Higher Education and K12 spectrum.*

*Superior learning experience and improved outcomes are at the heart of everything we do. This product is the result of one such effort.*

*Your feedback plays a critical role in the evolution of our products and you can contact us –* reachus@pearson.com. *We look forward to it.*

## An Evaluation of Liberal Theory (including Pluralism)

Some of the major attacks on liberal theory in IR came from the realist thinkers. They criticized liberal optimism about a peaceful, cooperative world. Realists like E. H. Carr, Hans J. Morgenthau, George Kennan and Arnold Wolfers saw the views of the liberals as 'idealistic' and accused them of misreading the actual situation prevailing in world politics, and nurturing false dreams about the world. According to Carr, there is little rationale to believe that nation-states wish to live in harmony and peace. On the contrary, conflict of interests of the nation-states is the reality in international politics. Nation-states do not cooperate in world politics because their opposing interests would leave limited options for them to search for peace and harmony. Clash of interests actually lead the nations to war. The two world wars bear testimony to this observation, think the realists. Carr, in his book *The Twenty Years' Crisis*, noted that profound conflict of interests between countries and people occur almost always in international politics. For instance, the developed nations, for their economic and political advantages, would prefer to continue with the prevalent international order, whereas the poor nations, due to their disadvantageous position in the international system, would like to alter the system. This and many other clashes of interests may lead to frequent conflicts in the world. The liberals are thus wrong in suggesting that nations try to share mutual interests and live in peace and harmony. The realists find international politics is a conflict zone, rather than cooperation among countries.

Hans J. Morgenthau, in his celebrated work *Politics among Nations: The Struggle for Power and Peace*, shattered the liberal 'myth' of a peaceful, interdependent, cooperative world based on democratic values. He started with a portrayal of human nature as self-seeking and self-interested. These selfish human beings cannot change their basic human nature as rulers of the state. As a consequence, the state also looks after its own interests and does not bother for others' interests. In international politics, Morgenthau does not find anything wrong in this attitude of the state. The main tasks of a country are to safeguard its own interests, loosely termed as national interests, and to provide security to its people. In these tasks, the rulers of the state cannot afford to practice morality. Morality can be practiced in the private domain, but not in statecraft. An ordinary individual can practice morality in private life, but the leader of a state cannot afford to go by ethical and moral principles if the interests of the country are at stake. International politics, like domestic politics, is a struggle for power where nations compete, and if required, conflict with one another for supremacy. There is little scope for cooperation, as the liberals suggest, in this international order. According to Morgenthau, 'interest backed by power' is the key word in international politics, and countries prefer to follow this policy rather than the policy of peace and harmony.

For realists like Carr, Morgenthau and Wolfers, the state is the most important actor in international politics. They oppose the pluralist view that individuals, groups, associations or institutions play significant roles in IR. World politics is essentially a game for the nation-states, who remain in a controlling position in international affairs. Further, neo-realists like Kenneth Waltz and John Mearsheimer oppose the pluralist view that institutions play important roles in IR. Institutions are not important in their own right; they acquire importance because nation-states either work through them or seek their assistance. Nation-states use the institutions to fulfill their own interests. The state is the main actor and the institutions are the less important players in IR. The pluralist view of interdependence among countries is also contested by neo-realists. They argue that in the long-term interdependence, a power game is involved. Advanced and powerful

# International Relations Today

## CONCEPTS AND APPLICATIONS

**Second Edition**

Aneek Chatterjee

Department of Political Science
Hooghly Mohsin College

Pearson

*Editor—Acquisitions*: Kaushal Jajware
*Senior Editor—Development*: Amrita Marik
*Senior Editor—Production*: G. Sharmilee



ISBN 978-93-530-6126-5

First Impression, 2018
Eighth Impression, 2022
**Ninth Impression, 2024**

Published by Pearson India Education Services Pvt. Ltd, CIN: 72200TN2005PTC057128.

**Head Office:** 1st Floor, Berger Tower, Plot No. C-001A/2, Sector16B, Noida 201301 U.P., India.

**Registered Office:** Featherlite, 'The Address' 5th Floor, Survey No 203/10B, 200 Ft MMRD Road, Zamin Pallavaram, Chennai - 600044.
Website: in.pearson.com, Email: companysecretary.india@pearson.com

*Compositor*: Cameo Corporate Services Limited
*Printed in India at Sai Printo Pack Pvt Ltd*

# Contents

# List of Tables, Figures and Boxes

## Tables



## Figures



## Boxes

# Preface to the Second Edition

*International Relations Today*: *Concepts and Applications* was first published in June 2010. The first edition was received well by students, teachers, scholars and researchers. The book has found place in the syllabi of more than hundred universities across India and South Asia, at the undergraduate and postgraduate levels, not only in Political Science and IR, but also in the curricula of Security and Military Studies. Civil service aspirants in many countries in South Asia consult this book regularly, and many civil service toppers have recommended this book as a 'must read' for International Relations (IR). The text has been cited in academic work in the US, UK, South Africa, Brazil, Portugal, Moldova, Lithuania, Pakistan, Iran, Iraq, Poland, Denmark, Austria and India. Some scholars have termed this book as a fundamental text in the discipline of IR.

The success of the inaugural edition has prompted the author and the publisher to make this book more comprehensive for the benefit of students and researchers. Two important theories in IR, namely, the English School and Critical Theory have been added to the existing 11 theories in Chapter 2, which analyses major theories in the discipline of IR. Foreign policies of major powers in the world today, namely, the US, China, Russia, Japan, Britain and India have been updated till the year 2018, to make the book contemporary and relevant. For instance, foreign policy of India has been updated to cover the premiership of Narendra Modi. Similarly, the US foreign policy analysis covered the presidency of Donald Trump, and Russian foreign policy discourse looked at the Putin years. Likewise, chapters on the UN; Nuclear and Security Issues; Regional Organizations; Other Inter Governmental Organizations; Post Cold War International Relations; International Political Economy and Recent Issues in IR have been upgraded to cover recent periods and events. I hope that students, researchers and teachers would find the new edition helpful and likeable.

I must thank Kaushal Jajware and Amrita Marik of Pearson Education for their unflinching support for the second edition of the book. As always, my wife Sarbani and daughter Prerna have been constant source of encouragement. Needless to say that responsibility of any error or omission in this edition of the book rests with the author. I sincerely believe that this edition, like the previous one, will also serve academic interests of students, teachers and researchers in the discipline and related areas.

Aneek Chatterjee

# Preface to the First Edition

International Relations (IR) is a changing and dynamic discipline. Today, the discipline is different in many ways from the discipline of IR immediately after the Second World War. The impact of globalization or terrorism on IR was almost negligible during that period. Moreover, the post–Cold War World order has thrown many challenges to the students of IR. Is the post–Cold War international order a unipolar or a multipolar one? Is globalization eroding the notion of state sovereignty? What would be the impact of energy crisis on world politics? Is the world moving towards economic integration? Is China going to pose an effective challenge to the might of the United States? What is the future of the SAARC or the NAM? What are the major theories in contemporary IR? These and many other pertinent issues require proper analyses in order to understand the nature of the discipline today. This book is a humble attempt at studying such issues. It is primarily meant for students of International Relations in colleges and universities. It would also help civil service aspirants and others interested in the discipline.

In the course of writing this book, I got immense help from several persons and institutions. All members of Pearson Education need special mention in this regard. I wish to particularly thank Praveen Dev, Debjani M. Dutta, Barun Kumar Sarkar and Arani Banerjee of Pearson Education for supporting this project from time to time. I also thank my colleagues and students in the Department of Political Science who raised many interesting questions and debated with me on many issues for providing intellectual stimuli that helped me in the course of writing. The excellent library facilities of Presidency College always boosted my desire to work for the book. My wife Sarbani and daughter Prerna, besides providing mental support, also helped me in computer work, which proved very helpful at times for a tiring person. My sincere thanks to them. Needless to say that the author is responsible for any error or omission in the book. If this book provides any help to students and teachers, I will consider my efforts successful.

Aneek Chatterjee

# About the Author

Aneek Chatterjee, Ph.D., teaches at the postgraduate department of Political Science at Hooghly Mohsin College, India. He has authored and edited nine books, and contributed several research articles in leading journals and edited volumes. Earlier, he served as Professor and Head of the Department of Political Science at Presidency University (formerly, Presidency College), Kolkata, India. Dr Chatterjee was a Fulbright Nehru Visiting Lecturer at the University of Virginia, US, in 2010–11. He also received the ICCR (Govt. of India) Chair professorship to teach International Relations in reputed foreign universities. Dr Chatterjee presented research papers in international academic conferences in France, Japan, Slovenia, the US, China, Australia, Hungary, Thailand and India, and visited many other countries for academic work. He sits in the editorial boards of three national/international journals; and acts as reviewer for many research journals in India and abroad.

as was a key figure among critical theorists and his views have influenced criti-
colonialt. Although Habermas never directly referred to international politics
primarily individual society, his ideas of communicative action, discourse
s of the relation between knowledge and human interests have strengthened
views within IR. The ideas of Habermas centre round radical democratiza-
s belief in the ideals of enlightenment led him to think that universal moral
the basis of resolution of conflicting claims in social and political life. For
modernity has achieved technological progress, it has not yet brought free-
nd emancipation of human beings. Therefore, he wishes to find a path where
nd progress can be united again under modern conditions (Yalvaç 2015). He
the human progress, as viewed by Marx, should also be reconstructed in a way
(illum) for social communication and mutual understanding among people,
o analysing society on the basis of labour and production. Habermas made a
osophy of consciousness to a philosophy of language, making a major shift in
ical tradition. The philosophy of language allows for the communication and
diverse identities and interests. This concept also facilitates a pluralist under-
I reality. This view brings Habermas closer to many postmodernist thinkers.
[illegible]
duced the idea of a 'pure communicative sections', defined as an 'ideal speech
h the actors can freely and truthfully communicate (Habermas, 1984, 1985). In
force of the better argument' prevails. Thus, rationality is formulated so that
imply a universality of norms but a discursive and procedural context of an
. History is re-conceptualized as a collective learning process whereby the
technical knowledge for domination of nature but also develops new
nation in the moral-practical sphere (Yalvaç, 2015).
Habermas's on communicative rationality to what he calls knowledge constitu-
erests (1972). This refers to the role of knowledge in achieving different forma-
tions. He argues that knowledge generated by positivism is not the only type
nied to fulfil the needs of social life. Positivism conceives of social problems
ems that require technical solutions. However, knowledge of the social world
not only on social control but also on communication and human emancipa-
15). Habermas made a distinction among 'technical cognitive interests' in
is seen as the basis for controlling one's environment, and 'practical cogni-
t seek to promote inter-subjective communication between different subjects;
e cognitive interests', regarding communication that deals with the conditions
and fulfilment and the conditions necessary to achieve autonomy and freedom.
In the post-positivist phase, emancipatory cognitive interests will help human
awareness the potential of autonomy and freedom.

## and IR

980s, a group of scholars involved with IR theory addressed new epistemological
uestions in IR under the influence of critical theory. Scholars such as Richard
Cox, Andrew Linklater, John Maclean and Mark Hoffman began to argue,
about the idea of emancipation of people in the world. Under the influence of

# 1 The Discipline of International Relations

International Relations (IR) is an important academic discipline and constitutes a significant area of modern social science. It is primarily considered as the study of the relations among nation-states. But this view is oversimplified, because contemporary IR covers a very broad subject-matter. Yet, for a basic understanding this view is helpful. The complex nature of contemporary IR is analysed later in this chapter. But before going into the details of its nature and scope, a look into the history and development of the study of IR is necessary. This chapter begins with a short history of IR as an academic discipline, as well as a practice of maintaining relations among political systems, states or pre-states.

## History and Evolution of International Relations (IR)

As an academic discipline, IR is not very old. Its systematic study started after the First World War, and universities in West Europe and the United States introduced separate courses on it from the 1920s. But as relations among states or pre-state political systems, the subject is very old. As the relation among nation-states, IR is believed to have developed with the Peace Treaty of Westphalia of 1648, which is considered as the creator of modern nation-states in Europe. But before the birth of modern nation-states, pre-state political systems had developed in different parts of the world. Relations among these pre-state political systems could be viewed, rather incoherently, as the beginning of IR. But this history of IR is a disputed one because the nature and pattern of interactions among pre-state political systems, or for that matter among the nation-states after the Treaty of Westphalia, raise controversies. It is now generally believed that immediately after the treaty was signed, no structured pattern of IR originated. And it was not before the French Revolution in 1789 that systematic interactions among nation-states or other types of political systems had developed. If the more recent history of IR—since the Treaty of Westphalia—is so controversial, it is not difficult to imagine that pre-state IR is subject to more disputes. Some of the known pre-state political systems that existed before the treaty were: (1) Sumerian city-states like Kish, Karsa, Ur, Lagash; and oriental city-states like Jericho, that existed before 2500 BC; (2) Greek city-states and (3) large empires in the West and the East. The nature and extent of interactions among pre-state political systems differed from time to time, making it difficult to systematize the history of IR in ancient times. Occassional and contradictory references to sporadic diplomatic ties among pre-state political systems did not help either in knowing the history of pre-state IR. It is believed that the Treaty of Westphalia encouraged the rise of the independent nation-states by recognizing territorial sovereignty. The treaty also led to the institutionalization of diplomacy and armies. But immediately after Westphalia, no structured pattern of IR had developed. IR, in a modern sense, started to develop when the European nation-state system, born out of the treaty, was transplanted later in the two Americas, Africa and Asia, through the routes of colonialism.

The nation-state system that emerged after Westphalia had undergone a long process of evolution and changes to assume the present nature. During its long process of evolution, this system was influenced, strengthened and also affected by several developments: socio-political, economic and scientific. The rise of capitalism, the Industrial Revolution, the French Revolution, the American War of Independence and colonialism influenced this evolving process till the end of the nineteenth century. In more recent times, since the beginning of the twentieth century, the two world wars; the decolonization process; nationalist movements in Asia, Africa and Latin America; globalization; postmodernism and IT (Information Technology) revolution exerted tremendous influence over the nation-state system. To keep pace with the changing times, nation-states have changed in character; but their basic nature has remained the same since the Treaty of Westphalia: it is a sovereign territorial unit of people sharing some common feelings, loosely identified as nationalism.

IR as a system of interactions among nation-states has also undergone changes from time to time, yet its basic nature has remained the same—it is a system where nation-states mainly interact and make the system operative. As an academic discipline, IR is mainly concerned with the study of such interactions that have assumed multi-dimensional character since the last century. Although primarily a study of the interplay among nation-states, the subject is no more confined only to states; it also deals with other non-state actors and their important roles in international politics and economy. Today, IR is also concerned with new and emerging issues like environment, globalization, terrorism and energy. The discipline also analyses the significance of non-state actors like international organizations, multinational corporations and non-governmental organizations. The importance of these non-state actors, along with nation-states and issues like environment, globalization, energy and terrorism, gradually came to acquire a significant place in the study of IR after the First World War. Thus, IR appeared as a structured and comprehensive academic discipline after the First World War; and as a separate branch of study, the subject was offered in European and American universities from the 1920s.

The study of IR as an academic discipline evolved further and matured significantly after the Second World War. With the process of decolonization almost complete, and the appearance of new states in Asia, Africa and Latin America, contemporary international politics assumed a new dimension after the war, a period when IR as an academic discipline progressed significantly. With the end of the Balance of Power system that had existed for three centuries, the post–Second World War international order was different; it saw the emergence of two non-European nuclear (weapon) superpowers, the United States and the Soviet Union, instead of the earlier five to six major non-nuclear (weapon) European powers. From the end of the Second World War (1945) to the end of the Cold War (1991), several issues gained prominence in IR. These are: strengthened existence of non-state actors as significant players in IR; energy; environment; terrorism; globalization and communication revolution. These issues helped to shape a new global order vastly different from those of the past. This new order in effect made the study of IR more dynamic, complex and broader in scope.

Although the world became unipolar after the Cold War, with the United States remaining the only superpower, the present international order has become more interdependent due to the spread of globalization, including international trade, information technology revolution, terrorism and environmental degradation. States are increasingly seeking cooperation from other states, as well as non-state actors, to adjust and compete in this world where states are largely dependent on one another. As an academic discipline, IR is also addressing these issues with more sincerity and articulation after the Cold War.

# Nature and Scope of IR

## Nature of IR

Is IR an independent academic discipline? The controversy that haunted modern IR for a long time since its emergence in the 1920s, revolved around its status as an independent academic discipline. Some scholars were unwilling to recognize it as a separate, autonomous academic discipline, and thought it to be largely dependent on subjects such as political science and history. The controversy that existed for more than four decades, till the 1960s, seems to have died down now with IR getting the recognition of an independent academic discipline. An autonomous academic discipline requires, mainly, a systematic body of theory, appropriate methodology, and a distinct subject matter. IR today is capable of meeting these criteria to exist and flourish as an autonomous discipline.

Without entering into this controversy (it does not exist anymore), it would be pertinent to identify the distinctive character of IR as an academic discipline. If political science is concerned with the 'politics', both formal and informal, of say, India, Britain, China or Australia, IR would be more concerned with the relationship between India and Britain, or China and Britain, or Australia and India, or among all of them. These relations may not be confined to political aspects only; they may cover economic, security, cultural or environmental issues. In other words, an IR scholar would not normally study the constitution or party system of any state; he would rather go for (international) relations of this particular state with others. A political scientist would be interested in the Government of India, or China, and its politics; but an IR scholar would be more interested in the foreign policies of India and China and their impact on relations between the two countries, rather than the domestic political systems in both countries.

Although this separation is not always absolute, as both the political scientist and the IR scholar may have to enter the 'other's area' for the sake of a proper study, but these 'visits' are now more for scholarly inputs rather than helpless dependence. And such inter-disciplinary visits are prerequisites for matured academic work. Similarly, IR scholars' areas of interest would ultimately differ from those of economists or historians, and they may follow different methodologies to study their subject. Interactions between IR and other social science disciplines have increased over the years, but the former's 'dependence' on the latter has been considerably minimized, thus helping it to emerge as an autonomous discipline with a distinct set of theories, methodology and subject matter.

## Theories and Methodologies

It is believed that there are four major theoretical traditions in the discipline of IR: liberalism, realism, theories based on international society approach, and theories rooted in international political economy. Recent approaches to counter earlier theories constitute the 'post-positivist' position in the discipline. Chapter 2 makes an elaborate analysis of the major theories in IR, based on these four theoretical traditions. However, it may be noted here that these theories have strengthened the claim of IR as an autonomous discipline. Methodologies in IR can be broadly classified into four types: traditional or classical, behavioural, positivist and post-positivist. While the traditional methodology revolved around historical, philosophical, moral or legal questions, the behavioural methodology wanted to base IR on scientific analysis. Traditional or classical methodology drew heavily from other disciplines like history, political science, philosophy and international law. It was based on knowledge and experience, rather than on hypotheses that could be tested. The behavioural method, on the other hand, wanted a systematic study of IR based on 'scientism', that is, use of appropriate scientific methods to study the subject. Behaviouralists wanted verifiable hypotheses and quantifiable data. They were concerned more with explanatory rather than normative approach. An example may bring out the difference between the two methodologies more clearly: classical methodology would be happy with the statement that 'democracy leads to peace', as this proposition is based on experience; behavioural methodology, on the other hand, would raise the question 'does democracy lead to peace?' and try to find an answer through verifiable data obtained from different democracies.

The positivist methodology in IR carries the legacy of behaviouralism, in more sophisticated ways. This method asserts on a precise, empirical approach based on logically related hypotheses that can be tested through scientific techniques, by using, if required, statistical or mathematical analyses. The 'game theory' in IR, analysed in Chapter 2, is an example of positivist methodology. The post-positivist methodology draws inspiration from the critique of behavioural and positivist approaches, and wants to assert that IR is not merely a field of techniques and meaningless scientism; it is also a vast area of knowledge without any short and specific agenda. Post-positivism is a very big umbrella that shelters several approaches like critical, postmodern, constructivist and normative approaches. One area of post-positivism, the normative approach, even wishes to revive the classical methodology in IR. More details on IR theories and methodologies would be provided in the next chapter. Methodologies in this subject are varied and constitute a fascinating area of study; and they also substantiate the claim of IR as an academic discipline.

## International Relations or International Politics?

Sometimes the terms 'international relations' and 'international politics' are used interchangeably to analyse issues related to the discipline. Such overlapping creates confusion among the young readers regarding the 'name' or 'title' of the discipline. It must, therefore, be made clear at the outset that the term IR has been globally accepted and recognized as the appropriate name for the discipline, as this term is broader in scope and more comprehensive than the term international politics. The former covers a vast range of interactions among states beyond political relations, and it also covers other non-state actors and their contributions to the international order.

Conversely, the latter refers only to the political events and aspects of the world, and may loosely refer to political interactions among nation-states. As stated at the beginning of this chapter, IR is primarily known as relations among states; but this view is oversimplified and inadequate. This discussion naturally leads the reader to expect a proper definition of the discipline.

### Definition of IR

Like many other social science disciplines, it is not easy to define IR in a few words. Although states and their interactions constitute the primary focus of IR, the discipline is concerned with many more issues like non-state actors, international political economy, international security, international environment, globalization, terrorism, area studies and military studies. Relations among states, in a broader sense, cover many such issues, yet leave out many more to be analysed separately. For instance, in a broader sense, international political economy, international security, globalization or environment, to cite a few, are somewhat linked to interactions among states; yet these issues may go beyond the sphere of relations among states. Non-state actors may also influence these issues profoundly. Therefore, IR being viewed as interactions among states is oversimplification, though helpful for a primary understanding. A broader and more comprehensive definition of the subject would be this: *International Relations as a branch of social science is concerned with relations among nations, and other issues like non-state actors, international political economy, international security, foreign policies of major powers, globalization, international terrorism, international environment and area studies.* This definition indicates that the scope and subject matter of IR has become vast today, unlike earlier times when IR was mainly concerned with nation-states and their interactions.

## Scope of IR

Like many other social science disciplines, IR has no definite boundary, and contemporary IR covers a very broad area of study. Creation of artificial and mandatory boundaries for the sake of making a discipline autonomous is not a necessity in any modern social science discipline, because inter-disciplinary exchanges can make all the disciplines enriched. IR also lacks specificity, and contemporary IR, particularly after the Second World War, has broadened its scope beyond limitations. From a preliminary study of government-to-government relations, the scope of IR has widened to include almost all aspects of international politics, and many areas of international political economy, international security, and environment. In 1947, the Council on Foreign Relations (CFR) in the United States identified five major areas of study in IR: (1) the nature and operation of the nation-state system; (2) factors that affect the power of a state; (3) the international position and foreign policies of the great powers; (4) the history of recent IR and (5) the building of a more stable international order. IR is now not confined only to these five areas; it has moved far and beyond.

A careful analysis of the report presented by the CFR in 1947 shows that many important issues covered by contemporary IR were not included in the report. For instance, the role and significance of non-state actors were not mentioned in its list; neither were mentioned the importance of international political economy (IPE) and environmental issues. But these issues and many others have gained prominence in IR over the years. Today, the study of IR broadly covers the following areas.

i. *Nation-states and their relations*: The operation of the nation-state system and relations among nation-states have always made international politics possible, and constituted the basic subject-matter of IR. These would continue to remain the primary area of study in the discipline.
ii. *Non-state actors*: The importance of non-state actors in the study of IR has been increasing over the years. Non-state actors like the multinational corporations (MNC), international non-governmental organizations (INGO), and the inter-governmental organizations (IGO) exert considerable influence in today's IR. So, these non-state actors are important ingredients of the study of contemporary IR.
iii. *International political economy* (IPE): International political economy is the study of IR with the help of economic activities and analyses. With the onset of globalization from the mid-1980s, a renewed interest in IPE has developed among scholars. Along with political and security angles, the study of IR is frequently analysed today with the help of economic views.
iv. *International security*: Security has always remained the primary concern of nation-states. The concern for security had led to war and peace in the past, and would continue to promote these in the future. A peaceful international order is always linked to the notion of international security that includes, among others factors, non-proliferation of weapons of mass destruction, and reduction of tension among states. Studies on war and peace and strategic studies in IR are also related to international security.
v. *Foreign policies of important powers*: Foreign policies of major and medium powers constitute important subject-matter of IR because these powers are the driving force in IR. When the balance of power system was prevalent, the study of foreign policies of major European powers was considered important. In contemporary IR, analyses of foreign policies of the United States, China, Russia, Japan and India may be useful as these states have become major actors in recent times.
vi. *Globalization*: This primarily refers to economic activities which have serious impact on political and social spheres. With the ascendance of liberal economy over mercantilist economy since the early 1980s, the term globalization has assumed increasing popularity and usage, and become significant in the study of IR. Although globalization and IPE are closely related, these are not identical, as subsequent chapters in this book would reveal.
vii. *International environment*: Environmental issues have now assumed greater significance in the study of IR than ever before because industrialization and technological progress have enhanced concerns for environmental safety all over the world. Environmental issues have made states across the world highly interdependent today because carbon emissions from industrial plants in one part of the world may affect other parts; or shortage of river water in a state may lead it to war with its neighbouring states. A stable and peaceful international order is dependent on environmental issues in today's world.
viii. *International terrorism*: Terrorist activities involving citizens of more than one country and having transnational impacts constitute international terrorism, an important area of study in IR. It is also referred to as 'cross border' terrorism. International peace and security are closely related to this issue.
ix. *Area studies*: Sometimes it becomes rather difficult to study international political, security or economic issues from a broader perspective. So area studies have become

popular nowadays. Under it, such issues concerning different areas of the world are taken up separately for analysis. For instance, West Asia, South Asia or Central Europe may be taken up for exclusive analysis under area studies, which has gained prominence in contemporary IR with increasing proliferation of regional organizations and free trade areas (FTA).

The expanding scope of IR lead to the view, and also to the controversy, that the discipline is becoming increasingly unmanageable, and that it lacks a clear conceptual framework. But this view is born out of pessimism about the discipline, and is not acceptable. Today, the subject has a definite and useful theoretical framework to support research in different areas. The broad scope may actually be helpful for it, because the varied subject matter may lead to more research and analyses, as well as greater specialization within the discipline. The broad scope of political science, physics or history, for that matter, has enriched these disciplines and helped them to grow further. There is little rationale therefore to worry about the expanding scope of IR; it will help the discipline to mature into a well-defined and enriched branch of modern social science.

## IR in Everyday Life

Students and the literate section of the society sometimes nurture a feeling that IR is far away not only from daily life, but also from domestic politics. They take IR as a subject of interest for governments and leaders, where an ordinary man has no role to play. They also think that it deals with issues which are 'international' in character, and are therefore remote from their private life, and even from national politics. But this idea is far from reality. IR is very much linked to domestic politics, as well as to our daily life. Its study not only enriches our academic knowledge and broadens our views about global affairs, it also helps us to understand daily life and domestic politics.

International security and international political economy, among other issues of IR, are closely linked to our daily life. A war, for instance, would affect our daily life profoundly. Our movements may be restricted, our freedom to turn on the lights in our houses may be curbed, and market prices may soar, affecting the normal rhythm of daily life. So, not only students of IR but every citizen would value the existence of peace in regional and international politics. Further, if the price of petroleum increases in the world market, our daily life would be affected because our kitchens would suffer as well due to the enhanced price of cooking gas. Such price hike may also become an issue in domestic politics. Moreover, the prospect of getting jobs after college education would depend on international economic and political conditions. At the time of economic recession or political turmoil, there may not be enough jobs. In an era of globalization, international economic crisis would definitely affect job prospects around the world, and normalcy in daily life.

Sometimes treaties among states may affect the life of of the common people. A bilateral treaty between two countries on sharing of the water of a certain river, for instance, may have profound impact on the daily life of the people living by the side of the river. The 'Ganga River Water Accord' between Bangladesh and India, signed in 1996, affected the life of many people in these two countries, besides having an impact on the relations between the two neighbours. Similarly, a multilateral trade or security treaty may also influence the life of the people living in countries that are party to the treaty. Nowadays, regional trade agreements like the SAFTA (South Asian Free Trade Agreement) or the AFTA (Asean Free Trade Agreement) influence the development of the economy of participating states. Such influence over the national economy may, in turn, affect our daily life. A bilateral or multilateral treaty may also fuel controversies in domestic politics. The Ganga River Water Accord generated controversies in domestic politics in both Bangladesh and India. The recent India–US Civil Nuclear Agreement (CNA) became a hot political issue both in Indian and American politics from 2005, when the treaty was conceived, to 2008, when the CNA was finally achieved. Not only political parties, but also ordinary citizens in the two countries got involved in the political debates generated by the agreement. All these examples provided here are indicative of the impact of IR in our daily life.

On the other hand, ordinary citizens also take part, knowingly or unknowingly, in IR. When people cast their votes in parliamentary elections, they actually take an active part in the formation of the government of their country. The government, in turn, formulates foreign policies of the country, along with domestic policies; and tries to protect national interests in world politics and maintain IR. Therefore, through the process of elections, every adult citizen everywhere takes part not only in domestic politics, but also in IR. Further, when people take part in an educational or cultural project sponsored by organizations like the UNESCO (United Nations Educational Scientific and Cultural Organization), they associate themselves, perhaps unknowingly, with international developmental activities. IR, as perceived in common parlance, is not a distant subject, far removed from our daily life. On the contrary, it influences the life of ordinary citizens, and in turn, also benefits from them. The discipline shares a symbiotic relationship with the ordinary person.

## QUESTIONS

1. Write a note on the history and evolution of IR as an academic discipline.
2. Analyse the nature and scope of IR.
3. Bring out the significance of IR in everyday life.

# 2 Important Theories in International Relations

## What Is a 'Theory' and Why Is It Required?

A theory is an analytical tool for understanding, explaining and making predictions about a given subject matter. It is a body of rules, ideas, principles or techniques to explain a natural event that can be put to test and is capable of predicting future events. A theory, in the scientific sense, is an analytic structure designed to explain a set of empirical observations. It is necessary because it acts as a guiding principle to systematically structure our observations. Different persons with different assumptions and perspectives may observe an event differently. A theory can tell us what to accept and what to ignore in our observations. Without the guidance of a theory, observers would be lost in the sea of facts and data, would be unable to systematically explain and structure their observations. A theory is unavoidable as it guides observers to systematically analyse their observations among a huge quantity of contradictory facts and data. It leads to an accurate and proper explanation of the subject matter.

## Theories in International Relations

Theories in International Relations (IR) attempt to provide a conceptual framework that would help to analyse properly different aspects of the discipline. Theory-building in IR proceeded, like in many other disciplines, with historical and contemporary developments taking place across the world. When nation-states and their relations were of prime importance, theories developed around the subject matters of the nation-state, such as war and peace. Later, when non-state actors and events came to influence IR thinking, various new theories such as behaviouralism, globalization and postmodernism concerning these areas developed. In a similar vein, future events taking place in the world would provoke many more theories in IR. Theories in IR, as in other social sciences, sometimes develop around values, and they may also contain visions about the future world, the world we prefer to see and live in.

Earlier theorists in IR were concerned with the survival of the nation-state system, because they had observed the holocaust of the First World War. IR, which developed as an academic discipline after the First World War, was mainly preoccupied with the nation-states and their interactions in its early days. As frequent wars were threatening the existence of nation-states, early IR thinkers developed theories on war and the ways to avoid war. Thus theories on peace also developed alongside theories on war. Concern with nation-states, their wars, interests and efforts for peace gave birth to theories like liberalism and realism. Later, when nation-states and their interplay became rather stale, new observations developed in IR. These generated theories like behaviouralism and globalization, which tried to focus on non-state issues in the discipline. At a still later stage, post-positivist theories developed, which sought to challenge all earlier theories. For instance, postmodernism, which comes under the huge umbrella of post-positivist theories in IR, claims that there cannot be any objective truth in IR; everything in IR or social sciences is subjective, built around human notions of values, ideas, emotions and beliefs. So, once these constructions (known as theories) based on so-called 'objective truth' are deconstructed, their hollowness gets exposed. Liberal ideas of cooperation and peace, or realistic ideas about conflict of interests, are actually subjective interpretaions, not to be taken as eternal 'objective truth', argue the postmodernists. According to them, every theory must be deconstructed to arrive at new conclusions. Although postmodernists were criticized as negativists, they were able to mark their presence in the sphere of theory-building in IR. So, theories in IR are numerous and varied as they progressed alongside courses of development that occurred in the world from time to time.

An important question is: which theory, among this variegated lot, is to be accepted as the most important? The answer to this apparently simple question would lead students of IR to a debate currently taking place in the discipline. One prominent view is: since a theory helps us to systematically structure our thinking of the world, it is necessary to identify the best possible theory that would help us in this direction. Another view holds that there is no need to identify any particular theory as 'important' or 'all-inclusive' in IR. As theories develop around human observations, these would be divergent. It is best to seek the help of all these theories on an 'issue-based approach'. In a social science discipline, it is difficult to formulate a 'principal theory' applicable to all problems. Different theories may be required to solve different kinds of problems. The debate continues among scholars in the discipline. With these preliminary ideas about theories in IR, we proceed to discuss some of the major theories in the discipline of IR.

## Liberal Theory (including Pluralism)

The evolution of liberal philosophy covers a vast period in history—from the Reformation Movement in the sixteenth century till today. During this long span of existence, liberalism came under the influence of various intellectual minds, trends and historical forces. It shattered the spiritual illusions nurtured carefully by the feudal society, and gave birth to a scientific and secular view of life. It helped to remove feudal superstitions and religious dogmatism, and brought reason, courage, confidence and self-respect. For these reasons, liberalism was associated with modernization of society and individual life. Liberal philosophers, beginning with John Locke in the seventeenth century, emphasized individual liberty and freedom, which could be sustained in a free civil society and within an encouraging state that would allow individual liberty and aspirations to flourish. Individual liberty, believed other liberal thinkers like Immanuel Kant, J. S. Mill and T. H. Green to name a few, could be nurtured best within a cooperative organization of people, like the state. An individual's liberty and freedom are not in contradiction to the creation and existence of the state; in fact these are ensured by a liberal, less interfering state. This view of the liberal, encouraging and less-intrusive state influenced scholars in IR; they developed a liberal tradition in IR thinking, which was later identified as the liberal theory in IR.

Liberal theory (or Liberalism) in IR is closely associated with the following ideas: (1) a modern liberal state that encourages human activities for the development of society; (2) state- and non-state actors as partners in the development process; (3) a peaceful state based on democratic principles as the best promoter of a peaceful international order; (4) free economic systems within the state and on an international level and (5) interdependent national and international orders. Liberalism is a product of history and courses of development in the international order. Early liberals like Norman Angell and Woodrow Wilson, who had witnessed the tragedy of the First World War, were concerned more with a peaceful international order based on cooperation among nation-states. This peaceful world order could only be ensured by peaceful, liberal-democratic nation-states which valued individual freedom and liberty, and promoted competitive economy. This period of early liberalism in IR which originated after the First World War was also known as utopian or idealist liberalism because the protagonists believed in an ideal world order free from conflicts and war. But with the emergence of Nazi Germany, fascist Italy and the failure of the League of Nations, idealist liberalism lost grounds to neo-realist theory (discussed in the next section of this chapter), which began to emerge from the late 1930s. However, liberalism in IR was revived with renewed vigour after the Second World War, as it generated newer ideas and thinking which enriched the study of the discipline.

Post–Second World War liberalism in IR developed into a multi-faceted doctrine. Authors like Robert Jackson and Georg Sorensen (2003) have identified four main branches of post–Second World War liberalism: sociological liberalism, interdependence liberalism, institutional liberalism and republican liberalism. The core idea of sociological liberalism refers to IR as the study of relations among individuals, groups and societies, in addition to the study of interactions among national governments. A. J. P. Taylor, John Burton and James Rosenau are the leading theorists of sociological liberalism which views IR also as the study of 'informal' relations among groups and societies beyond the more 'formal' relations between governments of different nation-states. Interdependence liberalism believes that with the advancement of science, technology and trade, nation-states get engaged in a complex web of interdependence. Liberal theorists like David Mitrany, Ernst Haas, Robert Keohane and Joseph Nye argue that modern states are welfare—and not security—organizations. The primary goal of these welfare states is to secure a cooperative international order based on mutual understanding. Non-state actors are important instruments of this cooperative international order which seeks to promote peace, and not conflict, in the world. Institutional liberalism holds the view that international institutions like the UNO (United Nations Organization), WTO (World Trade Organization), NATO (North Atlantic Treaty Organization), European Union (EU) help to promote cooperation among states in the world and strengthen efforts for international peace. Institutional liberals like Volker Rittberger, O. R. Young and Robert Keohane hold the view that international institutions help to reduce the possibilities of anarchy in the world by advancing cooperation based on mutual interests. Thus, for instance, an international institution like the WTO promotes economic interests of nation-states and help in achieving cooperation among countries of the world. This cooperative international order strengthens international peace. The basic idea of republican liberalism is that democracy and international peace are inseparable. Republican liberals like Michael Doyle, B. M. Russett, D. Lake and others believe that democracy ensures peaceful resolution of conflicts. A state where democratic cultures have taken firm root is less prone to violence and conflict, because it can solve its problems through dialogues and negotiations. Therefore, promotion of democracy in the world would ensure lesser violence and a peaceful international order that would be mutually interdependent for common economic and political interests.

This analysis of the liberal position in IR enables us to focus on the salient features of liberal theory in IR and its main protagonists. Box 2.1 highlights the basic assumptions of the liberal theory:

**Box 2.1 Liberal Theory in IR: Basic Assumptions and Leading Theorists**

**Early Liberalism (1920–late 1930s)**

**Basic Features**

- Nation-states are the main actors in IR.
- Cooperation among nation-states is essential for a peaceful world order.
- Nation-states that valued individual liberty and freedom in their domestic political systems can best ensure international peace.
- Relations among nations would help avoid war and establish peace in the world.

*Early Liberal Theorists*: N. Angell, W. Wilson. Also known as 'Utopian Liberalism', early liberalism lost grounds to neo-realism in the late 1930s.

**Post–Second World War Liberalism (1945–1970s)**

**Basic Features**

- Nation-states are not the only actors in IR; individuals, groups, societal organizations are also important actors.
- Technological advancement and economic interests bind the states in a complex web of interdependence. This interdependence promotes a cooperative international order.
- International institutions like the UNO, WTO, NATO and EU help to promote international cooperation and strengthen efforts for peace.
- Democracy and competitive economy can ensure international peace.
- Democratic states seek peaceful resolution of conflicts, and do not fight with each other.
- Competitive market economy keeps away security fears of nation-states, because commercial interests become the primary concern of states.

*Post–Second World War Liberal Theorists*: A. J. P. Taylor, D. Mitrany, E. Haas, R. Keohane, J. Nye, V. Rittberger, O. R. Young, M. Doyle, B. M. Russett.

## Neo-liberalism

Liberalism is a long historical tradition that continued its journey into the twenty-first century. With the onset of globalization and free trade in the late 1970s, a group of liberal thinkers argued that this new economic trend would have enormous impact on the nation-state and the international order. This group, known as neo-liberal thinkers in IR, emerged after the triumph of the 'New Right' in Britain and the United States during the late 1970s and 1980s. Neo-liberals like

C. B. Macpherson, T. Friedman, John Rawls, Francis Fukuyama and K. Ohmae argued, in different ways, against the Keynesian philosophy of state intervention in economic life. In an era of globalization, neo-liberal theorists in IR favoured a free play of economic forces, and a minimal role for the state in economic life. They argued that the former theory of *laissez faire* in trade could not remove the control of the state over economic life without hindrance. With the concept of the 'welfare state' gaining popularity after the Second World War, the state came to exercise a constant dominance in socio-economic life. The neo-liberals argued that the triumph of globalization renders the notion of state sovereignty vulnerable as 'free trade' introduced the idea of trade without national borders. They believed that globalization can help achieve true internationalism and a peaceful world order about which post–Second World War liberals remained so passionate and optimistic. They wanted a 'rollback' of the welfare state and protectionism in economic life, because these practices ultimately kill the enterprise and talent of the individual, and make the society incapable of achieving better results. So, a minimal state is required for economic liberalism, which in turn can pave the way for a cooperative international order based on peace, harmony and safeguard of human rights.

After the disintegration of the Soviet Union and the 'Socialist Bloc', the neo-liberal philosophy claimed to have gained more strength. They refer to the Soviet model of state intervention and protectionism in economic life to vindicate their arguments. According to the neo-liberals, state protectionism in economic matters not only affects human enterprise, they bring corruption, nepotism and inefficiency in socio-political life which may prove to be very detrimental to the state and the society. Conversely, economic liberalism of the 'minimal state' helps national and world trade to prosper with benefits reaching the grassroot level. Organizations like the WTO, APEC (Asia Pacific Economic Community), NAFTA (North American Free Trade Agreement), IMF (International Monetary Fund) and the World Bank, which help to promote free trade among nations, also promote world peace and security by enhancing the economic prosperity of the nation-states and the world. Globalization, represented by free market economy in the domestic sphere linked to international trade, has helped many underdeveloped states to achieve sufficient economic development, which in turn would positively affect socio-political development in these countries, think the neo-liberals. They believe that sufficient cooperation and interdependence among nation-states are possible through globalization. In the twenty-first century, it is not possible, and hence desirable, for any nation to isolate itself from world trade, and fully control its internal economic life. The neo-liberal view is not beyond criticism. It is discussed later in the chapter. In Box 2.2, we turn our attention to the basic assumptions of the neo-liberal theory in IR.

## Pluralist Theory

Pluralist theory in IR is a branch of the broader liberal theory. As the name suggests, this theory holds the view that in IR, individuals, groups, associations, institutions and organizations also play important roles apart from the state. In other words, this theory believes that every society is plural in nature, and the state is one among many institutions in the society. So, it is unwise to identify the state as the only important actor in IR; other organizations and institutions play vital roles in IR today.

The diversification of liberal theory into sociological, institutional and interdependence liberalism actually upholds the views of the pluralists. These branches of liberalism minimize

**Box 2.2** **Neo-liberal Theory in IR: Basic Assumptions and Leading Theorists**

**Basic Features**

- Economic liberalism is marked by free trade and globalization.
- Minimum state intervention in economic life—discarding of the Keynesian model.
- Failure of *Laissez faire* theory to remove state control on economic life.
- Rollback of the 'welfare' and 'protectionist' state as it breeds inefficiency and corruption.
- Free trade can ensure domestic and international peace and security because states are engaged in the economic development process, and shy away from war.
- Free trade can best thrive in a democratic political system as it secures human rights and basic freedoms of people.
- Disintegration of Soviet Union and the 'socialist bloc' marked the triumph of free market economy.
- In the twenty-first century, cooperation and interdependence of states are possible through globalization.

**Leading Theorists:** C. B. Macpherson, T. Friedman, J. Rawls, F. Fukuyama, K. Ohmae.

the excessive importance of the state in IR, and suggest that non-state actors are also very significant in IR today. Therefore, before identifying the general characteristics of the pluralist theory, it would be pertinent to know about these three branches (sociological, institutional and interdependence) of liberalism that form the core of the pluralist theory. The basic idea of sociological liberalism refers to IR as the study of relations among individuals, groups and societies, in addition to the study of interactions among national governments. Pluralists like R. Little, D. Nicholls and J. Burton agree with the theorists of sociological liberalism, and view IR as the study of 'informal' relations among individuals, groups, associations and societies beyond the more 'formal' relations between governments of different nation-states.

Institutional liberalism holds the view that international institutions like the UNO, WTO, NATO and EU help promote cooperation among states in the world and strengthen efforts for international peace. Pluralists like Krasner, Young and Underdal subscribe to this view of institutional liberals and add multinational corporations (MNCs) and non-governmental organizations (NGOs) to their list of non-state actors who play significant roles in IR today. Like the Institutional liberals, these pluralists also believe that international institutions, MNCs and NGOs help to reduce the possibilities of state-sponsored anarchy in the world by advancing cooperation based on mutual interests. Sometimes, activities of an international organization and an NGO may be pursued for the same end. Thus, while an international organization like the UNO promotes international peace by thwarting the evil designs of a country, an NGO like the Amnesty International helps in curbing excesses of the national governments and restoring human rights in the world, and through such activities, promotes the cause of international peace. Without adequate safeguard of human rights, international peace and security it is difficult to achieve in the modern world. Institutions and organizations beyond the state are engaged in promoting, knowingly or unknowingly, international peace and harmony, and getting increasing importance in international affairs. The pluralists provide theoretical support to these institutions, associations, groups and organizations in IR today. Interdependence liberalism believes that modern states are welfare organizations and not security organizations. The primary goal of these welfare states is to secure a cooperative international order based on mutual understanding. Pluralists like Rosecrance and Hoffmann believe that in this international order, it is not sufficient to engage the nation-states only; the involvement of non-state actors must be secured to make the world truly friendly, cooperative and peaceful. Non-state actors are important instruments of the present cooperative international order which is highly interdependent in nature.

Pluralists are against the monopoly of the state as an actor in international affairs. In all modern societies, plural forces for socio-political and economic activities are in existence, and working alongside the state. These bodies are not contrary, but complimentary, to the state. They are engaged in socio-political-economic development within the state. Some of these non-state actors are working outside the boundaries of the state on a global scale. They are engaged in different activities that ultimately help in securing international cooperation and harmony. The UNO has also recognized the role of the NGOs in developmental activities throughout the world. Pluralists believe that the contribution of these non-state actors in IR must be properly recognized, and given due importance. The recognition of non-state actors in IR would not only help in establishing a cooperative world, it would also curb the dangers of state-dominated international affairs.

This analysis of the pluralist theory helps us to identify some general characteristics of the theory. Box 2.3 highlights the features of the theory and the leading advocates of this theory.

**Box 2.3** **Pluralist Theory in IR: Basic Features and Leading Theorists**

**Basic Features**

- Pluralism is a branch of liberal theory in IR.
- Pluralism actually thrives on sociological, institutional and interdependence liberalism.
- According to pluralism, the state is not the monopoly actor in IR.
- Non-state actors like individuals, groups, institutions, associations and organizations are also significant actors in IR.
- International cooperation, peace and harmony require the involvement of non-state actors along with nation-states.
- IR is not only government-to-government interactions; it is also interactions among societies and non-state actors.
- MNCs and NGOs play crucial roles in international affairs today.
- A dependent world is the product of a close connection between state- and non-state actors.

**Leading Theorists:** R. Little, D. Nicholls, O. R.Young, A. Underdal, R. Rosecrance, S. Hoffmann.

## An Evaluation of Liberal Theory (including Pluralism)

Some of the major attacks on liberal theory in IR came from the realist thinkers. They criticized liberal optimism about a peaceful, cooperative world. Realists like E. H. Carr, Hans J. Morgenthau, George Kennan and Arnold Wolfers saw the views of the liberals as 'idealistic' and accused them of misreading the actual situation prevailing in world politics, and nurturing false dreams about the world. According to Carr, there is little rationale to believe that nation-states wish to live in harmony and peace. On the contrary, conflict of interests of the nation-states is the reality in international politics. Nation-states do not cooperate in world politics because their opposing interests would leave limited options for them to search for peace and harmony. Clash of interests actually lead the nations to war. The two world wars bear testimony to this observation, think the realists. Carr, in his book *The Twenty Years Crisis*, noted that profound conflict of interests between countries and people occur almost always in international politics. For instance, the developed nations, for their economic and political advantages, would prefer to continue with the prevalent international order; whereas the poor nations, due to their disadvantageous position in the international system would try to alter the system. This and many other clashes of interests may lead to frequent conflicts in the world. Liberals are thus wrong in suggesting that nations try to share mutual interests and live in peace and harmony. The reality is different in international politics: it is conflict rather than cooperation among countries.

Hans J. Morgenthau, in his celebrated work *Politics among Nations: The Struggle for Power and Peace*, shattered the liberal 'myth' of a peaceful, interdependent, cooperative world based on democratic values. He started with a portrayal of human nature as self-seeking and self-interested. These selfish human beings cannot change their basic human nature as rulers of the state. As a consequence, the state also looks after its own interests, and does not care for others' interests in international politics. Morgenthau does not find anything wrong in this attitude of the state. The main tasks of a country are to safeguard its own interests, loosely termed as national interests, and to provide security to its people. In these tasks, the rulers of the state cannot afford to practice morality. Morality can be practiced in the private domain, but not in statecraft. An ordinary individual can practice morality in private life, but the leader of a state cannot afford to go by ethical and moral principles if the interests of the country are at stake. International politics, like domestic politics, is a struggle for power where nations compete, and if required, conflict with one another for supremacy. There is little scope for cooperation, as the liberals suggest, in this international order. According to Morgenthau, 'interest backed by power' is the key word in international politics, and countries prefer to follow this policy rather than the policy of peace and harmony.

For realists like Carr, Morgenthau and Wolfers, the state is the most important actor in international politics. They oppose the pluralist view that individuals, groups, associations or institutions play significant roles in IR. World politics is essentially a game for the nation-states, who remain in a controlling position in international affairs. Further, neo-realists like Kenneth Waltz and John Mearsheimer oppose the pluralist view that institutions play important roles in IR. Institutions are not important in their own right; they acquire importance because nation-states either work through them or seek their assistance. Nation-states use the institutions to fulfill their own interests. The state is the main actor, and the institutions are the less-important players in IR. The pluralist view of interdependence among modern states is also contested by neo-realists. Neo-realists argue that within this apparent interdependence, a power game is involved. Advanced and powerful countries of the world create an atmosphere of interdependence to serve their political, economic and strategic interests. Every strong power in history would create this condition to fulfill its interests. That way, history is seldom changed, according to the realists; all history is the history of anarchy due to the politics of power and interest, played by nation-states.

Marxists—from Karl Marx and Frederick Engels to neo-Marxists, to thinkers influenced by the Marxist ideology, such as the World System theorists—have criticized the liberal theory in IR on several grounds. A general Marxist critique propagated by Marx himself and his friend Engels, and also by the neo-Marxists, points out flaws in the liberal idea of democracy and peace in IR. The idea of democracy advanced by the liberal thinkers was the bourgeois idea of democracy that only protected the interests of the bourgeois class. Similarly, the idea of peace in IR was mooted to maintain the existing status quo in the international order, controlled by the capitalists. The neo-Marxists also criticize liberal views on globalization and human rights. Globalization is not the panacea to all economic problems of the poor countries, because it would create economic inequality through capital outflow that would be controlled by the rich nations. Therefore, globalization would bring with it more economic and social disparity by widening the gap between the poor and the rich countries. Human rights, according to neo-Marxists, is nothing but the idea of bourgeois freedom, and it does not take into account the rights and freedoms of the toiling masses of the world. Further, protagonists of the World System Theory (WST) such as Immanuel Wallerstein, Andre Gunder Frank and Samir Amin believe that in the present international order there is a big gap between the rich industrial nations, whom they called the 'core' states, and the deprived poor states, identified as the 'peripheral' states. Globalization and the resulting economic disparity were behind this 'core–periphery' difference system where the core dominates and exploits the periphery in the current international order.

The liberals react differently to these criticisms. A group of 'weak' liberals, as identified by Jackson and Sorensen, accept many of the criticisms, and believe that the current state of IR needs changes and rich–poor disparity must be minimized. However, a 'strong' group of liberals, identified by Jackson and Sorensen, counterattack the critics by saying that the present state of IR reflects liberal optimism, as more nations are favouring an international order based on democracy, peace and interdependence. The pessimism of the realists and the Marxists, argue the strong liberals, has been rejected by the people in different parts of the world as they shared liberal optimism of a peaceful and cooperative international order based on the protection of democracy and human rights.

## Realist Theory

The tradition of realism is rooted in the writings of many ancient scholars. The classical realists believed that there was no permanent solution to the problems of national and international politics. Among them, Greek historian Thucydides is perhaps the oldest. While writing on the Peloponnesian War (431 BC–404 BC), he focused upon the conflicts and competitions among the Greek city-states. According to him, the states were unequal in terms of power. All states have to accept this reality of unequal power and act accordingly. If the states follow this 'reality' they will survive and prosper. He said that 'the strong do what they have the power to do and the weak accept what they have to accept'. In order to survive, a state has to apply the ethics of caution and prudence, foresight and judgment.

The Italian realist writer Niccolo Machiavelli urged rulers to be shrewd and ruthless. As the world was anarchic in nature, and a dangerous place to live, a ruler had to be brave like a lion and cunning like a fox. According to him, the survival of a state, preservation of its territorial integrity and political independence, and the welfare of its people depended largely on the manipulative powers of the ruler. Thomas Hobbes, the English political philosopher, talked about the 'state of nature' where government was absent. In this state of nature there was no rule of law. The fear of the people about getting hurt or killed forced them to unite and form a sovereign state. The sovereign state provided safety and security to its people, and defended itself from external attack. A government was thus necessary within a society in order to provide rule of law and security to the people against violence. But in the international sphere, the multiplicity of sovereign states might result in a state of anarchy that could endanger international security. Hobbes believed that even if war was the last resort for the resolution of an international conflict, such conflicts could be moderated through the enforcement of an international law. So an international law had to be framed by the sovereign states collectively, and its strict adherence was necessary for the states to survive and prosper.

Classical realists were of the opinion that people lived in a condition of total insecurity and lawlessness. This situation was altered by a powerful sovereign state with a strong government. However, in domestic politics as well as in international affairs, the problem of conflicts could not be solved permanently. Realists viewed conflicts and violence as integral parts of domestic and world politics. The ruler needs to be powerful to resolve conflicts in politics. The classical realists emphasized the primary value of power in statecraft. The concern for power of the ruler characterized classical realism. This belief in power was again reflected and reinforced in the writings of neo-classical realists of the twentieth century, such as E. H. Carr and Hans J. Morgenthau.

E. H. Carr's book *The Twenty Years Crisis* (1939) provided a scathing criticism of the liberal kind of 'utopian' politics. Carr denounced the liberal idea of abolishing war in international politics. According to him, conflicts between states were inevitable in international politics, because there was no international regulatory authority to curb conflicts and wars. We may wish to abolish wars between states, but wars will continue to be fought due to opposing interests of states, and the absence of any regulatory authority in the international system. Carr believed that 'power', not 'morality' would be the guiding force in international politics.

Morgenthau's realist theory rests upon the assumption that people are by nature self-interested and power-hungry. In his book *Politics among Nations: The Struggle for Power and Peace* (1972), Morgenthau wrote that humans by nature were political animals and they enjoyed power. The element of power can secure an individual's position in the society, and can place him in an advantageous position in comparison to others. Like the classical realists, Morgenthau also believed that 'politics is a struggle for power'. As political groups compete with one another to enjoy the fruits of power in domestic politics, similarly in international politics, states compete and fight for power. In international politics, the state must pursue power, because it is the only means for the furtherance of national interest. But, as did Thucydides and Hobbes, Morgenthau too argued that the state system creates international anarchy. He believes that the preservation of international peace and stability is possible only by individual states in the absence of any integrated world society. Here he defends the craving for power by individual states and tries to legitimize this urge for power in terms of morality and ethics. According to him, morality has two sides—private and public. He assigns one type of morality for the private sphere and an entirely different type of morality for the public sphere. Individuals in the private sphere can observe moral practices as much as they like, but a state cannot afford to preach morality if the safety and security of its people are in danger. In times of acute crisis, it may become imperative for a state to adopt certain means like spying or conspiring or waging full-scale war for ensuring the security of its people. Such an act may appear to be contradictory to private morality. Morgenthau urges scholars to separate political ethics from private ethics. An individual may not like war, but the leader of the state can never swear to not going to war if the interests of the people and the state are at stake. Let us analyse this distinction between private and public morality, as seen by Morgenthau, in more simple terms. Let us suppose 'B', the individual, does not like conflicts. As an individual, he can remain very faithful to this ethics, and may not hit or hurt others. But if 'B' assumes leadership of his nation, he cannot remain faithful to his 'ethics' of disliking conflicts. If the interests of his nation and people are harmed, he would have to involve himself in conflict or war to secure the interests of his nation and people. Political ethics on the one hand involves foresight, prudence, wisdom, courage, judgment; on the other, it involves cunning, maneuverability and shrewd diplomacy.

In order to understand Morgenthau's version of realism, it is necessary to know his 'six principles of political realism' as presented in *Politics among Nations*. These principles are as follows.

i. The law of politics is rooted in human nature which is self-seeking, self-interested and power-loving. This human nature has remained unchanged since ancient times.
ii. Politics is 'an autonomous sphere of action'. It is different from economics, ethics, religion or aesthetics. The concept of 'interest defined in terms of power' makes politics autonomous because the concept of 'power' can help to analyse all politics adequately.
iii. Interests of different states may vary from time to time. It is wrong to believe that the meaning and definition of interest is unaffected by the circumstances of time and space. The political and cultural environment determines the nature of interests of a state. This changing reality has to be recognized by all.
iv. There is a sharp difference between private morality and political ethics. A leader has to judge a political situation in the light of actual circumstances. Ethics in international politics is political or situational ethics, and therefore sharply opposed to private morality. Application of individual moral judgment is not possible for a leader. He has to take necessary steps considering wider political responsibilities. As a citizen, a person's action might be influenced by private morality, but the moment he acts as a leader, he has to follow political morality with prudence, taking into account the actual situation.
v. Political realism believes that aspirations of a particular state cannot become the governing law of the universe. This would amount to the imposition of a state's beliefs upon another. Such a situation is dangerous as it would undermine international peace and security. This might ultimately lead to the destruction of human civilization.
vi. Statecraft is a sober and uninspiring activity that involves a profound awareness of human limitations. Human nature as it is should be considered in international politics, rather than human nature as it should be.

Box 2.4 highlights Morgenthau's six principles of political realism.

The impact of behaviouralism and positivist philosophy in social sciences resulted in the emergence of a new line of realist thought during the 1960s and 1970s. Thomas Schelling, for

**Box 2.4** **Six Principles of Political Realism as Advocated by Morgenthau**

1. The law of politics is rooted in human nature which is self-seeking, self-interested and power-loving.
2. Politics is an autonomous sphere of activity, and does not depend on economics. The concepts of 'interest' and 'power' can make politics independent of other disciplines.
3. A state's interests are not fixed; they are changeable depending on time and space. This reality must be recognized in international politics.
4. Ethics in international politics is political or situational ethics, and therefore sharply opposed to private morality.
5. Political realism believes that aspirations of a particular state cannot become the governing law of the universe.
6. Statecraft is a sober and uninspiring activity that involves a profound awareness of human limitations. Human nature as it is should be considered in international politics, rather than the human nature as it should be.

example, came up with a newer version of realism, later identified as strategic realism. This could be considered as a part of neo-realism, which wanted to analyse international politics from an empirical point of view, making a departure from the normative tone of classical and neo-classical realism. To the classical and neo-classical realists, interest and power became 'norms' in both domestic and international politics. They believed that by analysing these concepts, all aspects of domestic and international politics could be studied adequately. Keeping the normative aspects of earlier forms of realism in the background, strategic realism tends to emphasize on empirical analytical tools for strategic thoughts.

Thomas Schelling, the chief exponent of strategic realism, is well aware about the crisis-ridden contemporary world. In order to avoid disaster, he talks about various mechanisms like strategies, moves and calculated actions to be followed by statesmen. For instance, a good strategy suggests that a state uses power intelligently, and not blatantly, while formulating a foreign policy, to avoid any catastrophe. Schelling is not bothered with the questions 'what is good?' or 'what is right?'; he is concerned more with the elements required for the success of a foreign policy. The crucial instrument for the success of a foreign policy is the military. It is a coercive apparatus that can scare an adversary. Coercion can force an adversary into bargaining. For Schelling, diplomacy is all about bargaining. War no longer remains a contest of strength in today's world of nuclear arsenals. Currently the 'threat' of war is more fearsome than actual war. Therefore, the 'threat' perspective is more important to him than the real war; and intelligent strategies require very calculative use of this threat perspective in foreign policy. Although Schelling justified intelligent strategies to be adopted by foreign policy-makers, he failed to analyse the role of values in such strategies.

Among contemporary neo-realist thinkers, Kenneth Waltz is particularly important. In his important work, *Theory of International Politics*, written in 1979, Waltz argued that to study IR one should begin with the system—the state or other political system—and ultimately come down to the individual actors. This is in opposition to the traditional realists' approach, whose basic premise was the individual human nature. For the neo-realists, the structure of the system and its relative distribution of power are the focal points of analysis. For instance, Kenneth Waltz places great importance on the structure of the system, on its interacting units, and on the changes occurring within the system. He sees the system and its structures as more important than individuals. Waltz's version of neo-realism is identified as the 'neo-realist systems theory' with emphasis on scientific analysis.

According to Waltz, all states are similar in their functional aspects, as all perform similar tasks such as promoting citizens' welfare, collecting taxes, formulating foreign policies and maintaining internal peace. What makes a state strikingly different from others is not its culture or constitution or ideology; it is rather the varying capabilities of the states that make them different from each other. Therefore, those states which are more 'capable' than others would control international politics. What naturally follows is that the great powers are the determining factors in the international political system. After the Second World War, the United States and the Soviet Union, two big and powerful nations, controlled international politics. The bipolarity that developed after the war was more stable than the multi polar nature of world politics that existed before it. During the bipolar period, the two superpowers were very keen on maintaining the system, because the system provided them with more advantages. According to neo-realists, leaders cannot act independent of the structures of the state. Conducting of foreign policy becomes essentially a mechanical and obvious task for leaders. They are compelled to operate within the confinements of the structures of the political system. While the focal point of strategic realism is the art of diplomacy and prudent strategies, neo-realism is more concerned with structure that dictates and determines policies. However, Waltz also stressed upon the notions of state sovereignty and national interest. But unlike neo-classical realists, Waltz does not see national interest as the core issue in international politics; for him, it acts as a guide to tell the statesman when and where to proceed. In other words, a statesman would have to depend on the structures of the state to formulate foreign policies; but in the making of foreign policy, national interest would guide him how to proceed. Therefore, according to neo-realism, there is no room for wisdom, intelligence, experience or astuteness of the decision-maker. What determines the behaviour of the state is the structure as a whole.

Contemporary economic and technological advancement have posed a challenge to realist thinking. Globalization, increasing privatization of state-owned enterprises, foreign investment, increasing significance of non-state actors, and the growth and importance of civil society have questioned the validity of the realist theory which views the state as the most important unit in international politics. What are the neo-realist responses to these challenges? Neo-realists like Kenneth Waltz, Stephen Krasner, Robert Gilpin and John Mearsheimer have provided answers to these challenges. From their writings, a few common responses to these 'crises' could be deciphered. First, neo-realists are sceptical about the impact of globalization throughout the world. They believe that globalization is a typically 'Western' concept, and its impact is limited to the developing nations of Asia, Africa and Latin America. Globalization, therefore, would not be a serious threat to nation-states and their interplay in IR. Secondly, neo-realists consider economic interdependence of the world as a myth. If capital flows are measured as a percentage of the GNP (Gross National Product), the level of economic interdependence in the world in 2000 is more or less equal to that of 1910. So, the neo-liberal claim that economic interdependence of the world has made the nation-state a minor player in international affairs is not tenable.

Thirdly, the neo-realists believe that both 'socialist' and 'market' economic models have produced very satisfactory growth rates. Soviet Union of the 1950s and Japan of the 1980s are good examples of this argument. The neo-liberal claim that only free market economy can achieve sustained growth is also not true. Fourthly, the nation-state is still the most preferred political unit in international affairs, and despite anti-statism, there is no strong rival to challenge and replace the state in IR. The nation-state still commands allegiance of the people and successfully manages conflicts to give its citizens a secured and peaceful life. The notion of state sovereignty, as Krasner (1999) points out, has not become wholly vulnerable to globalization. Finally, neo-realists think that military power is still the determining factor in international politics. Waltz's notion of 'capability' of a state rests on its military power. The more capable military power would remain in the controller's position in international politics. During the bipolar period, the United States and the Soviet Union were examples of this proposition. Today, the United States and China may be cited as examples of 'capable' states due to their military power. After identifying the major arguments of different schools of realism (classical, neo-classical, neo-realism), Box 2.5 summarizes the important characteristics of different trends of realism.

**Box 2.5** **Realist Theory in IR: Basic Features and Leading Theorists**

**Classical Realism**

**Basic Features**

- Classical realists were of the opinion that people lived in a condition of total insecurity and lawlessness. This situation was altered by a powerful sovereign state with a strong government.
- The ruler needs to be powerful to resolve conflicts in politics. Classical realists emphasized the primary value of power in statecraft.

**Leading Theorists:** Thucydides, Niccolo Machiavelli, Thomas Hobbes.

**Neo-classical Realism**

**Basic Features**

- Conflicts between states were inevitable in international politics because there was no international regulatory authority to curb conflicts and wars.
- The law of politics is rooted in human nature which is self-seeking, self-interested and power-loving.
- The concept of 'interest defined in terms of power' makes politics autonomous because the concept of 'power' can help to analyse all kinds of politics adequately.
- Ethics in international politics is political or situational ethics, and therefore sharply opposed to private morality.
- Aspirations of a particular state cannot become the governing law of the universe.

- Statecraft is a sober and uninspiring activity that involves a profound awareness of human limitations.

**Leading Theorists:** E. H. Carr, H. J. Morgenthau.

**Neo-realism**

**Basic Features**

- In the contemporary world, the 'threat' of war is more fearsome than actual war.
- For the neo-realists, the structure of the system and its relative distribution of power are the focal points of analysis.
- States which are more 'capable' than others would control international politics.
- Neo-realists are sceptical about the impact of globalization throughout the world.
- The neo-liberal claim that economic interdependence of the world has made the nation-state a minor player in international affairs is not tenable.
- The neo-liberal claim that only free market economy can achieve sustained growth is not true.
- Despite anti-statism, there is no serious rival to challenge and replace the state in international relations.

**Leading Theorists:** K. Waltz, T. Schelling, S. Krasner, R. Gilpin, J. Mearsheimer.

## An Evaluation of Realist Theory

Classical and neoclassical theories of realism were criticized by the liberals and the feminists for their narrow and partial views. For classical and neo-classical realists, power seems to be the only important element in international politics. This makes the theory very narrow and partial. It reduces other aspects of politics such as cooperation, peoples' freedom, nature of the government, values and beliefs of the people, and motivation of the leaders to a negligible level. Again, while highlighting the selfish and evil nature of man, the realists were discarding the human instinct of love and affection. This is only a partial view of reality. Critics argue that realism is a narrowly focused theory. The international scenario does not only reflect the collective behaviour of states in conflict. It also shows states sharing common interests, observing common rules and cooperating in a mutually dependent world. Besides states, there are other significant actors in the global society, such as NGOs, MNCs and INGOs, which are not taken into account by the realists.

Emancipatory theorists—who believe in the social emancipation of people—like Ken Booth and Andrew Linklater, criticize realism as an obsolete theory. They believe that power politics and defence strategies are no longer relevant in the contemporary world. Today security has become a local problem within disorganized, and sometimes failed, states. The scope and character of security has also changed. Security needs to be provided to the global community as a whole against threats such as ecological disaster, poverty, illiteracy, poor education and health facilities. The main thrust of the emancipatory theorists is not on physical security of the people, but on the more general and global problems.

The neo-realist ideas have also been countered by the neo-liberals and the constructivists. Schelling's strategic realism has come under attack from the constructivists. No strategy, however prudent, can be free from normative values. Emphasis on value-free strategies is as dangerous as emphasis on power. Moreover, Waltz's love for structures of the system appears to be partial again. It is not that structures only condition humans, it is also the other way round—humans build and change structures of the political system according to their convenience. But Waltz, due to his obsession for structures, failed to notice the immense potentialities of the individual and groups of people.

However, despite criticisms by many schools of thought in IR, realism continues to be an important theory in the discipline because of its emphasis on power and the significance of the state in international politics. Realism will continue to remain relevant as long as the states pursue power and remain the pivotal actors in world politics.

# The English School (International Society Approach)

## Origin and Intellectual Traditions

IR as an academic discipline was dominated by the Americans for a long time since its beginning around the year 1920. However, a group of scholars based in British universities in general, and London School of Economics and Political Science (LSE) in particular, delved into theoretical and practice-oriented issues in IR since the 1950s. With the establishment of the 'British Committee on the Theory of International Politics (BCTIP)' in January 1959 by Herbert Butterfield, articulation of views from Britain on the nature of international politics influenced the theoretical domain of IR. Scholars attached to LSE and other British universities and people associated with the BCTIP were also interested to find alternatives to realism and liberalism—the two dominant theories in IR at that point of time (that is, post–Second World War). Scholars such as Charles Manning, Herbert Butterfield, Martin Wight, Hedley Bull, Adam Watson, R. J. Vincent and others worked hard to develop an alternative approach to analyse international politics. Gradually these scholars came to be known as the English School in IR. Their views, although diverse, were termed in different ways, like the English School Theory in IR or the International Society Approach in IR, or liberal realism. But in this analysis, with a view to minimize confusion, the name English School Theory (EST) would be used.

The nature of international politics always attracted the attention of scholars. Is the nature of international politics conflict-prone, as claimed by the realists, or is it based on cooperation, as the liberals wanted us to believe? Theorists belonging to the English School tried to analyse the nature of international politics, taking cues from both realism and liberalism. This attempt at incorporating tenets from both realism and liberalism led the EST to be termed also as liberal realism. The English School does not discard realist postulates like states interacting in an anarchic international system, but combines that realist understanding with the idea of a human element emerging from the domestic sphere. The classical English school starts with the realist assumption of an international system that forms as soon as two or more states have a sufficient amount of interactions. In such interactions, anarchy may persist and form the core of enquiry in the process of analysing IR. But despite the existence of anarchy, states also form a society at the international level and develop rules to restrain conflict, with an urge to sustain this society of states.

There are three distinct philosophical traditions that influenced English School theorists in their attempt to analyse international politics. Martin Wight, a classical English School thinker, referred to these three traditions as realism, rationalism and revolutionism, represented by Machiavelli, Grotius and Kant, respectively. Wight believed that these three always operated simultaneously at the international level. Martin Wight and Barry Buzan, a leading protagonist of the EST in the later stages, identified these elements as first, the international system; second, international society; and third, world society. Buzan called these as English School's triad, based on Martin Wight's three traditions of the English School. Idea about these three will help to understand the EST in a significant way. According to Buzan, international system refers to an interaction of states for power. This struggle for power may lead to a conflictual nature of international system as envisaged by Niccolo Machiavelli (1469–1527), and later, by Thomas Hobbes (1588–1679). It puts international anarchy as the centre of IR theory and argues that states in the international system fights for power and supremacy. Therefore, international system, as advocated by the realists, also puts states as most important actor in international politics. Thus, international politics is anarchic in nature due to the conflict of states for power. This conflictual nature of international politics leads to an international system based on anarchy.

The second element, according to Barry Buzan, is international society that thrives on institutionalization of shared interests among states. Hugo Grotius (1583–1645) advocated about the nature of international politics as shared norms and institutions among states. This view was revived by the English School theorists. According to these theorists, shared interest and identity among states form the basis of international society. For the English School, rationalism rather than realism lies at the centre of IR theory. Rationalism puts the creation and maintenance of shared norms, rules and institutions as essential features of international society. Therefore, cooperation among states through shared norms, institutions and rules is also an important element of international politics, apart from the notion of an anarchic system. English School theorists prefer to call this coexistence of states (through shared interests) in international politics as international society.

Barry Buzan (2001) identifies the third element in international politics as world society, composed of non-state actors, individuals and the overall global population as a part of international arrangements. In simple words, the state is not the most important actor in international politics, as the realists believe; non-state actors and human beings, as an individual and a global community, are also important. This position was taken by Immanuel Kant (1724–1804) earlier, and English School theorists revived this Kantian logic (also identified as revolutionism) to analyse international politics. In the world society, the nature of international politics is confined not only to interaction among states (for power), but also to interaction among non-state actors and identities. Even, transcendence of the state into a transnational or global phenomenon is possible in a world society. This transnationalism (or revolutionism) forms the centre of IR theory. However, Buzan believed that this Kantian position was not developed enough by the English School scholars into sound conceptual clarifications.

Therefore, following Martin Wight's classification (which was later emphasized by Barry Buzan), the triad of English School tradition consists of realism (represented by Machiavelli), rationalism (represented by Grotius) and revolutionism (represented by Kant). Later, Wight added Giuseppe Mazzini (1805–72), a leading thinker of revolutionary nationalism, to his triad to make it a four-fold pillar of scholarly tradition for the English School (Wight and Porter, 2005). However, the English School followed Hugo Grotius and his ideas of international society more than the other three traditions. But in the EST, one may find a combination of all traditions. The EST believes that there is a society of sovereign states at the international level despite the existence of anarchy, and this society follows a set of rules to restrain conflict.

## Major Arguments

The position of the EST that there is a society of sovereign states bound by a set of rules despite the existence of anarchy, raises a few questions. How is it possible for the world to be anarchical and social at the same time? How is it possible for the sovereign states to be governed by a set of rules, known as international law? Post-classical English School theorist Hidemi Suganami raised these questions. Suganami attempted to find answers to these crucial questions from the writings of classical English School scholars such as C. A. W. Manning and Hedley Bull (Suganami, 2010). Both Manning and Bull acknowledged the fact that the world contained many entities other than states, which are not the only actors in international politics. All these different entities together form some sort of social system that exhibits complex interactions. However, Manning and Bull did not go much into this complex social system comprising different entities. Their interest was fixed on the formal structure of this international social order, which they viewed as an international society of sovereign states governed by international law (Suganami, 2010). Both Manning and Bull tried to analyse an international society of independent sovereign states, bound by international law. These states communicated among themselves through the institution of diplomacy.

But how a complex international social order of sovereign states is possible, alongside the existence of anarchy? Hedley Bull believes that states are not as vulnerable to anarchy as an individual human being is. For Bull (1977), anarchy has three meanings: absence of rule, disorder and confusion. For an individual, it is difficult to survive anarchy because all three notions of anarchy may follow one after another and threaten his/her existence. However, in the international society, the absence of rule may not be necessarily followed by disorder and confusion. Through the institution of diplomacy, states may diffuse disorder and confusion, if there is any absence of rule. But an individual human being may not be in a position to avoid disorder and confusion. Therefore, states are in a position to survive reasonably well without the kind of protection normally given to an individual within the boundaries of the state. Anarchy entails different connotations for an individual and for the international society. In the international society of sovereign states, anarchy is restrained through institutional arrangements such as diplomacy and a set of rules formed by states. These rules are termed as international law. As a consequence, an international society of sovereign states survives despite the existence of anarchy.

The next important puzzle before the English School theorists was to solve the issue of sovereign states governed by international law. To answer this puzzle, classical English theorists delved deep into the meaning and nature of sovereignty, especially at the international level. They made sharp distinctions in the meaning of sovereignty, as applicable to domestic and international politics. Manning and James believe that a state remains a sovereign state regardless of its international legal obligation so far as it does not become incorporated into another sovereign state (Suganami, 2010). At the international level, a state enters into treaties and legal obligations for various purposes. Sometimes a state enters into treaties and legal obligations to further its national interests. At other times, it may join any legal treaty or contract to help the world and its people to survive. International legal frameworks on environment or human rights may be cited as examples here. When a sovereign state enters into any international legal obligation, for the safeguard of its national interest or for the security of the existing world order, it does so as an independent state, without surrendering its sovereignty. In an international society of independent states, such legal obligations are important and necessary for the survival of the state concerned as well as of the world order. Here, a sovereign state adheres to international law willingly without surrendering its power to decide its own course of action. According to Manning and James, a sovereign state remains sovereign and independent in the international society of states till it is incorporated into another state. Sovereignty therefore is not a hindrance in accepting international law, in fact, adherence to international law may help a sovereign state to further its national interest and promote a sustainable international society.

## Pluralist and Solidarist Divide in the English School

Over the issues of international society and its activities, the English School is divided between a pluralist and a solidarist approach. Scholars such as Hedley Bull were apprehensive about realistic achievements of a society of states working in solidarity to uphold human rights or distributive justice for all in the world. In simple words, Bull believed that the international society of states had not become matured enough to work together to ensure human rights and justice for all people. According to Bull, from a realistic point of view, the world is still at a pluralistic stage where states disagree to achieve the so-called 'higher values' such as protection of human rights and justice (Bull, 2000). For instance, will all the states in the international society agree to use force against a state accused of violating human rights? A realistic answer at this point of time would be in the negative. Therefore, pluralists such as Bull, Vincent and Jackson believe that states, in reality, follow a 'live and let live' approach which should be acknowledged. In a society of sovereign states, not all will think in the same way; plurality and diversity will exist, and that diversity should be respected.

Solidarists, on the other hand, think that the international society must develop a consensus to punish states who fail to protect human rights and distribute justice for all. This is necessary for achieving the goal of a peaceful world order and also to restrain increasing sense of insecurity among people. They prefer humanitarian intervention by the international society against regimes accused of human rights violations or threatening global peace. Contemporary international law does not allow such intervention and use of force for these violations. Solidarists such as Nick Wheeler and others argue that international legal framework must be developed to thwart attempts of states and regimes which violate human rights of people and to ensure justice for all. This is important to achieve a peaceful and developed world where human rights, justice, order, economic and environmental stability would exist. Solidarists among the English School thinkers believe that after the end of the Cold War and superpower rivalry, we should move forward towards achieving an international society that would ensure justice, order, rights, economic progress and environmental protection for all people in the world. This kind of a world would minimize conflicts and help all sovereign states in the international society to live peacefully without insecurity. However, a pluralist like Hedley Bull doubts how much of the solidarist view of a peaceful world order could be achieved in reality.

According to Hidemi Suganami, a leading thinker of the English School, the pluralist–solidarist divide is not an insurmountable one. He thinks that the two sides disagree mainly on what is achievable in the contemporary society of states. Even pluralists would acknowledge, believes Suganami, the fact that there may be some regional groupings of states within which guarantee and protection of human rights may be possible. It may be true that the solidarist view of the international society may have more appeal in the post–Cold War world order looking for inclusive development, the pluralist concern about its feasibility in the contemporary world rests equally on strong foundations (Suganami, 2010). Despite the end of superpower rivalry, the world is still not in a situation where small-scale regional conflicts, or for that matter, large-scale conflicts, would be ruled out. Due to divergence of opinion and national interest, conflicts are possible. Ideologically, inclusive development and protection of human rights of all people of the world should be the goal of a post–Cold War world order; but the question remains, how much of this is achievable in reality today.

**Box 2.6** **English School Theory: Origin, Basic Features and Leading Theorists**

**Origin**

In the late 1950s; in Britain

**Basic Features**

- It wished to provide an alternative to liberalism and realism, the two major theories in IR prevalent after Second World War.
- This school incorporated tenets from liberalism and realism, but provided a new analysis of international politics.
- It believes that an international society of sovereign states is possible despite the existence of anarchy.
- Martin Wight's triad of English School traditions were: (i) realism, following Machiavelli; (ii) rationalism, following Grotius; and (iii) revolutionism, following Kant.
- Wight also added Mazzini later and analysed four intellectual traditions of the English School.
- The English School followed rationalism of Hugo Grotius and his ideas of international society more than the other three traditions.
- However, in EST, one may find a combination of all traditions.
- The EST believes that there is a society of sovereign states at the international level, despite the existence of anarchy, and this society follows a set of rules to restrain conflict
- It is divided between pluralist–solidarist views over the functional issues of the international society.
- The EST gained popularity in the post–Cold War period due to the end of superpower rivalry; and the wish to develop a world order based on protection of human rights, justice, economic and environmental security.
- How far is this world order achievable remains a question.

**Leading Theorists**

*Classical English School Theorists*: Herbert Butterfield, Martin Wight, C. A. W. Manning, Hedley Bull, Adam Watson, Alan James, John Vincent, Andrew Hurrell.

*Post-classical or New English School Theorists*: Barry Buzan, Richard Little, Nick Wheeler, Robert Jackson, Hidemi Suganami.

## A Critique of the EST

By taking a middle road between realism and liberalism, the English School helped in theorizing world politics from a balanced point of view, removed from the pessimism of realist theory and unnecessary optimism of the liberal theory. As international politics since the Second World War is not all about continuous conflict or unbroken peace, views of the English School theorists appear reasonable for analysing global politics. Their focus on both state and non-state actors as well as global population and governance has made the EST a very cogent and important theory in IR in recent times. Further, with the end of the Cold War and superpower rivalry, the danger of anarchy permeating world politics has minimized considerably. After the end of the Cold War, the world is looking to protect human security, economic freedom and environmental safeguards for all people of the world. With a view to achieve these goals, English School scholars prefer to resort to a normative approach, that is, adherence to international laws and legal framework. This way, EST revived normative traditions in IR theory making. Sovereign states of the world must come together to frame and follow international law for the protection of human rights, justice, order, economic freedom and environment. In other words, EST paves ways for the formation of international legal regimes to protect human rights and ensure distributive justice. Scholars of the English School keep faith on diplomacy as an instrument of communication among states. Today, international law and diplomacy are important instruments in the international society of sovereign states. Despite limitations, global governance and international regimes are getting increasing importance in global politics. EST does provide credence and strength to these factors in the post–Cold War international order.

However, there is a lack of clarity in EST over issues of international law and diplomacy. Realist thinkers point out factors such as inadequacy and applicability of international law. Although EST points out the significance of international law, the position of the English School on international law has nowhere been properly and adequately set out. Manning and Bull tried hard to analyse why sovereign states would follow international law, but there were flaws in their arguments. Will a sovereign state continue to follow international law if its national interest remains in danger? The answer would be in the negative. This question puts the efficacy of international law and international regimes in crisis. If it is accepted that in the post–Cold War period, sovereign states would cooperate among themselves and follow international legal framework for their economic interests and environmental concerns, they are also prone to violate international rules to safeguard their national interests. Further, as pluralists among English School theorists argue, diverse nature of the international society with divergent views and interests of sovereign states, make it less prone to solidarity in the present time.

Moreover, EST originated and flourished in the Western world where rule of law, state system and the urge for global citizenship have matured over a long period of time. English School thinkers, classical and post-classical, have put forward their arguments keeping in view Western states and their possible mode of interactions and functions. But a vast majority of states in the world and global population are non-Western. State system and views on international law in these regions are far from matured. Will the concept of international society of states get favourable grounds in these regions? EST faces a real challenge in these relatively new states. Enforcing human rights, justice and order from above, by an international society backed by international rule, as the solidarists in English School think, may not work in these regions. Domestic political considerations and matured handling of sensitive political issues are keys to success in these regions. Is the international society, and unclear international laws, matured enough to work for ensuring human rights and justice in the non-Western world? The EST could not provide any satisfactory answer to this crucial question.

# Critical Theory in IR

## Meaning and Origin

There are four major theoretical traditions in IR, as outlined in the section titled 'Theories and Methodologies' in Chapter 1. These are realism, liberalism, English School (international society) theory and post-positivist theories. Critical theory is an important part of post-positivism in IR. While the other three (realism, liberalism and English School) traditions have been analysed in this chapter, this section will proceed to examine the critical theory in IR.

Critical theory has challenged the mainstream understanding of IR and inspired the development of alternative forms of analysis and approaches. While there are many ideas and views about the meaning of the term 'critical', basically the term has been used to apply reason and critical insight in relation to the emancipation of human beings. Critical theory is committed to the development of a more just and equal world. It does not merely believe in providing theoretical suggestions for the formation of a just world, it wants socio-political actions for the creation of a more egalitarian world and emancipated human beings. This theory goes beyond theoretical boundaries to provide momentum for actions in challenging, resisting and disrupting existing power relations. Critical theory opposes the neo-realist and neo-liberal views of the world and its development, and tries to provide an alternative approach of analysing international politics. This approach, unlike others in the discipline, began with the help of concepts related to political economy, to analyse world politics.

Critical theory was initially influenced by the ideas of Kant, Hegel and Marx. These philosophers were instrumental in the development of the idea of critique, which to them was challenging the existing discourses and power equations. For Kant, critique was 'enlightenment'; to Hegel, it was 'spirit of history'; and to Marx, it was 'emancipation' (Yalvac, 2015). However, the influence of Karl Marx on early critical theorists was more pronounced. There is a rich variety of critical theory ranging from normative to structural to post-structural. Despite the existence of different varieties of critical theorizing, all strands were united in their critique of mainstream research agenda, and the positivist interpretation of world politics, questioning the concept of value-free theoretical and political enquiry. In simple words, critical theorists brought back the tradition of normative political interpretation, which was missing in the positivist phase with excessive emphasis on scientific and value-free analysis. As human beings, society and politics are not value-free; theories and related political actions must not be value–free either. Post-positivism does not believe in analysing social and political issues based on excessive and rigorous scientific tools. As an important part of the post-positivist approaches, critical theory reverts back to normative and value-oriented analysis minus excessive scientism.

Critical theory in social sciences owes a lot to the Frankfurt School. In 1923, Frankfurt Institute for Social Research was established; and subsequently it was attached to Frankfurt University in Germany. The institute remained functional till 1933 when the Nazis came to power. Afterwards, it became increasingly difficult for the Frankfurt School to continue working in Germany. Many leading scholars attached to the institute went to the United States, and this institution was established in New York City, affiliated to Columbia University. The term 'critical theory' became associated with this institute in the United States. After the end of the Second World War and the end of the Nazi rule, the Frankfurt School was re-established in Germany and it continued to operate there without any hindrance. The institute and its leading scholars, who were pioneers in making critical theory relevant for social sciences, were termed as the Frankfurt School. These scholars were Walter Benjamin (1892–1940), Max Horkheimer (1895–1973), Theodor Adorno (1903–69), Erich Fromm (1900–80), Herbert Marcuse (1898–1979) and Jurgen Habermas (1929–). German intellectual tradition and politics in particular, and European thinkers in general, influenced critical theorists. Apart from Kant, Hegel and Marx, the writings of Weber, Simmel, Nietzsche, Gramsci, Derrida and Foucault influenced different threads of critical scholars. German idealist philosophy and theology, and European psychoanalysis in a broader sense, exerted considerable influence on critical theory.

## Major Arguments

Critical theory put the idea of Marxian political economy at the centre of analysis, and early critical theory showed commitment to Marxian views of materialism and socialism. One of the major features of this stance was the belief that a social theory could not accept anything as given or unchangeable. All of social life is a corollary of the economic system; and the role of a social theory was to investigate the ways in which this changed and affected society and its people. A social theory is not only social and political, but a researcher's task is to examine economic, cultural and value preferences of the individual as well. When Max Horkheimer became director of the Institute for Social Research in 1930, he wanted the institute to carry out multidisciplinary studies cutting across traditional academic disciplines. He viewed critical theory as an approach that would examine all aspects of social life, not merely the structures, but also individual, consciousness and the community. As a consequence, the institute began working with ideas from philosophy, the social sciences, the arts, the humanities and other traditions. Horkheimer was critical of social scientists for eliminating philosophy from their analysis and limiting themselves to the study of specific aspects of social life, without considering the society as a whole with its structures and organizations. At the same time, he was critical of some branches of philosophy for limiting themselves to observable facts and the 'scientific method'. As a consequence of these critical tradition, early critical theorists did not resist from criticizing Marxism when it was mechanically materialist or too determinist. In other words, critical theorists saw knowledge in its entirety, not in fragments.

Jurgen Habermas was a key figure among critical theorists and his views have influenced critical theory in IR profoundly. Although Habermas never directly referred to international politics (his concern was primarily individual society), his ideas of communicative action, discourse ethics and analysis of the relation between knowledge and human interests have strengthened alternative critical views within IR. The ideas of Habermas centre round radical democratization of society. His belief in the ideals of enlightenment led him to think that universal moral principles can be the basis of resolution of conflicting claims in social and political life. For Habermas, although modernity has achieved technological progress, it has not yet brought freedom, solidarity and emancipation of human beings. Therefore, he wishes to find a path where human freedom and progress can be united again under modern conditions (Yalvac, 2015). He believes that historical materialism, as viewed by Marx, should also be reconstructed in a way to harness the potential for social communication and mutual understanding among people, rather than simply analysing society on the basis of labour and production. Habermas made a move from a philosophy of consciousness to a philosophy of language, making a major shift in Western philosophical tradition. The philosophy of language allows for the communication and understanding of diverse identities and interests. This concept also facilitates a pluralist understanding of social reality. This view brings Habermas closer to many postmodernist thinkers (Yalvac, 2015).

Habermas introduced the idea of a 'pure communicative sociation' defined as an 'ideal speech situation' in which the actors can freely and truthfully communicate (Habermas, 1984, 1985). In this situation, the 'force of the better argument' prevails. Thus, rationality is formulated so that it does not solely imply a universality of norms but a discursive and procedural context of an ideal speech situation. History is re-conceptualized as a collective learning process whereby the species not only acquires technical knowledge for domination of nature but also develops new norms of communication in the moral-practical sphere (Yalvac, 2015).

Habermas links his views on communicative rationality to what he calls knowledge constitutive interests (Habermas, 1972). This refers to the role of knowledge in achieving different forms of social arrangements. He argues that 'knowledge generated by positivism is not the only type of knowledge oriented to fulfill the needs of social life. Positivism conceives of social problems as technical problems that require technical solutions. However, knowledge of the social world should be based not only on social control but also on communication and human emancipation' (Yalvac, 2015). Habermas made a distinction among 'technical cognitive interests' in which knowledge is seen as the basis for controlling one's environment; and 'practical cognitive interests' that seek to promote inter-subjective communication between different subjects; and 'emancipatory cognitive interests', a guiding communication that deals with the conditions of distorted communication and the conditions necessary to achieve autonomy and freedom (Yalvac, 2015). In the post-positivist phase, emancipatory cognitive interests will help human beings in society to harness the potential of autonomy and freedom.

## Critical Theory and IR

Since the early 1980s, a group of scholars involved with IR theory addressed new epistemological and normative questions in IR, under the influence of critical theory. Scholars such as Richard Ashley, Robert W. Cox, Andrew Linklater, John Maclean and Mark Hoffman began to argue, in different ways, about the idea of emancipation of people in the world. Under the influence of emancipatory ideas ranging from Kant to Marx to Habermas, the group of IR scholars delved into the possibilities of achieving universal freedom and equality. Mainstream IR theories such as realism and liberalism remained essentially conservative in the sense that these theories wanted to continue with the maintenance of state power. Critical IR theory, on the other hand, sought to develop knowledge that might contribute to the progressive and emancipatory transformation of the international order. This theory wanted to know the historical structures of international power, and how changes could be made in these structures. In simple words, critical theory in IR is not just another scholarly discourse on the maintenance of the state and global power structures, but it was also a concerted attempt to bring changes in these power structures. Critical theory in IR is different from a 'traditional' theory (such as realism or liberalism) in terms of a practical purpose. This theory is critical to the extent that it seeks human emancipation, what Horkheimer called, 'to liberate human beings from the circumstances that enslave them'.

Mark Hoffman, Robert Cox and Andrew Linklater made significant contributions in introducing critical theory to the theoretical domain of IR as an academic discipline. Mark Hoffman's essay, *Critical Theory and the Inter-paradigm Debate* (1987), signifies one of the first efforts to introduce arguments of critical theory in the discipline of IR. Hoffman believed that limitations of critical theory must be underlined while presenting it as an important paradigm in the discipline of IR. Andrew Linklater, in his essay *The Question of the Next Stage in International Relations Theory* (1992), emphasized on the need for 'emancipatory ideas' to be included within the realm of IR theory. Human beings deserve to be made equal, free and emancipated domestically as well as internationally, an idea that 'traditional' theories such as realism, liberalism and English School failed to comprehend because of their excessive concerns with the state as a seminal actor in global politics. Linklater identified three areas of critical theory in IR: normative, sociological and praxeological. The first two (normative and sociological) spheres refer to the individuals, groups and states; shared moral commitments to international justice and freedom; and to the historical and social structures of the international system. The praxeological sphere refers to human governance, and how human actions are directed towards universal ideals of freedom, equality and justice. Linklater believed that open-ended dialogue between and among citizens enhanced chances for harmony at the international level. Whereas Robert Cox preferred to work with ideas of hegemonic and counter hegemonic discourses, Linklater drew on Habermas' discourse ethics and theory of historical development to identify the potential of modern states to move beyond the state system in the context of world order.

According to some scholars, critical theory in IR may be classified as per four general positions (Patrascu and Wani, 2015). First, neo-Gramscian works on global political economy and international politics, as reflected in the work of Robert Cox. Second, normative and explanatory theory as inspired by the Frankfurt School in general, and Jurgen Habermas in particular, and reflected in the work of Andrew Linklater. Third, postmodernist work, such as that of Richard Ashley, R. B. J. Walker, James Der Derian and M. Shapiro. Their studies were largely inspired by a range of postmodernist and poststructuralist philosophers, including Jacques Derrida and Michel Foucault. Fourth, the feminist work such as that of Jean Elshtain, Cynthia Enloe, Christine Sylvester and Ann Tickner. Feminist scholars were influenced by a very wide range of traditions (including Marxism, the Frankfurt School and postmodernism). All these strands, although diverse in perceptions, have a common element: critical in approach and analysis.

Arguments put forward by critical theorists such as Andrew Linklater help to identify, according to scholars (Patrascu and Wani, 2015), a few contributions of critical theory in the realm of IR as listed here:

i. Critical theory in IR contests the methodology of 'positivism' and wants to bring back normative traditions in analysis, theory and activism.
ii. It opposes the idea that the existing social structures of the world are immutable and tries to examine the prospects for greater freedom inherent within existing social relations.
iii. It endeavours to overcome the flaws in Marxism by emphasizing forms of social learning, following Habermas' reconstruction of historical materialism. This is done in conformity with 'emancipatory' ideas .
iv. The theory advances ideas of open discourse not only between fellow citizens but also between all members of the human race, with enlightenment and universalism as guiding principles.

Robert Cox believes that there are major differences between critical theory in IR and traditional theories in the discipline. He prefers to call traditional theories, such as realism and liberalism, problem-solving theories. Problem-solving theories have two main characteristics: first, a positivist methodology; and second, providing legitimacy to existing social and political structures. By contrast, as Richard Devetak points out, 'critical international theory starts from the conviction that cognitive processes themselves are subject to political interests and so ought to be critically evaluated. Theories of international relations, like any knowledge, necessarily are conditioned by social, cultural and ideological influence, and one of the main tasks of critical theory is to reveal the effect of this conditioning' (Devetak, 2001). In simple words, critical theorists believe that our knowledge is influenced by political, social and cultural interests; and critical theory in IR tries to unearth these influences. In this endeavour, critical theory in IR prefers a post-positivist methodology.

**Box 2.7** **Critical Theory in IR: Origin, Source, Basic Features and Leading Theorists**

**Origin**

Early 1980s

**Source**

*Early Intellectual Inspiration*: Immanuel Kant, George W. F. Hegel, Karl Marx, Max Weber, Georg Simmel, Friedrich Nietzsche, Antonio Gramsci.

*Later Intellectual Inspiration*

**Frankfurt School:** Walter Benjamin, Max Horkheimer, Theodor Adorno, Erich Fromm, Herbert Marcuse and Jurgen Habermas.

**Basic Features**

- Under the influence of emancipatory ideas ranging from Kant to Marx to Habermas, it delves into the possibilities of achieving universal freedom and equality.

- It wants to know the historical structures of international power, and how changes could be made in these structures.
- Critical theory contests the methodology of 'positivism' and wants to bring back normative traditions in analysis, theory and activism.
- It opposes the idea that the existing social structures of the world are immutable and tries to examine the prospects for greater freedom inherent within existing social relations.
- By emphasizing forms of social learning, following Habermas' reconstruction of historical materialism, it endeavours to overcome the flaws in Marxism.
- It advances ideas of open discourse not only between fellow citizens, but also among all members of the human race, with enlightenment and universalism as guiding principles.
- Critical theory believes that our knowledge is influenced by political, social and cultural interests; tries to unearth these influences; and prefers a post-positivist methodology.

**Leading Theorists:** Richard Ashley, Mark Hoffman, Robert W. Cox, Andrew Linklater, Jacques Derrida, Michel Foucault, Cynthia Enloe, Christine Sylvester and Ann Tickner (The last three for their contributions to feminist critical theory in IR).

## A Critique of the Critical Theory in IR

Critical theory in IR has added strength to the discipline in many ways. Following Habermas, critical theorists in IR have placed emphasis on 'emancipatory cognitive interests', which refers to conditions necessary to achieve autonomy and freedom of human beings. In the post-positivist phase, 'emancipatory cognitive interests' will help individuals harness the potential of autonomy and freedom. In other words, critical theorists wanted to see knowledge as impetus for activism for creating a world where justice, equality and freedom for all human beings prevails. Critical theory wants a closer relationship between new understanding in knowledge and political actions to use the new understanding for changing the existing world order. Any contribution that academic discourses could make to change the world would be through adopting the attitude of critique—by posing constant challenges to earlier narratives, and the power relations they project. Critical theory introduced this important element of constructive academic critique to the discipline of IR. Therefore, theoretical understanding has become more matured and relevant for our knowledge of the contemporary world, and ways to change it. Many issues of contemporary importance, such as identity politics, global economic processes and terrorism, could not be understood adequately with earlier theoretical resources available within the discipline. Critical theory has enabled scholars to develop a more matured understanding of the historical development of the world and its complex social processes.

These theoretical strengths notwithstanding, critical theory in IR has been subjected to many criticisms. One major critique against critical theory is its euro-centric and Western-centric bias. Like other major theories in the discipline (realism, liberalism, English School), critical theory was predominantly European and Western. Seen from this perspective, it offered nothing new. J. M. Hobson believes that even when it is critical of the West and Western imperialism, most Marxist analyses of IR, discourses on political economy and neo-Gramscian approaches suffered from an essentially euro-centric bias (Hobson, 2007). Contemporary world has witnessed the rise of non-Western societies like China, Brazil, South Korea and India. Social and political processes in these countries are different from the Western world. Critical theory, with its euro-centric understanding, would appear inadequate to address human interactions and possibilities of change in these societies. With ideas of development rooted in Western societies, critical theory seems to possess limited understanding of the development processes and their critique in non-Western societies. Thus, critical theory appears less inclusive, like other West-oriented theories, in covering socio-political processes in the postcolonial and developing world.

Further, critical theory failed to provide a definitive answer as to how emancipation of human beings would be achieved. There were many divergent views among critical theorists on the issue of relationship between understanding the world and ways to change it. Critical scholars appeared directionless about achieving a free and fair world, based on freedom, equality and justice for all, although they referred to these issues frequently. On the question of human emancipation, there were differences among normative, neo-Gramscian and post-structuralist views within the critical scholars. Moreover, critical theorists were also unsure about how knowledge could be transformed effectively into activism. Robert Cox candidly agreed that he was better placed to 'theorize' the world than to engage in a neo-Gramscian activism to organize a counter-hegemonic block (Cox, 2002), although he was not averse to the creation of this block. Habermas also saw dangers in crossing the limit between a theorist and an activist (Calhoun, 1997). In other words, critical scholars held divergent views about knowledge of the world and ways to change it. They were unsure about crossing limits between academia and active politics.

Feminist strand within critical theory questions masculine domination in the realm of thought in IR. Feminist critical theorists such as Cynthia Enloe, Christine Sylvester and Ann Tickner believe that history and structure of, and knowledge about, IR are all gendered. As observed later in this chapter, feminist scholars of IR have shown how the formation of the state and the 'international society' of states have helped the construction of gender differences through divisions such as private/public, state/society and domestic/international. Although critical about traditional theories in IR, feminist perceptions about social and political processes of the world and its possible changes differ from the normative and neo-Gramscian scholars within the critical realm of thought.

Despite all such divergent views about knowledge, human emancipation, state and non-state actors, communication and activism, critical theory was able to raise many vital questions about theories and methodologies in the discipline of IR. It proved successful in igniting the now famous 'fourth debate' in the discipline of IR, surrounding post-positivist ways of thinking, to analyse and change our contemporary world.

# Marxist Theory in IR

The Marxist theory in IR would be difficult to understand without a basic idea of Marxism. Broadly speaking, the writings of Karl Marx and his friend Frederick Engels constitute the basic premises of Marxism. Later on, the views of socialist leaders like Vladimir Lenin, Joseph Stalin, Mao Zhe Dong and several academicians and scholars were added to the Marxist political philosophy. The neo-Marxists have also added fresh dimensions to Marxist ideology to make it academically more rich, time-worthy and relevant in today's world. The following are a few basic tenets of Marxist political philosophy, as developed by Marx and Engels.

i. The Marxist idea of dialectical materialism holds the view that change is inevitable in nature and in society; and changes must be qualitative rather than merely quantitative.
ii. The Marxist view of historical materialism argues that in all hitherto existing societies (except primitive communism), there were class divisions among people based on their relations to property and means of production; and changes always took place through class struggles (clash of interests of opposing classes).
iii. Classes are mainly economic groupings of people based on their relation to the production process in the society. Thus, those who own the means of production belong to one class, and those who do not belong to another class.
iv. Although class divisions existed in all societies except in case of primitive communism, antagonism among classes reached its peak in the capitalist society, which ultimately was divided into two classes: the capitalists (the owning class) and the proletariat (the non-owning class).
v. Excessive production and profit motive of the capitalists led to severe exploitation of the proletariat in the capitalist society. Unable to bear with such extreme form of exploitation, the proletariat consolidates as a class on the basis of economic, political and ideological similarities, and wages a class struggle against the capitalists. In this class struggle, the proletariat wins and establishes, gradually, the socialist society which is free of classes and class divisions.
vi. The state was created by the owning class to safeguard its interests and to oppress the non-owning class through different mechanisms, such as the police. Therefore the state, in Marxist view, served the interests of the owning class and became a tool for oppression. When class division ends in the socialist society, the state will have no role to play in the society, and therefore, will 'wither away'.
vii. Proletariats all over the world are exploited, and therefore share common interests. They are not bound by national borders or national interests, because their agony everywhere in the world is the same—they are exploited to the tilt by the capitalists. The proletarian revolution is, therefore, international in character.
viii. Economic issues in the society constitute the base in Marxist political philosophy; every other aspect, such as politics, culture, education or religion, remain at the super-structural level, dependent on economic factors (the base).

Although the whole gamut of Marxist philosophy is not as simple as presented here, nevertheless these basic ideas would help us to properly understand the Marxist theory of IR.

The Marxist view of the world is determined by the rise of capitalism and its impact on human relations. At a certain stage in the development of history, Marx and Engels observed in their book *Communist Manifesto*, that capitalism played a progressive role in eradicating the irrational and superstitious feudal system and introducing rational and scientific ways of thinking. Yet, capitalism soon turned into a system that divided people on the basis of ownership of the means of production. The owning class, by means of its economic power, cornered state (political) power to safeguard its interests. With a view to augment production and garner more profit, the capitalists started exploiting the non-owning people by denying them basic economic, social and political freedoms. Through this process of exploitation, capitalism also brought about, unknowingly, solidarity in international working class movement. The rise of capitalism, therefore, was a turning phase in human history and IR, because it gave birth to possibilities of ending existing social relations and generating new ones that would help to create different and new IR.

The Marxist critique of the capitalist system is still much relevant in IR with the onset of globalization, which is viewed as a global movement of capital, goods and labour. It is possible for the rich capitalist states to control this global movement, and dominate in international politics. The liberal and neo-realist critics of Marxism wanted to prove that Marxism had made no contribution to the study of IR, because in the Marxist philosophy state, nationalism and cooperation or conflict among states had little relevance. If IR is primarily concerned with interactions among nation-states, the Marxist philosophy does not fit into it because it does not have any interest in nation-states, their struggle for supremacy, national interests and politics for power among states. But this criticism is not valid because classical and neo-Marxist thinkers proved quite relevant for the study of IR. Classical Marxist thinkers like Lenin and Bukharin developed the theory of imperialism, which they considered as an advanced stage of capitalism. At this stage of development of capitalism, new mercantilist states emerged. These states were willing to use force to achieve their economic and political goals, resulting in further crises in capitalism and estrangement of the proletariat from the capitalist system. Lenin and Bukharin argued that the First World War was the product of a desperate need for new markets for the surplus capital accumulated by the dominant mercantilist states. The tendency of the mercantilist state to find new outlets for its accumulated surplus capital led to a severe struggle among these states that shattered the promise of a peaceful international order, advanced by the liberals. Lenin's and Bukharin's views on imperialism—that it would create severe competition, even struggle, among states for markets, and shatter the notion of interdependence and peace among nations—thus served as a critique of the liberal position. Their study of imperialism also strengthened Marx's original proposition that developed capitalism would face increasing internal crises.

Contemporary Marxists have largely drawn from their classical comrades to build their ideas on development and underdevelopment. But they have also made some significant departures from the classical Marxists who believed in the progressive side of capitalism that would facilitate industrial development for all peoples. Dependency theorists, for instance, argued that 'peripheral' societies failed to achieve industrial development because of the dominant class interests of the capitalists in the 'core' and the 'periphery'. Underdeveloped peripheral societies must detach themselves from the world capitalist economy to achieve autonomous industrial development. This view is linked to the process of globalization as well, which the liberal thinkers claim would help in achieving unprecedented economic growth. The dependency theorists believe that due to the shared class interests of the capitalists in all parts of the world, globalization would not be able to bring about equal development for all people, and end exploitative tendencies of the 'core' over the 'periphery'. World System theorists like Wallerstein also disagreed with the classical Marxist view in the progressive role of capitalism to bring about industrial development in all parts of the world. But classical- and neo-Marxists share the view that class interests of the capitalists know no boundaries, and these are exploitative and dominant in all parts of the world. These exploitative class interests of the capitalists would create unbridgeable gap between the rich and the poor peoples of the world. The proletariat must rise above national interests to introduce change in this international order, and aim for a class-less society to achieve IR based on equitable relations among people. Present IR are dominated by the interests of the capitalists. This could be ascertained from the fact that capitalists of 'core' and 'peripheral' societies join hands to exploit the poor people, and to justify the existing international order. Only through the establishment of socialist class-less societies across the world, the present exploitative nature of IR could be changed. For that end, the proletariat of the world, cutting across national boundaries and national interests, would have to unite and struggle for change of the existing international order.

This analysis of the Marxist theory of IR helps us to identify the basic assumptions of the theory. They are presented in Box 2.8.

**Box 2.8** **Marxist Theory of IR: Basic Features and Leading Theorists**

**Basic Features**

- Marxist theory of IR is based on some of the main principles of Marxism, such as dialectical materialism, historical materialism and class struggle.
- The economically dominant class in almost every society cornered social and political power and exploited the poor people.
- Class division and exploitation of one class by another reached its peak in the capitalist society.
- Excess production and profit motive led to extreme exploitation of the proletariat in the capitalist society.
- Excess production also generates conflicts—among the capitalists for new outlets to sell the produced goods—and crises in advanced capitalism.
- The First World War was an example of such conflicts. Search for new outlets also resulted in imperialism.
- Marxist views on imperialism served as a critique of the liberal theory in IR that late capitalism brings in a cooperative and peaceful world order based on free-trade interdependence among states. Views on imperialism also strengthen Marx's original position that advanced capitalism would face internal crises.
- Neo-Marxists believe 'peripheral' societies remain underdeveloped due to common class interests of the capitalists in 'core' and 'peripheral' societies. Globalization could not generate equitable economic development for all people.
- Present international relations are dominated by capitalists across the world, and need to be changed.
- With the establishment of class-less socialist societies in every part of the world, new international relations based on equality of all people could be built.
- For bringing about such changes in IR, the proletariat must rise above national identities and national interests, because they have no state to serve their causes.

**Leading Theorists:** Karl Marx, Frederick Engels, Vladimir Lenin, Joseph Stalin, Mao Zhe Dong, Nikolai Bukharin, Leon Trotsky, Antonio Gramsci

## An Evaluation of Marxist Theory of IR

Major criticisms of the Marxist theory of IR came from the liberals and the neo-realists. The liberals think that with the disintegration of the Soviet Union, Marxist view of IR lost its relevance.

The end of the Soviet Union, according to the liberals, marked a triumph of capitalism over socialism, a reality the Marxists failed to comprehend. The present international order has been shaped according to the liberal-democratic ideology which the Marxists termed as capitalist philosophy. Whatever be the terminology, liberal-democratic or capitalist, the fact remains that the present world has never developed according to the Marxist view. With the eclipse of the Soviet Union, the socialist ideology has been declared as non-existent by the liberals.

Neo-realists like Kenneth Waltz have argued that for the proletariat, national identity comes before proletarian internationalism. Waltz believed that during the First World War members of the proletariat found that they had more in common with their own national bourgeoisie than with the proletariat of other states. In every country of Europe, the proletariat demonstrated nationalistic feelings manifested by its support for the state and for war. So, the idea of proletariat internationalism is absurd and based upon utopian premises. This major flaw in Marxism results due to economic reductionism, which identifies that economic interests of classes propel them to transcend national boundaries.

Not all these criticisms appear to be correct. For instance, the disintegration of the Soviet Union did not mark an end to socialism or a triumph of capitalism; it rather revealed the ugly face of party bureaucracy. The Communist Party in the Soviet Union usurped all power and allowed nepotism and corruption to enter into the party. As a consequence, the party was estranged from the people. Capitalist elements took the opportunity to replace a corrupt and weak party. Some contemporary, Western experts of IR—Andrew Linklater, for example—believe that Marxism has not lost its relevance after the end of the Soviet Union, and the onset of globalization. Linklater identified four major contributions of Marxism to the study of IR. First, the materialist analysis of history, and ideas of production, property relations and class, are immensely strong to oppose the realist views which hold that power and national interests constitute the core in international politics. Second, Marxism was concerned with international inequality generated by capitalist globalization. Third, the global spread of capitalist modernity helps in the development process of modern societies and the conduct of their IR. Fourthly, analyses of IR and globalization get a critical outlook from the Marxists. Globalization and international political economy (IPE) are analysed much objectively by the neo-Marxists, who believe that these are not ubiquitously beneficial for people. These views, in effect, strengthen the discussions on globalization and IPE.

It is wrong to assume that Marxism has no relevance in the study of IR. On the contrary, Marxist philosophy has been credited with generating a new series of critical theories in IR which attempt to analyse IR from a new angle distinct from the two main traditional schools of IR theory: the liberal school and the realist school. Marxist interpretation of the development of advanced capitalism proved somewhat right with controversies surrounding the concept of globalization in today's world.

## World System Theory

Some scholars of IR, Marxist in orientation, developed the WST to analyse the postcolonial international order where, according to them, regional class divisions and exploitation exist because of the capitalist nature of the world economy. For the protagonists of the WST, class divisions have assumed a regional character in the postcolonial world which is divided into 'core' and 'periphery' regions in terms of wealth accumulation and economic development. In the postcolonial international order, the rich industrial regions of the world form the core, and the vast impoverished third world regions constitute the periphery. Throughout centuries, the core exploited the periphery and accumulated wealth that helped the core regions to build industrial infrastructure. The core regions mostly manufacture goods by using capital which these regions have accumulated in plenty. The peripheral regions mostly supply raw materials and cheap labour to the core, but are neglected by the core as far as capital flow to the periphery is concerned. Thus, according to WST, the present world system is highly unequal because in this system the core dominates over the periphery by means of its economic strength. The core represents mostly the owning class, whereas the periphery represents mainly the non-owning class.

The core uses its economic strength to garner political power and to act as the centre in this new world system. The centre wants to shape this new world order according to its interests. The centre coerces the periphery to accept its diktats, and the periphery sometimes succumbs to such diktats. However, the core and the periphery are not strictly homogeneous categories. Internal crisis, which is typical in the capitalist economic system, may also affect the core. For instance, protagonists of WST like Immanuel Wallerstein, Andre Gunder Frank, Samir Amin and Giovanni Arrighi have pointed out that the two world wars and several other regional wars resulted due to the clash of interests of the core states over the right to dominate and exploit the periphery. The periphery again is not strictly an exclusive category. Within the periphery there may again be centres and peripheries. Thus, the city of Mumbai may be termed as a centre while rural Maharashtra may be described as a periphery. This distinction may also be there in the core regions. The city of Toronto, for instance, makes the centre whereas Winnipeg may form the periphery.

In WST there is also a notion of 'semi-periphery'. It is an area where some industrial bases have been built, manufacturing of goods has commenced on a moderate scale, and some accumulation of wealth has taken place; but compared to the advanced core regions they are minimal. But the semi-periphery is economically more developed than the periphery. For instance, Singapore or Taiwan may be considered as semi-peripheries as compared to Bangladesh or Bhutan which could be treated as peripheral states in the present world system. A semi-periphery is somewhere between the core and the periphery and may act as a bridge between the two. The former East Bloc countries could also be seen as semi-peripheries. The core tries to dominate both over the periphery and the semi-periphery in order to control the world system. The class struggle in today's world could take place between the core and the periphery; and in any such class struggle the semi-periphery and the periphery would be treated as one class because the interest of the two would converge against the vastly different capitalist interests of the core. Hence the capitalist class interest in the core.

Some Western scholars of IR like Edward Friedman and William Thompson suggest that there could be upward and downward mobility among the core, the semi-periphery and the periphery. According to them, it is possible for a semi-peripheral state to move upward and join the core. Similarly, a periphery can move upward and become a semi-periphery. Conversely, a core state may go downward to become a semi-periphery. But supporters of WST have never hinted at such possibilities. While it is arguably possible for a periphery to become a semi-periphery, it is difficult to imagine that any core state in today's world would go downward and turn into a semi-periphery. The high level of wealth accumulation of a core state may prevent it from going downward and turning into a semi-periphery.

Some IR scholars, influenced by Marxism, have developed the dependency theory to explain the plight of the third world countries. Some basic assumptions of the dependency theory come closer to WST, although these two theories are different in the long run. Mostly developed by Latin American scholars like Fernando Henrique Cardoso and Enzo Faletto, the dependency theory puts forward the argument that accumulation of capital in a third world country cannot sustain itself internally. They provided instances from Latin American countries to show that a nation's own capital was not adequate enough for its overall economic development. Due to its long colonial past, a third world country became perennially dependent on advanced states. A dependent country, even if it accumulates self-sustaining capital, must borrow foreign capital to produce goods, repay debts and build infrastructure for development.

Although the dependency theorists do not highlight the overall structural pattern of the world advanced by WST—like centre and periphery—they focus on the disadvantageous conditions of the peripheral states. For instance, the issue of economic development in a peripheral state is dependent on several conditions, some of which are internal, some external. Internal conditions include the class relationship within the society, the country's history, and the present political system. External conditions comprise the presence of foreign capital, the MNCs, and global economic and political preferences. The national government of a peripheral state has little control over these internal and external conditions, and as a consequence, its developmental efforts suffer. In this context, dependency theorists have coined the idea of 'enclave economy' in which foreign capital is invested in a peripheral country in order to extract raw materials like minerals and plantations, but the sale of products from these raw materials takes place in foreign lands. As a result, the local enclave (state) does not benefit economically, except some jobs for a small group of population. But its natural resources get depleted in the process and the enclave continues to suffer from lack of development. In another form of dependency that emerged in the postcolonial era, the local capitalist class controls production, sells products in local and foreign markets, earns profits, and reinvests these profits in (national) capitalist-controlled local production to earn more profits. This cycle helps to build a strong local bourgeois class which is not different in orientation from the foreign bourgeoisie, because its interests converge with the interests of the foreign capitalists. This class is more concerned with its own profits, makes haphazard industrialization within the state, and is not interested in the overall development of the country. These local capitalists constitute the centre within the periphery, while majority of the poor population and the areas which they inhabit remain the periphery within the periphery. As a consequence development suffers immensely in third world countries. This analysis of WST helps us to identify the basic features of the theory and its leading proponents. They are presented in Box 2.9.

**Box 2.9** **World System Theory: Basic Features and Leading Theorists**

**Basic Features**

- Influenced by Marxism and its idea of accumulation of wealth.
- Class divisions have assumed a regional character in the postcolonial world.
- The world is divided into 'core' and 'periphery' regions (in terms of wealth accumulation), a system in which the rich capitalist core regions dominate over the poor periphery, mainly the third world regions.

- Semi-periphery is not as advanced as the core, but ahead of the periphery in terms of wealth accumulation.
- There may be core (centre) and periphery within the 'core' and 'periphery' regions; the new class struggle would involve the core and the periphery.
- Dependency theory, which comes closer to WST, suggests that due to historical reasons, the third world remains dependent on external foreign capital.
- 'Enclave Economy' and national capitalists are responsible for underdevelopment in the third world region.

**Leading Theorists:** I. Wallerstein, A. G. Frank, S. Amin, F. H. Cardoso, E. Faletto (Dependency Theory).

## An Evaluation of WST

The WST has been criticized by the neo-liberals as a poor replication of Marxism and its ideas of wealth accumulation and class division. By indicating class division on a regional basis, WST has created further confusion. For instance, it is difficult to assume that capitalists of a region would always share same class interests and would transcend nationalism for common economic interests. For the neo-realists, nationalism is more important in international affairs than class conflicts based on common economic interests of opposing classes. In other words, neo-realists believe that causes of conflict in IR are rooted in power aspirations of nations, and not in class consciousness of people in a region. Moreover, the economic base of class has also been criticized by neo-liberals. Classes may also be formed on the basis of political power or social configuration (and not only on economic factors), in both 'core' and 'periphery' regions; but the proponents of WST have ignored this reality.

Wallerstein argued that capitalism failed to bring about industrial development in the periphery, but suggested that some industrial development had taken place in the semi-periphery. This view of Wallerstein, a leading protagonist of WST, remained quite unclear. A semi-periphery did not emerge overnight; it grew out of a periphery. If this proposition is correct, then it would not be difficult to assume that some wealth accumulation had taken place in the periphery itself, facilitating, in a very small scale, the process of industrialization in the periphery. In other words, roots of industrialization originated in the periphery, and flourished, to some extent, in the semi-periphery. Therefore, local capitalists did initiate some industrialization in the periphery. If one recalls core (centre) and periphery regions within a periphery as advanced by the proponents of WST, then the role of national capitalists living in the core area within the periphery could not be ignored.

The current trading pattern in the world, however, justifies some of the views of WST. The 'core' countries of the West export more manufactured goods, chemicals and machinery than their imports of these items. The 'periphery' regions of Asia, Africa and Latin America export more agricultural products, minerals and textiles; and import more machinery, chemicals and other important technologies from the West. As these items are more costly than agricultural and textile products, the periphery does not benefit much economically, and remains dependent on the core. The core uses its economic advantage to gain political mileage, and acts as the 'centre' in world politics. Therefore WST helps, to some extent, in analysing current trends in international affairs.

# Game Theory

Originally conceived by the Hungarian–American mathematician John Von Neumann, game theory has been widely applied in social sciences since the 1950s. At later stages, the theory was reinforced by the works of scholars like Osker Morgenstern, Anatol Rapoport, Martin Shubik and John Nash. The theory has been useful in analysing situations of conflict, competition and cooperation. It became popular with social scientists because for every society and every state, these issues are important. The theory also finds its application in IR, because conflict, competition and cooperation among nation-states form important areas of discussion in the discipline. Game theory helps in explaining and addressing social problems. Since games often reflect real situations—especially competitive or cooperative situations—they can suggest strategies or ways for dealing with such circumstances. As we may understand the strategy of players in a particular game, we may also be able to predict how people, political factions or nation-states will behave in a given situation.

Situations in the real world, including IR, may replicate any game. Just as players normally try to win games, people in real life also try to win or achieve their goals in competitive situations. However, both in games and in the real world, we have to follow a set of rules to pursue, and finally achieve, our interests or goals. Some games, like some real situations, are intensely competitive, where only one player can win. Chess is an example of such a game. Other games, like football or baseball, require cooperation to win. Similarly, in the real world, some situations demand cooperation even during times of hostility; because rivals here generally share common interests, and must cooperate to some degree for the sake of such common interests. During the Cold War, for instance, despite an intense East–West rivalry, America and the Soviet Union had to cooperate to achieve their common interest of averting a nuclear war.

Game theory usually supports a decision-making approach based on the assumption of rationality of players in a situation of competition. Each player tries to maximize gains or minimize losses under conditions of uncertainty and incomplete information. This situation requires each player to rank preferences, estimate probabilities, and try to discern what the other player is going to do. During the Cold War, both the United States and the USSR played such a game of 'one-upmanship'. Both wanted to maximize their gains, or at best tried to minimize their losses under conditions of uncertainty. The game theory suggests several types of games. For example, in a two-person *zero-sum* game, what one player (or actor) wins, the other loses; if A wins 7, B loses 7, and the outcome is zero. The 'Prisoner's Dilemma', analysed later, is an example of this zero-sum game. In a two-person *non-zero* or *variable sum* game, gains and losses are not necessarily equal; it is possible that both sides may gain. This is sometimes referred to as a *positive-sum* game. In some games, both parties may lose, and by different amounts or to a different degree. The so-called *n-person* game includes more than two actors or sides. IR today resembles, to some extent, the n-person game.

Game theory may help in examining strategic interactions among two or more participants. By using easy, sometimes numerical, models to study complex social (including international) relations, this theory can analyse the potential for, and dangers of, cooperative behaviour among distrustful and competing participants. It has five major concepts:

i. *players* or decision-makers;
ii. *strategies* available to each player, which take into account the potential behaviour of opponents;
iii. *rules* governing players' behaviour;
iv. *outcome*, each of which is a result of particular choices made by players at a given point in the game;
v. *pay-off*, accrued by each player as a result of each possible outcome.

The theory assumes that in any game each player would pursue strategies within a set of rules that help him or her to achieve the most profitable outcome in every situation, and get the maximum pay-offs. In the field of IR, nation-states are the players or actors who pursue strategies to achieve the most profitable outcome. In order to achieve a mutually productive outcome, the states must coordinate their strategies, because if each state pursues its greatest potential pay-offs, the shared outcome is unproductive. This confusion has been illustrated by the 'prisoner's dilemma' game. This and other games illustrate the potential for cooperation to produce mutually beneficial outcomes. However, they also highlight the difficulties of obtaining cooperation among distrustful participants, because each player is tempted to pursue his or her individual interests. Cooperation requires that both players compromise, and forego their individual maximum pay-offs. Yet, in compromising, each player risks complete loss if the opponent decides to seek the maximum pay-off. Rather than risking total loss, players tend to prefer the less productive outcome.

## Prisoner's Dilemma: An Example of the *Zero-Sum* Game

'Prisoner's dilemma' is one of the important games propagated by the game theory. It illustrates the paradoxical nature of interaction between two suspicious participants with opposing interests. In this hypothetical situation, two accomplices in a crime are imprisoned, and they enter into a pact not to betray one another and not to confess the crime. The severity of the punishment that each may receive is determined not only by their behaviour, but also by the behaviour of their accomplices. The two prisoners are separated and cannot communicate with each other. Each is provided with four possible outcomes:

i. if one confesses to the crime and puts the blame on the accomplice—thereby *defecting* from the pact—their sentence would be reduced;
ii. if one confesses, but their accomplice does not—that is, the accomplice *cooperates* with the pact not to betray each other—the first prisoner can strike a deal with the police and would be set free. But the information they provide will be used against the second prisoner, who would receive the maximum punishment;
iii. if both individuals confess to the crime—that is, both *defect* from their pact—then each receives a reduced sentence, but no one is set free;
iv. if neither confesses to the crime—that is, they *cooperate*—then each prisoner receives minimum sentence because of the lack of evidence. This option may not be equally attractive to

> either person, as the chance of striking a deal with the police and being set free at the expense of one's partner is wasted. Since the prisoners are not in a position to communicate with each other, the question of whether to 'trust' the other not to confess is the most crucial aspect of the game.

The game prisoner's dilemma can be used to examine complex situations in IR like strategic interactions and arms race between countries. If two rival countries build up their stock of armaments in uncontrolled ways, they increase the potential for mutual loss and destruction. For each country, the gain of arming itself is decreased because the costs of arming—financial costs, increased security tensions, greater mutual destructive capabilities—provide few advantages over the opponent, resulting in an unproductive outcome. However, each country has a choice here—either to cooperate to control arms build-up, with the goal of achieving mutual benefits, or defect from the pact and build armaments. The dilemma stems from the realization that if one country arms itself (defects) and the other does not (cooperates), the country that builds armaments will be considered stronger and will win the game. If both cooperate, the best possible outcome is a tie. This is better than the pay-off from mutual defection and an arms race, but it is not as attractive as winning. The temptation to beat one's opponent in the arms race is always present. The fear that one's opponent will give in to such temptations often drives both nations to arms, because not doing so risks total loss. The benefits of not arming can only be realized if one's opponent overcomes the temptation to win. Such trust is often lacking in international politics.

The supporters of the game theory cite the US-Soviet relationship as an example of the game 'prisoner's dilemma'. During the Cold War, the two countries never trusted each other. Each country spent astronomical amounts to arm itself, fearing that the other one was doing the same, and not wanting to lag behind. But the cost incurred in the arms race was so high that it eventually made one player (Soviet Union) to run bankrupt. Had both the nations trusted each other, much of the arms race—as also financial losses, and security tensions for both and also for the rest of the world—could have been avoided. However, the lessons initially drawn from the game 'prisoner's dilemma' can be discouraging. The game illustrates a zero-sum situation, in which one player must lose for the other to win. To keep from losing, each player is motivated to pursue a 'winning' strategy. The collective result is unproductive at best, and destructive at worst.

However, an extended version of the game 'prisoner's dilemma' game calls for repeated interaction, which enhances the probability of cooperative behaviour. The logic of this version of the game suggests that a player's strategy (to defect or cooperate) depends on his experience in previous interactions, and that that strategy will also affect the future behaviour of the opponent. The result is a relationship of mutual reciprocity. An actor is likely to cooperate if the opponent had wanted to cooperate previously, and is unlikely to cooperate if the opponent had not. The assumption that the game will be played again leads players (actors) to consider the consequences of their actions. An opponent may retaliate or be unwilling to cooperate in the future, if one actor always seeks maximum pay-offs at the expense of the other player. This analysis of the game theory leads us to identify some characteristics of the theory along with its main proponents, which are presented in Box 2.10.

**Box 2.10** **Game Theory: Basic Features and Leading Theorists**

**Basic Features**

- The theory is useful in analysing situations of conflict, competition and cooperation.
- Since games often resemble real situations—especially competitive or cooperative situations—they can suggest strategies or ways for dealing with such circumstances.
- The theory is useful for IR too, because conflict, competition and cooperation among nation-states form important areas of discussion in the discipline.
- The theory usually supports a decision-making approach based on the assumption of rationality of players in a situation of competition. Each player tries to maximize gains or minimize losses under conditions of uncertainty. During the Cold War, both the United States and the USSR played such a game. They both wanted to maximize their gains, or at best, tried to minimize their losses, under conditions of uncertainty.
- The theory suggests several types of games: two-person *zero-sum* game; two-person *non-zero* or *variable sum* (chicken) game; the *n-person* game which includes more than two actors or sides, etc. IR today resembles, to some extent, the *n-person* game.
- 'Prisoner's dilemma' is one of the important games propagated by the theory. It illustrates the paradoxical nature of interaction between two suspicious participants with opposing interests.
- The theory has five major concepts: players, strategies, rules, outcome and pay-off.

**Leading Theorists:** J. V. Neumann, O. Morgenstern, A. Rapoport, M. Shubik, J. Nash.

## An Evaluation of Game Theory

Game theory has not only contributed to the development of models of deterrence and arms race, but it has also provided the basis for work concerning the issue of how collaboration among competitive states in an anarchic world could be achieved. These models may provide insights into the strategic options and likely outcomes available to participants in particular situations. From such insights, decision-makers may assess the potential effects of their actions, and may make decisions that would help to achieve the desired goals. For example, deterrence theory has persisted in US defence strategies since the end of the Second World War. Deterrence assumes that a credible and significant threat of retaliation may curb an aggressor's behaviour. However, if two states recognize that their best interests lie in avoiding each other's retaliation, neither is likely to initiate hostilities. This was the guiding principle behind US–Soviet relations during much of the Cold War. The concept of mutual deterrence paved the way for arms-control measures and further cooperation. By highlighting strategic choices and potential collective outcomes, game theory helped in illustrating how a potentially destructive relationship could be managed and transformed to provide mutual benefits, including measures to control arms race and nuclear war.

The game theory fails to answer why states as actors are often irrational, and why they are guided by different notions of rationality. A central problem is that the rational decision for an individual actor such as the state may be to 'defect' and go it alone as opposed to taking a chance in collaborating with another state actor. Thomas Schelling has questioned the validity of the game theory in its zero sum form. He believes that the zero sum game has contributed very little to the solution of the problems such as limited war, surprise attacks, atomic blackmail and massive retaliation. He provides a detailed criticism of the game theory on this issue. According to him the essence of international politics lies in the existence of conflict and mutual dependence which demands some kind of cooperation and accommodation among states. This situation presupposes that there should be an interdependence of expectations. In other words, the choice of a state largely depends on what it expects from other states.

Schelling believes that since the range of alternatives is very large, bargaining becomes necessary. He holds that if bargaining results in the convergence of mutually consistent expectations, there would be suggestions exchanged by the players and that collaboration and accommodation can be carried on by basic motives of commitments, promises or threats. The concept of zero sum game is valid only in the case of war. But in the study of IR, war is not the only issue demanding analysis. In situations other than war, there are elements of cooperation and accommodation as well. These situations are mostly bargaining situations in which conflict and cooperations can be found. Bargaining situations are different from the zero sum game because the latter has no scope for collaboration.

Richard Snyder has warned against premature application of mathematical models to political problems. According to him, two factors contribute to the premature application of the game theory to politics. First, the game theory or certain games advocated by the theory might not be sufficiently developed to analyse all political problems properly. Second, political science or IR, in the reverse way, may not be ready yet to use many of the sophisticated models developed by mathematicians or statisticians. Therefore, it is wise not to be too euphoric about mathematical models provided by the game theory.

## Decision-Making Theory

The decision-making theory in IR seeks to focus on the decision-making aspects for analyses of policies of nation-states. The subjects of enquiry in this theory mainly relate to issues like how and why ruling elites of states behave in certain ways in IR. One of the key assumptions of the theory holds that political actions follow ways which the decision-makers as 'actors' want them to follow. Therefore, the 'how' and 'why' of a political action, and the reasons behind it, are the preferred areas of study in decision-making theory. In other words, the setting or background in which policy decisions are made is studied by the theory.

Decision-making theory in IR mainly focuses on foreign policy decisions of countries and the setting in which these decisions are taken. This setting or background has two sides: internal and external. The 'internal setting' includes personality of decision-makers; organizational structure and culture which may influence the decision-makers; values and aspirations (goals) of society; ideology of the party that runs the government and technological factors. The 'external setting' consists of broader political and economic systems prevailing in the world; dominant values, such as liberalism, socialism and free or restricted trade; and also technological factors. The theory gained tremendous popularity in social science disciplines like economics, sociology, business management, political science and IR. Decision-making theory, which came to IR in the 1950s, is still very popular because it anlyses interesting issues like how and why a nation behaves in a particular manner in IR, and reasons behind such behaviours. Theorists like Richard Snyder, H. W. Bruck, Burton Sapin, Harold and Margaret Sprout, Dean Rusk and Alexander and Juliette George have made important contributions in the study of decision-making in IR.

What do we gain by analysing decisions of nations, or, in other words, what is the purpose of the theory? This theory helps us to identify important structures in the political system of a nation where decisions are made. There may be formal or informal, and known or not-so-known structures where decisions are formulated. For instance, the Council of Ministers is a formal structure, but the 'kitchen cabinet' consisting of key members of the government is an informal one. Both structures may be associated with the decision-making proces. Again, the ruling party may be a known institution for decision-making, but the influential 'nucleus' within the party may be a little known caucus. Further, the systematic analysis of decision-making may lead to unearth certain behaviours or 'actions' of a certain state in the sphere of IR. Why India took military actions during the Kargil crisis? Which decisions led to such actions? What led the United States to attack Iraq? These and many other inquiries could be met by the decision-making theory. This theory sees the actions of the state through the actions of the decision-makers.

While the mindset of the decision-makers influence the decisions they make, actions taken on the basis of decisions consist of the manifest behaviour of the actors. In other words, decisions belong to the internal psychological world, whereas actions belong to the external, manifest world. On the basis of these two, decisions and actions, proponents of the theory have put emphasis on three foundations of decision-making. These are: (1) environmental factors; (2) psychological factors and (3) real actors behind decision-making. Environmental factors in the theory refer to a milieu that is composed of psychological and operational aspects which can set limits on the choice of the decision-maker. Harold and Margaret Sprout have examined the relationship between the environment and decision-making. They have analysed how the decision-makers view the environment, and how environment may remain outside the perception and estimate of the decision-makers. Put differently, a decision-maker may not have total control over the environment as the Sprouts have defined them. They are interested not in the origin of decisions, but rather in analysing decisions after they are taken in the context of the environment, and in the limits set by the environment. This approach helps in making a comparative analysis of decisions. For instance, a foreign policy, analysed with reference to environment, may be compared with another foreign policy, and measures for improvement may be suggested.

Proponents of psychological factors of decision-making take into account the personality traits of the decision-maker, and how these personality traits shape decisions and actions. Alexander and Juliette George have studied the personality factor of the former American President Woodrow Wilson, and anlysed how his personality influenced his decisions. Although the impact of the personality factor on the overall decision is not beyond doubt, it is not totally irrelevant either. Personality factors of leaders like Hitler, Stalin, Churchill, Mao and Indira Gandhi had profound impact on their decision-making and actions. But the impact of personality factors is dependent on the position of the decision-maker in the policy-making structure, nature of the decision and value orientations of the decision-maker. If the decision-maker occupies a central position in the policy making body, the impact of their personality on decision-making would be greater. Stalin's or Indira's personality would have been less pronounced on their decisions, if they did not occupy central positions in decision-making structures. The factor of personality is also dependent on the nature of the decision. Decisions which involve crucial national interests, such as the survival of the state, may have less personality imprints. Values, beliefs and attitudes of the decision-maker may shape their personality, and impact decision-making. A decision-maker, indoctrinated in Marxist ideology, would likely to go for a socialist political system. Further, a leader with an adventurous attitude may be inclined to make risky decisions. But it must be mentioned here that personality factors are subjective, and not beyond question in the process of decision-making.

Theorists like Bernard Cohen, Roger Hilsman and James Robinson want to concentrate on the real actors or the actual makers of foreign policy. Cohen identified five principal institutions in the making of foreign policy: (1) specific actors in the executive (Head of the Government, Foreign Minister and few other members of the cabinet and bureaucracy); (2) specific committees in the legislature; (3) concerned interest groups; (4) public opinion and (5) the mass media. He believes that these five agencies constitute the core actors in foreign policy-making. Hilsman believes that a foreign policy is the final outcome of a process of different objectives of the executive and the legislature. Therefore, to Hilsman, the executive and the legislature are the two real actors behind foreign policy. Robinson believes, following his case study on foreign policy-making in the United States, that the legislature is the core decision-maker in foreign policy issues. However, it should be noted here that the nature of 'core actors' in foreign policy making may vary from country to country, but the executive and the legislature play important roles in almost all political systems. Further, some individuals like the presidents, prime ministers, foreign ministers and some institutions like the executive, legislature, bureaucracy and mass media act as important 'actors' in foreign policy making.

A few models have been developed by the theorists based on their different approaches to the process of decision-making. Prominent among these models are rational goals-ends model, quagmire model and risk analysis model. According to the rational goals-ends model, objectives or goals are first decided by the policy maker; then the means to achieve these goals are decided upon. In deciding the means to realize objectives, policy makers go through 'rational' and 'comprehensive' steps before arriving at any final decision. These steps include all possible alternatives, analysed in a rational way as far as possible, and a comprehensive outlook that takes into account all inputs from different agents interested in foreign policy. Therefore, according to this model, decisions are rational policies to achieve certain objectives, as well as the means to realize these objectives. The quagmire model believes that big decisions are not made at any point by any single individual. Decisions are not also made for any long-term goal. Decisions are made in a piecemeal manner, in short ranges, and they are continued step by step. In that sense, decisions are incremental; a short-term decision may continue if the situation demands, and can be converted into a long-term decision. The American decision to involve itself in Vietnam was initially a short-term decision; but as things turned out, it ultimately became a long-term policy with incremental effects. This model is also known as the 'quicksand' or the 'incremental' model. In the risk analysis model, possible outcomes of each decision and action, and the risks involved, are thoroughly examined. The objective is to carefully analyse decisions and their possible effects when they are implemented. The risk analysis technique is very popular in management sciences and organizational behaviour where important decisions are scrutinized before they are put into practice. In IR, this technique has been adopted to examine foreign policy. These analyses of the decision-making theory may now help us to identify the basic assumptions of the theory, and some notable protagonists, as presented in Box 2.11.

**Box 2.11** **Decision-making Theory: Basic Assumptions and Leading Theorists**

**Basic Features**

- Political actions follow ways which the decision-makers as 'actors' want them to follow.
- 'How' and 'why' of a political action, and the reasons behind it, are the preferred areas of study in decision-making theory.
- This theory in IR mainly focuses on foreign policy decisions of countries and the setting in which these decisions are taken.
- This setting or background has two sides: internal and external.
- This theory helps us to identify important structures in the political system of a nation where decisions are made.
- There may be formal or informal, and known or not-so-known, structures where decisions are formulated.
- Based on decisions and actions, there are three foundations of decision-making: (1) environmental factors; (2) psychological factors and (3) real actors behind decision-making.
- There are three important approaches to the decision-making theory: (1) rational goals-ends model; (2) quagmire model and (3) risk analysis model.

**Leading Theorists:** R. Snyder, H. W. Bruck, B. Sapin, H. Sprout and M. Sprout, B. Cohen, A. George and J. George, R. Hilsman, J. Robinson.

The decision-making theory is useful in unravelling the actions of nation-states in IR. By focussing on foreign policy making and implementation, the decision-making theory helps to solve the puzzle of states' actions in international politics. The theory tries to meet, sometimes successfully, the how and why of a state's actions. There is no denying the fact that IR are still primarily interactions among states. In a community of states, the behavioural aspects of states make central issues in the study of IR. Why states behave in a certain manner? Why do they take particular actions? The decision-making theory tries to answer these questions by examining the foreign policies of states. Although it is not easy to grasp the totality of foreign policy, this theory nevertheless has provided ways to examine the intricate nature of foreign policy, and found out reasonable methods to study the complex web of international affairs. IR revolves around decisions, and the urge to properly study these important decisions has provided significant research orientations to IR scholars. Decision-making theory fulfills the need to study policy making and implementation which constitute crucial subject matters in IR.

But decision-making is very much a subjective element which is difficult to study from an objective value-free approach. The environmental factor or the personality factor can never be entirely objective. When the decision-making theory refers to the psychological 'internal' aspects of decision-making, it plunges into a world of the unknown. Here lies the greatest paradox of the theory. It aims to study foreign policy as objectively as possible, but refers to psychological factors or personality factors as important elements in decision-making. Is it possible to read a statesman's mind fully objectively? Can an individual who occupies the central position in decision-making be totally value free? These crucial questions go unanswered in the decision-making theory.

Are decisions fully rational, as suggested by the rational goals-ends model? Although decisions are products of rationality when they are made, but they may appear to be quite 'irrational' when they are put into 'action'. This complexity may create problems in studying both 'decisions' and actions of the state. If a 'rational' decision becomes an irrational action, the researcher would be in great trouble. America's Vietnam policy may be cited here as an example. When the United States got involved in Vietnam for the first time, the decision, taken after comprehensive discussions, appeared rational. But later on the same decision appeared to be irrational when the American public opinion condemned the Vietnam policy. Therefore, decisions are not always rational and objective, and they can never be studied fully objectively. But subjective assessment of foreign policy may create more difficulties in the study of IR. Due to this dichotomy, the decision-making theory fails to become an adequate theory to study the complex nature of IR today.

# Systems Theory

The systems theory owes its origin to biology, particularly to the writings of Ludwig Von Bertallanfy, a noted biologist of the 1920s. From biology, the systems theory came to anthropology, sociology and political science. Sytems theory in IR was first introduced in the mid-1950s by a group of American scholars. Since then, this approach has become popular in analysing the courses of IR. To understand this theory, it is necessary to know what a 'system' is. According to Bertallanfy (1968: 11), the founder of the systems theory, a system 'is a set of elements standing in interaction'. James Rosenau, a scholar of IR, believes that 'a system is considered to exist in an environment and to be composed of parts which through interaction are in relation to each other' (1961: 35). Proponents of the theory hold that every system has many components. First, every system has clearly identifibale 'elements'. The elements of the solar system are the sun and the planets. Similarly, the elements of international system are the nation-states. Second, a system must have a set of 'relationships' among elements. The elements must interact and remain interdependent to engage themselves in relationships. For example, the family may be called a system because its elements, the individual members, interact with one another and remain interdependent. In the international system, nation-states interact with one another, and are dependent on one another.

The third characteristc of a system is the concept of 'boundary'. This boundary separates a sytem from other phenomena like the broader environment and other systems. A systems theorist must know where a system begins and where it ends, and must have a clear notion of the boundary of a system. Without boundaries, a system is incomplete. However, everything around us does not constitute a system. For instance, people present in a supermarket at a particular time do not make a system, because they do not share any relationship and are not inderdependent. So, a system consists of three things: identifiable elements; relationship among elements; and clear notion of boundary. A system has sub-systems. For example, in the solar system, the earth and its satellite, the moon, constitute a sub-system. Similarly, in the international system, regional organizations—such as the ASEAN or the SAARC—form one type of sub-systems.

The proponents of the systems theory in IR believe that a scientific study of IR is possible if the interactions among nation-states and their levels of interdependence can be satisfactorily analysed. For instance, Morton Kaplan, one of the best known systems theorist of IR, holds that interaction and interdependence of nation-states are to be examined in order to have a good knowledge about the international system. This, he maintains, could be done with the help of six models of international system. These are: (1) balance of power system; (2) loose bipolar system; (3) tight bipolar system; (4) universal actor system; (5) hierarchical international system and (6) unit veto system. A few words about the six models are necessary to understand Kaplan's views.

The *balance of power system* works on the basis of interaction and interdependence among the major powers in international politics. Five to six major powers in the world, more or less equal in strength, maintain a balance in international politics by increasing and showing their strengths. Each state is aware of the strength of others, and is not normally inclined to alter the balance. For example, if state A knows that military and economic strengths of states B, C, D, E and F are equal to those of its own, it would not risk antagonizing them. This way a balance, though precarious, would be maintained in world politics. In fact, this balance of power system existed in the world for three-and-a-half centuries, from the seventeenth to the mid-twentieth century, when five to six major powers controlled international politics through understanding and negotiations. According to Kaplan, this system may get disturbed if any of the actors (states) does not follow the rules of the game, that is, if any actor gains strength tremendously, the balance may be destroyed. This would also mean a shift in the decision-making process of the actor towards more ambitious national interests.

According to Kaplan, the balance of power system, if destroyed, may result in a *loose bipolar system* where two states become dominant, and control world politics. After the Second World War, two main actors, the United States and the USSR, controlled world politics by leading opposing blocs of states. This system, which lasted till 1991, could be termed as a loose bipolar system. Under this system, the two superpowers were surrounded by groups of smaller powers and non-aligned countries. The attachment of non-aligned countries to either of the superpowers, according to Kaplan, made the system loose. Moreover, unlike the balance of power system, there were no set of rules to be followed by the leading actors of the system.

The *tight bipolar system*, which may develop after the collapse of the loose bipolar system, is different from the latter in several ways. Non-aligned states, who made the previous system loose, would not hang around with the principal actors. The system would operate only around two main actors, leading two tightly controlled super blocs. But the stability of the system would remain only when the states of the two super blocs are hierarchically organized. This presupposes tight control of the leaders of respective super blocs. If this hierarchy dissolves, it tends to give way to a loose bipolar system again.

The *universal actor system* may also develop after the loose bipolar system. Under this system, the universal actor, such as the UN, is powerful enough to control the national actors (individual states). This system would be a highly integrated system, possessing integrated mechanisms which would perform political, economic, judicial and administrative functions. The national actors would be allowed to pursue their objectives, but within the framework set by the universal actor. The system would work on the basis of the value structure of national actors to pursue their objectives through peaceful methods, and to avoid the threat of force. Prestige and rewards will be given to national actors, as also to individual human beings for adhering to the norms of the system. The universal actor would be able to restrict the national actors from resorting to war. But this system would witness initial instability because the national actors would like to pursue power to fulfill their objectives, but once the universal actor establishes its control, the sytem would stabilize.

In the *hierarchical international system*, one universal actor would control world politics. This system can be both directive and non-directive. If the international order is controlled by one national actor like Nazi Germany, this system would be directive. But if the controlling national actor follows principles of democracy, it would be non-directive. In the directive hierarchical system, there would be greater tension within the sytem as small actors would feel insecure and threatened. But in the non-directive hierarchical system there would be lesser tension due to the prevalence of democratic principles.

The *unit veto system* is one where all national actors are immensely powerful and can destroy one another. Under this system, all actors possess highly destructive weapons, such as WMDs, to finish others. It is a system similar to the state of nature described by Hobbes where all are selfish and quarrelsome, and target others.

Through these six models of interaction among nation-states, Kaplan elucidated his views about the international system. According to him, one political system can be distinguished from other systems by its rules which clearly specify areas of jurisdiction and methods of conflict resolution. He believes that physical force is necessary to make the political system survive because for conflict resolution, which is a major function of the political system, physical force may be ultimately required. Kaplan criticizes the realists for their emphasis on 'power', saying that the realist zeal for power failed to distinguish between the 'political' and the 'non-political'. The realists made power so ubiquitous that it included everything, even the family and the peer groups. But relationships in these groups are non-political, and therefore may remain outside the purview of power, unlike the nation-states.

The idea of an international system where nation-states are the main 'elements', and their interactions make the system survive, is not beyond controversy. Scholars like C. W. Manning support the idea of the international system resting on nation-states, whereas others like Kenneth Boulding and John Herz feel that the nation-state itself is facing many crises to remain a major 'element' in the system. Manning believes that the concepts of sovereignty, national interest, institutionalized diplomacy and international law make the nation-states very strong as pillars of the international system. But Boulding and Herz think that the impact of atomic weapons, globalization and stellite communication has made them weak and, therefore, the international system based on nation-states may not be identified as a proper system. Even Kaplan had doubts about IR being seen as a proper systematic discipline. He preferred to see IR as a sub-discipline of political science. However, it was he who made a thorough application of the sytems theory to the study of IR. We are now in a position to identify the basic assumptions of the systems theory in IR, and its main protagonists. These are presented in Box 2.12.

**Box 2.12** **Systems Theory in IR: Basic Features and Leading Theorists**

**Basic Features**

- The theory owes its origin to biology, particularly to the writings of Ludwig Von Bertallanfy.
- Sytems theory in IR was first introduced in the middle of the 1950s by a group of American scholars.
- A system is a set of elements standing in interaction; in IR, nation-states are the 'elements' engaged in interactions.
- A system consists of three things: identifiable elements, relationship among elements and clear notion of boundary.
- A system has sub-systems. In the international system, regional organizations—the ASEAN, the SAARC, for example—form one type of sub-systems.
- Proponents of systems theory in IR believe that a scientific study of international relations is possible if the interactions among nation-states and their levels of interdependence can be satisfactorily analysed.
- For Morton Kaplan, interaction and interdependence among states could be analysed in terms of six models of international system: (1) balance of power system; (2) loose bipolar system; (3) tight bipolar system; (4) universal actor system; (5) hierarchical international system and (6) unit veto system.
- C. W. Manning supports the idea of the international system resting on nation-states, whereas scholars like Kenneth Boulding and John Herz feel that the nation-state itself is facing many crises to remain major 'elements' of the system.

**Leading Theorists:** M. Kaplan, C. W. Manning, K. Boulding, H. Guetzkow.

## An Evaluation of Systems Theory in IR

The systems theory perceives IR as a system where nation-states are the main actors. But it is difficult to put the whole range of IR, which is not very organized, within the systems framework. IR is not only interactions among states, several non-state actors and individuals exert considerable influence on IR today. The systems theory failed to recognize their roles within the framework of the international system. It may envisage methodological problems, because the concept of 'elements' is not very clear here. The theory considered nation-states as 'elements' leaving out several important non-state elements of the international system which play significant roles in international politics today. Another methodological problem relates to the concept of 'environment' which is also not clear in this theory. Since the international system encompasses almost everything—from political to economic, to cultural, to scientific—what remains outside the purview of its scope? In other words, since IR discusses almost every problem in the world, what is left out as environment here? The idea of interaction of elements with environment, in the form of receiving inputs and providing outputs, sounds confusing. If the whole world is the subject-matter of study in IR, what remains as the environment? Therefore, the concept of environment is either absent or is very limited in the international system, as perceived by the proponents of the theory.

Among the six models of the international system advocated by Kaplan, three are highly improbable. The first among the three is the universal actor system where the universal actor is sufficiently strong to restrict national actors from using the threat of force or resorting to war. Is it possible for any universal actor like the UNO to restrict the ambitions of several national actors? If any national actor thinks that its national interest demands the use of force, it will not hesitate to use force. Moreover, what is the source of strength of the universal actor? Kaplan is not very explicit about the source. Is there any guarantee that all national actors would follow a value structure as propounded by Kaplan? In the final analysis, the universal actor system suffers from several defects, and it is unlikely to be a reality in IR. The hierarchical international system also suffers from maladies. It is difficult to achieve the non-directive hierarchical system based on democratic principles. We may respect and love democratic ideals, but there is little reason to believe that the whole international system would be run according to democratic values. On the contrary, directive hierarchical order like the Nazi rule would be more visible in international politics, because there would always be rogue states to break the normal preferences. Finally, the unit veto system resembling the Hobbes' state of nature is also an improbability in today's IR. Even if every state possesses highly destructive weapons, the whole world may not be destroyed, because that would be suicidal for every state, and would work against the national interest of every actor. On the contrary, anti-weapons movements would be strengthened, because that would save the world and the international system. After all, making the system survive may fulfill every actor's national interest.

But the systems theory in IR has made some notable contributions to the discipline. The systems theory made the study of IR more organized and focused. It also provided ways for the international system to survive, and adapt itself to changes. A system is an integrated one where all elements work to make the system survive. In the international system, the nation-states, knowingly or unknowingly, help the system to survive and progress. Moreover, the inputs the system receives from the environment help it to adapt to new and newer demands, and to accommodate itself to changes. This becomes manifest through the outputs produced by the system. Despite crises, the international system had survived and progressed. Systems theory of IR strongly sends the message that by adapting itself to changes, the international system would become an efficient system where the nations-states would be more engaged in cooperation and mutual development.

## Communication Theory

Communication theory in IR owes its origin to cybernetics, which is a systematic study of communication and control in organizations. The initial contributions towards the development of communication theory came from Norbert Weiner in the 1940s. He noted that major wartime advances in electronic communication, such as sonar, radar and radar-controlled anti-aircraft weapons, involved transfer of information. He identified that these communication processes in machines were similar to human, social and institutional processes. In other words, Weiner believed that basic similarities existed among electronic signals, human nerve cells and governmental functions. They are all goal-oriented systems which share and transmit information.

It was Karl Deutsch who followed Weiner's logic and brought the concept of cybernetics to study IR. Deutsch, the pioneer of communication theory in IR, pointed out that cybernetics was important to politics because it provided an alternative to power, which, according to him, was 'steering'. Modern politics, domestic or international, is not rooted in power as the realists suggest but in 'steering', believes Deutsch. A government's primary function, according to Deutsch, is to steer the nation and not to engage in power, which may be dangerous for the country.

In his book *The Nerves of Government: Models of Political Communication and Control*, Deutsch argued that cybernetics, as the study of communication and control, offers a general perspective on all kinds of politics. Communications remain at the centre of politics, and form the 'nerves of government'. The study of communications may help us to know how messages flow among decision-makers, and how such messages contribute towards making decisions. Cybernetics is applicable to any system that possesses adequate organization, communication and control; any system where messages are frequently transferred, retrieved, stored and responded. The international political system fulfills these criteria, and hence the study of communication flows help to analyse international politics. Transmission of messages, whether through electronic machines, human interactions or nerve cells, are always significant to any system—electronic, biological or social. Communication flow is also very important in international politics, and a proper study of these communications may bring out the core of international politics.

How does this communication network operate? Proponents of communication theory have identified several mechanisms through which flow of communication takes place. These are: (1) information; (2) entropy; (3) load; (4) lag; (5) distortion; (6) gain; (7) lead and (8) feedback. In order to understand the theory, a few words about these mechanisms of communication are necessary. *Information* is knowledge about events taking place in the system. In case of IR, it would mean knowledge about events and processes in the international system. Information is generally transmitted through communication and can be reproduced, stored, quantified and measured. This information is the backbone of any communication. The idea of *entropy* comes from thermodyanamics. It refers to the tendency of a closed system to decay. According to Wiener, every organized thing, whether a living being or a machines, is prone to decay. A closed political system is, therefore, prone to entropy and requires strong flow of communications. The concept of *load* refers to the gap between the goals of a political system and the information about its changing environment. The environment may put stress on the system. Any system, the international political system included, has to bear with load. If the system can take on the load, it can function efficiently. Conversely, inability to handle load may make the system vulnerable. Excessive demands may put stress on the system and create loads. For instance, the demand for equal rights of states may create load in IR and lead to conflicts.

The idea of load is dependent on the flow of informtion. The time taken between the realization of load (reception of information) and sending of response to it is called *lag*. In other words, it is the time taken by the decision-makers to respond to the information about load. The greater the lag, the more inefficient the system is. Conversely, an efficient political system could respond to the information about load more quickly. *Distortion* is an idea close to lag. It refers to the changes that take place in information when it is received and when it is responded to. The system would be in trouble if much distortion takes place. The concept of *gain* refers to the reaction of a system to load, and the amount of changes the system makes due to load. If the change is substantial the gain is more and vice versa. The idea of gain helps to measure the speed and extent of the decision-maker's reaction to load. For instance, if political or military measures are taken quickly in response to a sudden attack, it may amount to gain.

The idea of *lead* refers to the ability of an organization to assess elements of future stress, anticipate incoming loads and make necessary adjustments in advance. It provides information about future crises. A system that is more capable in making such predictions is more efficient than one which cannot secure 'lead'. *Feedback* is information about the success or failure of decision-makers' reactions to load. It may help to improve the responses to loads or crises. The quality of feedback that the decision-makers receive about their responses may bring out the effectiveness of the system. A self-regulatory system is more likely to provide quality feedbacks. Feedback helps to shape further decisions and responses, and is, therefore, an important-mechanism in the communication flow. *Learning* refers to accquiring and upgrading knowledge about the system, based on information. Load, lag, gain and feedback help to augment learning. The learning mechanism is a continuous process in the communication approach. It helps the organization to work against entropy and makes it stronger and more efficient. These are some of the important mechanisms of cybernetics, as presented by communication theory in IR. The efficacy of a government can be measured in terms of these mechanisms, as the following illustration would show.

The failure of the Indian Peace Keeping Force (IPKF) in Sri Lanka during 1987–89 could be analysed with reference to the communication theory. All governments depend on communication system for effective functioning. During the IPKF operations in Sri Lanka, at least six mechanisms of communication showed marked weakness. Information channels were poor. The Indian government had little knowledge when it agreed to send the IPKF to Sri Lanka that the force would be targeted and killed by the Tamil militants like the LTTE (Liberation Tigers of Tamil Ealam). The government was unable to secure lead as it failed to assess and anticipate future stress. Such poor information and failure to get lead created load on the government, which resulted in lag when the government responded in a slipshod manner. Moreover, due to weak feedback mechanism, the government was not in a position to corner any positive gain. As a consequence, the IPKF had to be withdrawn finally when there were huge setbacks in terms of killing of Indian soldiers, drainage on the exchequer, and overall political and military embarrasment. In this case, the change was insufficient and negative, resulting in lesser gain. As this example shows, it is possible to analyse issues in IR by the communication theory.

This analysis of the communication theory leads us to identify some basic assumptions of the theory and its important proponents. These are given in Box 2.13.

**Box 2.13** **Communication Theory: Basic Features and Leading Theorists**

**Basic Features**

- The theory is based on cybernetics.
- It holds that similarities exist among electronic signals, human nerve cells and governmental functions. They are all goal-oriented systems which share and transmit information.
- The theory believes that modern politics, domestic or international, is not rooted in power, as the realists suggest, but in 'steering'.

- Cybernetics is applicable to any system which possesses adequate organization, communication and control; and where messages are frequently transfered, retrieved, stored and responded.
- Communication and control (cybernetics) is very important in international politics.
- The theory identifies several mechanisms through which the flow of communication takes place: (1) information; (2) entropy; (3) load; (4) lag; (5) distortion; (6) gain; (7) lead and (8) feedback.
- It analyses issues in IR through these mechanisms of communication.

**Leading Theorists:** N. Weiner, K. Deutsch, J. Burton.

### An Evaluation of Communication Theory

Communication theory opens up new and unexplored areas in the study of IR. By focusing on the value of information and communication in international politics, this theory could provide an alternative to power politics. This alternative was the idea of 'steering', based on communication. The communication model was also able to replace traditional concepts of IR. According to John Burton, by focusing on the decision-making processes in the perspective of communication flow, this theory replaced the static concepts of balance of power, and the traditional notion of politics as a struggle for power. The idea of politics based on power proves the inability of the political system to make adjustments and changes according to the needs of time, thinks Burton. Communication theory, according to him, also helps in policy planning and policy analysis. In the nuclear age, it is important to know policies of states and how decisions are made and implemented by nations. This theory also helps to understand a state's reaction to issues and events in IR, as noted in the example provided earlier about the IPKF in Sri Lanka.

But critics of this theory contend that the model of cybernetics is not applicable to all political problems. Cybernetics is very helpful in engineering but not in IR, because IR does not constitute a 'system' in the real sense of the term. Unprecedented expansion of IR today is not suitable for the cybernetics model which works effectively in smaller circuits. Davis Bobrow, for instance, believes that not all issues in IR could fit into the cybernetics model. It would be cumbersome to examine all events and issues in IR in terms of the mechanisms of cybernetics such as load, lag, lead, entropy orgain. Moreover, steering does not cover every aspect of government activities, and sometimes the notion of 'power' helps to analyse a state's functions, especially when the state is dealing with national interest or security. Despite such criticisms, there is little doubt that the communication theory brought some fresh changes to the study of IR.

## Postmodernism

The origin of postmodernism could be attributed to a group of French philosophers like Jacques Derrida and Michel Foucault who challenged the idea of existentialism prevalent in France after the Second World War. Postmodernism emerged in France in the early 1950s, although it entered the study of IR in the early 1980s. It must be made clear at the outset that the term 'postmodernism' was never used by its proponents; rather they preferred to use terms like 'poststructuralism' and 'deconstruction'. However, the coinage postmodernism became increasingly acceptable throughout the world since the mid-1970s, possibly due to the proponents' attack on what was termed as 'modernism' after the Second World War. Postmodernism entered into the study of IR through the works of scholars like Richard Ashley, Jenny Adkins, Cynthia Weber, Rob Walker and David Campbell.

Postmodernist thinkers hold the view that scholars build, and live in, their own conceptual prisons. The most notable conceptual prison is that of modernity itself and the idea that modernization leads to progress and an improved life for humanity. Postmodernists attack the idea put forward by 'modern' thinkers that there can be objective knowledge of social issues. For the postmodernists, knowledge is not simply a cognitive factor; knowledge is also normative and political. According to Foucault, power and knowledge are mutually supportive, and they directly imply one another. It is therefore important to see how activities concerning power fit in with the social and political issues in the world. Postmodernists are critical of classical liberals like Kant who believed in 'knowledge' or 'enlightenment'. They are also critical of contemporary positivists who believe in the objectivity and superiority of 'science'. Both liberals and positivists believe in the advancement of human knowledge which postmodernists find limited and narrow, akin to a prison.

Like the postmodernists in general, postmodern IR theorists reject the notion of objective truth. They contradict the idea that there can be anything like the 'expanding knowledge' in our world. These notions are intellectual illusions that create subjective beliefs, like a religious faith. The liberals or neo-realists may claim that they have discovered the real truth about IR, but they actually live in the world of illusions created by their own intellectual dogmas. By attacking the modernist belief that knowledge can expand and improve, leading to continuous progress of the world, postmodernists have recognized human efforts to control the society and the world. They also reject the belief that appropriate institutions can be created to provide just and fair treatment to all people.

Through 'deconstruction', the postmodernists want to look at every accepted or settled idea with new lenses. Deconstruction is a process of radically challenging and unsettling accepted concepts, and providing fresh insights into them. In the field of IR, for instance, stable theories like liberalism or realism have been deconstructed by postmodernists like Ashley or Weber to prove that these theories were not suitable to explain the present international system. These theories were 'metanarratives' or accounts which claimed to have discovered the truth about the human world. But such claims are hollow and unfounded. Ashley, for example, argues that neo-realist claims about the everlasting anarchical nature of international politics are unfounded because there are no impartial grounds for judging them. Narratives or metanarratives are constructed by theorists and they are always prejudiced by their personal biases. Social science is never impartial or neutral; it is historical, cultural and political and therefore, biased. Ashley believes that the neo-realist knowledge about everlasting anarchy in the international order is biased because the neo-realists wanted to establish this 'fact' (anarchy) as an objective truth. This desire to find the objective truth may blind thinkers and compel them to declare facts of his choice as objective truths. As Jackson and Sorensen have observed, 'every theory, including neorealism, decides for itself what counts as "facts". There is no neutral or impartial or independent standpoint to decide between rival empirical claims. Empirical theory is myth. In other words, there is no objective reality; everything involving human beings is subjective' (2003: 251). According to postmodernists, there cannot be any stable or grand theory; everything must come under scrutiny because knowledge is intimately linked to power, the desire to prevail over others. This makes knowledge not universal, but susceptible to deconstruction.

Robert Walker, in his book *Inside/Outside: International Relations as Political Theory*, attempted to deconstruct the idea of state sovereignty. Walker's analysis led to a fresh inquiry into state sovereignty as a useful descriptive category to explain IR today. He suggested that modern political life was not only organized around sovereign states and sovereign boundaries of states; it questioned the notion of state sovereignty as the most accepted subjective category of IR today. New forms of political community and identity can emerge beyond the notion of sovereign states, and can become important subjective ideas of contemporary IR. Walker opposed the idea of accepting the sovereign state as the pivotal element of the present international system and unsettled the historic notion of primacy of sovereign states in IR. William Connolly also provided a postmodern critique of state sovereignty by challenging the accepted notion that the sovereign state possessed monopoly over the allegiances, identifications and energies of its members. State sovereignty, argued Connolly, was incompatible with democracy in an international order where globalization was believed to have broken national boundaries in the period of modernization. Globalization, state sovereignty and democracy are highly incompatible in contemporary IR, believes Connolly.

These postmodernist views help us to identify some basic features of what is called 'postmodern theory' of IR. These features, along with the leading postmodern thinkers, are presented in Box 2.14.

**Box 2.14 Postmodernism in IR: Basic Features and Leading Theorists**

**Basic Features**

- Postmodernism in IR emerged in the 1980s, although postmodernism as a social theory originated in the early 1950s in France when a group of scholars questioned existentialism, prevalent in Europe at that time.
- The term 'postmodernism' was never used by any thinker, but became acceptable due to its critique of modernity.
- Postmodernism challenged the notion that knowledge is eternal and leads to progress of the world; it also rejected the idea that there can be anything called objective truth.
- According to it, knowledge is intimately linked to power; no knowledge is impartial.
- Postmodernism believes in 'deconstruction', a process to challenge and unsettle accepted ideas; and to give fresh insights into stable ideas.
- It challenged accepted theories in IR, such as liberalism and realism, and held that these theories were biased by the personal preferences of their protagonists.
- It challenged the neo-realist view that everlasting anarchy in IR is an objective truth. It holds that this view too is not impartial or neutral as it is prejudiced by the beliefs of neo-realist thinkers.

- It challenged the liberal view that the idea of state sovereignty is an important subjective category of IR; new forms of political community and identity can emerge beyond the notion of sovereign states.
- Democracy, sovereign state and globalization, as advanced by modernists, are not compatible with one another, and these are inadequate to analyse contemporary IR.

**Leading Theorists:** R. Ashley, J. Edkins, C. Weber, R. Walker, W. Connolly, D. Campbell.

## An Evaluation of Postmodernism in IR

The contributions of postmodernism to the theory of IR are many. To begin with, it exposed the intimate connection between knowledge and power. What we know as universal knowledge is ultimately the ideas of the powerful in the society. Knowledge backed by political power normally becomes 'universal' knowledge, and acceptable. Postmodernists exposed this illusion, disguised as knowledge, by indicating that knowledge is prejudiced. Secondly, through the process of deconstruction, the postmodernists were able to give fresh insights into liberal notions of state sovereignty and neo-realist claims about anarchy as the objective truth in IR. State sovereignty is not the most important subject in the study of IR today, as claimed by the liberals. In the postmodern world, any account of international politics must also include transnational actors and movements that work outside and inside state borders. The ideas of democracy and state sovereignty are not at all compatible, think the postmodernists. They also burst the bubble created by the neo-realists about anarchy as an everlasting objective truth in IR. This view of anarchy is highly subjective, as it is clouded by personal choices of the neo-realist thinkers. Thirdly, postmodernists renewed the concept of the 'political' in IR by expanding its applicability beyond territories of the sovereign state. In other words, the term 'political' may also be invoked without referring to the sovereign state. For instance, there may be a political community or identity beyond sovereign states. Postmodernists broadened the sphere of the political which opened up several theoretical assumptions in the study of IR.

But there are also negative aspects of postmodernism. If every theory is prejudiced by personal preferences of its thinkers, what about the postmodern theory? Is it above bias or prejudice? If not, then why would we accept it? Postmodernism actually raised the possibility of falling in the trap created by its thinkers. Moreover, the process of deconstruction is not beyond question. Deconstruction can be worse than the original construction, and may generate confusions. The process of deconstruction would be unending as every new construction would attract deconstruction. This would simultaneously bring unending confusions in our analyses. Further, postmodernists in IR rejected narratives and metanarratives, and accused liberal and neo-realist thinkers of using metanarratives. Yet their deconstructions of earlier theories in the discipline were not dissimilar to metanarratives, as they reached certain conclusions which they also wanted to establish as 'facts'.

Scholars like Jackson and Sorensen hold the view that postmodernism can degenerate into nihilism—negativism for its own sake. They wrote, 'Criticism can be made merely for the sake of criticism. Narratives can be taken apart with nothing to take their place. Ultimately, postmodernists can become estranged from the social and political world that they seek to understand' (2003: 252). This over-critical attitude of postmodern theorists subjected them to scepticism, and made their theory controversial. This attitude was also labeled by liberals as dogmatic. In their efforts to reject dogmatism in earlier theories, postmodernists in IR were accused of confining themselves to new dogmas like deconstruction, and challenge to 'metanarratives' that ultimately became fetishes for the postmodernists. As a consequence, their views suffered from inadequacy and imbalance.

## Constructivism

Constructivism is not a new theory in IR, although it is often highlighted as a new discourse in the study of the subject. After the end of the Cold War, constructivism has been presented in a new light by a group of Western thinkers like Alexander Wendt, Nicholas Onuf, Peter Katzenstein and Friedrich Kratochwil. But the roots of constructivism could be traced back to the eighteenth century in thc writings of Italian philosopher Giambattista Vico, who argued that social and world history were shaped by human beings. States were also created by human beings, and relations among states did not develop naturally; they were built by men and women living in states. Contemporary constructivism argues in the same way, although with more sophisticated, and sometimes difficult, terminologies. Constructivism today does not accept the social world as something 'given', as a natural identity. It was created by human beings with their ideas, concepts and thoughts.

Constructivism therefore believes that our social world is not made essentially by material forces, external to human ideas and control; our world is made of human thoughts, beliefs and innovative ideas. Proponents of this theory contradict the material, scientific theories of the world, commonly known as the positivist approach in IR, and prefer instead an ideational view of our world. Human relations, including IR, have been constructed by men and women, because no natural law can govern politics and economics of the world; these are governed through laws devised by human beings. Every material manifestation in international affairs—cooperation, conflict, allies, enemies, interests, power—bears meaning given to it by humans. Nothing in IR is natural, created without human agency; everything is a product of conscious construction by human beings. Social structures, according to Alexander Wendt, are created through human ideas. There can be different, sometimes opposing, social structures in IR, but they are all dependent on human ideas. For instance, a 'security community'—for example, the NATO—is a social structure created by men; as also the 'security dilemma' of states, where one country views the other as its opponent or enemy.

Constructivism focuses on inter-subjective beliefs—such as ideas, assumptions or views—that are widely shared by people. These inter-subjective beliefs shape ways in which people build relations with others and conceive of themselves in society. For instance, the collective assumption of people of country A that country B is not friendly towards them may lead to an adverse relationship between states A and B. Constructivists also try to explore how these relations are formed and expressed. Constructivists like Finnemore and Sikkink have referred to state sovereignty as an expression of inter-subjective belief. According to them, state sovereignty has no definite material reality, but it exists only because people collectively believe in its existence, and act accordingly.

Human relations based on inter-subjective beliefs can be both cooperative and conflicting. There can be agreements or disagreements among people that may lead to cooperation and conflict. Constructivism tries to find out the causes behind such cooperation and conflict. But in its research, the constructivist approach differs from the positivist 'scientific' approach. The emphasis of constructivism in this case would be more on human ideas and beliefs, rather than on the so-called 'material' causes and events, normally advanced by positivists. For a constructivist, cooperation happens because people want to achieve it. In other words, a constructivist may see cooperation as agreements or adjustments of two minds or mindsets. For a positivist, on the contrary, cooperation may take place due to material advantages, such as economic benefits. For a constructivist, idea precedes matter; for the positivist, such as neo-realists, matter precedes ideas. A neo-realist, therefore, would establish anarchy as the reality in international politics; a constructivist, on the other hand, would search the roots of anarchy in human minds.

This discussion on constructivism helps us to identify some important features and leading protagonists of this theory, as are presented in Box 2.15.

**Box 2.15** **Constructivism: Basic Features and Leading Theorists**

**Basic Features**

- Originated in the eighteenth century; but often considered as a new theory because it was presented with renewed vigour after the end of the Cold War by a group of Western scholars.
- Early constructivism believed that our history and social world were created by human ideas and conceptions.
- Contemporary constructivism revived this argument after the Cold War, and holds the view that society, the world and human relations are not just natural or physical; they are shaped by human thoughts, ideas and beliefs.
- Contradicts the positivist 'scientific material' view of IR; prefers an ideational view of IR.
- All human relations including international relations are made through conscious human efforts, because international politics and economics are not governed by natural laws; these are controlled by man-made laws.
- Every material manifestation in IR bears meaning given to it by human beings.
- According to Wendt, social structures emerge through human ideas.
- Human relations, including international relations, depend on inter-subjective beliefs which shape different kinds of human relations.
- Cooperation or conflicts in IR are not due to material considerations; these are reflected through agreements or disagreements of human minds.
- Ideas precede matter in international relations.

**Leading Theorists:** A. Wendt, N. Onuf, P. Katzenstein, F. Kratochwil.

## An Evaluation of Constructivism in IR

The rise of constructivism has inspired many theoretical debates within the field of IR. Till the mid-1990s, the main theoretical debate within the discipline—it is still present—was between the neo-liberals and the neo-realists. In this debate, the major issues were cooperation, peace and interdependence among states, as opposed to conflict among, anarchy in, and security of the states. With the emergence of constructivism, new debates arose between rationalists—the group was influenced by idealist and realist thoughts—and constructivists; and between critical theorists—influenced by Marxism, liberalism and the Frankfurt School—and constructivists. The core debates in the discipline of IR today revolve around normative issues—put forward by constructivists—versus material forces—highlighted by rationalists and critical theorists; differences over the nature of social structures, and continuity and transformation in international politics.

As observed earlier, constructivists put emphasis on ideas as opposed to matters in the analysis of the international society. They also differ with others on the emergence and activities of social structures in international affairs. Examples have been provided in this respect in our analysis earlier (security community and security dilemma). The constructivists further believe that it is possible to make significant transformation in our theoretical and empirical approaches to the study of IR. For instance, important issues in discipline, such as security, state sovereignty, cooperation or conflict can be studied from a different perspective, without putting too much importance on physical or material factors. For example, conflicts between states can be viewed as ideational conflicts or antagonistic mental constructs of the ruling elites; and not always due to physical or material factors. Therefore, constructivism encourages new empirical research and new orientations in IR that, they believe, are different from neo-liberal, neo-Marxist and neo-realist approaches. With the rise of constructivism, ideational, normative issues strike back in the study of IR.

The emphasis on ideational issues is not beyond question. Are social structures mainly reflections of ideas? Are major activities and events in international affairs due to ideas, beliefs and conceptions of rulers? These questions may generate puzzles that are not easy to solve. Wendt analysed social structures with reference to human ideas and thoughts. But material needs may also propel the ruling elite to form social structures. Was NATO (a security community) formed due to the convergence of ideas of ruling elites, or was it formed due to the prevailing security (and, national) interests of participating states? It is not easy to answer this question. Did ideas precede security fears in this case; or ideas generated because of security fears? If the former is correct, then there would be another related question: is it possible to form ideas before every event in international politics? The answer probably would be negative. However, if the later is true with respect to the formation of the NATO, then material events in IR score over human thoughts and beliefs, a view which the constructivists would like to dislike.

Moreover, pursuing empirical research on the basis of ideas, thoughts and conceptions, termed as inter-subjective beliefs by the constructivists, is extremely difficult and prone to errors. Observation and analysis of these psychological traits are not easy, and may not be conducive to empirical research. Inter-subjective beliefs are uncertain because these may change from time to time. But everything in IR is not frequently changeable. Despite criticisms, the nation-states are still major actors in international politics, as they had been earlier. Now, is there any possibility that nation-states would give up their sovereignty in the near future and pave way for an altogether new discipline of IR? Are such immediate changes in ideas and conceptions of nation-states possible? The answer would probably be negative. Internal contradictions exist in constructivism. The theory propagates an ideational nature of IR based on inter-subjective beliefs. But the very nature of IR, as relations among nation-states, opposes inter-subjectivity in every sphere and calls for continuity in its basic structure—a community of states. Therefore, despite several positive contributions to the study of IR, constructivism falls short of being labelled as a grand theory in the discipline.

# Feminism in IR

Feminist theories of IR try to focus on the hitherto neglected role of women in global affairs. Although as a social theory feminism is not quite new, feminist theories of IR have proliferated mainly after the 1980s. It should be mentioned here that there are many forms of feminist social theory: liberal, Marxist, radical, postmodern and others. Similarly, feminism has many voices within the discipline. For instance, the critical theory in IR, in its Marxist tradition and postmodernism, has expressions for feminist causes. While feminism, influenced by Marxism, has highlighted the exploitation of women in society; postmodern feminists have focused more on gender, or on how divisions between the masculine and the feminine constitute a hierarchy of power by which the former subordinates the latter. However, these seemingly different lines of thought converge in the general issue of neglect of women in international affairs, and are broadly known as the feminist theories of IR.

These theories have pointed out that the history and structure of, and knowledge about, IR are all gendered. Some of the major issues that have traditionally dominated IR studies were relations among nations, war, peace, security, cooperation, diplomacy, foreign policy, propaganda and military. According to feminist theorists of IR, these issues reflect a masculine way of thinking. For instance, the realist idea of military security of nations in an international order based on anarchy is a masculine projection that conceals the existence of gender hierarchy in international politics. As Christine Sylvester has argued in her book *Feminist Theory and International Relations in a Postmodern Era* (1994), this realist concern for security tries to seek protection from an outside threat, with a view to ensure protection of a domestic jurisdiction that fixes continuous subordination of women. Further, feminist IR theorists argue that although wars have been largely caused and fought by men, women form the majority of civil casualties. Besides, women are providers of various support services (domestic, medical, psychological and sexual) during war and militarization. As Cynthia Enloe (1989) observed, women constitute reserve armies in home industries, transnational peace activists, soldiers as well as mothers of soldiers, and revolutionaries in national liberation struggles and civil wars. Enloe added the term 'international' to the now-famous radical feminist slogan 'personal is political' to make it 'personal is political, and international' to suggest that international politics involves personal identities and private lives which remain mostly unanalysed. Feminist scholars of IR have also shown how the formation of the state and the 'international society' of states have helped the construction of gender differences through divisions such as private/public, state/society and domestic/international. For instance, the division of private and public spheres within a state has been created by a patriarchal mindset which relegated women to household work that remain largely unnoticed, and unpaid.

Peterson and Runyan have argued in their book *Global Gender Issues* (1993) that women are a disadvantaged group in the world compared to men. According to them, women make up less than five per cent of heads of state and cabinet ministers; take home only ten per cent of their income, although they make for about sixty per cent of all working hours; nearly seventy per cent women in the world are illiterate; and nearly eighty per cent women are refugees. This high level of gender inequality has been patterned by a hierarchy of power in the international society in which men are superior to women. The authors argued that we live in a gendered world in which masculinity and the values associated with it—such as rationality, activity, strength—get more weight and status than femininity and its values—such as emotionality, passivity, weakness. They point out that a gender-sensitive analysis of international politics may bring the issue of gender inequality into focus and expose how the present international political and economic systems contribute to the subordinate position of women.

Globalization has not been able to alter the plight of women; rather it has enhanced the level of exploitation of femininity. According to Guy Standing (1992), a process of 'global feminization' has occurred alongside globalization in which many jobs, formerly dominated by men, have been given to women. But these jobs have become low-wage, contractual and insecure, with very few social benefits. Sassen (1991) points out that 'free trade' export processing zones in third world countries are heavily dependent on women's labour. Big cities which make important centres for global financial transactions are also reliant on a class of women workers, who are often underpaid than their male counterparts. Pettman (1996) argues that a darker 'underside' of globalization can be found in the significant growth of 'sex tourism', and in trafficking of women and girls for transnational prostitution. According to him, many developing economies get valuable foreign exchange through sex tourism and related 'activities' in the age of globalization.

Feminism in IR proved immensely helpful in focusing on women's plight and women's demands through gender-sensitive research and theories. These theories not only harp on the exploitation of women in the family, the state, and in domestic and international societies; they have material impact on decision-making. Several countries, for instance, have taken steps to integrate women in mainstream politics and economics. In several Indian states (provinces), one-third of the seats have been reserved for women in institutions of local governance, and a Bill is underway in the Indian Parliament for reservation of one-third seats in the Parliament for women. But these measures, although significant, have only a cosmetic value. Gender inequality can be eradicated only by altering the patriarchal social structure, and by empowering women socially and economically, across the world.

This helps us to identify the distinguishing features of feminism in IR and its leading advocates, which are presented in Box 2.16.

**Box 2.16** **Feminism in IR: Basic Features and Leading Theorists**

**Basic Features**

- Feminism in international relations points out that the history and structure of, and knowledge about, IR are all gendered.

- Postmodern feminists have focused more on gender, or on how divisions between the masculine and the feminine constitute a hierarchy of power by which the former subordinates the latter.
- Major issues in IR, such as war, peace, security, power cooperation, diplomacy, foreign policy, propaganda and military reflected a masculine way of thinking.
- The realist concern for security tries to seek protection from an outside threat with a view to ensure protection of a domestic jurisdiction that fixes continuous subordination of women.
- Feminist IR theorists argue that although wars have been largely caused and fought by men, women form the majority of civil casualties.
- Cynthia Enloe rephrased the radical feminist slogan to 'personal is political, and international'
- Feminist scholars of international relations have shown how the formation of the state and the 'international society' of states have helped the construction of gender differences through divisions such as private/public, state/society and domestic/international.
- Globalization has not been able to alter the plight of women.
- Gender-sensitive analysis of international politics may bring the issue of gender inequality into focus.

**Leading Theorists:** C. Enloe, C. Sylvester, V. S. Peterson, A. S. Runyan, G. Standing, S. Sassen, J. Pettman, J. True.

## Conclusion

Proponents of feminism in IR not only encourage gender-sensitive research and analysis, they also seek to move beyond fixed gendered ideas of the human society. Some theorists searched for emancipatory paradigms within the human society, and tried to provide alternative models of human relations. J. A. Tickner (1997), for example, noted that a feminist perspective could make IR richer by providing alternative models which may redefine the ideas of production and reproduction, rationality and human relationship. Such models, believes Tickner, would help in building our conceptions about individuals, states and the international society in a better way. They may help to view individuals and states as independent, yet connected, with multiple identities and relations. Individuals and states, if viewed as having autonomous spheres of activities, would not be engaged in a relationship based on hierarchy of power. Yet they must be connected for developing a better way of living. Individuals and states must have multiple relations, beyond any fixed gendered relationship of domination of masculinity. Therefore, feminist perspectives of IR may help the discipline to search for new ideas, conceptions and theories.

QUESTIONS

1. Why is a theory required? Write a note on the important theories in IR.
2. Make a critical analysis of the liberal theory in IR.
3. Examine the pluralist theory in IR.
4. Examine Morganthau's six principles of political realism.
5. Make a critical estimate of the realist theory in IR.
6. Analyse the major arguments of the English School theory in IR.
7. Make a critique of the English School in IR.
8. Examine the major arguments of the Critical Theory in IR.
9. Make a critique of the Critical Theory in IR.
10. Analyse the Marxist theory of IR.
11. Critically discuss the WST in IR.
12. Point out the significance of the game theory in IR.
13. Analyse the decision-making theory in IR.
14. Make a critical assessment of the systems theory in IR.
15. Write a critical note on the communication theory in IR.
16. Analyse the significance of postmodernism in IR.
17. Examine the theory of constructivism in IR.
18. Bring out the importance of the theory of feminism in IR.

the table. The high-income countries comprise the highly developed category with very high level of industrial and technological growth, and higher rates of literacy and life expectancy. The upper middle income nations make the developed category with significant industrial and technological progress, as also higher literacy rates and life expectancy. The next two are the developing categories with moderate or low literacy rates and life expectancy. However, it must be noted here that the GNI per capita may not be the most accurate tool of measurement of a country's economic growth. GNI per capita of countries with a big population may lag behind GNI per capita of countries with lesser population. GDP growth rates may also come into consideration in this respect. For instance, the growth of Indian economy sounds credible if one looks at GDP growth rates over the years than GNI per capita over the years. But we must also remember at this point that although there may not be any direct correlation between the GNI of a nation and its impact in international politics, it can never be denied that the 'high' and the 'upper-middle' income states enjoy advantageous position in world politics today due to their economic clout.

## The Role of MNCs

MNCs are very large organizations spanning across several countries. Normally a MNC has a particular country of origin, but it spreads its business worldwide, with rapid circulation of goods and capital. Although there is no fixed definition of MNCs, they share some similar chracteristics. They operate simultaneously in many countries, with fixed offices, facilities and employees in each of them. They operate within the parameters of the rule of law in each country. MNCs have assumed greater significance in international politics today because they have immense economic strength and exert profound political influence on the basis of their economic prowess. Before analysing the role of such a corporation in international politics today, it is important to know different types of MNCs operating in the present world. They can be broadly classified into three types: industrial corporations, financial corporations and corporations providing services. Industrial corporations produce their own goods in factories located all over the world, and sell them to various other industries and consumers locally as well as globally. They are giant corporations in terms of their revenue and areas of operation. Most of them are in the automobile, electronics, infrastructure, and oil and gas sectors. They belong to the highly developed industrialized states like the former G-7 countries. MNCs like General Motors, General Electric, Mitsubishi, Suzuki, Toyota, Sony, LG, British Petroleum, Wal-Mart and Exxon Mobil fall into this category.

Financial corporations are involved in financial business like banks, stock broking, asset management, portfolio management and mutual funds. Like industrial corporations, they also operate across boundaries. Financial giants like the HSBC (Hong Kong and Shanghai Banking Corporation), Standard Chartered, American Express Bank, Citi Bank, Deutsch Bank, JP Morgan and Merrill Lynch maintain transnational operations. Nowadays almost all financial corporations are engaged in multifarious financial activities like banking, portfolio management, stock broking and asset management, although they are subject to more stringent (domestic) legal restrictions than the industrial or 'service corporations'. With monetary transactions at the rate of $2.0 trillion per day around the globe, financial corporations are becoming increasingly important in today's IPE.

# 3 Basic Concepts

## State as an Actor in International Relations

The concept of 'state' is very important in the study of International Relations (IR). The subject of IR, in the traditional view, deals with the interaction among independent sovereign states. As the most important political institution in the society, the concept of the state has always attracted the attention of scholars—from ancient times to the present day. It has often been analysed by scholars from different—albeit sometimes contradictory—perspectives. But its basic identities remained largely unaltered. A state is a definite geographical territory comprising people who are politically organized and pay obedience to its authority. The modern idea of the nation-state is believed to be the product of the Treaty of Westphalia of 1648, which organized different political units in Europe on the basis of language. These units gradually came to be known as nation-states. The modern state, like earlier states, has some basic components: territory, people, government and sovereignty. But it has something more: (1) legal continuity of the national society; (2) institutionalized agencies and social changes; (3) law-enforcing agencies; (4) defence against external attack or internal insurgencies and (5) economic sustenance to its population. The state exercises sovereignty exclusively over its territory and its people, and is recognized by all other states in the international domain. Even today, in the face of expanding globalization, the state remains the primary and conventional political unit that plays a key role in international affairs.

The international system is a structured pattern of behaviour among different states in accordance with certain rules and mechanisms of interaction. The extent of influence in the international political sphere varies from one state to another. The most powerful nation would exert enormous influence in any particular international issue and try to manoeuvre the situation in its favour. In actuality, few states in the world possess a strong economy, a powerful military, sufficient territory, and adequate industrial and technological infrastructure, by means of which they can exert considerable influence beyond their territorial borders. Those who do are referred to as Great Powers. Historically, these powers have shaped the international order through economic and political power, through alliances, colonial hegemonies, wars, religious aggressiveness and such other methods, in order to perpetuate their influence.

Before the Second World War, some European states—Britain, France, Germany, Holland, Spain, Portugal—were considered as great powers as they largely shaped international politics. But the war hit them hard and their powers were reduced. Instead, two other nations—the United States of America and the Soviet Union—emerged as the two superpowers after the war, and began to exert their influence in international politics and shape the world according to their calculations. Due to their ideological and political rivalries, the world got distinctly divided into two warring camps. Scholars described this situation as the Cold War. However, the collapse of the Soviet Union marked its end. In the post–Cold War period, the United States remained the only superpower with sufficient economic and military strength. It is now trying to be the prime controlling power in international politics. Historically speaking, states dominating the sphere of IR have always remained the great powers of the world. At present, the world economy is dominated by a few rich states whose GDP (Gross Domestic Product) are substantially high, compared to other states. The United States, Japan, France, Britain, China, Germany and Russia estimate for about half of the world's GDP. The concentration of economic power, along with subsequent political clout, in the hands of these few states has resulted in their superiority in world politics today. They have become important actors in world politics, influencing and dominating IR. Besides the great powers, there are other states—medium and small powers—which often play significant roles in world politics. The smooth functioning of the international system largely relies on the interdependence and interplay of all these states. Despite several challenges to the state, such as scientific and technological development, information revolution, globalization, expanding arms market, increasing significance of multinational companies and non-government organizations, the state has been able to maintain its position as the key actor in contemporary international politics.

# Non-state Actors

Traditional thinkers considered the state as the most important actor in IR; but global issues today are no longer confined only to state-based politics, war or diplomacy. A wide range of issues—relating to trade and business, communication system, ethnicity, environmental pollution, human rights or religion—are also covered by the discipline now. Besides the state, the stage of IR is now occupied also by a group of non-conventional players, popularly known as the non-state actors; they have made their presence felt in various spheres of world politics. They often influence the course of international affairs, manipulate multilateral decisions and, in some extreme cases, can even supersede the states' policies and programmes. Interdependence among states across the world has made these non-state actors quite active and significant in international affairs. For convenient understanding, non-state actors may be classified into three main groups: (1) multinational corporations; (2) inter-governmental organizations and (3) international non-governmental organizations.

## Multinational Corporations (MNCs)

A multinational corporation (MNC) is a business organization rooted in a particular country with offices and factories in several other states serving the business interest of the organization. MNCs set up offices and factories in host countries (countries where they are operating) to expand their business; to earn profits through minimizing production and transportation costs; and to regulate the global flow of capital, goods and labour. The annual incomes of some of the big MNCs exceed those of many small states. With enormous economic clout, the MNCs have the ability to influence and alter the course of domestic and international politics, and have thus become very significant actors today. For more on MNCs, and their impact on international political economy, see Chapter 10.

## Inter-governmental Organizations

Inter-governmental organizations (IGOs) are very large groupings of different national governments. The United Nations (UN) system is one of the most prominent examples of an IGO. Apart from it, some other important IGOs are the World Trade Organization (WTO), the Non-Aligned Movement (NAM), the Commonwealth of Nations, the European Union (EU), the Association of South East Asian Nations (ASEAN), the Organization of Oil and Petroleum Exporting Countries (OPEC), the Arab League and the African Union (AU). The activities of such organizations differ according to their respective goals. Some are global (like the UN, WTO, NAM, Commonwealth of Nations) while others are regional (like the EU, ASEAN, AU) or functional (like the OPEC) in nature.

By far UN is the most important IGO in today's world. It comprises almost all the countries of the world. Since all its members are sovereign states, the UN cannot enforce its decisions upon a member-state without the latter's consent. But that does not minimize its role as the principal organization on the international platform working towards maintaining peace and security in the world. The UN was created to avoid the horror called war and sustain global peace—while avoiding the use of force in its efforts—and to serve the needs of member-states. It works as a forum for socio-economic development of its members, as well as a conflict resolution mechanism for them. It endeavours to promote global peace through international cooperation. Apart from its peace initiatives, the UN is also concerned with various other issues like the welfare of women and children, environment, health, food and agriculture, education and human rights. It is also involved in disaster management programmes, housing problems and population control programmes. Despite its functional weaknesses, the UN has been playing a major role in maintaining international peace and security since its formation, and has proved to be a very significant IGO of the times.

The significance of some other IGOs like the WTO, NAM, EU, ASEAN, AU and the Commonwealth of Nations has been detailed in different chapters of this book. Without being repetitive, reference may be made to another important IGO with strong economic and political influence in the contemporary world—the Organization of Petroleum Exporting Countries (OPEC). With its secretariat in Vienna, Austria, it is an association of major oil-producing countries of the world. Its member-states, currently eleven, produce nearly 80 per cent of the total crude oil in the world, and control more than half of the world's oil exports. Considering the importance of oil in today's civilization, one may easily realize the significance of this organization in contemporary international economy and politics. The OPEC started exerting its influence in international politics in the early 1970s, when it decided to stop supply of oil to countries that supported Israel in the Arab–Israel conflict of 1973. Since then, it has remained engaged in a much successful 'oil diplomacy', with a view to influence global politics.

## International Non-governmental Organizations

Among the non-state actors, international non-governmental organizations (INGOs) are slowly assuming prominence in international affairs. They are mainly non-profit-oriented organizations, private in nature, with roots in a particular country, but not connected with any national government. Although their resources are much less as compared to national governments, INGOs interact with social institutions, MNCs, local governments and also states, to reach their goals.

They have distinct interests which they try to promote. As they extend their area of action beyond their national frontiers, they behave like global pressure groups. These organizations have specialized functions as most of them work on specific agenda like environment, human rights, disaster management, child labour, women's rights, malnutrition, ozone layer depletion, etc. These issues have assumed global relevance now, and involve and affect people across the world. In order to increase global awareness, INGOs operate across state borders and involve as many people as possible. Greenpeace is one such INGO working towards safeguard of global environment. Amnesty International, formed in 1961, is another well-known INGO engaged in activities for the protection of human rights. At present, it has a large network comprising over one million members spread across 160 countries. However, these organizations do not always enjoy the cooperation of the nation-states, and often find it difficult to pursue their goals.

Extensive industrialization and urbanization after the Second World War, and its effect on the environment and on human life, has led to proliferation of INGOs particularly during this period. Dealing mostly with humanitarian and environmental issues, big INGOs attract attention worldwide. These organizations sometimes act as campaigners, striving to seek the attention of the decision-makers with a view to influence government policies. In other cases, they may try to influence international politics by working in sensitive areas like environmental degradation, health, child labour or human trafficking. The International Committee of the Red Cross has got worldwide recognition for its commendable work in the areas of health and human welfare. Some non-state actors like different religious groups had always influenced world politics to some extent. The Church of Rome, popularly known as the Vatican or the Holy See, with the Pope as its religious head, is seen as an influential religious actor in world politics. Although Vatican has been traditionally recognized as a sovereign state, the Pope is revered more as a religious head of the Catholics the world over. His frequent opposition to birth control policies stirred up a hornet's nest in world politics in recent times. Like the Pope, the Imams of large and influential mosques in different countries also play important roles in domestic and international politics. Religious organizations like the Vishwa Hindu Parishad and the Muslim League, and religious leaders like the Dalai Lama, with their large number of followers, can influence policy-making both at the domestic front and in foreign countries, thus having a great impact on IR. But no typical pattern can be attributed to the manner of influence exercised by religious non-state actors, as their ways of exerting influence vary according to time, place and conditions.

Apart from the recognized and accepted religious non-state actors like the Roman Church, the Vishwa Hindu Parishad, the Imams or the Dalai Lama, several fundamentalist groups thriving on religious sentiments have proliferated in recent times. These fundamentalist groups often resort to terrorist activities in the name of religion so as to draw attention of the people and the policy-makers. Some of them maintain an incredibly vast global network, and even go to the extent of challenging the authority of the state. Attacks by the terrorist group Al Qaeda on American embassies in Kenya and Tanzania, and its assault on the World Trade Center in September 2001, clearly show the wide range within which such networks operate. These attacks largely affected international politics. The state sometimes appears to be very helpless in the face of such terrorist attacks carried out by the fundamentalist groups. Fundamentalist and terrorist organizations are, therefore, also considered to be important non-state actors today, due to their impact—although negative—on international politics.

A study of IR would remain incomplete without any reference to the state and non-state actors, because of their impact on international politics. Although the state remains the principal actor in IR till this day, the role of non-state actors like the IGOs, the MNCs and the INGOs have also become very much significant in recent times. They often influence and manipulate the domestic and international policies of a state. IR thrive on a successful interplay between state and non-state actors.

# National Power

Power is an essential element in politics. It is often defined as the ability of its holder to extract compliance from others, and to make others behave according to the wishes of the holder. In the study of IR, the term 'power' usually refers to national power—the power a state possesses to obtain compliance from other states. The power a state or nation possesses is dependent on a host of factors like the national economy, natural resources, military capabilities, level of industrial growth, leadership and popular support for its government. A state may use its power to promote and protect its vital interests in international politics, to save its population from external aggression and to cooperate with other nations. But at times a nation may also misuse its power by trying to enforce its decisions upon others. The extent of its ability to use or misuse power depends upon the actual power of the state. By the study of national power, it is somewhat possible to know the power of a state, and its relative position, in terms of power, in international politics. National power varies in degree and nature from one state to the other.

## Elements of National Power

The national power of a state is the product of a number of elements. These are: (1) geography; (2) population; (3) natural resources; (4) popular support; (5) national character; (6) technology and military strength; (7) ideology and (8) leadership. These elements are dependent on one another, and their combined positive contributions can make a nation powerful. All the elements of national power are not measurable or quantifiable. Elements like geography, natural resources, population and to some extent economy are somewhat measurable. Elements like leadership, ideology or morale are intangible and difficult to measure, but they too contribute to the formation of national power to a large extent. All the elements, and not any one, should contribute positively for the development of a strong and significant national power. The different elements of national power are discussed below.

### Geography

The territorial limit of a state indicates its geography. Geographic factors include location, size, topography, climate, boundaries and physical features of a state. Location is an important factor related to geography. Since times immemorial, India has been guarded by the Great Himalayas in the north and surrounded by sea or ocean on the three other sides. It could thus enjoy some sort of protection and avoid frequent foreign invasion. The location of a state can also make it a land power or a sea power, as well as contribute to its strategic importance. Location also helps in the spatial relationship of a state to other land bodies in and around it. The size of a state may also determine its power. Historically, very small states could not become great powers. Conversely, only having a big territory cannot make a state powerful. Argentina, Brazil and Kazakhstan are all big in size, but they are not big powers. However, a state must have a considerably big territory to aspire towards a 'big power' label.

The climate of a state directly affects its agriculture, economy and population. Excessively hot or cold climates are never conducive to human survival. Such climatic conditions are also unfavourable for productivity and agricultural growth. Regions with cool and temperate climate and sufficient rainfall are best suited for increasing productive capacity and for prosperity. The United States, Japan, China and a few west European countries located in the cool temperate type of climate have emerged as big powers in the world today. In general, the rhythm of life in a particular country is largely regulated by the climatic factor. The physical shape of a state also determines its administrative efficiency, vulnerability to foreign attack, military power, and also its trade and commerce. A compact state like Spain, with a well-defined boundary and a centrally located capital, enjoy better strategic and administrative efficiency than an elongated state like Chile, situated in the western coast of South America. Geographical factors like location, climate and shape are considered important in realizing differences between the rich industrialized countries of the North and the relatively poor countries of the South in the world today.

## Population

The number of people inhabiting a state can be a boon or an obstacle for the development of a state. The trends in population growth, the sex ratio, the percentage of working people, and the literacy rate are some of the factors that can contribute to national power. A sizeable population proportionate to a country's resources is ideal for the power of a state, while a disproportionate population is normally considered an impediment. However, such a population can, at times, also prove to be a source of strength. Sustained economic growth in China over the last three decades has proved that a large population can be effectively turned into human resource. But China has enforced strict birth control policies to curb its growing population. It is not always easy for every country to manage a very large population. A country with a sizeable population like the United States, England, Russia or Japan can manage its people more efficiently than countries with large populations like India or Indonesia. An ageing population is also not conducive to national power. Conversely, a population with more persons in the working age (fifteen to fifty-five years) may contribute towards enhancing national power. The rate of literacy, industrial skills and technological know-how of a population may also indicate the power of a state. The United States, Japan and west European countries with high rates of literacy and industrially skilled people are ahead in terms of national power than the countries of the South with low rates of literacy and industrial skills.

An adverse sex ratio in population is an impediment for socio-economic growth, and affects national power. A country with a disproportionate male–female ratio in its population is more prone to crime and social unrest. Another factor affecting the growth of a nation is the status of women in the society. In a society where women are seen—vis-à-vis men—as mere progenitors and not as equal partners in, or contributors to, socio-economic growth, it is difficult to strive towards development. In order to limit the size of a family and to achieve prosperity, it is necessary to educate women and give them all the rights required for the betterment of her family and the society at large. The inferior social status of women in less developed countries is closely associated with their economic backwardness.

## Natural Resources

Natural resources not only include flora and fauna, but also minerals, cultivable soil for agricultural products and resources from the sea. They are not evenly distributed throughout the world; some states abound in them, while others suffer from scarcity. Of the various natural resources, fossil fuels (coal, oil, gas) are perhaps more important in today's world. Fossil fuels presently constitute about 95 per cent of global energy consumption. Countries rich in these fuels have an edge over others in terms of national power. They earn valuable foreign exchange by exporting these minerals, particularly oil, to other countries deficient in them. Oil is also used to get political mileage. The OPEC's 'oil diplomacy' is a case in point, which remained much effective in international politics since the early 1970s.

Mineral resources are also important, but they are not the essential preconditions for a state's industrialization and for its overall economic development. Japan and England are not very rich in minerals, yet they are highly industrialized and developed nations because other elements of national power are available in plenty in these countries. But it becomes easier for a country with abundant mineral resources to become a great power than a country with little mineral resources. The United States and the Soviet Union, which emerged as two superpowers after the Second World War, had plenty of mineral and other natural resources to support their industry and military. Self-sufficiency in oil and other natural resources helped the United States to remain a superpower, and Russia to aspire for a 'big power' status, after the Cold War. The United States is self-sufficient in crude oil, copper, aluminium, coal, iron ore, zinc and gypsum, while Russia is still a key exporter of minerals like coal, iron ore, manganese and copper. China has abundant mineral resources to support its growing economy and industrial infrastructure, and its big-power aspirations.

Certain agricultural products are peculiar to some typical climatic and soil conditions. Rubber, sugar, tea, coffee, cocoa and jute are produced only in a few countries across the world, although they are used by almost all the countries. But the producing states have not been able to manipulate and raise market prices as the products are less essential than crude oil or coal. Enough supplies of food grains are important for a nation to be powerful. While the United States, Russia, France and other Western countries are self-reliant for food grains, most of the third world countries are not. Food is a major problem in almost all the developing states. They spend a considerable portion of their meagre foreign exchange on importing essential food grains like rice, wheat, corns and vegetables. This consequently weakens their economy, and therefore their national power. On the other hand, self-sufficiency in food has helped India to achieve economic growth and to add to its national power.

Mere presence of large reserves of natural resources alone cannot make a state powerful. For that, it is necessary to utilize them properly to meet the requirements of industrialization, export and the people of the state. Along with these, positive contributions of other elements of national power are also required for a nation to become sufficiently powerful in international politics.

## Popular Support

Popular support is an intangible element of national power. A nation with a popularly elected government is likely to exercise greater power both at national and international levels. Its policies and programmes are mostly backed by people's support and hence their implementation becomes easier. But in case of authoritarian governments, policies and programmes are often forced upon the people without their consent. Today, almost all the powerful states in the world are largely based on popular support expressed by their democratic forms of governments. More and more countries like the former socialist states of east Europe, and several nations in Asia, Africa and Latin America are taking the route to democracy. Even China has shed its earlier rigid authoritarianism to allow public opinion to be expressed in matters of government and politics. It is seldom doubted that a government enjoying popular support can pursue its interests and exercise its power more effectively than one with little legitimacy among its people. Popular support may sustain a government or reject it. The quality of leadership, the nature of the government, and the contemporary situation may ultimately determine the kind of popular support a state enjoys. The support of the people cannot be something constant. Like tides and ebbs, popular support is subject to fluctuations, even if not at regular intervals.

## National Character

The national character of a state is the product of various factors like its history, culture, religion, politics, economy and even propaganda. The character of the people of a nation is not built in a day. It takes ages to develop it. Different nations have developed their spirits of loyalty, courage, faith and respect with regard to their individual political systems, which can never be stereotyped. The concept of national character is perhaps best explained when we say that the Japanese are technologically highly developed, or that the Germans are disciplined people, or that the Americans are respectful to democratic values, or that the Somali people are less manageable. It is a state of mind and spirit which defies any organized analytical study. National character has a bearing on national power to a great extent. The character of the people of a state may determine its power ambitions. A state with less determination to succeed may not achieve sufficient national power. A state may be homogenous or heterogeneous; it may have religious diversities or not; it may be racially united or multiracial; but every nation has its unique national character which is reflected through an underlying current of loyal, bold and faithful spirit of love for the country. National character ultimately generates devotion towards one's country. It is also expressed in the form of support towards the national government.

## Technology and Military Strength

Advances in technology in the last few centuries have profoundly changed the global society. Technological innovations in the field of transport and communication, information systems, production facilities, agriculture, industries, medicine, finance and weapons have brought about significant changes in the world. Man's quest for knowledge has resulted in remarkable technological advancement. It has largely contributed towards increasing a state's power. A technologically advanced state is today regarded as a powerful state. It is possible for a country with sufficient technological base to have advanced industries, better transport facilities and a strong military with the latest weapons. Technological advancement has always contributed towards reinforcing the military strength of states. Countries that could acquire the latest technologies were able to build a strong military. They were always ahead in the race for national power, because a strong military is always very effective for power ambitions. Today, information technology is considered as a new-generation technology, and countries that are advanced in information technology have an edge over others in terms of national power. Technology changes with time. Countries that can acquire new technologies fast remain ahead in the race for power in international politics.

### Ideology

Ideology is a set of beliefs about the society, its people and the political system, including the government. Ideologies have a great influence on the public psyche. They are consciously advocated by various machineries of the society like political parties, governments, interest groups and non-governmental organizations. People may subscribe to various ideological beliefs like totalitarianism, communism, capitalism, liberalism, anti-colonialism, democracy and even nazism or fascism. The importance of ideology in international politics could be ascertained from the fact that ideological differences between a 'liberal democratic' United States of America and a 'communist' Soviet Union resulted in a struggle for power and supremacy in the world, known as the Cold War, for four and a half decades. Ideology, if it becomes a fad, may create problems for states. A rigid commitment to any ideology can lead states to war. Ideology is further linked to national power because without the backing of national power, an ideology remains a passive and non-productive pattern of ideas in IR.

### Leadership

Another important element of national power is leadership. A well developed society with an integrated technology and a high morale can be possible only when there are leaders of great ability. Leaders not only instill values and beliefs among people, but can also guide the state towards prosperity and growth, which ultimately enhances national power. The decision-making process in every state is influenced by its leaders' personality traits, values and beliefs. On the one hand, an ambitious leader of an ambitious state may try to achieve national power through coercive means and eventually lead the world to a war. In recent history, Hitler's leadership is a prominent example. On the other hand, the leaders of a state can be innovative and form new ideas to change a political system or to sustain it, thus leading to the country's prosperity or decline. China's communist leaders built the concept of a 'socialist market economy' to put China on the road to economic prosperity, and to sustain communist rule with renewed public support. Former Soviet leader Mikhail Gorbachev introduced the policies of 'glasnost' and 'perestroika' to revive the Soviet society and economy; and these policies were instrumental for the end of the Cold War. The element of leadership is thus crucial to the power a state enjoys both in domestic and international politics.

National power is essentially a relative concept. It needs to be analysed in terms of powers of other states. Since the various important elements of national power are subject to change, the concept itself is not constant. A state may rise or fall from time to time in terms of power. Power relations between states may change due to wars, natural calamities, scarcity of resources, technological innovations, economic progress, and changes in leadership, military strength and alliances. Such changes affect the rise or fall in power of a state.

## Balance of Power

In international politics, nations compete with one another for supremacy. Their struggle for power may be overt or covert. Some scholars maintain that international society is anarchic in nature. From times immemorial, independent states waged wars for promoting their respective national interests.

They applied direct or indirect methods for gaining control over other states. Such methods include application of force or use of military strength, diplomacy, economic assistance, alliances and negotiations. Whether a state is large or small in terms of power is largely determined by its military power. States are the only bodies to own and use military power. But waging a perpetual war is not possible—even for the strongest state on earth—nor is it desirable. The objective of establishing peace, however, also requires the backing of power. All states want to achieve national power to fulfill their objectives in international politics. The improvement of its power position, both externally and internally, becomes the dominant objective of a state. The system of balance of power becomes important here. Balance of power is a system where five or six nations, more or less equal in terms of power, control world politics and maintain—knowingly or unknowingly—a kind of a balance in world politics.

The concept of balance of power originated with the emergence of the nation-state system in 1648, after the Treaty of Westphalia was signed. Its principles were most fully applied in eighteenth and nineteenth century Europe. The balance of power system remained very active during this period. Since early nineteenth century, Europe occupied the centre of power politics. Five major powers—Britain, France, Prussia, the Austro-Hungarian state and Russia—maintained a complex balance.

The term 'balance of power' has different meanings. So it becomes rather difficult to define the term. Scholars have attempted to define balance of power in different ways. According to George Schwarzenberger, such a balance produces a relatively peaceful and stable international system. Here states join or leave alliances so that a stable pattern of behaviour is preserved. Balance of power is only a particular manifestation of a general social principle, according to Hans J. Morgenthau. He has identified four usages of the term balance of power. These are: (1) a policy aimed at a certain state of affairs; (2) the actual state of affairs; (3) an approximately equal distribution of power and (4) any distribution of power among states including a dominance of power by one over the other. Sidney B. Fay provides the most cogent definition of the term when he describes balance of power as 'a just equilibrium in power among the members of the family of nations as will prevent any one of them from becoming sufficiently strong to enforce its will upon the others'. This system operates in what may be called in a 'negative way' in world politics. Here the states are more interested in curbing the powers of other states rather than limiting their own strengths. They are keen on ensuring a balance of power in their favour by trying to limit the powers of other states. This makes the system rather peculiar and unique in international politics. An analysis of the features of this system follows.

## Characteristics of Balance of Power

The balance of power system has several characteristics. To start with, it may either be simple or complex. If two states are possessing more or less equal military power, they would not wage war against each other, realizing that a war would result in nothing but a great loss of resources and human life. There would then be, in all probability, no war. This is an example of simple balance of power or a see-saw model of balance of power. The situation is different when more than two powerful states are involved. States want power for themselves; at the same time they have the fear of being dominated by other states. This sense of uncertainty forces the states to form alliances which are shifting in nature. There can never be any constant greater power or smaller power. Different powers in the system alter their relative power positions in relation to their economic growth. As a result, there is always a shifting pattern of alliances which maintains a kind of a balance of power. Thus, the balance of power system is not permanent; rather it is temporary and short-lived.

The balance of power is not a gift of any unknown entity. States cannot wait for it to happen. They endeavour to achieve balance through different means. They may form alliances to counter-balance the power of another group of states. For the sake of their own survival, the states may have to go to war or enter into diplomatic negotiations. Such activities may lead to a balance of power system. In order to be effective, this system has to be changing and dynamic. Otherwise, it would appear to be meaningless in a constantly changing world order.

The system of balance of power cannot be regarded as an instrument for preserving world peace. It aims at maintaining the sovereignty of nation-states; it does not necessarily maintain world peace. It had been observed in the past that an alliance waged war against another alliance of states fearing that the existing equilibrium might be disturbed. Moreover, it becomes difficult for a nation to assess whether a balance of power has been achieved at all. Until there is no aggression on the part of a nation-state, it could be presumed that a balance of power prevails. Therefore, the real test of the system is believed to be in the time of war. This system is primarily a game for the big powers, and the small states are mere spectators.

Balance of power system is neither suitable for democracy nor for dictatorship. Democracy is based on consensus. Public opinion in a democracy may not favour pursue of power. Further, democracy aims at social welfare, development and peaceful coexistence among nations. It may not want to play a game where a war could happen at any time. On the other hand, dictators always wants to see their states over and above others. They want to pursue power, but would not like to compromise on the question of sharing power with others. They would not tolerate any rival in the game of power. They would not like to see any 'friend' gaining equality in terms of power; and are ready to make such a 'friend' a rival by wishing to demolish them in war. In other words, a dictator does not want the existence of a more or less equal partner. Some critics point out that the balance of power system is no longer operative in the world today. After the Second World War, international politics revolved round a 'bipolar system' where the two superpowers, the United States and the Soviet Union, controlled world politics. Under such conditions, the principle of balance of power failed to function along its classical line that favoured the existence of five or six more or less equal powers, and their interactions in world politics. It is believed that this system ended with the Second World War after existing for nearly three centuries. But it must be noted here that it may stage a comeback in future, if the world witnesses the emergence of five or six 'equal' powers with their endeavours to control international politics.

## Methods of Balance of Power

Hans J. Morgenthau identified some methods of balance of power which made the system active and operative. The application of these methods depended on several factors like the political situation, distribution of power among states and threat from other states. Balance could be attained either by making another state less powerful or by enhancing the power of one's own state. There are mainly four methods balancing power, as identified by Morgenthau: (1) divide and rule; (2) compensations; (3) alliances and (4) armaments.

## Divide and Rule

Since ancient times, 'divide and rule' has been a method used frequently to weaken the opposition. It is an age-old policy—initially adopted by individual rulers, and later by nation-states—of making their competitors weak by dividing them territorially, ideologically or politically. The most classical example of this divide and rule policy used as a method for achieving balance of power is the one adopted by France. Since the early seventeenth century till the Second World War, France favoured either the division of Germany into a number of small independent states or preventing the creation of a unified Germany. France was apprehensive that a strong and unified state of Germany might cause a threat to France in world politics. History tells that France had always opposed the birth of a unified Germany. Morgenthau also cites the example of the former Soviet Union preventing the creation of a unified Europe, since the 1920s to the end of the Second World War. The Soviet Union feared that the concept of a unified Europe might strengthen the West Bloc and upset Soviet power. So, it always encouraged the ideological division of Europe into an 'east' and a 'west' bloc. This policy helped the Soviet Union retain its supremacy in world politics for a ling time.

## Compensations

Since early eighteenth century, compensation was applied as a crude device to maintain balance of power. It was entirely territorial in nature. The working of the principle of compensation was clearly evident when Austria, Prussia and Russia mutually settled among themselves territorial acquisition of Poland, which helped to maintain power equilibrium in central Europe. Morgenthau noted that the Treaty of Utrecht, signed in 1713 to end the War of the Spanish Succession, recognized compensation for the first time as a method of maintaining a balance of power in Europe. The treaty provided for the division of the Spanish occupations, in Europe and other parts of the world, between the Hapsburg and the Bourbon monarchies. This principle of compensation was used in Africa by the major colonial powers. Numerous treaties were signed by these European powers to delimit their spheres of influence and to establish their domination over the colonial territories for the purpose of maintaining balance of power.

## Armaments

States trying to maximize power always procured arms to gain an advantage over others. But procuring or manufacturing of arms required the existence of strong economic conditions. Historically, very few states could afford to procure enough armaments to deter competitors. Five or six great powers always remained ahead in the arms race in their quest for supremacy. Armaments provided for a precarious balance of power system, where five or six states wanted to procure more arms either to outsmart their rivals or to maintain parity with them. It was a situation where nation A tried to obtain more arms to outdo nation B, or to keep pace with nation B, and also with nations C, D and E. These nations (B, C, D and E) would do the same either to outsmart others in the race for armaments, or keep parity with them. A balance of power, although precarious, would thus be maintained. It is true that initiatives for disarmament existed alongside the race for arms, but these efforts failed to meet the desired levels of success due to the quest of different states for more power. Armaments provided for a balance of power in a negative way.

### Alliances

Formation of alliances to add to the strength of states, or to deter or weaken the opposition, had been a potent method of maintaining a balance of power in international politics. History provides many instances where several states entered into alliances to prevent the rise of a powerful state. Initially, most alliances were formed in response to a perceived threat; hence they were defensive in their orientation. By forming alliances, states could add to their power capabilities, and could also exert greater influence when bargaining with others.

Alliances may be of short-term interests; they may be issue-based; they may also survive for longer periods if formed for strategic purposes or based on commonality of interests. Alliances are not permanent in character. As the states are independent and sovereign, they can make or break alliances whenever necessary. Alliances are actually arrangements made for convenience. They are mainly formed to prevent any state or a group of states from becoming sufficiently powerful in international politics, and thus play a significant role in maintaining balance of power. The temporary nature of alliances actually helps the balance of power system to remain operative. Most alliances are formed on the basis of converging interests, threat from common adversaries, or similar ideological orientations. When national interests converge in alliances, they tend to be a little more cohesive and organized. But generally, most alliances within the balance of power system are fragile in nature because they are based on political calculations of participating nations.

A study of the balance of power system reveals that as a system it is temporary and fragile, like some of its methods, which in fact contribute to its ephemeral character. Although the system existed for almost three centuries, from the mid-seventeenth to the mid-twentieth century, it could be destroyed any moment. However, three hundred years do not make a very long period in the history of statecraft. As mentioned earlier, the balance of power system collapsed after the Second World War. It requires favourable conditions to remain operative. The post–Second World War conditions were not conducive for the system to remain active. However, the system may emerge again if all the conditions for the maintenance of balance of power become favourable.

## Balance of Terror

The term 'balance of terror' is used to refer to the arms race, both conventional and nuclear, between the United States and the Soviet Union after the Second World War. Both the superpowers were engaged in a frightening arms race, each trying to terrorize the other and its followers during their intense rivalry, popularly known as the Cold War. But a precarious peaceful relation existed between the two countries, and between the two camps led by them. Both avoided a direct confrontation because both were afraid of a nuclear war and its projected devastation. But they went on stockpiling weapons of mass destruction to deter the other nation from launching an attack, and also to terrorize the other nation. This situation was described as a 'balance of terror'. It was believed by many scholars and statesmen that the balance of terror had replaced the balance of power after the Second World War.

The manufacture and stockpiling of nuclear weapons by the two superpowers after the Second World War created a new reality in international politics. The whole world gradually realized that the use of nuclear weapons in any war could destroy the entire human civilization. The two superpowers realized that any possible war between them would be a nuclear war, and in that war, there would only be losers, and no actual winner, because the devastations after a nuclear war would severely affect both the countries and their achievements. So, each restrained itself from attacking the other, although weapons of mass destruction continued to be manufactured and stockpiled by each of them to instill a sense of fear in the minds of the other nation and its followers. A kind of a balance was thereby maintained between the superpowers. In 1955, this condition in post–Second World War international politics was rhetorically described by Lester Pearson, an American Diplomat, as the 'balance of terror'.

# Imperialism and Colonialism

As important concepts of IR, imperialism and colonialism are difficult to understand separately, because these concepts are overlapping and somewhat interchangeable. Some of the well-known definitions of imperialism seem like definitions of colonialism, and vice versa. In his classic *Imperialism: A Study*, J. A. Hobson failed to distinguish between the two and ended up defining colonialism, rendering injustice to the title of his book. Hobson had little choice to do otherwise, because the two concepts are almost similar. Imperialism is often linked to the building of an empire by an alien power in an alien land, and direct rule of that empire; colonialism refers to the annexation of territory by a foreign power, and rule over the people of that territory. So there is hardly any difference between the two concepts. Consider, for instance, a well-known definition of imperialism offered by Parker T. Moon: 'Imperialism … means domination of non-European native races by totally dissimilar European nations.' (Palmer and Perkins, 1953). This could well be the definition of colonialism if the word 'imperialism' is replaced by 'colonialism'. V. I. Lenin's views on imperialism as the highest stage of development of monopoly capitalism is frequently referred to analyse the concept of colonialism. Some scholars tend to distinguish between the two by arguing that imperialism is a broader concept, which implies the desire of a state to create and rule empires in different parts of the world. In comparison, according to them, colonialism is narrower as it refers to somewhat small administrative units, known as colonies. But this distinction gets blurred when both the concepts actually mean occupation of territories and direct rule of the people living within those territories against their will. The distinction gets erased due to the simultaneous usage of these two terms both by common men and scholars. For instance, the two-hundred-year-long British rule in the Indian subcontinent is referred to as both British Imperialism and British Colonialism, by wise men and by not-so-wise people. The two concepts are very similar and somewhat interchangeable. Henceforth, this study will use the term 'colonialism' to refer to both the concepts.

Colonialism is the practice of domination of one state over another through political, administrative and economic control. In the past, it was also a process of acquiring territories by the industrially advanced European powers in Asia, Latin America and Africa. The rise of capitalism in Europe from the twelfth to the fifteenth centuries, and the Industrial Revolution, also in Europe, later, gave birth to a group of capitalists who gradually found markets exhausted in their own countries and looked for markets abroad. Colonial or imperial expansion became the order of the day, and new and newer territories in Asia, Africa and Latin America were captured.

Advances in agriculture, industries and military made the European states stronger. Science and rational knowledge prospered in Europe simultaneously. The age of discovery witnessed the rise of colonial powers in Europe. England, France, Portugal, Holland and Spain established their colonial empires in direct competition to each other. The colonies were acquired through the use of trade, diplomacy and force. Portugal, for instance, reaped huge profit through lucrative 'spice trade'. Portugal maintained sea-borne empires in populated Asian and Latin American societies with ulterior financial motives. Britain, on the other hand, had both financial and political motives. At its peak from eighteenth to mid-twentieth century, Britain possessed colonial empires comprising more than one-fifth of the world's land surface.

Most of the colonies comprised 'native-coloured' people. The 'white' colonial masters looked down upon them as uncivilized, unruly, backward and barbaric. The relationship between the colonial masters and the native people was that of domination and subjugation. The masters rationalized that it was their obligation, the 'white man's burden', to civilize the backward masses. Christian missionaries were used to 'civilize' the native people, and allegations of religious conversions were raised against the colonizers. Considering the native population simply as a source of cheap labour, they exploited them by inducting them into the armed forces to fight their brethren, as well as to pursue colonial aggression in newer territories. By distinguishing the 'whites' from the 'coloured' in all spheres of socio-political life, a crude and extreme form of racism was practised by the colonial rulers.

Since a colony is a territory ruled directly by the colonial power, the local population had almost no voice in the government. In a passively intelligent manner, the European rulers gave the 'native elites' some major benefits in order to gain socio-political control. They attempted socialization with certain key local groups to extract loyalty to the colonial rulers. The cost was little, but the gain enormous. The European colonizers forced their language upon the local inhabitants, and also imparted education in it. The natives were considered culturally inferior to the colonizers. From the newly annexed colonial territories, minerals and other raw materials were extracted and shipped away to home countries to support industries. Instead of food crops, the colonizers insisted on cultivating exportable cash crops like indigo, sugarcane, jute, coffee and tea. Infrastructural facilities were built to serve the purpose of the colonial rulers rather than the local people. The colonial rulers practically cared a little for the colonized people.

The process of decolonization started after the Second World War in most parts of Asia, Africa and South America. The European colonial powers suffered heavily during the war. Their economies being hit hard, it became a burden for them to maintain large colonial empires. The economic and political costs of maintaining colonies were too high after the Second World War. Most colonizers lost interest and granted independence to many colonies in Asia, Africa and Latin America. In some former colonies, independence came through peaceful ways, while in some other, violence accompanied independence.

Political independence of the erstwhile colonies, however, could not solve their woes. Socio-economic problems continued to haunt the newly independent states as they were trying to stand on their feet. For these decolonized countries, the state-building process proved very difficult with little economic resources, vastly impoverished and illiterate people, and inadequate industrial and communication infrastructures. Fostering economic growth with a sustained development, and installing a democratic government with matured political institutions, remained a distant dream for them. A new form of dependency developed. For initiating their state-building process, the newly independent countries looked for resources, and the developed states of the West were ready to give these countries loans and economic assistance, with very high rates of interests, and reciprocal socio-economic benefits. The new states had little option to deny these loans, and they again became victims of exploitation at the hands of the rich states. Economic domination by the rich countries led to a new kind of indirect control over the poor states, a control that also pervaded the socio-political-cultural sectors in the developing world. This new form of domination, of the newly independent poor countries by the rich states, after the Second World War, came to be known as neocolonialism.

# Neocolonialism

A group of third world scholars had first used the term 'neocolonialism' in the early 1950s to describe the economic exploitation of the erstwhile colonies by the rich, industrially developed states. Neocolonialism is different from colonialism. Here domination is more indirect and exercised mainly through economic means like loans, grants, aids and other forms of economic assistance given by the rich states. Unlike colonialism, it is not direct political rule of a state by a foreign power, through annexation of territories. Neocolonial domination is mainly perpetuated by indirect methods in the guise of a 'donor' or a benevolent 'helper'.

The colonies of Asia, Africa and Latin America became independent within the first twenty-five years after the Second World War. These former colonies aspired to have free and politically stable societies with satisfactory levels of economic development. But their aspirations remained largely unfulfilled as they had to depend on the developed states for their survival. The problems created by colonialism continued, and in some countries, got worse. The advanced countries exploited the economic backwardness of the new independent states by giving them economic assistance, but subjugating them to their wishes and dictates. This novel form of indirect exploitation came to be known as neocolonialism. It is a system of legal political independence of the former colonies, but a de facto economic dependence of these countries on the rich states.

## Methods of Neocolonialism

Neocolonial domination is perpetuated through several methods—economic, socio-political and cultural. The following are the 'economic' methods of neocolonialism. (1) Loans, aids, grants and donations to poor countries. Such economic leverages are not without strings. Countries providing them extract socio-political benefits, besides charging huge interest rates. (2) Creation of debt traps through economic assistance. Poor nations which take loans from the advanced states at high rates of interest are often unable to repay not only the principal amount, but even the interests. So, the amount of loan, keeps on multiplying. The situation turns grim when poor states require fresh loans for developmental projects. They need to take fresh loans from rich states without repayment of the earlier loans. As a result, they become burdened with huge debts. Sometimes rich states 'waive' loans, but they ask for many favours before making such write-offs. The poor states cannot but have to agree to the conditions set by them, to come out of the 'debt trap'. (3) Sometimes, MNCs are accused of serving the interests of their parent states, mostly developed states of the West, in their exploitation of the people of the poor countries.

They employ cheap and unskilled labour and pay relatively less wages to them in host countries. During the Cold War, they were also accused of investing money to topple or install governments according to the likings of their parent states.

Here is a classification of the 'socio-political' methods of domination used by the neocolonial states. (1) Creation of social unrest in former colonies by dividing them territorially, or on ethnic and religious lines. India, Palestine, Congo and several other former colonies are instances in this regard. (2) Influencing domestic politics by bribing political parties, or arming and paying groups that can topple an 'unwanted' government, and install a 'preferred' one. (3) Assassination of local leaders who prove to be 'obstacles' to the political game plans of the neocolonial masters. (4) Helping splinter groups to carry out subversive and terrorist activities. (5) Installation of military bases near the former colonies to keep them under pressure, and to frighten their political elite with a view to make them succumb.

'Cultural imperialism' is another way in which neocolonialism is perpetuated. It is the way in which the indigenous culture of a state is supplanted by the foreign cultures of the dominant powers. 'Cultural' methods of neocolonialism may be classified as follows. (1) Encouraging use of the language of the dominant powers for educational, social and official purposes. (2) Establishing lavish cultural missions to attract the local people towards the alien culture. (3) Flooding the market with books, films, CDs and DVDs of games and films, and foreign newspapers. (4) Using satellite television channels to air popular TV programmes of the dominant countries. (5) Creating web sites, online search engines and social networking sites to attract more and more people and gain popularity. It is believed that neocolonial powers spend astronomical amounts to sustain cultural imperialism because this is a very potent, friendly and gentle method to 'infiltrate' a country and its culture. Neocolonial powers also reap huge profits through the business of entertainment and culture.

Many scholars like Andre Gunder Frank, Samir Amin and Wallerstein tend to believe that neocolonialism brings more miseries to the poor, peripheral states of the world. The methods of perpetuating neocolonialism are more subtle, yet sharper than those of colonialism. Sometimes an affected state and its people fail to realize that they are the targets of exploitation, and potential victims. However, it is argued by many, particularly in the West, that with the onset and expansion of globalization and information revolution, neocolonialism has become an outdated concept. But as long as the big divide between the rich North and the poor South exists, neocolonialism as a concept will remain alive, and its critics will continue to find many takers.

## Racism

The term 'race' refers to a group of people believed to have common ancestors, different from other such groups in their physical features. Racism is the discrimination or prejudice based on race. Sociologists define racism as enjoyment of privileges by certain groups over others on the basis of colour of the skin, hair and eye; and also height, sharpness of the nose and a sense of superiority of the group. Racism emerged out of culturally sanctioned beliefs that defend the advantages the whites enjoy because of the subordinated position—social, economic and physical—of the non-white people.

Racism raised its ugly head with the system of slavery that existed in North America since the advent of the early settlers who emigrated there. Gradually, it spread to other places. With the early settlers fully dominating the colonial territories in terms of number and economy, the native populations were pushed to the margins of the society. Australia, New Zealand and the United States provided leading cases of such societies. Soon, the control of the states was in the hands of the colonial settlers. The colonial rulers brought the ships of Africans who constituted cheap labour force in these territories. Till the eighteenth century, at least eight million slaves were transported to North and South America. The institution of slavery was legitimized, and in the United States slavery was governed by an extensive body of law. Each state had its own slave codes and body of court decisions. Slavery in the United States lasted till the end of the nineteenth century. During the age of slavery, the blacks were considered as intellectually inferior to the whites. Slaves were regarded as personal properties of their masters. Racial segregation, that formally separated blacks from whites, especially in South America, became a prevalent practice in other parts of the world, and existed till the twentieth century. US President Abraham Lincoln's 'Emancipation Proclamation of 1863' imposed legal prohibition on the practice of slavery in the United States. However, outlawing slavery did not eradicate racial discrimination overnight. Progressive human rights movements in twentieth-century America has worked for the establishment of equal rights by eliminating racial segregation.

History bears proof that racism caused pain, suffering and bloodshed. German dictator Adolf Hitler's persecution, enslavement and methodical elimination of the Jews, popularly known as the 'holocaust', and 'apartheid' policies in South Africa, were manifestations of racism. Hitler's belief in the racial supremacy of the Germans encouraged and justified Germany's aggression against non-German states during the Second World War and the holocaust. The Germans considered themselves the superior people, the Aryans, the 'master race' who enjoyed the right to oppress the racially inferior groups. For this kind of racism, six million Jews were either killed or made to work to death in Germany during this period.

A policy of racial discrimination was prevalent in South Africa even in the latter part of the twentieth century. South African racial segregation policy was adopted by the white minority governments against the black majority population until 1990. It came into force in South Africa in 1948. The 'superior' white European settlers imposed a political system in South Africa known as Apartheid (meaning apart-ness). This system separated the whites from the non-whites. The minority whites forced the non-white inhabitants to enjoy only restricted rights. No interaction was allowed between the whites and the non-whites. There were schools, colleges, railway stations, parks, public toilets, movie halls, restaurants and unskilled jobs meant exclusively for the non-white population. Their entry was restricted to the places meant for the whites only. So intermingling of races was strictly prohibited. Soon South Africa became a country tormented by racial atrocities. Not only was Apartheid prevalent in South Africa, but the blacks were killed brutally on the streets, playgrounds and even in the police stations. From 1948 to 1990, South Africa had an appalling record of cases of human rights violation. After his release from jail, Nelson Mandela, the black leader of South Africa, campaigned hard against Apartheid laws. Under tremendous international and domestic pressure, the South African government eventually abandoned the Apartheid policy and established a new regime under the leadership of Nelson Mandela.

Racism, although legally prohibited, exists in our mindset even today, in the form of social discrimination. The roots of racism lie deep within the foundations of different societies which distinguish people on the basis of colour of skin, or birth in a socially accepted 'superior' family belonging to a 'superior' group in the social hierarchy. Till this day, racism is practised indirectly in different parts of the world, causing resentment among the racially discriminated people. For instance, police brutality against racial minorities is common in many countries. Racial minorities also face political and economic discrimination, as well as social ostracism, in many parts of the world. The fight for equal rights and fundamental freedoms of all people, everywhere in the world, is thus far from over.

## QUESTIONS

1. Describe the role of the state as an actor in IR.
2. Analyse the significance of the non-state actors in IR.
3. What do you mean by national power? Discuss its main elements.
4. What is balance of power? Describe its characteristics.
5. Examine the important methods of balance of power.
6. Write a short note on balance of terror.
7. What do you mean by imperialism? Is it different from colonialism?
8. What do you mean by neocolonialism? Discuss the methods of establishing neocolonialism.
9. Write a note on racism in contemporary international politics.

agreements and setting up of institutional mechanisms for closer cooperation. Wen's visit to India was eventful.

Bilateral relations continued to be steady in 2011. This was manifested through several top-level visits by leaders of the two countries. Indian Prime Minister Manmohan Singh visited Sanya in Southeast China from April 12 to 15 to participate in the BRICS summit. On the sidelines, he also had a bilateral meeting with Chinese President Hu Jintao. In the same year, chief ministers of Bihar, Madhya Pradesh and Gujarat also visited China in June, September and November, respectively. Similarly, the Chairman of Xinjiang Autonomous Region and Party Secretary of Gansu also visited India as part of the MEA-ILD exchange and Distinguished Visitors Programme of the MEA. One of the highlights of the 'Year of Exchanges' was the visit of a youth delegation to China. Premier Wen Jiabao met and addressed the Indian youth. Several ministerial and official visits to China were made to participate in BRICS activities. For the first time, India–China Consultations on United Nations Security Council issues were held in March 2011. Leaders of the two countries have maintained regular contacts and have met frequently during international gatherings and meetings of multilateral forums in the recent past.[19]

The year 2012 was declared as the 'Year of India–China Friendship and Cooperation'. In this year, high-level official visits between the countries continued unabated. In early February 2012, the Indian Foreign Minister Salman Khurshid visited China. He met with important Chinese leaders and discussed bilateral issues. About his trip, Khurshid told the media:

> On the bilateral front, we have discussed our growing trade relationship. We are confident in our reaching the goal of US$ 100 billion by 2015. I have highlighted the need for initiating measures to balance our trade relations ... Specifically, we have agreed that the newly established working mechanism for consultation and coordination in border affairs will have its first meeting at an early date.[20]

Chinese Foreign Minister Yang Jiechi visited New Delhi in late February 2012 on an official trip and met with top Indian leaders. After his talks with the Indian Prime Minister Manmohan Singh, Jiechi informed the media:

> Under the current international and regional situation, China and India enjoy broad prospects for growth of bilateral ties. 2012 is an important year for the two countries to build on the past progress and usher in a better future. The two sides have agreed on programs of exchanges and cooperation, which will increase friendship between the two peoples, advance exchanges and cooperation in various fields and send a positive signal about the growth of the relationship.[21]

Chinese President Hu Jintao visited New Delhi for the BRICS summit in late March 2012. On the sidelines of the BRICS summit, the Chinese President met with senior Indian leaders and discussed bilateral issues. During his meeting with the Indian Prime Minister, the two leaders talked about enhancing economic, cultural and people-to-people exchanges.

Chinese Defence Minister and a member of the Central Military Commission General Liang Guanglie visited India during 2–6 September 2012. It was the first visit of a Chinese military general to India in eight years. General Liang Guanglie called on the Indian Prime Minister and the Defence Minister. The Indian and Chinese Defence Ministers had an extensive exchange of views on defence and military exchanges and cooperation between the two nations. They also discussed the regional security situation and international issues of common interest and concern. The two defence ministers agreed to work together to enhance mutual trust in the security field and continue to maintain peace and tranquillity in the India–China border areas.[22] A series of

# 4 Concepts and Techniques of Foreign Policy

It is almost impossible for any state to live in isolation from international politics in today's world. Interdependence among states has increased tremendously. Each state strives to establish healthy relations with other states. Consequently, a country's foreign policy has assumed enormous significance, much like its domestic policy. A country's image and prestige, as well as the survival of its government, very often rests on its foreign policy. Every state therefore wants to formulate a definite foreign policy to interact with fellow states in international politics. But a country's foreign policy is not an abstract phenomenon. It is very carefully formulated by the government in the national interest, taking into consideration various factors like the tradition and cultural heritage of the country, its socio-political history, ideas and thoughts of its leaders, and also the changing aspects of international politics. The formulation and implementation of a country's foreign policy is thus not an easy job, because several important issues are associated with it. These issues relate to the concepts and techniques of foreign policy, which are discussed in detail in this chapter.

## National Interest

An important concept associated with the formulation of a foreign policy is that of national interest. Since the term 'national interest' is used very frequently in domestic and international politics, its exact meaning remains vague. National interest may refer to several things at the same time. It may mean the aspirations of a country, its policies and programmes, as also emotions and debates surrounding them. An example here may help to illustrate. Let us say that India aspires to become a major economic force in the near future. The policies and programmes surrounding this aspiration may be said to be India's national interests. However, there could be a serious debate on whether this (becoming a major economic force) is India's only national interest. It may have other aspirations as well. For instance, India may also try to become a major military power in the near future. This particular aspiration, and the policies and programmes to achieve this dream, may also be said to be India's national interests. Therefore, the term national interest has various meanings. But a simple definition may be as follows: *National Interest is composed of different aspirations of the state, as also of the policies and programmes to fulfill these aspirations. National Interest is not a fixed singular notion; it is the collective product of a country's aspirations and interests.*

National interest is not a value-free concept; it is linked to values like morality and altruism. No country in the world can ignore all values to fulfill its aspirations. National interest, if value-free, may become a threat to international peace and security. Experts like Joseph Frankel,

Norman D. Palmer and Howard C. Perkins have pointed to the significance of values in the concept of national interest. A country's national interest can never be mechanical, inhuman and absolutely selfish. It must respect the interests of other nations as well. In this world, every country formulates and implements its foreign policy to protect its own national interest. In doing so, it can never harm the interests of other states. In other words, if every country tries to protect its national interest in an aggressive manner, war would be inevitable and the world would be a dangerous place to live in. It is precisely because of this danger that the national interest of a state cannot be completely value-free.

However, an important debate crops up here. If the purpose of a country's foreign policy is to protect its own national interest, how can it respect and accommodate the national interests of others? Would a country respect others' interests at the cost of its own interests? The notions of cooperation and compromise are very important to solve this debate. A country would first try to protect its own interests as far as possible, and only then try to accommodate those of others. In other words, while protecting its national interests, a country must also cooperate with others and accommodate others as far as possible. In our earlier example, India must first fulfill its aspiration of becoming a major economic force. But in doing so, it cannot suppress other countries having similar ambitions. Through mutual cooperation and compromise, all nations can effectively pursue their respective national interests. On the contrary, if each nation tries to follow its national interests aggressively, war would be the inevitable outcome. For a nation, war is the last resort. When all other avenues of cooperation and compromise are closed, a nation may go to war to protect its interests. But normally states try to cooperate with one another and pursue their respective interests in an atmosphere of peace, because a peaceful condition is the most ideal condition to pursue national interest. In order to establish peace, every nation must be prepared to sacrifice some of its aims and aspirations and accommodate others. National interest is thus never a value-free concept. Ethical, moral and altruistic issues are linked with it.

National interest is very well reflected in a country's foreign policy. A foreign policy is made and implemented to protect the national interest of a country. Since national interest is not value-free, a foreign policy cannot afford to be value-neutral as well. In other words, a foreign policy is never unnecessarily aggressive; it tries to respect values of mutual cooperation, understanding and peaceful coexistence. An aggressive foreign policy seldom succeeds in international relations. A flexible, accommodating foreign policy is more near to reality, and more likely to succeed. The success of a foreign policy depends on certain techniques and instruments as well. One such instrument of foreign policy is diplomacy.

## Diplomacy

Every foreign policy has two sides—one is the making (formulation) of the policy, and the other its implementation. If national interest is associated with the formulation part, diplomacy is linked with the implementation part of a foreign policy. For the success of a foreign policy, the role of diplomacy is very crucial. Diplomacy is that art which, throughout ages, has implemented foreign policy in reality. Put simply, foreign policy is applied through the instrument of diplomacy.

Diplomacy is an ancient instrument of foreign policy. The city-states of ancient Greece had diplomatic links with one another. According to the famous Greek political philosopher Thucydides, the ancient Greek city-states developed a very well-structured diplomatic link in around 500 BC. This ancient art is still alive in the twenty-first century, despite many challenges and transformations. Its basic norm has, however, remained the same: diplomacy is an instrument through which states maintain relations among themselves.

## Definition

It is possible to define the term 'diplomacy' in simple words. As already mentioned, it is an instrument through which countries maintain relations with one another. According to *The Oxford English Dictionary*, Diplomacy is 'the management of international relations by negotiation' or 'the method by which these relations are adjusted and managed'. Theoretically, diplomacy is different from foreign policy. A foreign policy is applied through diplomacy, but diplomacy has nothing to do with the making of foreign policy. In other words, the concept of foreign policy has a much wider perspective. Besides diplomacy, other instruments are required for the successful implementation of foreign policy. Diplomacy is one of the instruments for the application of foreign policy. In that sense, diplomacy as a concept is narrower in scope than foreign policy. After this analysis, a modern and simple definition of diplomacy may be attempted: *Diplomacy is the method of communication among governments for the maintenance of international relations.*

## Main Tasks of Diplomacy

Diplomacy as an instrument of foreign policy performs several important functions. Hans J. Morgenthau in his book *Politics Among Nations: The Struggle for Power and Peace* identified four major tasks of diplomacy. These are: (1) to determine the major objectives of the state, and the power actually available to fulfill these objectives; (2) diplomacy must assess the objectives of other states and the power actually available to fulfill these objectives; (3) diplomacy must assess to what extent these objectives are compatible with each other; (4) diplomacy must employ the means suited to the pursuit of its objectives. According to Morgenthau, 'Failure in any one of these tasks may jeopardize the success of foreign policy and with it the peace of the world'. In his analysis of these four tasks of diplomacy, he opines that the first major task of diplomacy is to assess the objectives and aspirations of one's own nation. These objectives must be determined in the light of the power actually available to the state to fulfill such objectives. If any nation sets objectives that it has little power to achieve, it would indulge in inept diplomacy. Therefore, every nation must set its objectives in accordance with its national power.

Further, it is not enough to assess one's own objectives and powers; diplomacy must also assess the objectives of other nations and the actual powers available to them to fulfill such objectives. This is the second major task of diplomacy. This is not an easy task, as assessing others' objectives and powers is extremely difficult. It involves guesswork, examining the available information in a pragmatic manner and shrewd calculations. Diplomacy must not view others' powers and objectives casually and, at the same time, it must not eulogize the powers and objectives of other nations. Therefore, this continuous assessment process is difficult, yet a vital function of diplomacy.

The third major function of diplomacy, according to Morgenthau, is to determine to what extent the objectives are compatible to each other. This means that a diplomat must continuously compare the objectives and powers of his nation with the objectives and actual powers of other nations. For example, Indian diplomacy must assess the objectives and powers of India with those of China or Pakistan or United States. This is again not an easy task, and it requires adequate efficiency to perform this function.

The fourth important task of diplomacy, as per Morgenthau's view, is to employ suitable means to fulfill the objectives of his nation. Diplomacy must employ all possible means to achieve its goals. A skilled diplomat will employ methods according to the demands of the situation. Diplomacy may engage in negotiation, persuasion, appeal or use the threat of force. An excessive emphasis on a particular method may be detrimental to foreign policy. Therefore, diplomacy uses a combination of means to fulfill a nation's objectives. A weak nation with little military power, however, cannot use the threat of force to fulfill its objectives.

Morgenthau analysed the functions of diplomacy in the context of power. Morgenthau, an exponent of the Realist Theory in International Relations, believed that political power is a key element in international as well as domestic politics. He tried to analyse international relations in terms of power. Therefore, in his analysis of the functions of diplomacy, Morgenthau also used the concept of power. But such an analysis of diplomacy in the light of power is not above controversy. Continuous assessment of powers and objectives may not be accurate. Even if a diplomat can assess the power of his nation, it is impossible for him to assess the powers of other nations very accurately. However, in Morgenthau's 'four tasks of diplomacy', the essential duty of a diplomat may be observed: a diplomat will always apply his reason and wisdom to assess his objectives and also that of other nations. In this context, it is necessary to analyse the functions of diplomats. Diplomacy as an instrument of foreign policy is actually put into practice by the diplomats. Countries communicate with one another mainly through diplomats, even in this age of technologically driven communication channels. Therefore, it is essential to know the functions of diplomats.

## Functions of Diplomats

Norman D. Palmer and Howard C. Perkins identified four major functions of diplomats. These are: (1) representation; (2) negotiation; (3) reporting and (4) protection of the interests of the nation and its citizens in foreign lands. These functions are essentially vital for the success of diplomacy, and require careful analysis.

### Representation

A diplomat represents his country in a foreign land. All diplomats are, in this sense, the chief representatives of their countries in an alien land. For example, the Indian Ambassador to the United States officially represents India in America. This function of representation is important as well as sensitive. The personality of diplomats, their conversational skills, behavioural patterns, social contacts in their place of posting, all are very crucial for their success as a diplomat and for the success of the foreign policy of their country. A diplomat bridges two countries, their own states and the states where they are working. Their main duties are to implement the foreign policies of their governments and to protect the national interests of their countries in the alien land. For exercising their duties successfully, they have to cultivate social contacts on foreign land. They must establish contacts, among others, with leading politicians, bureaucrats, intellectuals, the military and business persons. Through their social contacts, they can 'sell' the foreign policies of their countries successfully. But at the same time, they must be very careful about their social relationships, because these may be misused by vested interests. If diplomats do not cultivate their social relations carefully, their own images and the images of their countries may suffer. A diplomat's functions can be compared with that of a 'salesman'. Like a successful 'salesman', a successful diplomat has to develop an attractive personality and important social contacts to 'sell' their products. Here, their 'products' are their national interests and foreign policies. They must 'sell' the national interests of his country effectively in the foreign land. Their governments are heavily dependent on them for the successful implementation of their foreign policies and for the protection of their national interests. The function of representation is thus very important for the diplomats as well as for their country.

### Negotiation

An important technique of diplomacy is negotiation. The success of diplomacy depends upon successful negotiation. A successful diplomat, in other words, must be an able negotiator. He may have to participate in bilateral, trilateral and multilateral negotiations, and for each type he may have to adopt different approaches. In international relations, it is possible to solve problems or diffuse tensions through negotiation. The art of negotiation involves a diplomat's ability to influence others, his power of persuasion through conversational skills, knowledge about prevailing international politics, wisdom about how and when to move forward or backward. Diplomats have to be very good calculators of events, time and space. A problem that the diplomat faces as a negotiator is how much to compromise and how much to claim, without sacrificing his national interest. A skilled diplomat can strike a fine balance between the two. The success of a foreign policy and the prestige of a nation often depend on successful negotiation. Therefore, this function of diplomacy is very important as well as sensitive for the diplomat.

### Reporting

This is another significant function of the diplomat. According to Palmer and Perkins, the report that a diplomat sends from his place of posting to his native land can be treated as the 'raw material' for the foreign policy of his country. A diplomat must analyse the social, economic and political conditions of his country of work and send an unbiased report to his government. So, a diplomat must have adequate knowledge about the socio-economic-political milieu of his country of posting. Moreover, his reports can determine the course of bilateral relations. For example, the Indian Ambassador to the United States would submit periodical reports to the Government of India, citing not only the socio-economic-political conditions in the United States, but also issues like bilateral trade and commerce, the scope for Indian business in the United States and vice versa, and the future political and economic scenario in the United States. He would also report about the attitude of important political leaders and legislators toward India. His reports would also highlight, among others, the present scenario and the future possibilities of India–US educational, scientific, strategic and cultural exchanges. The Indian government would study his reports carefully and take policy decisions with regard to bilateral relations with the United States, based on such reports. This shows the significance of the function of the reportings of the diplomat. An objective, unbiased and impartial report is always treated as a very good source material for foreign policy.

### Protection of the Interest of the Nation and Its Citizens in Foreign Land

A diplomat has the responsibility to protect the interest of his nation and its citizens in his country of work. As per provisions of different bilateral and international treaties and agreements, a diplomat shall protect the interests of his nation and its citizens in a foreign land. The Indian Ambassador in Japan, for example, shall protect the interests of the citizens of India in Japan. Indian citizens can contact the Indian Embassy in Tokyo during any crisis or mishap like natural disaster, wreckage of ships or accidents. Similarly, American citizens can contact their embassy in any country for help during any kind of crisis—personal, natural or socio-political. A diplomat also tries to promote his nation in a foreign land. Diplomats endeavour to promote the culture, education, trade and commerce, tourism of their country in their land of work. For this purpose, they organize seminars, symposia, exhibitions, tours and investment or educational fairs in foreign land to attract local people towards their country. In these seminars and fairs, they highlight the policies of their governments and try to draw the attention of the local people towards these policies. Hence, this function is one of the significant aspects of successful diplomacy.

## Open and Secret Diplomacy

Diplomacy, since its inception to the later part of the nineteenth century, was a clandestine affair. So, for a very large period diplomatic activities were conducted secretly. It was believed that since diplomacy is integrally linked with national interest, it would be wise to keep it a secret for the benefit of the nation. There are myriad examples of secret treaties—products of secret diplomacy—in international politics. The Berlin Congress Treaty of 1878 was kept a secret. The Sykes-Picot Agreement between France and Russia in 1916 was also kept in the dark. Before that, the 'Entente Cordiale' (Treaty of Friendship) between Britain and France in 1904 was surreptitiously conducted. Even several provisions of the Yalta Agreement of 1945 were created behind the curtain. The causes for secret diplomacy, as revealed later, were national interest and war-time exigencies. But one definite reason behind secret diplomacy was the fear of adverse public reaction towards certain treaties or agreements. Because of this fear, several treaties that had the potential to ignite public passion were kept secret.

From the first half of the twentieth century, the demand for open diplomacy gained ground. People started to denounce secret diplomacy mainly for two reasons: the spread of democratic ideas and the hatred that a nation incurred due to secret diplomacy. Gradually the demand for treaties concluded in full public view, and ratified by the Parliament, gained popularity. Woodrow Wilson, the former US President, was an ardent supporter of open diplomacy. In his address before the US Congress in 1918, Wilson called for full public knowledge about every treaty or agreement signed by governments. After that, the Covenant of the League of Nations and the Charter of the United Nations proclaimed full support for open diplomacy. The complexities created in international politics by secret diplomacy during the First World War and before it also inspired people to support open diplomacy.

Open diplomacy has two features: (1) rejection of the conclusion of secret treaties; (2) conducting of diplomatic negotiations in full public glare. But experts like Joseph Frankel and others have questioned whether it is possible in reality to go for open diplomacy. Frankel supports the demand for the rejection of secret treaties, because secret treaties contradict the ideals of democracy. But he is sceptical about the success of open diplomacy. He feels that open diplomacy can bring embarrassment for a nation. Diplomats use various shrewd methods in diplomatic dialogues—they often utter what they do not mean, and do not utter what they mean. They may regularly retract from verbal promises made by them. They may have to do this for the protection of their national interest. But it would be impossible for diplomats to use all their shrewd calculations in full public glare. Once they promise something before the people, they would not be able to retract. Their national interests may then suffer, thinks Frankel. Several other experts like Harold Nicolson, Walter Lippmann, Palmer, Perkins, Sisley Huddleston and Morgenthau have described the concept of open diplomacy as unrealistic. According to these scholars, political leaders would propagate open diplomacy in order to get public support, but in practice they would follow the rules of secret diplomacy, because diplomacy and national interest are inseparable.

There is truth in the view that open diplomacy is not realistically possible even in this age of globalization and democracy. No democratic country can afford to bring all diplomatic negotiations to light. For national security purposes, all democratic nations keep some areas of diplomacy secret. But nowadays treaties are not kept out of public knowledge as most of them require the ratification of the national Parliament, although not all the details of diplomacy are brought to light. In fact, the debate on secret versus open diplomacy is still very strong. While democratic ideas demand open diplomacy, national security concerns support the rules of secret diplomacy. This debate would be stronger in the future with the spread of democratic ideals across the globe.

## Economic Diplomacy

Economic diplomacy has assumed enormous significance since the onset of globalization and gained popularity in every part of the world after the Cold War. *Economic diplomacy means enhancing cooperation with other states through increasing trade and commercial relations. Economic diplomacy avoids political differences, and places greater emphasis on strengthening friendship through economic cooperation.* During the Cold War, the bipolar nature of world politics created an atmosphere of political and military rivalry. The world suffered from the fear of a real, devastating war between the two superpowers, which were nuclear states. In this atmosphere of tension and rivalry, diplomacy was mainly dominated by political and military issues. The end of the Cold War in 1991 created a unipolar world where intense military and political rivalry were no longer witnessed. In the absence of bloc politics, nations gave more attention to economic diplomacy. In a changed international order after the Cold War, economic diplomacy gradually gained momentum in different parts of the world.

However, we must remember in this context that economic diplomacy began its journey immediately after the Second World War. The Truman Doctrine, the Marshall Plan or the Warsaw Pact were forms of economic diplomacy in some way or the other. The main aim of all these programmes and pacts was to strengthen relations with countries through economic assistance. Economic diplomacy was born during the Cold War, but gained momentum after it. As stated already, economic diplomacy sets aside political differences and concentrates on trade and commercial relations, following several techniques. It tries to enhance trade with other countries, creates investment opportunities, establishes economic zones and free trade areas for hassle free trade, and encourages free movement of labour and capital. The onset of globalization gave a fillip to economic diplomacy. By the 1980s, third world countries had started liberalizing their economies. This liberalization programme had presented an unprecedented opportunity to the developed world to engage in economic diplomacy with the third world countries. On the other hand, the third world countries also grabbed this opportunity and got themselves seriously involved in economic diplomacy with the developed world.

The best example of how economic diplomacy sets aside political differences is the recent US–China bilateral relationship. From the political point of view, the United States and China stand far apart. The United States has a liberal democratic political system, whereas in China a one-party system exists. American politicians and legislators complain regularly about violation of democratic and human rights in China. Official American documents like the Annual Human Rights Report, released by the State Department, regularly place China in the group of countries that violate human rights and democratic freedoms of the people. Yet China and the United States share a very strong economic relationship. At present (2010), the amount of American investment in China is more than ten times the amount of American investment in India. China's huge market and its socialist market economy have attracted American investment in a massive way. Despite political differences, the United States and China are engaged in serious economic diplomacy. The latter is now the fourth largest trading partner of the former. Therefore, it can be stated that economic diplomacy has set aside political differences between the two states. Other countries, especially India and Pakistan, can emulate this trend of economic diplomacy as provided by the United States and China. Economic proximity between these traditional rivals can obliterate political differences and can generate a new era of cooperation in South Asia. Nevertheless, economic diplomacy has definitely ushered in new optimism in international relations.

## Future of Diplomacy

In an age of spectacular development of information technology, the role and importance of professional diplomats are coming under scrutiny. Now two Heads of Government (HOGs) can directly communicate between themselves over telephone, fax, e-mail or video-conferencing and discuss necessary political and related issues. The services of a professional diplomat may not be necessary in this case. This trend has raised doubts over the future of diplomacy. For a long time, from the birth of diplomacy in ancient Greece to the Second World War, professional diplomats were the undisputed channels of diplomacy. But since the Second World War, due to the unprecedented development of science and technology, traditional notion of diplomacy faced a crisis. Moreover, with the spread of democratic ideals and growing demands for open diplomacy, the traditional form of diplomacy is also facing a crisis. Democratic institutions like the Parliament, media and peoples' organizations are trying to influence the process of diplomacy. The world of diplomacy is, therefore, no longer the exclusive domain of the professional diplomats only; science and technology and democratic ideals have made deep inroads into this exclusive world.

What is the role of diplomacy then? If the prime ministers of India and Britain can directly talk over telephone or video-conferencing and solve all problems, where does the diplomat fit in? This question may strengthen doubts about the future of diplomacy. But at this juncture, it must be pointed out that neither diplomacy nor the importance of the diplomats have dwindled over the years. When two HOGs are talking directly, they are also engaged in diplomacy; and in this case it is known as direct diplomacy. Moreover, when the prime ministers of India and Britain are talking over telephone, the groundwork and issues for such talks have been prepared by the diplomats, because the politicians are not always very well acquainted with every detail of foreign policies. This is why when the HOGs meet directly, they are accompanied by senior diplomats and bureaucrats. Moreover, every nation carries out diplomatic missions in other countries in order to maintain healthy relations with others, as well as to protect its national interest and implement its foreign policy in other nations. The role of the diplomats is very crucial in this context. If diplomacy had lost its relevance, countries would not have spent enormous sums to maintain diplomatic missions abroad. Even in this age of advanced information technology and globalization, diplomacy is mainly used by professional diplomats who use science and technology to sharpen the art. Diplomacy is not conducted by politicians frequently as they are not aware of its tricks and as they do not have the time to pursue it. If any politician tries to take too much interest in diplomacy, his political career and the interest of his state would suffer. Therefore, he prefers to leave it to the diplomat and seek his advice when meeting, or talking over phone to, fellow politicians from foreign lands.

# Propaganda

Propaganda is an important technique by which foreign policy aims to succeed. In ancient times, the ruling class used the technique of propaganda to influence people to accept its programmes and views. But scientific propaganda, according to Joseph Frankel, started its journey in the early twentieth century. Till the First World War (1914–18), the importance of propaganda in international relations was negligible. American and Western European scholars believe that during the inter-war period (1919–39), the former Soviet Union and Nazi Germany used propaganda extensively to garner support for their views and programmes. Since then, the use of science and technology for propaganda started in a huge way, and the journey of scientific propaganda began.

## Definition

The idea of propaganda was first initiated by the Roman Catholic Church. According to Frankel, the Church 'had institutionalized the propagation of faith through a special Sacred Congregation (*de propaganda fide*) from the title of which the word "propaganda" is derived' (Frankel 1977: 131). The British Government during the First World War, and later, Soviet Union and Germany, started scientific propaganda in support of their views and programmes. Propaganda may be simply defined as follows: *A systematic attempt to influence the minds and emotions of a target group for a specific purpose. For propaganda radio, TV, print media and Internet are used in modern times.*

Propaganda is different from diplomacy. In the first place, diplomacy is a government-to-government affair, whereas propaganda is aimed at the people of other states. For instance, during the Cold War, Soviet propaganda was aimed at the populace of the United States and West Europe; whereas American propaganda was aimed at the populace of the Soviet Union and East European countries. At the same time, the respective propaganda were also used to influence the minds of their own people as well. Secondly, diplomacy may sometimes consider the interests of other nations, but propaganda is intensely self-centred. It is not possible for any propaganda to highlight the policies and programmes of other nations. The sole purpose of a propagandist is to highlight the interest of his own nation and affect the minds of others. Propaganda only glorifies the propagandist nation, it does not think of others. Thirdly, while diplomacy has positive impact on international relations, propaganda contributes nothing positive to it. According to Frankel, propaganda, due to its selfish state-centric character, only contributes negatively to international relations. Self-seeking propaganda, glorifying the policies and programmes of a particular nation, may generate a negative mindset in other countries. This only breeds hatred and animosity in international relations. Diplomacy and propaganda are thus different, although they are both very useful arms of foreign policy.

## Techniques

A successful propaganda may effectively be compared with advertising and sales. Like an advertiser or a salesperson, propagandists must fix their target group and area of operation and have adequate knowledge about them (the area in this case is a state). A propagandist must analyse, like an advertiser, the demands, aspirations, emotions and fears of his target group, as also the socio-economic-political milieu of his area of operation, and invent appropriate methods of propaganda. Propaganda has several methods. Palmer and Perkins have summarized all these methods to finally provide four important techniques of propaganda: (1) methods of presentation; (2) techniques of gaining attention; (3) devices for gaining response and (4) methods of gaining acceptance. These techniques are analysed here.

## Methods of Presentation

The success of propaganda is highly dependent on the presentation of issues. The acceptance of any propaganda depends on its art of presentation. A propagandist can transform a lie or a half-lie into truth, and vice versa, through their ability of presentation. Palmer and Perkins cited a very good example of how Nazi Germany used a wrong document to ignite anti-Jew sentiments successfully among the Christians in Europe. According to them, Hitler's Nazi administration aptly exploited as 'proof' a document titled *Protocols of the Wise Men of Zion* to spread the message that the Jews were hatching a conspiracy against the Christians to rule the world. This propaganda created anti-Jew sentiments in Europe and served Hitler's purpose. However, it was discovered later that the infamous protocol was designed by a section of the Tsarist police to topple Tsarist rule in Russia.

During the Cold War, both the United States and the Soviet Union resorted to convincing propaganda. The Soviet Union, in all its official documents, projected the picture of a very strong and solid economy. It, however, became evident after the disintegration of the Soviet Union that the Soviet economy was in poor shape. The Soviet Union had to resort to such propaganda to protect its image of a superpower and to compete with the United States during the Cold War period. The purpose of a propagandist is to win the confidence of his target-group by any means. Before attacking Iraq in 2003, the United States had declared that it had 'clear evidence' to 'prove' that Iraq was stockpiling WMDs (weapons of mass destruction). But till date, no such 'evidence' has been found in Iraq. Behind this propaganda, the purpose of the United States was to mobilize public opinion against Iraq. The purpose was fulfilled. Several such examples could be cited from international politics to show how the art of presentation made propaganda successful.

## Techniques of Gaining Attention

After presentation, the next target of the propagandist is to gain the attention of his target group. The propagandist adopts various means to gain attention. To attract the attention of the government of another country, methods like TV or radio speech, open letters, protest marches are arranged. Where the target group is the people of another country, several other methods are followed. A very subtle yet sober method is to run educational and cultural missions in foreign lands to spread the policies and programmes of a particular state. Organizations like The United States Information Agency or the British Council are spread across the globe to implement the programmes and policies of the United States and the British governments respectively. Besides providing services like library facilities to the people in a foreign land, these missions also attract the attention of the local people towards the policies of their governments through seminars, exhibitions and workshops. In today's world, the technique of gaining attention through direct show of military strength has become almost obsolete. Yet, rich nations try to show their prowess indirectly. The posh, air-conditioned, sophisticated educational and cultural missions silently announce the economic prosperity of the United States or Britain. The rich industrial nations also promise to give economic or military assistance to other countries. Such promises are generally accompanied by extensive propaganda. Normally, declarations for economic or military assistance are made during the visits of the HOGs to a foreign land, because such visits are covered extensively by the media in both countries. Thus, when the US President visits India, several American assistance or cooperation programmes are normally announced before the American and the Indian media. The visits of the HOGs are now exploited by every country to gain attention to its foreign policy. During such visits, extensive propaganda on friendship and cooperation are taken up. Although propaganda is a continuous activity, it may become forceful at certain times, like the visits of HOGs. The availability of modern tools such as satellite TV, radio, internet, fax and mobile services has added more teeth to propaganda. Nowadays, even the terrorist groups are taking the benefits of modern methods to gain public attention toward their policies.

## Devices for Gaining Response

A major aim of propaganda is to elicit response from the target group. The propagandist follows various methods to elicit response. They use sentimental appeal, nationalism, the emotion of the people—of their own nations and that of others, too—as well as reason, to gain response to their propaganda. A very effective method is the use of slogans to ignite the passion of people. Slogans like 'Liberty, Equality, Fraternity' or 'Workers of the world unite' or 'Herr Hitler' touched the emotions of the people to a great extent and elicited tremendous response. In independent India, slogans like '*Garibi hatao*' (eradicate poverty) or 'Green Revolution' or '*Hum do Hamaare do*' (we are two, we have two) became very popular as well as effective to attract people's attention to different domestic programmes. Apart from slogans, the use of national flags, symbols and images are quite frequent in eliciting responses from the people. The American 'eagle', British 'lion' or Indian 'lion pillars of Asoka' (Asokastamva) can ignite a sense of nationalism. According to Palmer and Perkins, the 'Swastika' symbol of Nazi Germany generated intense nationalistic feelings and emotional attachments. Sometimes, charismatic appeal by individual leaders is used to garner response from the people. Mahatma Gandhi, Netaji Subhas Chandra Bose, Abraham Lincoln, Hitler and Mussolini, to name a few, had such charismatic appeal. Nowadays, the charisma of renowned personalities from the world of sports or of cinema, besides that of political leaders, is used to gain support for official policies. They are frequently used as a part of propaganda to elicit popular response as its impact over public opinion is quite high.

### Methods of Gaining Acceptance

A propagandist uses different methods to make his campaign acceptable to people. He tries to project himself as very friendly to his target group. If the propagandist can successfully convey the message that 'I am one of you,' his chances of getting accepted are always high. During elections, candidates use this strategy in all countries. Even politically and financially strong candidates try to establish a 'people's man' image of theirs to garner support. A clever portrayal of this image can help them win elections. The propagandist also invokes religion or sycophancy around a national icon, or talks in terms of morality, ethics and altruism to make his propaganda acceptable. In international relations, states also try to make their propaganda acceptable on similar lines. For example, India frequently refers to the Gandhian principle of non-violence and peaceful coexistence in its foreign policy. The United States of America termed its invasion of Iraq as 'humanitarian intervention', required urgently to establish human rights in Iraq. In this instance, the United States tried to make its policy acceptable to the world by invoking the principle of morality.

A propagandist has to adopt various methods, depending upon his target-group and area, to make his propaganda sharp and successful. Appropriate and meaningful propaganda is essential for the success of foreign policy and protection of national interests. Therefore, all nations try to have an effective propaganda machinery. Successful propaganda, however, is not an easy task. It demands intellect, money and adequate infrastructure. It is frequently observed that, in this, rich nations are ahead of poor nations who lack money and infrastructure to launch massive propaganda operations in support of their policies and programmes.

## Military and Foreign Policy

The role of the military is very significant to the implementation of any foreign policy. It is easy for a nation with a strong military to protect its national interest and successfully implement its foreign policy. History does not provide any example to the contrary. For nearly 300 years, when the system of 'Balance of Power' was prevalent in international politics, five to six European powers controlled the course of international politics. These European powers were Britain, France, Germany, Holland, Spain and Portugal. All these nations had great military strength. Their military and economic strength put them ahead of others in the race for the control of world affairs. They were strong in conventional arms than others. But, after the Second World War, with the introduction of nuclear arms, these European powers were no longer in a position to occupy a key role in world politics. Their economies were devastated by the war. And, they were not nuclear-weapon states when they fought the war. Consequently, their three-hundred years of domination of world politics was compromised and their role as determinants of world politics was reduced to the minimum.

Bipolarity became prevalent in international relations after the Second World War. The United States and the Soviet Union, the two military superpowers, took the lead as controllers of international politics. Both were nuclear powers. Simultaneously, they maintained big armies and huge reserves of conventional weapons. They used to spend enormous sums for the maintenance of their military and armaments. After the end of the Cold War, the United States has emerged as the only superpower. The United States is very strong militarily and economically. As a result, it can control international politics after the Cold War. Therefore, it has been observed in this brief analysis covering a period of four hundred years—from the beginning of the Balance of Power system to the end of the Cold War—that only nations strong in military could always control international politics; not states with weak military power.

It must be mentioned in this context that economic strength is necessary to establish a nation as a military power, because the maintenance of powerful and a big armed force is highly expensive. As discussed earlier, the European nations had to depart as leaders of international politics due to the devastation of their economies during the Second World War. It became impossible for them to maintain a strong military, and consequently, their power receded. The Soviet Union had to spend excessive money to maintain its status as a military superpower during the Cold War period. But subsequently, the Soviet economy was unable to afford this huge spending on its military. According to experts like Peter Calvocoressi and Norman D. Palmer, this was one of the causes for the disintegration of the Soviet Union. Therefore a strong military always demands an equally strong economy.

It is normally believed that the role of the military in foreign policy is limited in a democracy, because democracy ensures civilian rule. But this view is not altogether true. The role of the military is quite significant in the implementation (and making) of foreign policy in a democracy as well. A former US President declared after the Second World War that the future of America would be ruled by the politician-military-industry combine. His views were proved correct. In present-day America, the role of this combine is extremely significant not only in domestic politics, but in its foreign policy as well. During the long forty-five years of the Cold War, the US military played a crucial role in America's foreign policy. The military was frequently consulted for the making and the implementation of the American foreign policy during this time. After the Cold War, in recent times, the US military also played an extremely meaningful role in the US foreign policy with regard to Iraq, Afghanistan and other nations of the world. The military is a significant factor in the foreign policy of other democratic countries like Britain and India as well.

The military also plays a very active role in the making and implementation of foreign policy in other forms of government (one-party and totalitarian) as well. In the one-party systems of the former Soviet Union and east European socialist countries, as well as in present-day China, the role of the military in foreign policy has been quite prominent. During the Cold War, the Soviet military, like its American counterpart, was always consulted in foreign policy matters. China also gives importance to its military in the making of foreign policy and its implementation. For instance, the proposal to solve any problem at the China–India border, or any agreement between them on this issue, requires the endorsement of the Chinese (as also Indian) military. Although such an agreement is normally proposed and signed by civilian rulers, they seek the approval of the military before proposing or signing the agreement. This example shows the importance of the military in foreign policy matters in one-party, totalitarian and democratic political systems. Needless to say, the military is all-in-all in military dictatorships in case of both domestic and foreign policy matters. The men in uniform in such a system enjoy direct exercise of state power; theirs is the last voice in domestic as well as foreign policy issues.

The idea that the military is required only at wartime is not true. The example cited above—a proposal or an agreement between India and China to solve any border-related problem must be endorsed by the military—is not one from the period of any war. Such agreements may be signed during peace as well. If the military of both the countries do not support this proposal or agreement, be it at the time of war or of peace, the proposal would be dropped from the foreign policy agenda. Therefore, the role of the military is very crucial in foreign policy making and implementation during peace time as well. Military support plays an instrumental role in making a foreign policy successful. During a war; this help can be direct; at the time of peace, it can be either direct or indirect. In the latter case, people may or may not have any knowledge about it. In today's world, although any direct manifestation of power is seldom observed, yet every state wants to use its military as a 'backup force' behind its foreign policy. The presence of a strong military helps a state protect its national interests and pursue its foreign policy effectively.

## Making of Foreign Policy

A foreign policy is usually understood as a policy of a certain state. Therefore, we are acquainted with phrases like 'India's foreign policy,' 'China's foreign policy' or 'the foreign policy of France'. But, if we think deeply, we will realize that what is known as 'India's foreign policy' has been formulated by only a few individuals or a certain group of India, and not its entire population. Similar to a domestic policy, a foreign policy is also prepared by the ruling class or the government along with some influential people. Nowhere in the world is the foreign policy of a country formulated by its entire populace.

Which individual(s) or group is associated with the making of a foreign policy? A simple answer to this question is: a foreign policy is made by the government. But the government is usually a big group that may consist of even a hundred persons. Studies have shown that governments in different countries usually have twenty-five to a hundred persons. Does all of them share the same interest in the making of a foreign policy? Foreign policy is a specialized area. Neither does everybody have the same interest in it, nor is everybody adept at it. For example, one who becomes the Minister of Agriculture for the first time may not have any interest in the foreign policy or may not be consulted by the cabinet in this matter. Usually a few persons in the government are associated with the making of its foreign policy, the HOG and the Foreign Minister assuming the primary role. Apart from these two people, a few other senior ministers and bureaucrats actively participate in the process. The Parliament, some interest and pressure groups and the public opinion can also influence the making of the foreign policy of a nation. The roles of these important individuals, groups and institutions in the making of foreign policy are analysed below.

## Head of the Government and the Foreign Minister

The role of the HOG is immensely significant in the making of foreign policy. HOGs like the US President, the British and the Indian prime ministers or the German Chancellor are intimately associated with the making of the foreign policies of their respective countries. The head may consult some senior ministers in the cabinet for this task. If the HOG takes keen interest in foreign policy, or if he has the charisma of a leader with total control over the cabinet, he takes lead in the making of the foreign policy of his country. Jawaharlal Nehru, the first Prime Minister of India, played such a leading role in the making of the foreign policy of his country. Normally, the HOG consults his cabinet, but there have been instances when he completely ignored the cabinet and took decisions on their own. During the 1956 Suez Canal Crisis, for example, the then British Prime Minister had sent the British forces to the Suez ignoring his cabinet. But the head of a coalition government cannot afford to ignore his cabinet on decisions regarding foreign policy.

If the HOG is not an expert on foreign policy, or if he does not take an active interest in this area, his Foreign Minister becomes an important figure. The Foreign Minister must, in that case, inform the HOG about all policy decisions and get their approval regularly. Sir Earnest Bevin, Foreign Minister of British Prime Minister Clement Attlee, and John Foster Dulles, US Secretary of State, who was in the Eisenhower Cabinet, became key figures in the making of foreign policies of their respective countries. In India, Foreign Minister I. K. Gujral (he later became the Prime Minister) took complete control of foreign policy matters as his Prime Minister H. D. Deve Gowda had little interest in this regard. As Attlee, Eisenhower and Deve Gowda did not take keen interest in foreign policy matters as heads, their foreign ministers played key roles in this direction. But nowadays, almost all HOGs take active interest in the making of foreign policies because the futures of their governments are largely dependent on the success of foreign policies. With the help of the Foreign Minister, other senior ministers and bureaucrats, they prepare foreign policies for their governments.

## The Legislature

In many countries, the legislature plays a relatively smaller role in the making of its foreign policy vis-à-vis its role in domestic politics. The Parliament of a country is more powerful in the making of domestic laws than in the making of foreign policy. The legislatures of different countries enjoy different degrees of power over their respective foreign policies. For example, the legislature in the United States called the US Congress has more power in foreign policy matters than the legislatures of India and Britain. The US Senate is, in fact, the most powerful legislative body in the world in matters of foreign policy. In India and Britain, the lower chambers of the Parliament enjoy some power over foreign policy issues. Outside democratic political systems, the legislature enjoys very little power over foreign policy. In one-party systems like China, the political party has the last say in this respect. In military dictatorships, the Legislature, if it is functional, has either no power over foreign policy, or it just endorses the decision taken by the military rulers in foreign policy matters without any debate.

The legislature is usually a big debating house, where it is difficult to actually *make* the foreign policy. It debates more on foreign policy than making it. In biparty and multiparty democracies, the government defends its foreign policy in the legislature, whereas the opposition either criticizes or gives support to the government's foreign policy. The scope for similar debates is limited in one-party systems. Here, the legislature endorses decisions already taken by the party. Generally, the Legislature ratifies bilateral or international treaties and agreements. It also passes necessary laws and approves pertinent budgetary allocations for the effective implementation of foreign policy. But the legislature enjoys, in almost all political systems, a very important power of allocating money in relation to foreign policy. Because of this power, in many countries, the lower chambers of the legislature are nowadays gaining additional strength in foreign policy issues and consequently exerting more influence in such matters. For example, the US House of Representatives has now become more powerful in matters of allocation of money for the implementation of American foreign policy. The Lok Sabha, the lower house in the Indian Parliament, is also enjoying more power over budgetary allocation on foreign policy matters.

The legislature tries to exercise control over foreign policy through its committee system in several countries. The Senate Committee on Foreign Relations is a case in point. It can effectively exert its control over foreign policy through its power of investigation and hearing. It is believed in the United States that the chairman of this committee is more powerful than the Secretary of State, because the Secretary is accountable to this committee and can be grilled by its members. The External Affairs Committee of the Lok Sabha of India does not enjoy so much power, but it can criticize the foreign policy and caution the government about any weak or wrong step.

The power of the executive is increasing in every country. The government tries to control the making of domestic and foreign policies through the introduction of new laws and ordinances. If the party in power has a majority in the legislature, this control becomes easier. As a result, the power of the legislature is decreasing in almost all countries. It may, therefore, be observed that except in the United States, the legislatures in other countries have limited power in matters of foreign policy today.

## Interest Groups and Lobbies

The role played by interest groups in the making of foreign policy is emphasized nowadays. Interest groups like the chamber of commerce, peasant's organizations, other professional bodies, organizations for friendship between two countries (the Indian–American Friendship Council, for example) may play significant roles in the making of foreign policy. Although it is true that these groups play a more prominent role in the United States than in other countries, in an era of globalization, their importance is being increasingly felt in other countries as well. An example cited below may illustrate the significance of such groups in the making and implementation of foreign policy. In May 1998, the United States imposed economic and military sanctions on India and Pakistan for their nuclear tests. Due to the sanctions, export of wheat from the United States to Pakistan was stopped. As a consequence, the wheat-producing farmers of America incurred huge losses which amounted to nearly US $400 million. The farmers' organizations of the northwest region—where wheat is produced more—vociferously protested against this huge loss. They put pressure through their legislators in the US Congress to waive the provision of sanctions. Giving in to this pressure, the US Congress passed a law by which export of agricultural products to South Asian countries commenced again. This law was known as Agricultural Export Relief Act (AERA). This incident shows how the US foreign policy was forced to undergo changes due to the pressures put on it by certain interest groups.

In fact, in several countries, including India, the course of foreign policy making and implementation can be altered due to the active intervention of interest groups. There have been improvements in India–US relations recently. This, according to experts like Robert M. Hathaway and Dennis Kux, is the outcome of the positive role played by several interest groups like the American Association of Physicians of Indian Origin, the Indian American Friendship Council and the Asian American Hotel Owners Association. They try to influence the US Congress through their representatives, so that the American Congress passes India-friendly laws. So, the role of interest groups can never be ignored in foreign policy matters.

In our discussion of the influence of interest groups in foreign policy, the role of 'lobby' deserves special reference. Simply, the endeavour of the interest groups to influence the legislature and the government is known as 'lobbying'. In this sense, lobbying is a verb. An interest group associated with lobbying may be called a lobby. In other words, interest groups which try to influence the legislature and the government are known as lobbies. The India Caucus in the US House of Representatives is a lobby in this sense. The main purpose of this lobby is to influence the US Congress to adopt India-friendly attitude and to make pro-India laws. The activities of the India Caucus may be called lobbying. Lobbies are usually very active in the United States and West European countries. They try and successfully influence the making of foreign policy in these countries.

## Public Opinion

The impact of public opinion on foreign policy is not beyond controversy because public opinion as a concept is ambiguous. Public opinion refers to the opinion of the people. But the opinion of all the people can never be the same, and that way, very cohesive. Is public opinion a concrete and reasonable opinion? The answer would certainly be negative. Therefore, what is termed as 'public opinion' can never be the rational and organized opinion of all the people. It may be the opinion of only a section of the people who assume positions of leadership at various levels. In reality, public opinion is formed and expressed by several groups of people. Usually, these groups are the political parties and the pressure or interest groups. They organize and express what is known as public opinion.

A common man is more concerned with the domestic policies of a country than its foreign policy because the former affect their day-to-day life, with which they are more concerned. In case of foreign policy, public opinion is formulated and expressed by political parties and interest groups. The media also creates public opinion, but the influence of political parties and interest groups in the formulation of public opinion is perhaps stronger than the media. As very few citizens are actually concerned with foreign policies, political leaders and interest groups find it easy to influence public opinion. Often, the wishes of political leaders are expressed in the name of public opinion. Citizens are usually concerned about the protection of their national interests, and political leaders try to organize public opinion in favour of national interest. Thus, political parties and interest groups organize and express the latent desires of the people as public opinion.

Public opinion may become important in case of foreign policy. Frankel has given a very good example of how public opinion influences foreign policy. The British Government decided to join the European common market in 1961 but failed to do so due to lack of public support. Political parties and interest groups gradually steered British public opinion in favour of joining the common market by 1967. The British Government eventually joined the common market in 1967 with favourable public opinion. Here, British political parties and interest groups gradually organized different views of the people into a cohesive and concrete public opinion. In the modern world, the influence of public opinion over foreign policy is strongly felt in almost all countries where political life has attained a certain degree of maturity and sophistication.

QUESTIONS

1. Analyse the concept of national interest.
2. Define diplomacy. Examine the main tasks of diplomacy.
3. Analyse the main functions of diplomats in international relations today.
4. Write notes on open and secret diplomacy.
5. Analyse the notion of economic diplomacy.
6. Examine the future of diplomacy.
7. Define propaganda. What are the major techniques of propaganda?
8. Analyse the significance of the military in the making of foreign policy.
9. Examine the role of the Head of the Government and his Foreign Minister in the making of foreign policy.
10. Analyse the role of the Legislature in the making of foreign policy.
11. Write a note on the importance of interest groups and lobbies in the making of foreign policy.
12. How does public opinion influence the making of foreign policy?

# 5 The United Nations

The tragedy of the Second World War created in the minds of the people a deep resentment against war. Prominent leaders of the world felt it was necessary to form a world body consisting of all states to prevent further wars of this magnitude. As early as in 1941, attempts were made to form an international organization. After several rounds of discussion and negotiation, the United Nations Organization was finally established in 1945 with fifty-one member-states. It was, of course, not the first international organization in the world. After the First World War, a world body known as the League of Nations was formed in 1919. But it failed to maintain international peace and harmony due to its structural and functional weaknesses. The founders of the United Nations (UN) tried to avoid the mistakes made during the formation of the League of Nations. The UN, despite its shortcomings, has remained an effective and quite successful international organization for more than six decades. This discussion of the UN starts with the origin of the organization.

## The Origin of the UN

The London Declaration of 12 June 1941 could be credited with the first formal attempt at creating the UN when all the nations fighting against Hitler announced their intention to create a world free of wars, and based on social and economic equality. This declaration was soon followed by the Atlantic Charter of 14 August 1941, which stressed upon the need for establishing an international body designed to maintain peace and security in the world. On 1 January 1942, the anti-Axis coalition, then comprising twenty-six countries, met in Washington DC to affirm the Atlantic Charter. It was there that US President Franklin Roosevelt coined the term 'United Nations' to indicate the unity of the allied powers to fight against a common enemy. However, the Washington Declaration also stressed on the need to unite for peace and to move forward in that direction.

The next significant step in the formation of the UN was taken on 30 October 1943, when Britain, the United States, China and the Soviet Union announced in Moscow that they sincerely recognized the need to create, at the earliest feasible date, a general international organization, based on the principle of sovereign equality of all peace-loving states. This pledge in Moscow was soon followed by the Tehran Declaration of 1 December 1943, which sought the cooperation and active participation of all nations, large and small, to create a family of democratic states. A Great Power Conference was convened by the United States in 1944 at Dumbarton Oaks near Washington DC, which lasted for nearly three months, from August to October. After much discussion and negotiation, the Dumbarton Oaks Conference prepared a Draft of the Charter of the UN. During late 1944 and early 1945, this Draft Charter was discussed, debated and amended in a few more international conferences in Washington DC and Yalta. These conferences elaborately discussed the proposed structures and functions of the new international organization. The draft charter of the UN was finally signed by fifty-one states on 26 June 1945 in San Francisco, United States. After ratification by the signatory states' parliaments, as provided by Article 110 of the charter, the United Nations Organization, a world body designed to maintain international peace and security, was established on 25 October 1945.

Articles 1 and 2 of the UN Charter clearly elaborated the purposes and principles of the UN. Article 1 says:

> The purposes of the United Nations are: 1. to maintain international peace and security, and to that end: to take effective collective measures for the prevention and removal of threats to the peace.... 2. To develop friendly relations among nations based on respect for the principle of equal rights and self-determination of peoples and to take other appropriate measures to strengthen universal peace.

Article 2 says:

> The organization is based on the principle of the sovereign equality of all its members....

It further points out:

> All members shall refrain in their international relations from the threat or use of force against the territorial integrity or political independence of any state, or in any other manner inconsistent with the purposes of the United Nations.

The purposes and principles of the UN are best maintained through the activities of different organs of this international organization. Therefore, it is necessary to analyse the functions of the important organs of the UN.

# Important Organs of the UN

## The General Assembly

### Composition and Voting

Chapter IV of the UN Charter elaborates in detail the composition and functions of the General Assembly (GA), one of the most important organs of the UN system. Articles 9 to 22 therein contain details about the GA—its structure, activities, voting methods and procedures for convening sessions. Article 9 begins with the composition of the GA. It says, 'The General Assembly shall consist of all the members of the United Nations'. In 2009, the UN had 192 member-states. So, the GA also had as much members. Each member-state can send a maximum of five representatives to the Assembly but cast only one vote. The GA could have a maximum of 960 (192 × 5) individuals attending its sessions, but a maximum of 192 votes. According to Article 18 of the charter, 'Decisions of the General Assembly on important questions shall be made by a two-thirds majority of the members present and voting'. The charter also outlined the 'important questions' on which decisions of the Assembly require a two-third majority of the members present and voting. These questions are: (1) recommendations with respect to the maintenance of international peace and security; (2) the election of the non-permanent members of the Security Council; (3) the election of the members of the Economic and Social Council (ECOSOC); (4) the admission of new members to the UN; (5) the suspension of the rights and privileges of membership; (6) the expulsion of members; (7) questions relating to the operation of the trusteeship system and (8) budgetary questions. According to provisions of the charter, decisions on other questions shall be made by a simple majority of members present and voting. The GA, as per Article 21 of the charter, 'shall adopt its own rules of procedure. It shall elect its President for each session'. Nowadays, the regular session of the GA begins in the third week of September, under the charge of the President of the previous session. The first task of a new Assembly is to elect its own President to assume the Chair for the next twelve months. No President of the GA can represent any big power. A new Assembly also elects several vice-presidents and some chairmen for the standing committees. The regular annual session of the Assembly is held in New York. As per Article 20 of the charter, special sessions of the assembly may be convened by the Secretary-General at the request of the Security Council or a majority of the members of the UN.

## Major Functions

***Discussion and debate*** The GA is best known for its discussions and debates. It is considered to be the biggest and most important of all international platforms, where different countries across the world can exchange views. H. G. Nicholas calls it 'a talking shop', as it discusses and debates almost all events happening in the world. But, it does so under the authority of the charter, as Part 2 of Article 11 confirms: 'The General Assembly may discuss any questions relating to the maintenance of international peace and security.... Any such question on which action is necessary shall be referred to the Security Council by the General Assembly'. Any issue that has the potential to disturb world peace and security may be taken up for discussion and debate by the Assembly. This provision indicates that the Assembly may discuss anything under the sun. It also performs the duty of referring actions to the Security Council. For such reference, debates are necessary, and that is why debates constitute an integral part of the overall functions of the Assembly. Over the years, some very constructive debates on issues like international peace and security, disarmament, nuclear proliferation, cooperation, ecological questions and socio-economic matters had taken place in the Assembly. Viewed from a different angle, such debates have great educational and informative values. Attention of the people is drawn to several important issues affecting the world through these debates.

***Legislative functions*** A second important function of the GA is the codification and development of international law. This function, according to Nicholas, brings the GA nearest to the law-making activities of a national legislature. This is why this Assembly is often called a quasi-legislature. According to Article 13 of the charter, 'encouraging the progressive development of international law and its codification' constitutes an important legal activity of the GA. Article 13 further empowers the Assembly to make recommendations for the 'realization of human rights and fundamental freedoms for all without distinction as to race, sex, language or religion'. From the initial years of the UN, the GA has been very active in performing its quasi-legal functions. It established the International Law Commission in 1948 to codify international law. The same year, it also passed the Universal Declaration of Human Rights (UDHR) to set a general guideline for the protection of human rights all over the world. In 1965, it adopted a resolution on the elimination of all forms of racial discrimination. It further signed two contracts on human rights in 1966. All such endeavours show the degree of involvement of the GA to protect the basic rights and fundamental freedoms of the people anywhere across the world, through appropriate legal measures.

***Political functions*** The GA performs some political functions as well. Initially, the framers of the charter did not want to make the Assembly a politically active organ. The political functions of the UN were then largely assigned to the Security Council. The GA was seen as a 'deliberative organ' that could only discuss, debate, review and criticize. But it gradually came to gain a lot of importance, mainly because of the shortcomings of the Security Council in performing the duties entrusted to it. The GA passed the Uniting for Peace Resolution in 1950, during the Korean War. It contained a provision that the GA can meet in twenty-four hours if the Security Council is prevented by the veto from exercising its primary responsibility of maintaining international peace and security. This resolution empowered the Assembly to take important political decisions bypassing the Security Council. Equipped with this resolution, the Assembly pushed itself into the field of political activities which the charter intended to reserve for the council. Although the Assembly failed in sustaining its 'supremacy' achieved through the resolution in the later years, it nevertheless started dabbling in the political affairs of the UN after the Uniting for Peace Resolution was passed.

Other important political functions of the GA include peaceful and legally justified political settlement and peaceful political change by promoting new international order. The creation of Israel may be cited as a pertinent example. H. G. Nicholas thinks that the GA has shown notable inventiveness and flexibility in carrying out its political functions. According to him, '... if the test of the vitality of a political institution is its ability to devise new instruments to assist in its tasks, the Assembly comes out well.' (Nicholas 1975: 125).

***Elective functions*** The Assembly shares some important elective functions with the Security Council. It, along with the council, can elect the Secretary-General, the judges of the International Court of Justice (ICJ), and admit new members to the UN. It can also elect 10 non-permanent members of the Security Council and fifty-four members of the ECOSOC. In both the cases, principles of 'geographical equality' are maintained. The Assembly also elects members of the Trusteeship Council.

***Supervisory functions*** The GA controls and supervises the activities of almost all other organs of the UN. It is to the Assembly that the Security Council, the ECOSOC and the Trusteeship Council submit their reports. The Assembly also controls the Secretariat. The Secretariat has to submit periodic reports of its activities to the Assembly. The Assembly shares a symbiotic relationship with the Secretary-General. According to Nicholas, 'the Secretary-General, though in a true sense the servant of the Assembly, may also be its conscience and guide'. This supervisory authority has made the Assembly one of the most significant organs of the UN.

***Miscellaneous functions*** The Assembly has several other functions which may be together called the miscellaneous functions. It scrutinizes and passes the budget of the UN, fixes rates of subscription for member-states and discusses budgets of the specialized agencies. It has a role in the amendment of the UN Charter as well. The charter can be amended with the consent of a two-thirds majority of members of the GA along with the approval of all five permanent members of the Security Council. Therefore, any major reform proposal of the UN requires the support of a two-thirds majority of the GA.

These functions, as mentioned above, empower the GA to enjoy, along with the Security Council, a very prominent position in the UN system.

### Evaluation of the Role of the GA

The framers of the UN Charter wanted to make the Security Council the prime organ of the UN. But due to structural weaknesses, revealed starkly during the Cold War, the Security Council failed to live up to the expectations of the founders of the UN. For instance, the concept of 'great-power unanimity', sought to be achieved through permanent membership of the council, could not materialize due to rivalry between the two superpowers during the war. As a consequence, the concept of collective security (discussed in detail later in this chapter), to be achieved under the guidance of the council, also failed. This structural weakness of the council helped the GA to usurp some powers of the council as revealed by the Uniting for Peace Resolution. The Assembly, unlike the council, is a truly representative organ of the UN. All members of the UN are members of the Assembly. The Assembly has thus become a significant platform for discussion, debate and negotiation. The member-states take it as their very own organ, where they can express their grievances and make their voices heard. More and more states, particularly those of the 'developing' world, are making frequent use of the Assembly as their international platform for effective diplomacy. This reliance of the member-states on the Assembly has significantly enhanced its activities and responsibilities. It is true that, on many occasions, the Assembly had failed to meet its responsibilities and surrendered the advantages it had gained through the Uniting for Peace Resolution. It is frequently accused of being a cumbersome and garrulous body, with little effective power to keep its promises. It also requires some reforms (the reform proposals of the UN would be analysed in detail later in this chapter). But the deliberative and recommending functions of the Assembly are quite important. Because of them, the Assembly gets all the desired attention of the member-states, other organs of the UN, and, broadly speaking, of the whole world. These functions help the Assembly to fulfill the primary responsibility of the UN—maintenance of international peace and security—and in realizing the expectations of its members of becoming a part of world diplomacy.

## The Security Council

### Composition

The Security Council, a very important organ of the UN for maintaining international peace and security, has a very limited membership, unlike the GA. Article 23 of the Charter elaborately states the composition of the Security Council. According to this Article, the council shall consist of fifteen members—five permanent and ten non-permanent. In the original charter, the limit of membership of the council was set at eleven, with five permanent and six non-permanent members. But the provisions were amended in 1965 and the number of non-permanent members was raised from six to ten. So, the council now has fifteen members. Currently, the permanent members of the Security Council are the United States of America, Russia (it had taken the place of the former Soviet Union), Britain, France and People's Republic of China. The concept of big powers assuming permanent membership of the council was created by the founders of the UN to achieve big-power unanimity, which they thought would help adequately in maintaining international peace and security. The ten non-permanent members of the council are elected for a term of two years, on the basis of equitable geographical distribution. None of them is re-elected immediately after the expiry of its two-year term. Each member-state of the Security Council shall have one representative and one vote. The council, according to the charter, holds periodic meetings, as and when necessary.

## Voting

The system of voting in the Security Council, though controversial, needs a special mention. Article 27 of the Charter deals with voting in the council. It says that each member of the Security Council shall have one vote, and decisions of the council on procedural matters shall be made by an affirmative vote of nine members. Part 3 of Article 27 is very important in this context. It states: 'Decisions of the Security Council on all other matters shall be made by an affirmative vote of nine members including the concurring votes of the permanent members'. The word 'concurring' is extremely important as it means that if any permanent member of the council opposes any proposed resolution, the resolution shall be discarded. In other words, no proposed resolution of the Security Council shall be passed if it is opposed by any permanent member. This power of the permanent members to nullify a proposed resolution of the council is known as Veto Power. Although created by the founders to achieve great-power unanimity, it had nevertheless become very controversial during the Cold War.

## Major Functions

***Maintenance of international peace and security*** The Security Council has been entrusted by the Charter with the primary responsibility of maintaining international peace and security. Article 24(1) of the charter declares: 'In order to ensure prompt and effective action by the UN, its members confer on the Security Council primary responsibility for the maintenance of international peace and security'. For this purpose, a Military Staff Committee of the UN is placed under the control of the Security Council, although use of military power would be the last resort of the council and the UN. The council would try for peaceful settlement of disputes without the use of military power. For this end, the charter elaborately laid down provisions for Pacific Settlement of Disputes. A brief discussion on the different mechanisms for maintaining peace follows.

i. *Pacific settlement of disputes*: Chapter VI of the UN Charter endows all powers to the Security Council to go for pacific settlement of disputes between or among rival states. Settlement of disputes is to be primarily achieved through negotiation and conciliation. Article 33 of the charter says:

    > The parties to any dispute, the continuance of which is likely to endanger the maintenance of international peace and security, shall, first of all, seek a solution by negotiation, enquiry, mediation, conciliation, arbitration, judicial settlement, resort to regional agencies or arrangements, or other peaceful means of their own choice. The Security Council shall, when it deems necessary, call upon the parties to settle their disputes by such means.

Clearly, the emphasis is on peaceful settlement of all disputes, as Articles 34 to 38 also refer to such a mechanism for the maintenance of international peace and security.

ii. *Power of action in cases of threats to peace*: If efforts for pacific settlement of disputes fail, the Security Council can act accordingly to restore peace. Chapter VII of the charter (Articles 39 to 51) is full of appropriate methods of 'actions' of the council. Article 39 is very clear in this matter. It says: 'The Security Council shall determine the existence of any threat to the peace, breach of the peace, or act of aggression and shall make recommendations, or decide what measures shall be taken … to maintain or restore international peace and security'. But the council shall explore all other possible measures to deter threats to international peace before taking military actions. Articles 41 and 42 indicate to such measures. Article 41 states: 'The Security Council may decide what measures not involving the use of armed forces are to be employed to give effect to its decisions … These may include complete or partial interruption of economic relations and of rail, sea, air, postal, telegraphic, radio, and other means of communication, and the severance of diplomatic relations'. If all these measures prove to be inadequate in restoring peace, the council shall resort to military action, as per provisions of the charter, against the offender. For this purpose, all the members of the UN are requested by Article 43 of the charter to provide the Security Council with armed forces and the rights of passage. As per Article 46, 'Plans for the application of armed forces shall be made by the Security Council with the assistance of the Military Staff Committee'. The Security Council had to approve military actions for breach of international peace on several occasions in the recent past.

iii. *Power to work for disarmament*: Universal disarmament is a necessary condition to maintain international peace. The UN Charter gave the Security Council powers to exercise regulation of armaments. Article 26 empowered the council to work for the regulation of arms globally. The Security Council shall exercise these powers with the assistance of the Military Staff Committee, as per provisions of this article. The framers of the charter gave this power to the council to stop arms race that could disturb international peace and security.

iv. *Power relating to 'strategic areas'*: The Security Council has been empowered by the charter to supervise the strategic areas as part of its function to maintain international peace and security. The strategic areas fall under the Trusteeship System of the UN as provided by Chapter XII of the UN Charter. Article 83 says, 'All functions of the United Nations relating to strategic areas, including the approval of the terms of the trusteeship agreements and of their alteration or amendment, shall be exercised by the Security Council'.

***Elective functions*** The council shares some elective functions with the GA. Along with the Assembly, it elects new members to the UN, the Secretary-General of the organization, and judges of the ICJ. It sends its recommendations to the GA on these matters.

On the whole, the Security Council has been vested with enormous powers by the UN Charter to act in relation to its responsibilities as laid down in its Chapters VI, VII, VIII and XII.

## Evaluation of the Role of the Security Council

The founders of the UN wanted to make the Security Council the strongest of all UN organs. But the council could not fulfill the hopes of its mentors. Several structural and functional weaknesses are responsible for a largely ineffective council. To begin with the structural problems, the limited membership of the council had come under criticism. In an organization that has currently 192 member-states, the council involves only fifteen countries as its members, and they take all crucial decisions on issues relating to international peace and security. The decisions of the Security Council are, therefore, never the decisions of the majority of countries of the UN. Moreover, the concept of permanent membership to achieve great-power unity did not work at all due to Cold War politics. As a consequence, the council could not function as per expectations. Some of the great powers, identified six decades ago, at the time of the establishment of the UN, no longer enjoy that status in a new international order. Britain and France may fall into this category. Some other nations have become contestants in the great-power category. Germany, Japan, Italy, India, Brazil and South Africa, to name a few, have put forward their claims to be included as permanent members in a reformed council. Further, there is a strong view that permanent membership and veto powers are responsible for a crippled Security Council and they should be done away with. In an enlarged council with more members, no permanent membership should be allowed. However, there would be points and counterpoints on these issues, as they are controversial (these issues are analysed in detail under 'Reform Proposals' later in this chapter), but one point is accepted by all—the council certainly has structural weaknesses.

Functional weaknesses of the council stem from its structural inadequacy. The veto power of the permanent members, conceived originally to secure great-power unanimity, boomeranged during the Cold War, when neither the United States nor the Soviet Union could agree on major international issues. As a consequence, veto power was frequently used by the two superpowers and the council remained crippled. After the end of the Cold War, it is alleged from different quarters, the United States has been using the council to serve its own interests in a new unipolar world order. The Security Council, therefore, always became a pawn in the power game of influential nations of the world. This made the council ineffective, as its potentials could never be realized. H. G. Nicholas had rightly pointed out that 'of all the organs of the UN none has shown a greater discrepancy between promise and performance than the Security Council'.

## The Economic and Social Council

### Composition

It is not possible to maintain international peace and security without economic and social development of different parts of the world. The founders of the UN realized this very truth, and therefore created the Economic and Social Council (ECOSOC) with a view to secure socio-economic development of the world. Chapter X of the UN Charter deals with the composition, functions and powers of the ECOSOC. Article 61(1) of the Charter says: 'The Economic and Social Council shall consist of fifty-four members of the United Nations elected by the General Assembly'. Initially, the ECOSOC had eighteen members. The membership was subsequently raised to twenty-seven, and in 1973 it was further raised to fifty-four. Eighteen members of the ECOSOC are elected each year for a term of three years. A retiring member is eligible for immediate re-election. The principle of equitable geographical distribution is followed in electing members to the council. According to Article 61(4) of the Charter, each member of the ECOSOC shall have one representative. Every member has one vote. As per Article 67 of the Charter, decisions of the ECOSOC shall be made by the majority of members present and voting.

The ECOSOC has two sessions every year—the first is held in New York during April–May, and the second in Geneva in October or November. Like the GA, a President is elected for the year from a member-state which is not a great-power. Decisions of the council are taken on the basis of a bare majority of members present and voting.

### Functions and Powers of the ECOSOC

The ECOSOC may make or initiate studies and reports with respect to international economic, social, cultural, educational, health and related matters. It may also make recommendations with respect to any such matters to the GA and to the various specialized agencies. Article 68 of the Charter empowers the council to set up commissions in economic and social fields. The primary responsibility of the ECOSOC is to work for the development of economic, social, educational and cultural progress of the world. The council works in these fields, in collaboration with various specialized agencies. The ECOSOC, according to Article 63, can enter into agreements with any of the specialized agencies referred to in Article 57, as also coordinate the activities of the specialized agencies. Articles 57, 58 and 63 of the UN Charter gave the council the first of its duties, that of bringing the various specialized agencies into 'relationship with the UN' and coordinating their activities.

Specialized agencies working within the ambit of the ECOSOC cover a wide range of economic, social, cultural, health, educational and many other activities. Prominent among these agencies are the following: United Nations Educational, Scientific and Cultural Organization (UNESCO), United Nations Children's Fund (UNICEF), World Health Organization (WHO), Food and Agricultural Organization (FAO), International Monetary Fund (IMF), International Labour Organization (ILO), International Development Association (IDA), International Atomic Energy Agency (IAEA), International Civil Aviation Organization (ICAO). The activities performed by these agencies are highly commendable and valuable. Nicholas correctly observes that 'the scale of their operations is impressive'. Because of the noteworthy performance of these specialized agencies, ECOSOC has earned a good name among different organs of the UN.

Apart from the specialized agencies, several important functions of the ECOSOC are performed through special and regional commissions. The activities of these commissions could be ascertained from their names. The six special commissions of the ECOSOC are: (1) Statistical Commission; (2) Population Commission; (3) Commission for Social Development; (4) Commission on Human Rights and Sub-Commission on Prevention of Discrimination and Protection of Minorities; (5) Commission on the Status of Women and (6) Commission on Narcotic Drugs. The four regional commissions are: (1) Economic Commission for Europe; (2) Economic and Social Commission for Asia and the Pacific (formerly known as the Economic Commission for Asia and the Far East); (3) Economic Commission for Latin America and (4) Economic Commission for Africa. All these regional commissions have been working successfully for the economic and social development in their respective areas.

Article 71 of the UN Charter vests the ECOSOC with the power to cooperate with the non-governmental organizations (NGOs) for socio-economic progress of countries across the world. It says: 'The Economic and Social Council may make suitable arrangements for consultation with non-governmental organizations which are concerned with matters within its competence'. For effective cooperation with the NGOs, the ECOSOC has a Committee on Non-Governmental Organizations. This thirteen-member committee is the council's main body to cooperate with over a thousand NGOs worldwide, working in different areas related to the council's objectives and aims. The ECOSOC may call, in accordance with the rules prescribed by the UN, international conferences on matters falling within its purview.

### Evaluation of the Role of the ECOSOC

The ECOSOC is one of the most active of all UN organs. The contribution of the council towards social, economic and cultural development of the world is significant. The humanitarian and peace-loving ideals of the UN have been reflected more through the activities of the ECOSOC than through those of any other UN organ. But the council has certain limitations as well. Several scholars have pointed out that it is difficult for an organization with such vast networks of specialized agencies and commissions to properly coordinate among different bodies and function effectively. A good deal of the council's time is spent in supervising the works of the specialized agencies and in collecting information. It works in a cumbersome manner. It is also alleged that the council is at the mercy of the rich nations, as they dominate some of its important specialized agencies.

The council has probably been endowed with more duties than it can handle. It has to look after economic, social, cultural, educational, ecological, humanitarian, health and several other issues. Its list of activities would be very long. It works mainly through its commissions and specialized agencies. The activities of the agencies need to be coordinated by the council, which actually has limited effective control over them. As a consequence, the council shows lack of confidence in its dealing with them and is not equally successful in its different activities—it is very effective in some areas, but less accomplished in others. According to H. G. Nicholas, the ECOSOC is 'perhaps better on its economic than on its social side, better at a regional than at a global level, better … when there is a universally recognized need to be filled than when there are priorities to be determined in the allocation of scarce … resources'. The success of the council is sometimes overshadowed by its limitations. The council, like other UN organs, requires effective reforms for more efficient operation.

## The Secretariat

### Composition

The UN is a very big organization with numerous departments, offices and staff. The Secretariat has been created by the UN Charter to coordinate and control the activities of all UN departments, offices and personnel. Situated in New York, the Secretariat is the centre of all UN activities. Chapter XV of the UN Charter outlines the composition and functions of the Secretariat. Article 97 of the Charter says: 'The Secretariat shall comprise a Secretary-General and such staff as the organization may require'. The staff shall be appointed from different countries of the world. The principle of equitable geographical distribution is followed in the recruitment of personnel to the Secretariat. Article 101(1) of the Charter declares that the staff shall be appointed by the Secretary-General under regulations established by the GA. Article 101(3) says that 'highest standards of efficiency, competence and integrity' shall be maintained for selecting staff to the Secretariat. The staff shall not receive instructions from any authority external to the organization.

### Powers and Functions

The UN Secretariat is truly a polyglot organization. It performs numerous activities to keep the UN system in order. To begin with, it provides services similar to the 'office' of a polyglot Parliament. It explains and translates all the proceedings, resolutions, documents, minutes and information of the UN. It also provides library services and important legal and procedural assistance to different bodies and specialized agencies of the UN. Nearly half of its staff is engaged in this stupendous 'Parliament-type' activity of the Secretariat. Interpretation and translation of all proceedings of the UN is indeed a huge task that the Secretariat has to perform. This task is also very important to keep the members—as also the non-members—of the UN informed about the activities of the organization. The Secretariat is also responsible for the publication of various resolutions and debates in the official journal of the UN, and for conducting of scientific and other research related to the activities of the UN.

Another important function of the Secretariat is to gather information on different issues of global importance and providing them to UN bodies and members. This function is slightly different from the ones noted above and constitutes an important segment of the activities of the Secretariat. According to Nicholas, 'the collection, ordering and providing of information at the points where it is more needed and can produce its greatest effect, is one of the most important services that UN officials discharge'. Several UN organs, agencies, commissions and members are immensely benefited by this service.

The Secretariat is also known as the International Civil Service, as it extends some executive assistance to the UN. Prominent among them are technical assistance and pre-investment aid to developing countries. Introduced as a small operation in 1945, the technical assistance programme grew over the years into a sizeable scheme for providing expert advice and help to the developing countries. The Secretariat performs a quasi-executive function through the UN Field Service, which is an unarmed force that provides transport, maintains communication and looks after the security for UN commissions in the field.

An important function of the Secretariat is administering the administrators. As international civil servants, the UN bureaucracy must learn to rise above national interests. At the same time, they must know the art of maintaining effective liaison with member-nations, that include their native countries as well. In their activities, they must not show any bias towards their own countries. The administrators of the UN must be given proper instructions to adjust to their new roles at the UN, and also given necessary training. The Secretariat performs these tasks.

The UN Secretariat remains in constant touch with the Foreign Affairs Department of both the member- and non-member states. It takes opinions and suggestions from them, analyses these inputs and uses the results thus obtained as raw materials in the crucial decision-making process of the organization. Considering the complexities involved in this diplomatic as well as political function, it may be considered as one of the most important tasks of the UN Secretariat. In order to control and run an organization as big and as cumbersome as the UN, the Secretariat has to perform different kinds of functions—some much known, some not, some very important, others not so much.

## The Secretary-General

The Secretary-General (SG) plays a major role in the functioning of the UN Secretariat, and is also the most important person in the UN machinery. Article 97 of the UN Charter describes him as the 'chief administrative officer of the organization'. He is the pivot round whom all activities of the UN revolve.

## Appointment of the Secretary-General

Article 97 of the Charter also deals with the appointment of the Secretary-General. It states: 'The Secretary-General shall be appointed by the General Assembly upon the recommendation of the Security Council'. All the five permanent members of the Security Council must agree on a name before recommending it to the GA for possible consideration for the post of the Secretary-General. After such a name has been recommended by the Security Council, the GA meets and approves the name, sometimes through voting, if required. The Secretary-General is normally appointed for a term of five years, though the Charter has no mention of his tenure in office. They usually get a second term. No citizen of the five permanent members of the Security Council can become the Secretary-General. The present Secretary-General of the UN—the ninth in this position—is Antonio Guterres of Portugal. He assumed office on 1 January 2017. Table 5.1 shows a list of secretaries-general of the UN.

**Table 5.1** Secretaries-General of the United Nations

| S. No. | Name | Period in Office | Country |
|---|---|---|---|
| | Gladwyn Jebb (interim SG) | 24 Oct 1945–1 Feb 1946 | United Kingdom |
| 1. | Trygve Lie | 1 Feb 1946–10 Nov 1952 | Norway |
| 2. | Dag Hammarskjold | 10 April 1953–18 Sept 1961 | Sweden |
| 3. | U Thant | 30 Nov 1961–31 Dec 1971 | Burma (Now Myanmar) |
| 4. | Kurt Waldheim | 1 Jan 1972–31 Dec 1981 | Austria |
| 5. | Javier Perez de Cuéllar | 1 Jan 1982–31 Dec 1991 | Peru |
| 6. | Boutros Boutros-Ghali | 1 Jan 1992–31 Dec 1996 | Egypt |
| 7. | Kofi Annan | 1 Jan 1997–31 Dec 2006 | Ghana |
| 8. | Ban Ki-moon | 1 Jan 2007–31 Dec 2016 | South Korea |
| 9. | Antonio Guterres | 1 Jan 2017– Present | Portugal |

*Source*: http://en.wikipedia.org/wiki/Wili/Secretary-General_of_the_United_Nations/.

## Functions of the Secretary-General

As the Chief Administrative Officer of the UN, the Secretary-General has to perform many functions. For a comprehensive analysis, his major activities may be divided into these categories: political, administrative, financial and representative.

***Political functions*** The Secretary-General plays a major role in keeping the UN promise of maintaining international peace and security. It is his primary responsibility to see that world peace and security is not threatened. Article 99 of the Charter allows him to bring to the attention of the Security Council any matter which in his opinion may threaten the maintenance of international peace and security. It has been observed in the past that during times of political crises, UN secretaries-general tried their best to mitigate tension and restore a peaceful atmosphere. The Korean War, the Congo Crisis, the Vietnam War, the Suez Crisis, and the more recent Iraq and Afghanistan crises were sincerely handled by the respective secretary-general. They might not always have succeeded in diffusing the crises due to internal political differences (big-power rivalry within the UN), but their degree of involvement and commitment to restore peace were much praiseworthy. Under different secretaries-general, the UN performed extremely laudable works to fight the menace of colonialism, terrorism and racism. The office of the UN Secretary-General has always been sincerely involved in establishing democracy, right to self-determination, freedom, liberty, education and human rights all over the world. In carrying out their political functions, secretaries-general face a lot of obstacles. They have to manoeuvre through opposing political interests of states, disinclination to solve problems, red-tapism and, above all, resource crunch. Despite limitations, secretaries-general have always remained much committed to their political duties assigned to them by the UN Charter.

***Administrative functions*** The Secretary-General has to carry out a great deal of administrative functions. The general administration of the UN and the supervision of all its major organs have been entrusted to him. Article 98 of the Charter clearly states that 'the Secretary General shall act in that capacity in all meetings of the General Assembly, of the Security Council, of the Economic and Social Council, and of the Trusteeship Council, and shall perform such other functions as are entrusted to him by these organs. The Secretary General shall make an annual report to the General Assembly on the work of the organization'. He also keeps in touch with different organs, subsidiary agencies and member-states, but he does not seek or receive instructions from any government. According to Article 100 of the Charter, 'each member of the United Nations undertakes to respect the exclusively international character of the responsibilities of the Secretary General and the staff and not to seek to influence them in the discharge of their responsibilities'. Therefore, the Secretary-General has full autonomy to discharge his administrative functions.

***Financial functions*** The Secretary-General has significant financial responsibilities. He prepares the UN budget, allocates money to different departments and collects subscriptions from the member-states. He places the budget of the UN in a special session of the GA. He may also consider giving financial aid to underdeveloped countries. Without the approval of the Secretary-General, no money can be spent by any organ of the UN.

***Representative functions*** The Secretary-General is the chief representative and the chief spokesman of the UN. He represents the organization at various international forums, participate in important deliberations with different countries across the world. He serves as the main link between the UN and the rest of the world.

***Appointing functions*** The Secretary-General is an important appointing authority of the UN. He appoints the higher officials of the Secretariat and supervise their activities. He enjoys this authority on the basis of Article 101 of the Charter: 'The staff shall be appointed by the Secretary-General under regulations established by the General Assembly'. As the Chief Administrative Officer of the UN, it is his responsibility to see that the staff of the organization are properly appointed.

## A Brief Evaluation of the Role of the Secretary-General

The post of the Secretary-General is extremely important in the entire UN system. He is given a status equivalent to that of a member-state and enjoys, as the report of the Preparatory

Commission says, 'a quite special right which goes beyond any power previously accorded to the head of an international organization'. A lot of expectations are naturally put on a person who holds such an important post. But have the secretaries-general lived up to such expectations? Critics allege that their activities are influenced by powerful groups of countries within the UN. It becomes very difficult for them to act independently, bypassing group politics and red-tapism within and outside the organization. Consequently, they find it almost impossible to exert their views and get work done according to their wishes and plans. This proves to be an obstacle in their playing an effective role in the maintenance of international peace and security. However, it would be pertinent to point out that different secretaries-general have shown a marked desire to rise above group politics and work sincerely for the promotion of international peace and security. For instance, Secretary-General U Thant played a very constructive role in diffusing the Congo crisis, despite group politics within the organization. Similarly, Kofi Annan tried heart and soul to solve the Iraq and Afghan crises in recent times. Like other heads of important international organizations, the success of the Secretary-General also depends on his personality, his skills for negotiation, his manoeuvering ability and, of course, on his contacts with important members of the organization.

## International Court of Justice (The World Court)

### Composition

The Charter of the UN makes no mention of the composition of the International Court of Justice (ICJ), which has been renamed the World Court. But the statutes of the court say that it shall consist of fifteen judges, who are to be appointed for a period of nine years. Five judges are to be appointed every three years. Ad hoc judges may be added to the list of fifteen, if any party (state) in a case does not have one of its citizens as a judge. It may be mentioned here that only states—and not individuals or groups—can be a party to any case in the World Court. It is customary for every permanent member of the Security Council to have at least one judge from its country. The judges are appointed by the GA on the recommendation of the Security Council. There is no fixed qualification for the appointment of judges. To be considered for appointment as a judge, a person must be an expert in international law; should be eligible for appointment to the highest national court; should possess a morally sound character and should be a jurist of international repute. The salary and allowance of the judges are decided by the GA. After their appointment, the judges cannot take up any political or administrative posts. The court sits in The Hague, Netherlands.

### Functions

The jurisdiction of the court may be of three kinds—arbitrary, compulsory and advisory. Arbitrary jurisdiction prevents the court from bringing any dispute within its purview without the consent of the disputed parties. No state is bound to bring any dispute to the court. The compulsory jurisdiction of the court covers all subjects included in the Charter of the UN, different clauses of international treaties and contracts, and fixation of penalties for violating international laws and customs. By its advisory jurisdiction, the court may give advice to different organs of the UN. Article 96 of the Charter says: 'The General Assembly or the Security Council may request the court to give an advisory opinion on any legal question'. Other organs of the UN and specialized agencies may also seek advisory opinion of the court on legal questions.

Many member-states of the UN signed the 'optional clause' of the court whereby they agreed to use the court for certain types of cases. The contexts for such cases may be the following: (1) the meaning of treaty clauses; (2) all matters concerned with the field of international law; (3) the existence of any fact which, if established, would constitute a breach of international obligation and (4) the nature or extent of the payment that must be made for breaking an international agreement or obligation. This 'optional clause' is known as compulsory jurisdiction of the court, as discussed earlier.

In deciding its cases, the court applies: (1) international conventions, whether general or particular; (2) international customs; (3) general principles of law recognized by civilized nations and (4) judicial decisions and teachings of the qualified publicists of different nations all over the world.

### An Evaluation of the World Court

The World Court has so far been successful in deciding many cases. Some of the notable cases are the dispute between American nationals and the citizens of Morocco, the case regarding the nationalization of the Anglo-Iranian oil company, and the dispute between Portugal and India. The World Court achieved remarkable success in 1992, when it settled a complex border dispute between El Salvador and Honduras, that existed since 1961 and led to many clashes and a major war in 1969. The court's verdict to split territories and common water bodies was accepted by both the disputing countries. This verdict led to the major success story of the court in recent years. However, there are instances of failures as well. In several cases, the court's decisions were rejected by member-states. For example, Albania rejected the verdict of the court when it held Albania responsible for damaging a British ship. In 1979, Iran refused to accept the jurisdiction of the court over its seizure of the US Embassy in Tehran. Critics allege that the court's decisions are not always impartial, that judges often favour the countries they represent. Moreover, decisions are influenced by international politics. As Nicholas observes, 'If it gets too much involved in what are essentially political quarrels, the court might run the risk of appearing merely as the guardian instrument of the General Assembly'.

A major weakness of the World Court is that its decisions are seldom accepted by the member-states. Although all the members have signed the treaty that formed the court, only about one-third of them have signed the 'optional clause' in the treaty agreeing to give the court jurisdiction in certain areas. Among those who signed the 'optional clause', many tend to ignore its provisions if they contradict national interests. The United States withdrew from the 'optional clause' in 1986 when it was sued by Nicaragua, alleging CIA's (Central Intelligence Agency) involvement in the internal affairs of Nicaragua. Therefore, international political issues certainly affect the functions of the World Court.

# Collective Security

## The Concept and Its Application

The concept of 'collective security' refers to a situation where the security of a nation is the collective concern of all other nations. Although it sounds idealistic, the concept was first introduced in international relations by the League of Nations, established in 1920. Article 16 of the League Covenant declared that states engaged in an act of aggression shall 'ipso facto be deemed to have committed an act of war against all other Members of the League'. By the provisions of the Covenant, all members of the League were required to impose economic and diplomatic sanctions, and, if the Council of the League permitted, military actions against the aggressor. The UN, established after the Second World War, also retained the concept of collective security. Chapter VII of the UN Charter empowers the UN Security Council to initiate collective military action against an aggressor and help the aggressed nation. For maintaining international peace and security, an aggressor must be repelled by all members of the UN. According to Morgenthau, 'one for all and all for one' is the key phrase for collective security.

Although the UN retained the League's idea of collective security, it did not place extreme reliance on this idea as the sole mechanism to maintain international peace and security. It's Charter also allowed member-states to retain their sovereign rights to individual or collective defence in collaboration with other alliances outside the UN. The Charter does not prevent a state from helping itself when collective security measures taken by the Security Council are ineffective. As a sovereign country, every nation has the fundamental right to its own security. Moreover, the UN would also depend on 'preventive diplomacy', which seeks to prevent the outbreak of hostilities among nations in the first place. Preventive diplomacy has an edge over collective security because if the former is successful, the latter is not required. The UN thus has several provisions to maintain international peace, besides collective security.

Collective security was applied by the UN for the first time during the Korean War (1950–53). But the experience was not a good one for the UN. Although North Korea attacked South Korea on 25 June 1950, Cold War political calculations prevented having a consensus in the UN about the identification of the aggressor. The United States and its allies identified North Korea as the aggressor and called for severe military actions, but Soviet Union and its allies were not of the same opinion. China joined the war for North Korea, making the situation more complex and worse. However, the Security Council was still able to apply collective security provisions against North Korea only because Soviet Union temporarily absented itself from the council and could not veto the resolution (on collective security) of the council. But when Soviet Union returned to the council, the onus of collective security was on the GA. Rising to the occasion, the GA passed the Uniting for Peace Resolution in November 1950.

Although the Security Council applied collective security measures against North Korea—the aggressor in this case—not all members of the UN contributed military force for this collective action. As Morgenthau noted, 'South Korea, the country immediately concerned, and the United States provided about 90 per cent of the armed forces that fought in Korea'. While China, a great power, joined the war for the 'aggressor', several other states with significant military capabilities remained non-committal. The avowed purpose of collective security—repelling the 'aggressor' and restoring normalcy—could not, therefore, be achieved in the Korean War. The mechanism of collective security failed its first real test in the Korean War, and has never been applied ever since.

## Limitations of Collective Security

The Korean War starkly exposed the limitations of collective security as a mechanism for restoring and maintaining peace. The ideal situation for implementing this concept calls for united action on the part of all UN members against the 'aggressor'. Such collective action is hardly possible in reality, as the Korean War had exposed. There are several reasons for this. Firstly, there would be no common consensus as to the identity of the 'aggressor'. If nation A attacks nation B, nation A should be the aggressor according to collective security principles. But in reality, there would be no agreement among the member-states of the UN on the identity of A as the aggressor. If nations C, D, E, F and G identify A as the aggressor, nations H, I, J, K would not, or may even support A, while nations L, M, N, O, P, Q, R, S, T may remain silent and non-committal. Therefore, a collective action against A would not be possible. In the complex world of international politics, states are driven more by their national interests rather than by improbable principles. Secondly, what would happen if the military strength of the aggressor and its supporters are more than the collective force of the UN? Would it lead to another World War? The chances may not be ruled out. Thirdly, situations may not always be favourable for a country, even if it agrees on the identity of the aggressor, to contribute military forces for collective security. At a time when collective security is sought, its military may be required for domestic insurgencies or civil wars. In that case, the UN force would not have the required strength and the purpose of collective security may be defeated.

Due to these limitations, collective security has not only remained an idealistic concept, its application might also prove to be dangerous for international peace, as the second point above shows. It being a weak mechanism for the protection of world peace, the UN did not place much importance on it. This is clearly evident from the fact that the UN has never applied this mechanism after the Korean War. Rather, it relies more on the different forms of diplomacy (preventive or economic) for maintaining international peace and security at this moment.

## UN Peacekeeping

Peacekeeping activities of the UN are not clearly mentioned in the UN Charter. They have only been partially referred in chapters 6 and 7. After the Second World War, peacekeeping missions of the UN were initially undertaken as extensions of the collective security mechanism, where member-states were required to provide military forces to the UN. Such forces could be used in response to aggressions. Gradually, efforts were made to keep the UN force in a troubled area to maintain peace. Sometimes, the multinational UN force, popularly known as the Blue Helmets, had to stay in a war zone for decades. As a consequence, peacekeeping efforts of the UN became a continuous activity and assumed significance in the study of the UN system. Though initially it was an extension of the collective security system, peacekeeping has now assumed greater importance on its own.

The Blue Helmets are not required to fight wars. They are sent by the Secretary-General to a troubled area at the invitation of a host government and must leave the area if the government wants so. They do not meddle in any conflict, but remain armed to defend themselves against any possible attack. Their sole purpose is to monitor peace and dissuade contending parties from using force. They have a moral authority to monitor peace due to the fact that their presence was agreed upon by all the contending parties and authorized by a supreme global body. Nowadays, the Security Council controls peacekeeping operations, and it also recommends to the Secretary-General the deployment of peacekeeping forces in a troubled zone. Funds for peacekeeping operations must be approved by the GA. Such operations appropriate a large portion of the UN budget. By 2000, costs of peacekeeping reached $2.6 billion.

Peacekeeping faces serious challenges when there is a civil war, when a government collapses or when there is severe famine. All these happened in Somalia in 1993. In the absence of a proper government, there is no taker for UN peacekeeping in such cases. Moreover, prevailing civil wars expose the peacekeepers to the great dangers of being targeted, ambushed or killed. Peacekeeping, therefore, operates best when there is a ceasefire agreed upon by all contending parties. Since 1948, when the first peacekeeping operation was undertaken by the UN, numerous other such missions have been launched by this international body. Among them, sixteen peacekeeping missions are still continuing in different parts of the world. Table 5.2 lists ongoing peacekeeping operations by the UN.

The UN peacekeeping actually involves two major functions: observation and peacekeeping. Observers are unarmed military personnel sent to a troubled zone to watch the situation and report back to the UN. Observation is no easy job. Observers are required to monitor the prevalence of human rights and democratic principles in troubled areas, as also ceasefire or elections. In other words, they help in the process of transition from war to democracy. This function of observation proved immensely beneficial for Nicaragua and El Salvador after the Cold War. For purposes of peacekeeping, lightly armed military (they would not take an active part in conflicts) are sent to the troubled zone to dissuade warring parties and negotiate with their military leaders. They have a very sensitive role. They must make the conflicting sides feel that they are impartial. Peacekeeping efforts of the UN would have little chance of succeeding if considered biased by any side.

With the end of the Cold War, UN peacekeeping changed from traditional missions involving strictly military tasks to complex multidimensional activities aimed at building the foundations for sustainable peace. According to a UN report, 'Today's peacekeepers undertake a wide variety of complex tasks, from helping to build sustainable institutions of governance, to human rights monitoring, to security sector reform, to the disarmament, demobilization and reintegration of former combatants'. The report further observes that the 'nature of conflicts has also changed over

**Table 5.2** Ongoing UN Peacekeeping Operations (1948–2018)

| S. No. | Name of the Operation | Full Title | From | To |
|---|---|---|---|---|
| 1. | UNTSO | United Nations Truce Supervision Organization | May 1948 | Present |
| 2. | UNMOGIP | United Nations Military Observer Group in India and Pakistan | January 1949 | Present |
| 3. | UNFICYP | United Nations Peacekeeping Force in Cyprus | March 1964 | Present |
| 4. | UNDOF | United Nations Disengagement Force | June 1974 | Present |
| 5. | UNIFIL | United Nations Interim Force in Lebanon | March 1978 | Present |
| 6. | UNISFA | United Nations Interim Security Force for Abyei | June 2011 | Present |
| 7. | MINUSMA | United Nations Multidimensional Integrated Stabilization Mission in Mali | April 2013 | Present |

(*Continued*)

**Table 5.2** (*Continued*)

| S. No. | Name of the Operation | Full Title | From | To |
|---|---|---|---|---|
| 8. | MINURSO | United Nations Mission for the Referendum in Western Sahara | April 1991 | Present |
| 9. | UNMIK | UN Interim Administration Mission in Kosovo | June 1999 | Present |
| 10. | MONUSCO | United Nations Organization Stabilization Mission in the Democratic Republic of the Congo | July 2010 | Present |
| 11. | UNMIL | United Nations Mission in Liberia | September 2003 | Present |
| 12. | MINUJUSTH | United Nations Mission for Justice Support in Haiti | October 2017 | Present |
| 13. | UNMISS | United Nations Mission in the South Sudan | July 2011 | Present |
| 14. | UNAMID | African Union/United Nations Hybrid Operation in Darfur | July 2007 | Present |
| 15. | MINUSCA | United Nations Multidimensional Integrated Stabilization Mission in the Central African Republic | April 2014 | Present |

*Source*: 'Where We Operate', The U.N. Website https://peacekeeping.un.org/, as accessed on 02 March 2018 at 2pm IST

the years. Originally developed as a means of dealing with inter-State conflict, UN peacekeeping has been increasingly applied to intra-State conflicts and civil wars'.[1] Although the Blue Helmets still constitute the backbone of most peacekeeping operations, the many faces of peacekeeping now include administrators and economists, legal experts and police officers, election and human rights observers, specialists in civil affairs and governance, de-miners and experts in communications and public information.

## UN Peacemaking

UN peacemaking is different from UN peacekeeping. While peacekeeping operations started in 1948, UN peacemaking is a relatively new effort that was initiated after the end of the Cold War. In 1992, the then UN Secretary-General Boutros Boutros-Ghali proposed to create a UN peacemaking force that would not only monitor a ceasefire, but also enforce it in the case of a breakdown. This would require heavily armed military personnel (unlike the peacekeepers) who would have to enter into a battle with the violators of a ceasefire. Boutros-Ghali proposed a peacemaking force that would be very quick to respond, unlike the peacekeeping force that sometimes took several months to reach the troubled zone. Although Ghali's proposals were not enthusiastically accepted by all member-states, it nevertheless set the ball rolling for peacemaking efforts by the UN. Today, besides military measures, peacemaking also involves preventive diplomacy. As one UN report observes, 'the end of the Cold War created new opportunities to end civil wars through negotiated peace settlements. A large number of conflicts were brought to an end, either through direct UN mediation or by the efforts of others acting with UN support. The list includes El Salvador, Guatemala, Namibia, Cambodia, Mozambique, Tajikistan, Bougainville, Afghanistan, Sierra Leone, Burundi and the North-South conflict in Sudan. Research has credited expanded UN peacemaking, peacekeeping and conflict prevention activities as a major factor behind a 40% decline in armed conflict around the world since the 1990s. An undetermined number of potential conflicts have been defused through preventive diplomacy and other forms of preventive action'.[2]

In June 2007, a Peace Building Commission (PBC) was created by the members of the UN to support peace efforts in countries emerging from conflicts. The PBC is an important addition to the efforts of the UN at peacemaking after the Cold War. The commission, according to a UN report, 'plays a unique role in (1) bringing together all of the relevant actors, including international donors, the international financial institutions, national governments, troop contributing countries; (2) marshalling resources and (3) advising on and proposing integrated strategies for post-conflict peace-building and recovery and where appropriate, highlighting any gaps that threaten to undermine peace'.[3] The resolutions of the GA and the Security Council establishing the commission provided for the establishment of a Peace-building Fund and a Peace-building Support Office, which together form the UN peace-building architecture of today.

## Human Rights and the United Nations

Since its inception, the United Nations had always espoused the cause of human rights. The Preamble to the UN Charter has a special mention about human rights. It promised 'to reaffirm faith in fundamental human rights, in the dignity and worth of the human person, in the equal rights of men and women and of nations large and small … and to promote social progress and better standards of life in larger freedom'.

An early effort of the UN to safeguard human rights of the people all over the world could be traced back to the GA Resolution No. 217A, which created the Universal Declaration of Human Rights on 10 December 1948. Since then, the UN had always endeavoured to protect human rights and fundamental freedoms of the people around the globe. In its latest effort in this regard, the UN created a Human Rights Council to monitor human rights activities in 2006. UN documents related to human rights always reflected the changing and complex demands of human rights practices.

The human rights organizations of the UN can be broadly classified into two areas: (1) charter-based bodies and (2) treaty-based bodies. Charter-based bodies (Figure 5.1) owe their origin to provisions contained in the UN Charter, while treaty-based bodies (Table 5.3) derive their establishment to specific legal instruments.

Among the charter-based bodies, detailed in Figure 5.1, the Human Rights Council (HRC) now works as the apex body of the UN system responsible for the protection of human rights in the world. HRC is an inter-governmental body for strengthening the promotion and protection of human rights around the globe and for addressing situations of human rights violations and

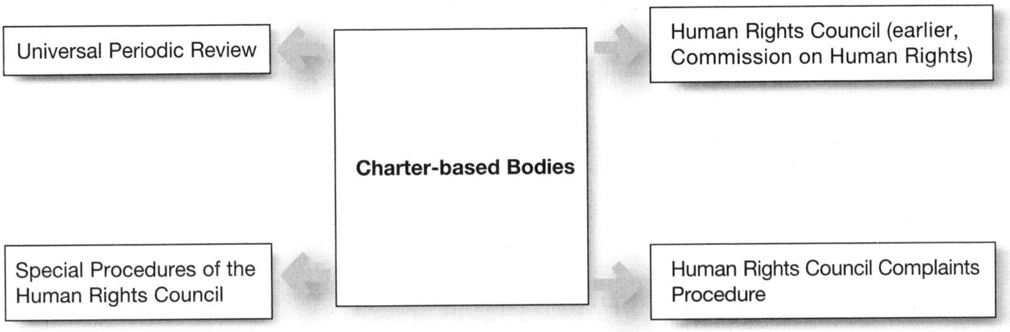


**Figure 5.1** UN Charter-based Bodies on Human Rights

**Table 5.3** UN Treaty-based Bodies on Human Rights

| S. No. | Name of the Treaty-based Body |
|---|---|
| 1. | Human Rights Committee |
| 2. | Committee on Economic Social and Cultural Rights |
| 3. | Committee on the Elimination of Racial Discrimination |
| 4. | Committee on the Elimination of Discrimination against Women |
| 5. | Committee against Torture |
| 6. | Committee on the Rights of the Child |
| 7. | Committee on Migrant Workers |
| 8. | Committee on the Rights of Persons with Disabilities |
| 9. | Committee on Enforced Disappearances |
| 10. | Subcommittee on Prevention of Torture |

making recommendations on them. It has the power to discuss all human rights issues and situations that require its attention throughout the year. It meets at the UN Office at Geneva. The council is composed of forty-seven member-states of the UN, which are elected by the UN General Assembly. The HRC replaced the former United Nations Commission on Human Rights.

The council was created by the UN General Assembly on 15 March 2006 by resolution 60/251. Its first session was held from 19 to 30 June 2006. In June 2007, HRC adopted its 'institution-building package' to guide its work and set up its procedures and mechanisms. 'Among them were the Universal Periodic Review mechanism which serves to assess the human rights situations in all United Nations Member States, the Advisory Committee which serves as the Council's "think tank" providing it with expertise and advice on thematic human rights issues and the Complaint Procedure which allows individuals and organizations to bring human rights violations to the attention of the Council'.[4] The HRC also works with the UN Special Procedures established by the former Commission on Human Rights and now assumed by the Council. 'These are made up of special rapporteurs, special representatives, independent experts and working groups that monitor, examine, advise and publicly report on thematic issues or human rights situations in specific countries'.[5]

There are nine treaty-based committees and one subcommittee on human rights at the UN today. Table 5.3 presents a detailed list of these committees. Among them, the Human Rights Committee is a body of independent experts to monitor implementation of the International Covenant on Civil and Political Rights by its state parties. All states parties are required to submit regular reports to the Committee on how the rights are being implemented. 'States must report initially one year after acceding to the Covenant and then whenever the Committee requests (usually every four years). The Committee examines each report and addresses its concerns and recommendations to the State party in the form of "concluding observations". In addition to the reporting procedure, Article 41 of the Covenant provides for the Committee to consider inter-state complaints'.[6] Further, the First Optional Protocol to the Covenant empowers the Committee with the 'competence to examine individual complaints with regard to alleged violations of the Covenant by States parties to the Protocol. The full competence of the Committee extends to the Second Optional Protocol to the Covenant on the abolition of the death penalty with regard to States who have accepted the Protocol'.[7] The Committee meets in Geneva and normally holds three sessions in a year.

The Committee on Economic, Social and Cultural Rights was established by the ECOSOC to supervise the implementation of the International Covenant on Economic, Social and Cultural Rights. The Committee meets three times every year in Geneva. States parties to the covenant are required to submit an initial report on the measures they have adopted and the progress made in achieving the rights recognized in the covenant within two years of its entry into force for the state party concerned and thereafter every five years.

The Committee on the Elimination of Racial Discrimination was established by Article 8 of the International Convention on the Elimination of All Forms of Racial Discrimination to overlook at the implementation of the convention. The Committee also meets twice each year in Geneva. As per Article 9, parties to the convention are required to submit an initial report on the legislative, judicial, administrative or other measures which they have adopted for the protection of rights enumerated in the convention within one year after its entry into force and thereafter every two years.

The Committee on the Elimination of Discrimination against Women is the body of independent experts to monitor the implementation of the Convention on the Elimination of All Forms of Discrimination against Women. This Committee consists of 23 experts on women's rights from around the world. 'Countries who have become party to the treaty (States parties) are required to submit regular reports to the Committee on how the rights of the Convention are implemented. During its sessions the Committee considers each State party report and addresses its concerns and recommendations to the State party in the form of concluding observations'.[8]

Another important treaty-based committee is the Committee against Torture, established by Article 17 of the Convention against Torture and Other Cruel, Inhuman or Degrading Treatment or Punishment. The Committee oversees the implementation of the provisions of the convention. The Committee meets twice each year in Geneva. Parties to the convention (states) are also required to submit an initial report on the measures taken under the convention within one year after its entry into force and thereafter every four years.

The Committee on the Rights of the Child is a treaty-based committee that was established by Article 43 of the Convention on the Rights of the Child to supervise the implementation of the convention. The Committee meets three times each year in Geneva. As per the conventions laid out in Article 44, parties to the convention need to submit an initial report on measures adopted and on the progress made on the enjoyment of those rights within two years of its entry into force and thereafter every five years.

The Committee on Migrant Workers, a treaty-based committee, was established pursuant to Article 72 of the Convention on the Protection of the Rights of All Migrant Workers and Members of Their Families to supervise the implementation of the convention. It meets twice every year in Geneva. Parties to the convention are required by Article 73 to submit an initial report on measures adopted and on the progress made on the enjoyment of those rights within one year of its entry into force and thereafter every five years. It held its first session in March 2004. The Committee will also, 'under certain circumstances, be able to consider individual complaints or communications from individuals claiming that their rights under the Convention have been violated once 10 states parties have accepted this procedure in accordance with Article 77 of the Convention'.[9]

The Committee on the Rights of Persons with Disabilities is a body of independent experts formed to monitor implementation of the convention by the states parties. All state parties are required to submit regular reports to the Committee on how the rights are being implemented. States must report initially within two years of accepting the convention and thereafter every four years. The Committee examines each report and makes suggestions and general recommendations on the report as it may consider appropriate and forwards these back to the state party concerned. 'The Optional Protocol to the Convention gives the Committee competence to examine individual complaints with regard to alleged violations of the Convention by States parties to the Protocol'.[10] This Committee meets in Geneva and holds two sessions per year.

The Committee on Enforced Disappearances is a treaty-based body of independent experts to monitor how the state parties implement the convention. All states parties are obliged to submit reports to the Committee on the application of these rights. States must report within two years of ratifying the convention. It examines each report and addresses its concerns and recommendations to the state party. In accordance with Article 31, a state party 'may at the time of ratification of this Convention or at any time afterwards declare that it recognizes the competence of the Committee to receive and consider communications from or on behalf of individuals subject to its jurisdiction claiming to be victims of a violation by this State Party of provisions of this Convention. In addition to the reporting procedure, Article 32 of the Convention provides for the Committee to consider inter-state complaints'.[11] The Committee meets in Geneva twice a year.

The Subcommittee on Prevention of Torture (SPT) and Other Cruel, Inhuman or Degrading Treatment or Punishment is a new treaty body in the UN Human Rights system. It has a preventive mandate focused on an innovative, sustained and proactive approach to the prevention of torture and ill treatment. The SPT started its work in February 2007. 'The SPT was established pursuant to the provisions of a treaty, the Optional Protocol to the Convention against Torture (OPCAT). The OPCAT was adopted in December 2002 by the General Assembly of the United Nations and entered into force in June 2006'.[12] The SPT is composed of twenty-five independent experts coming from different backgrounds and from various regions of the world. 'The SPT has two primary operational functions. First, it may undertake visits to States Parties, during the course of which it may visit any place where persons may be deprived of their liberty. Second, it has an advisory function which involves providing assistance and advice to

States Parties on the establishment of National Preventive Mechanisms (NPM), which OPCAT requires that they establish, and also providing advice and assistance to both the NPM and the State Party regarding the working of the NPM'.[13]

No discussion on Human Rights and the UN is complete without reference to the UDHR noted earlier. The preamble to the UDHR notes that 'disregard and contempt for human rights have resulted in barbarous acts which have outraged the conscience of mankind, and the advent of a world in which human beings shall enjoy freedom of speech and belief and freedom from fear and want has been proclaimed as the highest aspiration of the common people'. The UDHR, in thirty articles that seek to protect all kinds of human rights, has become a fundamental document of the UN in its efforts to safeguard basic rights and freedoms of all peoples around the world. Though the UDHR does not have the force of international law and sounds idealistic in today's context, it nevertheless sets a guideline for every member-state of the UN to follow some basic norms for the protection of human rights. In today's world, no state can claim to have a perfect record on human rights. As a result, the efforts of the UN to safeguard human rights and fundamental freedoms of the people have assumed increasing significance in our times.

# UN Reform Proposals

More than six decades have passed since the establishment of the UN. During this time, international relations and world politics have undergone radical changes. With the end of the Cold War, the bipolar nature of world politics and calculations based on this order have come to an end. Some of the post–Second World War major powers (such as Britain and France) have lost their earlier significance, while some new economic and political powers (like Japan, Germany, European Union, India, Brazil) have emerged. With these changes, demands for reforming the UN have naturally been made by various sections within and outside the UN system. The UN is contemplating sweeping internal reforms, both at the structural and functional levels, to adapt itself to the changing needs of time. However, major UN reforms would call for an amendment of the charter, which is an extremely difficult process. Minor reforms, which do not require amendment of the UN Charter, may be initiated quickly if member-states show political will to achieve them.

## Minor Reforms

i. *Financial reforms*: This is the most important in this category. It can galvanize the functioning of the UN to a great extent. At any point of time, about two-third members of the UN are in arrears. As a result, the UN faces severe financial crises and cannot perform many activities due to paucity of funds. Such crises of the UN can be averted if there is political will. Members may be compelled to pay their dues in time. Appropriate interests may be levied for late payments. Member-states in arrears should face unequivocal condemnation in the GA, the largest body of the UN. An alternative proposal could be that all aspiring members of the Security Council must clear their contributions to the UN, failing which their claims would not be recognized. All members must press—and be ready to accept—internal financial reforms with regard to budget ceilings, voting, allocation to programmes, costs of administration and staffing. Unorthodox means of raising finance must be explored. These may include consultancy and service charges, to be levied by ECOSOC and its specialized agencies, for any help to the non-government organizations (NGOs) and multinational corporations (MNCs). Costs might also be shared with regional associations benefiting from UN peacekeeping operations. But all these financial reform proposals, as said earlier, could be implemented only if there is genuine political will.

ii. *Peacekeeping operations*: The Military Staff Committee (MSC) system provided by the charter could never be used because of the Cold War. The ideal of collective security was also not very successful. Instead, there evolved an ad hoc system of peacekeeping, for intervention in disputes where the two superpowers agreed not to dabble. Instead of all permanent members (P-5) controlling the UN military operations (the ideal of collective security through great-power unity), peacekeeping almost always avoided any involvement of the P-5. Until recently, the non-permanent members financed almost all peacekeeping operations. The end of the Cold War has witnessed an increase in the UN peacekeeping operations. But the elaborate MSC system still remains non-operative. The former UN Secretary-General Boutros Boutros-Ghali had made some suggestions for improving the role of the UN in the maintenance of international peace and security. He had proposed the creation of a standing force, to be drawn from the defence forces of nations around the world, to be ready for instant deployment. However, the creation of a standing force would require amendments of the Charter and would be a complicated affair. An alternative, dependent upon the political will of the member-states, would be the creation of a rapid action force of nearly one lakh soldiers for a five-year term. The problem of financing peacekeeping operations could be solved if the governments paid for UN operations from their heavy defence budgets rather than from the more skimpy one of foreign affairs. Ghali also proposed a tax on arms sales, a levy on international air travel (which is dependent on the maintenance of world peace) and tax exemptions for private donations to the UN for peacekeeping operations. The peacekeeping cost needs to be compared with the much greater expense of not undertaking peacekeeping.

iii. *The Secretariat*: The Secretariat could be rejuvenated to a certain extent without amending the charter. One tenable proposal is to appoint the Secretary-General for only one seven-year term, instead of the present two five-year terms. It increases the temptation of the serving Secretary-General to use the end-phase of the first term as an election campaign to get re-appointed. Only one term in office would do away with such temptation and make the office-holder more independent and at the same time more responsible. The staff of the Secretariat should be minimized, and the Secretariat must be made a truly international civil service. Recruitment should be on merit and not on the whims of the national governments who use the UN as a charitable ground to distribute favours to retired politicians or relatives of the ruling elite. Recruitment should be preferably made at the lower levels. More women should be inducted in to the UN Secretariat. The staff must be made faithful to the promise they make at the time of joining the Secretariat, to avoid taking instructions from their national governments. The neutrality of the UN bureaucracy is absolutely necessary to make it a truly responsive international civil service.

iv. *Jurisdiction of the ICJ*: The ICJ is the prime legal body on the international platform. But, attendance at the ICJ is not mandatory for the member-states of the UN. Moreover, only about one-third of the members of the UN accept its jurisdiction. Some obvious reforms could be that attendance at the ICJ is made mandatory, all members are made to accept its jurisdiction, and greater use of the ICJ is made in the settlement of disputes among member-states.

## Major Reforms

Major reforms of the UN call for the reorganization of the principal organs that require amendment of the Charter. These reforms, though not easy to achieve, have generated a lot of debate and curiosity.

i. *The General Assembly*: It is the world's main political forum, the 'talking shop' of the UN. But it often talks without a purpose. It adopts non-binding resolutions which mainly reflect how the governments across the world think on particular issues. At present, this body is a unnecessarily big and cumbersome one with five representatives per nation. An important pertinent reform proposal is that representation should be based on the entire population of a nation, instead of the current five per nation. An alternative proposal is to make representation to the GA at a uniform two per nation. This proposal seems more tenable as representation on the basis of the population might foster a sense of inequality in the GA, leading to its further ineffectiveness. Two representatives per nation would reduce the size of the Assembly and make it more effective. The Assembly would be devoid of either some garrulous or some sleeping members. Another significant reform proposal is to make the resolutions of the Assembly binding. This would give teeth to this largest UN body, enabling it to share some power with the Security Council. The Assembly must sit frequently, preferably once in every two months. It would be easier for a smaller GA to sit frequently.
ii. *The Economic and Social Council (ECOSOC)*: This body is also unnecessarily large and complex. Currently, it has fifty-four members elected for a three-year term. The ECOSOC has six functional commissions, five regional commissions and 600 affiliated NGOs. There are sixteen autonomous specialized agencies, like the UNDP and WHO. There are also financial giants like the World Bank and the IMF. Additionally, there are subsidiary bodies such as the UNICEF and the UNEP. Due to this complex organizational structure, the ECOSOC suffers from lack of coordination between headquarters and field teams, leading to imprecise mandates and uneven results. There is a bigger problem of how the functional commissions and specialized agencies can be more effectively controlled by the ECOSOC. Specialized agencies have their own agenda, and every agency has its own governing board. Each has its own method of operation, its own objectives. This creates the problem of overlapping, and therefore confusion. One obvious choice for reform would be to go for some kind of centralization, with a streamlined 'authority'—a commissioner or administrator (to be appointed by the Secretary-General)—to guarantee accountability. But, given the decentralized organizational pattern of the UN, this kind of reform would be almost impossible to achieve. A more feasible proposal is that the specialized agencies should concentrate on their fundamental responsibility of collection of information, feasibility studies, programme design and specialist publication, leaving fieldwork to the UNDP. A slimmer ECOSOC is the need of the hour. I would prefer a thirty-member body with three-year terms. This would enable every ten members to retire after three years. The ECOSOC may take nominal charges from NGOs and MNCs for its services in the social, economic and cultural areas. This may help to solve some of the financial problems of this body. ECOSOC must also prepare effective guidelines for sustainable development, critical for any development policy.

iii. *The Security Council*: The issue of restructuring the Security Council has attracted enormous attention all over the world. How many members would a reorganized council have? How many of them could be permanent, how many non-permanent? Who would be the new permanent member, and on what grounds? Who among the existing five permanent members (P-5) are no longer regarded as great powers? Would the new permanent members enjoy veto power? If yes, what would be the consequences? All these intriguing questions are doing the rounds in world politics at this juncture. It is obvious that the P-5 are no longer the main countries across the globe, as they were in 1945, when the UN was formed. Britain and France are regarded by many scholars as the countries that need to be excluded from the P-5. But who would dare to exclude these veto-armed nations? A preferred choice for reforming the council would be to retain the P-5 and include some more permanent members. Germany and Japan are tipped to be the favourites because of their emergence as major industrial nations after the Second World War. They have also increased their financial contributions to the UN significantly. But if these two 'developed' countries are included, what about representation from the vast 'developing' world? Here arises the dilemma, because the aspirants from developing countries are many. The politics of reforms also revolves around this issue of inclusion of new permanent members from the developing world. Who among Brazil, India, Argentina, Nigeria, Mexico, Egypt, Indonesia, Pakistan and probably others, should be included from this vast terrain called the 'developing' world? One should also not forget some of the 'developed' aspirants like Italy, Canada and the European Union.

This brings us to the question of the composition of a revamped Security Council. A twenty-four-member council without permanent membership has been suggested by many experts like Richard Hudson and Frank Barnaby. This would enable each country to chair the council for one month during the two-year term of the membership of the council. The idea of permanent membership of the Security Council was mooted to achieve great-power unity that was thought necessary to preserve peace and security in the post–Second World War period. But that vision could not be materialized due to the superpower rivalry witnessed during the Cold War years. As a result, the concept of collective security failed miserably. As we know now, (the vision of) collective security failed because it contradicted the prime factor of national interest. The importance of national interest in world politics has not dwindled after the Cold War. This compels one to discard the ideal of any great-power bonhomie. This may be the reason to disfavour permanent membership in a revamped Security Council. The end of permanent membership will also solve the problem of veto power, the most widely condemned item in the UN system. There will be no veto power for the twenty-four non-permanent members of the reorganized council. The proposals for inclusion of new permanent members with or without veto are loaded with possible dangers. More veto-wielding permanent members would only exacerbate confusion and inefficiency in the council. Permanent members without veto would become second-class citizens, and lack in power to serve the council with confidence. Therefore, some reasonable recommendations for a revamped Security Council are as follows: (1) it would be a twenty-four-member body without permanent membership; (2) the term of each member would be two years, giving each member the chance to chair the council for one month; (3) no member would enjoy any special power (veto); (4) decisions would be taken by a majority vote of members present and voting, and the resolutions of the council shall be binding upon all the members of the UN; (5) the Security Council and the

GA must work in tandem through regular consultations and working parties. However, it should be noted here that any reform of the council would be difficult, because any member-state from the P-5 may flex its muscle, if the proposed reform goes against its interests.

## Other Reforms

The proposals for minor and major reforms are both based on retaining the UN's fundamental structure as an organization of nation-states. A third part of the UN reform spectrum consists of ideas based on recognizing the role of non-state actors within the UN system. The UN system must recognize the significance of the MNCs and the NGOs and allow them a greater role within the organization. The present world order began in 1648 with the Treaty of Westphalia, and subsequent emergence of the nation-states. But this system of nation-states as the principal actors in world politics cannot cope with many of today's problems. National governments prove to be too small for some problems and too large for others. Pollution and health hazards are now global problems beyond the control of any single nation-state. A new world order is evolving in which national governments have to share their responsibilities with international organizations like the MNCs and the NGOs.

The MNCs are the major global economic actors. They have greater liquid assets than all the major central reserve banks combined. With the introduction of free market economy almost everywhere in the world, they can move money around the globe even more easily. MNCs have themselves become global entities. The UN can take their help in solving some of its financial problems. They in turn benefit from the services rendered by the UN. Why could not the MNCs, then, be charged for providing such services? At present, the UN appears to be confused in handling the MNCs. More effective ways to cooperate with them would be to include them in some committees of the GA or as specialized agencies of the ECOSOC, allow them to work in specific fields, and charge fees from them for such work in addition to regular subscriptions.

NGOs have been involved in the functioning of the UN since its inception. They were present at the San Francisco Conference in 1945, which finalized the UN Charter. They got official recognition in Article 71 of the charter, which says that the ECOSOC could consult the NGOs. Such 'consultation' with the NGOs takes various forms at the UN. NGOs can attend meetings of bodies attached to the ECOSOC, such as the Commission on Human Rights or the Commission on the Status of Women, as also of the specialized agencies. Their papers are circulated at such meetings. They may seek permission to speak there. Permission may be granted to them depending on availability of time. The NGOs have, therefore, found a place among nation-states of the UN. The need of the hour is to strengthen their presence at the UN.

At present, the MNCs have no formal status at the UN, while the NGOs have only 'consultative' status. The new global order calls for more important roles for them in global decision-making and international law through participation in the UN system. A possible way to induct them into the system is to create two committees of the GA where representatives of MNCs and NGOs could express their views on proposed resolutions. This would enable them to share the same platform with national governments and open dialogue and areas of cooperation with these governments. The national governments would also learn to share their power with the MNCs and NGOs. In an era of globalization, the state and various non-state actors must learn to cooperate with one another. While such cooperation is taking place outside the UN, the largest international body of nation-states must also create opportunities for important non-state actors to air their voices and share their expertise within the UN system. In the new international order, MNCs and NGOs can never be left behind in any effort towards peace, security and development of the world.

QUESTIONS

1. Discuss the origin of the UN.
2. Analyse the composition and functions of the GA.
3. Discuss the composition and functions of the Security Council.
4. Write a note on the ECOSOC.
5. Analyse the role of the Secretary-General of the UN.
6. Make a critical estimate of the World Court (ICJ) of the UN.
7. Examine the idea of collective security.
8. Analyse the role of the UN in peacekeeping.
9. Bring out the significance of the UN in safeguarding human rights.
10. Write a note on the reform proposals of the UN.

## ENDNOTES

1. United Nations, http://www.un.org.
2. United Nations, *Op. Cit.*
3. *Ibid.*
4. UN HRC; http://www.ohchr.org/EN/HRBodies/HRC/Pages/AboutCouncil.aspx
5. UN HRC, *Op. Cit.*
6. *Ibid.*
7. *Ibid.*
8. *Ibid.*
9. UN HRC, *Op. Cit.*
10. *Ibid.*
11. *Ibid.*
12. *Ibid.*
13. UN HRC, *Op. Cit.*

# 6 Other Inter-governmental Organizations

## Non-Aligned Movement (NAM)

The end of the Second World War saw a new international order not known to the world earlier. The international system came to be dominated by two superpowers—the United States of America and the erstwhile Soviet Union, known officially as the Union of Soviet Socialist Republics (USSR). These two superpowers tried to influence other countries militarily, economically, as well as ideologically. Both the United States and the USSR were engaged in an intensified propaganda against each other and spent huge sums on it. They wanted to bring other countries to their respective spheres of influence, and for this purpose, they created security and economic alliances after the Second World War. As a consequence, the world became bipolar, and an intense bloc politics, where the two superpowers were engaged in building their own blocs, emerged. This led to mutual distrust, hatred and sharp rivalry between the two superpowers. The United States, in order to counter the spread of communism, encouraged West European nations to create the North Atlantic Treaty Organization (NATO), a military alliance, in 1949. The Soviet Union countered the NATO by forming the Warsaw Pact, another military alliance of East European nations, in 1955. Though these military alliances were initially formed in Europe after the Second World War, the Americans and the Soviets gradually tried to bring other Asian, African and Latin American countries under their military and economic influences. As a consequence, two 'supra national' blocs emerged in world politics. The world was sharply being split into a 'communist' part, and what the Americans called the 'free world'.

A parallel line of thought opposing this bipolar nature of the world was also evolving after the Second World War. Some developing nations defied the call of the superpowers to join their blocs, and nurtured the dream of a world free of bloc politics and the intense political tension associated with it. Some newly independent nation-states showed greater inclination to maintain their autonomy outside bloc politics. They felt that rendering allegiance to any of the superpowers would infringe upon their freedom to decide their own course after the much-awaited independence of their motherlands. Prominent among these newly independent developing countries was India, which rejected the idea of joining any bloc after the Second World War. Jawaharlal Nehru, the first Prime Minister of India, was opposed to militarism and preferred relying more on the age-old Indian traditions of non-violence and peaceful cooperation among nation-states. He was joined by Indonesian President Sukarno and Egyptian President Nasser, and they endeavoured to create a world free of bloc politics and military alignments. It was due to their efforts that the Non-Aligned Movement (NAM) emerged and gathered strength in world politics after the Second World War.

## Origin of the NAM

The idea of a non-alignment movement was conceived at the conference of Afro-Asian countries held in New Delhi in 1947. After India gained independence from British rule, it decided not to join any power bloc. Jawaharlal Nehru, the first Indian Prime Minister, took the initiative to encourage these Afro-Asian nations to fight against the evils of colonialism and imperial domination.

The term 'non-alignment' was first used by Nehru in a speech he delivered in 1954 in Colombo, Sri Lanka. In it, Nehru described the five guiding principles for China–India relations. These principles, known as '*panchsheel*' (five pillars), would later serve as the basis of the NAM. These were: (1) respect for each other's sovereignty and territorial integrity; (2) non-aggression; (3) non-interference in domestic affairs; (4) equality for all; (5) peaceful co-existence. But in its truest sense, the NAM took a proper shape at the Bandung Conference of Afro-Asian countries held in Indonesia in 1955. The attending twenty-nine nations declared their wish not to get involved in the Cold War and adopted a Declaration on Promotion of World Peace and Cooperation, which included Nehru's five principles. The Bandung Conference emphasized the need for emancipation of the people from colonial rule and urged the newly independent nation-states to stay away from bloc politics and adhere to the principles of nonalignment. This conference had built the base for the movement.

After Bandung, it took six more years to arrange the first non-aligned summit in Belgrade, the capital city of former Yugoslavia, in 1961. Meanwhile, erstwhile Yugoslav President Josip Broz Tito expressed his support to the NAM and invited the non-aligned countries to organize their first summit in Belgrade. Twenty-five countries participated at the Belgrade Summit. The basic thrust of this first non-aligned summit was on peace, socio-economic development of the underprivileged countries and disarmament of the world. The Belgrade Declaration on Peace evoked global response.

## Membership of the NAM

The Belgrade Summit clearly outlined the conditions required for a state to be declared a non-aligned state. The summit set five conditions, mainly based on *panchsheel*, for a state to become a member of the NAM. These are as follows:

i. a state willing to join the NAM must formulate an independent foreign policy aimed at establishing mutual cooperation among nation-states;
ii. it should support independence and right to self-determination of every nationality;
iii. it should not be a member of any military alliance created out of conflicts of big powers;
iv. if it enters into any bilateral or regional military alliance, such agreement or alliance must not be created out of conflicts of the big powers;
v. if it allows any foreign military base on its soil, such base must not be created out of the conflicts of big powers.

The underlying implication of all these five principles was that a non-aligned nation shall follow an independent foreign policy, shall support the independence of a nation and shall not enter into bloc politics. *It needs to be mentioned in this context that nonalignment does not imply neutrality. The NAM believes that neutrality is a negative concept and that as a policy it has little meaning.*

*Neutrality invokes passivity towards international politics. But a non-aligned movement means conscious and willing detachment from any power bloc; and therefore the movement is not at all indifferent to world politics.* The movement not only allows the nations to have greater manoeuvrability in their foreign policies but also to express opinion on any international issue independently. More and more countries joined the NAM to oppose the policy of alignment and bloc politics since the Second World War.

Since its first summit in Belgrade in 1961, membership of the NAM went on increasing. At present, NAM has 120 member-states. After the United Nations Organization (UNO), it is the largest organization of nation-states in the world, containing 55 per cent of the world population. Box 6.1 contains a list of the current members of the NAM.

**Box 6.1 Current Members of the NAM**

Afghanistan, Algeria, Angola, Antigua and Barbuda, Bahamas, Bahrain, Bangladesh, Barbados, Belarus, Belize, Benin, Bhutan, Bolivia, Botswana, Brunei, Burkina Faso, Burundi, Cambodia, Cameroon, Cape Verde, Central African Republic, Chad, Chile, Colombia, Comoros, Congo, Côte d'Ivoire, Cuba, Democratic Republic of the Congo, Djibouti, Dominica, Dominican Republic, East Timor, Ecuador, Egypt, Equatorial Guinea, Eritrea, Ethiopia, Fiji, Gabon, Gambia, Ghana, Grcnada, Guatcmala, Guinea, Guinea-Bissau, Guyana, Haiti, Honduras, India, Indonesia, Iran, Iraq, Jamaica, Jordan, Kenya, Kuwait, Laos, Lebanon, Lesotho, Liberia, Libya, Madagascar, Malawi, Malaysia, Maldives, Mali, Mauritania, Mauritius, Mongolia, Morocco, Mozambique, Myanmar, Namibia, Nepal, Nicaragua, Niger, Nigeria, North Korea, Oman, Pakistan, Palestine, Panama, Papua New Guinea, Peru, Philippines, Qatar, Rwanda, Saint Lucia, Saint Kitts and Nevis, Saint Vincent and the Grenadines, São Tomé and Príncipe, Saudi Arabia, Senegal, Seychelles, Sierra Leone, Singapore, Somalia, South Africa, Sri Lanka, Sudan, Suriname, Swaziland, Syria, Tanzania, Thailand, Timor-Leste, Togo, Trinidad and Tobago, Tunisia, Turkmenistan, Uganda, United Arab Emirates, Uzbekistan, Vanuatu, Venezuela, Vietnam, Yemen, Zambia, Zimbabwe.

Besides 118 regular members, the NAM offers 'observer' status to several countries and organizations within and outside the UN system. It also invites 'guests' to its summits. Like that of an observer, guest status is also given to states and organizations. Box 6.2 shows current observers and guests of the NAM. Members have the right to leave the organization. New members can also join the NAM provided they fulfill the criteria for becoming members.

## Organizational Structure of the NAM

The NAM, like other inter-governmental organizations, has no fixed organizational structure. It considers itself to be non-hierarchal in nature and no country enjoys any special privileges here. The organization does not have any constitution as many similar organizations do. This was done out of

**Box 6.2** **Observers and Guests of the NAM**

The following nations, along with some organizations, have observer status in the NAM:

Argentina, Armenia, Bosnia and Herzegovina, Brazil, Costa Rica, El Salvador, Kazakhstan, Kyrgyzstan, Macedonia, Mexico, Montenegro, Paraguay, People's Republic of China, Serbia, South Sudan, Tajikistan, Uruguay.

There is no permanent guest status in the NAM, but often several non-member countries are represented as guests at NAM summits. In addition, a large number of organizations, both from within the UN system and from outside, are always invited as guests.

the belief that with so many member-countries having so many diverse views and interests, any formal administrative structure would increase divisiveness in the organization. Members chair the different summits by official rotation. The Head of the State or the Head of the Government of the country where a NAM summit is held becomes the chairperson of the NAM for the next three years, or till a fresh summit is organized in another country. Thus, the head of the state or the government of a new NAM summit takes over as the new chairperson of the organization. The head of the state of Venezuela became the new chairperson of NAM in 2016.

Eighteen non-aligned summits were held from 1961 to 2019 in different parts of the world. A non-aligned summit normally takes place every three years, although political disturbances have caused cancellations of regular summits in the past. The details of the eighteen NAM summits held (and to be held) till 2019 are given in Table 6.1.

**Table 6.1** NAM Summits from 1961 to 2019

| S. No. | Summit | Year | Place | Country |
|---|---|---|---|---|
| 1. | First | 1961 | Belgrade | Yugoslavia |
| 2. | Second | 1964 | Cairo | Egypt |
| 3. | Third | 1970 | Lusaka | Zambia |
| 4. | Fourth | 1973 | Algiers | Algeria |
| 5. | Fifth | 1976 | Colombo | Sri Lanka |
| 6. | Sixth | 1979 | Havana | Cuba |
| 7. | Seventh | 1983 | New Delhi | India |
| 8. | Eighth | 1986 | Harare | Zimbabwe |
| 9. | Ninth | 1989 | Belgrade | Yugoslavia |
| 10. | Tenth | 1992 | Jakarta | Indonesia |
| 11. | Eleventh | 1995 | Cartagena | Columbia |
| 12. | Twelfth | 1998 | Durban | South Africa |

(*Continued*)

**Table 6.1** *(Continued)*

| S. No. | Summit | Year | Place | Country |
|---|---|---|---|---|
| 13. | Thirteenth | 2003 | Kuala Lumpur | Malaysia |
| 14. | Fourteenth | 2006 | Havana | Cuba |
| 15. | Fifteenth | 2009 | Sharm El-Shaikh | Egypt |
| 16. | Sixteenth | 2012 | Tehran | Iran |
| 17. | Seventeenth | 2016 | Margarita Island | Venezuela |
| 18. | Eighteenth | 2019 | To be announced | Azerbaijan |

During the Cold War, the NAM acted as a powerful alternative for a vast majority of nations who wanted to remain non-committal towards any power bloc. It not only promoted the interest of newly independent nations, but also tried to influence the decisions of the United Nations and other international bodies in favour of the developing countries. However, Western critics believed that in reality the NAM failed to play any successful role in international politics. They argued that hardly any member-nation could stay outside the influence of the two superpowers during the Cold War. As a consequence, according to Western critics, the movement was not truly nonaligned because several members became aligned to superpowers, making a mockery of the ideals of the movement.

There is possibly some truth in the view that the nonaligned nations could not remain isolated from bloc politics during the Cold War. Due to economic and political compulsions, several members of the NAM leaned towards either of the two superpowers during the Cold War, subjecting the movement to controversy. Despite such criticism, it may be said that the movement could provide the vast majority of developing nations with a very important platform to fight against economic and political exploitation by the developed nations. The NAM was successful in waging a continuous struggle against neocolonialism, use of armaments and economic inequality. It also encouraged the developing nations to pursue an independent foreign policy. Its popularity could be assessed from the continuous rise in membership during the Cold War. For the developing countries, the NAM was indeed an alternative to bloc politics, and a voice for the Third World, which the developing nations wanted to make survive. Although for political and economic compulsions many third world nations tilted towards the superpowers, yet they did not wish to see the end of the NAM. This desire on their part helped the NAM to continue as a significant organization even after the Cold War, although doubts were raised regarding its continued survival.

The end of the Cold War saw the end of bloc politics and of bipolarity in world politics. The disintegration of the Soviet Union helped the United States to emerge as the only superpower in the world. In the absence of bloc politics, what would be the relevance of the NAM, which originated only to counter the politics of alignment? This question became pertinent in the post–Cold War era, and leads to the discussion on the relevance of the NAM in contemporary international relations.

## Relevance of the NAM in Today's World

During the Cold War, nonalignment blossomed from a principle into a movement. However, doubts have been raised in the academic sphere about the relevance of the NAM since the end of the Cold War in1991. Momentarily, it seemed that with the end of the Cold War and the disappearance of the erstwhile bloc politics, the NAM had become marginalized. Scholars argued that the ideological and intellectual vigour of the movement had diminished in the absence of rival power blocs. But in reality the NAM has not lost its relevance after the Cold War; it has adopted new and newer policies relevant to the post–Cold War world order. These policies have helped the movement not only to survive, but to garner strength as well. Therefore, the survival and continuous significance of the movement cannot be questioned at the moment. This proposition can be strengthened by the fact that in the post–Cold War period nine successful summits were held by the NAM (1992, 1995, 1998, 2003, 2006, 2009, 2012, 2016 and 2019). At all of these summits, member-states of the NAM have stressed upon the continuous significance of the movement and outlined the altered role of the NAM in a new international order. The nine NAM summits held so far after the Cold War put emphasis on the social and economic progress of the developing nations, and the role of the NAM in these areas. From a primarily political orientation during the Cold War, the NAM has shifted its attention to socio-economic, ecological, health, anti-terrorism and related issues during the post–Cold War period. This does not mean that the NAM has dropped its political agenda; it is still a significant base for upholding the territorial integrity and sovereignty of the developing countries, as also an important platform to fight for the right to self-determination of oppressed nationalities. Alongside its political agenda, the NAM is also putting emphasis on other areas as mentioned above, because these issues have gained prominence in international relations after the Cold War.

A study of some of the proceedings of the last few NAM summits reveals the changing role of the NAM in the new international order. For instance, at the eleventh summit of the NAM held in October 1995 at Cartagena, Columbia, the then UN Secretary-General Boutros Boutros-Ghali identified the changing role of the NAM after the Cold War. Ghali told the summit: 'The end of the Cold War has freed the world of some of the political encumbrances that impeded its progress. The global society which is coming into being is rich with promise. But as we all know, it may also be fraught with dangers for the weakest and the most deprived . . . The Non-Aligned Movement more than any other entity, should therefore become active in this combat against exclusion from the fruits of progress, by fighting for economic and social development'. Ghali categorically invited the NAM-states to fight for socio-economic justice, because socio-economic problems of the developing world have not diminished with the eclipse of the Cold War.

The twelfth NAM summit at Durban in South Africa in September 1998 endorsed the new role expected to be played by the NAM at the dawn of the new century. In the Durban Declaration for the New Millenium, member-states of the NAM endorsed the altered role of the NAM in the context of globalization and free market economy. The Durban Declaration stated:

> We now stand on the threshold of a new era. An era that offers great opportunity yet possess special danger for the developing world. . . . Whilst globalization holds out the promise of prosperity, it brings with it severe challenges for the developing countries . . . Liberalization must not provide a cover for the protectionist policies of the rich and powerful . . . we must act positively to shape our future, advocating a new system of international relations that is both democratic and representative of all. . . .

Although the Durban Declaration outlined the brighter sides of globalization and liberal economy, it also sent out signals of caution about the negative influence of globalization and liberal economy on the developing nations. The declaration cautioned the developing nations about the economic disparity that might be created as a result of globalization and free market economy. The rich and developed countries might reap the fruits of liberal economy and globalization, warned the declaration. It also stated that the NAM should strive hard to remove the stark economic disparity between the developed and the developing world in the post–Cold War world. Finally, it outlined the role of the NAM in eradicating the dangers of the Weapons of Mass Destruction (WMDs) like nuclear, chemical, biological and radiological weapons, and urged the NAM countries to wage a fresh struggle against deadly diseases like AIDS, cancer and thalasemia, that have posed severe health hazards to the world.

The relevance of the NAM in the post–Cold War era became the focus of discussion in the thirteenth NAM summit held at Kuala Lumpur, Malayasia, in 2003. The Kuala Lumpur Declaration on Continuing the Revitalization of the Non-Aligned Movement emphasized on the role of the NAM in an era of globalization and communication revolution. The declaration called for a more strong and powerful non-aligned movement to meet the challenges of the new century. It stated:

> The future presents as many challenges and opportunities as the past and the movement must continue to remain strong, cohesive and resilient. The continued relevance of the movement will depend, in large measure, on the unity and solidarity of its members as well as its ability to adapt to these changes. In this regard, the process of the revitalization of the movement . . . must be given further impetus.

The future of the NAM shall depend on the unity of the member-states and on their mutual cooperation. Apart from this, the NAM has to face and accept new challenges of the new world. The long way travelled by the NAM, from Bandung to Havana, in the last fifty years has made it stronger and more resilient. It will also rise to meet new challenges in the future, as it had done in the past, because the NAM has adjusted itself remarkably to the demands of the new international order.

In the Havana Summit of 2006, the member-states of the NAM had stressed the need for giving new impetus to the movement, for putting in new efforts. This movement was launched during the Cold War to counter the hegemony of the superpowers. These states think that, in keeping with this objective, they must now work against a growing hegemony of the sole surviving superpower, the United States. They also called for multilateralism, the reform of the UN system and socio-economic development. The NAM also vowed to defend the rights of the peoples to peace, sovereignty and self-determination; oppose the use of war or the threat of its use in solving international problems. The movement upheld the rights of all countries to peacefully use nuclear energy, including the right to enrich uranium for producing electricity. It also rejected all terrorism against civilian populations.

A statement, issued by the NAM summit in Havana, called for the withdrawal of the Israeli occupation forces from the Gaza Strip and urged Israel to immediately release all detained Palestinian officials. About 3,000 delegates from over a hundred countries, including fifty-six heads of state or government and ninety foreign ministers, as well as other dignitaries and senior officials, attended the Havana summit. Two new members joined the movement in Havana—Haiti, and St. Kitts and Nevis—bringing the movement's membership to 118 nations, almost two-thirds of the members of the United Nations. At present, the membership has gone up to 120.

At the seventeenth summit of the NAM held during 17–18 September 2016 in Margarita Island of Venezuela, member-states released a 21-article declaration in which they reaffirmed their commitment to the promotion of human rights and disarmament of WMDs and recognized the importance of interreligious and intercultural dialogues. They also ratified their commitment to the founding principles of the NAM and the principles enshrined in the Declaration on the Purposes and Principles and the Role of the NAM in the present international juncture adopted in the fourteenth NAM summit in Havana.

These summits of the NAM have categorically identified its objectives in the backdrop of the current international order. *Firstly*, these summits have emphasized the need for more vigorous steps to tackle not only complex political issues but also socio-economic problems. With the end of the Cold War and the power blocs remaining no more, the increasing relevance of the movement could be felt when it continued to voice the plight of the developing world. The end of the Cold War did not put an end to the exploitative and restrictive tendencies of the rich and advanced countries. As a consequence, the poor nations continued to suffer. The prevailing political imbalance and socio-economic inequalities aroused grave concern in the NAM. As a result, it has now engaged itself in fighting neocolonialism, so that the developing nations are not exploited by the advanced countries. *Secondly*, in an age of globalization and liberal economy, the underdeveloped countries of the South are prone to more exploitation by the rich North. Although NAM recognizes the positive effects of globalization, it is aware of the dangers of liberal economy vis-à-vis the third world. So, it wants to secure the interests of the developing nations in a complex globalized world order. For this purpose, NAM is inclined towards achieving adequate economic growth rates in the under-privileged countries. *Thirdly*, the movement has planned to take appropriate steps to eradicate problems of poverty, illiteracy, health, environment and terrorism, because these problems have continued to affect the world since the Cold War. To fight these problems, nonaligned nations would also seek the support of the developed countries and express their desire to work together. *Fourthly*, NAM is supportive of dismantling nuclear arsenals. It has pledged to work for general and complete disarmament so that peace can be truly achieved in a world free of bloc politics. *Fifthly*, the unprecedented development of information technology (IT) has divided the world into two zones. This split in the field of IT is called the digital divide. The edge the developed nations acquired over the developing countries in the field of IT has given them added power in international political and economic spheres. Satellite communication, super computers, inter-continental ballistic missiles and other such facilities have provided extra mileage to the developed nations over the poor countries. Durban and Kuala Lumpur summits of the NAM have pledged to remove the digital divide from the world. *Sixthly*, apart from socio-economic issues, the NAM would also look into the political issues affecting the developing nations with equal emphasis and caution. In fact, it had criticized and protested against many political events that had occurred in the post–Cold War period. NAM condemned the United States for its military expeditions in Afghanistan and Iraq. The bombing of Kosovo by the NATO and the ethnic cleansing in Bosnia were bitterly criticized by the nonaligned nations in their summits after the Cold War. *Seventhly*, NAM wants to eliminate the painful phenomenon of debt trap, which the advanced countries create by means of providing loans and aids. For this purpose, NAM not only insisted on new economic measures for the development of nonaligned nations but also invited the international economic institutions and agencies to extend loan facilities at low interest rates to the developing nations. *Lastly*, NAM would extend material and moral support to the exploited people of the world in their fight for the right to self-determination and dignity. Since the rich-poor divide continues to exist in the world after the end of the Cold War, the relevance of the NAM as an organization representing the developing nations has grown over the years.

In the new international order, developing nations are ready to be more cooperative with each other on economic and political issues within and outside the framework of the NAM. So, the non-aligned nations have formed both big and small groups like G-15 or G-77 among themselves which interact and cooperate with each other on socio-economic and political issues. But this does not prevent the developing nations from entering into economic relations with the developed countries. The flexible organizational structure of the NAM is a great advantage in this respect. Though the NAM upholds the plight of the developing nations, it nurtures no animosity towards the developed ones, and calls for cooperation with the advanced world for the socio-economic benefit of the former. To maintain such flexibility, NAM has not imposed any constitution or legal parameters for its members. It rather encourages the nonaligned nations to maximize opportunities of meeting domestic economic needs while minimizing dependence on others. In order to have adequate economic growth as fast as possible, NAM sees no harm in cultivating economic and political relations among the nonaligned nations, as well as between them and the developed ones.

# Commonwealth of Nations

The Commonwealth of Nations, commonly known as the Commonwealth, is an association of independent states, most of which were former British colonies or their dependencies. In 2008, the commonwealth had fifty-three members, and barring Britain and Mozambique, other members were former British colonies or dependencies. The commonwealth is an association of independent sovereign states, and no member-state can impose its decisions over others. It is a voluntary political union of independent states, with members enjoying the right to leave the association. Though the British Monarch—presently Queen Elizabeth II—is the Head of the Commonwealth, her headship is purely nominal and symbolic. Member-states are not subject to the authority of the British monarch, as they joined the commonwealth voluntarily, while retaining the sovereignty of their countries. They voluntarily accepted the British Crown as the symbolic head of the organization which observes the principle of equality for all its members.

## Origin

The origin of the commonwealth could be traced back to the late 1880s when the British and the other colonial prime ministers had begun to hold regular conferences on common political interests. Such prime-ministerial meetings led to imperial conferences that began to take place since the late 1920s. These conferences were meetings where Heads of Government of the former British Empire assembled to discuss important political issues. The idea of the commonwealth developed from such conferences, where the independence of the self-governing colonies and dominions was recognized. The Balfour Declaration, made at the Imperial Conference in 1926, could be credited with the birth of the British Commonwealth. The Balfour Declaration of 1926, named after the British political leader Arthur Balfour, was a report that stated the relationship among governments of the British empire. It stated that Britain and its dominions are autonomous communities within the British empire, equal in status, in no way subordinate to one another in any aspect of their domestic or external affairs—though united by a common allegiance to the crown—and freely associated as members of the British Commonwealth of Nations. It should be kept in mind here that this Balfour Declaration of 1926 is different from the Balfour Declaration of 1917 relating to the creation of the state of Israel. The Statute of Westminster 1931, which is an Act of the British parliament, formalized the Balfour Declaration of 1926. Therefore, the British Commonwealth started its journey 'formally' in 1931.

After the Second World War, several British colonies in Asia and Africa became independent, and the vast British Empire dismantled gradually. As a consequence, the word 'British' was dropped from the earlier 'British Commonwealth' in 1949, in the meeting of prime ministers of the newly independent states in London, and the organization was renamed 'Commonwealth of Nations'. The statement that arose from this meeting, the London Declaration, is therefore treated as the fundamental document of the new commonwealth. In it, the newly independent countries agreed to accept the British monarch as their symbolic head, without surrendering their sovereignty. India took a lead in this regard. It declared that when it would become a Republic in 1950, it would have no problem in accepting the British monarch as the symbolic head, although the constitutional head would be the President of India. Other countries welcomed this stand of India and accepted the British crown as their symbolic head, although all of them had their respective Heads of the State. Thus, the new Commonwealth of Nations, an international organization of independent states with the British monarch as the symbolic head, started a new journey with the London Declaration of 1949.

## Membership

The issue of membership of the commonwealth changed from time to time as the organization evolved from an old union of British dominions to a new association of independent states. The Statute of Westminster, 1931, laid down the provision that membership required British dominionhood. The London Declaration changed this provision and stated that membership would be open to republics and monarchies who would accept the British crown as the head of the commonwealth. However, in the wake of decolonization, and movements for racial equality and socio-economic justice throughout the 1950s and 1960s, the Singapore Declaration of the commonwealth in 1971 stated that membership would be open to countries with declared policies of equality, peace, protection of human rights, liberty and free trade. It formed the basis for membership of the commonwealth, although these criteria for membership could not always be strictly enforced. The Harare Declaration of the commonwealth in 1991 vowed to enforce the criteria for membership adopted in the Singapore Declaration. The following is a relevant extract from it:

- We believe that international peace and order, global economic development and the rule of international law are essential to the security and prosperity of mankind;
- We believe in the liberty of the individual under the law, in equal rights for all citizens regardless of gender, race, colour, creed or political belief, and in the individual's inalienable right to participate by means of free and democratic political processes in framing the society in which he or she lives;
- We recognize racial prejudice and intolerance as a dangerous sickness and a threat to healthy development, and racial discrimination as an unmitigated evil;
- We oppose all forms of racial oppression, and we are committed to the principles of human dignity and equality;
- We recognize the importance and urgency of economic and social development to satisfy the basic needs and aspirations of the vast majority of the peoples of the world, and seek the progressive removal of the wide disparities in living standards amongst our members.

These principles were accepted as criteria for membership of the commonwealth. A Commonwealth Ministerial Action Group (CMAG) was created in 1995 to determine the issue of membership of countries on the basis of the Harare Declaration. At present, this declaration serves as the guiding document for membership of the commonwealth.

This was an analysis of how the criteria for membership of the commonwealth evolved. The criteria as it stands at present demands the following: (1) a member must be a sovereign state; (2) it must recognize the British monarch as the head of the Commonwealth of Nations; (3) it must adhere to the Harare principles; (4) it must accept the English language as the medium of communication in the commonwealth; (5) it must respect the wishes of the general population vis-à-vis commonwealth membership.

Fifty-three countries are members of the commonwealth at present. Box 6.3 shows the names of the member-states as in 2018. Applications from some countries for membership are being considered by the commonwealth.

**Box 6.3** **Current Members of the Commonwealth**

Antigua and Barbuda, Australia, Bahamas, Bangladesh, Barbados, Belize, Botswana, Brunei, Cameroon, Canada, Cyprus, Dominica, Fiji, Gambia, Ghana, Grenada, Guyana, India, Jamaica, Kenya, Kiribati, Lesotho, Malawi, Malaysia, Malta, Mauritius, Mozambique, Namibia, New Zealand, Nigeria, Pakistan, Papua New Guinea, Rwanda, St. Kitts and Nevis, St. Lucia, St. Vincent and the Grenadines, Samoa, Seychelles, Sierra Leone, Singapore, Solomon Islands, South Africa, Sri Lanka, Swaziland, Tanzania, Tonga, Trinidad and Tobago, Tuvalu, Uganda, United Kingdom, Vanuatu, Zambia.

## Structure

### Head of the Organization

In acordance with the London Declaration of 1949, the head of the commonwealth should be linked to the British monarchy. Queen Elizabeth II holds the position at present. However, it may be mentioned that the successor to the British crown does not automatically become the head of the commonwealth. They must be recognized by the member-states. This position of the head of the organization is purely a symbolic and nominal one. The Secretary-General of the commonwealth is the real executive head who looks after the day-to-day administration of the commonwealth.

### Commonwealth Heads of Government Meeting

Second to the nominal head, who remains at the top of the organization, is the biennial Commonwealth Heads of Government Meeting (CHOGM). This is the highest decision-making body of the commonwealth where heads of government of the member-states—like prime ministers and presidents—assemble for a few days to discuss matters of mutual interest.

CHOGM is the successor to the prime ministers' conferences, as also to the imperial conferences and colonial conferences dating back to 1887. Apart from the CHOGM, other ministers of the member-countries also meet regularly to discuss issues relating to their areas. As such, there are regular meetings like those of foreign ministers, education ministers, finance ministers or defence ministers. In these meetings, areas of cooperation and related matters are discussed. Important organizational decisions are taken in the CHOGM and other ministerial meetings.

### Commonwealth Secretariat

The Commonwealth Secretariat is the main coordinating body of the organization. Established in 1965, the secretariat is headed by the Secretary-General and located in London. As per new rules, effective since the CHOGM held in Cyprus in 1993, the Secretary-General is elected by the Commonwealth Heads of Government for not more than two four-year terms. Before 1993, a Secretary-General could enjoy a term of more than eight years. The present Secretary-General of the commonwealth is Patricia Scotland of Dominica, who took office in April 2016. The former Secretaries-General were Arnold Smith of Canada (1965–75), Sir Sridath Ramphal of Guyana (1975–90), Chief Emeka Anyaoku of Nigeria (1990–2000), Don McKinnon of New Zealand (2000–08) and Kamalesh Sharma of India (2008–16).

The main task of the secretariat is to facilitate cooperation among the member-states. It organizes commonwealth summits (CHOGMs), other ministerial meetings, meetings of the consultative committees and technical discussions. It plays a pivotal role in organizing the Commonwealth Games. In accordance with the principles and policies of the organization, the secretariat arranges for providing economic assistance to member-states for developmental activities. It also arranges for suitable measures to be adopted for technical development of the members. As the main coordinating body of the commonwealth, the secretariat also facilitates multilateral cooperation among member-countries. Like the secretariat of similar other organizations, the commonwealth secretariat also works as the continuing office of the organization.

## Main Objectives and Activities

The commonwealth activities pertain to almost all important areas of human life like education, health, economy, good governance, law, human rights, sports and cultural activities or gender issues. The objectives of the commonwealth, as outlined for the first time in the Singapore Declaration of 1971, were: (1) to promote democracy and human rights throughout the world; (2) to work for the economic development of the member–nations; (3) to achieve quality universal education in member countries; (4) to secure individual liberty and (5) good governance in commonwealth states. These objectives were subsequently reinforced by the Lusaka Declaration of 1979, which called for a fight against racism; the Langkawi Declaration of 1989, that put emphasis on environmental sustainability; and the Harare Declaration of 1991, that outlined in detail the main functions of the organization. The more recent Millennium Development Goals (MDG), adopted in 2003, also added new directions to the objectives and activities of the commonwealth.

In accordance with the Harare Declaration, a major objective of the commonwealth is to promote democratic principles throughout the world. The commonwealth sends experts to states which ask for its services. These experts help to promote democracy and strengthen democratic processes and institutions. The commonwealth also works towards conflict prevention. The Secretary-General plays an important role in this respect. The 'good offices' role played by them is the organization's primary mechanism for addressing political problems and conflicts. The commonwealth secretariat also makes arrangements for holding elections in member-states to strengthen democracy.

Universal, sustainable and high quality education for all citizens is another major objective of the commonwealth. The organization tries to ensure that every individual has access to high quality universal education, irrespective of age, socio-economic status or ethnicity. It works closely with ministries of education of the member-nations to promote this objective. It tries to use education to mitigate HIV and AIDS. The commonwealth also tries to secure gender equality in education. Further, the Human Rights Unit (HRU) of the commonwealth works to promote human rights in the world. The Harare Declaration observed: 'We believe in the liberty of the individual under the law, in equal rights for all citizens regardless of gender, race, colour, creed or political belief, and in the individual's inalienable right to participate by means of free and democratic political processes in framing the society in which he or she lives'. The commonwealth observes how does every member-state respond to its various issues related to human rights and democracy; it may suspend any of them showing poor performance in this regard. In the past, South Africa, Pakistan and Zimbabwe were suspended on these issues.

The commonwealth also works to achieve good governance in member-states. The Governance and Institutional Development Division (GIDD) of the commonwealth shoulders the primary responsibility of implementing the secretariat's mandate on public sector development. The Commonwealth Development Network (CDN) facilitates sharing of information among member-governments for good governance. Further, the Commonwealth Centre for E-Governance works as the nodal body in the use of information technology as a tool for strengthening good governance.

In the CHOGM of 2003 in Abuja, Nigeria, the commonwealth issued the 'Millennium Development Goals (MDG)'. The MDG highlighted the following activities as priority areas for the commonwealth in the new millennium:

i. eradicating extreme poverty and hunger;
ii. achieving universal primary education;
iii. promoting gender equality and empowerment of women;
iv. reducing child mortality rate;
v. improving maternal health;
vi. combatting HIV/AIDS, malaria and other diseases;
vii. ensuring environmental sustainability;
viii. developing a global partnership for development.

Since 2003, several projects have been undertaken in the member-states to implement the programmes highlighted by the MDG. For instance, in the area of economy, the commonwealth tries to alleviate poverty and strengthen economic growth in member-states through various measures. The secretariat works to achieve these goals through a range of programmes—at the macroeconomic level, through advocacy, consensus-building and policy advice; and through hands-on development assistance delivered via the Commonwealth Fund for Technical Cooperation. It provides debt management support and advice to its developing members. It also makes efforts to strengthen the investment climate in developing countries, particularly through promoting investment in small and medium enterprises (SMEs). The Commonwealth Secretariat also aims at fostering private sector development by providing assistance in the development of policies, laws and regulatory arrangements. It believes that such steps are necessary in an era of globalization.

Overall, it can be said that the activities of the commonwealth in implementing the MDG and other objectives of the organization are extremely commendable. Because of the good work of the commonwealth in social, economic, and political sectors, several problematic areas of its members could be successfully addressed.

# North Atlantic Treaty Organization (NATO)

The NATO was formed in 1949 as the first military alliance after the Second World War. It was conceived by some West European countries to combat the fear of aggression from Germany after the Second World War, although it eventually emerged as an anti-Soviet military organization under the impact of the Cold War. After the disintegration of the Soviet Union and the end of the Cold War, the NATO has been trying to move eastward to absorb the East European countries into the organization. The fundamental role of the NATO is to safeguard the freedom and the security of its member-states by political and military means. Article 5 of the North Atlantic Treaty declares that an attack on any of the member-states would be considered an attack on the organization, and repelled by all members. Today, the NATO is playing an increasingly important role in crisis management and peacekeeping.

## Origin

The 'ghost of Hitler' was haunting Europe for a considerable period of time after the end of the Second World War. Consequently, on 17 March 1948, five European countries—Belgium, France, Britain, Luxembourg and Netherlands—signed the Brussels Treaty to create a military alliance and consolidate their defence against any further aggression by any particular country. The Berlin blockade by the Soviet Union was another reason behind the signing of this treaty that is considered the precursor of the NATO. But very soon these five countries realized that any effort at military or economic resurgence of West Europe would not be complete without the support of the United States, because war-ravaged West European countries were not in a position to thwart the growing 'threat' of the Soviet Union. Therefore, efforts were made to include the United States into a wider security net in Europe. The United States also wanted this security alliance in Europe to counter the growing influence of the Soviet Union. After considerable discussion, the North Atlantic Treaty was signed on 4 April 1949, in Washington DC, to form the NATO. With the active engagement of the United States as a founder-member, this security organization started its journey as an anti-Soviet military alliance under the growing impact of the Cold War. The North Atlantic Treaty was signed by twelve countries—the United States, Britain, France, Belgium, Italy, Netherlands, Canada, Denmark, Luxembourg, Iceland, Norway and Portugal. In February 1952, Greece and Turkey joined the NATO, and subsequently several other states followed suit. After the Cold War, some of the former 'socialist' countries joined as well.

## Membership

Starting with an initial twelve, the membership of the NATO had come to be twenty-nine as of June 2018. Apart from full membership, the organization has 'partnership for peace' with a number of states who are called NATO-partners. This is a 'symbolic membership' that could be converted to full membership. Box 6.4 shows the present NATO-members.

**Box 6.4 NATO Member-Countries**

Albania, Belgium, Bulgaria, Canada, Croatia, Czech Republic, Denmark, Estonia, France, Germany, Greece, Hungary, Iceland, Italy, Latvia, Lithuania, Luxembourg, Montenegro, Netherlands, Norway, Poland, Portugal, Romania, Slovakia, Slovenia, Spain, Turkey, United Kingdom, United States.

Apart from these twenty-nine member-states, the NATO had several partners as of June 2018, as given in Box 6.5.

**Box 6.5 NATO Partner-Countries**

Armenia, Austria, Azerbaijan, Belarus, Bosnia-Herzegovina, Finland, Georgia, Ireland, Kazakhstan, Kyrgyz Republic, Malta, Moldova, Russia, Serbia, Sweden, Switzerland, Macedonia, Tajikistan, Turkmenistan, Ukraine, Uzbekistan.

Twenty-nine member-countries and twenty-one partner-countries together form the Euro Atlantic Partnership Council (EAPC). The fifty-member EAPC is a body that helps to maintain regular contacts between NATO-members and partners at different levels.

## Structure

The internal organization of the NATO is divided into three main structures—civilian structures, military structures, and agencies and organizations immediately subordinate to NATO-headquarters. The headquarters of the NATO is located in Brussels, the capital of Belgium.

### Civilian (Political) Structures

The North Atlantic Treaty, as also other agreements, outlined in detail the process of decision-making within the NATO. Each of the twenty-eight members sends a delegation or mission to the NATO's headquarters in Brussels. The senior permanent member—normally a senior civil servant or an experienced ambassador—of each delegation is known as the Permanent Representative of the concerned country to the NATO. All the permanent representatives together constitute the North Atlantic Council (NAC), a body which has effective political authority and powers of decision-making in the NATO. It meets at least once a week. The NAC also meets at higher levels from time to time, involving foreign ministers, defence ministers or heads of state or government. Major decisions regarding the NATO's policies are generally taken at these meetings. However, it is noteworthy that the council enjoys equal authority and powers of decision-making, and its decisions have the same status and validity, irrespective of the level at which it meets. NATO summits involving heads of state or government also take crucial decisions on many complex issues, enlargement of the organization, for instance. The meetings of the NAC are chaired by the Secretary-General of the NATO and, when decisions have to be taken, action is agreed upon on the basis of unanimity and common accord. There is no voting or decision-making on the basis of majority. Each nation represented in the council, or in any of its subordinate committees, retains complete sovereignty and responsibility for its own decisions.

Apart from the permanent representative, a second important member of each country's delegation is the Military Representative, a senior officer from each country's armed forces. All the military representatives together form the Military Committee (MC) of the NATO. It recommends to the NATO's political authorities the measures considered necessary for common defence of the area under the NATO's purview. Its principal role is to provide direction and advice on military policy and strategy. Like the council, the military committee too keeps meeting at a higher level of the chiefs of defence from time to time. The chief of defence is the most senior military officer in each nation's armed forces. Other important civilian structures in the NATO include Division of Political Affairs and Security Policy, Division of Operations, Division of Defence Policy and Planning, Division of Defence Investment, NATO Office of Security, and NATO Office of Resources. The NATO has an elaborate network of civilian structures which supervises all its socio-political activities. They are located in several member-states of the organization.

The Secretary-General is the chief executive of the NATO. He is elected for an initial four-year term, which may be extended in exceptional cases. He chairs the NAC, as well as all other important bodies of this orgnization. Table 6.2 shows a chronological list of the NATO Secretaries-General.

**Table 6.2** NATO Secretaries-General Since 1952

| S. No. | Name | Country | Period in Office |
|---|---|---|---|
| 1. | General Lord Ismay | United Kingdom | 4 April 1952–16 May 1957 |
| 2. | Paul-Henri Spaak | Belgium | 16 May 1957–21 April 1961 |
| 3. | Dirk Stikker | The Netherlands | 21 April 1961–1 August 1964 |
| 4. | Manlio Brosio | Italy | 1 August 1964–1 October 1971 |
| 5. | Joseph Luns | The Netherlands | 1 October 1971–25 June 1984 |
| 6. | Lord Carrington | United Kingdom | 25 June 1984–1 July 1988 |
| 7. | Manfred Wörner | Germany | 1 July 1988–13 August 1994 |
| 8. | Sergio Balanzino | Italy | 13 August 1994–17 October 1994 |
| 9. | Willy Claes | Belgium | 17 October 1994–20 October 1995 |
| 10. | Sergio Balanzino | Italy | 20 October 1995–5 December 1995 |
| 11. | Javier Solana | Spain | 5 December 1995–6 October 1999 |
| 12. | Lord Robertson of Port Ellen | United Kingdom | 14 October 1999–1 January 2004 |
| 13. | Jaap de Hoop Scheffer | The Netherlands | 5 January 2004–1 August 2009 |
| 14. | Anders Fogh Rasmussen | Denmark | 1 August 2009–1 October 2014 |
| 15. | Jens Stoltenberg | Norway | 1 October 2014–Continuing |

## Military Structure

The elaborate military structures of the NATO is headed by the Military Committee (MC). Under the MC, there are several bodies like International Military Staff (IMS), Allied Command Operations (ACO), Allied Command Transformation (ACT), and other NATO command and staff organizations. ACO and ACT control a large number of commands and divisions. Bodies like the Supreme Headquarters of Allied Powers Europe (SHAPE), currently located in Mons, Belgium, and Joint Force Commands (JFCs) in Brunssum and Naples, work under the supervision of ACO. Joint Headquarters, Lisbon, and other rapidly deployable corps headquarters also work under ACO. The ACT controls bodies like the Headquarters, Supreme Allied Commander Transformation (HQ SACT), Joint Warfare Centre (JWC) or NATO School of Military. There are strategic commanders responsible to the MC for overall direction and conduct of all military matters of the alliance within their areas of command. Before 2003, the Supreme Allied Commander Europe (SACEUR) and the Supreme Allied Commander Atlantic (SACLANT) were the strategic commanders. But the current arrangement is to separate command responsibility between ACO—responsible for NATO-operations worldwide—and ACT—responsible for transformation and training of NATO-forces.

## Agencies and Organizations

The NATO has nearly fifty agencies and organizations in its main structure, working in different important areas. These areas may be classified under the following broad categories: (1) Logistics; (2) Production Logistics; (3) Standardization; (4) Civil Emergency Planning; (5) Air Traffic Management and Air Defence; (6) Airborne Early Warning; (7) Communication and Information Systems; (8) Electronic Warfare; (9) Meteorology; (10) Military Oceanography; (11) Research and Technology; (12) Education and Training and (13) Project Offices. In each of these categories, again, there are several agencies and organizations working in various areas. All the different agencies and organizations under the NATO may be divided into two types—those working in the military and related areas, and those working in different fields to further the aims and objectives of the NATO.

## Functions of the NATO: A Critical Appraisal

Although the NATO was born out of the tensions of the Cold War, it was not involved in any possible military activities during the period. It had made intense military preparations to counter any military attack on its members, but it did not get any opportunity to engage in military warfare then. Ironically, most of the organization's military engagements took place only after the war. The end of the Cold War and the dissolution of the Warsaw Pact in 1991 removed its *de facto* main adversary. This caused a strategic re-evaluation of the NATO's purpose, nature and functions. As part of post–Cold War restructuring, the organization's military structure was reduced and reorganized. The changes brought about by the end of the Cold War on the military balance in Europe were duly recognized by the NATO and its members. France, which withdrew in 1966, rejoined the NATO's military committee in 1995, and had since then intensified working relations with the organization's military structure. However, France did not rejoin the integrated military command. It may be pointed out here that in June 2008, Nicolas Sarkozy, President of

France, had announced that France might also consider rejoining the integrated military command of the NATO. The country had, in fact, not always agreed to the NATO's policies during the Cold War; on several occasions during this period, it had openly opposed the organization's military ambitions during this period. After the war, in a changed strategic and political order, France has agreed to join the NATO's military committee.

The NATO got involved in its first military operation after the Cold War. In June 1993, it launched Operation Sharp Guard in former Yugoslavia to stop the ongoing civil war. This major military operation continued till October 1996. It provided maritime enforcement of the arms embargo and economic sanctions against the erstwhile Federal Republic of Yugoslavia. On 28 February 1994, NATO-forces shot down four Bosnian Serb aircrafts accused of violating a UN-mandated no-fly zone over central Bosnia and Herzegovina. NATO-air-strikes in 1994 helped bring the ethnic war in Bosnia to an end, although it raised intense criticism of the organization throughout the world. Russia, China and France opposed NATO-bombings in Bosnia and Herzegovina. With the signing of the Dayton Peace Agreement by the United States, NATO, Serb, Croatian and Bosnian leaders, ethnic war in Bosnia and Herzegovina ended in 1995. As per the terms of the agreement, the NATO deployed a peacekeeping force (PKF) in the region under Operation Joint Endeavor. This force stayed in Bosnia and Herzegovina from December 1996 to December 2004.

In March 1999, the NATO launched its first large-scale military operations in the Kosovo conflict. It was engaged in an eleven-week air strike called Operation Allied Force against what was then the Federal Republic of Yugoslavia, with a mission to stop the crackdown on Kosovo Liberation Army led by Serbia. The conflict ended on 11 June 1999, when Yugoslavian leader Slobodan Miloševic agreed to accept the NATO's demands. Bombings in Kosovo by the NATO also invited controversies within and outside the organization. France from within, and Russia, China and others from outside the organization, demanded that all its military operations must get the approval of the United Nations. But the United States, Britain and most other NATO-countries opposed efforts that would require the UN Security Council to approve the NATO's military strikes. They claimed that this would undermine the authority of the alliance, and would allow countries like Russia and China to exercise their Security Council vetoes to block NATO-operations. Such actions would jeopardize the purposes of the NATO and its efforts in bringing peace in different parts of the world.

The September 11 (2001) terrorist attacks on the United States encouraged the NATO to wage a war on terrorism. The organization has a three-stage mechanism to fight terrorism. First, it is a permanent consultative forum where collective decisions emerge from discussions. Second, this is backed by the NATO's strong military power. Third, the organization is part of an impressive network of cooperative relations with many partners to fight terrorism. The NATO has also engaged in a number of initiatives—political, operational, conceptual, military and technological—to combat the menace of terrorism. In this direction, it functions fully in line with the international laws, including human rights standards and humanitarian requirements. The North Atlantic Council (NAC), the highest decision-making body of the NATO, assumes a leading role in formulating NATO-policies to fight terrorism. Other NATO-bodies implement the decisions taken by NAC in this regard.

The NATO is also playing an active role in the reconstruction of Afghanistan. Its invovlement there is important because this is the first commitment of the NATO outside the Euro-Atlantic area in the organization's sixty-year history. Through its leadership of the International Security

Assistance Force (ISAF), the NATO is helping the Afghans establish a permanent system of representative government, and a system that would help foster self-sustaining peace and security. The NATO took over the command and coordination of ISAF in August 2003. Initially restricted to providing security in and around Kabul, the capital city of Afghanistan, NATO-led ISAF has gradually extended its presence and is now responsible for security across the whole country.

In a changed international political order after the Cold War, the NATO is trying to expand the organization through inclusion of several former 'socialist' countries of Europe. In order to make this expansion acceptable to the former 'East Bloc' countries of Europe, the NATO has identified several areas other than security in a wide-ranging programme of the organization in the post–Cold War period. Along with security issues, the NATO is also placing emphasis on economic development, democracy, human rights and anti-terrorism as some of the significant areas of activity after the Cold War. But the 'Eastward Expansion' of the NATO would remain incomplete without Russia's inclusion into the organization. Till date, Russia has not joined the NATO as a full member. It expressed its displeasure over NATO-air-strikes in Bosnia in 1995 and in Serbia in 1999. Though Russia is a partner-country of the NATO at present, it does not, however, hesitate to oppose the organization's military actions. The issue of Russia's becoming a full member of the NATO has thus remained a point of interest in the international political community during the post–Cold war period.

## QUESTIONS

1. Discuss the origin and significance of the NAM in international politics.
2. Do you think that the NAM is relevant in today's world? Argue your case.
3. Analyse the composition and functions of the Commonwealth of Nations.
4. Make a critical estimate of the NATO.

# 7 Cold War Politics and Beyond

International politics had undergone dramatic changes after the end of the Second World War. The domination of Europe in international politics had diminished, and new non-European powers emerged. Until the Second World War, several European states such as Britain, France, Italy, Germany, Portugal and Netherlands determined and controlled events in international politics. But the Second World War changed everything. Europe was most affected, as the war was fought in that continent. The long war damaged the economy of most European nations, and when it finally ended in 1945, these nations were devastated politically and economically. Europe, the centre of attention and power in international politics for a long time, failed to retain its former glory after the war. Instead, two non-European powers, the United States of America and the Soviet Union, emerged as the two most powerful nations in the world.

It could be argued here that both the United States and the Soviet Union had participated in the Second World War, and shared the pain, agony and, to some extent, devastation of the war with the European nations. How did they, then, emerge as centres of power after the war? It should be noted here that the United States entered the war against Germany in 1942, three years after it had started. The United States was not hit hard by the war. On the contrary, with a very strong economy, it pumped up large sums of money and arms in support of the Allied Powers during the war. It also shed its long-held isolationism, practised to avoid active engagement in world politics, to participate in the Second World War in favour of the Allied powers. Since, unlike Europe, the United States was not severely affected by the war, it could emerge as a superpower after the war with its very strong industrial, economic and military bases. It was the world's first nuclear power and also the first to use nuclear weapons during the war in 1945.

Soviet Union, on the other hand, was hit hard by the Second World War. Hitler attacked Soviet Union in 1941, and heavy war broke out in the Soviet territory. Millions of people died there, and the economy was also affected. But how did the Soviet Union overcome damages inflicted by the war and emerge as a superpower after the war? A few points could be cited as reasons behind this turnaround. First, the Soviet Union was the largest country in the world with a huge territory. The attack by Hitler could not shake the entire country. It was limited mainly to the European parts. Other areas of this vast country remained unaffected by this attack. Although Hitler's attack gave a jolt to the Soviet economy, it could not paralyse the industrial and economic infrastructure of this vast land, as it did to many small European nations. Second, under Joseph Stalin, the Soviet Union emerged as an industrialized state, with particular emphasis on heavy industries. A sound industrial base helped the country emerge as a military power as well, which, in turn, paved the way towards its becoming a superpower. Third, in 1949, within four years of the end of the Second World War, Soviet Union became a nuclear power, the second in the world after the United States. The possession of nuclear weapons certainly allowed it to gain superpower status. Finally, the weakness of Europe as a whole, and the division of Germany after the war, also helped Soviet Union emerge as a superpower in international politics.

The world thus witnessed the emergence of two superpowers, the United States and the Soviet Union, after the Second World War. Their possession of nuclear weapons made them more powerful than the earlier European states, which were only major powers with conventional weapons. During the course of the war, they helped each other. But when the war was over, they began to oppose each other in order to gain supremacy in world politics. Their rivalry during the next four and a half decades gave birth to the Cold War in international politics.

# Origin of the Cold War

The two superpowers, the United States and the Soviet Union, started to contradict each other over the issue of reconstruction of Europe after the Second World War. The United States chalked out a grandiose plan to revive the Western part of a shattered Europe. Immediately after the war, the US President Harry S. Truman sought the approval of the US Congress for providing an assistance of $400 million to Greece and Turkey. The foreign policy objective of the Truman administration, however, was to contain the spread of communism in West Europe. This objective was known as the Truman Doctrine. Under the $400 million package intended originally for Greece and Turkey, other nations of West Europe were also covered gradually. The Truman Doctrine paid special assistance to Italy and France, as they had a long history of socialist inclination, to prevent them from falling to communism. If the Truman Doctrine was a grand but indirect foreign policy strategy to contain a communist Soviet Union, the Marshall Plan, unveiled by Truman's Secretary of State George Marshall, was more direct and open in its aspirations. It wanted to bring the whole of West Europe under American influence through the means of economic diplomacy. The Soviet Union became apprehensive both about the Truman Doctrine and the 'Marshall Plan'. The Soviet leaders found in these plans the American design to make West Europe a satellite of the United States. To counter the US design, the Soviet Union started to give huge aids to the eastern part of Europe, which was geographically closer to the Soviet Union, to bring it into the Soviet fold. Germany, which was divided into four zones (under French, British, American and Soviet occupation) after the Second World War by the Potsdam Agreement, was also influenced by the two superpowers, and was ultimately divided into two parts—the Federal Republic of Germany (or West Germany) and the German Democratic Republic (or East Germany). Gradually, the whole of Europe became 'divided' into an East bloc, controlled by the Soviet Union, and a West bloc, controlled by the United States. This 'division' of Europe was known as the East–West Divide. Each of the two superpowers exercised enormous economic and political influence over their blocs in Europe and tried to prevent the other from gaining any foothold there. The Cold War originated.

Apart from political rivalry for establishing supremacy in world politics, the two superpowers had pronounced ideological differences. The Soviet Union, which was officially known as the Union of Soviet Socialist Republics (USSR) was born after the 1917 Bolshevik Revolution. It was the first socialist country in the world which adopted the socialist principles of Karl Marx and Friedrich Engels in its state system and economy. On the other hand, the United States of America followed liberal democratic principles in its state policy and economy. These two ideologies (Marxist socialism and liberal democratic) are contradictory to each other. When both the Soviet Union and the United States emerged as superpowers after the Second World War, they began to suspect each other of ideological expansionism. The United States had the fear that the Soviets would spread socialism, which had become quite popular in the world, to attract other nations to its bloc. The Soviets doubted American designs of providing economic aid to different countries as ploys to bring them to the US camp. While the Soviet Union labelled the United States as a 'neocolonial power' trying to dominate others through the 'politics of aid' and the appealing ideals of liberal democracy, the Americans described the Soviets as 'social imperialists' trying to dominate the world through the attractive and popular ideology of socialism. Thus, the cold war of mud-slinging and psychological conflicts between the two superpowers owed their origin to ideological differences as well.

The Cold War was no real war between the superpowers, although tensions and war-like situations always engulfed the United States and the Soviet Union. Every political, economic, diplomatic and propaganda initiative of one superpower was matched with a similar or more powerful initiative by the other. As a consequence, the two superpowers and their satellites were always tense and on high alert. The Cold War was riddled with the possibilities of a real war, although that did not happen during its span of four and a half decades, from 1945 to 1990. With the beginning of the war, the Balance of Power system, that existed in international politics for three centuries, also came to an end. Instead of five or six major powers controlling international politics under this system, now only two superpowers began to exercise their control in world politics. The East–West divide, created by superpower rivalry, made international politics clearly bipolar from 1945. This bipolarity co-existed with the Cold War in international relations until 1990.

# Evolution of the Cold War

The Cold War originated immediately after the Second World War in Europe. Gradually, it spread over to other continents. For a better and convenient understanding of the evolution of Cold War, a decade-wise analysis may be helpful.

## Cold War in the 1940s

After the Second World War, differences escalated between the two superpowers over issues like the reconstruction of Europe, future of Germany and establishing supremacy in international politics. The Truman Doctrine and the Marshall Plan aimed at perpetuating American supremacy in Europe. The Soviet Union did not sit idle. To counter these plans, it extended financial and security assistance to East European countries to attract them to the Soviet lobby. Soon Europe was 'divided' into two blocs—one led by the United States and the other by the Soviet Union. By 1947, the Cold War had spread its roots in the continent of Europe. The US policy of containment of communism began in Europe with the Truman Doctrine, and was subsequently reinforced by the Marshall Plan. The Soviets devised their own strategy of expanding socialism to East Europe through financing and militarizing the East Bloc. The United States took a major initiative of providing a security ring for west European countries by the creation of the North Atlantic Treaty Organization (NATO) in 1949. It was created to thwart any Soviet move to militarily dominate any Western Bloc country in Europe. It was agreed by the founding nations that all NATO-members would militarily help any member(s) attacked by an aggressor. In 1953, the Soviet Union formed the Warsaw Pact to counter the NATO and provide security guarantee to East European countries. The Cold War had got firmly entrenched in Europe by the beginning of the next decade.

## Cold War in the 1950s

The Cold War was not limited to Europe only. At the beginning of the new decade, with the outbreak of the Korean War in June 1950, the Cold War spread to Asia. After the Second World War, Korea was divided into a North Korea under Soviet influence, and a South Korea under American patronage. Though the two superpowers established their influence over the two Koreas after the Second World War, they openly opposed each other over Korea during the Korean War. On 25 June 1950, North Korea attacked South Korea. The United States demanded stern action against North Korea, the 'aggressor', and passed a resolution at the UN Security Council—in the absence of the Soviet Union—to initiate collective security measures against it. But when the Soviets returned to the council, the United States and its Western allies moved to the General Assembly and passed the Uniting for Peace Resolution to continue pressures on North Korea. They did it to avoid any Soviet veto in the Security Council. The Soviet Union opposed North Korea being identified as the 'aggressor' and promised to help its communist friend in the war. Another communist nation in Asia, the People's Republic of China, joined the war for North Korea in November 1950, making the scenario more complicated. The UN-sponsored mechanism of collective security did not succeed in the Korean War (for details see Chapter 5), and the two superpowers issued threats and counter-threats to contain each other in the Korean War. Finally, a cease-fire was declared in 1953, but the Korean War had, by this time, brought to light the bitter rivalry between the two superpowers for control over international politics.

The Warsaw Pact was created in 1953, under the leadership of the Soviet Union, to provide security assistance to the East Bloc countries. It was mainly a security treaty that contained the provision that if any country signing the treaty was attacked by others, all nations under it would come to the rescue of the attacked country. Through the treaty, Soviet Union, in effect, extracted the right to send its military to other East Bloc countries, because the Soviets had the strongest military in the region. Soon the Soviets got the opportunity to send its military to Hungary in 1956 to crush the Hungarian uprising for more democratic rights. Trouble started in Hungary in the spring of 1956, when several thousand students and intellectuals demonstrated against repressive domestic policies and demanded more freedom. They wanted Imre Nagy, who was Prime Minister of Hungary from 1953 to 1955, to be appointed the head of a new government, because Nagy was pro-liberal. He was also supported by the United States. Soviet troops arrived in Hungary within hours after the trouble began, and opened fire on the demonstrators. But the movement for liberal policies gradually got popular support. Under public pressure, Nagy was appointed the Premier on 24 October 1956. But the next day, Janos Kadar, a Soviet-backed communist leader who opposed the movement, was appointed as the First Secretary—a powerful political post—of the Communist Party, to counterbalance the appointment of Nagy. By early November, Soviet troops had started suppressing the movement ruthlessly, and Premier Nagy appealed to the Security Council for the withdrawal of Soviet troops from Hungary. The United States and Britain supported his appeal, but the Council failed to act due to a Soviet veto. The US camp then took the matter to the General Assembly and appealed for a settlement under the Uniting for Peace Resolution. Soon after, massive attacks by the Soviet military on the supporters of liberal policies and Nagy followed, and Imre Nagy had to flee the country. Subsequently, Kadar was made the Head of the Government by the Soviet Union, and Nagy and his supporters were executed. The Hungarian uprising remained a history of bitter Cold War politics between the two superpowers.

The same year, the Cold War shifted to Africa with the Suez Canal crisis. On 26 July 1956, Gamal Abdel Nasser, President of Egypt, announced that his government would nationalize the Suez Canal Company. Britain and France protested this decision because they had a stake in the Suez Canal through their oil and shipping companies. Israel also warned that the proposed nationalization would violate the Jordan–Israel armistice demarcation line. A Suez Canal Users Association was formed in London, mainly at the initiative of Britain and France, to stall the plans of nationalization. Hectic diplomatic activities also started and Britain and France urged the Security Council to take up the matter. From late September that year, the council called several meetings, and the UN Secretary-General met British, French and Egyptian leaders to break the deadlock. But nothing substantial happened. When Nasser, backed by the Soviet Union, stuck to his plans, Britain and France started air attack on Egypt in late October. The Council accepted a Yugoslav proposal, mooted at the behest of Soviet Union, to call an emergency meeting of the General Assembly, under the Uniting for Peace Resolution, to restrain Britain and France. On 15 November 1956, a United Nations Emergency Force (UNEF) was sent to Egypt. By that time, a cease-fire was achieved, mainly at the initiative of the United States. But the Suez Canal could not be reopened for commercial ships before late April 1957, because Egypt and UN authorities were working on the future control over the Canal. In accordance with an Egyptian government declaration on 24 April 1957, individual users of the Canal had to work out arrangements with Egypt for right to passage in the Canal, which, however, was denied to Israeli ships. Tension persisted in the region and the UNEF stayed back in Egypt. The superpowers were seriously involved in the crisis. It was again the issue of the West Bloc versus the East Bloc in the Suez Canal crisis.

The superpower rivalry did not remain limited to planet earth only; it reached outer space in the late 1950s. Both the United States and the Soviet Union launched ambitious space programmes during this period, which included spy satellites for monitoring enemy activities. Satellite-controlled missiles were also developed by the Soviets in 1957. This alarmed the United States, who developed similar weapons a year later. The advanced missile programmes of the two nuclear superpowers escalated the Cold War tensions. At large, the 1950s witnessed more intense rivalry between the superpowers in different parts of the world.

## Cold War in the 1960s

The decade began with serious crises over issues like shooting down of a US spy aircraft by the Soviet Union and problems in Congo. In 1960, the Soviets shot down an American spy aircraft called U-2 flying over the Soviet territory. A huge uproar was made by the United States over the issue, and a summit meeting between the Soviet leader Nikita Kruschev and the American President Dwight Eisenhower was cancelled mid-way. The issue further embittered the relationship between the two superpowers. The same year, Congo in Africa faced a sudden political crisis when the Belgians, the colonizers of Congo, finally handed over power to the Congolese on 30 June 1960. On 11 July 1960, Katanga, the richest province in Congo, declared secession. This led to a civil war in Congo, and Belgium rushed back its troops to protect its citizens living in Congo. The situation turned worse when South Kasai, another Congolese province, declared its intention to secede from Congo. Prime Minister Patrice Lumumba appealed for military help from Soviet Union, China, as also from Ghana, a neighbouring country. The Soviet Union was eager to help, promptimg the United States to support anti-Lumumba forces within Congo. President Kasavubu of Congo appealed to the United Nations (UN) for help, and the UN Secretary-General took special initiative to send a peacekeeping team—the United Nations Operations in Congo (UNUC)—to the troubled country. President Kasavubu and Premier Lumumba gradually fell out over the issue of bringing peace to Congo, as Lumumba was dismissed by Kasavubu. The civil war continued and the ONUC could hardly restore peace in the country. When the news of Lumumba's murder, allegedly by rival ethnic forces backed by the United States, arrived in January 1961, the civil war reached its peak. The ONUC had increased its forces with substantial contribution from the Indian military. The UN also sent a large number of civilians to negotiate peace. Gradually, the situation in Congo improved, and in August 1961, a Government of National Unity was formed under UN supervision. The ONUC continued its presence in Congo. The Congo crisis once again brought to light the severe political antagonism between the two superpowers.

In 1962, tensions escalated again over the Cuban Missile issue. In Cuba, a South American country geographically close to the United States, a communist government under the leadership of Fidel Castro came to power in 1959. A communist country next door irked the United States, while Castro remained apprehensive about an American attack. Therefore, relations between the two countries were hostile from the very beginning. In the summer of 1962, the Castro-government allowed the Soviet Union to install military bases on Cuban soil with medium-range ballistic missiles. An alarmed United States protested and complained that the ballistic missiles were targeted at the United States. The Americans also called for withdrawal of Soviet military bases from Cuba. US President John F. Kennedy warned the Soviets in October 1962 for launching offensive missiles in Cuba. Soviet President Kruschev denied that the purpose of the missiles was to attack the United States. As a security measure, the United States announced that it would search all westward-bound vessels within 800 miles of Cuba. The US Ambassador to the UN showed the Security Council photographic proofs of Soviet missiles in Cuba. Kruschev sent positive messages to the Americans in late October, stating his intentions to withdraw military bases from Cuba. The American President reduced the 800-miles embargo to 500 miles. President Kruschev repeated his promise to withdraw but wanted an assurance from the United States that it would not attack Cuba in future. The Soviets also wanted the removal of American missiles from Turkey installed in the late 1950s. President Kennedy agreed to both the Soviet demands after repeated negotiations between Soviet and American leaders and able mediation by the UN Secretary-General U Thant. President Kruschev withdrew all Soviet weapons by the end of 1962, and the United States removed its weapons from Turkey by April 1963. An imminent clash between the superpowers could be avoided.

In 1963–64, the United States became militarily engaged in South Vietnam, trying to prevent a takeover by the communists from North Vietnam. The American involvement in Vietnam actually started in 1961, when President Kennedy sent an 'observer' team to report what was happening there. One of the 'reporters' in a White Paper of 1961 asked for more military and financial aid to South Vietnam to prevent a takeover of the whole Vietnam by the Viet Cong, the communists. North Vietnam wanted to unite the two Vietnams under a communist rule. The Americans disliked this design and sent troops to prevent a military takeover. In early 1965, situations in Vietnam worsened with troops from the allegedly Soviet-backed North Vietnam crossing the 17th parallel and attacking South Vietnam. American President Johnson ordered the continuous bombing of military installations in North Vietnam. The American actions led to heavy civilian casualties. The United States decided to retain its troops in Vietnam due to the persistent fear of a communist takeover of the entire country. But the American leaders had to ultimately withdraw troops from Vietnam amidst severe domestic and international pressures. But it was engaged in Vietnam throughout the 1960s. During the 1960s, Vietnam witnessed a tense Cold War between the two superpowers.

It must be noted here that threats and counter-threats were used by both superpowers during the Cold War period as deterrent techniques to serve their purposes. The Cuban Missile Crisis remained a good example of this deterrent technique used by the superpowers. The Soviets threatened the United States with missiles in Cuba, to extract a promise from the Americans that they would not attack Cuba in future. This threat served the Soviet purpose. The United States, on the other hand, warned the Soviets of dire consequences for its 'adventures' in Cuba, to secure the withdrawal of Soviet military bases from Cuba. Threats, counter-threats, appeals, diplomatic negotiations—all methods were in fact applied by the superpowers as per the demands of the situation, during the Cold War. They also talked about reduction of arms. After the Cuban Missile Crisis was over, the United States and the Soviet Union signed, in 1963, a Limited Test Ban Treaty (LTBT) to put a moratorium on nuclear tests. Although the LTBT was not successful in reducing Cold War tensions, it was nevertheless a timely attempt to achieve peace.

A Hungarian-type uprising for democratic rights emerged in Czechoslovakia, a Warsaw Pact state, in 1968. This time, the Soviet military took no chance and crushed the uprising at the outset. The United States and its Western allies condemned the Soviet military action in Czechoslovakia and called the Soviets 'social imperialists'. For some time in 1968 and thereafter, Czechoslovakia remained the hot spot of Cold War rivalry between superpowers.

## Cold War in the 1970s

The United States, it appeared, fell behind the Soviet Union in the Cold War at the beginning of the 1970s. The Arab countries, backed by the latter, stopped supply of petroleum to the United States in 1973 because of America's support to Israel on the Palestine issue. As a result, the US economy became a bit shaky. In 1975, a US-backed government collapsed in South Vietnam, allegedly due to Soviet manipulations. Further, the collapse of the Shah government in Iran, which was actively patronized by the United States, put the Americans in an uncomfortable position in the Cold War. Encouraged by these American setbacks, Soviet Union decided to send its military to Afghanistan in 1979 to install a Moscow-backed government there. Although Soviet Union was initially successful in its mission, sending troops to Afghanistan proved to be disastrous for it later. In its Cold War political calculations, the country deemed it wise to control Afghanistan in order to effectively influence South and South-West Asia. It brought down the

Hafizullah Amin government and installed the Babrak Karmal government in Afghanistan in accordance with its plans. The United States and the Western Bloc were alarmed by the Soviet presence in Afghanistan. They made the presence of the Soviet Army there an issue to corner the Soviets in almost all international bodies. Moreover, the Americans began to help anti-Soviet dissident groups in Afghanistan with money and arms with a view to topple the Babrak Karmal government. The Talibans were among the dissident groups that allegedly received American help at that time.

The Soviet Union had to sustain its army in Afghanistan in order to maintain its lead in the Cold War. But it was beyond the calculations of Soviet leaders that they would have to sustain Soviet army in Afghanistan for a prolonged period. The initial plan was to install a Moscow-backed government in Afghanistan and gradually withdraw troops. But, as events turned out, several rebel groups opposing Soviet presence surfaced throughout Afghanistan and, backed by the United States, got engaged in armed insurgencies against the Soviet army. Now, Soviet Union was caught in an unenviable situation. An early withdrawal of troops would mean the fall of the Karmal government and the victory of the rebel groups supported by the United States. This would be detrimental to Soviet interests in the Cold War. Therefore, Soviet leaders decided to retain their army in Afghanistan. But it proved to be a very costly decision, both in material and in political terms. Maintaining a large army in Afghanistan was a huge burden on the Soviet exchequer. Moreover, as the stay became longer, the morale of the army kept sinking all the more, because many soldiers were being killed by the rebel groups. Politically, it became an embarrassment for the Soviet Union to patronize its troops in an independent sovereign country for a long period. Therefore, the Soviet plan to send its army to Afghanistan in 1979 was indeed a costly mistake. The Soviet Union finally withdrew its military from Afghanistan in 1989, ten years after it was sent. But by that time, the stay had drained the Soviet economy, the confidence of the army and the charisma of the Soviet Union as a superpower.

## Cold War in the 1980s

The Cold War reached its peak at the beginning of the 1980s due to the presence of the Soviet army in Afghanistan. American President Ronald Reagan, who assumed office in 1981, decided to increase the US Defence budget hugely, so as to counter the activities of the Soviet Union in more effective ways. Reagan wanted to give a lead to the Americans in the Cold War. He launched the 'star wars' programme that aimed at augmenting the production and the deployment of satellite-guided ballistic missiles and other modern weapons. The United States was also engaged in providing support to the rebel groups in Afghanistan. The clandestine presence of the United States in Afghanistan through dollars and guns escalated the Cold War to a great extent. The Americans also extended support to dissident groups opposed to Soviet-installed governments in Angola and Nicaragua. The United States support to rebel groups in Angola and Nicaragua led to civil wars in these two countries. The Reagan administration took it as a mission to oppose Soviet-backed governments in every part of the world. As a consequence, Cold War tensions and rivalry intensified in the first half of the decade.

In 1985, Mikhail Gorbachev assumed power in Soviet Union. He showed more interest in reviving a decaying Soviet economy and liberating the closed, party-controlled Soviet society, than in continuing the Cold War. Gorbachev had reasons to depart from his predecessors.

When he assumed office, the Soviet economy was in very bad shape due to the over-zealous policies framed by former Soviet leaders to stay ahead of the United States in the Cold War. The heavy Soviet Defence budget was a huge burden on the economy. Added to it was the prolonged presence of the Soviet troops in Afghanistan, which also cost the economy to a significant extent. Soviet Union, Gorbachev realized, was a military superpower, but not an economic one. The poor condition of the Soviet economy had its impact in the social sectors as well. People were getting restive, and demands for an open society and polity were gaining grounds. Consequently, Gorbachev concentrated more on economic and social reforms. He initiated Perestroika and Glasnost, two policies for economic and social rejuvenation. He also ordered the return of Soviet troops from Afghanistan, signaling his intention to end the Cold War. By 1985–86, signs of the end of the Cold War, because of Soviet disinterest to continue it, became apparent.

Therefore, if the first half of the 1980s witnessed escalated Cold War tensions, the second half was marked with the beginning of the end of the war. Gorbachev's policies of Perestroika and Glasnost brought sweeping changes in Soviet Union. Although these were domestic policies, they had far-reaching impact on the East Bloc countries as well. Under the influences of these two policies, demands for an open economy and an open society gradually strengthened in East Europe. Perestroika paved the way for the introduction of an open, market-oriented economy, first in the Soviet Union, and later in other East Bloc countries. Glasnost allowed freedom of speech and expression, right to self-determination by all nationalities and accommodation of different kinds of views, communist or non-communist. Under its impact, demands for multi-party democracy and separate states for different ethnic communities emerged. As a consequence, the one-party system broke down in the Soviet Union and other parts of East and Central Europe. Nationalism based on ethnicity, dormant so far, also surfaced. Soviet Union disintegrated into fifteen new independent countries. Some other East Bloc countries like Czechoslovakia and Yugoslavia also disintegrated. With the disintegration of the Soviet Union, there was no superpower to continue the Cold War, and the four and a half decade long Cold War finally came to an end in 1991.

## Causes of the End of the Cold War

The Cold War continued in international politics for a long time due to the desire of both the superpowers—the United States and the Soviet Union—to establish ideological and political supremacy all over the world. But when the latter started showing its disinterest in continuing with it from the mid-1980s, the war lost its intensity. From 1985—this is when Gorbachev became the supreme leader of the country—Soviet Union concentrated more on domestic economic and political reforms than on continuing with war. As said earlier, Gorbachev initiated two policies after assuming power—the Glasnost and the Perestroika, which, in the long run, became instrumental in bringing about the end of the Cold War. 'Glasnost' means 'open air' in its nearest English translation. Gorbachev wanted to introduce this sense of openness into the Soviet society and politics, which were considered to be rigid and closed. So far, freedom of speech and expression were believed to be absent in the Soviet society. There was very little scope for constructive criticism, for opposing political views in a one-party system. The party bureaucracy exercised high degree of vigilance in every sphere of social and political life in order to silence criticism and to punish the 'critics'. There was a sense of fear everywhere. The media in the Soviet Union was a puppet in the hands of the party bureaucracy. Under Glasnost, freedom of speech and expression, in the truest sense of the term, was allowed to the Soviet people. For the first time in Soviet history, people could speak out without fear. For the first time, a different political opinion was not considered a crime. Soviet media was also allowed, under Glasnost, to operate outside state-control. As a result, different news and views, other than those wished by the government, started to reach the Soviet society. The free media indulged in constructive criticism. With the permission given by the Gorbachev-administration for the use of satellite television in the country, the world reached the homes of the Soviet people. One could now easily feel an air of openness around them. Under the impact of the Glasnost, all kinds of change took place in the Soviet society. Free speech and free media allowed distressed voices, suppressed so far, to speak against party bureaucracy. Criticism was no longer drowned in fear. Different political groups started to emerge, and people started asserting their right to self-determination. Glasnost paved the way for the creation of a liberal society and a multi-party democracy, and the end of the one-party rule was imminent. It also allowed different ethnic communities living in the Soviet Union to express their demands. Nationalism based on ethnicity gained strength, and demands for separate states became very prominent. Non-Russian nationalities asserted their rights to self-determination and refused to be ruled by the Russians. As a result, Soviet Union disintegrated gradually and peacefully into fifteen independent states in 1991, twelve of which formed the Commonwealth of Independent States (CIS).

Like Glasnost, Perestroika too had a far-reaching impact . 'Perestroika', in the nearest English translation, means economic reforms, something which Gorbachev initiated to 'open' the Soviet economy. By the middle of the 1980s, when Gorbachev assumed office, the Soviet economy was in poor shape due to burdens of Cold War military and aid expenses to live up to a superpower status. But during the long period of the Cold War, the Soviet Union could not develop its industrial infrastructure in the modern sense of the term. Since the tenure of Stalin, almost all Soviet leaders concentrated mainly on heavy industries that could support weapons-related industries. So, modern industries like IT (information technology)-based sunrise industry, electronics or consumer goods industry did not develop much in the Soviet Union. The country also lagged behind in international trade. It had substantial trade relations with the East Bloc countries and some other 'friendly' countries like India. But these countries did not have sound economic bases. Moreover, it had practically no trade relation with the industrially and technologically developed West Bloc countries. Soviet earnings from international trade were, therefore, negligible. The 'closed' nature of the Soviet economy and absence of trade relations with the industrial world also contributed towards negligence of modern industrial infrastructures in the Soviet Union. Added to these were the burdens of maintaining a superpower status and the Cold War. Military expenses soared as the Soviet Union tried to maintain its superpower status through its very strong military power. But the Soviet economy was becoming increasingly unable to shoulder this burden. It was in disarray.

Perestroika aimed at reviving the Soviet economy and putting it alongside the mainstream world economy. Gorbachev freed the Soviet economy from its 'closed' state and opened it up to the world. Private business was allowed, foreign companies permitted to enter the Soviet Union, and foreign investments welcomed. The 'open' economy attracted investments from American and Western European multinational corporations since the huge Soviet market had great investment potential. Gradually, Soviet economy was transformed from a closed socialist-type economy to an open market-oriented economy. The arrival of American and Western investments to the Soviet market in turn softened the political outlook of these countries towards the Soviet Union. Economic interests gradually helped to weaken Cold War political rivalry. Therefore, the introduction of liberal market economy in Soviet Union under the impact of Perestroika contributed significantly towards the end of the Cold War.

While it is generally agreed that Gorbachev's policies, including Glasnost and Perestroika, were noteworthy factors behind the end of the Cold War, the answer to the most important question—'Why Gorbachev showed his disinclination to continue the Cold War?'—would be manifold. First, the Soviet economy was in shambles during the mid-1980s, when Gorbachev assumed power and was in no way capable of continuing the Cold War. Gorbachev was quick to realize this and had to signal the end of the war. Second, it could be assumed that the 'star wars' strategy of American President Ronald Reagan had de-motivating effects on the Soviet Union. Reagan's stupendous expenses on 'star wars' took the United States far ahead of the Soviet Union in the Cold War in the early 1980s. Gorbachev realized that it would be impossible to match American expenses on Cold War because of Soviet engagements in Afghanistan and the poor shape of the Soviet economy. So, he withdrew Soviet Union from the Cold War. Third, the closed, incapacitated Soviet economy would have in any case crumbled, with or without the onus of the Cold War. This desperate situation led Gorbachev to initiate Perestroika to instil life in the Soviet economy and discontinue the Cold War. After the end of the Cold War, a tendency towards unipolarity in international politics could be observed.

# Ethnicity and Nationalism in East Europe

Under the influence of Glasnost and Perestroika, winds of change started to blow in East Europe before the end of the Cold War. The right to self-determination of the people, suppressed so far under a closed political system, began to receive political support. Demands from different ethnic communities for a separate state started to emerge consequently. The whole of East Europe witnessed ethnic nationalism immediately before and after the Cold War. Under the impact of people's demands for a separate statehood, several new states were created in East and Central Europe, and the map of Europe changed. Nationalistic movements in East and Central Europe were noteworthy developments in the post–Cold War politics of Europe. This section will analyse ethnic nationalism in different parts of Europe after the Cold War.

## Ethnic Nationalism in Former Czechoslovakia

After the Second World War, Czechoslovakia emerged as a socialist state and signed the Warsaw Pact under the influence of the Soviet Union. Like other East Bloc countries, Czechoslovakia too followed Soviet political and economic models based on socialist principles. But, under the impact of Glasnost and Perestroika, winds of change also arrived in Czechoslovakia. From the early 1980s, resentment against one-party rule started to grow. Although similar resentment had been witnessed earlier, in 1968, when movements for democratic rights were scuttled by the Soviet military, the situation was different during the 1980s, due to the pervasive influence of the two policies. By 1989, when there were clear indications that the Cold War was nearing an end, the two principal ethnic groups in Czechoslovakia, the Czechs and the Slovaks, had started raising demands for the end of the one-party rule. This demand gradually gained strength and the movement for ending one-party rule spread throughout the country. Sensing the popular mood, the communist government in Czechoslovakia decided to hand over power to a non-communist government in a peaceful manner and resigned.

During the movement for democracy—and for an end to one-party rule—a Civic Forum was formed in the Czech-dominated northern part, under the leadership of Vaclav Havel, a noted writer, political activist and supporter of reforms in Czechoslovakia. In the Slovak-dominated south, another political organization, Public Against Violence (PAV) was formed. In December 1989, the Czechoslovak Parliament declared Havel as the new president of the country. He became the first non-communist president since the Second World War. The transformation from a communist to a non-communist government in Czechoslovakia was smooth and without any bloodshed. This peaceful transition later came to be known as the Velvet Revolution—a testimony of higher levels of political consciousness among the people of Czechoslovakia.

General elections were held in Czechoslovakia in June 1990. The Civic Forum in the northern part and the PAV in the southern part won the elections with huge margins. In July the same year, the Parliament of Czechoslovakia re-elected Havel as the president. Havel appointed Marian Calfa, a former communist leader, as the prime minister. The new government initiated economic reform programmes in the country. From a state-controlled economy, Czechoslovakia rapidly moved towards privatization. But this rapid transition created many economic and social problems. Poverty, unemployment, economic inequality, inflation escalated to unprecedented levels. In 1991, the rate of inflation reached an astronomical 58 per cent. As a consequence, social unrest also grew. The Slovak ethnic community blamed the Czech leadership for maintaining a huge economic disparity between the Czechs and the Slovaks.

In a multi-ethnic Czechoslovakia, the two principal ethnic communities were the Czechs and the Slovaks. They comprised 67 per cent of the total population. Between the two, the Czechs were a huge majority with 51 per cent of the total population. The Slovaks made 16 per cent of the population and the remaining 33 per cent comprised many nationalities like the Germans, Ukrainians, Hungarians and Bohemians. However, due to their numerical superiority, the Czechs were the dominant ethnic community with an overwhelming presence in the social, economic and political sectors. The Slovaks were always resentful of the Czech domination, and they expressed it on several occasions. However, Czechoslovakia survived as a nation on the basis of reconciliation between the two principal ethnic communities under the communist regime.

After the elections in 1990, poverty and unemployment rose sharply in the Slovak region. In 1991, unemployment reached 13 per cent in the Slovak region, but at the same time it was 2.7 per cent in the Czech region. This resulted in increased frustration and resentment against the Czechs among the Slovak people. The Slovaks alleged that the rich and developed Czech region was enjoying all the benefits of economic reforms. To remove this economic disparity, they demanded a separate state for themselves. Thus, ethnic nationalism in the Slovak region concentrated mainly around economic issues. President Havel tried his best to meet the demands of the Slovaks within the constitutional framework of Czechoslovakia. But the growing Slovak nationalism did not relent from its demand for a separate state. The Czechoslovak Parliament gradually agreed on the demand for a separate state for the Slovaks.

Another general election took place in Czechoslovakia in June 1992, this time mainly on the issue of two separate states for the Czechs and the Slovaks. In the Czech region, the conservative Civil Democratic Party (CDP) won the elections. Vaclav Klaus, the leader of the CDP, was a staunch supporter of market economy. In the Slovak region, Vladimir Meciar's Movement for a Democratic Slovakia (MDS) won convincingly. President Havel called Klaus and Meciar after the elections to decide the future of Czechoslovakia. Meciar, a hard-core Slovak nationalist, stuck to the demand of a separate state for the Slovak people, a demand that also helped him win the election. In July 1992, the Slovak National Assembly, the regional Legislature of the Slovaks, declared sovereign existence for the Slovak area. In the National Parliament, Slovak parliamentarians opposed another term for President Havel, who was a Czech. Havel failed to muster sufficient majority for another term as president and resigned from office.

Meanwhile, after several rounds of discussion, Klaus and Meciar decided that Czechoslovakia would be split into two states. On 31 December 1992, two separate states were born out of the former Czechoslovakia—the Czech Republic and Slovakia. Ethno-nationalism, generated by economic disparity, was the reason behind the birth of two new nations in East Europe. But the disintegration of Czechoslovakia was unique in the sense that it was totally based on discussions and consensus, without any bloodshed. In Czechoslovakia, the aims and aspirations of two principal nationalities were met successfully through peaceful negotiations. This showed the extremely advanced political culture of the people of former Czechoslovakia. The two new nations, Czech Republic and Slovakia, have now joined the European mainstream and are striving for increased economic developments. They are also engaged in constructive cooperation among themselves.

## Ethnic Nationalism in Former Yugoslavia

Unlike Czechoslovakia, ethnic nationalist movements in former Yugoslavia were not at all peaceful. Different ethnic communities in Yugoslavia were engaged in bloody civil wars after the breakdown of the socialist regime. However, ethnic problems in Yugoslavia started much earlier, mainly after the death of Josip Broz Tito. In order to understand ethnic problems in Yugoslavia, it is necessary to know the demographic and socio-economic characters of this former socialist country. After the Second World War, Federal Republic of Yugoslavia (FRY) was created with six republics: Bosnia-Herzegovina, Croatia, Macedonia, Montenegro, Serbia and Slovenia. Under Serbia, there were two autonomous regions: Vojvodina and Kosovo. Before and during the early periods of the Second World War, from 1918 to 1941, Yugoslavia was under a monarchical system. During 1941–42, Yugoslavia was under Nazi control; a royal government in exile was created in early 1943. The Democratic Federal Yugoslavia, proclaimed by Josip Broz Tito and recognized by the Allied powers, came into being in mid-1943, during the Second World War. After the war was over in 1945, Tito established his authority, and the FRY was finally proclaimed. The FRY initially followed the Soviet model and became a socialist state. Tito was first the Prime Minister, and later the President of the FRY. He was the supreme leader of Yugoslavia for thirty-five years, from 1945 to 1980. Under him, rapid industrialization and urbanization took place in Yugoslavia, and it became a prosperous country. Tito also joined the NAM later, although he never deviated from the official path of socialism. Tito was a very able and pragmatic leader, and under his long rule, separatist ethno-nationalism remained strictly under control. In fact, ethno-nationalism could hardly be observed in FRY during his tenure.

A unique feature in Yugoslavia's social life was the presence of different ethnic communities which were mixed and scattered all over the country. It was unique in the sense that in FRY no particular ethnic community resided in a particular place, like in many other European countries. They were highly intermingled and scattered all over. As per the 1991 Census—the first after the Cold War—8.5 million Serbians lived outside Serbia, in Bosnia and Croatia. Likewise, 20 per cent of the Croats lived outside Croatia, mainly in Bosnia and Vojvodina. Therefore, in Yugoslavia, ethnic communities lived in a mixed form, and, as in former Soviet Union and Czechoslovakia, they did not particularly live in their 'own' states. For this reason, separatist nationalism became very violent in Yugoslavia, as different ethnic and religious communities took up arms against one another within a particular state. The mixed demographic character of the FRY could be ascertained from another instance, taken from the 1991 Census. In Bosnia, as per the Census, 44 per cent identified themselves as Muslims, 31 per cent called themselves Serbs, 17 per cent called themselves Croats and only 5 per cent identified themselves as Yugoslavs. Owing to this highly intermingled population, the civil war in Bosnia took an ugly and violent turn.

Ethnic communities in FRY were separated from one another on the basis of language and religion. From the beginning of the Second World War to its disintegration, FRY had three official languages—Serbo-Croatian, Slovenian and Macedonian. The Serbs, the Croats and the Montenegrins used the Cyrillic alphabet for the Serbo-Croatian language, while the Muslim Slavs wrote the same language in the Latin alphabet. Those who used the Cyrillic alphabet considered themselves superior to others and took special pride in their script. Language was thus a source of ethnic differences in former Yugoslavia. Religion also created differences among ethnic groups. For instance, Serbs, Macedonian Slavs and Montenegrins were orthodox Christians; while Croats and Slovenians were Roman Catholics. There were also divisions among Muslims. Albanians and Muslim Slavs were 'Sunnis', while the rest identified them as 'Shias'. Religion also played a role in the use of alphabets in former Yugoslavia. For example, the orthodox Christians used the Cyrillic alphabet, and the rest used the Latin. All these differences created divisive senses among the people of former Yugoslavia.

Separatism could not, however, raise its ugly head during the tenure of Josip Broz Tito, mainly because of his able leadership, the one-party system under socialism, and satisfactory levels of economic development in FRY. However, after the death of Tito in 1980, there was a serious crisis of leadership in the country. The successors of Tito were not only inefficient, they were highly partial as well. They were extremely loyal to their *own* ethnic communities, a dangerous trend in a multi-ethnic country like Yugoslavia. In the absence of efficient leadership, the rate of economic growth declined, developmental projects suffered and the leaders of the six republics blamed one another for the decay. This had never happened during Tito's tenure. As a fallout of economic decline, all kinds of social unrest began to surface. Slovenia and Croatia, the two economically advanced provinces, alleged that other underdeveloped provinces of the South were burdening their economies. In 1988, Slobodan Milosevic, the Serb nationalist leader, started a movement for an independent state. He suspended the autonomous status for Vojvodina and Kosovo and pressurized the Albanian majority living in Kosovo to accept Serb supremacy. Milosevic's policies created tremendous panic among the non-Serbs living in former Yugoslavia, and they tried to resist his desire to bring the whole of Yugoslavia under Serb domination. This led to the beginning of fierce and bloody ethnic conflicts in Kosovo, Bosnia and other regions of former Yugoslavia.

The Communist Party in Yugoslavia was formally dismantled in January 1990. After the end of the one-party rule, leaders of different provinces began to foment ethnic nationalism.

Milosevic's extreme Serb nationalism created severe resentment in economically prosperous Slovenia and Croatia. People as well as leaders of these two provinces felt that extreme Serb nationalism would be detrimental for their economic and ethnic interests. Afraid and resentful of Serb domination over Yugoslavia, the republics of Croatia and Slovenia declared independence on 25 June 1991. Earlier, they had conducted a referendum for separate statehood, which was overwhelmingly supported by Slovenians and Croats. In 1992, the European Community (EC) recognized the independence of these two states. Two other republics, Bosnia and Macedonia, also declared independence at the end of 1991 and appealed for recognition from the EC. When the EC and the United States recognized Bosnia and Macedonia in April 1992, fierce ethnic wars started in these two republics. In Bosnia, Serbs, Croats and Muslims targeted one another in a bloody civil war seldom witnessed before. Each community had its agenda of ethnic cleansing in this civil war. Millions died and millions were displaced in Bosnia due to this civil war. The fierce civil war continued from 1992 to 1995. Finally, peace was restored in Bosnia in December 1995, when leaders from the United States, the NATO, Serbia, Croatia and Bosnia signed the Dayton Peace Accord to end the civil war in Bosnia. Hatred based on ethnicity, and the desire of all ethnic groups to annex territory, made the civil war in Bosnia bloody and violent.

On 27 April 1992, Serbian leader Milosevic declared that Serbia and Montenegro would henceforth be known as the Federal Republic of Yugoslavia (FRY). With this announcement, Milosevic tried to fulfill two wishes—first, to make Serbia and Montenegro the legal heir of former Yugoslavia; second, to accept, legally, the disintegration of Yugoslavia. But the UN, the EC and several states refused to accept Serbia as the inheritor of Yugoslavia. Following this, FRY was renamed Serbia and Montenegro in February 2003. Therefore, former Yugoslavia was initially split into five states due to ethnic nationalism. These five states are Slovenia, Croatia, Macedonia, Bosnia-Herzegovina and Serbia-Montenegro. It may be noted in this context that Kosovo declared its independence from Serbia on 17 February 2008. Although Kosovo's independence was recognized by several countries, several others, including Serbia and Russia, refused such recognition. Russia threatened to veto Kosovo's membership of the UN. So Kosovo has very little chance to become a UN-member in the near future as its independent status remains controversial at present.

Many reasons could be cited for the disintegration of Yugoslavia. These are: (1) extreme form of nationalism; (2) ethnic hatred; (3) crisis of leadership (after Tito's death); (4) non-uniform economic development (northern provinces like Slovenia and Croatia were more developed than the southern provinces) and (5) the unwillingness of different ethnic communities to live in a united Yugoslavia. All these factors led to severe ethnic conflicts in different parts of Yugoslavia. In all, four civil wars took place on the basis of ethno-nationalism in Yugoslavia. The first of these civil wars took place in Slovenia. It lasted only for ten days during June–July 1991, and there was very little casualty. The second one happened in Croatia, during the periods July– December 1991 and May–June 1995. The rate of casualty in the second war was more than Slovenia; thousands died and thousands were rendered homeless. But the third civil war in Bosnia was more violent. Millions died and about 2.5 million people were rendered homeless. Kosovo witnessed the fourth civil war from March to June 1999. Milosevic's repressive policies towards the Albanians and his desire to establish Serb supremacy gave the civil war horrific proportions. Kosovo attracted the attention of the whole world, and to resist Milosevic's Serb army, the NATO resorted to massive bombing in Kosovo. To safeguard the Albanians from Serb militia, the NATO called its mission in Kosovo a 'humanitarian intervention'. Kosovo created quite a stir in international politics in 1999.

## Ethnic Problem in the Russian Federation

Ethnic nationalism, mainly spearheaded by the Chechen people, has remained an irritant for the Russian Federation (henceforth, only Russia) for some time. At present, Russia is the largest country in the world in terms of territory. As per the 1999 Census, the Russian population is 14.6 crores, comprising over a hundred ethnic communities. The Russians constitute the largest ethnic community with 82 per cent of the total population of the country. The second largest ethnic community, as per the 1999 census, is Tatar, constituting 4 per cent. Among other ethnic communities, notable in terms of population are Ukrainians, Chuvashes, Germans, Buryats, Jews, Yakuts and Chechens. Russia has twenty-one autonomous republics (henceforth 'provinces', for easy understanding) and some of these provinces are named after the principal ethnic community living there. For example, in the Tatar province, the Tatars; in Yakut, the Yaukuts, and in Buryat, the Buryats are principal ethnic communities. But the Russians, numerically far superior to other ethnic groups, have a sizeable presence in all provinces. In fact, they are the majority ethnic community in several provinces, and have occupied important positions in the political and economic sectors. Other ethnic communities are resentful of this Russian domination.

In Chechnya, however, the Russians are not a majority; and the Chechens outnumber the Russians to be the majority ethnic community. After the disintegration of the Soviet Union, Chechnya became one of the twenty-one autonomous republics of Russia. Under former Soviet Union, Chechnya was in the autonomous republic of Chechen-Ingush. When Soviet Union was being split into fifteen independent states, Chechnya reiterated its demand for a separate statehood. In 1991, within months after the formation of the Russian Federation, Chechnya declared its independence. But the Russian government under President Boris Yeltsin—the first post–Cold War government in Russia—rejected this declaration and urged Chechen leaders to stay within Russia. It considered the Chechen demand for a separate statehood dangerous because such demands could incite separatist movements in other provinces as well, especially in non-Russian majority provinces like Tatar, Chuvash, Buryat or Yakut. Historically, Chechnya could never identify itself with the Russian culture, because its religion, language, social practices, all were different from those of the Russians. The Chechen language originated from the Nakh language group of the Caucasus region. The Chechens, for this reason, also identify themselves as 'nokhchiis'. For long, the Arabic script was used to write in the Chechen language. In 1920, the Latin script replaced the Arabic and is now used to write the language. The Russian language, on the other hand, is a part of the broader Indo-European language group, and originated from its Slav branch. The Chechens are thus linguistically different from the Russians. Their religions are different too. The Chechens are Muslims, mainly Sunnis. For a long time, religion had helped the Chechens maintain an identity separate from that of the 'Christian' Russians. Due to differences in language and religion, the Chechens considered themselves culturally different from the majority Russians in former Soviet Union.

The Chechens never accepted Russian domination lying down. In 1944, Soviet leader Joseph Stalin accused the Chechens of conspiring with Nazi Germany to topple the Soviet government. As a punitive measure, Stalin sent the Chechen leaders to exile in Central Asia. The autonomous status of the Chechen-Ingush region was also scrapped at that time. However, in 1957, this status was restored. The Chechens and the Russians shared a history of antagonism for long. After the disintegration of Soviet Union, their rivalry reached its peak. At the beginning of

1991, when the split of Soviet Union became imminent, Dzhokhar Dudayev, the Army Chief of Chechnya, demanded the end of Soviet rule in Chechnya and 'expelled' the Soviet army and the government officials from there. In October 1991, Dudayev won the election in Chechnya and became the President. Chechnya declared its independence before the 'official' disintegration of the Soviet Union in November 1991; but Dudayev was unable to obtain recognition for an independent Chechnya from other countries. The new Yeltsin-government of Russia urged the Chechen leaders to abandon demands for a separate statehood, and promised greater autonomy for Chechnya within the Russian Federation. Negotiations continued throughout 1992 and 1993 for providing greater autonomy to Chechnya, but the Chechen leaders never deviated from their demand for a separate state. As a consequence, talks between the Yeltsin- and the Dudayev-government failed. With the problem of ethnic nationalism becoming too serious in Chechnya in 1994, the Russian military was sent to tackle the situation. In a battle between the Russian and the Chechen armies, more than 40,000 people died. In February 1995, the Russian army captured Grozny, the capital of Chechnya. Dudayev fled, but terrorist activities continued. Dudayev was ultimately killed in 1996 in a rocket attack launched by the Russian army.

In May 1996, Russian President Boris Yeltsin and Chechen leader Zelimkhan Yandarbiyev signed a cease-fire. But this cease-fire failed to bring peace in Chechnya as the Russian army and the Chechen rebels continued to fight among themselves. Grozny was devastated and 300,000 Chechens took shelter in other parts of Russia. Russia reiterated its plans to give more autonomy to Chechnya. But the Chechen leaders rejected the offer and continued their fight. In August 1996, the Chechen rebels 'liberated' Grozny from the Russian army. In late August, a peace accord was signed between Aleksandr Lebed, Security Adviser to the Russian President, and the Chechen rebel leaders. By this accord, both sides accepted to postpone the question of Chechen statehood till 2001. It was decided that Chechnya would enjoy extreme autonomy till 2001, but the issue of separate statehood would be decided after that year. As per the peace accord, Russia withdrew its troops from Chechnya in December 1996.

The Chechen people and a section of the Chechen rebels could not accept the peace accord, as they found it insulting to Chechen nationalism. In the elections held in January 1997, Yandarbiyev was defeated and Army Chief Aslan Maskhadov elected the new President of Chechnya. In May the same year, Maskhadov signed another treaty with Yeltsin. But this new treaty actually retained the provisions of the treaty of August 1996. This resulted in Maskhadov being termed a traitor by the Chechen rebels and losing his authority, although he could not be removed from presidency immediately. Violent nationalism returned to Chechnya in mid-1997, and the province witnessed frequent and continuous armed battles. In 1999, the rebels captured Dagestan, and declared Chechen-Dagestan an Islamic state. Moscow sent troops and 'liberated' Dagestan, but terrorist activities continued. During August–September 1999, Chechen rebels bombarded Moscow and two other cities of Russia. In retaliation, Russian troops entered Chechnya again and captured Grozny in December 1999. Thereafter, once again fierce battle ensued between the Chechen rebels and the Russian army.

In May 2000, Russian President Vladimir Putin announced that Chechnya was an integral part of Russia, and all federal laws would be implemented in the autonomous republic of Chechnya. Putin decided to remove Maskhadov from Chechen presidency and install Akhmad Kadyrov as the new President. Maskhadov did not agree and began to openly instigate the rebels. Putin's declaration that Chechnya was an integral part of Russia violated the provisions of the August

1996 and May 1997 peace accords which decided to postpone the issue of Chechen statehood till 2001. Under the circumstances, rebels fighting for the cause of a Chechen state escalated their activities with Maskhadov as their new mentor. In October 2002, Chechen rebels forcibly captured a theatre in Moscow and detained 800 Russian people, including women and children. They threatened to blow up the theatre along with all the detainees if their demand for a separate Chechen state was not accepted. A special task force of the Russian military eventually rescued people trapped inside the hall by transmitting gas inside the hall, although 129 people—this included rebels as well—were killed in this operation. In November 2002, the Putin-government announced that a referendum would be held in Chechnya for the proposed Chechen Constitution which prescribed increased autonomy for Chechnya within the Russian federal system. The referendum was held in March 2003. Moscow declared it as being very successful while the Chechen rebels saw it as a great failure. Normalcy suffered between claims and counter-claims, and peace could not be restored in Chechnya. In September 2004, Chechen rebels captured a school in Beslan near Moscow and detained nearly a thousand people, including children and teachers. They demanded withdrawal of all Russian troops from Chechnya. The Russian army entered the school and recaptured it from the rebels, but not before a total of 350 persons, including rebels, were killed. This incident of Beslan was later compared with the '9/11' terrorist attacks in the United States on 11 September 2001.

Chechnya continues to remain an irritant for the federal government in Russia, which prefers to include Chechnya as part of the federation. Chechens, on the other hand, consider Russian domination over Chechnya as forced and without popular support. They continue to consider themselves a separate ethnic community with little similarity with the Russians; they continue to struggle for an identity separate from that of the Russians. Ethno-nationalism inspired the Chechens to voice their demand for a separate state for Chechnya, which the Russians rejected for fear of more such demands from other non-Russian nationalities. Ethno-nationalism, which remained dormant under socialist regimes, dominated the political scenario of East and Central Europe after the Cold War.

# Post–Cold War World Order

The four and a half decade long Cold War (1945–90) marked an important phase in recent international politics. This war was responsible for the bipolar nature of world politics, in which the two superpowers behaved like separate poles and contradicted each other on almost every issue and in every part of the world. The ideological and political differences between the Soviet Union and the United States acted towards sustaining bipolarity in international politics during this period. With the disintegration of the Soviet Union in 1991, Cold War ended and bipolarity in world politics also ceased to exist. International politics had undergone remarkable changes after the end of the war. The Russian Federation was acknowledged as the successor of the former Soviet Union by the international community. It was given a permanent seat at the UN Security Council, in place of the Soviet Union. Russia also retained nearly 85 per cent of the nuclear capability of the former Soviet Union. With Cold War political calculations disappearing, Russia and the United States started effective cooperation between themselves in the economic, political and security spheres.

Other notable developments in world politics that took place after the Cold War were the unification of Germany, the creation of the CIS, and the divisions of Czechoslovakia and Yugoslavia. Bipolarity and Bloc politics there being no more, East and West Germany got united into one Germany, and the Berlin Wall—it divided the city of Berlin and symbolized the onset of the Cold War—was demolished to mark the end of the war. Among the fifteen sovereign states created out of the Soviet Union, twelve formed the CIS, marking the beginning of a new era of cooperation and friendship. As noted earlier, Yugoslavia was initially split into five independent states amidst ethnic violence, and Czechoslovakia was divided into two sovereign states peacefully. This shows that the internal map of Europe was altered after the Cold War. In other parts of the world, countries were adjusting to their roles in a new world order which was markedly different from that of the previous four and a half decades. The days of bipolarity were over; political calculations on the basis of bipolarity had to be changed.

What was the nature of this new world order? In the absence of the Soviet Union, the United States emerged as the only superpower with formidable economic, military and political clouts. It appeared that there was no nation that could successfully counter the might of the United States. Therefore, the new international order immediately after the Cold War was described by scholars as a unipolar world, with the United States as the remaining superpower (Russia no longer remained a superpower), exercising unobtrusive control over world politics. Thus, bipolarity was replaced by unipolarity after the end of the Cold War.

At the end of the first decade of the twenty-first century, the question regarding the unipolar nature of the present international order may be re-examined. Is the world strictly unipolar today? Today, there are some powers in the international order which can pose a challenge to the superiority of the United States. China is believed by many to be one such power. It has a very strong military, the second strongest in the world. China is a permanent member of the UN Security Council and a nuclear-weapon state. Besides, China has achieved spectacular economic growth during the last two decades. If this rate of economic growth is sustained by China, it may emerge as a counter-balancing force to the United States in the near future. The European Union (EU) is also surging ahead despite different odds. A united Europe, as history has proved, could be a force to reckon with. This regional organization has one of the most powerful economies in the world at present. So, the EU is most likely to figure in any future power calculations, Russia has inherited most of the military might of former Soviet Union. As mentioned earlier in this chapter, it has retained almost 85 per cent of the nuclear weapons of the Soviet Union, as well as the permanent membership of the UN Security Council. Russia is now an emerging economy, and if it can continue with its current economic growth rate, this largest country on earth would certainly emerge as a great power. Finally, a united Germany has the potential to be a power to notice. It is one of the most industrially developed nations in the world and a major contender for a permanent seat in a revamped UN Security Council. In future, Germany too may play a crucial role in international politics. Considering the rise of these forces, a situation of bipolarity—United States versus China or United States versus Russia—or balance of power may once again emerge in world politics in the near future.

International politics is ever-changing; it is dynamic. It had never accepted any particular order as permanent. Before the Second World War, the balance of power system existed for a long period. After the war, there was change in this balance and a new bipolar world order set in. After the Cold War, the bipolar system made way for a unipolar one in world politics. At present, the United States is the sole superpower and the pivot around which this unipolar world politics revolves. But there are some powers, as has been just mentioned, which can pose a threat to the US supremacy. All this makes the current international order loaded with multipolar characteristics, where more than one power may exercise influence in world politics. Bipolarity or another balance of power system may mark international politics once again in the future. Considering all this, it would not be unwise to describe the present international order as 'unipolar with multipolar tendencies'.

QUESTIONS

1. Describe the origin and different phases of the Cold War.
2. Write short notes on:
   (a) Marshall Plan.
   (b) Truman Doctrine.
   (c) Cuban Missile Crisis.
   (d) Bloc Politics.
3. Analyse the causes of the end of the Cold War.
4. Examine the causes behind ethnic nationalism in former Czechoslovakia.
5. Why did Yugoslavia disintegrate? Explain in details.
6. Write a note on the ethnic problems in the Russian Federation.
7. How would you describe the post–Cold War world order?

# 8 Security and Nuclear Issues After the Second World War

The use of nuclear technology for warfare was unknown to the world before the Second World War. With the use of hydrogen bombs in Hiroshima and Nagasaki during this war, the devastating effects of nuclear weapons came to light. It became evident that nuclear weapons had far more destructive powers than conventional weapons, and a nation's ability to produce nuclear weapons would give it an advantage over others in terms of national security and international importance. The United States was the first nation to acquire and use nuclear weapons, but was soon followed by the Soviet Union that produced its own nuclear device in 1949. Soon a race for acquiring nuclear weapons started around the world and it posed a serious challenge to the maintenance of international peace and security after the Second World War. With two superpowers possessing nuclear weapons, the Cold War became intense and international security was in real danger. The dreadful event of a nuclear war between the two superpowers during the Cold War continuously threatened the goal of a peaceful world that the United Nations (UN), and other world leaders had envisioned. The world was facing an unprecedented security crisis with the advent of nuclear, radiological, chemical and biological weapons (these are together referred to as 'weapons of mass destruction' or WMDs) and the consequential politics surrounding the WMDs. The post–Second World War international order was new to such politics, and efforts started soon to deal with this new threat to global security and peace. Among the WMDs, nuclear weapons initially constituted the most dangerous threat to the world. As a consequence, Nuclear Nonproliferation Regime (NPR) was one of the first attempts to make the world free of WMDs after the Second World War.

After the Hiroshima and Nagasaki tragedies, when the awesome and destructive power of nuclear weapons became apparent, some nations were keen on pursuing policies that would prevent the spread of nuclear weapons. After the Second World War was over, in 1946, the United States advocated the Baruch Plan (designed by the American atomic scientist Bernard Baruch) that called for international control over all nuclear weapons. But the Soviet Union, still in pursue of its first nuclear bomb, as also due to the apprehension of West Bloc's supremacy in nuclear politics, rejected this plan. In 1953, the US President Eisenhower proposed an 'atoms for peace' plan to the UN General Assembly. This proposal reflected the ideals of the earlier Baruch Plan. In 1957, following the Eisenhower proposal of 1953, the Atoms for Peace Treaty (APT) came into force. The Soviet Union, already a nuclear power, agreed to sign the APT. The APT also created, in 1957, the International Atomic Energy Agency (IAEA) that was given the task of monitoring the use of nuclear energy. The IAEA, an autonomous body affiliated to the UN, was later assigned the work of ensuring that nuclear materials used for energy production are not diverted towards military activities. The Baruch Plan, the APT and the creation of the IAEA marked the beginning of what is today called the Nuclear Nonproliferation Regime (NPR).

# The Nuclear Nonproliferation Treaty

After the Cuban Missile Crisis in 1962, a Partial Test Ban Treaty (PTBT) was signed in 1963 in Moscow banning all nuclear tests in the atmosphere, under water and in space. While the United States, Soviet Union and Britain signed the Treaty, France and China did not, reducing greatly the effectiveness of the PTBT. But the quest for complete global disarmament continued under the NPR, and the two superpowers were involved in these efforts. After the Chinese nuclear explosion in 1964, the Soviet Union and the United States began to favour stringent nonproliferation norms. American president Lyndon Johnson and Soviet leader Nikita Kruschev, along with other world leaders (prominent among them was Frank Eiken, the Foreign Minister of Ireland), started working on a treaty that could prevent the spread of nuclear weapons around the world. Finally, the Nuclear Nonproliferation Treaty (NPT) was mooted. The treaty was opened for signature in 1968, although it entered into force in March 1970. Ireland and Finland were the first countries to sign this treaty. Till date, 189 countries have signed it, while India, Pakistan and Israel have declined to sign. North Korea signed the treaty, but withdrew from it in 2003. The NPT is a multilateral treaty mutually agreed upon by the ratifying countries. Initially, it was conceived for a period of twenty-five years with the provision for review every five years. But the signing states decided by consensus to extend the NPT indefinitely and without any conditions at the Fifth Review Conference of the NPT in 1995 in New York City.

The NPT has three major thrust areas, sometimes described by scholars as the three 'pillars' of the treaty. They are: (1) nonproliferation; (2) disarmament and (3) the right to peaceful use of nuclear energy. Provisions have been enumerated in the treaty to achieve these three objectives. When the treaty came into force in 1970, there were five declared nuclear-weapon-possessing countries in the world—the United States, the Soviet Union, Britain, China and France. These five states were described as the Nuclear Weapons States (NWS) by the treaty. The remaining signatories to the treaty were refereed to as non-nuclear-weapon states. After the disintegration of the Soviet Union, the Russian Federation has become the sole successor of the Soviet Union as a NWS.

## Important Articles of the NPT

Experts consider the NPT a major arms control device since the Second World War. This necessitates a brief analysis of the important articles in the NPT in order to realize its essence. In Article I, the NWS pledge not to transfer nuclear explosive devices or the means to produce them to non-weapon states. Article II obligates the non-weapon states not to receive nuclear explosive devices or attempt at acquiring them. It also prohibits non-weapon states from receiving any kind of assistance for the manufacture of nuclear weapons. Article III requires all non-weapon states to conclude an agreement with the IAEA for the application of the safeguards of the agency on all nuclear activities, and for accounting for all nuclear materials. Article IV, in its two sections, gives all signatories the 'inalienable right' to research, produce and use nuclear energy for peaceful purposes. It further provides:

> All the Parties to the Treaty undertake to facilitate, and have the right to participate in, the fullest possible exchange of equipment, materials and scientific and technological information for the peaceful uses of nuclear energy. Parties to the Treaty in a position to do so shall also co-operate in

> contributing alone or together with other States or international organizations to the further development of the applications of nuclear energy for peaceful purposes, especially in the territories of non-nuclear-weapon States Party to the Treaty, with due consideration for the needs of the developing areas of the world.

By Article VI of the NPT, all the signatories, particularly the NWS, pledge to work towards cessation of the nuclear arms race and universal nuclear disarmament. They also pledge to work for a 'treaty on general and complete disarmament under strict and effective international control'. Article X contains the provision of withdrawal from the treaty. It allows each party to the treaty to withdraw from it with three months' notice. The provisions contained in the NPT make it a legal document designed to encourage nations in making political commitment to abstain from acquiring nuclear weapons. However, it may be pointed out, the NPT is only a voluntary commitment without adequate mechanism for enforcement.

## India, Pakistan and the NPT

As noted earlier, India and Pakistan have not signed the NPT despite the treaty being ratified by 189 other nations. What are the Indian and the Pakistani positions vis-à-vis the NPT? Although these two countries of South Asia share some common perceptions about the NPT, they had put forward separate arguments for their refusal to sign the NPT. Both are of the opinion that the NPT is inherently discriminatory as it had created imbalances in the possession, use and distribution of nuclear energy. Further, the treaty had placed the NWS in an advantageous position vis-à-vis non-weapon states. It also failed to address the security concerns of the non-weapon states of the developing world. Apart from these common grounds, India and Pakistan had taken different paths for their refusal to sign the NPT.

India had been opposing the NPT on several grounds. Indian views on NPT could be succinctly summarized as follows: (1) the treaty is discriminatory as it allows the NWS, the nuclear 'haves', to gain absolute control over nuclear energy. It is possible for them to use the provisions in the treaty to deprive the non-weapon states of the important nuclear technology; (2) the NPT provides little security cover to the non-weapon states. These countries feel militarily threatened, and are extremely wary that nuclear weapons could be used against them to gain political mileage; (3) there must be a comprehensive, genuine and non-discriminatory ban on all nuclear tests, in the spirit of Article VI of the NPT. But unfortunately, Article VI had been violated several times by the NWS. As a result, complete disarmament could not be achieved; (4) nuclear issues in South Asia are not strictly regional in nature; they may have extra-regional effects. So, such issues there must not be addressed separately. Before denuclearization of South Asia, a global nuclear disarmament is absolutely necessary; (5) India would only recognize an impartial non-proliferation regime supported by a universal nuclear disarmament.

The Pakistani leadership had, time and again, made it clear that Pakistan would not sign the NPT unilaterally unless India was made to sign it. In fact, they think that India should be pressurized to sign the NPT jointly with Pakistan. Like India, Pakistan views the treaty as a biased one. Unlike India, Pakistan contends that the nuclear issue in South Asia is a regional issue and could not be solved by singling out Pakistan as the sole proliferator. They view India as a major nuclear proliferator in South Asia, and believe that Pakistan's acceptance of the NPT is very much dependent on India's joining the NPR, because India is a security threat to Pakistan.

The NPT, in their view, would not succeed in South Asia unless India is made to sign the treaty. This is why Pakistan linked its ratification of the treay to India's signing it.

# The Comprehensive Test Ban Treaty

The PTBT and the NPT, signed during the Cold War, were not completely successful in achieving universal nuclear disarmament. Superpower rivalry and tension during this period hindered satisfactory progress in nuclear disarmament until 1991. Signatories to the PTBT held an amendment conference in 1991 to discuss a proposal to convert the PTBT into an instrument seeking to ban all nuclear-weapon tests everywhere—in the atmosphere, under water, in space and underground. With strong support from the UN, negotiations for a Comprehensive Test Ban Treaty (CTBT) began at the Conference on Disarmament in Geneva in January 1994. The Final Draft, agreed upon by 127 states, was presented to the UN General Assembly (UNGA) on 10 September 1996. The treaty was opened for signature on 24 September 1996 at the UN Headquarters.

The CTBT consists of a preamble, seventeen articles, two annexes and a Protocol. The Protocol describes verification procedures and contains two annexes. The preamble to the CTBT stresses the need for 'continued systematic and progressive efforts to reduce nuclear weapons globally' with the ultimate goal of their elimination and of 'general and complete disarmament under strict and effective international control'. It recognizes that 'the cessation of all nuclear weapon test explosions and all other nuclear explosions . . . constitutes an effective measure of nuclear disarmament and non-proliferation in all its aspects'.

## Important Provisions in the CTBT

Article I of the CTBT outlines the 'Basic Obligations' of the treaty. Section 1 of the Article says: 'Each state party undertakes not to carry out any nuclear weapon test explosion or any other nuclear explosion, and to prohibit and prevent any such nuclear explosion at any place under its jurisdiction or control'. Section 2 therein declares: 'Each State party undertakes, furthermore, to refrain from causing, encouraging, or in any way participating in the carrying out of any nuclear weapon test explosion or any other nuclear explosion'.

Article II describes 'the Organization' of the CTBT to ensure the implementation of the treaty and provide a forum for consultation and cooperation.

Article III provides for 'National Implementation Measures' for the treaty. It requires each state party to take necessary measures to implement its obligations under the treaty, including the establishment of a National Authority for liaison with the organization and other state parties.

Article IV, along with the Protocol, establishes the 'verification regime' for the CTBT. Such a regime—consisting of the International Monitoring System (IMS), the International Data Centre (IDC), consultations and clarifications, on-site inspections and confidence-building measures—'shall be capable of meeting the verification requirements of the Treaty' on its entry into force.

Article VI of the CTBT provides for 'Settlement of Disputes' and elaborates the mechanisms by which disputes concerning the application or interpretation of the treaty may be settled. Subject to certain conditions, the International Court of Justice may be requested to give an advisory opinion.

Article VII refers to the 'Amendment Procedures' of the treaty. It says that each state party has the right to propose amendments to the treaty, the Protocol or the annexes to the Protocol at any time after the treaty's entry into force. The proposed amendment requires the approval of a majority of states parties at an amendment conference with no party casting a negative vote.

Article VIII, which enumerates 'Review of the Treaty' provisions, stipulates that a conference to review the operation and effectiveness of the treaty would be held ten years after its entry into force, 'unless otherwise decided by a majority of the States Parties'. Such review would take into account 'any new scientific and technological developments'. Further review conferences may be held with the same objective at intervals of ten years thereafter, or less, if the conference so decides in the preceding year.

Article IX declares that the treaty is of unlimited duration.

Article XIV of the CTBT remained the centre of controversy with its provisions for 'Entry into Force'. It said that the treaty would enter into force 180 days after the forty-four state parties have deposited their instruments of ratification with the Secretary-General of the UN, 'but in no case earlier than two years after its opening for signature'. To enter into force, the CTBT must be ratified by the forty-four countries that, in 1996, possessed nuclear research or power reactors. If the treaty has not entered into force 'three years after the date of the anniversary of its opening for signature', the Secretary-General of the UN, as Depositary of the Treaty, could, at the request of a majority of states that had ratified it, convene a conference to examine the situation and to 'decide by consensus what measures consistent with international law may be undertaken to accelerate the ratification process' in order to facilitate the treaty's early entry into force.

Article XVI declares the UN Secretary-General s as the treaty's Depositary.

Finally, Article XVII contains the provision that the texts in thetreaty are equally authentic, irrespective of their being in Arabic, Chinese, English, French, Russian or Spanish.

## CTBT: The Current Position

Article XIV of the CTBT, as mentioned earlier, states that in order to enter into force the treaty must be ratified by all forty-four countries that, in 1996, possessed nuclear research or power reactors. The status in 2010 is that forty-one of these forty-four countries have signed the treaty but only thirty-one have ratified it. Non-signatories include India, North Korea and Pakistan. The United States, which led the effort to conclude a CTBT and was the first to sign the treaty, remained, along with China, among those who had signed the treaty but not ratified it. The Bush (Jr) administration had actively resisted the CTBT's logic. The treaty now has 180 signatories but has not entered into force because the United States and eight other CTBT-countries, including China, Egypt, India, Iran and Israel, have failed to ratify it. The United States has not yet ratified the CTBT, and a ratification seems unlikely, given the US Senate's strong reservations about it. The Obama administration tried to secure consent from the Senate for ratification of the treaty, but was not successful. The Trump Administration has not moved much with it.

On 24 September 2009, thirteen years after the CTBT opened for signature on the same day in 1996, representatives from 103 countries participated in an Entry into Force Conference in New York City to discuss issues pertaining to facilitation for 'entry into force' of the treaty and nonproliferation. The two-day conference began on the same day as the UN Security Council started deliberations on nuclear nonproliferation and disarmament issues at Heads of State level. Among the 103 countries that attended the conference were eighty-six ratifying, thirteen signatory and two non-signatory states (Saudi Arabia and Trinidad and Tobago). The Final Declaration of the conference called on the non-signatories and the non-ratifying nations to sign and ratify the CTBT in order to facilitate entry into force of the treaty. It contained a special appeal to those nations whose ratification was necessary for making the treaty a legally binding instrument. The simultaneous meeting of the Heads of State at the UN Security Council, chaired by the US President Barack Obama, also called upon all states 'to refrain from conducting a nuclear test explosion and to sign and ratify the Comprehensive Nuclear-Test-Ban Treaty (CTBT), thereby bringing the treaty into force at an early date'.

The Entry into Force Conference of the CTBT held in New York on 25 September 2009—this is the last till date—aroused hopes, as did the earlier ones, for the treaty to enter into force. However, an early ratification of the treaty would be extremely difficult, given the opposition of the CTBT by three of the forty-four countries that attended the 1996 Conference. India, Pakistan and North Korea have not yet signed the treaty, and until they sign and ratify it, it can never become a legally binding instrument. Moreover, important powers in today's world, like the United States and China, have not ratified the treaty. Debates are going on in these countries over the issue of its ratification. The US Senate did not ratify the treaty earlier. It would not be an easy task for the Obama administration to persuade the Senate to ratify the treaty. Further, India and Pakistan are undecided about signing the CTBT. China too has not shown great enthusiasm in ratifying the treaty, although it signed it. Considering all these factors, it could be concluded that the future of the CTBT is uncertain, and like the PTBT and the NPT, it would not be an effective instrument for disarmament in the present world.

## CTBT and India

India joined the Conference on Disarmament (CD) that began in Geneva in January 1994. The conference deliberated over a CTBT as part of the overall disarmament process. From the very beginning, India had been opposing the draft of the CTBT on several grounds. To begin with, it alleged that the draft did not address India's security concerns. Nuclear activities were continuing unabated in India's neighbourhood, but the text of the draft did not bother to address the issue of security concerns for countries like India. Further, India objected to the Entry into Force (Article XIVE) clause of the CTBT Draft saying that it would put unwanted obligations on India. The mandatory signature of the forty-four states for the CTBT to enter into force was not acceptable to India because it viewed the CTBT as another flawed instrument like the NPT. Since India had not signed the NPT earlier, it would contradict its position on nuclear issues if it agreed to sign the CTBT.

India also objected to the verification regime referred to in the draft. The CD deliberated on the procedures to penalize defaulters after the treaty came into force. But who would identify the defaulters? What kind of international monitoring system was necessary for legal action? India was concerned about these issues while objecting to the draft. Moreover, India did not like the close linkage between the NPT and the CTBT. The Preamble to the NPT made specific references to the completion of a comprehensive test ban treaty and the linkage was discussed frequently ever since negotiations on the NPT started. Failure of the NPT signatory-states to fulfill the obligations outlined in Article VI of the treaty in fact increased the gap between nuclear 'haves' and 'have nots' in terms of nuclear capability and security. The linkage between the NPT and the CTBT would only exacerbate this discrimination, argued India.

India further viewed the CTBT as only an instrument to cap the nuclear programmes of the developing countries, while it would have practically no control over the nuclear activities of developed nations with sophisticated technologies. India also had reservations about linking universal disarmament with proliferation issues. Since the time of Jawaharlal Nehru, all Indian leaders called for a total universal disarmament of all weapons. Excessive emphasis on nuclear nonproliferation only reveals an evil design to stop nuclear activities of developing nations, while the developed countries would continue to test weapons in sophisticated laboratories. Therefore, a CTBT would indulge in further discrimination between the NWS and non-weapon states. Considering all these factors, India vetoed the draft text of the CTBT on 20 August 1996, saying that the text did not serve the purpose of promoting the realization of universal disarmament goals. It refused to sign the treaty.

# The FMCT and the MTCR

## FMCT: An Unfinished Story

A Fissile Material Cut-off Treaty (FMCT) has not yet been materialized, although proposals in this direction had been mooted in 1993. In December 1993, the UN General Assembly passed a resolution on fissile material cut-off, calling for the negotiation of a nondiscriminatory, multilateral and internationally and effectively verifiable treaty banning the production of fissile material for nuclear weapons or other nuclear explosive devices. The resolution wanted the International Atomic Energy Agency (IAEA) to provide assistance in examining verification arrangements. The CD agreed by consensus in March 1995 to establish an Ad Hoc Committee with a mandate to negotiate a cut-off treaty based on that resolution. In May 1995, at the NPT Review and Extension Conference, the participants agreed to seek 'the immediate commencement and early conclusion' of cut-off negotiations. However, despite the widespread international backing for an FMCT, formal negotiations on cut-off have not yet commenced. The Indian and Pakistani nuclear tests of 1998 again aroused the demand for an FMCT in the Western world, but deadlock persisted over the FMCT thereafter. As a consequence, the FMCT continue to remain a goal, not a reality.

The main objectives of the FMCT are: (1) to secure a comprehensive ban on any further production of fissile material for any nuclear explosives; (2) to bring all production facilities that are not subject to any international inspections under a strict verification and monitoring regime; (3) to make the world safer from nuclear weapons; and (4) to make it obligatory for the parties to the FMCT not to produce fissile material for any nuclear devices and give an undertaking to accept verification and monitoring regime.

All these objectives, except the third, have generated intense controversies and led to a deadlock over FMCT. While there is general agreement that the world must be made safer from nuclear weapons, there are controversies over the issue of a blanket ban on the production of fissile materials, and on inspection of production facilities. India, for instance, believes that all sovereign countries have an inalienable right to engage in research, and in production and use of nuclear energy for peaceful purposes. Fissile materials used for civilian purposes must be differentiated from materials used for nuclear explosives. In fact, FMCT controversies begin with the ambiguous definition of a 'fissile material' for nuclear explosives, as well as the recycling facilities of these materials. The US position, for example, is that some uranium and plutonium fuels become wastes after single use and they must be disposed of. The Indian, French and Japanese positions, on the other hand, are that the spent fuel must be treated as a 'resource' and needs to be recycled. Until controversies over these important issues are resolved, the FMCT will continue to remain elusive as an instrument of disarmament.

## MTCR: Another Step Towards Nonproliferation

The Missile Technology Control Regime (MTCR) is a voluntary association of sovereign states which share the goals of nonproliferation of unmanned delivery systems capable of delivering WMDs. The MTCR seeks to coordinate national export licensing efforts aimed at preventing their proliferation. It was established in April 1987 by seven countries—Canada, France, Germany, Italy, Japan, the United Kingdom and the United States. Since then, the number of MTCR-member-countries has risen to thirty-four, all of which have equal standing within the regime. The current members of the MTCR are Argentina, Australia, Austria, Belgium, Bulgaria, Brazil, Canada, Czech Republic, Denmark, Finland, France, Germany, Greece, Hungary, Iceland, Ireland, Italy, Japan, Luxembourg, Netherlands, New Zealand, Norway, Poland, Portugal, Republic of Korea (South Korea), Russian Federation, South Africa, Spain, Sweden, Switzerland, Turkey, Ukraine, United Kingdom and the United States of America.

### MTCR Guidelines

Guidelines issued by the MTCR define its purpose and provide the overall structure and rules to guide the member-countries and those wanting to adhere unilaterally to the guidelines. Further, The Equipment, Software and Technology Annexe (ESTA) is designed to assist in implementing export controls on MTCR Annexe items. The ESTA is divided into Category I and Category II items. It includes a broad range of equipments and technologies, both military and dual-use—used for military as well as industrial and commercial purposes—that are relevant to missile development, production and operation. Member-countries exercise restraint in the consideration of all transfers of items contained in the ESTA. All transfers are considered on a case-by-case basis. Category I items include complete rocket systems (including ballistic missiles, space launch vehicles and sounding rockets) and unmanned air vehicle systems (including cruise missiles systems, target and reconnaissance drones) with capabilities exceeding a 300 km/500 kg range/payload threshold; production facilities for such systems; and, major sub-systems including rocket stages, re-entry vehicles, rocket engines, guidance systems and warhead mechanisms. Utmost restraint is applied in the case of Category I items.

Category II items include complete rocket systems (including ballistic missiles systems, space launch vehicles and sounding rockets) and unmanned air vehicles (including cruise missile systems, target drones, and reconnaissance drones) not covered in item I, capable of a maximum range equal to or greater than 300 kilometres. Also included are a wide range of equipments, materials and technologies, most of which have uses other than for missiles capable of delivering WMDs. Members of the MTCR enjoy greater flexibility in the treatment of Category II transfers, compared to category I transfers, although within the parameters of restraint. The MTCR guidelines declare that the regime is 'not designed to impede national space programmes or international cooperation in such programmes as long as such programmes could not contribute to delivery systems for weapons of mass destruction'.

The MTCR has stipulated that partner-(member) countries should obtain the following undertakings before the transfer of a controlled item: (1) a statement from the user specifying the use and end use location of the proposed transfer, if necessary accompanied by documents explaining its business activities and organization; (2) an assurance explicitly stating that the proposed transfers will not be used for any activities related to the development or production of delivery systems for WMDs; and (3) wherever possible and if deemed necessary, an assurance that a post shipment inspection may be made by the exporter or the exporting government. All the partners have also agreed that their consent will be secured in a manner consistent with their national laws and practices, and prior to any retransfer to a third country of the equipments, materials or related technologies.

The partners of the MTCR have also affirmed the principle that membership of the regime does not involve the right to obtain technology from another partner or any obligation to supply it. Members are expected to exercise appropriate accountability and restraint in their trade with fellow partners. Member-countries may also encourage all other countries to observe the MTCR guidelines on transfers of missiles and related technologies as a contribution to the building of a safer world. A third country may choose to adhere to the guidelines without being obliged to join the group, and a few have done so. MTCR and its members may get involved in conducting technical exchanges and broader dialogues on proliferation issues with non-member countries.

## MTCR: The Balance Sheet

Since its establishment in 1987, the MTCR has been successful in helping to stop or slow down ballistic missile programmes of many countries. For instance, Argentina, Egypt and Iraq abandoned their joint Condor II ballistic missile programmes. Further, South Africa, Brazil, South Korea and Taiwan either shelved or eliminated missile or space launch vehicle programmes. Poland and the Czech Republic destroyed their ballistic missiles, in part, to enhance their chances of joining the MTCR. At the annual meeting of the MTCR in Oslo in July 1992, the member-countries agreed to expand the scope of the regime to include nonproliferation of unmanned aerial vehicles (UAVs) for all WMDs. Prohibited materials have been divided into two categories, which are outlined in the ESTA of the MTCR.

In October 1994, in order to achieve greater uniformity in the enforcement of the MTCR guidelines, the member-countries established a 'no undercut' policy, which meant that if one member denied the sale of some technology to another country, then all the members must adhere to that decision. In 2002, the MTCR was supplemented by the International Code of Conduct (ICOC) against Ballistic Missile Proliferation, also known as the Hague Code of Conduct. The code calls for restraint and care in the proliferation of ballistic missile systems capable of delivering WMDs. The ICOC, initiated by members of the MTCR, took the principles of the regime, expanded upon them and offered membership to all nations with less stringent restrictions. Now, 117 nations enforce export controls to curb the proliferation of UAVs.

The MTCR was also able to encourage some non-members to follow its guidelines. For instance, China has agreed to abide by the original guidelines and annexe of 1987. Some other countries like Israel, Romania and the Slovak Republic have agreed to abide by the MTCR without joining it. These countries have decided to maintain export controls consistent with the regime. The MTCR, however, has its limitations. It is alleged by the member-states that it failed to contain countries like Iran, North Korea, India and Pakistan in their bid to advance their missile programmes. These countries, with varying degrees of foreign assistance—some of which come from MTCR member-states—have developed and deployed medium-range ballistic missiles with a range of 1,000 kilometres and are in the process of building missiles with much greater ranges. These countries (not MTCR-members), as alleged by member-states, engaged in the transfer of missile technology in the global arms market. North Korea, for example, is suspected to be the primary source of ballistic missile proliferation in the world today. Iran has allegedly supplied missile production items to many Middle-East countries, Syria in particular. As the MTCR is a voluntary association, and the decision to export missile technology is the sole responsibility of each member-country, the regime has, in effect, limited control over transfers of controlled items. Monetary and political considerations often get precedence over associational norms in the MTCR.

## WMDs and the Present World

WMDs constitute an unprecedented threat to international security and the human civilization. Efforts have been made since the Second World War to make the world free of WMDs. In 1972, a Convention on the Prohibition of the Development, Production and Stockpiling of Bacteriological (Biological) and Toxin Weapons and on their Destruction, generally referred to as the Biological Weapons Convention (BWC), was signed in London, Moscow and Washington DC to prohibit the development, production and stockpiling of biological and toxin weapons. More than 165 states have signed and ratified it. Article 1 of the BWC declares:

> Each State Party to this Convention undertakes never in any circumstances to develop, produce, stockpile or otherwise acquire or retain: (1) Microbial or other biological agents, or toxins whatever their origin or method of production, of types and in quantities that have no justification for prophylactic, protective or other peaceful purposes; and (2) Weapons, equipment or means of delivery designed to use such agents or toxins for hostile purposes or in armed conflict.

The Geneva Protocol of 1925, for the first time, banned the use of bacteriological elements in warfare. But it was not before 1969 that a comprehensive draft, prepared by Britain and aimed at complete elimination of biological weapons, was taken up for negotiation. The UN lent out its support, and the General Assembly passed a resolution in 1971 supporting the proposed BWC of 1972. The BWC that entered into force in March 1975 also pledged that each member-country shall destroy all existing stocks of biological weapons, and no member-country shall engage in the transfer of materials required for the production of such weapons. India, like many other countries, has signed and ratified the BWC and has destroyed all its stockpile of biological weapons.

Since its entry into force, the BWC has been holding periodic review conferences. These conferences aimed at strengthening the convention through giving suggestions on issues like verification procedures, confidence-building measures, appointment of experts and other protocols to help the BWC keep pace with changing times. However, recent technological developments have posed a serious challenge to the convention. The biotech revolution, for instance, brought with it severe problems for the BWC. Biotechnology has made it possible to create 'designer bugs' that may be used as biological agents for military purposes. It is almost impossible to confront these designer bugs that could specifically target any particular racial, religious or ethnic group. Poor states which cannot afford to build costly nuclear weapons can take this comparatively cheaper route of biotechnology for the purpose of warfare. Therefore, a major arms control challenge of the present world is to combat newer forms of biological weapons that could be built following the biotech revolution.

Like biological weapons, chemical weapons too constitute a real threat to international security in the present world. These weapons are also considered as WMDs. They contain highly detrimental chemicals that can disable and kill people. Different chemicals are used in different chemical weapons to affect the nervous system, the respiratory system, the blood, the skin or other parts of the human body. After the holocaust of the First World War, that witnessed the use of mustard gas resulting in lung damage and skin eruptions, the Geneva Protocol of 1925 banned the production and use of chemical weapons. But it is difficult to exercise effective control on such usage as these can be produced using methods similar to those for producing pharmaceuticals, pesticides, gases and other items required for civilian and medical purposes. It is also difficult to locate production sites producing chemical weapons, because these could be present under the guise of civilian chemical facilities, as also because they deny chemicals or equipments wanted by a suspected nation. Chemical weapons are cheaper to manufacture, and therefore possessed by several states, including the poor ones. Therefore, elimination of chemical weapons, along with other WMDs, is the greatest challenge of our times.

In order to meet this challenge, a Convention on the Prohibition of the Development, Production, Stockpiling and Use of Chemical Weapons and on their Destruction, popularly known as the Chemical Weapons Convention (CWC), was signed on 13 January 1993 in Paris and New York City. It became operational from April 1997. As of February 2018, 192 states, including the original 165 signatories, have become parties to the CWC. India too has signed and ratified the CWC and destroyed its whole stockpile of chemical weapons by April 2009. This convention is currently administered by the Organisation for the Prohibition of Chemical Weapons (OPCW), and the UN Secretary-General is its depositary. As per the CWC stipulations, the OPCW must be informed of any plant having, or expecting, an annual produce of more than 200 tonnes of chemicals (chemicals falling under any of the three categories identified by the CWC) or thirty tonnes, if the chemical contains sulfur, phosphorous or fluorine. Over the years, the convention has made strict verification provisions and is in a position to sanction violators, including non-parties to the convention. The OPCW is mainly entrusted with the task of verification.

The international nonproliferation regime, with its various arms like the PTBT, NPT, CTBT, FMCT, MTCR, BWC and CWC, has been much active in fulfilling its dream of achieving a weapon-free world since the Second World War. In some cases, the regime has been successful in realizing its targets. The BWC and the CWC, for instance, have been working satisfactorily towards reducing the dangers of biological and chemical weapons from the world. Till 2009, most of the member-states of the UN have become parties to the BWC and the CWC, and have committed themselves to abide by the provisions in the two conventions. Some states, such as China, Libya and North Korea, have expressed reservations about the stipulations mentioned in the conventions. But that has not proved to be detrimental to the functioning and progress of the BWC and the CWC. Several states have already destroyed their stockpiles of biological and chemical weapons, and more and more states are willing to do so under the guidance of these conventions.

But similar success cannot be attributed to other instruments of the nonproliferation regime like the NPT, CTBT, MTCR and FMCT. At least ten states important in terms of nuclear weapons have either not signed, or signed but not ratified, the CTBT. India, Pakistan and North Korea have signed neither the NPT nor the CTBT, rendering these two instruments almost ineffective. Six other countries—the United States, Indonesia, Iran, Israel, China and Egypt—have signed but not ratified the CTBT. While the future of the CTBT and the FMCT remain uncertain, the MTCR has also not evoked the confidence of major nations like India, China and Japan. Both the CTBT and the FMCT are still in their formative stages, and it would take more time and more acrimonious deliberations among countries to finally make them legally binding instruments. It is thus evident that the nonproliferation regime has not been totally successful in its mission. This is due to some flawed provisions in instruments like the NPT, the CTBT and the MTCR, and also due to differences in treatment among nations as contained in the provisions of these instruments. Unless these deficiencies are addressed, the NPT, the CTBT and the MTCR could not receive universal acceptance. While disarmament is the need of the hour and a weapon-free world the primary target of our times, non-discriminatory instruments of disarmament are also very important to secure a world free of lethal weapons.

QUESTIONS

1. Make a critical estimate of the NPT.
2. Analyse the Indian position vis-à-vis the NPT and the CTBT.
3. Write notes on the FMCT and the MTCR.
4. Examine disarmament efforts in the contemporary world.

# 9 Regional Organizations

Regional organizations have proliferated all over the world after the Second World War. States of a particular region form regional organizations to forge economic, security and political cooperation among themselves. Although the primary motive of several regional organizations after the Second World War was to achieve security guarantee for their members, after the Cold War, in an altered international milieu, such organizations have mainly focused on economic development of the region through meaningful cooperation among member-states. Through the creation of Free Trade Area (FTA), regional organizations are trying to achieve purposeful economic cooperation among members. Moreover, they cater to the needs, desires and aspirations of the people of a particular region. Therefore, the study of regional organizations has assumed an important place in the discourse of International Relations. In this chapter, several such organizations would be taken up for analysis, and the discussion would begin with the SAARC, the regional organization of South Asia.

## South Asian Association for Regional Cooperation (SAARC)

### Origin and Members

The SAARC is a comparatively newer regional organization in terms of its establishment. It was formally established on 8 December 1985 in Dhaka, the capital of Bangladesh. However, the preparation for forming a regional organization in South Asia started earlier, in early-1980, when the then President of Bangladesh Ziaur Rahman put forward such an idea. After several rounds of discussion and deliberation, the SAARC was formally launched in 1985 with seven members—Bangladesh, Bhutan, India, Maldives, Nepal, Pakistan and Sri Lanka. Afghanistan joined SAARC in 2007. These eight states of South Asia form the SAARC at present. China, Iran and Myanmar have expressed their wishes to join the SAARC as members. Their candidatures for full membership are under consideration and subject to unanimous approval by current SAARC-members. Apart from these members, the SAARC has provided 'observer' status to Australia, China, European Union, Iran, Japan, Mauritius, Myanmar, South Korea and the United States. Russia has expressed its desire to be an 'observer'.

## Objectives of the SAARC

The Charter of the SAARC, signed by the Heads of Government (HOGs) of the member-states, has outlined in detail the objectives of the organization. They are: (1) to serve the people of South Asia and to develop their standards of living; (2) to work for economic, social and cultural development of the region, and to ensure dignity of life for every individual; (3) to create an atmosphere of unity and confidence among states in South Asia; (4) to realize others' problems through mutual trust and cooperation; (5) to establish mutual cooperation in economic, social, cultural, scientific and technological areas; (6) to enhance cooperation with other developing countries of the world; (7) to increase mutual cooperation among member-states in order to protect the interests of South Asia in different international bodies and (8) to seek increased levels of cooperation with all international organizations and other regional organizations.

## Administrative Structure of the Organization

Like other regional organizations, the SAARC too has an elaborate administrative structure to run the organization. At the top of this structure is the meeting of the HOGs of the member-states. Known as the SAARC Summit, this meeting of the HOGs is held once a year, and it draws up the policies, programmes and activities of the organization for the year. In reality, the SAARC summit approves policies formulated by the Council of Ministers, which comes next in the organizational hierarchy. The council consists of Foreign (External Affairs) Ministers of member-states, and it meets twice a year to formulate and devise methods of implementation of the policies and programmes of the organization. The Charter of the SAARC has enlisted five major tasks for the Council of Ministers. These are: (1) to formulate policies for the organization; (2) to determine levels of cooperation among member-states; (3) to identify new areas of cooperation; (4) to create new infrastructures for the organization as per requirements and (5) to take decisions on matters of general interest to member-states. The council is, in effect, the main decision-making body of the SAARC. The next in the administrative hierarchy is the Standing Committee. It is composed of foreign secretaries of every member-state. This committee is mainly responsible for the implementation of SAARC policies and programmes, which it analyses and supervises throughout the year. It sends an annual report to the Council of Ministers. The charter has provided for a Secretariat of the organization. This is the main office of the SAARC, located in Kathmandu, the capital of Nepal. It is responsible for coordinating SAARC activities in the region. The Secretariat is headed by a Secretary-General.

Apart from these main bodies, the SAARC Charter has instructed the formation of several committees, such as the Technical Committee and the Action Committee, for smooth implementation of SAARC programmes and policies. These committees would comprise experts from the economic, social, cultural and educational, scientific and technological, and ecological fields. As per the directives of the charter, the SAARC has formulated thirteen technical committees in different areas to spread its activities throughout the region. The areas for which these committees had been set up include agriculture, communication, education, culture and sports, environment, meteorology, health and population, prevention of narcotic drugs, rural development, science and technology, tourism, transportation and women's welfare. Apart from these committees, the SAARC has also set up five regional centres to spread its programmes. These are located in Dhaka, for the promotion of agriculture and information, and for Meteorological Research; in Kathmandu, for the prevention of tuberculosis; in New Delhi, for documentation; and in Islamabad, for human resource development. Further, the SAARC is engaged in commendable work in areas of child welfare, anti-terrorist activities, food and agriculture.

## SAARC Summits

Since its formation on 8 December 1985, nineteen SAARC Summits had taken place (till May 2018) in different parts of South Asia. Table 9.1 enlists different SAARC Summits held since 1985.

**Table 9.1** SAARC Summits from 1985 to 2018

| S. No. | Summit | Year | Place | Country |
|---|---|---|---|---|
| 1. | First | 1985 | Dhaka | Bangladesh |
| 2. | Second | 1986 | Bangalore | India |
| 3. | Third | 1987 | Kathmandu | Nepal |
| 4. | Fourth | 1988 | Islamabad | Pakistan |
| 5. | Fifth | 1990 | Male | Maldives |
| 6. | Sixth | 1991 | Colombo | Sri Lanka |
| 7. | Seventh | 1993 | Dhaka | Bangladesh |
| 8. | Eighth | 1995 | New Delhi | India |
| 9. | Ninth | 1997 | Male | Maldives |
| 10. | Tenth | 1998 | Colombo | Sri Lanka |
| 11. | Eleventh | 2002 | Kathmandu | Nepal |
| 12. | Twelfth | 2004 | Islamabad | Pakistan |
| 13. | Thirteenth | 2005 | Dhaka | Bangladesh |
| 14. | Fourteenth | 2007 | New Delhi | India |
| 15. | Fifteenth | 2008 | Colombo | Sri Lanka |
| 16. | Sixteenth | 2010 | Thimphu | Bhutan |
| 17. | Seventeenth | 2011 | Addu City | Maldives |
| 18. | Eighteenth | 2014 | Kathmandu | Nepal |
| 19. | Nineteenth | 2016 | Islamabad | Pakistan |
| 20. | Twentieth | 2018 | — | Sri Lanka (proposed to be held) |

As Table 9.1 shows, SAARC summits were not held regularly (once every year) due to political disturbances in member-states, and also due to political tensions between the two largest states in the organization, India and Pakistan. The longest interval between two summits occurred between the tenth (1998) and eleventh (2002) summits. This was due to the nuclear tests in India and Pakistan, and the Kargil crisis between these two states.

After the end of the Cold War, the SAARC placed renewed emphasis on economic coordination and development of the member-states. If it committed itself to socio-cultural issues in the 1980s, it placed special importance on economic issues in the 1990s. This could be ascertained from the fact that in 1993 the members signed a SAARC Preferential Trading Arrangement (SAPTA) to facilitate free trade among South Asian states. SAPTA became operational in 1995. It was the first significant step towards building up a FTA in South Asia as it pledged liberal trade among member-states. It announced tariff concessions on more than four thousand items of trade. It also encouraged trade with less or no duties. SAPTA remained effective till 2004, when it was converted, as per provisions of the Arrangement, into an agreement on South Asian Free Trade Area (SAFTA) at the twelfth SAARC summit in Islamabad. The SAFTA Declaration categorically stated that the agreement owed its inspiration to the successful operation of the SAPTA. For a thorough discussion of the FTA in South Asia, the agreement on SAFTA must be analysed carefully.

## Agreement on South Asian Free Trade Area (SAFTA)

The SAFTA Agreement (henceforth, only SAFTA) was signed in 2004, but it came into force from 1 January 2006. Article 3 of agreement states the objectives. It says that the agreement would facilitate trade and economic cooperation among the SAARC-states. These are various methods by which such cooperation could be enhanced: (1) by removing trade barriers and facilitating free movement of goods among SAARC-states; (2) by creating an atmosphere of fair competition for free trade and providing equal opportunities to all member-states; (3) by providing for adequate and proper administrative infrastructure to make the SAFTA operational, and to sort out differences; and (4) by providing for appropriate machineries to extend to all member-states the benefits of the agreement. Article 3 also enumerates the main principles regarding the governance of the SAFTA. It says the SAFTA shall be governed in accordance with the following principles: (1) the SAFTA would be governed by the provisions of this agreement and also by the rules, regulations, decisions, understandings and protocols to be agreed upon within its framework by the contracting states; (2) these states would affirm their existing rights and obligations with respect to the World Trade Organization and other treaties or agreements to which such states are signatories; (3) the SAFTA shall be based and applied on the principles of overall reciprocity and mutuality of advantages in such a way as to benefit equitably all contracting states under contract; (4) the SAFTA shall involve free movement of goods between states, inter alia, through elimination of tariffs, para-tariffs and non-tariff restrictions on the movement of goods, as also through other equivalent measures; (5) the SAFTA shall entail adoption of trade facilitation and other measures, and the progressive harmonization of legislations by the contracting states in the relevant areas and (6) the special needs of the least-developed contracting states shall be clearly recognized by adopting concrete preferential measures in their favour on a non-reciprocal basis.

The agreement, in its twenty-five articles, elaborates details of free trade in the South Asian region. For instance, Article 7 discusses in detail the measures required to be taken for implementation of Trade Liberalization Programme in South Asia. It contains provisions as well as methods of tariff reduction used by SAARC-states in order to implement the SAFTA. Article 10 contains provisions for developing adequate and appropriate infrastructure to create a FTA in the region. The special provisions for least-developed economies in the SAARC are declared in Article 11. The provisions for special concessions for Maldives are outlined in Article 12. Article 16 elaborates in detail the safeguard measures for the SAFTA, while Article 20 contains provisions for resolution of differences among contracting parties. Article 21 gives rights to the contracting parties to withdraw from the SAFTA. Article 24 states in detail the procedures for amending the agreement.

The creation of the SAFTA at the twelfth SAARC summit was undoubtedly a major step in forging regional economic integration in South Asia. In an era of globalization and trade liberalization, economic cooperation among states must be given due priority. Further, nations of a particular region may strive to achieve regional economic development through the creation of FTA. The success of ASEAN and EU in achieving economic development through FTA bears testimony to this proposition. FTA also helps individual states of a region towards economic development, because trade within a particular region is cost-effective and it can save valuable foreign exchange for a particular state. As a consequence, intra-regional trade actually benefits all the states of the region. Considering all these advantages, the creation of the SAFTA was indeed a welcome step towards regional economic integration in South Asia. This agreement may also facilitate a SAARC Customs Union and a common currency (such as euro), which the SAARC has plans to achieve in the future.

But the success of the SAFTA became dependent on the political relationship between the two principal states of the region, India and Pakistan. It, or even the SAARC, could not make much headway due to political rivalry between the two major states in the region. Since its inception, the SAFTA as well as its predecessor SAPTA had practically remained dwarfs in regional trade. More than a decade had passed since the introduction of the SAPTA in 1995, but trade among SAARC-states remained abysmally low; intra-regional trade accounted for only 5.5 per cent of total trade of SAARC-members in 2008. This shows how SAARC-members are reluctant to instill life into the SAFTA. Politics is getting precedence over economics in South Asia, while the trend is just the opposite in other parts of the world. Cross-border terrorism, political instability in several member-states, political rivalry between two principal states, and, above all, the reluctance of political elite in the region to go for meaningful economic integration are some of the reasons for the no-show of the SAFTA.

But there is tremendous potential for the SAFTA, provided there is the will to harness it. Business organizations like the Federation of Indian Chambers of Commerce and Industries (FICCI) opined that the total intra-regional trade among SAARC-states, which was around US $7 billion in 2005, could be doubled by 2012 provided the existing tariffs were reduced within the stipulated time frame of the SAFTA (as reported by Media Division of FICCI, New Delhi on 3 January 2006). The agreement holds huge potential for intra-regional trade growth because over 90 per cent of the imports by South Asian states come from outside the region and a major part of exports of South Asia go to states that are not part of the SAARC. Nearly 5,500 tariff lines under the SAFTA have been liberalized and are expected to move towards zero tariffs for non-LDCs (least developed countries) by the year 2013 and for LDCs by 2016. But unless the tariff lines cover items, which have trade potential and member-states have small sensitive lists, the very purpose and objectives of this agreement may remain unfulfilled.

The SAFTA may also enhance the attraction of South Asia as an FDI (Foreign Direct Investment) destination due to concepts like integrated market and liberalized trade. The foreign investors can set base in one country of the region and cater to the supply chain of the entire region. If South Asia becomes an integrated market, it can draw a much higher FDI for the entire region with a huge market size of over 1.5 billion people. The reduction in tariff rates as planned by the SAFTA can multiply trade and commerce only if it is complemented and supported by adequate infrastructure and trade facilitation measures by member-governments. This includes improving and strengthening the network of transportation in roads, railways, air and seas; harmonization of custom regulations; quality standards; easy visa regulations, and; dispute settlement mechanism. But all these shall depend on the will of the political elite of the region. The ASEAN and the EU have overcome many political differences in order to achieve meaningful economic integration. The SAARC can do the same provided there is the inclination of the member-states to make it a forceful regional organization.

## The SAARC Social Charter

At the twelfth SAARC summit in Islamabad in 2004, Heads of Government (HOGs) of member-states signed the Social Charter, originally conceived at the tenth SAARC summit in Colombo in 1998. This charter is an elaborate document that contains provisions of cooperation among member-states in the social sector that includes different areas like health; education; human resource development; youth mobilization; welfare of women and children; poverty alleviation; population stabilization and rehabilitation of drug addicts. It is an ambitious guideline that directs the SAARC and its member-states to forge significant cooperation in social sectors to improve the quality of life of the people of South Asia. The Charter, in its twelve articles, recognizes the urgent need to improve the social conditions of the people, which are inseparably linked to economic development of the region. The opening paragraphs of the charter reiterate the need to create a concerted platform for this regional organization to work for social progress of the South Asian region in words like these:

> Observing that regional cooperation in the social sector has received the focused attention of the Member States and that specific areas such as health, nutrition, food security, safe drinking water and sanitation, population activities, and child development and rights along with gender equality, participation of women in development, welfare of the elderly people. Youth mobilization and human resources development continue to remain on the agenda of regional cooperation.... Convinced that it was time to develop a regional instrument which consolidated the multifarious commitments of SAARC Member States in the social sector and provided a practical platform for concerted, coherent and complementary action in determining social priorities, improving the structure and content of social policies and programmes, ensuring greater efficiency in the utilization of national, regional and external resources and in enhancing the equity and sustainability of social programmes and the quality of living conditions of their beneficiaries, the Member States of the South Asian Association for Regional Cooperation hereby agree to adopt this Charter.

Article II of the Social Charter is important in this context as it outlines the principles, goals and objectives of this ambitious programme. It says:

> In the light of the commitments made in this Charter, States Parties agree to: place people at the center of development and direct their economies to meet human needs more effectively; fulfill the responsibility towards present and future generations by ensuring equity among generations, and protecting the integrity and sustainable use of the environment; recognize that, while social development

> is a national responsibility, its successful achievement requires the collective commitment and cooperation of the international community; integrate economic, cultural and social policies so that they become mutually supportive, and acknowledge the interdependence of public and private spheres of activity....

Clearly, the objectives are noble and the SAARC would aim to fulfill these objectives. In a region of acute poverty, social discrepancy and gender inequality, the SAARC Social Charter is a step towards the right direction.

Some of the goals of the Charter have been realized, although many more areas need to be covered carefully. In the field of education, the establishment of a South Asia University in New Delhi will help foster increasing interactions among students, teachers and academics in the region. Further, the creation of a SAARC Development Fund (SDF) will also help realize the goals outlined in the Charter. Under the social window of the SDF, projects on women empowerment, maternal and child health, and teachers' training would be implemented. In the fifteenth SAARC summit held in Colombo in August 2008, leaders emphasized the need to implement the objectives of the Charter quickly. The Declaration following this summit noted:

> The Heads of State or Government underscored the imperative to make steady progress in the implementation of the SAARC Social Charter and directed the Member States to complete the National Plans of Action with a perspective of seeking to transform current challenges into opportunities. They further directed the National Coordination Committees (NCCs) to recommend activities in conformity with the Social Charter and to introduce an efficient and effective monitoring and evaluation mechanism for reviewing the progress in the implementation of the Social Charter. The leaders emphasized the need to implement the selected regional and sub regional programs and projects to complement national implementation efforts. They urged that such activities be suitably accommodated in the SAARC calendar. They called for people's participation in strategy initiatives, planning and implementation to ensure people's responsibility and ownership. The leaders directed to develop a policy on the protection of rights of the senior citizens for their geriatric care taking into account existing national policies of the Member States.

But mere lofty rhetoric would not help the cause of social development programmes of the SAARC. Concrete and effective actions are required by member-states to implement the ideals of the Charter. It is pleasing to note that the SAARC is trying to achieve the goals identified in the Social Charter in a planned and phased manner.

## Future of the SAARC

The SAARC is a relatively young regional organization burdened with immense social, economic and political problems. It is the world's largest regional organization in terms of population, but the smallest in terms of intra-regional trade. In a region infected with poverty, social inequality, religious fanaticism, illiteracy, unemployment, terrorist activities and political rivalry among members, this organization faces a real challenge in achieving social and economic integration. The numerous problems speak for the slow progress of the SAARC in achieving its cherished goals. Despite the SAPTA and the SAFTA, economic integration and development of the region are yet to be fulfilled; despite signing of the Social Charter, upliftment of the poor and the underprivileged of the region remains a dream. Persistent political rivalry between the two principal states of South Asia has also affected the progress of the SAARC. But the organization exists, and slowly but steadily moves forward towards its goals. This is the most optimistic point. Despite odds and intense political problems, the organization is alive and taking new and newer initiatives for regional development. The member-states have already realized the importance of having a greater regional platform to initiate dialogues and discussions on regional problems that could only be tackled through mutual cooperation, and not individually by single states.

Chambers of commerce in the region feel that the SAFTA has immense potential, which could be realized if appropriate measures are taken for its proper implementation. Though the contribution of this agreement in the economic life of the region is not yet apparent, the picture may be different in the future. If zero tariffs are achieved by 2016, and other targeted goals realized by that period, the SAFTA may enhance intra-regional trade significantly and contribute towards economic development of the region. Similarly, the objectives outlined in the SAARC Charter are slowly yielding results, as analyses in the previous pages have shown. The formal declaration after the fifteenth SAARC summit in 2008 pointed out significant achievements in areas like women empowerment; child development; transportation; education; science and technology; tourism; environment; and information and communications technology development. These are undoubtedly brighter patches in the not-too-exciting history of the SAARC. If such achievements are sustained, and more are added to this list, and if there is political will on the part of member-states, this regional organization will continue to flourish in the future.

# Association of South East Asian Nations (ASEAN)

## Origin and Members

The ASEAN was born in 1967 in Bangkok. Five states of South East Asia formed the ASEAN mainly for political and security purposes. These five states were Thailand, Malaysia, Indonesia, Philippines and Singapore. They came together to form a regional organization to seek a security cover against any apprehended threat from China and Japan, the two powerful nations in the region. Although ASEAN later turned into a successful economic organization, its origin was linked to security fears of its founding members. For seventeen long years, the organization consisted of the initial five members. From 1984, the number of members started to increase. That year, Brunei Darussalam (Brunei, in short,) joined and became the sixth member. Vietnam joined in 1995 and Laos and Myanmar in 1997. Cambodia became the tenth member—the last so far—of the ASEAN in 1999. The permanent Secretariat of this regional organization is located in Jakarta, the capital city of Indonesia. Throughout the year, it coordinates various activities of the organization in different parts of the world.

## Objectives

The Bangkok Declaration of 1967, which founded the ASEAN, elaborated the main objectives of the organization. It said that the ASEAN would work for regional peace, stability and economic development of South East Asia. Further, the organization would engage itself in maintaining and advancing the rich cultural heritage of the region. In the first ASEAN Summit held in Bali, Indonesia, in 1976, some fundamental principles of the organization were announced. The member-states signed a Treaty of Amity and Cooperation (TAC) there. This treaty outlined the fundamental principles of the ASEAN, which must be respected by all members. These fundamental principles are: (1) mutual respect for the independence, sovereignty, territorial integrity and national identity of member states; (2) recognition of the rights of member-states to live independently without external interference and pressure; (3) non-intervention in the internal affairs of member-states; (4) peaceful resolution of differences among member states and (5) increasing meaningful cooperation among members.

## Organizational Structure

The ASEAN has a very strong organizational structure that has contributed immensely towards its success. At the top of this structure belongs the ASEAN Heads of Government (AHG). It is the apex body which takes all major policy decisions of the organization. This body meets 'formally' every three years. This formal meeting of the AHG is also known as the ASEAN Summit. But the AHG sits every year 'informally' to make policies and review programmes of the organization. In both its 'formal' and 'informal' meetings, crucial policy decisions are adopted and ASEAN activities reviewed and analysed. Table 9.2 highlights ASEAN Summits

**Table 9.2** ASEAN Summits and 'Informal Summits' from 1976 to 2019

| S. No. | Summit | Place | Country | Year |
|---|---|---|---|---|
| 1. | First Summit | Bali | Indonesia | 1976 |
| 2. | Second Summit | Kuala Lumpur | Malaysia | 1977 |
| 3. | Third Summit | Manila | Philippines | 1987 |
| 4. | Fourth Summit | Singapore | Singapore | 1992 |
| 5. | Fifth Summit | Bangkok | Thailand | 1995 |
| 6. | First Informal Summit | Jakarta | Indonesia | 1996 |
| 7. | Second Informal Summit | Kuala Lumpur | Malaysia | 1997 |
| 8. | Sixth Summit | Hanoi | Vietnam | 1998 |
| 9. | Third Informal Summit | Manila | Philippines | 1999 |
| 10. | Fourth Informal Summit | Singapore | Singapore | 2000 |
| 11. | Seventh Summit | Bandar Seri Begawan | Brunei Darussalam | 2001 |
| 12. | Eighth Summit | Phnom Penh | Cambodia | 2002 |
| 13. | Ninth Summit | Bali | Indonesia | 2003 |
| 14. | Tenth Summit | Vientiane | Laos | 2004 |
| 15. | Eleventh Summit | Kuala Lumpur | Malaysia | 2005 |
| 16. | Twelfth Summit | Cebu | Philippines | 2007 |

*(Continued)*

**Table 9.2** *(Continued)*

| S. No. | Summit | Place | Country | Year |
|---|---|---|---|---|
| 17. | Thirteenth Summit | Singapore | Singapore | 2007 |
| 18. | Fourteenth and Fifteenth Summits | Cha-Am Hua Hin | Thailand | 2009 (in March and October, respectively) |
| 19. | Sixteenth and Seventeenth Summits | Hanoi | Vietnam | 2010 (in April and October) |
| 20. | Eighteenth and Nineteenth Summits | Jakarta (May) Bali (November) | Indonesia | 2011 |
| 21. | Twentieth and Twenty-first Summits | Phnom Penh | Cambodia | 2012 (in April and November) |
| 22. | Twenty-second and Twenty-third Summits | Bandar Seri Begawan | Brunei Darussalam | 2013 (in April and October) |
| 23. | Twenty-fourth and Twenty-fifth Summits | Nay Pi Taw | Myanmar | 2014 (in May and November) |
| 24. | Twenty-sixth and Twenty-seventh Summits | Kuala Lumpur | Malaysia | 2015 (in April and November) |
| 25. | Twenty-eighth and Twenty-ninth Summits | Vientiane | Laos | 2016 (both in September) |
| 26. | Thirty and Thirty-first Summits | Pasay | Philippines | 2017 (in May and November) |
| 27. | Thirty-second and Thirty-third Summits | Singapore | Singapore | 2018 (in April and November) |
| 28. | Thirty-fourth and Thirty-fifth Summits | To be Announced | Thailand | 2019 (in March/ April and October/November) |

and Informal Summits since 1976, the year when the first ASEAN Summit took place at Bali, Indonesia. The table shows that ASEAN summits, both formal and informal, have been held regularly since 1995, although in the initial years, which could be termed as years of consolidation for the organization, summits were not held on a regular basis. Since the year 2009, ASEAN Summits are being held semi-annually, due to increasing organizational activities in recent times.

Next to the AHG in the organizational structure comes the ASEAN Ministerial Meeting (AMM). Normally, foreign ministers of member-states meet every year in this forum to review and implement policies and programmes of the organization. But other ministers may also meet under the AMM depending upon issues and programmes. For instance, if the ASEAN decides to have a programme on environmental issues, ministers of member-states related to environment matters would meet under the AMM. A body functioning parallel to the AMM is the ASEAN Economic Ministers (AEM). In this body, Economic Ministers of member-states meet once or more in a year to discuss the economic policies and programmes of the organization. ASEAN's tremendous emphasis on economic activities could be observed from the creation of the AEM alongside AMM. As per norms of the organization, both these bodies place their joint reports to the AHG during the ASEAN summit.

Next in the organizational hierarchy comes the Sectoral Ministers Meeting (SMM). In this body, ministers related to near-economic activities meet as per requirements to formulate programmes and review activities. Under the SMM falls ministries like commerce and industry, tourism, transport, agriculture and forestry. Parallel to this body remains other Non-Economic ASEAN Ministerial Meetings (N-E-AMMs). In this forum, ministers of non-economic departments meet as per requirements to plan and review agenda. Under N-E-AMM comes ministries like health, education, social welfare, science and technology, and labour. Therefore, ministers of health of member-governments can meet and discuss issues at the N-E-AMM. There is another body called the Joint Ministerial Meeting (JMM). This forum normally meets before the ASEAN summit. Under JMM, foreign and economic ministers of member-states meet before the summit to coordinate the policies and programmes of these two important departments in the ASEAN agenda.

To supervise the activities of the ASEAN all the year round, a Secretary-General is elected by member-states for a term of five years. The Secretary-General is appointed by the AHG on the recommendation of the AMM. They submit their report to the AHG, and remain accountable to this body. They preside over the meetings of the ASEAN Standing Committee (ASC). The ASC coordinates activities of different bodies of the ASEAN throughout the year, and also maintains contact with member states. Next to the ministerial-level bodies in the organization, there is an extensive network of official-level bodies like Senior Officials Meeting (SOM), Senior Economic Officials Meeting (SEOM), Other ASEAN Senior Officials Meeting (OASOM) and ASEAN National Secretariats (ANS). The ANS are located in the foreign ministries of the member-governments, and their main task is to implement ASEAN programmes in their respective states. ASEAN Committees in Third Countries (ACTC) are responsible for promoting programmes of this regional organization in non-member states. The success of the ASEAN in recent years has been possible due to this extensive and very strong organizational network.

## Other Collaborative Forums

Apart from this main organizational structure, the ASEAN has also developed—with non-members—very important international collaborative forums to promote its interests. In its initial years, the ASEAN had provided the 'dialogue partner' label to ten states and organizations. These are: Australia, Canada, China, European Union (EU), India, Japan, South Korea, New Zealand, Russia and the United States. The dialogue partners are also known as the ASEAN-10. In 2006, it was given observer status at the UN General Assembly. In response, it made the UN a dialogue partner the same year. It further extended its cooperation to the three major countries of South East Asia—China, Japan and South Korea—to create the ASEAN-3 in 1999. Although the ASEAN was initially apprehensive about China and Japan on grounds of security, with its increasing emphasis on economy, it felt the necessity to establish cordial relations with these three major economies of the region. Its economic success also drew these three states towards establishing ties with this organization and creating ASEAN-3. In 1994, it created the ASEAN Regional Forum (ARF) with twenty-two nations. The purpose for the creation of the ARF was to work for peace, security and economic development in the Asia-Pacific region. Ten ASEAN members, along with ten dialogue partners and two observers (Mongolia and Papua New Guinea), came together to create the ARF. The membership of the ARF has increased. With five new members included, the total in 2010 is twenty-seven. These five new members are Bangladesh, North Korea, Pakistan, Sri Lanka and Timor-Leste. In 2005, an East Asian Summit (EAS) was created under the auspices of the ASEAN with sixteen member-states which include ASEAN members, ASEAN-3, and India, Australia and New Zealand. The EAS was a prerequisite to a proposed East Asian Community (EAC). So far, three East Asian Summits were held in 2005, 2006 and 2007. The fourth summit took place in 2009. Further, the ASEAN has completed Free Trade Agreements (FTA) with China, Japan, South Korea, Australia and New Zealand. It has plans to launch an ASEAN Economic Community by 2015. The signing of the FTA with different countries has given a big boost to an already flourishing ASEAN economy. ASEAN has also established diplomatic relations with several individual nations in the world. This extensive network of international collaborative mechanism has benefited the association in significant ways like strengthening its economy, and consolidating its political standing in a new international order after the Cold War.

## ASEAN Free Trade Area and Related Free Trade Agreements

At the fourth ASEAN Summit in Singapore in 1992, the ASEAN Free Trade Area (AFTA) was launched. The ASEAN had earlier created the ASEAN Preferential Trading Arrangement (APTA) in 1977. The AFTA has given tremendous boost to regional economy as well as to individual national economies. In 1993, a year after the launch of the AFTA, the volume of intra-ASEAN trade was US $43.26 billion. It increased to US $80 billion in 1996. In 2006, the volume of intra-ASEAN trade reached a staggering US $352.75 billion (all figures from the web site of the ASEAN Secretariat). In comparison, intra-SAARC trade was a little over US $7 billion in 2006. In 2008, the volume of intra-regional trade in the ASEAN amounted to more than 50 per cent of the total trade of the member-states, while it was 15 per cent in 1967, when the association was formed. Compared to that, intra-regional trade in the SAARC was 5.5 per cent of the total trade of SAARC-members in 2008.

The organization has created the ASEAN Comprehensive Investment Area (ACIA) to encourage free flow of investment within the ASEAN. The ACIA aims to achieve the following: (1) elimination of investment impediments; (2) streamlining of investment processes and procedures; (3) enhancement of transparency; (4) immediate grant of national treatment to ASEAN investors; (5) undertaking of investment facilitation measures and (6) opening of all industries for investment, with a few exclusions. Full realization of the ACIA—with the removal of temporary exclusion lists in manufacturing, agriculture, fisheries, forestry and mining—is scheduled to be achieved for most ASEAN members by 2010 and for Cambodia, Laos, Myanmar and Vietnam by 2015. The ASEAN has concluded free trade agreements with China, South Korea, Japan, Australia and New Zealand. Further, free trade agreements with India and the EU are on the anvil.

## The ASEAN Charter

The members of the ASEAN launched the ASEAN Charter in Jakarta on 15 December 2008. It was earlier signed by member-states at the thirteenth ASEAN Summit in Singapore in November 2007, with the aim of moving closer to an 'EU-style community'. The charter turned the ASEAN into a legal entity and aims to create a single FTA for the region encompassing 500 million people. Some of its objectives are: (1) respect for the independence, sovereignty and territorial integrity of member-states; (2) peaceful settlement of disputes; (3) non-interference in internal affairs of member-states; (4) right to live without external interference; (5) establishment of a human rights body and an unresolved dispute mechanism, to be decided at ASEAN summits; (6) development of friendly external relations with international organizations like the UN and (7) increasing the number of ASEAN summits to twice a year and the ability to meet in emergency situations.

The ongoing global financial crisis (2008–09) was referred to in the charter as a threat to the goals envisioned by the charter, but the ASEAN was convinced that the crisis could be overcome.

## The ASEAN: An Evaluation

When the ASEAN started its journey in 1967, the region of South East Asia was much diverse politically, culturally and in its socio-economic areas. The region had a communist giant like China, an economic stalwart like Japan with its pro-capitalist leanings, emerging economies like Singapore and South Korea, and vastly poor areas like Myanmar, Laos, Vietnam, Cambodia and Thailand. The founding members of the ASEAN wanted to avoid both China and Japan, the regional bigwigs, and representatives of the communist and the capitalist world. But the success of the organization was in great doubt without these regional powers. Initially, through the mechanism called the ASEAN, the founding members wanted to have a security cover around themselves to thwart any possible aggression from China or South Korea, or economic suzerainty by Japan. But gradually, when these fears started to lessen, the ASEAN concentrated more on economic activities and the turnaround began to be noticed. The economic integration of this greatly diverse region gradually helped to eliminate political and security differences, and instilled confidence in member-states as well as non-member countries of the ASEAN about the prospects of this organization.

The success of the ASEAN in economic integration has been noteworthy. The steady growth of intra-ASEAN trade over the years remains a testimony to this proposition. Members also benefited from intra-ASEAN trade and foreign direct investment into the region which was quite significant since the 1980s. But the ASEAN's records in non-economic areas have not been as spectacular. Its interaction with civil society institutions and its role in the promotion of democracy and human rights among member-states are not very satisfactory. Its role in facilitating a democratic government in Myanmar is negligible. It is true that the ASEAN works on the principle of non-interference into members' internal affairs. However, it could pressurize Myanmar in several other ways to establish democracy and human rights in that country. The Bali Concord II, adopted by the ASEAN in 2003, upheld the notion of 'democratic peace' which asserted members' faith in democracy to establish regional peace and stability. The rule of Military Junta in Myanmar is contrary to the pledge of Bali Accord II. It is alleged by critics that ASEAN business has been managed through close interpersonal contacts among the political elites only, which often show a reluctance to institutionalize and legalize cooperation that can undermine their regime's control over regional cooperation. As a consequence, interaction of the ASEAN with civil society institutions remained at its minimum.

In spite of such criticisms, it should be acknowledged that the success of the ASEAN has outweighed its defects. Its achievements, especially in economic areas, have been recognized by all major states of the world, and international organizations including the UN. It is expected that its charter would go a long way in eradicating the shortcomings of the ASEAN and make it a very successful regional organization. The promise in the charter to create a human rights body and a dispute resolve mechanism could bring in expected changes in the organization. Nevertheless, the ASEAN has already made a mark as an important regional organization, and it should be remembered for what it has achieved over the years and not for what it could achieve.

# The European Union

## Origin

Today's EU came into existence in 1993, after the Masstricht Treaty—signed in 1991 in the Dutch city of Masstricht to form the EU—was ratified by the national parliaments of twelve signing countries. The recent Lisbon Treaty that was signed by member-states in Lisbon, the capital of Portugal, in December 2007, made the EU more efficient and effective to take on the challenges of the twenty-first century. The treaty finally came in to effect in December 2009. It made several significant reforms in the structural and functional areas of the EU, to make it a new-look organization compared to what it was after the Masstricht treaty. The reforms made by the Lisbon Treaty will be analysed later, but before that, we must know about the origin of the EU.

The formation of the EU was the outcome of a long historical process that started after the Second World War. The formation of a regional organization in Europe for economic growth after the Second World War was the brainchild of two French politicians, Jean Monnet and Robert Schuman. They planned the formation of this organization to control and enhance business related to coal and steel, the two principal items for industrial development at that time. This idea, which later came to be known as the Schuman Plan (Schuman was the Foreign Minister of France), was materialized through the creation of the European Coal and Steel Community (ECSC) in 1950. France, Germany, Italy and three Benelux countries—Belgium, Netherlands and Luxembourg—joined hands to form the ECSC. Its purpose was to bring the coal and steel industries of these six countries under one regulatory authority to maintain uniform rates in buying and selling of coal and steel, and to control these industries in the six countries. The ECSC was largely under private control, and its management used to keep close links with the Labour Unions of coal and steel industries.

In 1952, the six members of the ECSC formed a European Defence Community (EDC) by another treaty. The objective of the EDC was to create a Unified Military Command in Europe with contribution of defence personnel from members of the ECSC and other willing states. But the unified military command could not be created due to differences of opinion between France and Britain. The ECSC countries also attempted to form a European Political Community in 1953, but this plan too failed due to differences among member-states. A major step towards a unified Europe was the Treaty of Rome of 1957. By this treaty, the ECSC countries formed two very important regional organizations of Europe, the European Atomic Energy Community (also known as the Euratom) and the European Economic Community (EEC). It may be mentioned here that the ECSC was the first regional organization in Europe after the Second World War, and its members endeavoured to build the concept of a 'unified Europe'. It was due to their efforts that the Euratom and the EEC were formed. The EEC later came to be known as the Economic Community (EC), and also as the Common Market of Europe, where trade without barriers, political or economic, could be carried out. It was considered the real predecessor of today's EU, because the concept of economic integration on a regional basis was introduced for the first time in the EEC. The idea of FTA, which became popular in the era of globalization, was mooted successfully in Europe by the EEC. Similar to the EEC, the EU today is also trying to achieve economic integration for Europe.

In accordance with provisions in the Treaty of Rome, a Customs Union was created by the ECSC members in 1969. The main objective of this union was to achieve a unified rate of tariffs for its members. The concept of common market was also introduced by these members, and the common market facilitated the unhindered movement of goods, labour and capital among the six countries. In 1960, a Common Agricultural Policy (CAP) was created by the EEC to regulate agriculture-related activities and business. The idea of the common market gradually became popular in Europe, and three more nations, Britain, Ireland and Denmark, joined the EEC in 1973, Greece joined in 1981, and Portugal and Spain in 1986. The community started to become truly 'European' with the joining of new members.

The Treaty of Rome (1957) was drastically amended in 1986, and the Single European Act thereby passed to expedite the process of a unified Europe. In 1987, the European Parliament was made more representative by allowing more members to become part of it. The European Court of Justice (ECJ), established in 1957, was also strengthened. It was given the power to annul any national law that might contravene the Single European Act. Experts consider the ECJ more powerful than the International Court of Justice of the United Nations. The amendments made in the Treaty of Rome in 1986 immensely helped in consolidating the concept of the integration of Europe, and paved ways for the creation of a EU.

In 1991, twelve EEC members met in Masstricht to further strengthen the concept of an integrated Europe. These twelve members were Belgium, Britain, Denmark, France, Germany, Greece, Ireland, Italy, Luxembourg, Netherlands, Portugal and Spain. A treaty was signed in Masstricht to change the name of the EEC to EU. It was decided that this treaty would come into effect after the national parliaments of the twelve signing members ratified it. This ratification process took two more years, and the EU came into existence on 1 November 1993, after the ratification process was complete. In 1995, the Schengen Treaty was signed by members of the EU to facilitate borderless travel, which effectively means travel across the member states with a single passport. The Masstricht Treaty not only created the EU, it also outlined the future programmes of the organization. It set three major goals for the EU. The first of these goals was the creation of a monetary union for the EU, whose main objective would be to introduce a common currency for member-states of the union instead of separate national currencies. Accordingly, 'euro', a common currency, was introduced in 1999 in several member-states. It replaced the earlier national currencies (like Franc, Lira or Marc) of these states. At this moment, euro has been adopted by nineteen member-countries of the EU, and more are likely to introduce this common currency. The second goal set by the treaty was the creation of a European Police Agency (EPA) to check various types of crimes, mainly in the border areas. The third objective is to achieve political and military unity of Europe. A unified military command and a common foreign policy for member-states are parts of this objective. But this third goal would be difficult to realize for the EU because it might infringe upon the sovereignty of member-states. Nevertheless, the introduction of the euro in several states and the creation of the EPA are major achievements on the part of the EU, which has consolidated itself as a regional organization, helped immensely by sixty-eight years (1950–2018) of invaluable experience in regional integration in modern times.

## Membership and Organizational Structure

From twelve in 1993, the membership of the EU has risen to twenty-eight at present. Membership will expand further as a few candidates like Croatia, Macedonia and Turkey will join the union soon. The present twenty-eight members are: Austria, Belgium, Bulgaria, Cyprus, the Czech Republic, Croatia, Denmark, Estonia, Finland, France, Germany, Greece, Hungary, Ireland, Italy, Latvia, Lithuania, Luxembourg, Malta, the Netherlands, Poland, Portugal, Romania, Slovakia, Slovenia, Spain, Sweden and the United Kingdom. The EU has named Albania, Bosnia-Herzegovina, Montenegro and Serbia as potential candidates. To join the EU, a country must meet the Copenhagen criteria, defined at the 1993 Copenhagen European Council meeting. These criteria include: (1) a stable democracy which respects human rights and the rule of law; (2) a functioning market economy capable of competition within the EU and (3) the acceptance of the obligations of membership, including EU law. Evaluation of a country's appeal for membership and fulfilment of the criteria is the responsibility of the European Council. It must be noted in this context that in June 2016, a referendum was held in Britain on the issue of Britain's continuity as a member in the EU. As a majority of the voters (51.89 per cent) wanted Britain to leave the EU, British Prime Minister Theresa May, a leading proponent for the country's exit from the union, initiated legal procedures in March 2017 for the same. Till this process is completed, the United Kingdom is counted as a member of the EU.

The organizational structure of the EU is rather simple as compared to the extensive and complex one of the ASEAN. At the top of this structure is the European Council, consisting of Heads of Government (HOGs) of the member-states. At present, twenty-seven HOG from twenty-seven member-states make the European Council, which is the highest decision-making body of the organization. The council is headed by a system of rotating presidency, with every member-state assuming the responsibility of the President of the European Council for six months. Next to the European Council in the organizational hierarchy is the Council of Ministers, consisting normally of foreign ministers of member-states. It adopts policies and programmes for the EU and places them for approval with the European Council. In the Council of Ministers, other ministers may join and discuss policies depending upon the agenda. Thus, if there is an agenda on health, health ministers of all member-states may join this council. After the Council of Ministers in the organizational structure comes the European Commission, which is the pivotal organ of the EU. The commission now consists of twenty-seven commissioners from member-states, appointed for a term of four years, with provisions for re-appointment. It supervises the activities of the union throughout the year. The commissioners nominate one person as the President of the Commission from among them. The responsibility for implementation of the policies adopted by the European Council lies with the Commission. The council meets the President of the European Commission twice a year to discuss implementation of the policies and programmes of the union. The commission also controls the staff of the EU, known as the Eurocrats. The headquarters of the EU is situated in Brussels, the capital city of Belgium.

Apart from these three bodies (European Council, Council of Ministers and European Commission), other prominent institutions in the EU are the European Parliament, the ECJ, and the Economic and Social Committee. The European Parliament has been given some powers recently. The 785 members of the European Parliament (MEPs) are directly elected every five years by citizens under the union. Although MEPs are elected on a national basis, they sit according to political groups rather than their nationality. Each country has a set number of seats. The Parliament and the European Council form and pass legislation jointly, using co-decision, in several areas of policy. The Parliament also has the power to reject or censure the budget of the European Commission and the EU. The President of the Parliament also carries out the role of the speaker in the Parliament and represents it externally. The President and the vice-presidents are elected by MEPs every two and a half years. The judicial branch of the EU consists of the ECJ and the Court of First Instance (CFI). Together, they interpret and apply the treaties and the laws of the union. The CFI deals mainly with cases taken by individuals and companies directly before the EU's courts; and the ECJ with cases taken by member-states and institutions, as also cases referred to it by the courts of member-states. Decisions of the CFI can be appealed against at the ECJ, but only on a valid legal point. Member-states of the EU are responsible for their own territorial defence.

## The EU Today

The EU has traversed a long way since its formation with the Masstricht Treaty of 1993. Several new members have joined the organization, many new policies and programmes were undertaken, and norms and laws were changed to keep pace with time. A few more treaties were signed by member-states to meet new challenges faced by the EU. Prominent among these was the Amsterdam Treaty, which was signed in 1996 and became effective in 1999. This treaty called for the creation of more jobs within the EU, sustainable development of the environment, and protection of consumer rights. The Treaty of Nice, which came into force in 2003 (and was signed in 2001), wanted to make the union more efficient and streamlined. For this purpose, it proposed a reduction in the number of Eurocrats, which was nearly 15,000 at the beginning of the twenty-first century. The Lisbon Treaty, that came into effect in December 2009, has given more power to the European Parliament and the ECJ. The salient features of the treaty, that made important reforms in the EU, are given in Box 9.1.

Today's EU is an economic powerhouse. Since its origin, it has established a single economic market across the territories of all its members. Considered a single economy, this regional organization generated an estimated nominal gross domestic product (GDP) of US $16.48 trillion

**Box 9.1** **Major Reforms of the EU Introduced by Lisbon Treaty (2009)**

i. *A more democratic and transparent Europe*: The treaty has provided for a strengthened role for the European Parliament and national parliaments, more opportunities for citizens to have their voices heard and a clearer sense of who does what at European and national levels. It explicitly recognizes, for the first time, the possibility for a member-state to withdraw from the union.
ii. *A more efficient Europe*: The treaty, with simplified working methods and voting rules, streamlined modern institutions for a EU of twenty-seven members and an improved ability to act in areas of priority for today's union.
iii. *A Europe of rights and values, freedom, solidarity and security*: It also promoted the union's values, by introducing the Charter of Fundamental Rights into European primary law, and providing for new solidarity mechanisms, and ensuring better protection of European citizens.
iv. *Europe as an actor on the global stage*: The treaty seeks to achieve this goal by bringing together Europe's external policy tools, both when developing and deciding new policies. The treaty gives Europe a clear voice in relations with its partners worldwide. It harnesses Europe's economic, humanitarian, political and diplomatic strengths to promote European interests and values worldwide, while respecting particular interests of the member-states in foreign affairs.

Adopted with changes from the web site of the EU http://europa.eu./lisbon_treaty/glance/index_eu.htm/. Retrieved on 28 March 2010.

(based on purchasing power parity or PPP) in 2016, amounting to over 20 per cent of the world's total economic output in terms of purchasing power parity. This makes the EU the largest economy in the world on the basis of nominal GDP and the second largest trade bloc economy in the world based on PPP valuation of GDP. It is also the largest exporter of goods, the second largest importer and one of the biggest trading partners to several large countries such as India, China and Brazil. More than one-third of the 500 largest corporations in the world (Fortune 500 companies), measured by revenue, have their headquarters in the EU. The euro, within a decade of its introduction in 1999, has become one of the strongest currencies in the world. The success of the EU in achieving economic integration in the continent could be ascertained from the fact that more and more countries are showing interest in joining it. Many of these countries include the former East Bloc nations who want to be part of the mainstream economic development process of Europe today, and they have found in the union a very effective forum to realize their economic and political objectives.

However, there are grey areas within the EU. In August 2017, unemployment in the union stood at 7.6 per cent while investment was at 21.4 per cent of GDP; inflation was 2.2 per cent and public deficit –0.9 per cent of GDP. Moreover, there is a great deal of variance in annual per capita income within individual EU states, ranging from US $7,000 in poorer states (mainly in the East) to US $69,000 in rich countries. Compared to the EU average, the US GDP per capita is 35 per cent higher and the Japanese GDP per capita is approximately 15 per cent higher. The union currently imports 82 per cent of its oil, 57 per cent of its gas and 97.48 per cent of its uranium demands (all statistics in this section are from the official EU website). There is the concern that this organization is largely dependent on other countries, primarily Russia, for its energy sources, and any adverse relations with Russia may hinder its progress. The financial crisis in Greece in 2010 also posed challenges to the EU. Differences between France and Germany over the ways to resolve the crisis, and EU's role in this matter, made the EU appear like a disunited organization. Despite these shortcomings, the EU has emerged, due to its success noted earlier, as one of the most successful regional organizations in the world, with important economic and political clout in international affairs.

## The Future of the Union

The dream of a unified Europe is nothing new. Through ages, statesmen and the political elite have tried to achieve this dream. This desire could be noticed in Bismarck and Garibaldi; the aggression of Napoleon and Hitler also reflected their desire to bring the whole of Europe under their command. This dream has survived across ages in some form or the other, and the EU was its latest manifestation. But at the same time, it is also true that Europe could never be unified politically or economically despite several attempts. The idea of a unified Europe had always remained out of bounds. This dichotomy leads one to ponder over the future of the EU, its acceptability in all parts of the continent and its possible challenges. It is now well known that the formation of the union was never an easy task. Member-states had prolonged debates in domestic political circles before becoming part of either the EEC or the EU. Britain is a case in point. The conservative government of Margaret Thatcher was reluctant to join the EEC fearing that a common market might be detrimental for Britain's developed economy. Later, the Labour Government of John Major decided to join the EEC. In 2016 again, the Theresa May government in Britain held a referendum on the issue of Britain's membership in the EU. As a majority of voters wanted to leave, Prime Minister Theresa May initiated legal procedures in March 2017 for Britain's withdrawal from the EU. Whether the EU stands to lose or gain from the British exit (popularly known as Brexit) will be assessed in the future; however, this is surely a jolt to the concept of a 'single Europe'. Further, the introduction of a Customs Union or a common currency faced several hurdles. Even today, the euro has not been accepted by several member-states; notable among them are Britain, Denmark and Sweden, considered as leading economies in Europe. Unless a uniform bank interest rate is introduced, inflation is controlled and national income achieves some sort of parity in member-states; it would be difficult to introduce euro in all states, especially in the developed ones. This poses a challenge to the concept of a single monetary union in the EU.

Politically, Russia's lukewarm response to be a part of the EU may prove to be a serious hurdle in its march to the East. If Russia does not join eventually, the union's dream of a unified Europe would get a severe jolt, not only politically but also economically, because it is dependent on Russia for its energy resources. Moreover, a militarily powerful non-member like Russia may bring in trouble for it. Along with Russia, a few former Soviet states have also stayed away from the EU casting doubts about its acceptability. Further, the EU's slow progress in achieving a unified military command and a common foreign policy highlights the unwillingness of member-states to place it above national interests.

Despite these challenges faced by the EU, it must be remembered that it is not a supranational organization. It pays due respect to the sovereignty and territorial integrity of member-states, and, like any other regional organization, does not impose its will upon the members. The EU is also considering a proposal under the Lisbon Treaty to allow members to withdraw from the organization. But more and more countries in Europe, including former East Bloc nations, are joining it. This reveals the growing credibility of the organization. Besides its goal of economic integration of Europe, it has also been focusing on socio-political, cultural, educational, scientific and environmental development of the 'Euro zone' that consists of territories of member-states. The activities of the union not only benefit itself, it helps the member-states as well, particularly the developing ones. Since the formation of the union, members with weaker economies have reaped rich benefits through preferential and barrier-less trade with the developed parts of Europe. The developed economies have also been benefited because new and large markets have opened up for them through the EU. The success of the EU as an economic organization is attracting both non-members and third parties in other parts of the world. Consequently, it is growing and is poised to expand further in the coming years.

# The African Union

## Origin and Membership

Today's African Union (AU) is the continuation of the earlier Organization of African Unity (OAU), established on 25 May 1963 in Addis Ababa, capital of Ethiopia. The main objective of the OAU was to achieve unity among African nations and to work for the development of the region. It started its journey in 1963 with thirty-two member-states. Its name was changed to the African Union at its Durban Conference in 2002. Currently, the AU has fifty-five member-states, including three suspended ones. Almost all states in the African continent are its members. Box 9.2 lists the current members of the AU.

**Box 9.2** **Current Member-States of the African Union**

Algeria, Angola, Benin, Botswana, Burkina Faso, Burundi, Cameroon, Cape Verde, Central African Republic, Chad, Comoros, Côte d'Ivoire (Ivory Coast), Democratic Republic of the Congo, Republic of the Congo, Djibouti, Egypt, Equatorial Guinea, Eritrea, Ethiopia, Gabon, Gambia, Ghana, Guinea-Bissau, Kenya, Lesotho, Liberia, Libya, Malawi, Mali, Mauritius, Morocco, Mozambique, Namibia, Niger, Nigeria, Rwanda, Western Sahara (SADR), São Tomé and Príncipe, Senegal, Seychelles, Sierra Leone, Somalia, South Africa, South Sudan, Sudan, Swaziland, Tanzania, Togo, Tunisia, Uganda, Zambia, and Zimbabwe.

The three suspended members are Mauritania (suspended after the coup d'état of 2008), Guinea (suspended after the coup d'état of 2008) and Madagascar (suspended after the Malagasy political crisis of 2009). Morocco left the OAU in 1984, but joined the AU again in 2017. South Sudan joined the organization in 2011 after it seceded from Sudan and became an independent state. A member must adhere to the principles and objectives of the African Union which are to promote cooperation among member-states through mutual respect of each member's sovereignty and territorial integrity.

## Organizational Structure

The AU works mainly through ten principal institutions. They are: (1) the Assembly; (2) the Executive Council; (3) the Commission; (4) the Pan-African Parliament; (5) the African Court of Justice; (6) the Permanent Representative Commission; (7) the Specialized Technical Commissions; (8) the Economic, Social, and Cultural Council; (9) the Peace and Security Council and (10) the Financial Institutions. As their names suggest, these bodies work in different fields that include social, cultural, political, economic, technical, peace and security, legal and juridical areas. The first three institutions are the administrative bodies of the AU. The Assembly remains at the top in the organizational hierarchy, and is composed of the HOGs or Heads of State of member-states. It meets once a year to make policy decisions for the organization. Next comes the Executive Council (EC). It is a forum of foreign ministers and other ministers (depending on the issue under consideraton) and is responsible for implementing the policies taken by the assembly. The EC meets twice a year to review the works of the AU, and recommends issues to the assembly for consideration. In reality, the EC is the main policy-making body and the assembly merely approves its decisions. The Commission is the third important administrative body of the AU. Formerly, it was known as the Secretariat. It supervises the activities of the union throughout the year. The Chairperson of the commission (formerly the Secretary-General) is the administrative head, and coordinates work among different bodies of the AU. The commission is accountable to the assembly. It has its headquarters in Addis Ababa.

The Pan-African Parliament under the African Union, situated at Midrand, South Africa, is composed of 265 elected representatives from all the fifty-three member-states. Apart from discussion, debates and legislation over matters related to the union, the Parliament also ensures civil society participation in the functioning of the union. The African Court of Justice has been set up to give its ruling in disputes over interpretation of AU treaties. The Permanent Representatives' Committee consists of nominated permanent representatives of member-states; it decides the work to be done by the Executive Council. The Peace and Security Council (PSC) intends to work as a collective security mechanism and plans to facilitate early warning arrangement for timely and effective response to conflict and crisis situations in Africa. Other responsibilities of the PSC include prevention, management and resolution of conflicts; and post-conflict peace-building and development of common defence policies. The PSC has fifteen members elected on a regional basis by the assembly.

The Economic, Social and Cultural Council is an advisory organ composed of professional and civic representatives from member-states. Specialized Technical Committees (STC) have been proposed to be set up, and they are not yet functional. The ten proposed areas on which STC would be set up are: (1) energy, natural resources and environment; (2) trade and customs;

(3) labour and social affairs; (4) rural economy and agricultural matters; (5) monetary and financial affairs; (6) industry, science and technology; (7) transport, communications and tourism; (8) health; (9) education, culture, and human resources and (10) transport, communications and tourism. Financial institutions have also been proposed. These include: (1) the African Central Bank in Abuja, Nigeria; (2) the African Investment Bank in Tripoli, Libya; and (3) the African Monetary Fund, to be located in Yaounde, Cameroon. Eventually, the AU aims to have a single currency (the Afro), like the euro.

## The AU (and the Former OAU) at Work

The main purpose of establishing the OAU was to achieve unity among African nations and to speed up the process of de-colonization in the African continent that had started after the Second World War. The OAU was not a military coalition like the NATO; it was founded with the aim to achieve political unification in Africa, although it also endeavoured to achieve economic integration in the continent after the Cold War. But political unification of a continent torn in conflicts and civil wars was not an easy proposition. The OAU struggled a lot in its initial years to survive as an effective regional organization. For instance, it was practically divided over the issue of civil war in Angola. Angola, which was under Portuguese rule for a long time, became independent in 1974. But soon after the Portuguese relinquished power, different political groups in Angola were engaged in a bloody civil war to capture state power while Cold War politics added fuel to the fire. One political group known as the Popular Movement for the Liberation of Angola (MPLA) was supported by the Soviet Union and its allies; while opposing groups like the National Front for the Liberation of Angola (FNLA) and the National Union for the Total Independence of Angola (UNITA) was aided by the United States and its allies. In 1975, the OAU organized a vote over the issue of formation of the government in Angola, where the organization's internal squabbles came to light. Half of the members supported the MPLA while the other half supported the FNLA and the UNITA. As a consequence, the union was not in a position to solve the crisis in Angola. Its lack of unity also came to the fore over issues like military intervention in Katanga province of the then Zaire (now Congo) in 1977–78; Somalia's attack of Ethiopia in 1978 and war between Uganda and Tanzania in 1978–79. Further, in 1981, Morocco, along with a few members, opposed the inclusion of western Sahara into the organization with the status of an independent nation. The animosity over the issue reached such a point that Morocco relinquished membership of the OAU. These events substantiate the fact that the OAU was not very successful in achieving unity in African continent in the 1970s and 1980s.

But the history of the OAU is not altogether a story of failures. In 1965, it succeeded in resolving border disputes between Algeria and Morocco. It was able to solve border conflicts between Somalia and Ethiopia, and between Somalia and Kenya, during 1968 and 1970. It played a much commendable role in the process of de-colonization in Africa in the 1960s and 1970s, as also thereafter. During this period, the OAU actively helped countries like Guinea Bissau, Angola and Mozambique in their freedom struggles against Portuguese rule. It was mainly due to its efforts that these three states got independence in 1974. Moreover, it fought intensely the menace of Apartheid in South Africa, Zimbabwe and Namibia. South Africa was suspended from the OAU for practising Apartheid. In 1994, it regained its membership of the organization after it officially announced the end of Apartheid policies. In 1986, the OAU formed the African Commission on Human and People's Rights with a view to safeguard human rights and the fundamental freedoms of the people of Africa. All these activities of the OAU immensely helped the member-states as well as the people of Africa, and contributed towards strengthening African unity.

With the aim to facilitate economic integration of Africa through free trade, the members of the OAU formed the African Economic Community (AEC) in 1994. The 1990s was, in fact, a decade of resuscitation for the OAU under the able leadership of the then Secretary-General Salim Ahmed Salim. He was instrumental in the introduction of new economic and social policies in the organization and for bringing about dynamism in its functioning. In 1992, Salim created a Peace Fund to encourage its member-states in avoiding political conflicts and working towards establishment of peace. The main purpose behind the creation of this fund was to rehabilitate victims of political conflicts, to dissuade states from engaging in political conflicts, and to campaign for peace. In 1993, the OAU also sent a peacekeeping force to stop civil war in Liberia. Salim, a popular leader from Tanzania, served three terms as the Secretary-General of the OAU. Under his efficient leadership, the organization scaled new heights to achieve political unity and economic integration—its principal goals—in Africa.

## An Evaluation of the AU

The AU, and the OAU, its immediate predecessor, had many daunting tasks before them. Realizing programmes like de-colonization, anti-apartheid, or political and economic integration of Africa were indeed great challenges for the organization. The OAU also had to tackle problems like intense political rivalries among member-states or civil wars among opposing political groups within the territories of a number of member-states. At times, these political crises threatened to divide and break the organization. But it continued to act as an umbrella organization which tried to provide peace and security to its members. The performance of the OAU was mixed in this regard—it failed to bring peace to warring zones on several occasions; while at other times, it was able to provide peace and security to the people of troubled areas in Africa. It helped many African states to achieve freedom from colonial rulers, to fight the menace of apartheid, and to strive towards economic development. The 1970s and the 1980s were troubled times for the OAU, mainly due to socio-political problems in the member-states. This was also the period of consolidation and maturity for the organization. In comparison, since the 1990s it was a period of progression when the OAU launched several new economic and socio-political programmes; the union changed its name in 2002.

If the OAU dealt mainly with socio-political issues, the African Union concentrated more on economic issues, keeping pace with the changing demands of time. The future plans of the AU to establish a monetary union for Africa—along the lines of the EU—include the creation of a FTA, a customs union, a single market, a central bank and a common currency. The union aims at having a single currency for Africa by 2023. Its emphasis on economic issues may usher in new hopes for an economically poor Africa, which lags behind several of its states in terms of GDP. The GDP of all these states stands at a nominal US $500 billion—which is lower than that of many of them individually—while they together had a debt of US $200 billion in 2017. Africa, an economically backward continent, needs strong economic policies for resurgence, and the AU is working positively in that direction.

Emphasis on economic programmes does not in any way undermine the challenges faced by the AU in social and political spheres. Africa is still in political turmoil with severe political crises in Zimbabwe, Sudan, Somalia and Mauritania. Political rivalry among warring groups, leading to problems of governance, is the main reason behind political crises in these states. Keeping in with one of its objectives—to 'promote peace, security, and stability in the continent'—the PSC of the AU is actively engaged in negotiating peace through peacekeeping operations in these areas. Social problems like illiteracy, poverty, health hazards and environmental degradation, to name a few, are real challenges for the union. Africa ranks very high in cases of malaria and AIDS, as also in the rate of literacy and level of poverty. The union has proposed specialized technical committees (STCs) to deal with such issues. Hopefully, with the guidance of the AU, Africa would be able to resolve these problems in the future.

The African Union has not been as successful as the EU or the ASEAN, because it had to face more political problems within the organization than the earlier two. The process of economic integration started much earlier in the EU and ASEAN, and they reaped great benefits from such programmes. The AU started the process of economic integration as late as 1994; it would take some time more to get the benefits of these policies. At the eighteenth Ordinary Session of the Assembly of Heads of State and Government of the African Union, held in Addis Ababa, Ethiopia, in January 2012, a decision to establish a Continental Free Trade Area (CFTA) was adopted. The CFTA was expected to be operative in 2017. However, it would take some more time for the CFTA to be effective. As observed earlier, due to social and political problems, the AU could not initiate the process of economic integration during the 1970s and 1980s. However, since the early 1990s, it has taken measures to achieve such integration, as well as to address socio-political problems of the continent. The results are yielding slowly. The union itself has become more consolidated as an organization in recent years, and is taking specific initiatives for the development of Africa. If this trend continues, the AU would emerge as a strong regional organization in years to come.

# North American Free Trade Agreement (NAFTA)

## Origin and Members

The North American Free Trade Agreement (NAFTA) is a trilateral trade agreement among three North American states—the United States, Canada and Mexico. It entered into force on 1 January 1994, after it was ratified by the parliaments of the three nations in 1992. This agreement superseded the Canada–United States Free Trade Agreement, made in 1988. Today, the NAFTA is considered to be one of the most powerful trade blocs in the world because two of its members—Canada and the United States—are among the strongest economies of the globe. It controls the entire spectrum of present North American trade. Since it became operative in 1994, it has been updated with two major additions, the North American Agreement for Economic Cooperation (NAAEC) and the North American Agreement for Labor Cooperation (NAALC). A much recent addition was the Security and Prosperity Partnership of North America, designed to foster cooperation on issues of national security. The NAFTA Secretariat is an independent agency, responsible for impartial administration of provisions of dispute settlement in the NAFTA. It has a section each for Canada, Mexico and the United States, each headed by a national secretary, and each having an office in the respective national capitals—Ottawa, Mexico City and Washington DC. The secretariat is accountable to the NAFTA Free Trade Commission, which comprises ministers responsible for international trade in the three NAFTA partner-states.

## Objectives

The objectives of the NAFTA have been elaborated in Article 102 of the agreement. The article states:

> The objectives of this Agreement, as elaborated more specifically through its principles and rules, including national treatment, most-favoured-nation treatment, and transparency, are to: (a) eliminate barriers to trade in, and facilitate the cross-border movement of goods and services between the territories of the Parties; (b) promote conditions of fair competition in the free trade area; (c) increase substantially investment opportunities in the territories of the Parties; (d) provide adequate and effective protection and enforcement of intellectual property rights in each Party's territory; (e) create effective procedures for the implementation and application of this Agreement, for its joint administration and for the resolution of disputes; and (f) establish a framework for further trilateral, regional and multilateral cooperation to expand and enhance the benefits of this Agreement.

It was decided at the time of its formation that the NAFTA would gradually phase out all tariff reductions by the year 2008. This has been done successfully. The removal of tariff barriers had boosted trade in North America, as earlier Mexico used to avoid American and Canadian goods because of higher tariff rates. Intra-regional trade has now increased significantly.

## The NAFTA and Regional Trade

Trade relations among Canada, Mexico and the United States have broadened substantially since the implementation of the NAFTA. According to data released by the US Trade Representative (USTR), the overall value of intra-North American trade has more than tripled since then. The USTR adds that regional business investment in the United States rose by 117 per cent between 1993 and 2007, as compared to a 45 per cent rise in the fourteen years prior to the implementation of the NAFTA. Trade with NAFTA-partners now accounts for more than 80 per cent of Canadian and Mexican trade, and more than a third of US trade. In a report entitled 'Top US Export Markets: Free Trade Areas and Country Fact Sheets' released in the summer of 2008, the US Department of Commerce noted that 'overall trade in goods among the United States, the Canada and Mexico has grown from $297 billion in 1993 to $930 billion in 2007, an increase of 213 per cent'. Citing the positive impact of the agreement on regional trade, the report also noted that export of US goods to Canada and Mexico grew from US $142 billion in 1993 to $385.4 billion in 2007, an increase of 171 per cent. Similarly, import of goods from Canada and Mexico into the United States grew from $151 billion in 1993 to $523.9 billion in 2007, an increase of 247 per cent. A Council on Foreign Relations' (a reputed think tank in the United States) recent report observes:

> Economists largely agree that NAFTA has provided benefits to the North American econo-

> mies. Regional trade increased sharply over the treaty's first two decades, from roughly $290 billion in 1993 to more than $1.1 trillion in 2016. Cross-border investment has also surged, with U.S. foreign direct investment (FDI) stock in Mexico increasing in that period from $15 billion to more than $100 billion.[1]

Member-states have largely benefited from the NAFTA. Since 1994, Mexico's GDP has increased at an average annual rate of 2.7 per cent, which is lower than those of the United States (3.3 per cent) and Canada (3.6 per cent). Since the implementation of the agreement, Mexican exports to the United States have quadrupled from $60 billion to $280 billion per year. US exports to Mexico have also increased sharply—more than triple—as Mexico's economy has grown. Trade liberalization between Mexico and the United States has not only brought about a great change in Mexican business, it has directly benefited the Mexican people. For instance, the Council on Foreign Relations (CFR) thinks that the deal has led to a dramatic reduction in prices for Mexican consumers; it refers to GEA, a Mexico City-based economic consulting firm, which estimates that the cost of basic household goods in Mexico has halved since the implementation of the agreement.

Like the United States and Mexico, Canada—leading exporter of goods to the United States—too has experienced economic growth since implementation of the NAFTA. In fact, since 1994, its GDP has grown at a rate faster than those of the other two. Between 1994 and 2003, Canada's economy showed an average annual growth rate of 3.6 per cent, compared to 3.3 per cent in the United States and 2.7 per cent in Mexico. Canadian employment levels have also shown steady gains in recent years, with overall employment rising from 14.9 million to 15.7 million in the early 2000s (data obtained from the CFR report). The NAFTA has thus strengthened regional trade and helped the member-states to develop their economies further. According to the CFR report mentioned earlier, 'In the years since NAFTA, U.S. trade with its North American neighbors has more than tripled, growing more rapidly than U.S. trade with the rest of the world'.[2] This refers to a period from 1993 to 2016.

## Controversies Over the Agreement

There emanated controversies from all member-states over the actual success of the NAFTA. Canada protested over several provisions in the text of the agreement. It found chapters 11, 19 and 20 controversial and called for amendments in them. Chapter 11 allows corporations or individuals to sue Mexico, Canada or the United States for compensation if any action taken by those governments adversely affect their investments. Chapter 19 subjects crucial NAFTA-issues (such as antidumping and countervailing duty (AD/CVD) determinations) to bi-national panel review instead of the conventional judicial review practised in other FTA. Chapter 20 provides a procedure for inter-state resolution of disputes over the application and the interpretation of the NAFTA.

Further, the CFR report cites several scholars who argue that the deal has not proved beneficial for Mexico. According to the report, these scholars believe that economic growth has been poor in Mexico, averaging less than 3.5 per cent per year or less than 2 per cent on a per capita basis since 2000. Today unemployment rate is higher than what it was when the treaty was signed; and half of the country's labour force sustains a living in invented jobs in the informal economy, a figure 10 per cent higher than in the pre-NAFTA years. Some critics single out Mexico's farm industry, saying the agreement has crippled Mexican farming prospects by opening competition to the heavily-subsidized US farm industry. Although such criticisms are contradicted by supporters of the NAFTA, they nevertheless point towards the weak areas of this trilateral agreement. In the run-up to the American presidential elections in 2008, Democratic Party nominees Barack Obama and Hillary Clinton also sought revisions in the NAFTA to make it more time-friendly and progressive. According to the CFR report cited earlier:

> Critics of the deal (NAFTA), however, argue that it is to blame for job losses and wage stagnation in the United States, driven by low-wage competition, companies moving production to Mexico to lower costs, and a widening trade deficit. The U.S.-Mexico trade balance swung from a $1.7 billion U.S. surplus in 1993 to a $54 billion deficit by 2014.[3]

This kind of negative perception about NAFTA prompted President Donald Trump of the United States to talk about renegotiation of the deal and, if possible, to terminate it. In an interview to *Reuters* on 17 January 2018, President Trump was quoted as saying, 'We're renegotiating NAFTA now. We'll see what happens. I may terminate NAFTA'.[4] President Trump's comments came less than a week before trade negotiators from the United States, Canada and Mexico were scheduled to meet in Montreal for the sixth rounds of negotiations to update NAFTA.

## The Future of the NAFTA

The NAFTA is the largest trading bloc in the world in terms of combined purchasing power parity (PPP), GDP of its members and the second largest by nominal GDP comparison. It is a unique trilateral agreement where two of the world's most developed economies joined hands with a third world economy (Mexico) for boosting regional trade and business. Unlike the EU, the ASEAN or the AU, the NAFTA is primarily an economic bloc, which was formed with economic objectives. At its inception in 1994, it had set target to gradually phase out tariff barriers in trade latest by 2008. The target was achieved. This shows the commitment of member-states towards the agreement.

As noted earlier, the NAFTA has significantly benefited regional trade and helped member-states to develop their economies. Many had believed that Mexico, a relatively weak economy in the organization, would benefit the most from agreement. As data given earlier reveals, the NAFTA proved immensely beneficial not only for Mexico, but for Canada and the United States as well. However, it is true that the agreement could not realize all its expectations, and there are reservations about its contribution towards the economic development of member-states, especially Mexico. Criticisms notwithstanding, the NAFTA has consolidated remarkably well as an organization in the last fifteen years, and has become one of the strongest trading blocs in the world. It achieved its most important goal of removing all tariff barriers by 2008; and this would hopefully help it make better progress in the future. The years ahead are of crucial importance—the actual power of this organization could be assessed better now when there are no tariff barriers. If the United States finally withdraws from NAFTA citing American interests, the trade regime would surely get a jolt. Canada and Mexico are in favour of continuing with the NAFTA. President Trump also wanted to follow a flexible approach towards his withdrawal proposal.[5] Therefore, the future of NAFTA hangs in balance. If it wishes to exist as a noteworthy trade regime in North America, as well as in the world, it must try to remove trade imbalances among participating countries.

QUESTIONS

1. Make a critical estimate of the SAARC as a regional organization.
2. Write a note on the SAFTA.
3. Describe the composition and functions of the ASEAN.
4. Analyse the significance of the EU as a regional organization.
5. Examine the role of the African Union as a regional organization.
6. Give a brief account of the NAFTA.

## ENDNOTES

1. Backgrounder by James McBride, https://www.cfr.org/experts/james-mcbride and Mohammed Aly Sergie, https://www.cfr.org/experts/mohammed-aly-sergie. Last updated October 4, 2017, 'NAFTA's Economic Impact'. Accessed on 11 February 2018.
2. *Ibid.*
3. Backgrounder by James McBride and Mohammed Aly Sergie, https://www.cfr.org. Last updated October 4, 2017, 'NAFTA's Economic Impact'. Accessed on 11 February 2018.
4. Business News, January 18, 2018 / 6:22 AM / 2 MONTHS AGO. 'Exclusive: Trump Says Terminating NAFTA Would Yield the 'Best Deal' in Renegotiations. Jeff Mason, https://www.reuters.com/journalists/jeff-mason and David Lawder, https://www.reuters.com/journalists/david-lawder; https://www.reuters.com/
5. *Ibid.*

# 10 International Political Economy

Political Economy is not too new a branch of study in social science. It developed with the spread of capitalism in Europe, as also with the progress of academic discourses on capitalism, spearheaded by scholars like Adam Smith, David Ricardo, Karl Marx, Friedrich Engels, Max Weber and others. It attempts to analyse the impact of economic activities on politics and statecraft, and how economy and politics interact with one another. Likewise, International Political Economy (IPE) is the study of international relations on the basis of economic activities taking place around the world and their analyses. With the onset of globalization from the mid-1980s, a renewed interest in IPE has developed among scholars. Along with political perspectives and issues of security, the study of international relations today involves economic analyses. The continuing significance of trade and commerce in international relations; the increasing impact of economic institutions like the World Trade Organization (WTO), the International Monetary Fund (IMF) and the Free Trade Agreements (FTA); and the growing importance of multinational corporations (MNCs) in world politics, have been instrumental in the revival of interest in IPE in recent times. Now IPE constitutes one of the most significant areas in the study of international relations.

IPE itself is much vast in scope. It includes several issues like international trade regime, international monetary regime and international investment regime, with emphasis on economic institutions, organizations and activities; FTA among nation-states; economic development and disparity in different countries; globalization; the North–South divide and the future of capitalism and socialism. Almost all of these issues generated academic debates and gave birth to a host of theories in IPE. Of the different issues of IPE, this chapter proposes to analyse the global economic order after the Second World War; the international economic order as it exists today; and future economic trends of the world. The discussion begins with the international economic order after the Second World War that had largely contributed towards the development of the present global economic order.

## From Bretton Woods to the WTO

When the Second World War was nearing its end, with the defeat of the Axis powers in sight, leaders of the winning combination started discussions on the post–Second World War global politics and economy. In July 1944, 730 delegates from forty-four allied nations met in Bretton Woods, New Hampshire (United States), at the United Nations Monetary and Fiscal Conference to discuss and plan the world economic regime after the war. At the concluding stages of the conference, the delegates signed the 'Bretton Woods Agreement' to monitor the international economic system after the war. With a view to regulate the international monetary system, the delegates at Bretton Woods established the IMF and the International Bank for Reconstruction and Development (IBRD), which are part of the World Bank Group today. These organizations started to function in 1945 after the agreement was ratified by the participating countries. A major feature of the Bretton Woods Agreement was the necessity for each country to adopt a fiscal policy that would maintain the exchange rate of its currency within a fixed value. In other words, the main purpose of this agreement was to prevent currency disorders and to stabilize exchange rates through a regulated economic system. The IMF was created to bridge temporary imbalances of payments. Thus, for the international economy, leaders at Bretton Woods favoured a system of regulated market with tight controls on the value of currencies. Although there were disagreements on the methods of implementation of this regulated system, all agreed on the necessity for tight controls, given the experience of the Great (economic) Depression of the 1930s and the setback to European economy during the Second World War.

The theoretical position behind the Bretton Woods Agreement was strengthened by the Keynesian economic model, named after noted American Economist John Maynard Keynes, who favoured a controlled market economy with state intervention. Free trade with reduced tariff rates and liberal market economy were favoured by the Keynesian school of economists, but the state would not be invisible in these economic activities. In the international economic system, a high degree of cooperation among states was emphasized by the agreement; but to control this cooperation, institutions like the IMF and the IBRD would act as watchdogs. The global economic crises in the period between the first and the second world wars were attributed to a lack of cooperation among nation-states, as also the absence of any effective regulatory authority to monitor the global economic order. The agreement wanted to overcome these deficiencies of the inter-war period by establishing such cooperatives and monitoring agencies. Through such endeavours, it actually founded the modern international economic system that still thrives on cooperation among nation-states, although private economic actors play a significant role in today's IPE.

In the lines of the Bretton Woods system that aimed to establish international trade, monetary and investment regimes, a new mechanism known as the General Agreement on Tariffs and Trade (GATT) was created in 1947. The GATT was a part of the international trade regime while the IMF and the IBRD were parts of international monetary and investment regimes respectively. Earlier, plans to launch an International Trade Organization (ITO) had failed in 1946. Although mooted in 1947, the GATT finally became operational on 1 January 1948 when twenty-three countries signed the agreement. These countries were: Australia, Belgium, Brazil, Burma, Canada, Ceylon, Chile, China, Cuba, Czechoslovakia, France, India, Lebanon, Luxembourg, Netherlands, New Zealand, Norway, Pakistan, Southern Rhodesia, Syria, South Africa, the United Kingdom and the United States. It should be remembered in this context that the GATT was not an organization, it was a treaty. Its main objective was to reduce barriers in international trade. This was achieved through the reduction of tariff barriers, and through quantitative restrictions and subsidies on trade by executing a series of agreements. From its first round of talks in Annecy in 1949—excluding the 1947 round in Geneva that established the agreement—to its concluding round in Uruguay in 1993 (started in 1986), the GATT achieved around 45 per cent tariff reductions on several items in world trade. In terms of monetary value, around US $1,200 billion worth of tariff concessions were achieved by the agreement by 1993. Starting with twenty-three members-states in 1948, 123 members participated in the Uruguay round of negotiations. Besides tariff reduction, the GATT also negotiated on issues like non-tariff measures, rules, services, intellectual property, dispute settlement, textiles, agriculture, labour standards, environment, competition, investment, transparency and patents.

The Uruguay round of GATT negotiations decided to establish the WTO that would replace the GATT as the main body to monitor international trade regime. The WTO became operational in 1995 after the Marrakesh Agreement was signed. Since its inception in 1993, it has been acting as an important body to monitor and control international economic activities. The 153 member-states of organization represent 90 per cent of world trade. The details of WTO-membership, its purposes, organizational structure and impact on world economy and politics are analysed in this chapter.

# World Trade Organization (WTO)

## Objectives and Membership

The WTO is primarily an organization for the liberalization of international trade. It is also a forum for governments to negotiate trade agreements. Those member-states which face trade barriers and want them removed or lowered can negotiate at the WTO. Such negotiations may help to liberalize trade. But the organization is not all about liberalizing trade; in some cases its rules may support maintaining trade barriers in order to protect consumers' rights or to prevent the spread of diseases. The WTO set of rules mostly covers agreements, negotiated and signed by the member-states. These documents provide the legal ground rules for international trade and commerce. They are actually contracts, binding governments to keep their trade policies within agreed limits. Although contracted by member-governments, the WTO does not confine itself to governmental trade only; it also seeks to help private producers of goods and services, exporters and importers to conduct their business. At the same time, it encourages governments to meet their social and environmental commitments. A major purpose of the WTO, according to its official web site (http//www.wto.org) is as follows:

> To help trade flow as freely as possible ... so long as there are no undesirable side-effects ... because this is important for economic development and well-being. That partly means removing obstacles. It also means ensuring that individuals, companies and governments know what the trade rules are around the world, and giving them the confidence that there will be no sudden changes of policy. In other words, the rules have to be 'transparent' and predictable.

Moreover, resolving conflicting interests among trading nations is another important objective of the WTO. The dispute settlement mechanism, according to its agreements, includes some neutral procedures based on an agreed legal foundation. As per the official web site, 'WTO members have agreed that if they believe fellow-members are violating trade rules, they will use the multilateral system of settling disputes instead of taking action unilaterally. That means abiding by the agreed procedures and respecting judgments'. Unlike the GATT, the WTO now has an elaborate mechanism and a definite time frame to settle disputes. The Dispute Settlement Body (DSB) of the organization is responsible for resolving differences among trading parties.

The WTO currently has 164 members (as of December 2017). The 123 states that attended the Uruguay round of the GATT became its founder-members in 1995. Forty one more nations joined subsequently. Box 10.1 lists the current members of the WTO.

**Box 10.1 Current Members of the WTO**

Afghanistan, Albania, Angola, Antigua and Barbuda, Argentina, Armenia, Australia, Austria, Bahrain, Bangladesh, Barbados, Belgium, Belize, Benin, Bolivia, Botswana, Brazil, Brunei, Bulgaria, Burkina Faso, Burundi, Cambodia, Cameroon, Canada, Cape Verde, Central African Republic, Chad, Chile, China, Colombia, Republic of Congo, Costa Rica, Côte d'Ivoire, Croatia, Cuba, Cyprus, Czech Republic, Democratic Republic of Congo, Denmark, Djibouti, Dominica, Dominican Republic, Ecuador, Egypt, El Salvador, Estonia, European Union, Fiji, Finland, France, Gabon, Gambia, Georgia, Germany, Ghana, Greece, Grenada, Guatemala, Guinea, Guinea-Bissau, Guyana, Haiti, Honduras, Hong Kong (China), Hungary, Iceland, India, Indonesia, Ireland, Israel, Italy, Jamaica, Japan, Jordan, Kenya, Korea (Republic of), Kuwait, Kyrgyz Republic, Laos, Latvia, Lesotho, Liberia, Liechtenstein, Lithuania, Luxembourg, Macao (China), Macedonia, Madagascar, Malawi, Malaysia, Maldives, Mali, Malta, Mauritania, Mauritius, Mexico, Moldova, Mongolia, Montenegro, Morocco, Mozambique, Myanmar, Namibia, Nepal, Netherlands, New Zealand, Nicaragua, Niger, Nigeria, Norway, Oman, Pakistan, Panama, Papua New Guinea, Paraguay, Peru, Philippines, Poland, Portugal, Qatar, Romania, Russia, Rwanda, St. Kitts and Nevis, St. Lucia, St. Vincent and the Grenadines, Samoa, Saudi Arabia, Senegal, Sierra Leone, Singapore, Slovak Republic, Slovenia, Solomon Islands, South Africa, Spain, Sri Lanka, Surinam, Swaziland, Sweden, Switzerland, Tajikistan, Chinese Taipei, Tanzania, Thailand, Togo, Tonga, Trinidad and Tobago, Tunisia, Turkey, Uganda, Ukraine, United Arab Emirates, United Kingdom, United States, Uruguay, Vanuatu, Venezuela, Vietnam, Yemen, Zambia, Zimbabwe.

As of December 2017, the WTO has twenty-three states as observers. All the members have joined the WTO as a result of negotiation. Membership in this organization, as stated in the official web site of the WTO, means:

> ... a balance of rights and obligations. They enjoy the privileges that other member-countries give to them and the security that the trading rules provide. In return, they had to make commitments to open their markets and to abide by the rules—those commitments were the result of the membership (or "accession") negotiations.

Membership in the WTO is gained through a long accession process that involves several rounds of negotiation between the aspiring member and other existing members and WTO bodies. For legal reasons, the European Union (EU) is officially known as the European Communities in the business of the WTO. The EU is a WTO-member in its own right, as are each of the other member-states.

## Organizational Structure and Voting

The WTO has a very elaborate organizational structure. At the top remains the Ministerial Conference (MC), that acts as the highest decision-making body of the organization. It is composed of representatives (ministers) of all the members of the WTO and meets at least once every two years. Since the establishment of the organization in 1995, seven MCs have been held so far, the first being in Singapore in 1996. The first conference provided an opportunity to members to plan and declare the major initiatives of the organization. It addressed, among other issues, the continuation of negotiations for a higher level of liberalization in the services sector. It also adopted the Comprehensive and Integrated WTO Plan of Action for least-developed countries. At the end of the conference, the ministers adopted the Singapore Ministerial Declaration. It reaffirmed WTO-members' support of the multilateral trading system and set out the WTO work programme for the next few years. The second conference was held in Geneva, Switzerland, in 1998, and the third in Seattle, United States, in 1999. The fourth conference in Doha, Qatar, in 2001 needs special mention because the Doha Development Agenda (DDA) or the Doha Round was launched here. It also included China as the 143rd member of the WTO. The DDA wanted to make globalization more inclusive and help the world's poor, particularly by slashing barriers and subsidies in farming. It comprised boosting trade liberalization as well as making of new rules, with commitments to strengthen substantial assistance to developing countries. The fifth ministerial conference was organized in Cancun, Mexico, in 2003. It aimed at reaching agreements on the DDA. But the North–South divide over economic issues became pronounced in this conference with G-20 countries (led by China and India) from the South resisting moves by the Northern countries (led by the United States and Britain) to impose trade terms as per their design. As a result, negotiations at this conference reached a deadlock. The sixth MC took place in Hong Kong, China, in 2005. Here members agreed to phase out all their agricultural export subsidies by the end of 2013, and terminate any cotton export subsidies by the end of 2006. This conference accorded a few concessions to developing countries that included an agreement to introduce duty-free, tariff-free access for goods from the least-developed countries. Several other important issues were left for further negotiation to be completed by the end of 2010.

The General Council comes next in the organizational hierarchy. In effect, it is the real executive head of the WTO, meeting regularly to carry out the functions of the organization. The council has representatives (usually ambassadors or their equivalent) from all member-states and has the authority to act on behalf of the MC. It has its office at the headquarters of the WTO in Geneva. The council has several committees, working groups and working parties under its control. Some important committees are: (1) Committee on Trade and Environment; (2) Committee on Trade and Development (with Subcommittee on Least-Developed Countries); (3) Committee on Regional Trade Agreements; (4) Committee on Balance of Payments Restrictions and (5) Committee on Budget, Finance and Administration. The names of the committees are suggestive of their functions and programmes. The council also has Working Parties on 'accession' of new members to the organization. Further, it has Working Groups on these: (1) trade, debt and finance and (2) trade and technology transfer. Under the broader umbrella of the General Council, three different councils exist. These are: (1) Council for Trade in Goods (CTG); (2) Council for Trade-related aspects of Intellectual Property Rights (CTIPR) and (3) Council for Trade in Services (CTS).

The CTG has committees in the following areas under its jurisdiction: (1) market access; (2) agriculture; (3) sanitary and phytosanitary measures; (4) technical barriers to trade; (5) subsidies and countervailing measures; (6) anti-dumping practices; (7) customs valuation; (8) rules of origin; (9) import licensing; (10) trade-related investment measures and (11) safeguards. It also has a working party on state-trading enterprises. The CTIPR has no committees, working parties or working groups attached to it. The CTS has committees on trade in financial services, and specific commitments. It also has working parties on domestic regulation, and General Agreement on Trade in Services (GATS) rules.

The General Council also meets as the Trade Policy Review Body. The negotiations under the DDA take place in the Trade Negotiations Committee (TNC) and its subsidiaries. This includes negotiations on agriculture and services that began in early 2000. The TNC also operates under the authority of the council. Each year, new chairpersons for the major WTO-bodies are approved by the council. The General Council has thus been entrusted with myriad tasks and given enormous powers to effectively manage and control the activities of the WTO.

Each member-state in the WTO has one vote, but voting has never taken place in the organization. Decisions are generally made by consensus in order to find the most widely acceptable decision. However, it requires a long time and several rounds of negotiation to reach general consensus. Sometimes, it becomes difficult to arrive at a consensus, and negotiations fail. But since trade-related issues are linked to national interests, the WTO has relied on consensus decision-making. However, in reality, negotiations at the WTO are conducted through a process of informal negotiations between small groups of states. Such negotiations are widely known as 'Green Room' negotiations (named after the colour of the WTO Director-General's office in Geneva), or 'Mini-Ministerials,' when they take place outside the organization.

## Main Functions of the WTO

Among many functions of the WTO, the following are important: (1) assisting and developing transitional economies; (2) providing specialized help for export promotion; (3) extending cooperation in global economic policy-making; (4) monitoring implementation of the agreements covered and (5) maintaining the basic principles of international trade. An analysis of these functions would highlight the major activities of the WTO today. A discussion on these functions follows.

### Assisting and Developing Transitional Economies

About 75 per cent of the total WTO-membership belongs to developing states. Developing states like China, Brazil, India, Mexico, Indonesia and others play an increasingly significant role in the organization. The WTO pays due attention to the special needs and problems of developing and transitional economies. Such assistance may cover anything from providing help in dealing with negotiations to joining the WTO and fulfilling its commitments to providing guidance as to how to participate effectively in multilateral negotiations through training and workshops. Developing states, and particularly the least-developed among them, are furnished with trade and tariff data relating to their individual export interests and to their participation in WTO-bodies. New members with transitional economies immensely benefit from these services.

### Providing Specialized Help for Export Promotion

The WTO offers specialized help for export promotion to its members through the International Trade Centre that was established by the GATT in 1964. Now, it is jointly operated by the WTO and the United Nations, the latter operating through the UN Conference on Trade and

Development (UNCTAD). The centre receives requests from member-states, especially developing states, for assistance in formulating and implementing export promotion programmes as well as import operations and techniques. It is actively engaged in taking actions after receiving requests from the members. The centre provides information and advice on export markets and marketing techniques. It also assists in establishing export promotion and marketing services, and in training personnel required for these services. The centre's help is freely available to the least-developed states. The WTO's commitment to upliftment of the world economy is effectively fulfilled through this function.

## Extending Cooperation in Global Economic Policy-making

A major aspect of the WTO's mandate is to cooperate with the IMF, the World Bank and other multilateral institutions to achieve greater coherence in global economic policy-making. At the Marrakesh Ministerial Meeting in April 1994, a separate Ministerial Declaration was adopted to fulfill this objective. The declaration recognizes the link between different aspects of economic policy, and the responsibility of the WTO to maintain and improve cooperation with international organizations like the IMF and World Bank involved in monetary and financial matters. It also took account of the impact of trade liberalization on the growth and development of national economies. It says that this is an increasingly important component in the success of the economic adjustment programmes which many WTO members are undertaking in an era of globalization.

## Monitoring Implementation of the Agreements Covered

The WTO oversees about sixty different agreements which have the status of international legal documents. Member-governments must sign and ratify all WTO agreements on accession. Some of the important agreements that the organization monitors are discussed here. (1) GATS: The GATS was created to extend the multilateral trading system to the service sector, in the same way as the GATT provided such a system for merchandise trade. The agreement entered into force in January 1995. (2) Agreement on Agriculture (AoA): The AoA came into effect with the establishment of the WTO at the beginning of 1995. It has three central concepts or 'pillars': domestic support, market access and export subsidies. (3) Trade-Related Aspects of Intellectual Property Rights Agreement (TRIPS): The agreement on TRIPS sets down minimum standards for many forms of intellectual property (IP) regulation. It was negotiated at the end of the Uruguay Round of the GATT in 1994. (4) Agreement on Technical Barriers to Trade (TBT): The TBT Agreement is an international treaty of the WTO. It was negotiated during the Uruguay Round of the GATT, and entered into force with the establishment of the WTO in 1995. The treaty ensures that 'technical negotiations and standards, as well as testing and certification procedures, do not create unnecessary obstacles to trade'. (5) Sanitary and Phytosanitary (SPS) Agreement: The SPS Agreement on the Application of Sanitary and Phytosanitary Measures was also negotiated during the Uruguay Round of the GATT and entered into force with the establishment of the WTO in 1995. Under this agreement, the organization sets constraints on members' policies relating to food safety (bacterial contaminants, pesticides, inspection and labelling) as well as animal and plant health (imported pests and diseases). Through monitoring and implementation of the agreements covered, the WTO tries to maintain a practice of fair trade across the world.

### Maintaining the Basic Principles of International Trade

The WTO is committed to maintain certain basic principles in the conduct of international trade. They are: transparency; reciprocity; respect to commitments, non-discrimination among member-states and safety measures. The principle of transparency requires member-states to publish their trade regulations, to respond to requests for information by other members and to notify changes in trade policies to the WTO. The principle of reciprocity prevents members from taking unilateral trade-liberalizing policies. It reflects the commitment of the WTO to secure multilateral trade negotiations for equal access to foreign markets and trade gains. Respect to commitments is the principle that requires a member-state to fulfill its tariff commitments with regard to other members or partners. The Ceiling Bindings, enumerated in the Schedule of Concessions of tariffs, must be respected by member-states of the WTO. The principle of non-discrimination followed by the WTO has two major components: the Most Favoured Nation (MFN) rule, and the National Treatment Policy (NTP). The MFN rule requires that a WTO-member grants the most favourable conditions for trade in a certain product type to all other WTO-members. In other words, a WTO-member must provide the same conditions on all trade to other WTO-members. The NTP refers to equal treatment of imported and locally-produced goods to tackle non-tariff barriers to trade. Finally, the principle of safety measures allows member-governments to restrict trade under specific circumstances to prevent malpractices and discrimination.

The WTO also acts as a Dispute Settlement Body (DSB). The General Council of the organization has been entrusted with these two important tasks. Dispute settlement is considered as one of the significant contributions of the WTO in a multilateral international trading system; the organization thus has an elaborate dispute settlement mechanism. All WTO-members have agreed to use the multilateral system of settling disputes instead of taking action unilaterally. The dispute settlement process of the organization involves the panels of the DSB, the WTO Secretariat, the Appellate Body, arbitrators, independent experts and many specialized institutions. The WTO is currently engaged in the Doha Round of trade negotiations launched in 2001. Issues like tariffs, non-tariff measures, agriculture, labour standards, environment, competition, investment, transparency and patents come under the purview of this round. Discontent prevails among member-states over issues under negotiation in the Doha Round here. In accordance with its principles, the WTO is trying to follow the policy of non-discrimination in the Doha Round.

## WTO: An Appraisal

Since its establishment in 1995, the WTO has generated a lot of controversy over its trade-liberalizing policies and the methods of implementing these policies. Whether free trade is an answer to economic backwardness is a much-debated issue. The economies of several modern industrialized states were developed in the nineteenth and early twentieth centuries, although with trade barriers. The United States and Western European states are examples in this regard. After satisfactory and sufficient levels of economic development, these states have opted for free and liberal trade. Whether a newly independent state with immature political and economic infrastructure can afford trade without restrictions remains a controversial theoretical issue today. Leaving aside newly independent states, whether all developing economies can follow liberal trade policies with unrestricted exposure to international markets also remains doubtful. These controversies lead to a schism about the very concept of the WTO. People interested in the affairs of the WTO can broadly be categorized into two groups: 'defenders' and 'opponents' of the WTO. It appears that neither group is happy about the organization. The defenders, normally supporters of liberal trade, comprise the rich industrialized states. They are wary of the WTO because of its 'level playing field' policies that are reflected through principles like the MFN and the NTP. The opponents, usually the developing states, complain about discriminatory policies of the WTO that, they allege, favour the rich countries. They cite the example of unequal negotiations in the WTO, where bargaining depends on the strength of the economy and the size of the market. This kind of negotiation harms the interest of smaller developing economies. All these controversies had paralysed negotiations of the organization in the recent past. The Seattle Ministerial Conference in 1999 eventually failed, while the Cancun Ministerial Conference in 2003 witnessed severe animosity between the rich North and the poor South over trade-related issues.

The WTO's policies related to environment, labour and intellectual property rights (IPR) have also drawn criticism from different corners. Over environmental issues, the North–South divide is clearly pronounced. The industrialized North alleges that environmental safeguards are not properly maintained in third world industrial zones, while the Southern states complain that 'greenhouse effect' is at its maximum in developed states because polluting emissions are very high in industrialized states. The WTO-negotiations on environment did not prove to be effective in settling such disputes. Labour unions condemn the WTO for lacking in protection of labour rights. With the spread of globalization and free trade, labour rights require stringent protection. But the WTO has not been very successful in this area, allege different labour unions around the world. The IPR has also become a significant, though controversial, issue in the organization. The TRIPS Agreement, that sets down minimum standards for many forms of intellectual property regulations, was considered unnecessary in international trade by several economists. Non-trade agenda like the TRIPS may dilute real trade issues in the WTO. Further, member-states are not much satisfied with TRIPS-regulations. The French have been alleging that free trade in films would actually destroy French cinema, which the French perceive as a cultural icon. The TRIPS may not be enough to prevent such cultural intrusions.

It appears, therefore, that the WTO has become the perennial 'whipping boy' in the discussions of IPE. However, it has many 'successes'. The DSB has earned accolades for settling more than a hundred disputes in its short period of existence. Member-states see in this body a fair and impartial mechanism whose rulings are enforceable and acceptable. Developing states are now frequently using this forum against the might of powerful economies, because the DSB, on several occasions, had upheld their pleas against strong economies. The DSB has thus earned the confidence of member-states, both rich and poor. Further, the WTO has successfully concluded negotiations on liberalizing international markets in financial services, maritime services and telecommunications, with global accord. The liberalization process was due to be completed in the Uruguay Round, but was deferred for later negotiations. This has enhanced the credibility of the organization as a body for liberalizing trade.

An international trade regime is necessary in the age of globalization. But how this trade regime would represent itself and operate are important issues. In the early years of its existence, the WTO showed less maturity and tactlessness in handling trade-related issues, and presented itself as the extended arm of American trade interests. As a result, it could not initially generate much enthusiasm among developing states. The Seattle and the Cancun demonstrations against its policies were reflective of this trend. But now more and more developing states are willing to join the organization. This is not only because isolation is impossible in global trade, but also due to the increasing acceptability of the WTO as a mature custodian of the present world trade regime. Whatever be the general merits of free trade, the organization must view it with an open-minded approach, sans big-power influence. The developing states must also learn to adapt themselves to the concept and the practice of free trade that seems irreplaceable in the near future. They must not always raise their accusing finger towards stronger economies. The WTO is gradually earning their respect because it has handled many of their problems in a matured way, without big-power influence. This is important for its future because developing states make 75 per cent of its membership.

# Economic Order of the Present World

It is not easy to describe the present world economic order in a few words. This order is characterized by different factors like the existence of different types of national economies with different levels of economic development; international trade, monetary and investment regimes, as well as institutions and activities associated with them; tendency towards economic integration, regional and international; non-state economic activities spearheaded by the MNCs; free trade and globalization. Some of these issues—for instance, international trade regime with a focus on the WTO—have been discussed earlier in this chapter; while some others—for instance, trade and regional economic integration (like the EU, ASEAN or NAFTA); international political and economic integration (the UNO or WTO); globalization and theories concerning IPE (like liberalism, pluralism, Marxist theory, world systems theory [WST])—have been taken up in other chapters. In this section, the remaining issues of importance in IPE today, like divergent national economies with high level of income disparity, the role of MNC in the present economic scenario, and the North–South divide, would be highlighted.

## The Divergent Economic Order

Today's world is characterized by a high level of income disparity among states, and also by different levels of economic development. After the Second World War, different levels of economic development achieved by nation-states have led to a hypothetical division of the world into 'highly developed', 'developed' and 'developing' states. These categories are also loosely referred to as the 'first world', the 'second world' and the 'third world' respectively. The most-industrialized nations, generally known as the G-8 countries, and some others are the highly developed world today. The developed world comprises mostly the former East European bloc states and some others; while the remaining majority is termed as the developing third world. The development of a country is measured in terms of socio-economic indicators like rate of literacy, life expectancy, gross national income and gross domestic product. A country's level of development or economic growth is important in international politics because it may determine a country's stature and performance in international politics. It has been observed in international politics since the Second World War that nations with developed or growing economies have played the role of major actors. Levels of economic development thus assume increasing significance in international relations today.

The divergence in today's world economic order can be assessed by Gross National Income (GNI) per capita. The World Bank has divided countries into 'high income', 'upper-middle income', 'lower-middle income' and 'low income' categories based on GNI per capita as in 2016. Table 10.1 shows income disparity among nations in today's world.

**Table 10.1** Income Disparity Among Nations in the Present World

| High-income Countries with GNI Per Capita of US $41,208 or more | Upper-middle-income Countries with GNI Per Capita between US $8,177 and US $41,208 | Lower-middle-income Countries with GNI Per Capita between US $2,079 and US $8,177 | Low-income Countries with GNI Per Capita between US $ 612 and US $2,079 |
|---|---|---|---|
| Australia, Austria, Bahrain, Belgium, Canada, Denmark, Finland, Germany, Iceland, Ireland, Luxembourg, Netherlands, Norway, Singapore, Sweden, Switzerland, United Kingdom, United States | Antigua and Barbuda, Argentina, Bahamas, Barbados, Brazil, Brunei Darussalam, Chile, China, Costa Rica, Croatia, Cyprus, Czech Republic, Estonia, Greece, Grenada, Hungary, Israel, Italy, Japan, Kazakhstan, Kuwait, Korea (South), Latvia, Lithuania, Malaysia, Maldives, Malta, Mauritius, Mexico, Nauru, New Zealand, Palau, Panama, Poland, Portugal, Romania, Russian Federation, Saudi Arabia, Seychelles, Slovakia, Slovenia, Spain, St. Kitts and Nevis, St. Lucia, Trinidad and Tobago, Turkey, United Arab Emirates, Uruguay | Albania, Algeria, Angola, Armenia, Azerbaijan, Belarus, Belize, Bhutan, Bolivia, Bosnia, Botswana, Bulgaria, Cape Verde, Columbia, Dominican Republic, Ecuador, Egypt, El Salvador, Fiji, Gabon, Georgia, Guatemala, Guyana, Honduras, Indonesia, Iran, Iraq, Jamaica, Jordan, Kosovo, Laos, Lebanon, Macedonia, Moldova, Mongolia, Montenegro, Morocco, Namibia, Nicaragua, Nigeria, Papua New Guinea, Paraguay, Peru, Philippines, Samoa, Serbia, South Africa, Sri Lanka, Sudan, Surinam, Tonga, Tunisia, Turkmenistan, Tuvalu, Ukraine, Uzbekistan, Vietnam | Bangladesh, Benin, Burkina Faso, Cambodia, Cameroon, Chad, Congo, Ethiopia, Ghana, Guinea, Haiti, India, Kenya, Kyrgyzstan, Mali, Mauritania, Myanmar, Nepal, Pakistan, Rwanda, Senegal, Solomon Islands, Tajikistan, Tanzania, Uganda, Yemen, Zambia, Zimbabwe |

*Source*: World Bank; https://data.worldbank.org/indicator/NY.GNP.PCAP.CD. Retrieved on 3 February 2018.

It is beyond doubt that many High-income countries in column 1 in Table 10.1 such as United States, United Kingdom, Germany, Canada, Australia, Singapore and a few European nations are important actors in international economy and politics today. They exert considerable control over global politics and economy. Upper-middle-income countries such as China, Russia, Brazil, Japan and Saudi Arabia are also significant economic and political powers in the world today. Many South Asian countries such as India, Nepal, Pakistan, Bangladesh and a few African nations belong to the Low-income group of countries, presented in column 4 of the table. The high-income countries comprise the highly developed category with very high level of industrial and technological growth, and higher rates of literacy and life expectancy. The upper-middle-income nations make the developed category with significant industrial and technological progress, as also higher literacy rates and life expectancy. The next two are the developing categories with moderate or low literacy rates and life expectancy. However, it must be noted here that the GNI per capita may not be the most accurate tool of measurement of a country's economic growth. GNI per capita of countries with a big population may lag behind GNI per capita of countries with lesser population. GDP growth rates may also come into consideration in this respect. For instance, the growth of Indian economy sounds credible if one looks at GDP growth rates over the years than GNI per capita over the years. But we must also remember at this point that although there may not be any direct correlation between the GNI of a nation and its impact in international politics, it can never be denied that the 'high' and the 'upper-middle' income states enjoy advantageous position in world politics today due to their economic clout.

## The Role of MNCs

MNCs are very large organizations spanning across several countries. Normally a MNC has a particular country of origin, but it spreads its business worldwide, with rapid circulation of goods and capital. Although there is no fixed definition of MNCs, they share some similar chracteristics. They operate simultaneously in many countries, with fixed offices, facilities and employees in each of them. They operate within the parameters of the rule of law in each country. MNCs have assumed greater significance in international politics today because they have immense economic strength and exert profound political influence on the basis of their economic prowess. Before analysing the role of such a corporation in international politics today, it is important to know different types of MNCs operating in the present world. They can be broadly classified into three types: industrial corporations, financial corporations and corporations providing services. Industrial corporations produce their own goods in factories located all over the world, and sell them to various other industries and consumers locally as well as globally. They are giant corporations in terms of their revenue and areas of operation. Most of them are in the automobile, electronics, infrastructure, and oil and gas sectors. They belong to the highly developed industrialized states like the former G-7 countries. MNCs like General Motors, General Electric, Mitsubishi, Suzuki, Toyota, Sony, LG, British Petroleum, Wal-Mart and Exxon Mobil fall into this category.

Financial corporations are involved in financial business like banks, stock broking, asset management, portfolio management and mutual funds. Like industrial corporations, they also operate across boundaries. Financial giants like the HSBC (Hong Kong and Shanghai Banking Corporation), Standard Chartered, American Express Bank, Citi Bank, Deutsch Bank, JP Morgan and Merrill Lynch maintain transnational operations. Nowadays almost all financial corporations are engaged in multifarious financial activities like banking, portfolio management, stock broking and asset management, although they are subject to more stringent (domestic) legal restrictions than the industrial or 'service corporations'. With monetary transactions at the rate of $2.0 trillion per day around the globe, financial corporations are becoming increasingly important in today's IPE.

Several MNCs sell services to the people across the world. These service corporations exist, among others, in travel and tourism (mostly airlines), fast food, hotel, media and retail grocery sectors. Airlines like British Airways, Air France, Air Canada and Emirates maintain offices and staff in several countries across the globe to sell their services to people and reap profit from such services. Fast food chains like McDonald's and Kentucky and soft drinks giants like Pepsi and Coca Cola operate all over the world and earn huge sums of money through such operations. Hoteliers like Hyatt, Marriott and the Taj Groups have business interests in several countries. Media houses like the CNN and the BBC also reach out to people in different corners of the globe. Retail grocery chains like AM-PM, Lawson, Safeway supermarkets are also big MNCs operating in different countries. However, it is to be noted here that service corporations are smaller than industrial and financial corporations in terms of revenue and area of operation. But they are growing at a rapid pace and may soon catch up with other MNCs.

The role of the MNCs in international relations and IPE is highly controversial. Many analysts see them as 'agents' of their countries of origin (home country) and their governments. According to this view, the MNCs clearly have the political agenda of perpetuating the interests of its home country in other parts of the world. Thus, for example, General Motors is seen not as a purely business organization, but one that also tries to serve US national interests. A more radical view considers a national government as an 'agent' of MNCs. According to this view, the national government tries to protect and upheld the interests of the MNCs no matter how exploiting and detrimental these interests might be. The national government sees the MNC as a 'pride' for the country and tries to back it in all its ventures in different parts of the world.

A related view, mainly echoed by the Socialist School, considers the MNCs as perpetuators of neocolonialism. According to this view, MNCs help their national governments to dominate a state, especially a poor one, first through economic measures with the ultimate aim to subjugate it politically. The economic strength of the MNC is used by its home state to install or overthrow a political regime in another state with a view to bring the state under the home state's sphere of political influence. It is also believed by this school that the MNCs fund political groups, even terrorist outfits in other countries, in order to serve the interests of its home country. Although there is limited or no specific proof behind such belief, MNCs are alleged to have interests beyond purely trade and commerce in different parts of the world.

A contrary view, mainly propagated by the Liberal School of political thinkers, considers the MNCs as very important non-state actors in today's global economy. In this view, they cater to the needs of the people around the world and they are not bound by the interests of any particular country. Their only allegiance is towards their business and not towards any country. They may have countries of origin, but they pay loyalty only towards their clients and stakeholders in all parts of the globe. They are motivated by profits, and not by any political interests. In fact, according to this view, serving political interests actually harm the MNCs and they are aware of the detrimental effects of politicization. So, they resist indulging in politics and concentrate on their business, because their business interest require a very stable and peaceful international order. They are truly economic players and they actually strengthen the world economy through their commercial activities.

The MNCs are very powerful independent actors in the IPE. The annual income of many such corporations exceeds the national income per annum of several individual states. Several MNCs have a higher annual income compared to the annual revenue earned by the UNO, the largest inter-governmental organization (IGO) in the world. These comparisons bring to light the economic prowess of the MNCs in today's world. In an era of globalization, they have contributed towards global interdependence through the flow of capital and services across boundaries, as also through the creation of global infrastructure of facilities and communication networks. Although it is true that several MNCs have more economic power than many states in the world, when compared to strong industrialized states, their economic might appears to be small. The IPE is still controlled by economically powerful states, but all such states today have giant MNCs contributing towards the growth of the national economies. Therefore, the increasingly significant role of the MNCs towards the growth of national as well as global economy can never be underrated in today's world.

## The North–South Divide

The economic order of the present world is characterized by a huge gap in capital accumulation, technology, and overall standards of living between the advanced post–industrial countries of the North and the poor less-developed countries of the South. Although terms like the 'North' and the 'South' have a latent geographical connotation, they are not used in the study of the IPE in a strict geographical sense. Advanced countries south of the equator, like Australia and New Zealand, are considered part of the North in the discourses of IPE. In the terminology of the IPE, North is thus synonymous to technologically advanced rich post–industrial countries of the first world, whereas South is associated with the poor, less-developed countries of the third world. The erstwhile 'second world' countries of the East Bloc (during the Cold War period) have been gradually amalgamating into either the North or the South on the basis of their economic development. However, irrespective of conceptual ambiguity over terminology, the fact remains that the vast majority of the world's population today live in abject poverty in the South. More than a billion people in sub-Saharan Africa, South and Central Asia, Latin America and Central America live in extreme poverty without access to basic needs like food, shelter, water, sanitation, education and health care. On the contrary, people in the rich North are affluent with high levels of income, employment and social security. But why is this disparity? Scholars of international relations hold different opinions on the issue of this large gap between the North and the South. But before analysing the theoretical position on the North–South divide, a discussion on the problems of the South would be necessary.

## Problems of the South

The countries of the South share some common problems, although each country has its own 'peculiar' problem. The major problems of the South can be broadly classified into two types—economic and socio-political. To begin with the economic problems, most countries of the South could not follow an indigenous path of economic development due to long colonial rule. The colonial masters started to do their economic planning such that they suited only the needs of the colonizers, and not those of the native people. Consequently, economic activities were limited within a few areas of the country, as they failed to reach all parts of the land. After independence, countries of the South were left with legacies of colonialism, and in most cases the new political elite, due to lack of experience, followed the economic model thrust upon the state by the colonizers. Further, after independence—primarily after the Second World War—the countries of the South confronted a bipolar world of contrasting political and economic ideologies represented by the two superpowers—the United States and the Soviet Union. Due to political compulsions, many countries of the South followed either the capitalist or the socialist economic models without taking into consideration the socio-cultural background of the country. In other words, the new political elite also imposed an economic model for which the country might not have prepared itself. The result was utter confusion and lack of proper economic development. In some countries that chose 'mixed' economy, the public sector faired poorly due to over-protectionism and the culture of providing unplanned subsidy by the state. As a result, economic progress suffered immensely.

The newly independent states of the South carried enormous social and economic burdens due to oppressive colonial rule. Poverty, unemployment, population explosion, illiteracy, lack of health care and housing, and many other problems haunted these new states from the very beginning. Developmental efforts required a stupendous amount of money; these new states also did not possess that. So the ruling elite faced a great dilemma of fixing priorities for state-building through socio-economic development. For instance, a drive to remove illiteracy would have affected industrialization and vice versa. In this manner, economic development and the state-building process faced many obstacles in the South.

Industrialization and urbanization were haphazard in the countries of the South due to lack of funds and proper planning. The agriculture-based economy in these states mostly required agro-based industries, which in turn would have benefited vast rural areas and prevented migration of rural people to a few urban locations. But in many countries agro-industries were neglected. The rural people flocked to a few industrial pockets in urban areas in search of jobs. Such migration created undue pressure on the urban socio-economic infrastructure and gave birth to slums, poverty, crime, and demographic and environmental imbalance. A related problem was uncoordinated development of industry and agriculture. Due to lack of adequate funds, countries of the South could not lay coordinated emphasis both on industry and agriculture. Both these sectors suffered, because when industry was preferred, agriculture was neglected, and vice versa. Economy as a whole suffered in the long run.

In many states of the South, after independence, colonial exploitation continued in other forms. One form of such exploitation by the rich North was the creation of the 'debt trap'. The newly independent countries of the South required huge sums of money for their socio-economic developmental projects. The rich countries were too willing to lend this money to the poor South to 'help' them in their state-building activities. Money was lent at high rates of interest. The states of the South could not but borrow in order to sustain developmental activities. But many of them were not in a position to repay even the interests, let alone the principal amounts. The interests accumulated over years, as the loan amounts reached astronomic figures. A debt trap was thereby created, and the borrower had to give all kinds of economic and political benefits to the lender in its territory. This trap was a potent method of neocolonization perpetuated by the rich North over the poor South. Neocolonization is disguised exploitation in the name of providing help to poor countries for their socio-economic development. This mechanism of the debt trap was very much prevalent in IPE since the Second World War, and remained effective till the mid-1990s.

Socio-political problems in the South are not isolated phenomena; they are linked to economic problems and vice versa. For instance, political instability in less-developed countries has created obstacles for economic development. Frequent changes of government, political clashes between rival groups, civil war in some states, military or civilian dictatorship in some others—all these have created conditions of social unrest not favourable for economic progress. Steady economic development requires political stability, which remained a distant dream in many countries of the South.

The colonial rulers paid little attention to the creation of a coherent and peaceful society through the development of social sectors like education, health, housing and sanitation. On the contrary, the colonizers encouraged social divisions in the South to perpetuate their rule. Ethnic, religious, linguistic and caste differences among people were shrewdly exploited by the colonizers to segregate communities from one another, with a view to prolong their rule. They instigated one community against another so that lack of developmental work in the social sectors could be ignored by the people. The fragmented society created by the colonizers continued to exist after independence, and posed a severe hindrance to economic development and political governance in many states of the South. The colonizers did not create general facilities related to education, food, health care and housing for all. Countries of the South remained poverty-stricken and illiterate without access to the basic needs of life. Long periods of colonial rule made these countries largely backward compared to their counterparts in the North. The dearth of proper developmental activities in the social sector had created a backlog that many new states in the South inherited from their colonizers. Post-independence, it became impossible for a new state to clear the backlog and achieve parity with Northern countries.

In many countries of the South, due to a late start in the state-building process, proper political infrastructure has not yet developed. Here, political infrastructure refers to the institutions and processes that a mature political system normally possesses—like a democratically elected government and parliament; an independent election commission to conduct free and fair elections; the existence and importance of the constitution, as well as the opposition party; importance of the public opinion; free press and judiciary and rule of law. Needless to say, many states of the South do not have this political infrastructure. So, authoritarian rule prevails instead of democratic governance with no or little freedom for the press and the common man. Socio-economic development suffers in this condition.

The problems of the South and the wide North–South divide attracted the attention of scholars of international relations all over the world towards identification of the causes of this disparity. Different views exist on this huge gap between the advanced North and the less-developed South, which could be linked to several important theories in the discipline of international relations. A brief analysis of these different views is necessary for a proper understanding of the North–South divide.

## IR Theories and the North–South Divide

Marxist scholars analyse this disparity in terms of division of society into economic classes, mainly owners and non-owners. The fact that every society is controlled by the rich owning class who oppress the poor non-owning class holds true for the international order too. Since the time of Lenin, several Marxist scholars have opined that the poverty of the South is the direct fallout of accumulation of wealth by the rich capitalists of the North. The accumulated wealth is recycled in industries of the North to earn more profits and to buy workers there. The Dependency Theory and the WST, considered offshoots of the Marxist theory, link colonization by the rich North to the ultimate impoverishment of the South. WST scholars like Immanuel Wallerstein, Andre Gunder

Frank and others believe that the rich North has become the 'core' in international politics and economy by extracting raw materials from their colonies over centuries. Through such exploitation, the erstwhile colonies of the South have become the 'periphery' in the international system. The core continues to dominate the periphery because of its advantageous position in the present international order as well. As a result of this exploitation, the core gets all the blood while the 'periphery' remains anemic. The Dependency-theorists believe that it is not possible to sustain a country's economic growth only with internal resources. The capitalist path of development has created an interdependence of capital outflow, where the rich countries need to give loans and the poor ones are compelled to borrow to sustain their respective economies. But this interdependence is not marked by equality, as there is a perceptible imbalance in power relations between the North and the South, which is highly tilted, obviously, in favour of the North.

Liberal theorists, on the other hand, relate the impoverishment of the countries of the South to their failure to accumulate wealth and manage their economic and political systems effectively. According to the liberal view, the countries of the South have got enough time following independence to revamp their economy. But due to political instability and lack of adequate infrastructure, they failed to improve their economy. In an interdependent world economy, there exists ample scope for a developing economy to reap the benefits of globalization and capital outflow to become a developed one, think the liberals. Political stability and development of socio-economic infrastructure are prerequisites for economic prosperity. Many South-East Asian countries have achieved development in this way. Liberal feminist theorists, on the other hand, point out the central role of women in the process accumulation of wealth in both the North and the South. They believe that women's role in the accumulation of wealth in the North had not been properly recognized. It is time to focus on the role of women in the economic development of a country. In both the North and the South, women could play a pivotal role in the process of economic development through wealth accumulation and redistribution.

The North–South divide is a controversial area in the study of IPE today. This is evident from the fact that at present this debate is linked to many theoretical issues in the discipline of international relations. While theoretical issues of International Relations were discussed in detail in Chapter 2, theories concerning the North–South divide were taken up for a short analysis earlier in the present chapter. Having understood the North–South divide and the theoretical issues related to it, another question that concerns us at the present moment pertains to the future of the current international economic order. The next section tries to highlight this important issue.

## Future of the World Economic Order

Since the Second World War, the state system has been playing a very important role in IPE. In other words, states provide the key to the international economic system. This is apparent from the creation of the UNO, the IMF and the World Bank as parts of the UN system, and from the WTO where states are the major constituents. Despite criticism by the liberals, the state's leading role in IPE can hardly be ignored at the moment. In fact, the state's dominant role in economic activities could be observed more in the poor South than in the rich North. Economic activities are guided and protected by the state more effectively in the South than in the North. However, with the onset of globalization, mainly from the early 1980s, more and more private players have become very active in economic matters throughout the world. Although private players had remained involved in economic activities in the rich North, and in a few states of the South, since the Second World War, their increasing importance in economic affairs all over the world today can be attributed to the phenomenon of globalization. Thus, two parallel but linked actors are very active in IPE today: the states and the private corporations.

It is also argued today that with the presence of large interdependence among different states in the global economy, the post–Second World War distinction between national economy and international economic system is getting blurred. As national economies try to integrate more with the international economic order, the barrier is more frequently and consciously breached today than in earlier times. The concept of free trade across borders is gaining momentum, but not without risks. Increasing interdependence in the global economy may bring some relief to domestic economies through the inflow of capital and goods, but it may deprive people from getting vital social and economic security provided by the state. Global economic interdependence may allow national governments to shift some of its responsibilities to private and international actors, but the social costs of this transfer may bring disaster for people, particularly in the states of the South. At the same time, unilateral protectionism is also not possible in our times because it would rob a state's economy of competitiveness, and the desire to grow further and integrate itself with the international economic order.

This brings in a major dilemma in IPE of our times. Internationalization of economic activities, free trade and privatization may be necessary; but how far they can be stretched is the burning question today. The great economic recession in the United States and West Europe in 2008, mostly due to the failure of the private banking system, put a big question mark on excessive interdependence and privatization. The state had to finally step in and announce subsidy to overcome the crisis in the United States. The economic recession also posed a serious challenge to the liberal idea of free trade and internationalization in economic activities. The economic recession in 2008 proved that the liberal views of IPE, which seem to be very popular now, are not flawless and need to be reassessed further. Interdependence among global economic activities has not been effectively matched by global cooperation on ecological, health and demographic issues. This has further widened the North–South gap which may not prove to be healthy for IPE in future.

In future, international politics will thrive on economic and social inequalities between the North and the South. The growing North–South divide will increasingly challenge the wisdom of liberal economic ideas of free trade, privatization and globalization. If more than half of the world's population is deprived of the basic amenities of life, capitalist economy will be put to a litmus test. In that case, it may shift its current preference of growing internationalism to more regional trade blocs, concentrating in North America and Europe. The vast areas of the South may look back primarily to domestic economic affairs, shunning internationalism. The North–South divide may re-establish the distinction between national economy and international economic system, because no economic ideology can succeed if it divides the people on the basis of socio-economic parameters.

QUESTIONS

1. Make a critical estimate of the role of the WTO in the contemporary world.
2. Write an essay on the economic order of the contemporary world.
3. Write short notes on:
   (a) IMF.
   (b) TRIPS.
4. Analyse the role of MNCs in the contemporary world.
5. Examine the causes of the North–South divide.
6. How do you see the future of the world economic order?

# 11 Foreign Policies of Major Nations: India, The United States, China, Russia, Japan, England

## PART I

## India's Foreign Policy

### Origin and Philosophical Base

The foreign policy of any nation is the reflection of its tradition, cultural heritage and socio-political and economic conditions. Indian foreign policy is no exception. It draws inspiration from the age-old tradition of the land, its rich cultural heritage, as well as from the comparatively recent socio-political and economic experiences. India's foreign policy is imbibed with ideas of peace, universal brotherhood, non interference and non-violence. The philosophical basis of India's foreign policy is rooted in its rich cultural heritage that rests on Buddha's tolerance, Emperor Ashoka's non-violence, Sri Chaitanya's love for humanity and Kabir's religious harmony. Moreover, Guru Nanak's idea of ritual-free religion, Tagore's internationalism, Gandhi's faith in non-violence and Nehru's socialist inclination also had profound impact on India's foreign policy at its formative stage. Further, the tragic experience of the Second World War and the use of atom bombs in Hiroshima and Nagasaki led India to put its faith on non-violence and peace. The bloc politics of the post–Second World War period—characterized by the East–West divide, bi-polarity and the Cold War that led to continuous tension and war-like situations in the world—was deeply resented by India as it chose the path of non-alignment in its foreign policy. In recent times, India's foreign policy has been influenced by globalization and the idea of free market. Earlier, it was also influenced by the ideas of socialism, democracy and liberalism. Thus the philosophical base of Indian foreign policy owed its origin to the cultural heritage, socio-political and religious views of different personalities, prevalent international and domestic ideologies, as well as internal and external socio-political and economic events.

As a nation-state, India emerged in 1947, after independence from colonial rule. Any analysis of India's foreign policy begins from 15 August 1947, the day India became independent. But in effect, the origin of modern India's foreign policy could be traced back to 1946, when the Interim Government was formed to oversee the process of gaining independence. Jawaharlal Nehru, the leader of the government, and later the first Prime Minister of India, had started envisioning the foreign policy of independent India in 1946. The Second World War had just ended, and the spectre of a Cold War was prominent by that time. With his socialist inclination and utmost resentment for bloc politics, Nehru was conceptualizing the ideas of non-alignment in 1946. In a radio address to the people in 1946 as leader of the Interim Government, Nehru espoused the idea of non-alignment. In his address he said: 'We propose as far as possible to keep away from the power politics of groups, aligned against one another, which have led in the past to world wars and which may again lead to disaster on an even vaster scale'. The policy of non-alignment was thus considered as a part of India's foreign policy before independence.

The foreign policy of a state mainly has two sides to it—the first is the 'policy side', the second the 'application side'. The policy side consists of the philosophical or theoretical base of foreign policy. Generally, this part remains unaltered. The philosophical or theoretical base of foreign policy is built upon the tradition, culture, social and political history, and political ideas of great personalities of the state. The application side, on the other hand, is developed on the basis of the changing contours of national and international politics. As such, it is more pragmatic and dynamic as it has to constantly adjust itself with the changing demands of the times and politics. The application side of a state's foreign policy may not always reflect the ideologies contained in the policy side. For instance, one aspect of the theoretical base of India's foreign policy is the policy of nonalignment. But in its application, India's nonaligned policies were not beyond doubt during the Cold War period. Further, one theoretical premise of the US foreign policy is non-interference in the internal matters of sovereign independent states. But in the application of US foreign policy, one might also question if the Americans were true to this idea of non-interference during and after the Cold War. Actually, the theoretical side of a foreign policy relates to the 'idealistic plane', whereas the application side relates to the 'realistic plane'. Keeping these distinctions in mind, we proceed to discuss the basic principles of India's foreign policy.

## Basic Principles of India's Foreign Policy

The philosophical or theoretical base of India's foreign policy relates to its basic principles. Here is a brief discussion of these principles.

i. The architect of India's foreign policy, Jawaharlal Nehru believed that wars had become irrelevant in an age of nuclear weapons because any war in future would be a nuclear war that could cause immense destruction in the world. So, every state should avoid war in the nuclear age, and follow the path of peace and friendship. India denounces war and calls for peace among nation-states of the world.
ii. Following the ideologies propounded by Lord Buddha, Asoka and Gandhi, India believes in practising non-violence in the world. It believes that violence can only increase violence in international politics. Two world wars and several regional wars are testimony to this belief. So, India calls for tolerance in international affairs and avoiding any form of violence in the international order.
iii. An integral part of India's foreign policy is respect for and recognition of every state's sovereignty and territorial integrity. Every state reserves the right to determine its own course of action without external interference. India strongly reaffirms its faith in this right and believes that sovereignty and territorial integrity of each state must be preserved at any cost.
iv. India believes in harmonious coexistence with all states, especially with neighbouring countries. It always put faith in the importance of maintaining friendly, cordial relations with its neighbours. Cooperation among states all over the world, and particularly in the neighbourhood, has become more of a necessity in an era of growing terrorism. So India

wants to resolve its problems with its neighbours and also with other countries peacefully, through dialogues and negotiation, without external intervention. This is India's stand with regard to its problems with Pakistan on the Kashmir issue, and also other disturbing issues like abetting terrorism on Indian soil, drug-trafficking and ethnic issues. India firmly believes in peaceful resolution of differences among different states across the globe.

v. Belief in peace in the neighbourhood is integrally associated with India's faith in regional cooperation. India has always vowed for cooperation with its South Asian neighbours, and worked positively towards the creation of the South Asian Association for Regional Cooperation (SAARC). It is sincerely committed towards the principle of regional peace and cooperation, and is very much interested in upholding and furthering the objectives of the SAARC.

vi. Likewise, India is committed to maintain and respect the purposes and principles, and abide by the decisions of the UNO and other world organizations. It believes that world bodies like the UNO are striving hard to maintain peace and security in the world, and every state must assist the UNO in this difficult task. World organizations also help states to sit and exchange their ideas on a common platform, and assist the developing countries to air their voices at the international forum. They also help poorer countries economically. This faith in world organizations has led India to join the Commonwealth of Nations and other inter-governmental organizations without surrendering its sovereignty.

vii. India also adheres to and upholds all international treaties, conventions, and statutes to which India is a party. As a responsible member of the international community, India considers it to be a duty to respect and follow international treaties and conventions. It also respects, as far as possible, other international treaties and arrangements to which it is not a party, for its desire to maintain international peace and security. However, India's accountability to these treaties is limited and optional.

viii. Finally, the principle of nonalignment, as mentioned earlier, has remained a basic ingredient of India's foreign policy from the very beginning. Nehru believed that bloc politics would only result in utmost rivalry and war-like situation in the world. It would also infringe upon the freedom of sovereign states to decide their individual courses of action, and lead them to become satellites of superpowers. Therefore, India preferred not to align with the prevalent blocs in world politics, a path it believed was the best for the newly independent developing countries. The country's commitment to nonalignment did not wane a bit with the end of the Cold War, when the very survival of the Non-Aligned Movement (NAM) was questioned. India believes that after the Cold War, the NAM can be effectively used to fight social and economic injustice, terrorist threats and environmental problems, and menaces like the digital divide. The NAM is still very significant in international affairs, and India continues to put its faith on nonalignment as an important principle of India's foreign policy.

## Evolution of India's Foreign Policy: The Cold War Period

This section, as well as the next, contains analyses on the evolution of India's foreign policy during the Cold War and thereafter, on the basis of the terms of different prime ministers of India since independence.

## Jawaharlal Nehru (1947–64)

Since 1947, when independent India started its journey, India's foreign policy had traversed a tumultuous path and remained a major area of academic interest. In this section the evolution of Indian foreign policy during the last six decades would be analyed according to the tenures of different Indian prime ministers. Jawaharlal Nehru, as Head of the Interim Government in 1946, and as Prime Minister thereafter for a long time, was the man who primarily shaped Indian foreign policy during its formative years. Nehru and his team provided the ideological base to India's foreign policy and guided India's international relations for a considerable period of time. The term of Nehru (1947–64) thus remained an important and crucial era in the history of India's foreign policy. Nehru believed that wars had become redundant in the nuclear age, and peace and cooperation had become the key issues in international politics. Nehru wanted India to play a big role in this new peaceful international order. Friendly and cordial relations with neighbours were a priority area for him. He welcomed the creation of the Socialist People's Republic of China in 1949, and extended an olive branch to the new republic. He believed that India and China, two big states in Asia, and two great civilizations, would be able to shape the destiny of modern Asia through their cooperation. With other neighbouring states like Nepal, Ceylon (now Sri Lanka), Burma (now Myanmar) and Afghanistan, he wanted to pursue friendly and peaceful relations based on mutual understanding. Although India and Pakistan had developed acrimonious relations over the issue of Kashmir, Nehru was in favour of maintaining tolerance with regard to Pakistan. He even developed friendly relations with Britain, putting aside colonial hangovers.

His unflinching quest for peace led Nehru to seek 'political' solutions to all problems rather than 'military' ones. He never wanted the military as a backup force to foreign policy. In fact, he was opposed to the idea of a strong defence policy for India, as he believed that the balance of power existing in international politics was a covert guarantee for India's security.[1] However, Nehru's views were not always shared by other world leaders. His policy of nonalignment was viewed with suspicion initially by both the superpowers, and India was unable to develop close contacts with either the United States or the Soviet Union. Although for strategic reasons and Cold War political calculations, Soviet Union later came closer to India, that proximity mainly boomed during the post-Nehru period. Nehru's friendly gestures towards China was also not met with equal reciprocity as China started accusing India of meddling in the Tibet issue, and 'controlling' what China described as large parts of 'Chinese' territory. Much to Nehru's shock and bewilderment, China attacked India in 1962, and humiliated a militarily weak India. Nehru's China policy, viewed from an impartial angle, failed. India's defeat in the war of 1962 also put a question mark over Nehru's defence policy. It revealed starkly that it was very difficult for a militarily weak and economically backward state to play the role of a global leader.

Nehru was a visionary and an ideologue. He preferred to see India assuming the position of a leader of the developing nonaligned states. He wanted India to lead the struggling people of the developing world. But during Nehru's time, the country was not militarily and economically strong enough to assume such a role. Nehru was not much concerned about the big powers and their estranged relations with India; he wanted to place his country as the leader of the third world. So he wanted to endear China more than the United States, the Soviet Union or France. As a developing and a socialist state, China drew his attention more than the United States or the Soviet Union. So Nehru was very upset when China attacked and humiliated India.[2] Among the major powers, Nehru's India was able to develop cordial relations only with Britain, as India's relations with the United States, the Soviet Union and France were distant; and with China, it was adversarial.

But at the same time, Nehru earned for India and for himself what was perhaps a very special position of ideological leadership, through the policies of nonalignment and peaceful tolerance. Nehru's India was able to provide an alternative to bipolar politics to the vast majority of states in the developing world through the policies of nonalignment that gradually grew into a movement. Although nonalignment was questioned by the superpowers, it gave Nehru and India a preeminent position in international politics. Nehru would be acknowledged as an architect of India's foreign policy, and a founder of the NAM. India's foreign policy still follows the path shown by Jawaharlal Nehru in many respects.

### Lal Bahadur Shastri (1964–66) and Indira Gandhi (1966–77 and 1979–84)

After Nehru's death in 1964, Lal Bahadur Shastri became the Prime Minister of India. Unlike Nehru, Shastri was not a foreign policy person; he concentrated more on domestic affairs, his forte, leaving foreign issues to specialists and experts. Shastri's government mainly followed the foreign policies pursued by the previous government of Nehru, albeit with an important departure: Shastri started military preparedness for India. India's defeat in the war with China in 1962 was fresh in Shastri's mind as he ordered military build-up for his country. The Indian military put up a reasonably satisfactory performance during India's war with Pakistan in 1965 over the issue of Kashmir. Shastri did not have enough time to shape India's foreign or domestic policies. At the behest of Soviet leaders, he had gone to Tashkent, Soviet Union, in 1966 for post-war talks with Pakistan. He died there prematurely.

Indira Gandhi, the daughter of Jawaharlal Nehru, was chosen the Prime Minister of India by the ruling Congress Party after the untimely death of Lal Bahadur Shastri. Indira's premiership was divided into two parts—the first from 1966 to 1977 and the second from 1979 to 1984. She got plenty of time to guide and shape India's foreign policy. She did not alter the theoretical base founded by her father, although she made important changes to the 'application side'. For instance, it was Indira who made India a forceful regional power with a very strong military. If her father nurtured the vision of making India the ideological global leader, she wanted to see a militarily strong India ready to fulfill her national interests. In fact, she abandoned her father's policy of equidistance from both the superpowers and gradually became close to the Soviet Union. Realizing that alienating both the superpowers would not help India's national interests, she decided to move closer to one of them, although she continued to proclaim her faith in nonalignment. Indira Gandhi was the first Prime Minister of India to successfully separate the 'application side' from the more theoretical 'policy side' in India's foreign policy.

Unlike her father who liked to pursue a 'macro' approach in foreign policy, Indira preferred a 'micro' approach as she wanted to visualize India as a regional power rather than as a spiritual world leader. To realize this vision, Indira concentrated on economic development and military build-up. The process of building a strong military for India, which started during Shastri's tenure, got tremendous boost during Indira's first tenure. India gradually became a regional power with a reasonably strong military during her time. India's military might was demonstrated in the 1971 war with Pakistan, a war that India won convincingly for the first time. The moment of glory for Indira's foreign policy also arrived in 1971, when the government was successful in achieving maximum international support for India's position in the East Pakistan crisis. India's military action against Pakistan in 1971 helped to form the state of Bangladesh, a step considered a diplomatic success for Indira Gandhi's government. Three and a half months before the military involvement in East Pakistan, the government concluded a twenty-year 'friendship treaty' with the Soviet Union in August 1971, considered another landmark in Indira's foreign policy, which in effect was a security guarantee for India from the superpower. Through this Treaty, Indira was successful in neutralizing the fear of American intervention in favour of Pakistan in the 1971 crisis.

Riding on her success in 1971, Indira Gandhi actually commanded the Simla Agreement of 1972 with a weak and vulnerable Pakistan. This agreement, which mainly provided for peaceful settlement of all unresolved problems between the two countries, was another 'success' for Gandhi's foreign policy. Now she was in total command, as India was also on a high from a diplomatic point of view. A confident Mrs Gandhi, in her quest to see India as a permanently strong power in Asia, decided to conduct India's first nuclear explosions in the deserts of Pokhran, Rajasthan, in May 1974. The Indian nuclear tests raised hue and cry, particularly from the American nonproliferation lobby, as India's relations with the United States, already not much cordial, plummeted to a new low. Whether or not these nuclear tests of 1974 helped Indira Gandhi's government remained a debatable issue; but there was little doubt that going nuclear was a very bold step for India at that point of time.

In her first tenure (1966–77), Indira Gandhi's foreign policy was successful in achieving its goals. India was established as a strong regional power and Indira proved—as she had wanted—that only a strong state can fulfill its national interests. India's diplomacy vis-à-vis Pakistan was tremendously successful in the war of 1971 and in the Simla Agreement of 1972. Although a little hesitant initially, Indira ultimately took the bold step of establishing close political and security relations with the superpower Soviet Union at the risk of getting flak from the opposition parties for deviating from the path of nonalignment. She wanted to be close to the Soviet Union to fulfill her foreign policy goals, although she alienated the United States in the process. During her first tenure, Indira angered the Americans for many reasons. First, the American position in the East Pakistan crisis of 1971 was markedly different from the Indian position. The United States did not want India to wage a war against Pakistan, an American ally in South Asia. Second, India's friendship treaty with the Soviet Union, a Cold War adversary of the United States, did not go well with the Americans. Third, the Americans considered India's nuclear tests of 1974 a violation of the international nonproliferation regime spearheaded by the United States, and opposed India's efforts to earn the 'nuclear weapons state' status. India and the United States thus developed antipathy for each other during Indira Gandhi's first tenure as the Prime Minister of India. At this point of time, Indira did not bother much about the United States as she deliberately went the Soviet way, realizing that one of the superpowers must be endeared to fulfill India's national interests.

During her second tenure (1979–84), Indira improved relations with the United States, although her liking for the Soviet Union continued. One reason for India's growing attention towards the United States was the presence of a strong community of Indian immigrants there, with over 3,00,000 people in 1981.[3] They influenced the gradual change in India's antipathy towards the United States. Although differences between the two countries over political, economic and security issues continued, a more matured Indira was now less hostile towards the United States as more and more young Indians were preferring the United States as their destination for a job or for higher education. The change in the Indian attitude about the Americans had actually started in the early 1980s, during Indira Gandhi's second tenure. However, relations with Pakistan and China continued to be adversarial, as both were contenders to India's regional power ambitions, and they were engaged in arms transfers and nuclear-power-related transfers to put India under pressure. With Britain and other Western powers, India's relations were of a 'not too close, not too far' nature, because Indira, like her father, maintained close relations with the socialist East. She was nevertheless able to retain India's leadership role in the NAM, despite India's proximity to the Soviet Union. Mixing these two apparently opposing trends—closeness to a superpower and following nonalignment at the same time—was another diplomatic marvel during Indira's tenures as the Prime Minister of India. In the overall analysis, Indira Gandhi was able to command respect for India from the international community by cementing India's position as a strong regional power, and through forceful diplomacy that was successful in achieving India's national interests.

## Morarji Desai (1977–79) and Charan Singh (1979)

After the fall of the Indira Gandhi government in 1977, Morarji Desai of the Janata Party formed the first non-Congress, and the first coalition, government in India. Desai was known in the West as a person with soft attitude towards the United States and the Western world. This image of the Indian Prime Minister helped to bring the United States closer to India. Desai was also keen on breaking the perceived Soviet-tilt in India's foreign policy. Encouraged by Desai's policy stance, the United States also showed its interest in strengthening relations with India. US President Jimmy Carter paid an official visit to India in January 1978. He was the first American President to visit India in nineteen years, after President Eisenhower's visit to New Delhi in December 1959. Desai and Carter signed the 'Delhi Declaration' on 3 January 1978, that called for, among other issues, improved cooperation between the two nations, speeding up the process of global disarmament, and the need to remove economic disparity among nations of the world. Desai paid a reciprocal visit to the United States in June 1978, signalling warmth in bilateral relationship. This was the first reciprocal visit of the leaders of the two nations in a single calendar year. The visit was indicative of an improved relationship between the United States and India. The United States became the largest trading partner of India, and Indo-US two-way trade registered impressive growth during the Desai premiership.

The Desai government also endeavoured to improve relations with China. In 1979, India's Foreign Minister Atal Behari Vajpayee went to China on an official visit, the first high-level visit after the war of 1962. Vajpayee's visit revived hopes that normalcy would prevail in India–China relations. Vajpayee met Deng Xiaoping, the supreme leader of China, who offered him a package solution for border disputes between the two states. This package included the proposal from Deng that China would accept the McMohan line in the Eastern sector, if India recognized 'legitimate' Chinese claims in the Western sector. Vajpayee told Deng that India would sincerely consider the proposal. With Pakistan, always a foreign policy challenge for India, the Desai government concluded the Sallal Dam Agreement in 1978 over the controversial issue of sharing of Chenab river waters. The conclusion of the agreement sent positive signals to Pakistan that India was willing to improve relations. The Janata government of Morarji Desai was indeed keen on improving relations with all of India's neighbours in order to erase the label of a 'big brother', a label India's neighbours preferred to bestow on India earlier. The Desai government was able, to some extent, to give the message to India's neighbours that India was interested in maintaining a healthy relation with all its neighbours.

The Desai government fell in July 1979 due to internal feuds among coalition partners, and Charan Singh became the new Prime Minister of India. Charan Singh was in office only for six months. During this short span, it was not possible for him to determine the course of India's foreign policy. So he decided to maintain the status quo. But his government had to face a diplomatic challenge when the Soviet troops entered Afghanistan on 27 December 1979. The United States expected India to condemn what the Americans termed as Soviet 'invasion' of Afghanistan. But the Charan Singh government was late in its reactions. When it finally called the presence of Soviet troops in Afghanistan undesirable, the United States said that the Indian statement was too soft and evasive. With a fragile coalition and a resurgent Congress party waiting in the wings to assume power, Charan Singh was in dilemma to issue a forthright statement condemning Soviet presence in Afghanistan.

In January 1980, Indira Gandhi came back to power to assume premiership for a second tenure, with a comfortable win in the parliamentary elections. As mentioned earlier, she tried to improve relations with the United States during her second term. But her pro-Soviet image continued to prove a hindrance in her efforts. During this term, she was not able to make substantial changes to India's foreign policy. She nurtured close relations with the Soviets, India's biggest supplier of defence equipments and its security partner. India's neighbours again developed doubts about India's foreign policy, which they believed would rest on 'big power' ambitions under the guidance of Indira Gandhi.

## Rajiv Gandhi (1984–89)

After the tragic assassination of Indira Gandhi in October 1984, her eldest son Rajiv Gandhi was chosen by the Congress Party as the Prime Minister of India. In the parliamentary elections of January 1985, Rajiv Gandhi won a landslide mandate to consolidate his position as the leader of the Congress Party, and of India. As the youngest Prime Minister, Rajiv wanted to see a technologically equipped and economically strong India. He visualized a modern India through the information technology revolution. He understood that India should cultivate better relations with the technologically advanced United States and the Western world. Although Rajiv did not deviate much from the foreign policy of his mother, he nevertheless tried to endear the United States, a trend that was manifest in India's foreign policy during the second tenure of Indira Gandhi as the Prime Minister of India. The perceived Soviet-tilt in India's foreign policy was also present during Rajiv's tenure, as the young Indian Prime Minister paid his first official visit to the Soviet Union. But the Soviet visit was soon followed by a visit to the United States where Rajiv was able to establish very good personal relations with the American President Ronald Reagan. Rajiv's personal chemistry with the Soviet leader Mikhail Gorbachev was also excellent. He was thus successful in improving relations with both the superpowers.

During his official visit to the United States in June 1985, Rajiv persuaded the Americans to sell Cray XMP-24 supercomputers to India, a feat considered as a diplomatic 'success'. The Americans did not usually give these supercomputers, important for meteorological research, to countries outside the US lobby. Further, Rajiv was invited to address a joint session of the

US Congress, an honour not accorded to his mother or grandfather during their official visits to the United States. This showed that the Americans gave him importance. India, under Rajiv Gandhi, also extended friendly warmth to China. Rajiv personally visited China in 1988; he was the first Indian Prime Minister to visit the country after Jawaharlal Nehru. His visit did help to ease relations with China. The most significant outcome of the visit was the decision to set up a Joint Working Group (JWG) to study border problems. It was decided that the JWG would meet every year, alternately in Beijing and New Delhi. India would be led by the Foreign Secretary in the JWG, while China would be led by its Vice Foreign Minister. The JWG met several times since 1988, and was instrumental in suggesting various measures to diffuse border problems between two states. The creation of the JWG was a major achievement of Rajiv's visit to China. During his stay there, the two governments also concluded a few agreements on cooperation in civil aviation, science and technology, and cultural exchange programmes. This visit initiated a whole new process of top-level official visits between the two countries.

Despite many successes, there was a grey area in Rajiv's foreign policy. His government decided to send the Indian Peace Keeping Force (IPKF) to Sri Lanka, as per the provisions of the 1987 Indo-Sri Lanka Accord that Rajiv had signed with J. R. Jayawardene, the Sri Lankan President. The IPKF was sent to Sri Lanka to maintain peace and normalcy in the strife-torn island, ravaged by the ethnic Tamil problem. But the IPKF experience was horrific for India as thousands of Indian military personnel died or was injured in clashes with Tamil insurgent groups. Such casualties demoralized the military. Moreover, the expenses to maintain the IPKF in Sri Lanka cost the Indian exchequer heavily. The IPKF experience in Sri Lanka proved that it was difficult for an external army to control ethnic violence in an alien territory. The IPKF had to be eventually withdrawn from Sri Lanka in late 1989, with its mission remaining unaccomplished. The IPKF episode put India in a spot, as other neighbours smelt in it a hegemonic attitude shown by the 'big brother' of South Asia. It also remained as a negative chapter in an otherwise successful foreign policy pursued by the government of Rajiv Gandhi.

## V. P. Singh (1989–90) and Chandra Sekhar (1990–91)

After the parliamentary elections of December 1989, the National Front—a coalition of several parties—formed the government with external support from the Left parties and the Bharatiya Janata Party (BJP). Vishwanath Pratap Singh, who was chosen as the leader of the National Front, became the Prime Minister of India. As he was more comfortable with domestic politics, his Foreign Minister I. K. Gujral mainly steered his government's foreign policy. Gujral believed that it was important for India to maintain very cordial relations with its South Asian neighbours. The V. P. Singh government decided to withdraw the IPKF from Sri Lanka, to send a message to all South Asian countries that India was not interested in playing the role of the 'big brother' in the neighbourhood. The Sri Lankan government welcomed this decision, as India's image as an 'equal partner' improved among South Asian states.

However, Foreign Minister I. K. Gujral's sincere efforts notwithstanding, relations with Pakistan did not improve much during the premiership of V. P. Singh. One reason for the deterioration of relations with Pakistan was enhanced terrorist activities in the Kashmir valley which, the Singh government alleged, had Pakistan's active support. The terrorists abducted the daughter of the Home Minister in the Singh Cabinet, and demanded release of some of their colleagues locked in different jails, in exchange of her release. The Singh government had to yield to this demand.

Further, tension between India and Pakistan reached a great height as both the states increased the number of troops along the border, as reports of conflicts in the border areas poured in. Tension at the border led to a war-like situation. In an effort to diffuse tension, an anxious US President sent his special envoy Robert Gates to both India and Pakistan. China and the Soviet Union also appealed to the leaders of both the states to reduce troops along the border. Finally, both the states reduced troops along their border under international pressure, but relations between them continued to suffer.

In August 1990, Iraq attacked Kuwait with a view to capture Kuwait, and international politics heated up over the issue. V. P. Singh sent his Foreign Minister to Iraq to ensure the safety of Indian nationals living in the Persian Gulf region. Gujral met the Iraqi leader Saddam Hussein to discuss possible evacuation of Indian citizens from the Gulf region, and also other issues. The United States expressed its displeasure with the Gujral–Saddam meeting, although this did not cast a shadow on India–US relations. In September–October 1990, the V. P. Singh government allowed American fighter planes to refuel in India on their way to the Gulf. This decision of the Singh government created domestic political turmoil. Probably the V.P. Singh government realized the importance of the United States in the backdrop of a changing international order with the Cold War nearing an end. This might have prompted it to take sensitive decisions like allowing US mediation over Kashmir (through Robert Gates) and refuelling facilities for American fighter planes.

In November 1990, the V. P. Singh government fell due to internal political crises. An eager Chandra Sekhar assumed premiership with the support of the Congress (I) Party led by Rajiv Gandhi. The Chandra Sekhar government remained in office only for six months (till May 1991), including two months as caretaker government (from March 1991). So, it was not possible for Chandra Sekhar to take new initiatives with regard to India's foreign policy. In fact, the minority Chandra Sekhar government, with the support of only fifty Members of Parliament, had to constantly work under the threat of being toppled over by Rajiv Gandhi's Congress (I) Party that was waiting in the wings to take over power. It had neither the time nor the desire to experiment with India's foreign policy. It followed the policies of the former Singh government in external affairs. Chandra Sekhar's government also allowed refuelling facilities for American fighter jets. Rajiv Gandhi threatened to withdraw support from the government over this decision. This government also supported the controversial resolution of the UN Security Council that wanted to impose very rigid economic sanctions on Iraq. However, the Chandra Sekhar government, dependent on support from the Congress (I) Party for its survival, could not last long, as the minority government fell in March 1991. Chandra Sekhar's government was the last Cold War-period government in India.

## India's Foreign Policy After the Cold War

### Narasimha Rao (1991–96): The First Indian Prime Minister After the Cold War

In the parliamentary elections of 1991, the Congress (I) won a thumping majority and formed the government. Its supreme leader Rajiv Gandhi was assassinated during an election campaign, and the huge sympathy wave among the electorate brought back the Congress (I) to power. P. V. Narasimha Rao was designated as the Prime Minister by the party. He became the first post–Cold War Prime Minister of India. The end of the Cold War brought several important changes to the international order. To begin with, the end of the Cold War signalled the end of the bipolar nature of world politics that existed for forty-five years, and also the era of bloc politics in international relations. Second, with the disintegration of Soviet Union, the United States remained the only superpower in international politics. Third, the impact of globalization on international economy and politics became more pronounced than it was during the Cold War. Fourth, every state, now exposed to a new international order, started the process of redesigning its foreign policy with a view to adjust with the new international system. The Rao government in India also faced the challenge to suitably reshape India's foreign policy to make it more time-worthy. The new government appeared ready to face the challenge.

Within two months of assuming power, the Rao government took a very bold step to reform India's economy. The government, possibly under the pervasive impact of the process of globalization, decided to go for liberalization of the Indian economy. Rao's Finance Minister Manmohan Singh announced on 24 July 1991 that India's economy would be liberalized from unnecessary bureaucratic control and red tapes to make it more dynamic and competitive. He declared that foreign direct investments (FDI) would henceforth be encouraged; and the licensing system in industries, considered by many as the real obstacle to growth of the economy, would be abolished. The Rao government primarily identified ninety industries for each of which upto 51 per cent of shares would be sold to foreign investors. Manmohan Singh also announced that the Rao government would modernize, and if necessary privatize, weak public sector enterprises to make them more competitive and profit-oriented. This economic liberalization programme, launched by the Rao government, aimed—for the first time since India's independence—at opening up the Indian economy to the international market and removing protectionist policies for industries. It was a significant departure from the so-called 'mixed economy' model introduced by Nehru and followed by India for more than four decades.

Although the economic reform programme of Narasimha Rao's government was very much a part of the new government's domestic policies, it proved to be significant for India's foreign policy as well. The United States and other industrialized nations of the world welcomed India's economic liberalization and hinted at more investments in the Indian market. In fact, data showed that FDI in India increased significantly within two years of India's economic reforms. In 1990, total American investment in India was US $20 million. It rose to US $110 million in 1993.[4] The industrialized nations of the world began to express their interests in the Indian market for the first time since India's independence.

The Rao government realized that in the new international order after the Cold War, economics would be the determining factor for political equations. Moreover, to draw the United States—the only remaining superpower—closer to India, economy would be the best instrument. During the Cold War, due to India's Soviet-tilt, the United States and other industrialized nations of the West Bloc did not develop noteworthy trade relations with India. Now in a changed international order, the Rao government decided to go for a market economy that could attract American and other foreign investors to India. This policy was successful, as the United States, encouraged by India's economic reforms, constituted the US-India Commercial Alliance (USICA) in 1995 and declared India as the 'big emerging market' the same year. There could be no denying the fact that India's economic reforms, launched by the Rao government, brought the United States and other industrialized nations closer to India after the Cold War.

The government, under Narasimha Rao, also strived hard to improve relations with India's neighbours. The Prime Minister made an official visit to China in 1993. During this visit, the two sides discussed important bilateral issues like the determination of the Line of Actual Control (LAC) and reduction of troops along the border. Rao's visit helped to alleviate some of the bitterness existing in India–China relations. Government of India signed the important Mahakali Treaty with Nepal, facilitating generation of hydro-electricity and its export to India. This treaty helped to reaffirm Nepal's faith in India. In 1995, Prime Minister P. V. Narasimha Rao signed the South Asian Preferential Trade Agreement (SAPTA) along with other Heads of Government of the SAARC states, to boost the idea of free trade within the SAARC. The government also engaged itself in economic diplomacy with Sri Lanka. In late 1994, India and Sri Lanka announced the plan for setting up of thirty joint venture industries in both the countries. By 1995, thirteen joint venture initiatives started in Sri Lanka, and another seventeen were ready to be launched in the two countries. Through such economic diplomacy, the government was able to break the ice in its relation with Sri Lanka that had deteriorated after the sending of the IPKF to the island-state.

The Rao government tried to bolster India's security and strategic programmes. It launched an ambitious ballistic missile technology programme and tested successfully the Augmented Satellite Launch Vehicle (ASLV) and the Polar Satellite Launch Vehicle (PSLV) in 1992. In 1994, India tested 'Prithvi', a short-range ballistic missile that was subsequently developed into an intermediate-range ballistic missile (IRBM). An indigenously-built IRBM 'Agni' was also successfully launched in 1994 for India's security purposes. Although India's ballistic missile programme angered the United States, which was proclaiming nonproliferation as one of its foreign policy agenda, it did not affect the relations much due to improved trade and economic relations between the two countries. Overall, the Rao government was successful in meeting the challenges posed to India's foreign policy by the altered international order after the Cold War. The Rao government could be credited with the introduction of a new trend of economic diplomacy in India's foreign policy.

## H. D. Deve Gowda (1996–97) and I. K. Gujral (1997–98)

After the parliamentary elections of May 1996, the BJP emerged as the single largest party with 160 seats. Its leader Atal Behari Vajpayee was invited by the President of India to form the government. But Vajpayee could stay in office only for thirteen days, as he resigned during discussions on a vote of confidence in the Parliament. The President then invited the National Front–Left Front coalition to form the government. After long deliberations, the coalition nominated H. D. Deve Gowda, a former Chief Minister of Karnataka, as the new Prime Minister of India. He took charge on 1 June 1996. He selected an experienced I. K. Gujral as the Foreign Minister in his cabinet.

The Deve Gowda government put maximum emphasis on better relations with India's neighbours. During its short tenure, India's relations with neighbours like Bangladesh and China improved significantly. On 29 November 1996, India and China signed a very important agreement on Confidence Building Measures (CBM) in New Delhi during the visit of the Chinese President Jiang Zemin to India. Zemin's visit was the first ever official visit by a Chinese President to India. Article 1 of the agreement on CBM declared that neither India nor China would use military power against the other. Deployment of minimum force in border areas was also proposed in the CBM. During this historic visit of Zemin, the two countries also signed three more agreements: (1) agreement to cooperate in prevention of drug trafficking and related crimes; (2) agreement to maintain the Indian Consulate in Hong Kong and (3) agreement to use sea routes between the two countries for trade and communication. A high-level delegation also accompanied President Zemin to explore close cooperation in areas like culture, science and technology, trade and commerce.

India's bilateral relations with Bangladesh, the Eastern neighbour, also showed marked improvement during the tenure of Deve Gowda. The Prime Minister requested Jyoti Basu, the veteran communist leader and Chief Minister of West Bengal, to visit Bangladesh and discuss the controversial issue of sharing of the water of the Ganga river. Basu's able diplomacy and the positive attitude shown by the two governments led to another historic agreement between India and Bangladesh. This agreement, 'the Ganga Water Accord, 1996', was signed on 12 December 1996 by Deve Gowda and his Bangladeshi counterpart, Sheikh Hasina Wajed. This important agreement helped the two nations to settle an age-old controversial issue between them. Deve Gowda and Gujral also extended their cooperation to Pakistan. But their efforts failed because of the internal political crisis in Pakistan with the removal of the Benazir Bhutto government in November 1996. India's economic relations with the United States, the only superpower, improved during the premiership of Deve Gowda, although differences over security-related issues like the CTBT persisted.

In the Deve Gowda cabinet, foreign policy was mainly steered by I. K. Gujral, the experienced Minister for External Affairs. Gujral always put emphasis on improving relations with India's neighbours. In order to achieve better relations among neighbours, and to secure peace in South Asia, he formulated a set of policies that later came to be known as the 'Gujral doctrine'. These were the main principles of the Gujral doctrine: (1) as the largest nation in South Asia, India must show a big heart. With neighbours, India must not ask for reciprocity, but should give all that it can in good faith and trust; (2) no South Asian country would allow its territory to be used against the interest of another country; (3) no country would interfere in the internal affairs of another and (4) countries of South Asia must settle all their disputes through peaceful bilateral negotiations. Gujral analysed in detail these policies, which he believed would help to build peace in South Asia, in a speech he delivered in London in August 1996. The Gujral doctrine remains a significant contribution of the Deve Gowda government to India's foreign policy in recent times.

Due to internal political crises, and pressures from the Congress Party, Deve Gowda was replaced by Gujral as the leader of the ruling coalition in April 1997. The latter took over as the new Prime Minister of India on 21 April 1997. External affairs is an area Gujral was comfortable with; and as Prime Minister he kept the Ministry under him. Since he was the commander in Deve Gowda's foreign policy matters, it was important for him to continue the previous government's policies in external affairs. So, after taking over charge as the Prime Minister, Gujral continued his efforts to improve relations with neighbours with a view to promote peace and security in South Asia. He attended the Ninth SAARC Summit in Male, Maldives, where he also had a special meeting with his Pakistani counterpart Nawaz Sharif. The two leaders discussed ways of settling outstanding problems between the two countries. In June 1997, India and Pakistan met again in Islamabad, this time at the Foreign Secretary level. The 'Joint Statement' issued after the meeting contained some definite proposals for solving the Kashmir dispute. It was decided at the Foreign Secretary level meeting that the two sides would form JWG to discuss outstanding problems in Kashmir, and take necessary steps to resolve them. The issues to be discussed by the JWG were also highlighted by the joint statement. These were: (1) peace and security; (2) Jammu and Kashmir; (3) Siachen Glacier; (4) Wulgur Dam, and the Tulbul Project; (5) 'Sir Creek' area; (6) terrorism; (7) drug trafficking; (8) trade and commerce and (9) cooperation in other areas. Through this joint statement of 1997, both India and Pakistan showed genuine and sincere efforts to solve the Kashmir problem for the first time since the Simla Agreement of 1972. The Gujral doctrine was India's source of inspiration behind this statement.

The Gujral government also wanted to improve relations with the United States. In September 1997, the Indian Prime Minister went to New York to address the session of the General Assembly at the UNO. He also met the US President Bill Clinton to discuss bilateral issues. Clinton assured Gujral that the United States had no intention to mediate in the Kashmir problem, as reported by a section of the media, without India's approval. This assurance by the US President helped to clear India's doubts about the United States and brought back faith, an important element in bilateral relations. During Gujral's premiership, three high-level visits to India by American dignitaries took place. The US Secretary of State Madeleine Albright, Commerce Secretary William Daley and Under Secretary of State Thomas Pickering paid official visits to India from October to December 1997. The visits of these three top-level American dignitaries within a short span of time brought out the fact that the United States was considering India with importance. In fact research showed that during Gujral's short tenure as the Prime Minister (from 21 April 1997 to 18 March 1998), India's relations with the United States improved significantly.[5] The Gujral government was able to improve India's relations with Pakistan and the United States, two of the difficult terrains in India's foreign policy.

## Atal Behari Vajpayee (1998–99 and 1999–2004)

After the twelfth parliamentary elections in India, held in February–March 1998, the National Democratic Alliance (NDA), a coalition of several parties, came to power. The biggest coalition partner (in terms of number of seats), the BJP nominated its leader Atal Behari Vajpayee as the Prime Minister of India. Vajpayee took over charge on 19 March 1998. The BJP, in its Election Manifesto, promised that the party would reconsider India's nuclear options if it came to power. In order to fulfill this promise in its Election Manifesto, the Vajpayee government tested nuclear bombs in the deserts of Pokhran on 11 and 13 May 1998. Pokhran was also the site of India's first nuclear tests in 1974. So, the May 1998 tests came to be known as Pokhran II. Tension mounted in the South Asian region after these tests. Pakistan declared that India's nuclear tests were dangerous for Pakistani security and that they would also conduct similar tests to ensure their security. At the end of May 1998, Pakistan conducted nuclear tests in the Chagai Hills region of Balochistan province. The nuclear tests by two arch rivals of South Asia not only escalated tension in the region, it also created unprecedented concerns all over the world. The nuclear nonproliferation regime, so enthusiastically championed by the United States and other western powers, was put to a real test. India's Prime Minister Vajpayee announced that India's nuclear tests were conducted only for deterrence, and India sincerely believed in the policy of 'no first use' of nuclear weapons.

The May 1998 nuclear tests by India and Pakistan had very adverse effects on bilateral relations between the two neighbours. The peace process initiated by the previous Gujral government got a jolt due to the nuclear tests. India's relations with the United States also suffered due to Pokhran II. President Bill Clinton condemned India's nuclear tests and imposed economic sanctions on

India under the US Nuclear Nonproliferation Laws of 1994. The Clinton administration was very annoyed both with India and Pakistan as their nuclear tests challenged the nonproliferation efforts of the American government. President Clinton's nonproliferation policies were questioned by the US Congress and the media. India's nuclear tests and subsequent American sanctions on India took bilateral relations to a very low. Under the sanctions, economic aids to India from the United States and other financial institutions were stopped, and severe restrictions were put on military sales and exchanges to India. The Vajpayee government called the sanctions unfortunate, but at the same time reiterated that Indian economy was resilient enough to tide over the crisis. On the whole, India–US bilateral relations suffered tremendously after Pokhran II in an atmosphere of mistrust and suspicion, reminiscent of the Cold War times.

But doors of diplomacy were kept open both by India and the United States after Pokhran II. Within a month of India's nuclear tests, the two sides began top-level official discussions with a view to reduce tension and ensure security in South Asia. From 11 June 1998, India and the United States were engaged in diplomatic talks that ultimately led to the longest-ever diplomatic dialogues between the two nations spanning almost three years. In these diplomatic talks, the Indian side was led by Jaswant Singh, the Deputy Chairman of the Planning Commission, and later the Foreign Minister of India; while the American side was led by Strobe Talbott, the US Deputy Secretary of State. Singh and Talbott met in different parts of the world like New Delhi, Washington DC, Rome and Frankfurt, to participate in a total of twelve rounds of negotiations from June 1998 to February 2001. These diplomatic negotiations helped immensely to normalize relations between India and the United States. Under American persuasion, India and Pakistan also agreed to resume talks in order to reduce tension in South Asia. In February 1999, Indian Prime Minister Vajpayee took a bus to Lahore (in Pakistan) to meet his Pakistani counterpart. The two leaders signed the Lahore Declaration on 21 February 1999. This declaration proposed several measures to restore confidence and normalize relations between the two nations.

The peace process initiated by the Lahore Declaration, however, did not last long as tension mounted again over the issue of intrusion of Pakistani troops in the Kargil region of Kashmir in India in May 1999. Relations between the two neighbours deteriorated again over exchange of fire between troops of the two countries in the Kargil region. The Kargil conflict virtually led to an 'undeclared war' between India and Pakistan. The world, and especially the nonproliferation lobby, became very worried about the Kargil conflict because it could get transformed into a nuclear war between India and Pakistan. As a consequence, the G-8 nations quickly condemned Pakistani intrusion into the Kargil areas and identified Pakistan as the aggressor. The Clinton administration in the United States also condemned the presence of Pakistani forces in Kargil and requested Nawaz Shariff, the Pakistani Prime Minister who was summoned to Washington DC, to withdraw troops from the region. For the first time since the Second World War, the United States showed its preference for India over Pakistan on the Kargil issue. Under US pressure, and also due to the valiant efforts of the Indian military, Pakistani troops had to finally depart from the Kargil region in July 1999.

India's foreign policy faced severe challenges during the first tenure of Vajpayee as the Prime Minister of India (excluding an earlier stint for thirteen days in 1996) due to Pokhran II and the Kargil crisis. But there were some rays of hope in an otherwise critical situation that India's foreign policy faced during this period. The Lahore Declaration with Pakistan and the American support to India during the Kargil crisis could be identified as positive gains for India's diplomacy.

The Vajpayee government resigned in the wake of a vote of confidence in the Indian Parliament in April 1999 and faced the 13th parliamentary elections in September–October 1999. The NDA coalition was voted back to power by the Indian electorate, and Vajpayee took charge as the Prime Minister for a second tenure (excluding the thirteen-day stint) on 11 October 1999.

The foreign policy pursued by the Vajpayee government during its second tenure became more matured and sharp. This government was able to significantly improve relations with the United States, Russia, Pakistan, the ASEAN, the EU, Nepal and Iran. It also reestablished diplomatic relations with Afghanistan, that were cut off during Taliban rule in that country. In March 2000, the US President Bill Clinton paid an official visit to India for five days. Clinton was the first American President in twenty-two years to visit India, after President Carter's visit in 1978. Vajpayee and Clinton signed a very comprehensive and futuristic bilateral agreement, the 'US–India Relations: A Vision for the 21st Century' on 21 March 2000 in New Delhi. This agreement came to be known as the 'Vision Document' in diplomatic circles. It outlined in detail, the scheme of close cooperation between the two countries in political, economic and security spheres. It was declared that the Heads of Government of the two nations would meet at least once a year to discuss bilateral matters and to sort out differences. Further, an Annual Foreign Policy Dialogue under the leadership of two foreign ministers would take place alternately in New Delhi and Washington DC. The document also contained an elaborate scheme to institutionalize close cooperation between the two largest democracies. Some of the important institutions created by it were: (1) US–India Financial and Economic Forum; (2) US–India Commercial Dialogue; (3) US–India Working Group on Trade and (4) US–India Science and Technology Forum. The Vision Document signed by Vajpayee and Clinton remained the most comprehensive agreement ever in the bilateral diplomatic history. It contributed immensely towards the development of India-US relations during the Vajpayee tenure, and also thereafter. For instance, high-level official visits and dialogues started regularly between the two countries after the signing of the Vision Document. Vajpayee paid a reciprocal official visit to the United States in September 2000, the first reciprocal visit in a single calendar year after twenty-two years. Other top-level dignitaries started visiting each other's nation regularly, and the institutions created by the Vision Document met as per schedule after 2000. It could thus be observed that the 'Vision Document' contributed to a great extent towards the improvement of India–US relations.

Russian President Vladimir Putin visited India in October 2000. During his visit, Russia and India signed defence cooperation agreements through which Russia promised to supply important arms and aircrafts to India. This visit by the Russian President helped the two countries to revive close cooperation in security affairs, observed during the Soviet era. Putin and Vajpayee emphasized the creation of a multipolar world after the end of the Cold War. In November 2001, Vajpayee visited Russia. During his visit, Vajpayee and Putin signed the Moscow Declaration to start close cooperation in trade, security and political spheres. The declaration also urged the international community to strengthen the UN system to fight new challenges like terrorism and environmental degradation. Vajpayee also visited England the same month to renew friendship and cooperation between the two countries. In July 2001, President of Pakistan Pervez Musharraf visited India with a view to normalize relations between the two neighbours. Vajpayee and the Pakistani President had a summit meeting in Agra to discuss bilateral issues. But the summit did not yield any positive result due to Musharraf's uncompromising attitude on the issue of Kashmir. However, the Agra Summit did manifest the intentions of the two nations to improve relations.

In order to pursue India's 'Look East' policy, launched in the early 1990s with sincerity and vigour, Vajpayee visited Vietnam and Indonesia. There he signed trade and commercial agreements with both the states, giving boost to government and private investments to and from these countries. As part of the Look East policy, the Vajpayee government established close trade and political relations with the ASEAN. India had very little connection with the ASEAN earlier; but this government was able to strengthen them, with its renewed emphasis on this policy. The Vajpayee government was also the first to establish very close relations with the EU. In June 2000, the first India–EU summit took place in Lisbon, the capital city of Portugal. Since then regular summits have been taking place between the two. At present, India's trade with the EU covers nearly 25 per cent of total Indian trade; but initiatives for better relations with the EU started during Vajpayee's second tenure as the Prime Minister of India. So it could be observed that Vajpayee was able to pursue a more matured and focused foreign policy in his second term, because several new and unexplored areas in India's foreign policy, as discussed here, were cultivated with good results during this period.

## Manmohan Singh (2004–09 and 2009–14)

In the fourteenth parliamentary elections of India, no political party got a majority mandate, with the Congress Party emerging as the single largest party in the Parliament. The United Progressive Alliance (UPA), led by the Congress, formed the government with external support from the Left parties. The Congress party nominated veteran Manmohan Singh to head the UPA government. He took over as the Prime Minister of India on 22 May 2004. Natwar Singh assumed charge as the Foreign Minister in the Singh cabinet, but was later replaced by Pranab Mukherjee, another senior leader of the party. The first Manmohan-government was in office from May 2004 to May 2009. A few bold and novel initiatives in foreign policy matters were taken during this period. One of such initiatives was the plan made by India and the United States in a joint statement issued on 18 July 2005, during Manmohan's official visit to the United States, to enter into cooperation in the area of civil nuclear energy. (This plan is hereafter referred to as CNEC: civil nuclear energy cooperation.) The CNEC proposed to make the two countries true partners in nuclear cooperation, rather than adversaries. The United States promised that through the CNEC, the Bush (Jr) administration would seek agreement from the US Congress to adjust American laws and policies with a view to implement the CNEC. It also promised to work with friends and allies to convince international regimes to enable full civil nuclear energy cooperation and trade with India. The Indian government on its part agreed, among other issues, to identify and separate civilian and military nuclear facilities and programmes, and place India's civilian nuclear facilities under IAEA (International Atomic Energy Agency) safeguards voluntarily; and continue with India's unilateral moratorium—declared after Pokhran II—on nuclear testing. The CNEC was a very bold initiative undertaken by India and the United States in the background of India's refusal to sign the NPT and the CTBT, and India's nuclear tests only seven years ago, in 1998. The Manmohan government believed that the CNEC would help India to join the international nuclear mainstream, from which India had remained officially cut-off due to India's refusal to sign the NPT and the CTBT.

Indian Prime Minister Manmohan Singh and US President George W. Bush (Jr) formally signed the CNEC Agreement on 2 March 2006, during Bush's official visit to India from 1 to 3 March 2006. As per the agreement, India would open up fourteen of its twenty-two

(65 per cent) nuclear reactors to IAEA safeguards. By 2014, India would also separate all civilian reactors from military reactors, and place them under IAEA safeguards. In return, India would be given recognition as a *de facto* nuclear-weapons state; and nuclear-related supplies to and from India would be accepted by the Nuclear Suppliers Group. The CNEC Agreement created a storm in domestic politics and landed the Manmohan government in trouble with the ultimate withdrawal of support from the Left parties. However, the government survived with support from the Samajwadi Party, and the CNEC Agreement was finally put into effect from October 2008. It was a major achievement of the first Manmohan government, because India–US strategic partnership, heralded by the earlier Vajpayee governments, was cemented through this agreement. Further, India could join the international nuclear mainstream for the first time through the agreement, and the country would be able to harness the potential of vital nuclear energy, required for a developing nation like India.

During his first tenure as the Prime Minister, Manmohan Singh also put emphasis on improving relations with India's neighbours, other important powers and regional organizations. The Manmohan government entered into a trilateral agreement with the governments of Bangladesh, India and Myanmar in January 2005 in Yangon. By this agreement, India wanted to pursue both trilateral and bilateral cooperation to promote, develop and implement projects and forums to augment the utilization and development of energy resources and related infrastructure in the region. The President of Pakistan, Pervez Musharraf, visited India from 16 to 18 April 2005 to discuss bilateral issues. He and Manmohan made a positive assessment of the progress that had been made so far through confidence-building measures, people-to-people contacts, and enhancing areas of interaction; and they agreed to build on the momentum already achieved in bilateral relations. The two leaders also addressed the issue of Jammu and Kashmir and agreed to continue these discussions in a sincere and purposeful manner to achieve a final settlement. They agreed to pursue further measures to enhance interaction and cooperation across the LoC, including agreed meeting points for divided families, trade, pilgrimages and cultural interaction. Unlike his last Agra Summit with Prime Minister Vajpayee, the Pakistani President was more flexible this time, and a bit mellowed, probably due to domestic political crisis, and discussed on a wide range of bilateral issues. India and Pakistan continued their bilateral negotiations at different levels throughout the major part of Manmohan's first tenure.

Hu Jintao, the President of the People's Republic of China, paid an official visit to India from 20 to 23 November 2006. During his visit, the Chinese President met several Indian leaders and had important talks with the Indian Prime Minister Singh on bilateral issues. A Joint Declaration, issued in New Delhi on the occasion of Hu's visit, identified a 'ten-pronged' strategy to improve relations between the two big neighbours. This ten-pronged strategy referred to the following:

i. ensuring comprehensive development of bilateral relations;
ii. strengthening institutional linkages and dialogue mechanisms;
iii. consolidating commercial and economic exchanges;
iv. expanding all-round mutually beneficial cooperation;
v. instilling mutual trust and confidence through defence cooperation;
vi. seeking early settlement of outstanding issues;
vii. promoting trans-border connectivity and cooperation;
viii. boosting cooperation in science and technology;

ix. revitalizing cultural ties and nurturing people-to-people exchanges; and
x. expanding cooperation both at the regional and the international front.

As many as thirteen agreements were signed by the two countries in different areas. President Hu Jintao's visit was said to be successful in the joint declaration. Although this official claim was not beyond debate, it was nevertheless true that the visit of the Chinese President helped to chart a new futuristic course in India–China bilateral relations.

The foreign ministers of India, China and Russia met at Harbin, China, on 24 October 2007 to discuss trilateral cooperation and global political and economic issues. This was only the third stand-alone trilateral meeting of foreign ministers, the first one having taken place in Vladivostok in June 2005, and the second in New Delhi in February 2007. Although these countries have been meeting regularly since 2002, most of the meetings have been held on the sidelines of multilateral gatherings. In the Harbin meeting, the three foreign ministers reiterated that the economic development of China, India and Russia made a major contribution to maintenance of peace and development of the region and the world, and proved beneficial to the process of multipolarity in the international order. The 'joint communiqué' issued after the meeting observed that with their continuous development and growing role in international affairs, China, India and Russia would further contribute to world peace, security, stability and prosperity. This trilateral-meeting mechanism among the three important states in international politics gathered momentum during the first tenure of Manmohan Singh as the Prime Minister of India.

The Russian President Dmitry Medvedev visited India in December 2008. This visit was in conformity with a series of top-level visits by the leaders of the two countries. As Prime Minister, Manmohan Singh visited Russia in December 2005; the India–Russia JWG to Combat Terrorism met in October 2006; and the former Russian President Vladimir Putin visited New Delhi in December 2007. These top-level visits and cooperation between the two countries strengthened bilateral relations between India and the Russian Federation. In 2006, the Manmohan government established a strategic and global partnership with Japan to harness the full potential of the age-old India–Japan relations. As part of this policy, an annual India-Japan summit between the Heads of Government was planned. Accordingly, Manmohan Singh and Taro Aso, Prime Minister of Japan, met in Tokyo on 22 October 2008 for the India-Japan Annual Summit. They held the view that both the countries, as major countries of Asia with common values and interests, must strengthen bilateral cooperation as well as cooperation in regional and multilateral areas with the objective of promoting peace, stability and prosperity in Asia and the world. They also expressed satisfaction at the growth of bilateral trade which was projected to reach US $20 billion by 2010. The two leaders welcomed the satisfactory progress achieved in case of the Economic Partnership Agreement (EPA) and the Comprehensive Economic Partnership Agreement (CEPA). They expressed hope that the agreements would be mutually beneficial and contribute to harness the true potential of economic partnership. Further, the two prime ministers shared the opinion that nuclear energy could play an important role as a safe, sustainable and non-polluting source of energy in meeting the rising global energy demands; and expressed the view that international nuclear disarmament and non-proliferation efforts must be reinforced. They also reiterated the importance of achieving a world free of nuclear weapons. The 'India-Japan Strategic and Global Partnership' was another major foreign policy initiative of the Manmohan Singh government.

An India–UK strategic partnership was also launched in 2004, and the Manmohan government worked hard to strengthen this partnership. The Annual India–UK Summit was held in New

Delhi in January 2008 between Manmohan Singh and Gordon Brown, Prime Minister of United Kingdom. Brown supported, on behalf of his people, the India–US Civil Nuclear Agreement, and reaffirmed his country's commitment to help India to join the international nuclear mainstream. He wished to establish close strategic links with India, as well cooperation in the areas of nuclear energy. The two leaders expressed satisfaction at the growing cooperation between India and United Kingdom in economic, educational, scientific and defence areas. Nicolas Sarkozy, the President of France, visited India in January 2008 and discussed strategic and economic partnership with India. Singh and Sarkozy announced an ambitious plan to achieve bilateral trade of a total of Euro 12 billion by 2012. Sarkozy also expressed satisfaction at the growing India–EU trade relations, and expressed hope that this relation would grow further during the French Presidency of the EU from July 2008. In this context, it must be noted that India-EU relations achieved significant growth during the first tenure of Manmohan Singh as the Prime Minister of India. For instance, India–EU trade has doubled just in four years, from Euro 28.6 billion in 2003 to over Euro 55 billion in 2007.[6] India and the EU are also cooperating in areas like defence and strategy, climate change, education and culture, and health, and contemplating to have a Free Trade Agreement between them.

A proper scrutiny of India's foreign policy during the first tenure of Manmohan Singh (2004–09) revealed that the Singh government was successful in establishing close relations with the United States, the sole superpower in today's world, and with all major states and regional organizations that are important in the international order of the times. The Singh government established close strategic and political partnership with Japan, United Kingdom, France and Russia as the preceding analysis noted. With important regional organizations like the ASEAN and the EU, the Singh government was able to strengthen economic and political connections. India's relations with neighbours like China, Pakistan, Bangladesh, Myanmar, Nepal and Sri Lanka also improved during this period. Therefore, it could be observed that India's foreign policy passed through a brighter phase during the first tenure of Manmohan Singh as the Prime Minister of India.

The second tenure of the Manmohan Singh government began in May 2009. During this phase, the government continued with the good work it had done earlier to bolster India's foreign relations. The annual meeting of the foreign ministers of India, Russia and China took place in Bengaluru, India, on 27 October 2009. In this meeting, the three ministers expressed satisfaction at the growing cooperation among the three countries in different spheres, and resolved to further strengthen the trilateral cooperation in economic, strategic, environmental and energy-related areas. The tenth India-EU summit took place in New Delhi on 6 November 2009, and the Indian side was led by Manmohan Singh. At the summit, the leaders discussed regional and global issues, and the means to strengthen India-EU relations. The leaders expressed satisfaction over the rapid expansion of the relationship between India and EU, including very strong trade relations, and hoped that it would grow to be deeper and stronger, founded on a global, strategic and mutually beneficial partnership. On 16 June 2009, leaders of Brazil, Russia, India and China (BRIC) met in Yekaterinburg, Russia, to further their cooperation. The four countries reiterated their resolve to continue close cooperation in economic, energy-related, and environmental issues, and to maintain peace and stability in the world. BRIC is a very important forum of four growing economies of the world, and their cooperation is necessary for a better world of tomorrow.

The US Secretary of State Hillary Clinton visited India in July 2009. After her meeting with the new Indian Foreign Minister, S. M. Krishna, a Joint Statement was issued in New Delhi on 20 July 2009. The statement noted:

> [Both Clinton and Krishna] agreed to strengthen the existing bilateral relationships and mechanisms for cooperation between the Government of Republic of India and the Government of the United States of America, while leveraging the strong foundation of economic and social linkages between our respective people, private sectors, and institutions. Recognizing the new heights achieved in the India–U.S. relationship over the last two Indian and U.S. Administrations, they committed to pursuing a third and transformative phase of the relationship that will enhance global prosperity and stability in the 21st century.[7]

The two countries resolved to further strengthen their cooperation in defence, civil nuclear energy, education, science and technology, economy and climate change. The leaders of the Group of Five (G-5), that includes India, China, Brazil, Mexico and South Africa, met in L'Aquila, Italy, on 8 July 2009, and separately issued 'political' and 'trade' declarations after the meeting. The political declaration noted:

> [T]he global economic crisis in its multiple dimensions, including social, employment and food and energy security risks, non traditional threats to security such as diseases and epidemics, as well as the challenges posed by climate change, underscore our fundamental interdependence and the imperative of enhancing cooperation to achieve equitable and sustainable development for all.[8]

The G-5 was a notable initiative of the Manmohan government during its second tenure, which was commonly referred to as the UPA II government (2009–14). However, during its second term in office, the Manmohan government's performance in foreign affairs was not as bright as its first term. The government was more preoccupied with domestic political crises, spearheaded by corruption charges levelled against members of the cabinet. But a trilateral security arrangement among the United States, Japan and India, which began at the end of 2011, provided a silver lining in an otherwise lacklustre foreign policy initiative. This security arrangement manifested India's willingness to augment its presence in multilateral forums. The effort also signalled India's wish to have more cooperation with Japan, a major Asian economy. The UPA II government could not also give a final shape to the much hyped India—US Nuclear Agreement. This created some irritants in bilateral relations. With neighbours and other major powers such as China, Russia, Britain and EU, no significant improvement in relations took place during the second tenure of the Manmohan Singh government.

## Narendra Modi (2014–)

Narendra Damodardas Modi, a BJP leader, assumed office of the Prime Minister of India in May 2014. Modi headed the NDA coalition, although BJP on its own got majority in the 2014 Indian Parliamentary elections. Prime Minister Modi, unlike some of his predecessors, had a special liking in foreign policy matters; and his foreign policy initiatives began next door, with efforts to improve relations with India's neighbours. He invited Heads of Governments of SAARC nations to New Delhi for his swearing-in ceremony, with a view to send messages to neighbours that India was willing to have closer links with them. Modi's 'Neighbourhood First' policy was successful in generating positive vibes in South Asia. Relations with Bangladesh witnessed an upswing with ratification by India of the Land Boundary Agreement that had been pending for forty years. Ties with Sri Lanka also got a boost, largely due to a change in domestic leadership in that country with Maithripala Sirisena replacing Mahinda Rajapaksa as President. The Indian Prime Minister wasted no time in improving relations with Sri Lanka, by paying an official visit to that country in March 2015, the first visit by an Indian Prime Minister to the island nation in thirty years. With Afghanistan, relations remained friendly. In June 2016, Modi visited Afghanistan where he was conferred with the country's highest civilian award. Prime Minister Modi assured the Afghan people and their leadership that India would always stand by the nation in times of any crisis. The Afghan President Ashraf Ghani had also visited India in April 2015 and again in September 2016. These visits amply manifested cordial relations between the two neighbours.

However, relations with Pakistan did not witness any major change due to continuing mistrust and schism. Cross-border terrorist activities continued unabated. Further, flash strikes by security forces of both nations along the Line of Control (LoC) escalated tension between the two. As a consequence, bilateral relations suffered. India's relations with Nepal did not improve much during Narendra Modi's first four years in office (2014–18), partly because India got entangled in domestic politics of these countries. India needed to follow a more cautious approach during the adoption of Nepal's new constitution. In contrast, with Bhutan, Modi continued to pursue friendly relations. He preferred Bhutan as the country for his first foreign visit as Indian Prime Minister, which was never done in seventy years of India's diplomatic history. This visit in June 2014 also manifested the fact that India was taking Bhutan as a serious partner in its quest for a peaceful South Asia. Modi's visit was also a tribute to the country's continued support to India in all aspects of foreign relations, including counter-terrorism initiatives.

Prime Minister Modi's foreign policy proved to be more effective with major powers during 2014–18. The new Indian Prime Minister worked hard to strengthen relations with the United States. He has visited America five times till 2017 and established close personal rapport with Barack Obama and the US Administration. Obama also became the first US President to visit India twice during his tenure, which includes his presence in India's Republic Day Celebrations (the first US President to do so) in 2015 as the Chief Guest. These visits by the two Heads of Governments were indicators of improved relationship between India and the United States. Donald John Trump assumed office as the forty-fifth American President on January 2017. During his election campaigns, Trump called himself a 'big fan of India' and praised Modi as a decisive leader, raising hopes of closer cooperation between the two countries. The Indian Prime Minister paid an official visit to the United States in June 2017 when he met the new American President and discussed bilateral and global issues. The two leaders resolved their commitment to deepen the strategic partnership between the countries and advance common objectives. With growing trade relations and increasing impact of the Indian diaspora in the United States, India–US relations will continue to expand during the remaining period of Modi's premiership.

India's relations with Japan continued to be cordial during Modi's tenure. The signing of the civilian nuclear cooperation agreement with Japan in November 2016, a pending issue for a long time, was a notable achievement. The Indian Prime Minister also established good personal rapport with Shinzo Abe, the Japanese Prime Minister. During Abe's visit to India in 2015, Japan promised to support India with US $15 billion for constructing high-speed railway system in the country. The Modi government has been instrumental in building India's ties with Japan into a strategic partnership. Further, Modi's 'Act East Policy' helped to strengthen India's relations with the ASEAN and East Asia. ASEAN–India trade had grown nearly ten times from FY 2001–02 to FY 2015–16. ASEAN nations' renewed focus on India could be viewed as a positive impact of the 'Act East Policy'.

India's bilateral relations with Russia also improved during Modi's first four years in office. He visited Moscow on 23–24 December 2015 for the sixteenth Annual Summit meeting between the heads of governments of the two nations. Seventeen new documents covering a wide range of cooperation were signed by the two countries during Modi's visit to Russia. Prime Minister Modi and President Putin also adopted a joint statement entitled 'Shared Trust, New Horizons' during this visit. The Russian President also travelled to India in October 2016 for the seventeenth Annual Summit meeting. During this meet, the Indian Prime Minister reiterated that Russia would remain India's major defence and strategic partner. President Putin reaffirmed Russia's continued commitment to the Special and Privileged Strategic Partnership with India. Under the Modi government, India's relations with Russia were further energized. Prime Minister Modi visited Russia again in June 2017 during his four-nation trip to Europe. The eighteenth Annual Summit meeting between India and Russia was held in St. Petersburg where Modi and Putin talked extensively about the special strategic partnership between the two nations. Five agreements, including a crucial pact on setting up two more atomic power plants at Kudankulam in Tamil Nadu, were signed during Modi's visit. A joint statement issued during the visit observed that India and Russia complemented each other in the energy sector and both countries will strive to build an 'energy bridge'. It also noted that the future of Indian–Russian cooperation holds great promise across a wide spectrum covering nuclear power, nuclear science and technology.

Modi also took initiative to improve relations with Britain. He visited Britain between 12 and 14 November 2015. During the visit, the Indian Prime Minister and his counterpart signed a 'Vision Statement' which contained fundamental principles on which UK–India partnership would be built and also outlined a roadmap for deepening cooperation. British Prime Minister Theresa May travelled to India in November 2016. This was her first trip outside Europe as Prime Minister of Britain. She was accompanied by a large trade delegation. During May's meeting with Modi, the two leaders emphasized on strengthening trade and business relations. However, provisions for easing of British visa restrictions for Indian professionals and students were not sorted out during May's visit. The British Prime Minister attended the India–UK Technology Summit and assured more cooperation in the sphere of science and technology between the two nations. May also labelled India as a 'closest friend of Britain' during the trip.

But China remained a tough challenge for Indian foreign policy during this period. China's increasing military and economic prowess made it politically more assertive in global politics. As a consequence, China tried to thwart India's efforts to impact international politics. China's refusal to allow India's entry into the Nuclear Suppliers Group could be cited as a case in point. Moreover, China's proximity with Pakistan made Indo-China relations somewhat difficult. Beijing's active support for Pakistan, notably with the US $46-billion China–Pakistan Economic Corridor (CPEC) that crossed territories claimed by India, led to further stress in bilateral relations. The recent One Belt One Road (OBOR) policy, undertaken by the Chinese government, raised apprehensions in India. OBOR aimed to build roads (by China) along the sensitive Indian border areas. This did not go down well with the Indian administration. Chinese and Indian national interests contradicted many a times during 2014–18. Despite growing trade relations, and bilateral visits and exchanges, China–India ties could not be free from misgivings and apprehensions.

Modi's foreign policy initiatives, therefore, yielded mixed results during this period, as the preceding analysis indicates. However, there was little doubt that Indian foreign policy became more assertive under the premiership of Narendra Modi.

# PART II

# Foreign Policy of the United States of America

## Origin and Evolution

The United States, the only remaining superpower after the Cold War, has a long political history. The territory, known as the United States today, was discovered in the early sixteenth century by John Cabot, an Englishman by birth. Cabot reached the East coast of America and established a settlement in Maryland, Virginia. Before Cabot, another sailor, Christopher Columbus, reached the nearby islands of West Indies in 1492. So it was Cabot and not Columbus who discovered America. As Cabot was a British, he ultimately handed over the power to rule Virginia to the British monarch Henry VII, and a British colony, the first foreign colony in America, was set up in Virginia. Gradually other foreign powers reached different parts of America and set up their colonies. In the Southwest, near the present Florida, Spain established its rule. The French people occupied Novo-Scotia, the Dutch-captured areas around the Hudson Valley, while the Swedish set up their colony in Delaware. The first official colony in America was set up in 1607 at James Town. By 1732, the number of formal official colonies rose to thirteen, all ruled by European powers. In 1664, the British defeated the Dutch and captured the Dutch-ruled areas. Similarly, they also captured the Spanish colonies and established British rule over a vast area of America. Finally, the Englishmen defeated the French in the Anglo-French war of 1763, and established their sovereignty over the whole of America.

Anger and frustration over British rule began to be noticed in all thirteen colonies, and protest movements started all over America. The dissident leaders in all colonies gradually established close links among themselves bypassing political differences. They also set up a combined armed force to fight the British rulers. On 4 July 1776, leaders of the thirteen colonies signed a declaration proclaiming independence from British rule. This day (July 4) is now treated as Independence Day in the United States. Although America got freedom from British rule in 1776, it took eleven more years to start the constitutional process in the territory. In 1787, the constitution was adopted and the United States of America, consisting of thirteen former colonies, was officially formed. The constitution became effective from 4 March 1789. The two Houses of the American Parliament (Congress), the House of Representatives and the Senate met separately for the first time in April 1789. On 30 April 1789, George Washington took charge as the first President of the United States, and John Adams assumed office as the first Vice President of the country. Gradually, states were reorganized in the United States and today, the US Federation consists of fifty states. An abundance of natural resources, spectacular development of agriculture and industry, science and technology, and above all, human endeavour, have made the United States the only economic, political, military and technical superpower in the world.

The political history of the United States is, therefore, more than 230 years old (from 1776), and its constitutional history is more than 220 years old (from 1787). But in its long constitutional history, the US foreign policy mainly followed a policy of isolationism—willful abstinence from the main currents of international politics. From 1789 to 1940, the United States never involved itself actively in international politics, although it maintained diplomatic ties with several countries. For more than 150 years, US foreign policy had an 'isolationist phase', with much less active involvement in international politics outside the continent. It was not before the Second World War that the United States took active interest in international politics. It wanted to follow the policy of non-involvement in the Second World War as well. Franklin D. Roosevelt, who became the US President in 1933, announced on 5 September 1939—two days after the Second World War started—that the United States would remain neutral in the war. However, the United States changed its decision later and joined the war. Hitler and Mussolini declared war on the United States on 11 December 1941, after the Japanese military bombed Pearl Harbor on 7 December 1941. All these events compelled the United States to break its isolationism and join the war. From 1941, the United States got involved with the main currents of international politics.

The Second World War ended in 1945. The same year, Harry S. Truman became the American President after the death of Roosevelt. Remarkable changes took place in international politics after the Second World War. The erstwhile major powers of Europe were hit hard by the war and their economies were devastated. As a consequence, they could not retain their supremacy in international politics, and Europe, long considered as a centre of power in international relations, failed to sustain its preeminent position. Instead, two non-European powers, with nuclear arms and strong industrial and military bases, emerged as new superpowers in international politics. The United States, along with the Soviet Union (not strictly a European power with vast territories in Asia), were the two new superpowers in the world and they emerged as the controllers of international politics after the Second World War. President Truman and his administration were new to a superpower status for America, but adjusted well to play the leading role in world politics. Truman and his Secretary of State, George Marshall, declared grandiose plans to 'revamp' the economy of West European states, many of which were American allies during the war and American supporters after it. Overtly, the 'Truman Doctrine' and the 'Marshall Plan' were American policies to help its friends, but the Soviet Union saw in them clandestine designs to spread American influence in Europe, and efforts to thwart the 'march' of communism in the continent. These two policies of the United States, and the issue of the division of Germany earlier, were believed to be among the reasons for a Cold War between the two superpowers, which the United States had to sustain for four and a half decades after the Second World War. American foreign policy was very much influenced, directly or indirectly, by the events of the Cold War that existed from 1945 to 1990.

It would not be untrue to state that the foreign policy of the United States (and also of the Soviet Union) was centered on Cold War issues for four and a half decades. All American Presidents during the Cold War period, from Truman to George Bush (Sr), framed their foreign policies to counter the Soviet Union and its possible 'advantage' over the United States in world politics. The creation of the NATO, the American positions over the Korean War, the Suez crisis, the Cuban Missile Crisis, the Hungarian uprising, the Czechoslovak uprising, the Vietnam War, and the 'Star Wars' programme could be cited as some of the instances of how Cold War political and strategic calculations dominated American foreign policy for more than four decades. Many writers like Randall B. Ripley and James M. Lindsay believe that the US foreign policy suffered from a Soviet obsession during the Cold War. America's (and Soviet Union's) relations with other countries outside the two 'blocs' (West and East) were also influenced by Cold War rivalry. For instance, America's relations with states 'A' or 'B' were termed as a counter-Soviet alliance, and Soviet Union's ties with states 'C' or 'D' were seen as anti-American lobby. America, for instance, viewed India—not belonging to any bloc—with suspicion during the Cold War period due to India's proximity to the Soviet Union. Sometimes non-political exchanges related to culture, sports, science and education were viewed in political light and categorized as anti-American (or anti-Soviet) activities. It would not be an overstatement to say that American foreign policy largely suffered from a kind of fixity during the Cold War period; it used to view the shadows of the Soviet Union everywhere, and tried to frame America's policies to counter this ubiquitous presence of its rival.

## US Foreign Policy After the Cold War

The disintegration of the Soviet Union and the end of the Cold War brought new challenges for American foreign policy. The Soviet-obsession, found largely in this policy during the Cold War, had to be changed; and at the same time, the policy had the responsibility to sustain the new-found role for the United States (the only remaining superpower) in the world. A new international order after the Cold War also necessitated changes in this policy. The immediate post–Cold War world order was mainly based on the following conditions: (1) the emergence of the United States as the only superpower; (2) end of bipolarity and bloc politics; (3) end of American and Western fear about the spread of socialism and (4) an apparent end to military rivalry with the decline of bipolarity and bloc politics. US foreign policy was new to such conditions and it had the responsibility to adjust itself and protect American interests in this new international order.

Foreign policy planners in the United States were ready to take up the challenges posed by the post–Cold War international order. In a new altered scenario, American foreign policy placed emphasis on the following issues: (1) nonproliferation of the weapons of mass destruction (WMDs) in the world; (2) protection of human rights; (3) economic diplomacy; (4) counter-terrorism and (5) security assistance programme (SAP). But it should be remembered at this point that these issues were not refreshingly new in American foreign policy. They were also given importance in US foreign policy during the Cold War period. For instance, the Truman Doctrine and the Marshall Plan were parts of economic diplomacy during the Cold War. The SAP also featured in the US foreign policy during that period. Some of these old issues were taken up and given new looks in the American foreign policy after the Cold War. As such, no radical changes were introduced in the foreign policy of the United States after the Cold War; the new policy continued to work through the amalgamation of some old and some new issues. In fact, in the absence of the 'Soviet-factor', foreign policy planners in the United States were trying to adopt some issues which would give American foreign policy a global acceptance after the Cold War. Their objectives were fulfilled to some extent by the adaptation of these issues in American foreign policy after the war. Consequently, these issues were highlighted in the post–Cold War US foreign policy.

At the time of the end of the Cold War, George W. Bush (Sr) was the American President. The Bush administration zealously pursued nonproliferation policies. The US Foreign Policy Department worked hard to contain the spread of the WMDs. After Bush (Sr), Bill Clinton took office as the US President. Clinton served two terms in office, from 1993 to 2000. His administration was the first significant American foreign policy planner after the Cold War. During his presidency, nonproliferation of WMDs became an important element of American foreign policy. The Clinton administration declared different countries of the world as nuclear 'rogues' and 'threshold' states. For instance, North Korea and Iraq were declared as nuclear rogue states. India, Pakistan, Israel, South Africa, Brazil and Argentina were termed as nuclear 'threshold' states. The United States also identified South Asia as a 'nuclear hot spot', along with North Korea and Iraq, and engaged in diplomatic talks with India and Pakistan—North Korea and Iraq did not respond to such talks—to encourage nonproliferation in these countries. It was believed that the Clinton administration was successful in persuading the Narasimha Rao government to abandon its nuclear testing programme in 1994–95 (although specific evidences were not available). The United States also engaged itself in diplomatic dialogues with other nuclear 'threshold' states to prevent proliferation of WMDs.

During its second term, the Clinton presidency also pursued vigorously the nonproliferation agenda. However, it failed to restrain both India and Pakistan from testing nuclear weapons in May 1998. An enraged American President imposed 'economic sanctions' on both India and Pakistan immediately after their nuclear tests under the 'Arms Export Control Act' (AECA) passed by the US Congress in 1994. American economic and military transfers to both India and Pakistan were prohibited under the AECA. President Clinton saw the nuclear tests by India and Pakistan as a challenge to his nonproliferation policies around the world, and therefore acted quickly to impose sanctions under the Act. The creation of the AECA in 1994 and its imposition on India and Pakistan for the first time in 1998, clearly indicated the Clinton administration's emphasis on nonproliferation issues after the Cold War. The next American Presidents George Bush (Jr) and Barack Obama continued the American policy of nonproliferation of WMDs in the post–Cold War world order. In a speech in Prague on 5 April 2009, President Obama said: 'We will reduce the role of nuclear weapons in our national security strategy and urge others to do the same.... To reduce our warheads and stockpiles, we will negotiate a new Strategic Arms Reduction Treaty with the Russians this year'. Clearly, the priority of the Obama administration is to secure nonproliferation of nuclear weapons.

Protection of human rights and fundamental freedoms of the people around the world has found renewed importance in the American foreign policy after the Cold War. Concern for human rights is nothing new in this policy. For instance, the US State Department has been placing the Annual Human Rights Report (AHRR) before the American Congress since 1977 for discussions on human rights conditions around the world. The report contains human rights practices and abuses in every individual country. On the basis of this, the US Congress often decides American assistance to individual countries. The importance of this report has enhanced greatly after the Cold War because the label of 'biased evaluation', put on it during the Cold War by the non-Western bloc, has been removed. The AHRR is now considered as an important, mostly unbiased, document on human rights. The US Congress puts a bar on American financial and security assistance to those countries accused of human rights violations by this report. Sometimes, American diplomatic relations suffer with countries accused of human rights violations by the AHRR. Normally, the United States tries to avoid relations of economic, political or security-related significance with countries alleged by the AHRR of violation of human rights. But there are exceptions in case of important powers. For instance, China is almost regularly accused by the report of gross violations of human rights. Going by normal practices, the United States would need to 'avoid' any significant relationship with China. But after the Cold War, American economic and political ties with China have been growing significantly. US–China two-way trade is almost ten times more than US–India bilateral trade. Although the US Congress admonishes China almost regularly for human rights violations, the attraction of a huge market in China is impossible to ignore for the American private and government businesses. The market potentiality of China provides an explanation for the 'soft' American attitude towards China, although at the same time, the United States takes a very 'hard' stance in case of smaller countries (and markets) like North Korea, Libya, Sudan, Iraq, Iran, Serbia—all accused by the AHRR of human rights violations. This proves that for an economic and industrial giant like the United States, trade and business interests often score over human rights issues. However, American human rights policies have become much liberal after the Cold War, in the sense that human rights issues are used less for political purposes today than they used to be during Cold War times.

Another important feature of US foreign policy after the Cold War is the importance on economic diplomacy. Economic diplomacy is not new to this policy. But this issue has been given more weight by American foreign policy planners in the wake of globalization. Economic diplomacy places importance on trade and business, keeping aside political considerations. After the Cold War, the United States worked hard to pursue policies of economic diplomacy with different states. Enhancing trade and commercial relations with other countries, providing investment opportunities to American capital in different parts of the world, increasing American financial assistance for industrialization and developmental activities in other states, all these constitute integral elements of American economic diplomacy. With the onset of economic liberalization in many developing countries after the Cold War, economic diplomacy has proved to be a very useful tool for American foreign policy. Such liberalization has provided an unprecedented opportunity to American business to spread its wings in different parts of the world. The United States has strengthened its presence through capital investment, trade and commerce in many developing states, including China, India and the former Socialist bloc countries. Improved economic ties with many countries have helped the United States to erase political differences. For instance, a very strong US economic relationship with China helped both countries to overlook political differences. The United States also had political and strategic differences with India in the post–Cold War period over issues like the Indian nuclear tests and signing of the CTBT. But India–US relations have grown stronger after the Cold War, mainly due to strong economic ties between the two countries. In fact, all American administrations after the Cold War have successfully used economic diplomacy as an effective instrument of foreign policy to serve American national interests in different parts of the world.

Counter-terrorism constitutes another important aspect of US foreign policy after the Cold War. The 9/11 terrorist attacks on the United States have strengthened American counter-terrorism policies. The Bush (Jr) administration declared a 'war on terrorism' after the 9/11 incidents and vowed to fight the menace throughout the world. Bush's 'war on terrorism' contained four major policies: (1) no compromise with terrorism and terrorists, and no exchange or settlement with terrorists (like release of detained terrorists or economic exchanges); (2) judicial trial of terrorists for crime against humanity; (3) isolation of countries providing help to terrorists from the international community, and pressurizing these countries to abandon their harmful activities and

(4) provision of all kinds of assistance to states engaged in the fight against terrorism. The Bush (Jr) administration also declared an 'anti-terrorism assistance programme' that contained, among other things, military training, exchange of information and security assistance to countries involved in the war on terrorism. Further, a 'rewards for justice' programme announced by the Bush Administration sought to exchange information about international terrorists with friendly states, and give rewards of upto US $25 million for information on international terrorists, and assistance to capture them. The Obama administration also stepped up American efforts on counter-terrorism. For instance, Obama's 'Af-Pak Policy', announced in March 2009, sought to eliminate terrorist groups like the Al Qaeda and the Talibans from Afghanistan and Pakistan and provide massive economic and security assistance to these countries to eliminate terrorist activities from their soil.

SAP became an integral part of US foreign policy after the Second World War. Almost 50 per cent of American assistance to different countries during the Cold War period came under this programme, which was considered crucial for American strategic interests to counter Soviet influence. However, after the end of the Cold War, the future of the programme was hotly debated in the United States. In the absence of the Soviet Union, whether it would be wise for the United States to spend huge amounts on the SAP became a controversial issue. But all American Presidents after the Cold War preferred to continue with the programme, and the US Congress approved the budget on the SAP from time to time. The continuance of the programme by all American administrations during the post–Cold War period proved the importance of the SAP as an element of American foreign policy in recent years.

The SAP contains several programmes like Foreign Military Financing (FMF), Economic Support Fund (ESF), International Military Education and Training (IMET) and Cooperative Threat Reduction (CTR). About 95 per cent of the SAP-money is spent on FMF and ESF. President George W. Bush (Sr), the first US President after the Cold War, lobbied hard to retain the SAP after the Cold War. Bush considered SAP as a very significant part of US defence strategy. He identified three areas in the American Defence Strategy which could be bolstered by the SAP. They were: (1) meeting crisis situations; (2) reorganization and (3) presence of US military in other countries as per requirements. He believed that the SAP would be very useful to protect vital American interests, mainly in these areas. After Bush (Sr), all post–Cold War American Presidents lent their support for the SAP and continued to consider it as an integral part of American security policy. After the Cold War, the SAP was used to strengthen democratic processes in East Europe, help counter-terrorism and anti-narcotic activities around the world, strengthen the maintenance of international peace and security, and above all, protect American national interests. The US Congress also allocated enough money to keep the SAP going during the post–Cold War period.

American foreign policy after the Cold War mainly rested on the five pillars, as mentioned in the second paragraph of this section. America's foreign relations after the Cold War were largely guided by these five policies. For instance, US–China relations are dominated by economic diplomacy, whereas American diplomacy with Sudan, Libya and North Korea hinges on human rights issues. Further, American relations with many countries in the Middle East, Russia, Afghanistan and Pakistan are mainly guided by the SAP. But it should be remembered here that no country's international relations are dependent on any particular foreign policy issue, and the United States is no exception in this regard. America's international relations are also dependent on a combination of foreign policy issues. As such, nonproliferation issues, economic diplomacy and the SAP may be applied together for maintaining America's relations with another country. Sometimes American foreign relations with a country may be guided by a combine of three, four, or all the five policies outlined here, depending on the time, the situation, and the US national interests.

## US–India Relations After the Cold War

America and India did not have a close relation during the Cold War. Mutual disbelief and misunderstanding dominated bilateral relations from 1947 to 1990. The United States did not trust India or its policy of nonalignment due to India's Soviet-tilt. It considered India as a Soviet 'stooge' during the Cold War. India, on the other hand, then viewed the United States as a neo-imperialist and neo-colonial power with the ultimate motive to dominate the world. America's 'soft' attitude towards Pakistan also alienated it from India. Such mutual disbelief and mistrust during the Cold War created differences between the two largest democracies. American diplomat Dennis Kux said US–India relations during the Cold War to be 'estranged'. However, the end of the Cold War created new opportunities for both India and the United States to come closer and renew their relationship. There were several reasons for such opportunities: (1) the disintegration of the Soviet Union; (2) India's economic liberalization; (3) the increasing economic and political clout of Indian Americans in the United States; (4) the emergence of the United States as the only superpower and (5) no special treatment of Pakistan by the United States due to the end of Cold War political calculations. It was believed by experts in both countries that the presence of these opportunities would help the two nations to forge a strong relationship after the war.

Some of the opportunities were used significantly after the Cold War by both governments to strengthen US–India relations. For instance, India's economic liberalization in 1991 helped to initiate close economic ties between the two nations. The United States welcomed India's economic reforms and American investment in the Indian market enhanced to a great extent. US–India two-way trade also registered significant growth. In 1991, the total volume of US–India bilateral trade was US $5,070 million. The volume of bilateral trade rose to US $14,353.80 million in the year 2000. This amount grew further to US $28,140.70 million in 2009 (till September 2009).[9] In 1991, total American investment in India was US $97 million. It grew to US $900 million in 2000 and US $1,802.0 million in 2008–09 (April 2008–March 2009).[10] These data indicate that India's economic reforms gave a boost to US–India trade and American investment in India. In fact, India–US economic relations got significantly strengthened after India's economic liberalization, and became the driving force behind an overall close relationship.

The emergence of the United States as the only superpower after the Cold War, along with the disintegration of the Soviet Union, also helped US–India relations. Foreign policy planners in India were quick to realize that it would not be prudent for India to continue its estrangement with the world's only superpower. This realization led India to come closer to the United States. On the other hand, the absence of the Soviet-factor and Cold War political calculations led the United States to befriend India, an emerging market for American business, and a big power in Asia. Mutual trust, missing in bilateral relations for a long time, began to grow in US–India relations after the Cold War. The Indian Americans also played a big role in strengthening bilateral relations.

The highly educated and economically well-off Indian Americans constitute the second-highest earning community—after the Japanese Americans—in terms of per capita income in the United States. As successful individuals in different walks of life, the Indian Americans started becoming actively involved in American politics as well. Many of them are now important members of the two leading political parties in the United States. In 1992, the Indian Americans formed the 'Congressional Caucus on India and Indian Americans', popularly known as the 'India Caucus', to influence America's India-policy inside the US Congress. Although the India Caucus has its limitations, it nevertheless was successful in influencing American decision to back India during the Kargil crisis in 1999. It also played an important role in achieving the US–India Civil Nuclear Agreement. Overall, the contribution of the Indian Americans in forging a strong bilateral relationship after the Cold War could hardly be ignored.

President Bill Clinton paid an official visit to India in March 2000. This visit was historic because Clinton was the first American President to visit India in twenty-two years (after President Carter's visit in 1978). He was the fourth US President in fifty-three years (1947–2000) to pay an official visit to India. This visit was seen as the outcome of a close relationship between the two countries after the Cold War. On 21 March 2000, US President Clinton and Indian Prime Minister Vajpayee signed the 'Vision Statement' (VS) in New Delhi. This statement became a significant document in bilateral diplomatic history as it provided a detailed outline of the areas of closer cooperation between the two nations in future. The VS announced institutional mechanisms to expedite cooperation in different fields. These are some of the institutional mechanisms created by it: (1) US–India Financial and Economic Forum; (2) US–India Commercial Dialogue; (3) US–India Working Group on Trade; (4) Joint Consultative Group on Clean Energy and Environment and (5) US–India Science and Technology Forum. The statement also declared that the Heads of Government of the two countries would meet regularly—at least once a year—to augment cooperation. Further, Annual Foreign Policy Dialogue at the ministerial levels would take place to ensure close cooperation. The VS also suggested the creation of 'High Level Coordinating Groups' to monitor progress in bilateral cooperation. Vajpayee paid a reciprocal visit to the United States in September 2000. This was the first reciprocal visit to the United States—after Morarji Desai's in 1978—in twenty-two years; it signalled a markedly improved US–India relationship. After these reciprocal visits in 2000, bilateral relations witnessed gradual upswing, and the signing of the Civil Nuclear Agreement between George Bush (Jr) and Manmohan Singh on 2 March 2006 in New Delhi was the outcome of this upsurge in US–India relations after the Cold War. Since 2000, the Heads of Government and other important leaders of the two countries have been meeting regularly and very intense cooperation in different fields have been taking place between the two largest democracies in the world.

There were, however, apprehensions in some quarters about the sustenance of a strong US–India relationship under the Barack Obama administration, due to Obama's anti-outsourcing policies, affinity for China, and the Af-Pak policy that sought to reinstate Pakistan as central to US strategic and counter-terrorism policies. US Secretary of State Hillary Clinton's delayed visit to India in July 2009, which 'finally' took place several months after she visited other 'important' Asian countries, added fuel to such speculations. But during Manmohan Singh's official visit to the United States in November 2009, President Obama called India 'indispensable' for the United States and assured that close links with India in economic and strategic areas would continue. Earlier, the American President had hinted that he was committed to take the Civil Nuclear Agreement to fruition.

During the visit, Singh said that US–India relations rested on 'five Es' at the concluding stages of the first decade of the twenty-first century. The five Es that Manmohan highlighted were: Economy, Energy, Environment, Education and Empowerment. He believed that these five Es would guide future US–India relations along with defence, security and counter-terrorism. President Obama had expressed considerable admiration for India since he took office in January 2009. His official visit in November 2010 signalled India's importance to the US administration. During his stay, President Obama reiterated once again America's commitment towards building an economic and strategic partnership with India. The two nations have overcome many crucial hurdles (like India's nuclear tests; US sanctions on India, etc.) in the recent past, but their relationship never remained hostage to such obstacles and it moved ahead. Our bilateral relations has attained considerable strength since the year 2000. In that context, President Obama's visit to India added a fillip to relations between the two nations.

The bonhomie in India–US relations continued after Narendra Modi assumed office as Prime Minister of India in May 2014. Under his leadership, India–US relations continued to develop into a 'global strategic partnership', based on convergence of interests and mutual trust. As per a report of the Ministry of External Affairs (MEA), government of India, 'Regular exchange of high level political visits has provided sustained momentum to bilateral cooperation, while the wide-ranging and ever-expanding dialogue architecture has established a long-term framework for India–US engagement'.[11] The frequency of high-level visits and exchanges between India and the United States has gone up significantly in recent times. Prime Minister Modi visited the United States from 26 to 30 September 2014. During this visit, the Indian Prime Minister held meetings with the American president, members of the US Congress and also members of President Obama's cabinet. The Indian prime minister also reached out to the American commerce and industry, civil society and think-tanks, and the Indian diaspora in the United States. During this visit, the two sides set up a contact group for advancing the full and timely implementation of the Civil Nuclear Cooperation Agreement, and to resolve pending issues. This visit also facilitated the creation of an India–US investment initiative, with a special focus on augmenting FDI, portfolio investment, capital market development and financing of infrastructure. According to the MEA, 'The visit also succeeded in reaffirming India's strategic priorities in critical spheres of high technology, security, counter-terrorism and defence'.[12] During the visit, a VS and a joint statement were issued.

President Barack Obama visited India from 25 to 27 January 2015 as the Chief Guest at India's Republic Day. During the visit, the two sides issued a Delhi Declaration of Friendship and adopted a Joint Strategic Vision for Asia-Pacific and the Indian Ocean Region. Both sides elevated the strategic dialogue between their foreign ministers to Strategic and Commercial Dialogue of Foreign and Commerce Ministers. Indian Prime Minister Narendra Modi again visited the United States from 23 to 28 September 2015. During this visit, he held a bilateral meeting with President Obama, interacted with leaders of business, media, academia and the provincial leaders in the United States. Economic relations between the two countries have also progressed well in recent years. From a modest US $5.6 billion trade in 1990, India–US bilateral trade reached US $62.11 billion in the FY 2015–16. Several Indian companies are now investing in the United States. These include Tata Group, Wipro, Reliance, Piramal and many others. However, India–US bilateral trade relations need to be augmented further, with a target of US $100.0 billion by the year 2020.

During Narendra Modi's June 2017 visit to the United States, bilateral relations were evaluated and analysed for further growth by the Indian and American leaders and officials. Modi met the new US President Donald Trump and discussed bilateral and international issues. This meeting was important in the context of changing global power equations where a more assertive China was trying to put forward its policies such as OBOR and CPEC. Prime Minister Modi and the US President Trump agreed to strengthen the strategic partnership between the two nations and cooperation on sensitive global issues. India and the United States have the potential to be natural allies in the future due to changing global power equations, being observed at this point of time.

# PART III

# Foreign Policy of the People's Republic of China

## Origin and Evolution

Today's People's Republic of China (PRC) has a rich political history. One of the most ancient civilizations, China's political history is nearly seven thousand years old. During this long political history, China was under various rulers and political systems. It had dynastic rulers who ruled the land for long periods. Notable among them were the Shang, the Chou and the Manchu dynasties. The Manchu rulers governed China for a very long period, from 1661 to 1911. They were able to create a large territory that included Tibet, Mongolia and Sinkiang. But at a later stage, the Manchu rulers were unable to govern and protect this large empire. Inefficiency, corruption and extravagance of the later Manchu rulers led to the downfall of the Manchu dynasty. This unstable situation was exploited by different foreign powers to proclaim their dominance in different parts of China. The Russian, German, British and Japanese forces occupied these parts. But it should be remembered at this point that entire China never came under any particular foreign rule; parts of the land were occupied by different foreign rulers at different times. To protest against the presence of foreign rulers, and the corruption in Manchu rule, the Boxur Revolt was led by Sun Yat Sen during 1895–1900. Although this revolution was not totally successful, it nevertheless inspired people to unite against foreign rule and the Manchu dynasty.

After the end of Manchu rule, Sun Yat Sen became the leader of China in 1912. Since then, China experienced a republican system instead of the earlier monarchical system. Before the First World War, Sun Yat Sen relinquished power in favour of Yuan Shi Kai, although Sen and his Kuomintang Party were very influential in China during this period. During the First World War, Yuan Shi Kai declared himself as the Emperor of China reviving possibilities of returning to a monarchical system again. However, after the death of Shi Kai in 1916, the Kuomintang appointed Li Yuan Hang as the President of China, and declared China as a Republic. The tremors of the Bolshevik Revolution in Russia in 1917 were also felt in China, and the Chinese Communist Party was set up in Shanghai, the largest Chinese city, in 1920. Several members of the Kuomintang joined the Communist Party under the influence of the Bolshevik revolution, and socialism.

After the death of Sun Yat Sen in 1925, Chiang Kai Shek assumed leadership of the Kuomintang party and China. Kuomintang preferred to call itself a nationalist party with the aim to create a unified China, and Chiang Kai Shek became, as the undisputed leader of his party, the harbinger of this aim. But Chiang had problems to realize the dream of a unified China. Among these problems, Japanese aggression, internal political and administrative corruption, and the increasing popularity of the Communist Party under the leadership of Mao Zhe Dong were prominent. Since 1935, Mao was pressurizing the Kuomintang government for rapid land reforms programme in favour of the peasants. Mao and his Communist Party started to concentrate on rural areas working on the welfare of the rural people, mainly peasants. This focus on rural areas yielded tremendous results as the popularity of Mao and his party soared in a largely rural, agro-based China. Before the Second World War, the communists gave issue-based support to the Kuomintang to fight Japanese aggression; but their ideological differences continued.

Gradually the Chinese Communist Party (CCP) emerged as an organized, popular and respectable political outfit, and during the Second World War they became a formidable political force in China. There were several reasons behind the phenomenal growth of the CCP: (1) Mao's very able leadership; (2) call for land reforms and establishment of rights of the peasants; (3) support from the 'socialist' Soviet Union and (4) a corrupt Kuomintang rule. Mao was trying to topple the Kuomintang regime, and training the communists to fight the Kuomintang. In 1946, a civil war started in China between the communists and the Kuomintangs. The United States supported the Kuomintang regime through military and economic assistance. But the communists who were more organized and efficient (in guerilla warfare) won the civil war, and created the modern Peoples' Republic of China on 1 October 1949. Chiang Kai Shek fled to Formosa (now Taiwan). The modern Chinese state (PRC) was born in 1949 and Mao Zhe Dong became its supreme leader. From 1949 till his death in 1976, Mao Zhe Dong was the undisputed leader of the PRC, and the chief architect of China's foreign policy.

## Foreign Policy of China Under Mao Zhe Dong (1949–76)

Mao's revolutionary background and faith in socialism influenced his foreign policy agenda. America's assistance to the Kuomintang regime during the civil war in China, and later in Taiwan, led him to locate the United States as an adversary. He believed that after the Second World War, when European imperialism had taken a backseat, the Americans had assumed the role of a neo-imperialist and a neocolonialist. Mao's PRC was very critical of the American role in Taiwan and in other parts of the world, where the United States was allegedly trying to interfere in the domestic affairs of states through economic and security assistance. American interference in the Korean War in 1950 angered Mao, and China's relations with the United States plunged to an abysmal low after the Korean War. At various times in his leadership, Mao openly labelled the United States as an imperial and neocolonial power. Understandably, China's relations with the United States were much strained from the beginning. Mao was also sceptical about other Western European powers like Britain, France, West Germany and Italy for their perceived anti-communist ideological positions. As a committed person to socialist ideologies, Mao was deeply resentful of the West Bloc, and almost turned China away from the Western world. China thus had very little relationship with the West European states, which were viewed as harbingers of capitalism and agents of the United States by Mao and his PRC. So China's relations with the United States and other Western powers were very cold and distant during the Mao era.

Mao's PRC went on a bonhomie with the Soviet Union, the first socialist state in the world, a superpower and a supporter of the Chinese communists during China's civil war and thereafter. Ideological proximity and material support brought the Soviet Union closer to China. Moscow gave huge economic and technological assistance to China after 1949, when the state-building process was going on in full swing. China was creating its industrial and transport infrastructure with Soviet assistance during this time. But the Soviet–China proximity did not last long, as differences emerged from the mid-1950s, overtly on the issue of transfer of poor Soviet technology to China, but covertly over the broader issue of leadership of the Socialist bloc. The Sino-Soviet rift became very pronounced by the early 1960s as both China and the Soviet Union accused each other to be a 'social imperialist'. China strongly condemned the Soviet role in the Cuban Missile Crisis of 1962. The same year, the two countries levelled charges of illegal occupation of territories around their borders against each other. China also severely criticized the presence of Soviet troops in Czechoslovakia in 1968 to curb a popular movement against the communist government. From the mid-1960s, China tried to be close to the East Bloc countries, only to arouse further Soviet suspicion. The Soviet Union viewed this Chinese zeal as designs to curb the Soviet influence in the East Bloc countries. However, China was able to develop close relationship with Albania by the mid-1960s. An angry Soviet Union stopped economic and technological assistance to Albania as a retaliatory measure. The Sino-Soviet rift continued throughout the 1970s and the 1980s, as both the socialist countries tried to provide leadership to other socialist states during this period, and viewed the other with suspicion and mistrust. US President Richard Nixon's visit to China in 1972 further fuelled the suspicion. Soviet leaders alleged that China was trying to build an unholy nexus with the United States to marginalize the Soviet Union in international politics. China's relations with the socialist superpower were thus mostly adversarial in Mao's time.

Mao's China provided support to the anti-colonial struggle in the developing states with the desire to become the leader in those states. For this purpose, China supported the NAM and participated in the Bandung Conference in 1955 that formally created the NAM. China also became friendly with India, and the two big countries of Asia went along well for some time. But from the late 1950s, border disputes and the issue of Tibet created serious differences between the two countries which ultimately led to the 1962 Indo-China war. During the initial years after the formation of the NAM in 1955, China was keen on becoming a leading nation in the NAM. But differences with India—and later with Indonesia—and the broader issue of leadership of the Socialist bloc refrained Mao from taking very active interest in the NAM. Instead, China concentrated on building good relations with some other Asian states like Burma (now Myanmar), Nepal, and Pakistan. Foreign policy analysts in India viewed this Chinese move with suspicion, a latent design to isolate India and strengthen anti-India sentiments in these countries. However, China's efforts to become a leader of the third world failed, as it could not take leadership in the NAM, and as it developed acrimonious relations with many third-world countries.

After 1965, China's relations with Indonesia and many other countries in Africa and Latin America deteriorated. Indonesian President Suharto alleged that China was instigating the communists in Indonesia with a view to create internal disturbances in the country. Suharto severed diplomatic relations with China. Three African states, Burundi, Ghana and Central African Republic, cut off diplomatic relations with China in 1965–66. Kenya also condemned the aggressive 'socialist imperialism' of China during this time. Mao's China also failed to develop close connections with the developing countries of Latin America. It tried to woo Cuba to come out of Soviet influence by condemning Soviet role in the Cuban Missile Crisis; but Fidel Castro, the supreme leader of Cuba, remained committed to the Soviet Union during and after the crisis. China's aim to lead the third world against the 'imperialistic' policies of the two superpowers was not realized, as Mao's China got estranged from several third world countries.

Viewed from an objective standpoint, Mao's foreign policy was not very successful. He isolated both the superpowers and developed adversarial relations with them. With important states of the third world like India, Indonesia and Yugoslavia (all leaders of the NAM), Mao's China developed very antagonistic relations. China also remained isolated from the industrially developed Western European countries due to Mao's apathy for these 'capitalist', formerly colonial powers. Mao, who was supposed to develop cordial relations with the poor states for his support to the anti-colonial freedom struggle in poor countries, also isolated poor countries in Africa, Asia and Latin America. The Soviet influence over East Europe was a deterrent for Mao to make any significant impact in East Europe, although he tried and succeeded to establish close links with one or two smaller states in the region. But he failed to bring them out of the Soviet ring. The ideological underpinning of Mao's foreign policy, to avoid the 'colonial' and 'imperial' powers, did not help China economically or politically, as China got estranged from the industrially developed United States and the West. The confusion in Mao's foreign policy was manifested further when China got entangled in bitter rivalries with a 'socialist' Soviet Union, and 'nonaligned' India and Indonesia, and other developing countries of the third world with whom Mao's ideology should have gone well. Instead, Mao's China was soon termed as politically ambitious, with an eye to leadership in the socialist bloc, and the third world. This China aroused suspicion in the world, and as a consequence, failed to win friends. During Mao's tenure, China remained largely estranged in international relations.

## China's Foreign Policy After Mao (1977–91)

China's foreign policy during the Cold War years could be classified mainly into two parts: first, the Mao era (1949–76); and second, the Deng era (1978–97). This proposition clearly refers to the fact that after the death of Mao Zhe Dong, China's domestic and foreign policies were controlled by another supreme leader, Deng Xiao Ping. Although Deng officially assumed leadership in 1978, succeeding Hua Guo Feng, who took over leadership for a very short period (1976–78) after Mao's death, Deng's rise in Chinese politics could be noticed from 1977. From 1977 till his death in 1997, Deng Xiao Ping remained the most prominent figure in Chinese politics. Consequently, Chinese foreign policy was also controlled by Deng during this period. He made significant departures from Mao's policies, both in domestic and international spheres. Mao's foreign policy was loaded with ideological issues like distance from the 'capitalist' and 'imperialist' states, spreading the message of socialism, supporting 'revolutionary' communist and nationalist movements around the world. Deng's foreign and domestic policies were considered more pragmatic than ideological. Deng was the architect of economic reforms in China which opened hitherto closed Chinese doors to the industrially developed Western world. Chinese economic reforms helped Deng to pursue a more realistic and internationally acceptable foreign policy.

Deng realized that it would not help China much to isolate both the United States and the Soviet Union simultaneously. For China's economic development, the United States, Western

European states and an industrially developed Japan were crucial and more welcome than the socialist rival, the Soviet Union. China could no longer afford to ignore the Western states as 'capitalist' and 'imperialist' powers. In 1979, Deng's China established diplomatic relations with the United States. Apart from economic interests, a common adversary (the Soviet Union) also brought China and the United States closer. American President Richard Nixon tried to break the ice in Sino-American relations by visiting China in 1972. But differences between the two nations persisted over Taiwan—which China claimed as its territory but the United States considered as a sovereign independent country—and Mao's label on the United States as an 'imperialist' power. Therefore, Sino-American relations continued to be indifferent during the Mao period. It was Deng who broke real grounds to establish closer links with the United States and other developed states of the West.

Deng used economic diplomacy to attract these states towards China. In 1979, China opened up its economy, allowing private business to proliferate and foreign investment to come. Deng made a very new experiment for China. He retained Communist Party's control over Chinese politics and the state, but transformed Chinese economy into a liberal market economy. A new Chinese Constitution was introduced in 1982 to facilitate liberal economic developments in China. Deng's China created Special Economic Zones (SEZ), mainly in the coastal areas, to give special privileges to foreign investors. Now, the industrially advanced states, apathetic to China for long for its 'closed door' policies, felt encouraged and got attracted to China. The socialist market economy (SME) that Deng introduced in China was a new model in international politics and economy. It retained one-party control in Chinese politics and society, but allowed deregulation of the economy. Although there were initial schisms about the SME, it gradually proved to be a huge success and made Deng, the conservative pragmatist, the undisputed leader of modern China.

Deng's foreign policy, must, therefore, be analysed in the context of the SME and his conservative pragmatism. The success of the state-controlled liberal economy in China, manifested through its economic growth rate, made China a very attractive destination for foreign investments. American, Japanese and west European private business started to enter China in a big way from the early 1980s, paving ways for the relegation of political differences to the background. China's annual average economic growth rate for the decade 1960–70 was 5.2, and for 1970–80 it was 5.5. During the next decade (1980–90), when SME was operating, China's annual growth rate rose to a staggering 10.3, almost double the average growth rate of the earlier two decades (source: International Monetary Fund). Therefore, Deng's China was economically stronger than Mao's China, and it was easier for an economically open and strong China to conduct international relations with more determination, zeal and success. As China shed its ideological bias to invite foreign investments from the 'capitalist' and 'imperialist' states of the West, these industrially developed nations also changed their views about a 'rigid' and 'closed' socialist state in Asia. Gradually China's relations with the Western world improved, as China began to play, from the early 1980s, a significant role in mainstream international economics and politics. Mao's China also wanted to play a major role in world politics, but could not fulfill its desires due to China's closed economy and adverse international relations; but Deng's China, economically open and strong, could play this desired role more easily, as China became more acceptable to the rest of the world.

China's relations with the Soviet Union also improved after Mikhail Gorbachev came to power in the USSR in 1985. Border trade between the two socialist giants went up and got strengthened by the late 1980s. Gorbachev paid an official visit to China in May 1989. Before his visit, the Soviet Union announced the withdrawal of 5,00,000 Soviet troops from its borders with China. Chinese leaders welcomed this Soviet gesture. In 1990, Li Peng, Prime Minister of China, visited the Soviet Union. A ten-year vision on close cooperation in trade, economic and technological areas between the two countries was announced during Peng's visit. With 'glasnost' and 'perestroika' taking shape, the Soviet Union also opened up and shed its earlier hostility towards China. As a consequence, Sino-Soviet relations began to improve. Deng also reached out to third world countries, including India, to assess possibilities of improved trade and commerce. By the early 1990s, when Cold War was nearing its end, China secured its place in the international order as a rapidly growing economy, a strong military, and a more open state with a realistic view of the world. China's journey towards a major power status continued after the end of the Cold War.

## China's Foreign Policy After the Cold War

China maintained its spectacular economic growth after the Cold War and continued to use economic diplomacy as its major thrust in international relations. Although an ageing Deng Xiao Ping resigned from all official posts in 1991, he remained as the central figure in Chinese politics, and virtually controlled the party and the state in China till his death in 1997. The SME brought economic gains for China, which subsequently helped China in conducting international diplomacy more effectively. After the Cold War, the United States remained the only superpower in an altered international order. Deng's pragmatic China wanted to be close to the world's only remaining superpower. The United States also wanted to forge strong economic relations with China because of its emerging market. Mutual interests brought these two countries close after the Cold War. In 1994, the United States granted the 'Most Favoured Nation (MFN) in Trade' status to China. Despite persistent criticism in the US Congress about human rights violations in China, the United States did not hesitate to grant MFN status to China for trade and economic interests. By 1998–99, China became the fourth largest trading partner of the United States with bilateral trade reaching US $94.9 billion at the end of 1999. Sino-US two-way trade was only US $2.4 billion in 1979.

In 2001, China entered the World Trade Organization (WTO), backed heavily by the United States. Since then, it has become a major player in the WTO, supporting interests of the developing states. Sino-US trade continued to escalate in the new century as well. Two-way trade reached a substantial US $409.2 billion in 2008.[13] The United States emerged as the top trading partner of China in 2008 and 2009, with Japan emerging as the second largest trading partner in 2009. These data revealed how China had used its economic diplomacy after the Cold War to bring former adversaries close towards China. Despite occasional American concern for an authoritarian political system, and violation of democratic and human rights in China, the US–China economic relations remained very strong after the Cold War, and these would continue to remain strong in the future for mutual trade and business interests. Strengthened economic relations also helped Sino-American political relations to improve after the Cold War. Top-level mutual visits by the leaders of the two nations continued after the war. American President Barack Obama visited China in November 2009. The US–China joint statement issued during Obama's visit acknowledged China's leading role in world politics, and particularly in Asia.

The statement, which raised eyebrows in India, clearly indicated that China occupied a dominant role in Asia. It appeared to highlight the new Democratic Administration's preference for China. This preference may also strengthen US–China political relations in future.

With Gorbachev becoming the President of the Soviet Union, Sino-Soviet relations began to improve. China's relations with the new Russian Federation continued to grow after the Cold War. In 1991, the Sino-Russian Border Agreement was signed apportioning territory that became controversial during the Sino-Soviet border conflict during the Cold War period. In 1992, Russian President Boris Yeltsin visited China, and signed economic and defence agreements with China. After Gorbachev's visit to China in 1989, leaders of the two states continued to pay mutual visits. These top-level visits helped to normalize relations between the two countries. Russian President Vladimir Putin visited China in 2000, and signed three important economic and trade agreements with China. In 2001, Russia emerged as the top supplier of defence equipments to China. Also in 2001, the close relations between the two countries were formalized with the 'Treaty of Good Neighbourliness and Friendly Cooperation', a twenty-year strategic, economic and arguably, an implicit military, treaty. Before this treaty was signed, the two countries joined Kazakhstan, Kyrgyzstan, Tajikistan and Uzbekistan to form the Shanghai Cooperation Organization (SCO), a multilateral forum for economic and strategic cooperation.

The Russian government also agreed to transfer Tarabarov Island as well as one half of Bolshoy Ussuriysky Island to China in 2004, ending a long-standing border dispute between the two countries. The transfer had been ratified by both the Chinese and the Russian parliaments. The official transfer ceremony was held on 14 October 2008. This event was a big leap forward in bilateral relationship between China and Russia, and could act as a confidence-building measure in the future. Two-way trade between the two countries also registered significant growth in recent times. Sino-Russian trade volume was US $33.4 billion in 2006. It reached a healthy US $56.8 billion in 2008. During his visit to Russia in 2007, Chinese President Hu Jin Tao told Russian journalists that he was very optimistic about bilateral trade reaching US $80 billion by 2010.[14] Russian President Dimitry Medvedev also expressed similar hopes during his state visit to China in 2008.[15] Although the total volume of present China–Russia trade is not as large as the volume of Sino-American trade, it is encouraging to note that China–Russia two-way trade has gained momentum after the Cold War. It appears from the analyses made here that both countries are now eager to forge strong economic and political relations in a changed international order after the Cold War.

China also improved its relations with Japan, a close neighbour and an economic giant, after the Cold War. Under the SME, China allowed Japanese companies to do business in the country. This Chinese gesture helped to ease tensions between the two Asian neighbours. In 1992, Japanese Emperor Akihito visited China. This was the first visit to China by any Japanese Emperor after the Second World War. Naturally, this visit aroused great interests in the two countries and helped to improve relations. In 1993, Japan's erstwhile Prime Minister Hosokawa expressed regrets on behalf of his people for Japan's aggression over China during the Second World War. His regrets softened Chinese sentiments towards Japan. The two states are now politically and economically very close. Top-level mutual visits by the leaders of the two states are taking place regularly. In 2006, Shinzo Abe, Prime Minister of Japan, visited China. During his talks with the Chinese leaders, Abe stressed on cooperation in bilateral trade and investment. Chinese Premier Wen Jiabao visited Japan in 2007 and held talks on various areas of cooperation between the two states.

Chinese Foreign Minister Yang Jiechi visited Japan in November 2009 and met Japanese leaders. Japan's Foreign Minister Okada welcomed Yang on his official visit to Japan, and stated that Japan and China had engaged in dialogues on a variety of issues between their counterparts and that he would like to further promote active cooperation not only in bilateral relationship but also in regional and global issues. As mentioned earlier, Japan had emerged as the second largest trade partner of China in 2008 with a total trade volume of US $266.8 billion.[16] Clearly, mutual economic interests had paid dividends in Sino-Japanese bilateral relations which improved significantly after the Cold War.

China also endeavoured to improve its relations with the ASEAN, the regional organization with strong economic credentials. China is an important part of the ASEAN + 3 mechanism that also includes Japan and South Korea as non-members of the ASEAN. China and the ASEAN now hold regular summits, also known as the 10 + 1 mechanism. On 24 October 2009, the Twelfth China–ASEAN Summit (10 + 1) was held in Hua Hin, Thailand. Chinese Premier Wen Jiabao and the leaders of ASEAN-countries attended the summit. The two sides reviewed the joint efforts to tackle the international financial crisis and other challenges faced by the two sides over the past one year, expressed their will to forge cooperation and seek common development, and reached broad consensus on deepening comprehensive cooperation. The China–ASEAN Free Trade Area (FTA), to be completed by 2010, would become another important milestone in the history of relations between the two sides. The current relationship between China and the ASEAN is featured by stronger mutual trust, closer ties in different areas, and the will to work for peace and security in the Asia Pacific region. China has also enhanced its cooperation with the EU. China's relations with EU were established in 1975, and are currently guided by the 1985 EU–China Trade and Cooperation Agreement. At present, apart from regular political, trade and economic dialogue meetings between China and the EU, there are over twenty-four sectoral dialogues and agreements, ranging from environmental protection to industrial policy, to education and culture. The Twelfth EU–China Summit took place in Nanjing, China, on 30 November 2009. The joint statement issued after the summit acknowledged the role played by EU and China in fostering peace and harmony in the world, and called for increasing cooperation between the EU and China in the areas of trade, security, environment, education and culture. As a group, the EU emerged as the largest trade partner of China in 2008. China's relations with the developing nations of Asia, Africa and Latin America also improved after the Cold War in an atmosphere of free market economy and changed political calculations. China is helping many developing states to improve their industrial and social infrastructure through economic and technological assistance. On the whole, an economically resurgent China is now playing the role of an important actor in world politics after the Cold War.

## China–India Relations After the Cold War

Two years after India gained independence in 1947, the People's Republic of China emerged as a new socialist country in Asia. Therefore, the modern Indian state and the new socialist state in China began their journey almost simultaneously. Initially, the two big Asian neighbours shared a cordial relationship among themselves. Jawaharlal Nehru, the first Prime Minister of India, welcomed the creation of a socialist China as a victory in the struggle against imperialism and colonialism. Nehru's socialist leanings encouraged him to establish close connections with China. China reciprocated by sending its leader Zhou Enlai to India, and the two countries declared that their friendship would be guided by the 'Panchsheel' (five principles) which essentially called for mutual respect for each other's sovereignty, territorial integrity and the policy of non-interference. In 1955, China joined the conference of Afro-Asian states in Bandung, and supported the endeavour of these states to remain non-aligned in a sharply divided bipolar world perpetuated by the Cold War. India hailed the Chinese stance in Bandung.

The bonhomie, however, did not last long. By the late 1950s, differences over border issues and Tibet's accession to China emerged between the two states. Both China and India accused each other of illegal occupation of territory. China further alleged that India was instigating the separatist Tibetans by giving shelter to the Dalai Lama, the Tibetan religious leader. From 1957, border skirmishes between the armies of the two states began. The two states went to war in 1962, in which China won convincingly. China's victory in this war with India helped to fulfill, to some extent, a few political designs of China. These were: (1) to teach India a lesson on the issue of Tibet; (2) to nullify the Indian position on the border issue; (3) to scuttle India's desire for leadership of the third world and (4) to harm Nehru's image as a global leader. After the 1962 war, diplomatic relations were cut off, and the two states distanced themselves from each other. As a consequence, during the 1960s and the 1970s, Sino-Indian relations remained very low. Ambassadorial relations between them were restored in 1979, after the visit of the Indian Foreign Minister Atal Behari Vajpayee to China that year; but bilateral relations did not improve much after the visit, the first top level visit by any leader of the two countries since the war of 1962.

In 1981, China's Foreign Minister Huang Hua visited India. It was decided during Hua's visit that China and India would resume talks to resolve border problems. Accordingly, seven rounds of talks were held between the two countries from 1981 to 1987 in New Delhi and Beijing. But due to the inflexible attitude of both states, the talks failed. Sino-Indian relations did not improve till the late 1980s. With Indian Prime Minister Rajiv Gandhi's visit to China in 1988, bilateral relations started getting back to normalcy. It was decided during this visit that the two states would form JWGs to continue dialogues to resolve outstanding border issues. The annual meeting of the groups would take place alternately in the capital cities of the two states. These groups were successful in reducing tension in the border areas. For instance, after an agreement reached in the JWG meeting in 1993, the two states reduced troops in the border areas. As a result, tensions subsided along the 4,000 km border between the two countries. After the JWG meeting in 1996, China and India announced a series of confidence-building measures to restore peace in border areas. Further, in the eleventh meeting of the JWGs in 1999, the two states agreed to work for regional peace and security and reduction of nuclear weapons, alongside border problems. Till 2002, the JWG met fourteen times in Beijing and New Delhi, and proved to be a very useful and successful mechanism for bilateral talks. Apart from the creation of the JWG, the two states also signed important agreements on cooperation in civil aviation, exchange of technology and cultural delegations. Rajiv Gandhi's visit to China helped to normalize relations between the two Asian neighbours. It also paved the way for further top-level reciprocal visits by the leaders of the two states.

Chinese Premier Li Peng visited New Delhi in December 1991. Peng was the first Chinese Prime Minister to visit India in thirty-seven years after Zhou Enlai visited India in 1954. It was also the first top-level visit from China after the Cold War. Three important agreements were signed during Peng's visit: resuming border trade; cooperation in space research and opening of consulate offices in Mumbai and Shanghai. Peng's visit was hailed as a success by the media in the two countries. Indian Prime Minister Narasimha Rao visited China in 1993. During his visit, Rao and the Chinese leaders agreed to reduce tension and restore peace along the LAC. An Expert Committee comprising diplomats and military personnel from the two countries was also formed to assist the JWG in bilateral talks. In 1992, President of India R. Venkataraman visited China, while Indian Vice President K. R. Narayanan paid an official visit to China in 1994. From the Chinese side, Li Ruihan, a top leader of the CCP, visited India in 1993, and the Chairman of the National Peoples' Congress (NPC) Qiao Shi visited India in 1995. Since high-level visits are always important in bilateral relations, these reciprocal visits helped to improve Sino-Indian relations after the Cold War.

Chinese President Jiang Zemin paid a very successful visit to India in 1996. His was the first-ever visit to India by a Chinese President. Four important agreements were signed between the two countries during his visit. These were: (1) agreement on confidence-building measures in the military along the LAC; (2) agreement concerning the maintenance of the consulate office of India in the Hong Kong Special Administrative Region in the PRC; (3) agreement on cooperation for combating illicit trafficking in narcotic drugs and psychotropic substances and other crimes and (4) agreement between the two countries on maritime support. The visit initiated a process of cooperation between the two countries in new and newer areas. In April 1998, General Fu Quanyon, Chief of the Chinese Army, came to India and met senior Indian leaders, including Prime Minister Vajpayee, to discuss defence and security issues concerning the two states. India's Foreign Minister Jaswant Singh visited China in June 1999 to discuss bilateral issues. So there was a spurt of high-level visits between India and China throughout the 1990s. The two neighbours shed many of their differences in this decade, and endeavoured to forge an amicable relationship between them. The effort continued into the new century with Indian President K. R. Narayanan's official visit to China in May 2000, and the visit of Li Peng, Chairman of the Standing Committee of the NPC, to India in January 2001.

Two-way high-level visits continued, showing improvements in bilateral relations, and the Chinese Premier Zhu Rongji came to India in January 2002. Agreements on trade, science and technology, and environment were signed during Rongji's visit. In June 2003, Atal Behari Vajpayee visited China again, this time as the Prime Minister of India. Vajpayee met President Hu Jintao, Premier Wen Jiabao and other Chinese leaders during his stay in China. The two states agreed to strengthen mechanisms for bilateral cooperation, and decided to create Joint Study Groups (JSGs) consisting of experts from the two nations to explore trade and business opportunities. It was also decided during Vajpayee's visit that the defence ministers of China and India would exchange regular visits to monitor security issues, including border problems.

Wen Jiabao paid a reciprocal visit to India in April 2005 and met Prime Minister Manmohan Singh and other Indian leaders. During his visit, the two sides issued a joint statement, establishing a 'Strategic and Cooperative Partnership for Peace and Prosperity'. Chinese President Hu Jintao visited India in November 2006. India and China issued a joint declaration, outlining a ten-point strategy to intensify cooperation in all areas and to give greater strength to strategic and cooperative partnership between India and China. Manmohan Singh visited China in January 2008. A joint document entitled 'A Shared Vision for the 21st Century of the Republic of India and the People's Republic of China' was issued during the visit, highlighting common positions on various international and bilateral issues. Prime Minister Singh visited China again in October 2008 to participate in the Seventh Asia–Europe Summit held in Beijing on 24–25 October. India and China have stepped up functional cooperation in all areas. The two foreign ministries have instituted dialogue mechanisms on issues relating to counter-terrorism, policy planning and security, besides strategic dialogue and regular consultations. There are also close cooperation in areas as diverse as water resources, judiciary, science and technology, audit, personnel, finance, and labour.[17] India and China are now also parts of important multilateral groupings like the BRIC (Brazil, Russia, India, China) and the BASIC (Brazil, South Africa, India, China) which try to protect the interests of group members in other international political, economic, environmental or trade forums. This reflects the desire of the two states to work more closely in bilateral and multilateral mechanisms.

A major area of satisfaction in bilateral relations is the increasing trade volume between the two countries. China–India trade, which totalled US $13.6 billion in 2004, rose to US $51.8 billion in 2008.[18] China is already a leading trade partner of India. But there is ample scope for radical improvement in bilateral trade. In 2008, the total volume of China–India trade constituted less than 2 per cent of total Chinese trade, and less than 6 per cent of total Indian trade. This grey area in bilateral trade requires attention, because these two Asian neighbours are the most developing economies in the world today. They must pay more attention to each other in terms of trade. However, the pace of growth in bilateral trade since 2004 may be viewed with optimism.

Despite noteworthy improvement in China–India relations during the post–Cold War period, it would not be wrong to mention that the relationship suffers from lack of trust. Border problems are persistent irritants in bilateral relations, with occasional claims on each other's territories. The Tibet issue often comes back to affect the relationship. For instance, the visit of Dalai Lama to India in November 2009 drew Chinese criticisms about India's 'designs'. Moreover, India fears that a militarily and economically strong China might prove to be a security threat for it. India cited the presence of a nuclear neighbour (China) as a security threat and as the justification for Pokhran II in May 1998. Chinese security-related supplies to Pakistan further exacerbate Indian schism.

The President of India Pratibha Patil paid an official visit to China from 26 to 31 May 2010. In Beijing, she held talks with Chinese President Hu Jintao and met with NPC Chairman Wu Bangguo and Premier Wen Jiabao. The Indian President attended the reception to mark the sixtieth anniversary of diplomatic relations between the two nations. Chinese Premier Wen Jiabao visited India from 15 to 17 December 2010. During his visit, Premier Wen met with President Patil, Prime Minister Manmohan Singh, Vice President Hamid Ansari, UPA Chairperson Sonia Gandhi and the leader of the opposition, Sushma Swaraj. Six agreements were signed during Wen Jiabao's visit. These agreements covered areas such as green technologies, media exchanges, hydrological data, cultural exchange and banking. During the visit, a bilateral trade target of US $100 billion was set to be achieved by 2015. A Strategic Economic Dialogue and a CEO Forum were also established and the year 2011 was declared as 'Year of India–China exchange'. The establishment of hotline between the Indian Prime Minister and the Chinese Premier, a mechanism of annual Foreign Ministers Meeting and a regular high-level exchange mechanism were also announced. Considering all these agreements and setting up of institutional mechanisms for closer cooperation, Wen's visit to India was eventful.

Bilateral relations continued to be steady in 2011. This was manifested through several top-level visits by leaders of the two countries. Indian Prime Minister Manmohan Singh visited Sanya in Southeast China from April 12 to 15 to participate in the BRICS summit. On the sidelines, he also had a bilateral meeting with Chinese President Hu Jintao. In the same year, chief ministers of Bihar, Madhya Pradesh and Gujarat also visited China in June, September and November, respectively. Similarly, the Chairman of Xinjiang Autonomous Region and Party Secretary of Gansu also visited India as part of the MEA-ILD exchange and Distinguished Visitors Programme of the MEA. One of the highlights of the 'Year of Exchanges' was the visit of a youth delegation to China. Premier Wen Jiabao met and addressed the Indian youth. Several ministerial and official visits to China were made to participate in BRICS activities. For the first time, India–China Consultations on United Nations Security Council issues were held in March 2011. Leaders of the two countries have maintained regular contacts and have met frequently during international gatherings and meetings of multilateral forums in the recent past.[19]

The year 2012 was declared as the 'Year of India–China Friendship and Cooperation'. In this year, high-level official visits between the countries continued unabated. In early February 2012, the Indian Foreign Minister Salman Khurshid visited China. He met with important Chinese leaders and discussed bilateral issues. About his trip, Khurshid told the media:

> On the bilateral front, we have discussed our growing trade relationship. We are confident in our reaching the goal of US$ 100 billion by 2015. I have highlighted the need for initiating measures to balance our trade relations ... Specifically, we have agreed that the newly established working mechanism for consultation and coordination in border affairs will have its first meeting at an early date.[20]

Chinese Foreign Minister Yang Jiechi visited New Delhi in late February 2012 on an official trip and met with top Indian leaders. After his talks with the Indian Prime Minister Manmohan Singh, Jiechi informed the media:

> Under the current international and regional situation, China and India enjoy broad prospects for growth of bilateral ties. 2012 is an important year for the two countries to build on the past progress and usher in a better future. The two sides have agreed on programs of exchanges and cooperation, which will increase friendship between the two peoples, advance exchanges and cooperation in various fields and send a positive signal about the growth of the relationship.[21]

Chinese President Hu Jintao visited New Delhi for the BRICS summit in late March 2012. On the sidelines of the BRICS summit, the Chinese President met with senior Indian leaders and discussed bilateral issues. During his meeting with the Indian Prime Minister, the two leaders talked about enhancing economic, cultural and people-to-people exchanges.

Chinese Defence Minister and a member of the Central Military Commission General Liang Guanglie visited India during 2–6 September 2012. It was the first visit of a Chinese military general to India in eight years. General Liang Guanglie called on the Indian Prime Minister and the Defence Minister. The Indian and Chinese Defence Ministers had an extensive exchange of views on defence and military exchanges and cooperation between the two nations. They also discussed the regional security situation and international issues of common interest and concern. The two defence ministers agreed to work together to enhance mutual trust in the security field and continue to maintain peace and tranquillity in the India–China border areas.[22] A series of other important high-level visits took place between the two countries in 2012. All these visits manifested the fact that India and China were eager to maintain close contacts at the political level and wanted to engage each other in different areas of bilateral cooperation. India–China political relations also got enhanced and strengthened by various mechanisms.

A change of government in India in the year 2014 did not alter efforts for close connection between the two neighbours. However, a few intriguing issues bothered bilateral relations when the new government, under the leadership of Narendra Modi, assumed office. The new Indian Prime Minister paid a three-day official visit to China from 14 to 16 May 2015. The visit was undertaken at a time when India–China relationship assumed a 'complex' character with the two Asian giants viewing each other with schism. A few key irritants affecting ties were a decades-old unresolved border problem and a mounting trade deficit that threatened to cross US $40 billion in 2015. Added to this was China's announcement of US $46 billion in investments in an economic corridor through Pakistan and a section of disputed Kashmir areas, which fuelled Indian suspicion. In the backdrop of these issues, Modi's visit aroused considerable diplomatic and academic interests. During the visit, the two sides have come up with some noncontroversial, yet important pacts to boost bilateral relations. These agreements covered areas from business to security, to the issue of trade deficit and e-visa.

During Indian Prime Minister's visit, Chinese and Indian firms signed agreements worth more than US $22 billion in deals on 16 May 2015. The two nations signed twenty-one deals in areas ranging from telecom, steel, solar energy and films. India and China also decided to set up a hotline between the military headquarters of the two countries. It was decided that to build trust between the two militaries, China's Vice Chairman of the Central Military Commission will visit India and India's Defence Minister will go to China regularly. There will also be an increase in the number of meetings between border personnel and commanders at all sectors of the India–China border areas. Joint counter-terrorism activities involving two naval forces and militaries were also proposed. It was also agreed that a 'task force' will look at ways to reduce the trade deficit that was US $38 billion in 2013–14 and expected to be in the range of US $ 40–45 billion in FY 2014–15. The task force was also supposed to examine India's complaints regarding problems faced by Indian IT and pharmaceutical companies to enter the Chinese market. It will also look into complaints about problems faced by Chinese firms to invest in India. In a bid to boost tourism and advance people-to-people ties, Modi announced electronic visa on arrival facility to Chinese nationals. The announcement was expected to increase two-way flow of people as the years 2015 and 2016 have been designated 'Visit India' and 'Visit China' years, respectively.

Despite such laudable efforts at improving bilateral relations, the year 2017 saw renewed tensions between the two neighbours over the area of Doklam—a disputed border land between China and Bhutan, which is closer to India. Both China and Bhutan claim the ownership of Doklam, but India supports Bhutanese claim. On 16 June 2017, Chinese troops and engineers arrived in Doklam for constructing a road very close to Indian borders. Two days later, on 18 June, nearly 300 Indian troops arrived in the area. The two sides continuously issued diplomatic statements justifying their respective positions in Doklam. Bhutan also stated that the disputed territory belonged to Bhutan, and any Chinese construction in the area would be uncalled for. Indian and Chinese troops continued to stay in the area as tension escalated. Finally, troops were withdrawn in late August. Peace was restored, not only in Doklam, but also in India–China relations. On 5 September 2017, Indian Prime Minister Narendra Modi and Chinese President Xi

Jinping held hour-long discussions on the sidelines of the ninth BRICS summit that took place in Xiamen City, China. The two leaders agreed on a 'forward looking' approach to see that Doklam-like stand offs did not occur again. Both Modi and Jinping reiterated that maintaining peace in border areas was a prerequisite for cordial bilateral relations. Border tensions and trade deficit (from the Indian point of view) are the two areas of concern at this point of time (i.e., in 2018) in the relationship between the two Asian powers.

# PART IV

# Foreign Policy of the Russian Federation

## The Post–Cold War Dilemma

The Russian Federation, the largest country in the contemporary world, emerged after the disintegration of the Soviet Union in 1991. It is one of the fifteen independent countries created from the former Soviet Union. Today's Russian Federation (henceforth, only Russia) is twice as big as the United States and China, and six times bigger than India. Russia has retained permanent seat in the UN Security Council, and inherited a large portion of nuclear arsenals from the Soviet Union. Russia is now an emergent economy, a multiparty democracy and very rich in energy resources. So it is believed to have all the capabilities of emerging as an important power in world politics. The present foreign policy of Russia is geared to take up the 'big power' role in international politics. After the end of the Cold War, with the disintegration of the Soviet Union in 1991, Russia entered the Commonwealth of Independent States (CIS) along with eleven other former Soviet republics. However, immediately after the Cold War, it was struggling to find its proper role in world politics. During this period (1991–99), it concentrated more on domestic political and economic reconstruction, and pursued a modest, not-too-ambitious foreign policy, unlike the former Soviet Union.

## The Yeltsin Period: An Incoherent Beginning

Boris Nikolayevich Yeltsin was the first post–Cold War President of Russia. The Yeltsin administration had to give more time to build the 'new look' Russian Federation, which was passing through a transitional phase after the disintegration of the Soviet Union. Yeltsin tried to give a new dimension to Russian foreign policy as he made major departures from the preceding Gorbachev era. In early 1992, Russian Foreign Minister Andrey Kozyrev announced that Russian foreign policy would differ from foreign policy under Gorbachev's 'New Thinking' because now democratic principles would drive it instead of the earlier 'socialist' principles. These new democratic principles would give Russia the opportunity to engage itself in the global peace process in a new international order after the Cold War. Kozyrev also emphasized that the basis for the new foreign policy would be Russia's national interests rather than the so-called class interests of the workers of the world that theoretically dominated Soviet foreign policy for a long time. For two years (1992–93), Russian foreign policy was generally low key and conciliatory towards the West with endorsement of many Western positions in world politics.

Pressing domestic problems faced by the Yeltsin government were determining factors behind this 'low key' foreign policy.

But this departure from the traditional socialist policies, and conciliatory attitude of the Yeltsin government towards the West, raised severe public debates. Ultranationalists and communists criticized the new foreign policy as detrimental to Russian national interests. Some of them argued that Russia should not follow a low-key foreign policy with a 'soft' attitude towards the West. Foreign policy issues, along with other pressing domestic problems, were troubling the Yeltsin government immediately after the end of the Cold War. In response, the Yeltsin government came up with a comprehensive foreign policy document in 1993 to allay criticisms that the government's initial foreign policy measures were sketchy and lacked imagination. This document, approved by the Russian Parliament in April 1993 and named as the 'Foreign Policy Concept', was the first major official foreign policy document of the Russian Federation.

The 1993 Foreign Policy Concept (FPC) declared Russia as a great power with several foreign policy priorities. These priorities were: (1) protecting the sovereignty and unity of the state, with special emphasis on border stability; (2) ensuring national security through diplomacy; (3) providing favourable external conditions for democratic reforms in Russia; (4) mobilizing international assistance for the establishment of a Russian market economy and assisting Russian exporters; (5) protecting the rights of Russians abroad; (6) furthering integration of the CIS and pursuing friendly relations with other neighbouring and nearby states, including those in Central Europe; (7) continuing to build friendly relations with all other countries and (8) ensuring Russia an active role as a great power. The FPC also called for enhanced ties with Asia-Pacific countries to balance relations with the West. Through the FPC, the Yeltsin government placed greater emphasis on the protection of Russia's vital interests. The FPC of 1993 was Yeltsin's answer to his critics and an attempt to place Russia as a great power in the new international order. It also refrained from pursuing open pro-Western policies.

Yeltsin was President of Russia for two terms: the first from 1991 to 1996; and the second from 1996 to 1999. During his first term in office, Yeltsin was rather unsure about the role Russia would take in international politics. He began in 1991 with a conciliatory foreign policy that manifested a soft attitude towards the United States and the West; but soon changed his position—as the FPC of 1993 makes evident—under increasing criticism from his rivals in Russian politics. From 1993–94, he started to espouse Russian nationalism and began to talk in terms of Russia as a great power. In his first State of the Federation Address to the Russian Parliament in February 1994, Yeltsin noted that as a great country, Russia was capable of preventing any global war, cold or hot, and Russia would also prevent the proliferation of WMDs. What is worth notable here is Yeltsin's emphasis on Russia as the single main actor to prevent future global wars. Through his reference to the possibility of global war, Yeltsin tried to appease the Russian military and other conservatives within Russia that the United States and the West still remained a threat. He also opposed the expansion of the NATO to include Central European states leaving out Russia. He put emphasis on making the CIS an economic union with a common market and a common security system with guarantees on human rights. He warned that Russia would not tolerate any harm to its national interests.

The nationalist rhetoric of 1993–94 mellowed down in favour of conciliatory policies again in 1995–96. In his State of the Federation Address of February 1995, Yeltsin highlighted a cooperative and conciliatory foreign policy for Russia. He outlined Russia's cooperation with the Group of Seven (G-7) industrialized states, the Organization for Security and Cooperation in Europe (OSCE), the UN and the NATO. He announced Russia's sincere intention to adhere to arms control agreements and hinted at possible reductions in Russian armed forces. Yeltsin, however, continued with Russia's objection to the enlargement of the NATO and called it a threat to European security. He also announced that in 1995–96 Russian foreign policy would be peaceful and committed to the principle of 'real partnership in all directions' with the United States, Europe, China, India, Japan and Latin America. Russian foreign policy, Yeltsin declared in his address, would be guided by a 'balance of interests' with respect to the CIS and the Western world including the United States.

During his second term in office, Yeltsin was troubled by recurring health problems, domestic political turmoil, more intense separatist movements in Chechnya and a weak economy. As a result, he had to continue with conciliatory policies towards the West with occasional outbursts of Russian nationalism. For instance, during the 1999 Kosovo war, he strongly opposed NATO military operations and warned of possible Russian intervention and a resumption of the Cold War, if NATO deployed ground troops to Kosovo. He also had differences of opinion with the American President Bill Clinton over Moscow's military intervention in Chechnya which, according to the American President, resulted in huge civilian casualties. Clinton requested him to stop military operations in Chechnya, which he refused. But at the same time Yeltsin relied heavily on the Americans and US-supported financial organizations for the reconstruction of the Russian economy. He sought help from the International Monetary Fund (IMF), the World Bank and from the US Treasury Department for Russia's economic revival. During his presidency, Russia received more than US $40 billion from international financial organizations. His government was also accused of embezzling these funds, and other financial corruptions.

Yeltsin's foreign policy, like his domestic policies, was marked by inconsistency and incoherence. Russia was searching for its proper identity and place in world politics during the Yeltsin presidency. Although it inherited the legacy of the former Soviet Union, Russia was unsure of its status in the new international order. It wished to bask in the superpower glory, and wanted to play a big-power role in international politics. However, the world at large, and Russia itself, was sceptic about its big-power status in international politics. With a struggling economy, a nascent and weak democracy, pressing domestic problems and an ailing but obstinate President, Russia's transition from a socialist political system to a liberal democracy was arduous. It had to take conciliatory policies towards the West, yet wanted to pursue big-power ambitions. These incoherent policies did not help Russia to assume the leading role that it wished to follow in international politics during the Yeltsin period.

## The Putin Presidency: A Resurgent Russia

Vladimir Vladimirovich Putin assumed Russian Presidency in 2000, and served two tenures; first during 2000–04, and second, during 2004–08, lasting till May 2008. Putin was a more assertive leader than Yeltsin. This observation could be substantiated by the progress of the Russian economy, considerable domestic political stability, and a more focused and assertive foreign policy. During Putin's eight years as the President, Russian economy grew at an average 7 per cent, making Russia the seventh largest economy in the world in terms of purchasing power. The country's GDP (Gross Domestic Product) increased six-fold between 2000 and 2008, and the poverty level (people living below the poverty line) decreased from 30 per cent in 2000 to 14 per cent in 2008. Putin enjoyed a very high approval rating from the Russians, an average of 65 per cent during his presidency, the highest enjoyed by any leader in the world (as per public opinion surveys), because he was credited with bringing political stability to the country and restoring rule of law. In international affairs, Putin firmly placed Russia as a leading state and earned respect for it; a dream that his predecessor Yeltsin nurtured, but failed to achieve. This was possible through an assertive foreign policy backed by a resurgent economy. During his presidency, Russia emerged as an able competitor to the United States and Europe.

The theoretical foundation of Putin's foreign policy was laid in the 'Foreign Policy Concept of the Russian Federation' (FPCRF), approved and issued by the President on 28 June 2000. This sixteen-page document clearly stated the foreign policy objectives of the Putin government, and Russia's priorities in the new international order in the twenty-first century. Section 2 of the FPCRF, entitled 'The Modern World and the Foreign Policy of the Russian Federation', stated:

> There is a growing trend towards the establishment of a unipolar structure of the world with the economic and power domination of the United States. In solving principal questions of international security, the stakes are being placed on western institutions and forums of limited composition, and on weakening the role of the U.N. Security Council. The strategy of unilateral actions can destabilize the international situation, provoke tensions and the arms race, aggravate interstate contradictions, national and religious strife. . . . Russia shall seek to achieve a multi-polar system of international relations that really reflects the diversity of the modem world with its great variety of interests.

Clearly, the pronouncements are assertive. By naming the United States as the power wishing to perpetuate its dominance in international affairs, Putin's FPCRF denounced such tendencies and said that Russia was in favour of a multipolar world. These pronouncements sounded like resumption of the Cold War by the Putin administration, although it was proved later on that Putin was not interested in another Cold War; rather he wanted Russia to be strong and resilient, both in economic and security terms.

Putin's foreign policy was forthright, yet moderate. Russia conveyed its opinions clearly without antagonizing other important powers. For instance, Putin condemned American attacks on Iraq in 2003 and called for removing economic sanctions from Iraq. But his views did not affect US–Russia relations. The Russian President had very good personal equations with George W. Bush (Jr). In fact, Bush waived economic sanctions on Iraq after the war was over in 2003. Before the Iraq war, Putin allowed coalition military bases in Central Asia during the US-led military operations in Afghanistan in 2001, despite objections from the ultranationalists in Russia. This instance showed that Putin's opposition to the United States was issue-based, and not chronic. He signed the very important 'Strategic Offensive Reduction Treaty' (SORT; also known as the 'Moscow Treaty') with Bush in Moscow on 26 May 2002. According to the treaty, both the United States and Russia would reduce 1,700 to 2,200 operationally deployed nuclear warheads each. The SORT, a significant step towards nonproliferation, would expire on 31 December 2012.

The moderate but assertive foreign policy pursued by the Putin government earned respect for Russia from the international community. Putin objected to Kosovo's plan for separation from Serbia, and warned the United States and European powers not to encourage Kosovo's cessation. At the same time, he was credited with improving Russia's relations with the EU. He opposed NATO's expansion programme, but also formed the NATO–Russia Council. These instances revealed stark pragmatism in Putin's foreign policy. He understood correctly that Russia would require economic help from the United States and other European powers. Therefore, he did not blindly oppose these nations to appease Russian nationalists. Yet he never missed any chance to condemn American 'dominance' in international politics, and projected the image of a constructive critique of the United States in international relations. This moderate foreign policy yielded tremendous results for Russia.

During his eight years as the President of Russia, Putin's foreign policy achievements were significant. Russia regained its status as a leading global power during the presidency of Putin. Sustained economic growth, coupled with assertive domestic and foreign policies, led to Russia's enhanced international prestige and acceptance. It had emerged as the world's biggest energy base, producing more oil than Saudi Arabia. Almost the whole of Europe is dependent on the export of natural gas from Russia. The growing arms and commodity items exports have made Russia the third largest reserve of foreign exchange in the world. Russia is now included in the group of the most rapidly developing emerging economies, the BRIC. Russia under Putin formed several multilateral forums like the Sanghai Cooperation Organization (SCO), NATO–Russia Council, Collective Security Treaty Organization (CSTO), Quartet on the Middle East (QME) and the EU–Russia Common Spaces, to increase its presence and importance in international politics. It also continued with its strong presence in other important international forums like the UNO, CIS, WTO, G-8, OSCE and the APEC (Asia Pacific Economic Cooperation). Russia's active involvement in all these forums indicated Putin's desire to achieve a big-power role for his country.

Vladimir Putin faced foreign policy challenges as well. Anti-Russian regimes in neighbouring states like Kyrgyzstan, Georgia and Ukraine emerged for some time to threaten Russia's security and its foreign policy initiatives in neighbouring countries. But Putin successfully met these challenges and made Russian position secure in Central Asia and East Europe. A failed 'tulip revolution' initiated by anti-Russian groups in Kyrgyzstan in 2005 turned into a nightmare for the local population. The failure, accompanied by killings and chaos in the capital and other cities, frightened the local elites and population; but at the same time it strengthened Russia's position in Central Asia. Earlier, the much publicized 'rose revolution' in Georgia in 2003, and the 'orange revolution' in Ukraine in 2004–05 (these were also known as 'colour revolutions') that destabilized Russia-friendly governments in these countries, lost their sheen and gradually the political elite close to Russia came to power in Georgia and Ukraine. These failed revolutions in effect ensured the success of Putin's foreign policy in neighbouring states. Putin warned the United States and West European powers not to meddle in Georgia and Ukraine, and the situation never went out of Russia's control. The Americans, with limited strategic interests in Georgia and Ukraine, also restrained themselves because they did not wish to antagonize Putin due to increased American political and business interests in Russia. Putin and his Russia commanded more respect from the international community compared to Yeltsin and his Russia of the 1990s.

The foreign policy of Putin had its shortcomings as well. Russia, despite strong economic growth, failed to emerge as a major trade partner for many of its important neighbours like China, Japan and Kazakhstan. With industrial nations like Germany, Italy, England and Canada, Russian trade remained insignificant during the Putin period. Further, Russia's trade volume with important regional organizations like the EU and the ASEAN did not assume significant proportions during the Putin presidency. Russia in 2009–10—when Putin was the Prime Minister and a main figure in the Medvedev government—seemed to have lost its earlier political influence in many neighbouring states, especially in Georgia and Ukraine, with the proliferation of anti-Russian forces in these states. However, negative points in Putin's foreign policy are outweighed by the positive points. Without reviving the Cold War and significantly antagonizing the West, Putin was very successful in establishing Russia as an important actor in international politics.

## The Medvedev Presidency

Dimtry Anatolyevich Medvedev took over as the Russian President on 7 May 2008, after Putin finished his two terms in presidency, the maximum allowed at a stretch by the Russian Constitution. He was appointed as the Prime Minister in the new government. Medvedev was widely known as the person groomed by Putin to take over the mantle after him. He continued with Putin's policies in domestic and foreign affairs, although he often showed sparkles of his individuality in dealing with internal and external issues. Unlike Putin, Medvedev was not known in Russian politics as a person comfortable with foreign policy; he was more a 'domestic' politician. He was largely dependent on Putin and the Russian foreign ministry for external affairs. But he gradually attained control in foreign policy matters as well.

Like his predecessors, Medvedev also issued a Foreign Policy Concept (FPC) on 31 July 2008, that outlined foreign policy priorities of his government. It contained six priority areas that Russia wished to follow in international relations. These were: (1) the emergence of a new world order where Russia would work for a multipolar world instead of a unipolar world; (2) the primacy of law in international relations; (3) strengthening international security; (4) international economic and environmental cooperation; (5) international humanitarian cooperation and protection of human rights and (6) information support for foreign policy activities, by which Russia would demand correct and accurate information on foreign policy activities pursued by different states in the world. The FPC of 2008 contained nothing unique as compared to the FPCRF issued by the Putin government in 2000. The former also opposed the expansion of the NATO and called for equitable relationship between Russia and the NATO in the Russia–NATO Council. It objected to the inclusion of Georgia and Ukraine in the NATO and the projected expansion till the borders of Russia. The FPC stated that 'Russia calls for building a truly unified Europe without divisive lines through equal interaction between Russia, the EU and the United States. This would strengthen the positions of the Euro-Atlantic States in global competition'. It also stressed on increasing cooperation with the CIS, the EU, Japan, China, the two Koreas, the ASEAN, and several West European, African and Latin American states.

Medvedev met US President Barack Obama in April 2009 during the Group of 20 (G-20) Leaders' Summit in London. The two presidents issued a joint statement after their bilateral meeting which was cordial and positive. Medvedev and Obama agreed to pursue verifiable reductions in their huge nuclear arsenals. By agreeing to verifiable reductions, Medvedev made a departure from the earlier Putin administration, which did not go for the verifiable reduction clause after the SORT, signed in 2002. Both Medvedev and Obama reiterated their commitment to a nuclear-weapon-free world, and vowed to work together to achieve the goal. They underscored the need for enhanced cooperation between their nations to meet the demands of the new international order. The statement noted: 'We, the leaders of Russia and the United States, are ready to move beyond Cold War mentalities and chart a fresh start in relations between our two countries ... Now it is time to get down to business and translate our warm words into actual achievements ... ' The tone of the statement was very positive and underlined the desire of the Medvedev government to improve relations with the United States.

Medvedev, like Putin, continued the policy of economic diplomacy for Russia. He also used the resurgent Russian economy and strong energy resources to establish Russia's position in international politics. Russia under Medvedev continued as the largest arms and energy exporter in the world. But Medvedev gradually came out of the shadow of Putin in foreign and domestic policy matters, and put the stamp of his own personality in these areas. For instance, Medvedev wanted the dismantling of a moribund OSCE in favour of more active security and cooperation mechanisms for Europe, and proposed a European Security Treaty. He established a Customs Union with Belarus, and proposed similar unions with other CIS-countries. Medvedev is no longer another Putin in a different garb; he is a different mind as well. Time is not yet ripe to scrutinize the success or failure of Medvedev's foreign policy, because he has been in office for nearly two years (as of March 2010). But Russia under Medvedev is doing well in economic development and international affairs, although the process of building a democratic Russia is far from over.

Vladimir Putin again became President of the Russian Federation on 7 May 2012 for a six-year term, as the tenure of Russian Presidency was extended from four to six years. Putin's foreign policy was not much different from his earlier term. He nurtured cordial relations with India and China, but proved a hardliner in former Soviet states of Georgia and Ukraine. Russia also intervened in the Syrian civil war in September 2015, following a request by the Syrian government. It is believed that the Russian President shares a good rapport with the new US President Donald Trump, although the United States supported sanctions against Russia in recent times. Russia under Putin is trying to regain its important place in global politics and economy. Russia joined the WTO in August 2012, after Putin assumed presidency for a third term. However, Russian economy faced a crisis from the later part of 2014, when rouble collapsed due to a decline in the international price of oil, and some Western sanctions against Russia. The country is trying to come out of its present economic impasse, as Putin has imposed internal economic restrictions through several presidential decrees. On the international front, Russia is focusing more on South-East Asian countries for increased trade and business, rather than depending on the west. Politically, many European countries have condemned US-backed sanctions against Russia in recent times.

## Russia–India Relations After the Cold War

India had strong and friendly bilateral relations with the former Soviet Union. The Russian Federation, since its formation in 1991, also developed cordial relations with India. After the end of the Cold War, the two countries began to think afresh about forging a close relationship in the backdrop of a new international order. During the first term of Boris Yeltsin as President of Russia, the relationship started to take a new shape. It took a while to consolidate bilateral relations as both Russia and India were new to the post–Cold War situations. However, the two sides began working sincerely on bilateral relations from 1992–93. During the January 1993 visit of Yeltsin to India, the two countries signed agreements that promised to herald new economic and defence cooperation between the two states.

A new Treaty of Friendship and Cooperation, which replaced the Indo-Soviet Treaty of Friendship of 1971, was signed during Yeltsin's visit. The new treaty dropped security clauses present in the 1971 treaty because both India and Russia felt that they were not necessary in the changed international order. Yeltsin announced that Russia would provide cryogenic engines for India's space programme under a US $350 million deal between the Indian Space Research Organisation (ISRO) and the Russian space agency, Glavkosmos. The Russian President expressed strong support for India's position on Kashmir. A defense cooperation agreement aimed at ensuring the continued supply of Russian arms and spare parts for India's military, and at promoting the joint production of defence equipment, was also signed during Yeltsin's visit. Prime Minister of India Narasimha Rao and the Russian President agreed that bilateral trade, which had fallen drastically during 1991–92, would get a boost following the resolution of the dispute over India's debt to Russia. Earlier in May 1992, the two countries decided to abandon the 1978 rupee-rouble trade agreement in favour of the use of hard currency. Although the cryogenic engine deal did not materialize, the visit of Yeltsin helped indeed to set the ball rolling, as it ushered in a new era of close relationship between India and Russia.

Narasimha Rao visited Russia in July 1994. He and Yeltsin signed declarations to continue close bilateral cooperation, and supply of Russian arms and military equipment exports to India. His visit yielded positive results for India. Apart from ensuring the continuation of Russian defence-related exports to India, he was able to restore the sale of cryogenic engines to India, which was seen as a diplomatic victory in Indian foreign policy circles. In December 1994, Russian Prime Minister Viktor Chernomyrdin visited New Delhi to discuss bilateral issues with Indian leaders. Eight agreements were signed between the two countries during his visit. These agreements covered military and technical cooperation from 1995 to 2000, trade, merchant shipping, promotion and mutual protection of investments, and cooperation in outer space. The success of Chernomyrdin's visit was hailed by the Indian and the Russian media as a return to warmer ties between the two countries. Regular top-level visits and close cooperation in different areas of bilateral interest have been continuing since Chernomyrdin's visit to India.

The two countries inched closer and enhanced their cooperation at the turn of the new century. In October 2000, President Valdimir Putin of Russia visited India. India and Russia signed ten agreements in all during his visit. The most important agreement signed personally by Indian Prime Minister Vajpayee and the Russian President was the declaration on strategic partnership between the two countries. This declaration was very significant for the two countries as New Delhi and Moscow instituted an inter-governmental commission for military-technical cooperation under the co-chairmanship of the two defence ministers. Both sides have committed themselves not to participate in any military, political or other arrangements or armed conflicts threatening either side. Under the strategic partnership, long-term and diversified Indo-Russian cooperation would be organised in the sphere of metallurgy, fuel and energy, information technology and communications. Defence and military-technical cooperation arrangements would be put in place in a long-term perspective with special emphasis on cooperation between defence forces of the two countries. India and Russia would cooperate in the peaceful uses of nuclear energy and outer space. Putin assured the Indian leaders that Russia was willing to share cutting-edge defence technologies with India—an unprecedented commitment that went a long way to cement security partnership between the two states. The other agreements related to increased cooperation across the spectrum of political, economic, defence, technological and cultural spheres.

Prime Minister Atal Bihari Vajpayee paid an official visit to Russia in November 2003. A joint declaration was issued during the visit and the Indian Prime Minister signed several agreements on bilateral cooperation with the Russian President in Moscow on 12 November. The agreements covered the spheres of science and technology, space, earthquake research, expansion of bilateral trade and defence supplies. The declaration referred to an agreement between the two countries on war against terrorism. Both Vajpayee and Putin affirmed a consistent and uncompromising approach on tackling terrorist threat. Russia endorsed the Indian position on resuming a dialogue with Pakistan, agreeing that an end to cross-border terrorism was necessary to initiate a purposeful dialogue. The declaration recommended a concrete and time-bound action plan under the aegis of the UN for the earliest restoration of democracy and sovereignty in Iraq. Both leaders also agreed that the role of the UN should be restored in dealing with problems of peace and security in the global context. They also agreed, as per the joint declaration, that all support should be given to the transitional government in Afghanistan to enable it to emerge as a stable country free from external interference. India and Russia further agreed that the future international order should be based on multi-polarity, and must be determined by collective and multilateral processes rather than unilateral initiatives. The declaration also reiterated that closer India–Russia cooperation in the fields of defence, space, and science and technology would be intensified and expanded in the near future.

With the Congress Party assuming power in New Delhi in 2004, it was hoped that India–Russia relations would get another fillip, considering Congress Party's traditional preference for Moscow. Regular top-level visits continued after 2004, along with closer bilateral cooperation in different areas. The new Indian Prime Minister, Manmohan Singh, visited Russia in the first week of December 2005 for the annual summit meeting with the Russian President, Vladimir Putin. During Singh's visit, India and Russia signed some important agreements. These were: (1) agreement on reciprocal protection of intellectual property rights in military technical cooperation; (2) space exploration cooperation agreement; (3) agreement on cooperation in the field of solar physics and solar terrestrial relationships; (4) agreement on implementation of programme for military and technical cooperation till 2010. However, contrary to expectations, the visit was low-key and yielded little significant results; and compared to Manmohan's highly successful visit to the United States in July 2005, when India and the United States planned the civil nuclear agreement, his December 2005 visit to Moscow appeared to be just another routine diplomatic exercise.

The visit of Dmitry Medvedev, the new Russian President, to India in December 2008 yielded more positive results. He was the first world leader to visit India after the 26/11 terrorist attack on Mumbai. Obviously, terrorism was pushed to the top of the agenda. The joint declaration, signed by the Russian President and Prime Minister Manmohan Singh, urged the international community to provide all assistance to India to bring to justice the terrorists who executed attacks on Mumbai. One of the major achievements of the visit was the new thrust on the proposed Indo-Russian peaceful nuclear cooperation. Apart from signing an agreement for construction of four more reactors at the Kudankulam plant in Tamil Nadu, where Russia was in the final stages of building two reactors, both sides expressed their desire to build additional reactors there, as well as to go for new nuclear plants elsewhere in India. During Medvedev's visit, India and Russia also signed a deal totalling US $700 million for Russian nuclear fuel supply to India. The joint declaration further appealed to the international community to resolve the Iran issue through peaceful means, dialogue and negotiations. While requesting all sides for demonstrating flexibility and restraint, Russia and India upheld Iran's right to conduct research, production and use of nuclear energy for peaceful purposes in accordance with the terms of the NPT and its other international obligations. The Medvedev visit of December 2008 would be remembered for preparing the groundwork for the Indo-Russian Civil Nuclear Cooperation Agreement, signed next year, and also for strengthening defence ties between the two countries.

Manmoham Singh paid an official visit to Russia in December 2009 for the annual summit meeting with the Russian President. The landmark civil nuclear cooperation agreement between India and Russia was signed on 7 December 2009, after talks between Singh and Medvedev in Moscow. The two leaders, in their joint statement, described the agreement as 'pathbreaking' and expressed hope that the agreement would deepen and strengthen the already existing nuclear cooperation between the two countries. By the terms of the agreement, the Russians would build twelve to fourteen nuclear reactors in India. The agreement with Russia was believed to be much more advantageous to India than the 123 agreements India signed with the United States, especially because the new agreement contained assurances on uninterrupted supplies of uranium to India for the atomic reactors and on transfer of nuclear technology. The two sides also signed agreements on extending their long-term military cooperation programme for another ten years, till 2020. Singh and Medvedev also discussed regional issues, including the situation in Afghanistan, in which both the countries have a stake and favoured a 'stable and prosperous' Afghanistan. This visit of Manmohan Singh was highly successful, considering the positive outcome that the visit yielded for India.

Prime Minister Manmohan Singh visited Russia again in December 2011, to participate in the twelfth Annual Bilateral Summit. Five agreements were signed during the visit. These agreements included two protocols, two memoranda of understanding and one pact related to exchange in education. One agreement between the two countries related to an intergovernmental initiative on the production of forty-two more Sukhoi-MKI 30 jets by Hindustan Aeronautics Limited. The Department of Science and Technology, government of India, and the Interregional Association Siberian Federal District, Russian Federation, signed a protocol of intentions aimed at facilitating development and application of technologies for the utilization and safe management of fly-ash in the Siberian Federal District; experience sharing; investment projects and mutual exchange of scientific personnel. Another fifth agreement signed during Manmohan's visit was an educational exchange programme between the Ministry of Education and Science of the Russian Federation and the Ministry of Human Resource Development of India. The purpose of this agreement was to boost cooperation in the field of education via inter-institutional arrangements. Russia also supported India's bid for a permanent seat in the United Nations Security Council as well as its intentions to join the SCO. India also welcomed Russia's entry to the WTO.

President Vladimir Putin of the Russian Federation visited India on 24 December 2012 for the thirteenth Annual India–Russia Summit. He held discussions with the Indian Prime Minister Manmohan Singh and President Pranab Mukherjee. The leader of the opposition in the Lok Sabha, Sushma Swaraj, and Sonia Gandhi, Chairperson of UPA, also called on the Russian President. The year 2012 marked sixty-five years of the establishment of diplomatic relations between India and Russia (earlier Soviet Union). To commemorate the occasion, ten bilateral documents were signed during Putin's visit. These included a joint venture to set up a modern industrial facility to manufacture Russian helicopters in India to promote the development of a high technology-based domestic aerospace industry, a joint collaboration to manufacture pharmaceuticals in Russia and an IT agreement for developing software, systems integration and emergency response systems to help in producing niche products. The two nations also entered into contracts for the supply of seventy-one Mi-17 helicopters and forty-two Sukhoi-30 MKI fighter jets worth US $3.5 to US $4 billion.

The new Indian Prime Minister Narendra Modi visited Moscow from 23 to 24 December 2015 for the sixteenth Annual Summit. During Modi's visit, seventeen new documents covering a wide range of cooperation in civil nuclear energy, defence, hydrocarbons, satellite navigation, railways, solar energy, visa simplification, Ayurveda and media were signed by the two countries. Prime Minister Modi and President Putin also adopted a joint statement entitled 'Shared Trust, New Horizons' during this visit. Besides the annual summit meeting in December 2015, the Indian Prime Minister met the Russian President on the sidelines of the SCO Summit in Tashkent (Uzbekistan) on 24 June 2016. The Prime Minister of India visited Ufa in Russia to participate in the seventh BRICS summit on 8–9 July 2015. On 15 February 2016, India assumed the presidency of BRICS. The summits of this group provide a forum for regular interaction between the heads of governments of India and Russia.

Russian President Vladimir Putin visited India in October 2016 for the seventeenth Annual Summit between the two nations. The Russian President met the Indian prime minister in Goa (also the venue of the eighth BRICS summit). The two leaders discussed extensively on different issues and areas of bilateral cooperation. The joint statement issued during the visit noted that the two leaders reviewed the Special and Privileged Strategic Partnership between India and Russia. They pledged to pursue new opportunities in economic ties, achieve sustainable development, promote peace and security, strengthen inclusive and transparent global governance and provide global leadership on issues of mutual interest. Indian Prime Minister Narendra Modi visited Russia again in June 2017 during his four-nation trip to Europe. The eighteenth Annual Summit meeting between India and Russia was held in St. Petersburg where Modi and Putin talked extensively about the special strategic partnership between the two nations. Modi's visit also marked the seventy years of partnership between the two nations. Five agreements, including a crucial pact on setting up two more atomic power plants at Kudankulam in Tamil Nadu, were signed during Modi's visit. A joint statement reiterating the need for closer cooperation in different areas, including global security, was also issued during the visit.

India and Russia have established IRIGC or the India–Russia Inter-Governmental Commission. One of the two IRIGCs is on trade, economic, scientific, technological and cultural cooperation, and the other is on military technical cooperation. Both the IRIGCs meet annually. In addition to the IRIGC, there are other bodies that conduct economic relations between the two countries. These include the Indo–Russian Forum on Trade and Investment, the India–Russia Business Council, the India–Russia Trade, Investment and Technology Promotion Council and the India–Russia Chamber of Commerce. All these mechanisms are aimed at strengthening bilateral relations between the two traditional friends.

# PART V

## Foreign Policy of Japan After the Cold War

Japan enjoyed a big-power status in the world from the middle of the nineteenth century till the Second World War. After its victory in the Russo-Japanese war of 1905, Japan came to be recognized as a major power, and remained as an important international actor ever since. Following its defeat in the Second World War, it lost its status as a great power in military terms, but regained the status of an economic great power since the 1960s. Today, Japan is restricted by the provisions of its constitution to develop its military force; although Japan is a very strong economy—the second largest in the world after the United States in terms of nominal GDP—and a very active member of the G-8 industrial nations. In 1947, devastated by the Second World War, Japan adopted a new pacifist constitution which proclaimed liberal democratic policies. Article 9 of the constitution of 1947 forbids the use of force as a means to settle international disputes. This article also prohibits Japan from maintaining an army, navy or air force. The Japan Self Defence Forces (JSDF), assigned to maintain security of the country, is an extension of the police force, and do not strictly fall into the category of an organized military. This unique position of Japan, a very strong economy but without any substantially recognized military, makes Japan an 'unbalanced' major power in the present international order.

Japan became an American ally after the Second World War. Its close strategic connection with the United States remained a significant issue in its foreign policy since the war. A Japan–US Security Treaty was signed in 1951 at the end of occupation of Japan by the Allied Forces. This treaty made Japan dependent on the United States for the maintenance of its security. This treaty was replaced by the Treaty of Mutual Cooperation and Security between Japan and the United States, signed in 1960. Under the treaty, both parties assumed an obligation to maintain and develop their capacities to resist armed attack and to assist each other in case of armed attack on territories under Japanese administration. Article 6 of the treaty contained a 'status of forces agreement' on the stationing of American forces in Japan. The Agreed Minutes to the treaty noted that the Japanese government must be consulted before any major changes in deployment of US forces in Japan or before the use of Japanese bases for combat operations other than in defence of Japan itself. The 1960 US–Japan Security Treaty not only provided a security cover for Japan, but proved very important to maintenance of peace and stability in East Asia. This treaty also helped Japan to develop a very close relationship with the United States, which continues till today. All post-War Japanese governments relied on a close relationship with the United States as the foundation of their foreign policy and depended on the mutual security treaty for strategic protection. Today, Japan and the United States share strong political, economic and security relations, and act as close allies in international affairs.

Japan has not remained dependent on the United States alone, but successfully diversified its foreign relations to develop close connections with many other states, especially the important ones. For instance, Japan developed friendly relations with its neighbours. It signed a peace and friendship treaty with the People's Republic of China in 1978. Bilateral relations between the two neighbours developed rapidly after the treaty was signed. The Japanese extended significant economic assistance to China in various modernization projects. Japan has maintained close economic—but not diplomatic—relations with Taiwan. Today, a substantially strong bilateral trade relationship exists between the two states. This policy of strong trade relations, without diplomatic ties, with Taiwan has in fact helped Japan to build good relations with China, an important neighbour, and a major power in the world today. Since 2000, China has emerged as a significant import and export destination of Japan. With South Korea, Japan shares strong strategic and economic interests. The ties between them improved continuously since an exchange of visits by their political leaders in the mid-1980s. As an American strategic ally, Japan supports the US and South Korean positions on containing nuclear activities of North Korea. Japan, the United States and South Korea coordinate closely and consult trilaterally on policies towards North Korea. Japan strongly supports the American position that North Korea should sign the NPT, and abide by the rules of the IAEA. It also supports, along with South Korea, American policies to freeze North Korean nuclear programme. Japan's relationship is stronger with South Korea than with North Korea. Today Japan has limited commercial and political ties with North Korea. Due to the North Korean nuclear programme which Japan sees as a threat to peace and security in the region, Japan's normalization of relations with North Korea received a jolt in the mid-1990s.

Japan's relationship with the ASEAN is very cordial now. After initial schism about each other, Japan and the ASEAN established informal dialogue relations in 1973, which were later formalised in March 1977 with the convening of the ASEAN-Japan Forum. Since then Japan-ASEAN relations have been growing to cover economic, strategic, political, cultural and educational, and science- and technology-related areas. After the Cold War, relations between Japan and the ASEAN have been further strengthened by the signing of the 'Tokyo Declaration for the Dynamic and Enduring ASEAN-Japan Partnership in the New Millennium', along with the 'ASEAN-Japan Plan of Action', at the ASEAN-Japan Commemorative Summit held in December 2003 in Tokyo, Japan. The ASEAN and Japan are also closely involved in different cooperation frameworks such as the ASEAN Plus Three (APT) process, the ASEAN Regional Forum (ARF) and the East Asia Summit (EAS). Japan acceded to the Treaty of Amity and Cooperation (TAC) in Southeast Asia in July 2004 in Jakarta, Indonesia. This gave impetus to the promotion of peace and stability in the region. Trade relations between the ASEAN and Japan have continued to grow and strengthen. The total volume of trade between the two grew from US $173.1 billion in 2007 to US $211.4 billion in 2008, an increase of 22.1 per cent. ASEAN exports to Japan increased by 22.8 per cent from US $85.1 billion in 2007 to US $104.5 billion in 2008. ASEAN imports from Japan for the same period also grew from US $87.9 billion to US $106.8 billion, that is, by 21.5 per cent. At present, Japan is the largest trading partner of the ASEAN with a share of 12.4 per cent of the total trade of the association.

Japan's relations with Russia are carrying the hangover of the Cold War times. Relations are not very cordial due to the inability of both states to resolve their territorial disputes over four islands in the Pacific. These islands, known as the Southern Kuriles in Russia and the Northern Territories in Japan, were seized by the Soviet Union after it declared war on Japan on 8 August 1945, forcing about 17,000 Japanese residents to flee. Japan wants to get back the islands—a demand that the Russians are not going to meet easily—due to the proximity of these islands to Russian oil regions. The stalemate prevented conclusion of a peace treaty after the Second World War, and continued to affect bilateral relations since that time. The United States supports Japan on the issue of the Northern Territories and recognizes Japanese sovereignty over the islands. However, Japan and Russia have made some progress in developing other aspects of the relationship.

For instance, commercial relations between Japan and Russia have been growing over the years. Trade between the two states increased from US $5 billion in 2000 to US $20 billion in 2007, and is expected to reach US $40 billion by the end of 2010. But the two countries would need to resolve their territorial disputes to achieve a stronger relationship.

Beyond its immediate neighbours, Japan has pursued a more active foreign policy in recent years, recognizing the responsibility that accompanies its economic strength. It has been successful in strengthening ties with the Middle East, which provides most of its oil. Japan is also active in Africa and Latin America and has extended significant support to development projects in these regions. It is strongly in favour of UN reforms, and a major contender for a permanent seat in the UN Security Council. For this purpose, Japan is actively working in tandem with Germany, India and Brazil, the other aspirants for a permanent seat. Since its joining the UN in 1956, it has remained intimately involved in UN activities. Japan contributes 11 per cent of the total UN budget, the second largest contribution after that of the United States. Its relations with the EU is very strong. The EU–Japan annual summit meetings (ASM) constitute elaborate framework for close cooperation, and cover important areas like foreign policy, economy, environment, culture, and science and technology. The eighteenth ASM was held in May 2009 in Prague where the two sides discussed important bilateral issues like trade and environmental cooperation. The EU ranks second in Japanese exports, and third in Japanese imports. Among the twenty-seven members of the EU, Germany, France and the United Kingdom are the top three trading partners of Japan. In 2016, EU–Japan trade reached €124.6 billion.

After the Cold War, internal political debates over Article 9 of the constitution of 1947 and Japan's role in international affairs have been continuing. The Japan Socialist Party (JSP) and the Japan Communist Party (JCP) are in favour of scrapping Article 9, and a more independent role of Japan in international relations. They believe that the JSDF is unconstitutional and should be dismantled. However, the Liberal Democratic Party (LDP) and the Democratic Party of Japan (DPJ) think that Article 9 of the Constitution of 1947 ensures that Japan plays a peaceful role in international politics under the security cover of the United States. This peaceful foreign policy has yielded good results for Japan since the Second World War and should be continued. Throughout the post–Second World War period, Japan concentrated on economic growth while generally taking a passive, low-profile role in world affairs. This policy was highly successful and allowed Japan to grow as an economic power. Although Japan is capable to present a strong military backed by nuclear weapons, it is restricted from doing so by the provisions of Article 9. There is no indication that Japan might violate Article 9 and emerge as a military power, because as a strong economic power, it enjoys great attention in international affairs.

## Japan–India Relations After the Cold War

Historically, Japan and India shared a close relationship for a long time. With the introduction of Buddhism in Japan in the sixth century, exchanges were believed to have started between the two. Buddhism brought with it shades of Indian culture to Japan and the process of cultural interactions began. After the Second World War, the two countries signed a peace treaty and established diplomatic relations in April 1952. This treaty was one of the first peace treaties that Japan signed after the war. For some time in the post-war period, raw materials from India—coal and iron ore in particular—helped Japan in its industrialization programme, and in its recovery from the devastation of the war. After Japanese Prime Minister Nobusuke Kishi's visit to India in 1957, Japan started providing aid loans to India in 1958, as the first yen aid extended by the Japanese government. Since 1986, Japan has remained the largest aid donor of India.

The Japanese Constitution of 1947, known also as the 'pacifist constitution', discouraged Japan from playing an interventionist role in international politics. Playing a politically passive role during the Cold War, it was possible for Japan to develop cordial relations with many states, including India. During this period, India–Japan relations were cordial, and the latter was the largest aid donor to India. Japan was one of the few countries in the world to initiate economic diplomacy as a potential tool in international relations. The two countries continued to enjoy a cordial relationship even after the Cold War. But the nuclear tests carried out in India in 1998 elicited very strong reactions from Japan, leading it to cancel any kind of economic, strategic or technological assistance to India for some time. With its horrific experience of nuclear bombs at Hiroshima and Nagasaki during the Second World War, Japan had been strongly advocating a nuclear-weapons-free world. In this background, these tests did not go well with the Japanese political elite; Japan imposed economic sanctions on India in May 1998. However, with continued dialogues and diplomatic negotiations between the two countries, economic sanctions were waived and normalcy was restored in mutual relations in 2000. Barring this nuclear hiccup, Japan–India relations remained cordial after the Cold War.

In August 2000, Japanese Prime Minister Yoshiro Mori's visit to India laid the foundation for closer Japan–India relations in the new century. The two states signed the 'Global Partnership between Japan and India in the 21st Century' during Mori's visit. This agreement called for better exchange and cooperation in economic fields between the two countries, including information technology (IT). Tokyo and New Delhi further agreed to facilitate comprehensive dialogue and wider cooperation by way of increasing regular bilateral visits of important ministers and leaders of the two states. Since Mori's visit, annual meetings of top leaders of the two states have been taking place regularly. India's Prime Minister Atal Behari Vajpayee visited Japan in December 2001. This was the first visit to Japan by an Indian Prime Minister after nine and a half years, during which both countries agreed to cooperate on a variety of issues such as terrorism, Afghanistan, and disarmament and non-proliferation, both from regional and global perspectives. After the summit meeting between the two prime ministers, the 'Japan-India Joint Declaration' was announced as a guideline for future partnership between these two states of Asian. In July 2002, Indian Defence Minister George Fernandes visited Japan. 2002 also marked fifty years of political relations between India and Japan. Ways of strengthening military and political ties, and improving cooperation on bilateral issues and border problems between India and Pakistan, were discussed during Fernandes' visit to Japan. The Indian Defence Minister held discussions on bilateral cooperation with his Japanese counterpart General Nakatani, Japanese Prime Minister Junichiro Koizumi and Foreign Minister Yoriko Kawaguchi.

Top-level visits, considered as important instruments of bilateral diplomacy, continued between India and Japan. In April 2005, Koizumi visited India as Prime Minister of Japan; and Prime Minister of India Manmohan Singh paid a reciprocal visit to Japan in December 2006. During this visit, Japan agreed to engage in discussions with India on civilian nuclear cooperation under 'appropriate' international safeguards. Although Japan stopped short of any direct support to the landmark Indo-US nuclear deal, it said that international civilian nuclear energy cooperation should be enhanced through 'constructive approches' under appropriate IAEA safeguards. Prime Minister of Japan Shinzo Abe visited India in August 2007. During his visit, Abe and Manmohan Singh agreed to take forward the growing relationship between the two countries. They agreed that Japan and India shared universal values of democracy, open society, human rights, rule of law and market economy, and that the two states also shared common interests in promoting peace, stability and prosperity in Asia and the world. Based on this recognition, the two leaders reaffirmed that the Japan–India partnership is a bilateral relationship with the largest potential for growth. Following Singh's visit to Japan in October 2008, Japan and India signed the 'Joint Statement on the Advancement of the Strategic and Global Partnership between Japan and India'. This statement aimed at promoting cooperation in a wide range of fields such as politics, economy, environmental protection, energy security and climate change. The 'Joint Declaration on Security Cooperation between Japan and India' was also signed during the visit to strengthen security cooperation between the two countries.

Prime Minister of Japan Yukio Hatoyama visited India in December 2009 as part of the annual bilateral summit meetings. The joint statement issued after the summit between Hatoyama and Manmohan Singh focussed on different areas of bilateral cooperation. According to the statement, the two prime ministers took note of the status of the Economic Partnership Agreement (EPA)/Comprehensive Economic Partnership Agreement (CEPA) negotiations, with a view to conclude a mutually beneficial agreement at the earliest. They hoped that economic relations between India and Japan would develop further after the conclusion of the EPA/CEPA. They shared the view that Japanese Official Development Assistance (ODA) would continue to play a significant role in alleviation of India's poverty, economic and social infrastructure development, and human resource development. The two prime ministers reaffirmed their commitment to realize a comprehensive reform of the UN Security Council, and vowed to continue with their cooperation with the G-4 and other like-minded countries in this regard. The two prime ministers reaffirmed their resolve to work together in the framework of regional cooperation, and the Indian Prime Minister lauded the sincere initiative taken by Prime Minister Hatoyama for an East Asian community.

Indian Prime Minister Manmohan Singh paid an official visit to Tokyo from 24 to 26 October 2010 for the Annual Bilateral Summit. According to the Indian MEA, 'This landmark visit has imparted a further momentum and continuity to the India–Japan Strategic and Global Partnership'.[23] He also held extensive talks with his Japanese counterpart. Naoto Kan, who is Japan's Minister for Foreign Affairs and Minister for Economy, Trade and Industry of Japan, also met the Indian prime minister. Opposition Leaders from Liberal Democratic Party, New Komeito Party and Your Party also called on Manmohan Singh. In December 2011, Japanese Prime Minister Yoshihiko Noda paid a three-day official visit to India. The two prime ministers signed a joint statement entitled 'Vision for the Enhancement of Japan–India Strategic and Global Partnership upon Entering the Year of the 60th Anniversary of the Establishment of Diplomatic Relations' between the two nations. This statement declared,

> In the context of the two countries commemorating the 60th anniversary of the establishment of diplomatic relations in 2012, the two Prime Ministers reaffirmed that Japan and India enjoy deep mutual understanding and vibrant people-to-people contact as the relationship is based on universal values such as democracy, human rights and rule of law, as well as wide-ranging strategic and economic interests. They stressed the need to enhance the Strategic and Global Partnership for peace and prosperity.[24]

They also expressed satisfaction at ministerial-level and other policy dialogues such as those between foreign ministers and defence ministers of Japan and India. The two prime ministers welcomed the entry into force of Japan–India CEPA on 1 August 2011. Asserting that CEPA is an important milestone in the trade and economic relations between the two countries, they expressed hope that CEPA will further strengthen their economic engagement in terms of trade in goods, services, investment and contribute immensely to mutual prosperity.[25]

Prime Minister of India Manmohan Singh visited Japan again in May 2013 for the Annual Bilateral Summit. During the visit from 27 to 30 May, a joint statement signed by Manmohan Singh and the Japanese Prime Minister Shinzo Abe was issued in Tokyo. The joint statement entitled, 'Strengthening the Strategic and Global Partnership between India and Japan Beyond the 60th Anniversary of Diplomatic Relations' expressed satisfaction at the steady growth of political exchanges, dialogue and policy coordination between the two countries. The joint statement reaffirmed the importance of civil nuclear cooperation between the two authorities in the governments to work towards its early entry into force. The joint statement reaffirmed the importance of civil nuclear cooperation between the two countries, while recognizing that nuclear safety is a priority for both the governments. In the joint statement, the two nations vowed to accelerate the negotiations of an Agreement for Cooperation in the Peaceful Uses of Nuclear Energy towards an early conclusion.[26] The two prime ministers welcomed the signing of the memorandum between the Department of Atomic Energy of India and the Ministry of Economy, Trade and Industry of Japan on cooperation in rare earths industry in India.

The Indian Prime Minister Narendra Modi visited Japan from 30 August to 3 September 2014 for the ninth Annual Summit Meeting with his Japanese counterpart Shinzo Abe. During the visit, the two sides decided to upgrade the relationship to a 'Special Strategic and Global Partnership' and launched an India–Japan Investment Promotion Partnership under which Japan announced its intention to invest in India approximately US $35 billion over the next five years. The following agreements were signed during the visit: (i) Memorandum on Defence Cooperation and Exchanges between the Indian Ministry of Defence and the Ministry of Defence of Japan; (ii) Memorandum of Cooperation between the Ministry of Health and Family Welfare of the Republic of India and the Ministry of Health, Labour and Welfare of Japan in the Field of Healthcare; (iii) Memorandum of Cooperation in the Field of Women and Child Development between the Ministry of Women and Child Development of the Republic of India and the Ministry of Foreign Affairs of Japan; (iv) Framework of Cooperation between Ministry of Road Transport and Highways Government of India and Ministry of Land, Infrastructure, Transport, and Tourism of Japan in the Roads and Road Transportation Sector; (v) Memorandum of Understanding between Ministry of New and Renewable Energy, Government of India, and Japan Bank of International Cooperation and (vi) Confirmation of the intention regarding the Partner City Affiliation between City of Varanasi and City of Kyoto.[27] The foreign minister level eighth Strategic Dialogue was held in New Delhi on 17 January 2015. The two foreign ministers reviewed all aspects of the bilateral Strategic and Global Partnership and discussed regional and international issues of mutual interest. Bilateral Foreign Office Consolation was also held between Japan's Deputy Foreign Minister Shinsuke Sugiyama and Indian Foreign Secretary S. Jaishankar in New Delhi on 6 April 2015.

A historic India–Japan Civil Nuclear Agreement (CNA) was signed in Tokyo on 11 November 2016 during Indian Prime Minister Narendra Modi's three-day trip to Japan. This agreement was a pending issue for many years. The CNA will allow the two countries to engage in exchange of nuclear-related technology. This deal makes India the first non-NPT signatory to enter into a nuclear agreement with Japan. Japanese Prime Minister Shinzo Abe visited India during 13–14 September 2017 and held fruitful discussion with his Indian counterpart. A joint statement welcoming the significant deepening of bilateral relations in the past three years in political, economic and strategic areas was also released. The two nations have developed firm foundation of common values and traditions as well as have an emerging consensus on contemporary issues of peace, security and development.

In fact, India–Japan relations have attained maturity over the years. The two countries have developed several important mechanisms to boost bilateral relations. The Annual Bilateral Summits between the prime ministers, and other institutional mechanisms for dialogues and cooperation such as the Annual Strategic Dialogues, Annual Defence Dialogues, Two plus Two Dialogues and exchange visits by parliamentarians and leaders indicate healthy and satisfactory political relations between the two significant Asian countries in the new century. After the initiation of these institutional mechanisms, Japan and India have engaged each other more in recent times. As observed, both nations try continuously to explore new areas of cooperation through these dialogue mechanisms. However, one area that needs special attention is trade between two countries. Indo-Japan trade relations have not achieved its true potential till date. Total volume of two-way trade between the two nations was US $18.5 billion in FY 2012–13 and has dropped down to US $13.5 in FY 2016–17. This was due to a significant fall in Indian exports to Japan in FY 2016–17. In FY 2012–13, Indian exports to Japan stood at US $6.1 billion. In contrast, this came down to US $3.8 billion in FY 2016–17.[28] Historically, Indian imports from Japan have remained behind Indian exports to Japan. As a consequence, trade deficit (from the Indian context) continued during the last five financial years (i.e., FY 2011–12 to FY 2016–17) between India and Japan. The two countries must pay more attention to this area to sustain an otherwise bright India–Japan relations.

# PART VI

# Foreign Policy of England After the Cold War

England enjoyed great-power status in international politics for a long time, from the early sixteenth century to the end of the Second World War. After the war, England's powers were diminished because its economy was hit hard due to the war; and its colonies all over the world became free of British control, depriving it of essential resources to sustain its economy. In comparison, the United States and the Soviet Union emerged as strong economic and military superpowers after the Second World War, relegating England to a lesser-power status in international politics. British economy and foreign policy became largely dependent on the United States, its ally before and after the war. This dependence continued during the Cold War and also thereafter. All the important bases of British power for centuries actually started eroding before the Second World War, leaving Britain to remain satisfied with a medium-power status today.

Britain rose to great-power status from the early sixteenth century due to its five strengths: geography, sea power, trade, imperial interests and balance of power. For a long time, British diplomacy depended heavily on these factors to establish Britain's supremacy in world politics. Of these five 'strengths', imperial interests and balance of power ended with the Second World War. The vast British empire, in the form of colonies in almost every part of the world, went out of British control after the war. For almost three and a half centuries Britain did not allow any other power to dominate in Europe, and maintained a balance of power in the continent through its command as holder of the balance. But the system of balance of power also came to an end after the Second World War with the rise of two superpowers possessing nuclear weapons. The end of the balance of power system also marked the end of British political command in the world. With unprecedented development in the field of science and technology from the early twentieth century, several European states—such as Italy, Germany, France, Portugal and Spain—started competing with England as important sea powers and trading states. So Britain's dominance as a sea power and a trading state faced challenges before the Second World War. The advantage of the British geography—its 'insularity' from the rest of the European continent—remains valid till today; although in an age of spectacular progress in military technology, such insularity is not enough to gurantee total security for Britain. British economy, traditionally dependent on sea power and trade, found many competitors after the Second World War—such as Japan, the United States, Italy and the USSR—and lost grounds. All these factors led to Britain's 'fall from grace' as a great power in world politics.

During the Cold War, Britain wished to play the role of an important actor in international politics, and succeeded to some extent, with the help of the United States. With common bonds of heritage, language and culture, Britain and the United States remained strong allies before and after the Second World War. Like the United States, Britain's post-war foreign policy was preoccupied with the task of thwarting the 'advancement' of communism and the Soviet Union in the world. Britain was an active member of the West Bloc and the NATO, and formed an anti-Soviet group with the United States and other West European countries during the Cold War. For this reason, Britain's relations with the socialist countries of East Europe, Africa, Asia and Latin America were distant, and sometimes antagonistic. But it must be pointed out at this point that Britain did not always support the United States blindly during the Cold War. It expressed its reservations about the American policy on China, and put forward the view, as early as in 1950, that trade with China must be augmented. With impressive and increasing volumes of Sino-American and Sino-British trade today, Britain's views proved right in the long run. Britain also opposed American policies during the Suez Canal Crisis and the Vietnam War. Moreover, Britain tried to expand its sphere of influence in the world, independent of the United States, through the Commonwealth. Britain was able to establish close political, economic and cultural links with more than a hundred states in the world through the commonwealth system. Although the commonwealth is a much heterogeneous movement now, with lesser British control, it nevertheless helps British foreign policy to cultivate closer ties with many states, and has proved to be beneficial for British diplomacy for a long time. As a permanent member of the Security Council, Britain played a very important role in international affairs during the Cold War. In 1979, during the premiership of Margaret Thatcher, Britain successfully resolved the Rhodesian crisis leading to the establishment of Zimbabwe. Thatcher, the last Prime Minister of Britain (1979–90) during the Cold War, also won the Falklands War against Argentina in 1982 to re-establish British control over the Falkland islands that Argentina had captured for a brief period.

British victory in the Falklands War reminded the world that Britain was not a spent force and could preserve its national interests effectively.

John Major of the Conservative Party was the first post–Cold War Prime Minister (1990–97) of England. The Major government pursued a moderate foreign policy for Britain, perhaps appropriate with the changing international order. Major and his team did not seek a very proactive role for Britain in the new world order immediately after the Cold War. However, the first Gulf War in 1991 and the Masstricht Treaty for a revamped EU were tough foreign policy challenges for the Major government. The Major administration attempted to ratify the treaty with stiff opposition from the Labour Party, and a section of his own Conservative Party. A nationalistic Major ultimately showed his disinterest in the policy of a single European currency, opting to retian the 'pound sterling' for Britain. But the Masstricht Treaty and the issue of a united Europe raised political storms in Britain, bringing out the shaky position of the Major government on foreign policy matters. However, Major showed some determination during the first Gulf War by sending British troops to defend Kuwait, and by persuading the American President Geoge Bush (Sr) to support 'no-fly zones' in Northern Iraq with a view to prevent Iraqi aircrafts from flying over the area to attack rival aircrafts. This policy proved very effective during the first Gulf War. Major also initiated the Northern Ireland peace process by opening talks with the provisional Irish Republican Army (IRA) in 1993. He paved the way for the Belfast Agreement, also known as the 'Good Friday Agreement', between Britain and Northern Ireland which sought to end London's direct control over Northern Ireland. The agreement was finally signed in 1998 after John Major left office.

Anthony Charles Lynton Blair, popularly known as Tony Blair, of the Labour Party served as British Prime Minister from 1997 to 2007. Unlike John Major, Blair was more assertive in foreign policy matters. Under him, Britain preferred an 'interventionist' role in international politics. During his two terms in office (1997–2002 and 2002–07), Blair mainly pursued a three-pronged foreign policy: assertive interventionism; close ties with the United States and placing of Britain at the helm of European affairs. The Blair government's interventionist preferences could be ascertained from Britain's active involvement in NATO attacks on Kosovo and Serbia in 1999 in the wake of ethnic conflicts in these regions. Blair persuaded the US government of Bill Clinton to attack Kosovo and Serbia with a view to contain Slobodan Milosevic and his Serbian forces. The Blair administration also made England an active player in the 'humanitarian intervention' in Afghanistan in 2001 and in Iraq in 2003. The British military joined hands, mainly with its American counterparts, to launch massive attacks on disruptive forces in Afghanistan and Iraq. In all these operations—Kosovo, Serbia, Afghanistan and Iraq—the Blair government cooperated closely with the United States to achieve its foreign policy goals of making Britain a principal actor in international politics again. Blair was an ardent advocate of US–UK partnership to secure and promote Britain's national interests. Immediately after taking over as Prime Minister, Blair declared in a 'Foreign Policy Speech' in November 1997: 'our aim should be to deepen our relationship with the U.S. at all levels. We are the bridge between the United States and Europe. Let us use it'.[29] After the 9/11 terrorist attacks on the United States, the Blair government began to work in close partnership with the United States in counter-terrorism activities. This cooperation became stronger after suicide bombers attacked civilians in London in 2005. During his two terms in office, Blair used the policy of maintaining close rapport with the Americans, the sole superpower in the world, and engaging them in all major areas of bilateral diplomacy.

The Blair government, with a view to securing a prominent role for Britain in European affairs, took active interest in matters related to the EU. Britain worked hard towards achieving a European Monetary Union, and the Blair government asked the British Treasury to assess the possibility of adopting the euro. After careful assessment, the government decided to defer the adoption of euro for Britain when the single currency was introduced in many countries of Europe in 2002. But it hoped that the currency would be introduced in Britain in future. The Labour government also endorsed the Nice Treaty in 2002 which sought to strengthen the EU by revamping its internal structure. Further, it signed the Brussels Reform Treaty in 2007 that wanted to extend the powers of the union. The Belfast Agreement was initiated by the former John Major government to bring peace to Northern Ireland. After assuming office, the Blair government signed this treaty in 1998. This agreement formed a part of Blair's policy to brighten England's image in Europe. In deference to the Belfast agreement, the Tony Blair government helped to restore the 'Stormont', the Northern Ireland Parliament, in 2007. During his two tenures, Blair visited almost every part of Europe—including several areas in East and Central Europe—to restore Britain's close ties with these countries which were affected in many cases by Cold War politics. Blair's euro-centric policies helped in many ways to reestablish Britain at the helm of European politics after the Cold War.

James Gordon Brown of the Labour Party assumed charge as the Prime Minister of England in June 2007, after Tony Blair resigned from office. Brown continued with the foreign policy priorities of the Blair government, seeking closer ties with the United States and an active role in European and international politics. Although Brown was committed to the Iraq War, he ordered withdrawal of British combat troops from Iraq in 2008. Wanting to improve relations with China, he paid an official visit to the country in July 2008. There he expressed hope that England–China economic relations would continue to be strong, and the volume of bilateral trade would touch US $60 billion by the end of 2010. Although British sympathisers of the Tibetan unrest in 2008 wanted Brown to send a strong message to China, he could not satisfy them fully as he attended the closing ceremony of the summer Olympics of 2008 in Beijing on 24 August 2008. Brown was in favour of building closer ties with China, a booming economy and an important power in today's world politics.

British relations with Russia suffered a setback when the Brown government expressed support to the people of Georgia during the South Ossetia War of 2008 between Russia and Georgia. The British Foreign Secretary, David Miliband, visited the Georgian capital Tbilisi to meet the Georgian President and said that the British government and people stood in solidarity with the Georgian people. The opposition party in Britain accused the Brown government in October 2009, during a Westminster Hall debate on a 'frozen relationship' with Russia that was reminiscent of the Cold War disengagement between the two countries. Although Brown met with his Russian counterpart Medvedev twice in 2009, the relationship appeared far from cordial. With Japan, the Brown government nurtured a traditionally close relationship, and further strengthened it. It signed the Lisbon Treaty in December 2007, which sought to reform the EU by amending the earlier Masstricht Treaty. The Lisbon Treaty aroused severe political controversies in Britain, and the opposition Conservative Party was against signing it. However, the treaty was ratified by the British Parliament in July 2008, signalling an important foreign policy victory for the Brown government. However, in the May 2010 General Elections, the Labour Party did not fare well and Brown resigned. Davis William Donald Cameron, the leader of the

Conservative Party, became the new Prime Minister of Britain on the basis of a new coalition between the Conservatives and the Liberal Democratic Party. The Cameron government became the first coalition government in the United Kingdom since the Second World War.

David Cameron served as the Prime Minister of a coalition government in Britain from 2010 to 2015. Following a victory of the Conservative Party in the 2015 parliamentary elections, Cameron continued as Prime Minister, this time of a single Conservative Party government. During his tenures, Cameron had to face the legacy of financial crisis of the early 2000s, and his government had to take several austerity measures in domestic politics. Internationally, his government introduced a referendum for Britain's continued association with the EU, and intervened in the Libyan civil war. Britain participated in the UN-backed military action in Libya, but his government could not intervene in the Syrian civil war. He was the first British Prime Minister to lose a foreign policy vote on a proposed British military action against Syria.

Over the question of Britain's continuity as a member of the EU, the referendum introduced by the Cameron government supported the country's exit. David Cameron, who supported Britain's continuity as a member of the EU, resigned as leader of the Conservative Party, and as the Prime Minister of Britain after the referendum verdict favoured an exit. Cameron was Britain's Prime Minister in two terms from 11 May 2010 to 13 July 2016.

Theresa Mary May of the Conservative Party assumed office of the Prime Minister of Britain on 13 July 2016. May, considered as a hardliner, became only the country's second woman Prime Minister after Margaret Thatcher. Within a year of assuming office, Theresa May called for a parliamentary election in Britain which was held in June 2017. The election produced a hung Parliament, but May survived as the Prime Minister with the support of the Democratic Unionist Party of Northern Ireland. May established good political relations with the United States, and she went slow on Brexit (Britain's exit from the EU). Her government supported Saudi intervention in Yemen and rationalized arms sales to Saudi Arabia. She also condemned the action of Myanmar military against the Rohingyas, describing it as 'ethnic cleansing'. May did not support easing of visa restrictions for Indian students and professionals, an issue raised by India for some time.

British foreign policy in the post–Cold War period suffered from a major dilemma, caused by its close links with the United States. Criticism arose within and outside England that British foreign policy was nothing but another face of American foreign policy. To remove this 'American' tag, policy planners in Britain had been searching for a 'British' identity in their foreign policy since the end of the Second World War. But due to several reasons, their policy could not come out of the American sphere of influence. Demands of 'realpolitik', alliance sentiments, advantages of partnership and Britain's incapacity to carry on its international ambitions alone are some of the reasons for Britain's dependence on the United States in foreign policy matters. The reliance of three successive Labour governments (Blair and Brown periods) on the United States bears testimony to such observations. The Blair government faced intense domestic criticism for its role in Afghanistan and Iraq, for its failure to check human massacre in Rwanda, Bosnia and Serbia. The opposition Conservative Party and the media accused it of earning a bad name for Britain by aligning with the United States in military operations across the world. This criticism forced the Brown government to withdraw combat troops from Iraq; but due to Britain's economic and strategic interests, it also remained heavily dependent on the

United States. British foreign policy thus often suffers from an identity crisis, and it would continue to haunt policy makers in Britain in future.

## England–India Relations After the Cold War

For over six decades since India's independence in 1947, relations between India and England have remained reasonably strong. History, democracy and shared values have contributed to the uniqueness of these relations. Much of Indian public life has been structured around British laws, ideas and values. This includes the field of education, industry and the media. Indian political and legal institutions, constitutional government, free press, civil service, modern universities and research laboratories have all been fashioned through British influence. Britain contributed at various levels in India's developmental projects after the country gained independence. But by the late 1980s, India and Britain began viewing each other as genuine partners, free from the hangover of the colonial experience. After the Cold War, the relationship moved beyond culture, curry and cricket, as Britain became India's foremost trading partner. In the twenty-first century, Britain and India are engaged in a meaningful bilateral relationship mutually beneficial for both states.

The new century heralded close cooperation between the two states as top-level bilateral visits continued facilitating a multi-faceted relationship. Indian Prime Minister Atal Behari Vajpayee visited Britain in November 2001. At a joint press meet with British Prime Minister Tony Blair, Vajpayee noted bilateral cooperation in the area of counter-terrorism. He observed that Britain was the first country to ban six terrorist groups operating in the subcontinent and thanked the British Prime Minister for this positive action. Vajpayee told the British press that both Britain and India have been familiar with the ugly face of terrorism for long before the incident of 9/11, and they must to go beyond Al-Qaeda in their global war against terrorism and target all its sponsors, who finance, train, equip and harbour terrorists. Blair paid a return official visit to India in January 2002. He was the first British Prime Minister in twelve years to visit India, although many important leaders from Britain came to India during this period. In New Delhi, Blair focussed on the importance of resumption of a 'comprehensive' dialogue between India and Pakistan. He opined that for talks to be meaningful, all terrorist activities should stop. 'There are two sides to the equation. On the one hand, there has to be complete rejection of terrorism and an end to support to it in any form. And then meaningful dialogue can begin', Blair told the media persons in New Delhi. Clearly counter-terrorism agenda got preference as an agenda in bilateral relations in the aftermath of the 9/11 terrorist attacks on the United States.

Indian Prime Minister Manmohan Singh visited Britain in September 2004 and met his British counterpart and other leaders. During the visit, Blair and Singh signed a joint declaration entitled 'India–UK: Towards a New and Dynamic Partnership', which envisaged annual summits between prime ministers and meetings between foreign ministers of the two states. Since 2004, the prime ministers of Britain and India, as well as their foreign ministers have been meeting regularly, initiating new chapters in bilateral relationship. The declaration also outlined areas for future cooperation in civil nuclear energy, space, defence, counter-terrorism, economic ties, science and technology, education and culture. Blair mooted the idea of India joining G-8 discussions. At his invitation, Manmohan Singh visited England in July 2005 for the 'G-8 plus 5' Gleneagles

Summit, where Heads of Government of five emerging economies (India, China, South Africa, Brazil and Mexico) were present along with G-8 leaders. This was a good opportunity for India to get entry in to the 'rich industrial club' of the world.

Tony Blair visited India in September 2005 in his capacity as the President of the EU, for the EU–India Summit on 7 September, and also for the second UK–India bilateral summit held on 8 September in Udaipur, Rajasthan. The two prime ministers focused on measures to be adopted in trade and investment exchanges, in the new and promising area of healthcare, and also in the area of services. They also agreed to intensify cooperation in areas of science and technology and the knowledge sector, in which both our countries have special strengths. Several memorandums of understanding (MOU) and agreements were finalized during the summit. These related to: (1) cooperation in the area of hydrocarbons, which is important for energy policies of the two states; (2) an MOU on sustainable development; (3) an agreement on intellectual property rights; (4) an agreement on co-production of films and (5) a new air services agreement. Blair reaffirmed his commitment to India's candidature for the permanent membership of the expanded UN Security Council. Singh told him that the Government of India had decided to create a chair named after Jawaharlal Nehru at Cambridge University. He also welcomed Blair's initiatives regarding education, that aimed at more student exchanges and better academic relationships between the two nations at the university level. Prime Minister Singh visited Britain again in October 2006 for the third UK–India annual summit.

The fourth UK–India annual summit was held in New Delhi in January 2008, during the visit of the British Prime Minister Gordon Brown. After the summit, the two sides issued a joint statement on India–UK Strategic Partnership. The two sides also agreed to cooperate in developing collaboration between small and medium enterprises, entrepreneurs and venture capitalists. It was agreed to establish an Education Forum to work towards an early conclusion of an educational partnership agreement and to enter into an MOU on an Indo-UK Higher Education Leadership Development Programme to develop leadership skills in higher education. The two prime ministers also agreed to promote cooperation in civil nuclear energy and would work towards a bilateral agreement for this purpose. Gordon Brown informed Manmohan Singh that Britain supports the India–US civil nuclear cooperation initiative.

British Foreign Minister David Miliband paid a three-day official visit to India in January 2009. His visit was marked by controversy as he linked terrorism to the 'unresolved' problem of Jammu and Kashmir. The Indian Foreign Ministry expressed its reservations over Miliband's views and said that India did not need unsolicited advice on internal issues in India such as that of Jammu and Kashmir. The opposition in India, BJP, saw the visit as a disaster, while the Conservative Party, the opposition in Britain, called it as damaging for UK–India relations. However, Miliband's views that were expressed in the British newspaper *The Guardian* (issue dated 15 January 2009) were said to be personal and unintended; they did not want to hurt Indian sentiments. Apart from this hiccup that did not affect bilateral ties, Britain–India relations remained cordial after the Cold War.

Economic relations between India and Britain have strengthened over the years through increased trade and investment flows. The volume of two-way bilateral trade was US $11 billion till February 2009, and is expected to cross US $15 billion by the end of 2011. Britain's cumulative investment in India from April 2000 to March 2009 was nearly US $6 billion. In 2010, it is the fourth largest investor in India. India has emerged as the third largest foreign investor in Britain and the second largest overseas investor in London and Northern Ireland, in terms of number of acquisitions or investments. It is the second largest creator of jobs in Britain with over 500 Indian companies opening offices there. London Stock Exchange hosts fifty-two Indian companies, with a combined market capitalization of £9 billion. The strong Indian diaspora living in Britain acts as a catalyst for stronger bilateral ties. The population of Indians living in Britain is estimated to be 1.5 million, mostly engaged in 'white collar' jobs and business. The Indian community is now very active in British politics, and is capable of impacting the courses of bilateral relations.

During her visit to England in October 2009, President of India Pratibha Patil asserted that India and Britain have now emerged as 'natural partners' in the twenty-first century. At present, the two countries are negotiating a civil nuclear cooperation agreement, which will take a definite shape in the near future. This agreement would further boost relations between the two countries. Britain-India relations have immense potential for growth. For instance, trade relations between the two countries may scale new heights. Both Britain and India are focusing on this area, aiming at trade worth US $50 billion in the near future. Both Britain and India have a parliamentary democratic set up, with free society and media. Indian students join several British universities every year and act as cultural linkages between the two countries. The large English-speaking middle class in India would welcome stronger and more stable bilateral relations with one of the world's oldest democracies.

British Prime Minister David Cameron visited India in July 2010. This prepared the ground for 'Enhanced Partnership for the Future', which was defined by a high-level economic and technological cooperation and closer coordination on many regional and global issues. The British prime minister was accompanied by the largest ever delegation to India since 1947. During the visit, the two governments announced a deal between BAE Systems, Rolls-Royce and India's leading aerospace company Hindustan Aeronautics Limited (HAL) to supply fifty-seven Hawk trainer aircraft to India. Cameron opined that the deal was a pointer to Britain's new economic foreign policy in action, and he identified India as a leading partner in this policy.

High profile bilateral visits from India and Britain became a regular feature since 2010. Through these visits, the two countries demonstrated their intention to strengthen cooperation. Engagements between the two nations continued after the new government took office in India in May 2014. British Foreign Secretary, William Hague, and Chancellor of the Exchequer, George Osborne, jointly visited India during 7–8 July 2014. They held meetings with the new Indian Prime Minister, Narendra Modi, and External Affairs Minister, Sushma Swaraj, to discuss political, strategic and economic issues as well as matters relating to Indian students in the United Kingdom and skill development.[30] The new Indian Prime Minister also met his counterpart David Cameron on the sidelines of the G-20 Summit in November 2014 in Australia and discussed issues of mutual interests. Indian External Affairs Minister visited Britain during 16–17 October 2014 to inaugurate the Regional 'Pravasi Bharatiya Diwas' where she had bilateral meetings with the British deputy prime minister and foreign secretary. The Indian Minister of State for External Affairs, V. K. Singh, visited London from 3 to 4 December 2014 to attend the London Conference on Afghanistan.

Nirmala Sitharaman, Minister for Commerce and Industry in the Modi cabinet, visited London from 18 to 20 January 2015 for the tenth JETCO. Indian Finance Minister Arun Jaitley travelled to Britain from 13 to 14 March 2015 to unveil the statue of Mahatma Gandhi in British Parliament Square. British Foreign Secretary, Philip Hammond, came down to India from 12 to

13 March 2015 for bilateral consultations.

PM Narendra Modi went on a tour of Britain from 12 to 14 November 2015. During this visit, along with his British counterpart, he endorsed a VS setting out the fundamental principles on which UK–India partnership would be built on as well as outlined a road map for deepening cooperation. Indian Finance Minister Arun Jaitley visited the United Kingdom again in January 2016 to attend the eighth India–UK Economic and Financial Dialogue.

British Prime Minister Theresa May visited India in November 2016. This was her first trip outside Europe after assuming Prime Minister's office. She was accompanied by a large trade delegation. During her meeting with Modi, the two leaders put emphasis on strengthening trade and business relations. However, provisions for easing of British visa restrictions for Indian professionals and students were not sorted out during this official visit. She also attended the India–UK Technology Summit and assured more cooperation in the sphere of science and technology between the two nations.

Over the years, the two countries have developed several mechanisms for closer cooperation. These are as follows:

i. Foreign Office Consultations (FOC), which are held annually between the foreign officials of the two nations;
ii. Joint Working Group (JWG) on counter-terrorism and strategic dialogue;
iii. India–UK Round Table where multi-faceted bilateral issues are discussed every year;
iv. India–UK (JETCO);
v. India–UK financial dialogue;
vi. India–UK investment summit;
vii. India–UK education forum for forging closer partnership in the field of education; and
viii. UK–India Education and Research Initiative (UKIERI).

Despite the existence of these mechanisms, bilateral trade and investment is not as bright as could be expected. The total volume of India–UK trade stood at US $14.33 billion in the FY 2014–15. In the preceding financial year (i.e., FY 2013–14), it was US $15.81 billion. In FY 2011–12, total volume of bilateral trade was US $15.71.[31] These data show that there was a fall in bilateral trade volume during FY 2014–15. In fact, India–Britain trade volume remained lower than the actual potential of the two countries. It is high time that the two nations pay due attention to this area.

QUESTIONS

1. Analyse the basic principles of Indian foreign policy.
2. Trace the evolution of Indian foreign policy.
3. Analyse American foreign policy after the Cold War.
4. Examine Chinese foreign policy in the backdrop of the post–Cold War world.
5. Make a critical assessment of the Russian foreign policy after the Cold War.
6. Bring out the essence of the Japanese foreign policy after the Cold War.
7. Examine the foreign policy of Britain after the Cold War.

## ENDNOTES

1. See, in this context, Harish Kapur, *India's Foreign Policy 1947–92: Shadows and Substance* (New Delhi: Sage, 1994), 22.
2. See, in this context, Dennis Kux, *Estranged Democracies: India and the United States—1941–1991* (New Delhi: Sage, 1994), 208.
3. See, in this context, Dennis Kux, *Estranged Democracies*, 381.
4. M. Granger Morgan, K. Subrahmanyam, K. Sundarji, and Robert M. White, 'India and the United States', *The Washington Quarterly*, Vol. 18(2), Spring 1995, 161.
5. See, in this context, Aneek Chatterjee, 'Beyond Expectations: Remarkable Development in India–U.S. Relations During the Gujral Premiership', *Jadavpur Journal of International Relations*, Vols 11–12(2008), 25–46.
6. European Commission: Trade, http://ec.europa.eu/trade/creating-opportunities/bilateral-relations/countries/india/.
7. Ministry of External Affairs, Government of India, http://www.meaindia.nic.in/.
8. *Ibid.*
9. US Census Bureau, Foreign Trade Service, http://www.census.gov/foreign-trade/.
10. Department of Industrial Policy and Promotion, Ministry of Commerce and Industry, Government of India.
11. Ministry of External Affairs, Government of India, 2016, 'India–United States Relations'. Available at https://www.mea.gov.in. Accessed on 13 September 2016.
12. Ministry of External Affairs, Government of India, *Annual Report: 2014–15* (New Delhi: Government of India, 2015), 114.
13. For all Sino-US trade statistics, see http://www. census.gov/foreign-trade/.
14. *Xinhua*, Chinese News Agency
15. *Ibid.*
16. Ministry of Foreign Affairs, Japan, http://www.mofa.go.jp/.

17. Ministry of External Affairs, Government of India, http://www.meaindia.nic.in/.
18. *Ibid.*
19. Ministry of External Affairs (MEA), Govt. of India, *India-China Bilateral Relations,* http://www.mea.gov.in/. Retrieved on 3 May 2013.
20. MEA, Government of India, *Opening Remarks by EAM at Media Interaction in Beijing,* 9 February 2012, http://mea.gov.in/. Retrieved on 5 May 2013.
21. Ministry of Foreign Affairs of the Peoples' Republic of China, *Indian Prime Minister Manmohan Singh Meets with Visiting Chinese Foreign Minister Yang Jiechi,* http://www.fmprc.gov. Retrieved on 5 May 2013.
22. *Ibid.*
23. Ministry of External Affairs, India, *India–Japan Relations.* Available at http://www.mea.gov.in/. Accessed on 2 November 2013.
24. MOFA, Japan, *Vision for the Enhancement of Japan–India Strategic and Global Partnership upon Entering the Year of the 60th Anniversary of the Establishment of Diplomatic Relations.* Available at http://www.mofa.go.jp/. Accessed on 2 November 2013.
25. MOFA, *Op.Cit.*
26. MEA, India (2012), "Joint Statement on Prime Minister's visit to Japan: Strengthening the Strategic and Global Partnership between India and Japan beyond the 60th Anniversary of Diplomatic Relations", [on line] http://www.mea.gov.in/bilateral-documents.htm?dtl/21755/Joint+Statement+on+Prime+Ministers+visit+to+Japan+Strengthening+the+Strategic+and+Global+Partnership+between+India+and+Japan+beyond+the+60th+Anniversary+of+Diplomatic+Relations; retrieved, December 12, 2013.
27. Ministry of External Affairs, Government of India, *Annual Report: 2014–15* (New Delhi: Government of India, 2015), 37.
28. Export–Import Data Bank, Ministry of Commerce and Industry, Government of India.
29. 'British Foreign Policy Since 1997', Research Paper 08/56 (London: House of Commons Library, 2008).
30. Ministry of External Affairs, Government of India, *Annual Report: 2014–15* (New Delhi: Government of India, 2015), 104.
31. Export–Import Data Bank, Ministry of Commerce, Government of India.

# 12 Recent Issues in International Relations

A study of international relations deals with several emerging issues that have a profound impact on international politics, economy, security and environment. In a complex and changing international order, issues like globalization, terrorism, energy or ecology have assumed increased significance and require careful academic analysis. In fact, no discourse on IR is now complete without any reference to these important issues. In this concluding chapter, these emerging issues in IR are taken up for sincere analysis; it starts with the issue of globalization, a much debated and significant aspect of the present world.

## Globalization

### Meaning of the Term

It is indeed impossible, and perhaps improper to provide a fixed definition of globalization because the term is used in economic, social, political, cultural and many other areas. We come across phrases like 'globalization of civil society', 'globalization of American culture' or 'globalization of cricket'. In such phrases, the worldwide expansion of, let us say, American culture or of cricket, have been emphasized. In that sense, globalization refers to the worldwide presence and importance of a certain phenomenon, like civil society, or cricket, or American culture. But having kept all these myriad meanings of globalization in mind, we must note that in the study of IR, the economic and political connotations of globalization are important. In fact, if one says that globalization is primarily an economic concept, one would not be wrong. In today's world, globalization primarily refers to economic activities which have serious impact on political and social spheres. In these examples, if one says that globalization of American culture or cricket has economic interests involved, one would not be wrong again. With the ascendance of liberal economy over mercantilist economy since the early 1980s, the term globalization has assumed increasing popularity and usage, and primarily refers to economic activities on a worldwide basis.

Globalization today mainly refers to expansion of economic activities like trade, and movement of capital and goods and labour, beyond borders. The socio-political impact of such economic activities can hardly be ignored. The process of globalization may affect domestic as well as international economy, and may have spill-over repercussions on national and international politics. For example, business process outsourcing (BPO) from the United States to India created political controversy in the United States and became a campaign issue in the 2008 presidential elections. Similarly, the growing popularity of Japanese automobile and electronic goods in the United States was a matter of concern for the Americans. Further, the controversy over the merits and demerits of globalization is very livid in international politics. Considering all these issues associated with the term, a workable (not fixed in any sense) definition of globalization may be provided:

> The term 'globalization' primarily refers to economic activities like trade, movement of capital, goods, labour, and communication system across boundaries facilitating higher levels of interconnectedness in the world. These economic activities have great impact on socio-political sectors nationally and internationally.

The ubiquitous and influential nature of (economic) globalization has led to the use of the term in every other area, like globalization of baseball, globalization of rock music, globalization of civil society or globalization of Hindi films. The term is used today in all activities on a worldwide scale.

## Globalization: Different Views

With increasing popularity and importance of globalization, the term globalization drew different and contradictory views from different scholars around the world. One view that supports globalization and mainly comes from the rich industrial North, holds that globalization has benefited the world immensely. The idea of the integrated global market helps the rich and the poor at the same time. According to this view, if the rich get cheap labour from the global market, the poor would have continuous access to capital and goods. The growing access to markets worldwide would help the rich and the poor alike. Supporters of this view believe that globalization has ultimately brought the fruits of liberal economy to people all over the world. Free and competitive trade would break the shackles of state-controlled, subsidized, idle economy that is not growth-oriented. The process of globalization would ultimately integrate national economies into an interconnected global market, and the fruits of this interconnectedness could be shared by all states, rich and poor. A free, growth-centered, liberal economy would help the poor state to move on the path of unprecedented economic development, thereby narrowing the gap between the rich and the poor. The supporters of globalization also believe that from an economic point of view, national boundaries are becoming less important. The global market is making national geography irrelevant. Today, an increase in the price of petroleum in the global market can hit Indian domestic kitchens. Further, any embargo on BPO to India by the US government may affect American private business as the cost of labour would then go up in the United States. So if India, a poor country, suffers in the first example, the United States, a rich nation, gets affected in the second example. Thus globalization is a great leveller, claim the supporters of globalization.

The benefits of globalization, according to its supporters, can be best observed through the revolution in information technology (IT) in recent years. The IT revolution has indeed made the world very small, facilitating unprecedented levels of communication around the globe. Every part of the world, rich or poor, is enjoying the fruits of this IT revolution. An e-mail bridges the North and the South of the world within seconds; a great deal of information in almost all areas, from medical sciences to tourism, to movies, to higher education, is exchanged daily across the world. This revolution has also given a boost to trade and commercial activities all over the world, according to supporters of globalization. For instance, N. R. Narayana Murthy, the founder of Infosys Technologies Limited, and a pioneer of IT revolution in India, had stated in clear terms that economic liberalization in India (in 1991) had proved to be a boon for IT and software industries, and many other industries in India.[1] The IT revolution has also increased interconnectedness in the world to a great extent, paving ways for greater economic and social cooperation across the globe. It also posed a challenge to the concepts of state-controlled economy, state boundary and state sovereignty which had become vulnerable due to the IT boom.

A second view, which mainly comes from the underdeveloped South and from some scholars of the advanced North, criticizes globalization and its ways for the economic woes of the world. According to these critics, the fruits of globalization are not enjoyed universally, but mainly by the rich states, due to their superior control over the flow of capital and the communication system. The North–South divide has not been obliterated; on the contrary, it is very much pronounced and visible in today's world. Millions of people are still excluded from the purview of globalization, and they suffer in silence. The view that an integrated world market has replaced national economy is altogether wrong. The state still has, and must retain, enough control over the national economy in the third world to move it towards people's benefit. A profit-oriented global market can never think of the benefit of all the people in the world; only a state-guided national economy can think of the benefit of the indigenous people. Globalization, according to these critics, has not generated an unbiased, integrated, free world market; it has rather created antagonistic, rival, regional economic blocs in Europe, America and Asia. These regional economic blocs would fight against one another for the control of markets in different parts of the world. Therefore, principles of free trade, that regional economic groups claim to follow, must not be seen as a boon; they may actually lead to more squabbles in the world.

A third view comes from a group of scholars who believe that the problem lies not with globalization itself, but with how it has been managed. These scholars believe that globalization, if managed properly, can be immensely beneficial for the people. The notion of globalization only as an economic activity must be changed to make it more humane. As Joseph Stiglitz, a leading proponent of this view writes:

> One of the reasons globalization is being attacked is that it seems to undermine traditional values. . . . Economic growth—including that induced by globalization—will result in urbanization, undermining traditional rural societies. Unfortunately, so far, those responsible for managing globalization, while praising these positive benefits, all too often have shown an insufficient appreciation of this adverse side, the threat to cultural identity and values.[2]

Stiglitz therefore recommends 'globalization with a more human face' to reap its benefits. Sincere reshaping of the current form of globalization is required to give it a more human face. The changes that he suggests for reshaping the current form of globalization are: (1) reforming the international financial system with drastic changes in the work of the global financial institutions like the IMF, the WTO and the World Bank; (2) adopting policies for sustainable, equitable and democratic growth; and (3) altering the capitalist view of 'development' where the industrially advanced countries 'guide' the process of development of the weaker nations. The less-advanced countries must assume responsibility for their own development. Globalization, if properly managed, can boost democracy, civil society and sustainable development with a human face, believes Stiglitz.

Contradictory views on globalization reflect people's interest in it all over the world. Globalization aroused the interest of scholars as well as the common man because it touches everybody's daily life. Very few concepts have generated so much interest and controversy in recent years as globalization had done. This phenomenon has made an enormous impact on international and domestic trade, democracy, civil society and the notion of sovereignty of the state. This idea of state sovereignty faced a new challenge with the march of globalization. Global free trade and communication revolution, among other phenomena, posed a threat to the state. The next section of this chapter analyses the position of the nation-state vis-à-vis globalization.

## Globalization and Sovereignty of the State

Globalization, with emphasis on an integrated and interconnected world, is believed to have dealt a severe blow to the concept of state sovereignty. The free movement of capital, goods and labour around the world; the free flow of communication across state boundaries; the mighty presence of the MNCs; and related events have raised questions about the supremacy of the notion of sovereignty of the state. It is believed that in this age of free trade and communication revolution, the role of the state has been minimized. With increasing and strong presence of non-state actors like the MNCs, the NGOs and the IGOs, the once-powerful state is no longer in a position to exert its strong control over economic, social, and trans-national activities. Also, the demand for a limited state—once the leading demand behind *laissez faire*—has been rejuvenated in the West, because, according to the proponents of globalization, free trade requires a minimal state. Further, the state has limited control over the world wide web of communication, and related information system; it has practically no control over intercontinental ballistic missiles that can strike targets with immaculate precision across boundaries. Therefore, according to the supporters of globalization, the state has been rendered helpless in many situations, and the notion of state sovereignty has become vulnerable in our times.

Elements of truism could be found in these arguments. Due to the pressure of external and internal forces, the state has been facing a crisis precisely since the Second World War. With the advent of nuclear weapons, the expanding commercial activities of the MNCs, and the international financial system introduced by the Bretton Woods Conference, the state began to face external competitors after the Second World War. Internally, the maturity of the civil society, the unprecedented rise of pressure and interest groups, and growing politicization of the society, challenged the supremacy of the state after the war. Consequently, the notion of the state as the all-important controlling power in the society started to erode. Further, in the era of globalization—that began in the 1980s, in the modern sense of the term—the concept of an integrated world based on trade without barriers, and the spectacular IT revolution made the world a truly small place. The state also appeared to be small in terms of its power as it had little control over the course of international trade, and communication flow. Moreover, the growing menace of international terrorism, and in some countries, internal terrorism, also made the state appear helpless and vulnerable. All these factors made the idea of the impenetrable state a phenomenon of the past.

It is true that in an interconnected world, the state can never remain isolated to enjoy its absolute sovereignty over groups, citizens, associations and institutions. The state needs to follow the international economic, political or environmental order to remain engaged internationally. It is almost impossible for a state to ignore the international economic or political regulations. Isolation is almost impossible in today's world. But having noted all these, it must be mentioned that the state is not completely lost today. Apart from retaining its sovereign control over revenue collection, currency, defence and foreign policy, the state also retains its sovereign voice as far as international economic or political regimes are concerned. The state has the right to oppose, and if necessary reject, any stipulation imposed by the UNO or the WTO, or the IMF. But one important factor must be remembered at this point—the state referred to is not a homogenous category here. It is easier for a strong state to oppose or reject any regulation from an international body, whereas it is very difficult for a weak state to do the same thing. But here too a weak state has the sovereignty to go for shrewd diplomacy in order to bring the situation in its favour. In other words, a weak state may try to garner support from some of the stronger states to oppose the targeted regulation and may finally become successful in rejecting it. In another situation, if the strong states are not inclined to support, the weak state may get the support of several other weak states, and together they could oppose the regulation. International diplomacy would not be bereft of examples of such possibilities. Therefore, a state has several options at its disposal to deal with the international community.

Internally, the state should not view the rise of the civil society or group politics as antagonistic factors. It must follow the democratic methods of dialogue, negotiation and peaceful settlement in order to meet their demands. In the age of globalization, a democratic state has the best chance to preserve its sovereignty compared to an autocratic state. A pluralistic society is not opposed, but complementary to the state. Internal terrorism may be countered by the state through socio-economic development of the estranged people. For combatting international terrorism, states need to join hands with one another. In the final analysis, an integrated world does not replace an international system based on sovereign equality of the nation-states. As observed in Chapter 10, the post–Second World War international economic and political orders continue to remain essentially state-oriented till today. States are the most important players at the UNO, WTO, IMF, World Bank and other international bodies, and although strong states are more visible in these organizations, the voices of the weaker states are not always submerged in them.

States are not completely helpless even in the age of globalization. In the third world, the state is, and needs to be, in the steering position for socio-economic developmental efforts, because equitable distribution of socio-economic resources cannot be left at the hands of private agencies. The 'welfare' role of the state can never be fully surrendered. In order to have 'globalization with a human face', the state cannot be totally sidelined. The state has not lost its control over MNCs, NGOs, IGOs and the IT revolution; it has only allowed them to stay reasonably free. This is also true for the advanced world, where state initiative is required to combat social and economic crises. The great financial recession in the West in 2008 required the intervention of the state in the United States, Britain and many other advanced countries. Further, new problems of the age of globalization, like international terrorism and environmental degradation, can never be tackled effectively without the active and leading participation of the state. The state is thus very much visible, and will continue to be seen in future in many spheres of domestic and international activities with its sovereignty retained firmly. The state has been willingly sharing many of its tasks with non-state actors since the Second World War, because it suited the interests of the state in a changing world order. So, the sovereignty of the state would melt down only to the extent the state would want it to dissipate.

## Environment

Environmental issues have assumed greater significance in the study of international relations today than ever before because industrialization and technological progress have enhanced concerns for environmental safety all over the world. Like globalization and IT revolution, environmental issues too have made states across world highly interdependent today because carbon emissions from industrial plants in one part of the globe may affect other parts; a leakage in a nuclear power plant in one state of Europe, for instance, may create airborne radioactivity throughout the continent and even beyond, causing serious health hazards; shortage of river water in a state of Africa may lead it to a war with neighbouring states. Many more instances could be provided to show that environmental issues have now assumed global character, and constitute an important area of study in International Relations. Environmental issues cover a vast area from pollution leading to global warming and climate change, to demographic alteration including population explosion, to sharing of natural resources, to the question of international peace and security, and many more. Some of these important issues are taken up for analysis in this section.

## Global Warming and Climate Change

Rapid and increasing industrialization in the world have led to the problem of global warming and climate change in recent years. Industrial emissions in different parts of the world have created a Green House Effect that significantly affected the rise in global temperature. When industrial and transport gases, mainly carbon dioxide, methane, nitrous oxide and chlorofluorocarbons (CFCs) are released into the atmosphere, they act like glass panes in a green house normally built to save plants in very cold climates. These gases in the atmosphere allow solar radiation falling on the earth, but absorb and reflect back to the earth's surface the long-wave infrared part of the radiated solar rays. This way the heat radiated from the earth's surface is trapped, causing tremendous increase in global temperature. The consequential impacts are dangerous. Rise in temperature would melt the age-old ice caps of the polar region causing increase in sea-level in different parts of the world. The densely populated regions along the sea coast all over the world would be inundated. Many island-states face the danger of disappearing from the world map. Further, melting down of the ice covers in the high mountains would cause rivers to rise and flood vast areas, causing irreparable devastation on earth. Global warming results in severe climate change in many parts of the world, causing unprecedented floods, droughts, cyclonic storms and widespread disruption of the ecological system.

Apart from industrial and transport gases, global warming is also caused by rapid *deforestation* of the earth. In many regions, forests have been removed for the sake of urbanization and industrialization. Resources from forests are also used for various industries. As a result, trees and forests are becoming lesser in number. Tropical rain forests in Brazil, for example, are on the wane. Reduction of forests is causing global warming since trees absorb carbon dioxide and emit oxygen. Lesser trees would mean more carbon dioxide on earth and rise in global temperature. A related and equally serious problem is the depletion of the *zone layer* over the earth. This layer, which exists over the earth's surface at a height between ten and thirty-five kilometres, prevents harmful ultraviolet (UV) rays of the sun from reaching the earth. Some industrial emissions, mainly CFCs, interact with the ozone layer and break it down, causing holes in the layer through which UV rays of the sun reach the earth. These rays are dangerous. They cause skin cancer in human beings and many animals, and agricultural crops are destroyed; biodiversity (huge diversity of plant and animal species on earth) is disturbed, and the earth's ecological system is severely affected.

Global warming and climate change have serious repercussions on international relations because states have started to blame one another over the issue of industrial and transport emissions. The states of the South blame the rich industrial North for maximum emissions, while the advanced Northern states accuse the less-developed countries of the South of poor safety measures in their industrial plants, which they think cause huge emissions. Within the North as well as the South, states blame one another over issues like emission, sharing of natural resources, and displacement and migration of people due to ecological disorders. Side by side, there are international efforts—these are analysed later in this chapter—to tackle problems related to environment. International Relations and studies related to it are, therefore, immensely influenced by environmental issues.

## Demographic Issues

Growth in world population, particularly in the poor South, is a major area of concern for the environmentalists. The world population, which is around 7.5 billion at present, is expected to reach around 11.8 billion by the year 2100, according to the UN estimates. About 95 per cent of the population growth would take place in states of the South, putting maximum pressure on their resources, both natural and created. Several states of the South may face problems like shortage of food, housing, employment; lack of adequate roads and transportation; and health hazards, if agricultural, social and industrial infrastructures are not properly developed. More people with limited resources would create enormous pressure on the environment, and escalate social tension. Although many states have adopted policies to curb population growth, the rate of success in this regard varies from one state to another. In China, for instance, the rate of population growth has decreased fast, whereas in states like Pakistan and Nigeria it has not been equally fast.

Some years ago, population growth was explained in terms of falling death rate, while the birth rate remained steady, due to advancement in medical sciences. While this argument is still valid for population growth in some states, the birth rate is also decreasing in most of the states of the world due to governmental policies to arrest population rise. However, the gap between the rates at which the birth rate and the death rate decrease is important with respect to the analysis of population growth. In a state where this gap is wide, population growth would take place more steadily than in a state where this gap is narrow. Demographic issues cover many interesting yet intriguing aspects. It has been observed in several states of the South that when economy grows faster than population, the total number of poor people may actually increase. This mainly happens when fruits of economic growth are enjoyed by a minority in the population. Therefore, arrest of population growth is not the only goal of a state, distribution of resources in a more or less just manner is more important in order to achieve reduction in poverty.

Rise in population affects a state's economy and environment in several ways. Unchecked growth in population leads to low per capita income in a state, which in turn hampers economic development. Low per capita income may lead to less purchasing power, which ultimately affects the domestic market. Further, a rising population fosters acute competition for economic resources, and those who are deprived of economic means may get involved in social crime and violence. In many poor states of the South, perpetual social violence due to inadequate economic resources have crippled socio-political systems, and in turn severely affected economic development. A rising population would also put severe pressure on natural resources like water, land, minerals, forests and seas, leading to serious imbalance in the ecological system. It would be more prone to health hazards because a weak economy cannot guarantee health security for all people. Thus, in the long run, population growth puts immense pressure on the economy and the environment, leading to social and political tensions, health hazards and poverty.

## Environment and International Peace

International peace and security are now much dependent on environmental issues; and environment, in turn, can be sustained through international peace. Environmental issues like sharing of river water and territories, or forest and sea resources, or climate change, may affect international peace and security. States go to war over these issues. One of the principal reasons behind the long war between Iran and Iraq from 1980 to 1988 was the issue of control over Shatt-al-Arab, a common water body spanning across the two states. The mountainous Kashmir valley remained a bone of contention between India and Pakistan for more than six decades and led to two large-scale wars and one undeclared war (two full wars in 1947–48 and 1965; and the recent Kargil 'War' in 1999). Territorial occupation has been the main source of conflict between the Palestinians and Israelis for nearly seven decades. The Caspian Sea, the largest inland water body in the world—with its abundant natural resources, including oil and gas—was a point of controversy between former Soviet Union and Iran, and after the Cold War, among the states surrounding the Caspian Sea. Today, there is a North–South divide not only over economic issues, but also over the question of climate change. As already noted, the North and the South accuse each other of maximum emissions that lead to environmental degradation. Global warming and climate change, if not tackled effectively, might lead to more conflicts in the world in future, and threaten international peace and security.

Present-day world politics has a great and serious impact on environmental issues. Many scholars working on environment blame international politics for global warming and climate change.[3] In order to protect their national interests in world politics, and gain economic benefits, several states are not paying enough attention to the issue of environmental degradation. Further, wars and conflicts wreck havoc on the environment across the globe. The world has not forgotten the dropping of atom bombs on Hiroshima and Nagasaki, and the resulting devastation of environment and population, both human and animal. In the more recent Gulf War in 1991, Iraqi military burnt oil wells in Kuwait and also spilled oil in the Gulf, causing unprecedented ecological disasters and health hazards. In almost all conflicts, regional or global, the warring parties deliberately degrade the environment to garner advantage over the opposition. They set fire to forests, level villages and towns, damage agricultural lands, poison river water, spray harmful gases, and resort to many other tactics that are detrimental to our ecological system. The environment is deliberately damaged during wars. Environmental safety is, therefore, highly dependent on international peace and security.

## International Efforts to Safeguard the Environment

Today's world is much concerned about environmental degradation because it threatens the very existence of life on earth. Apart from national governments, inter-governmental organizations (IGOs) like the UNO, as well as several NGOs, hold regular meetings and summits to discuss environmental issues and take necessary steps to safeguard the environment. Notable among the more recent international efforts to save our environment are the UN Environment Program (UNEP) launched in 1989; UN Conference on Environment and Development held in Rio de Janeiro, Brazil in 1992 (popularly known as the 'Earth Summit'); International Conference on Population and Development held in Cairo, Egypt, in 1994; International Conference on Natural Disaster Reduction in 1994; Second UN Conference on Human Settlements (Habitat II) in Istanbul, Turkey, in 1996; the Millennium Assembly of the UN in New York in 2000; and the UN Climate Change Conference in Copenhagen, Denmark, in December 2009. The Rio + 20 Conference, held in Rio de Janeiro in 2012, under the auspices of the UN and the UN Sustainable Development Summit in New York in 2015 continued global efforts for the protection of environment. The Energy and Resources Institute (TERI) organized the World Sustainable Development Summit in New Delhi in 2018. This marked another laudable initiative on environment protection in recent times. Table 12.1 presents a list of important conventions, conferences and summits on environment and related issues, held recently in different parts of the world.

**Table 12.1** Important International Conferences on Environmental Protection (1973–2018)

| S. No. | Name of the Convention/Conference/Summit | Year |
|---|---|---|
| 1. | International Convention for the Prevention of Pollution from Ships (MARPOL) | 1973 |
| 2. | Convention on Long Range Transboundary Air Pollution | 1979 |
| 3. | UN Convention on the Law of the Sea (UNCLOS) | 1973–82 |
| 4. | International Convention for the Regulation of Whaling | 1989 |
| 5. | UN Framework Convention on Climate Change | 1992 |
| 6. | Convention on the Prevention of Marine Pollution by Dumping Wastes and Other Matter (London Convention) | 1972 |
| 7. | Montreal Protocol on Substances that Deplete the Ozone Layer | 1987 |
| 8. | Vienna Convention for the Protection of the Ozone Layer | 1985 |
| 9. | Basel Convention on the Control of Transboundary Movements of Hazardous Wastes and Their Disposal | 1989 |
| 10. | Convention on Wetlands of International Importance (Ramsar) | 1971 |
| 11. | Convention on Biological Diversity | 1992 |
| 12. | Convention on the International Trade in Endangered Species of Wild Flora and Fauna | 1973 |
| 13. | UN Conference on Environment and Development (Earth Summit), Rio de Janeiro | 1992 |
| 14. | International Conference on Population and Development, Cairo | 1994 |
| 15. | UN Global Conference on the Sustainable Development of Small Island Developing States | 1994 |
| 16. | International Conference on Natural Disaster Reduction | 1994 |
| 17. | Conference on Highly Migratory Fish Stocks | 1995 |
| 18. | World Food Summit | 1996 |
| 19. | Second UN Conference on Human Settlements (Habitat II), Istanbul | 1996 |

*(Continued)*

**Table 12.1** *(Continued)*

| S. No. | Name of the Convention/Conference/Summit | Year |
|---|---|---|
| 20. | Earth Summit + 5 | 1997 |
| 21. | General Assembly Special Session on Small Island Developing States | 1999 |
| 22. | UN Workshop on Energy Efficiency, Global Competitiveness and Deregulation | 2000 |
| 23. | The Millennium Assembly of the UN, New York | 2000 |
| 24. | The UN Climate Change Conference, Copenhagen | 2009 |
| 25. | The UN Conference on Sustainable Development (also known as Rio + 20), Rio de Janeiro | 2012 |
| 26. | UN Sustainable Development Summit, New York | 2015 |
| 27. | World Sustainable Development Summit (organized by TERI), New Delhi | 2018 |

It could be ascertained from the table that national governments, IGOs and NGOs all over the world are seriously concerned about environmental problems and they try to resolve such problems. For this purpose, several conferences, conventions and summits were held in different parts of the world on different aspects of environmental and related issues. The names of conferences, conventions and summits outlined in the table are indicative of the issues taken up for discussion there. For instance, the Earth Summit convened by the UN in Rio de Janeiro, Brazil, in 1992 was one of the biggest conventions ever held on environment and development, involving people from over a hundred states. The UN Climate Change Conference, held in Copenhagen in December 2009, is the biggest conference on environmental degradation so far, attended by 195 states. The 'Copenhagen Accord', agreed upon at the conference, recognized that climate change is one of the greatest challenges of our times and that actions should be taken to keep any increase in temperature below two degrees Celsius. The Rio + 20 Conference was held in Rio de Janeiro in 2012. The UN organized this event 20 years after the Earth Summit was held. It was attended by nearly 200 nations. But it should also be noted at this point that only international conferences and summits are not enough to address problems related to environment; the issue of economic development across the globe is integrally linked to this. The poor states lack enough resources to tackle problems associated with environmental degradation, although they have the desire to address them. Such problems would not, hence, be effectively resolved if underdevelopment and poverty continue to affect world economy in a similar manner in future.

# Energy

Generally speaking, issues related to energy resources come under the broader theme of environment. But the increasing importance of energy in international politics in recent years demands a separate analysis of energy resources. Like globalization, energy issues determine the twists and turns in international politics today. They have assumed greater significance in the study of international relations. Among several natural resources, energy resources are very important for modern post–industrial economy. Energy resources like oil, coal, natural gas, hydroelectric and nuclear power are crucial for the survival of today's sophisticated industrial economy.

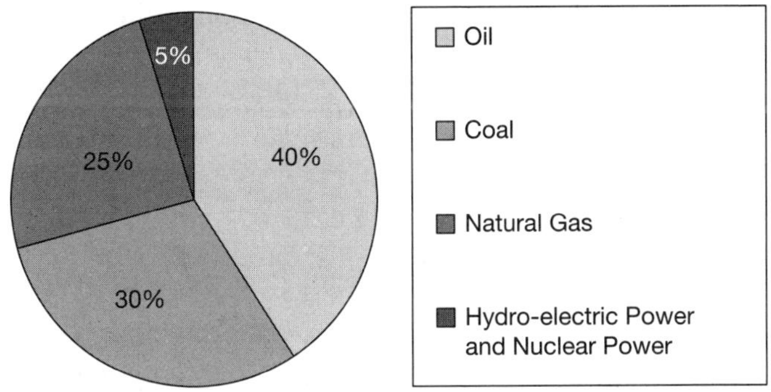


**Figure 12.1** Major Energy Resources of the World

Of different energy resources, oil constitutes about 40 per cent of world energy consumption, followed by coal that makes for about 30 per cent. Natural gas constitutes about 25 per cent, and hydroelectric and nuclear powers make for another 5 per cent of world energy consumption in 2010. The following chart illustrates current major energy resources in the world. Countries having sufficient energy resources may have the potential to become driving forces in international economy and politics. Conversely, countries having little energy base may not play the role of important actors in international politics.

Trading in energy has assumed significant proportions all over the world and will continue to grow in future. Subsequently, marketed energy consumption will also rise worldwide by 2030. In 2006, marketed energy consumption in all energy resources was 472 quadrillion British Thermal Units (BTU). This will rise to 678 BTU, an increase of 44 per cent, by 2030. This rise will take place due to increased consumption of major energy resources like oil and other petroleum products, coal, natural gas, electricity, biofuels and nuclear energy. Table 12.2 highlights the projected increase in global marketed energy consumption of some significant items from 2006 to 2030.

**Table 12.2** Increase in World Marketed Energy Consumption (2006–2030)

| S. No. | Energy Resource | 2006 (in Quadrillion BTU*) | 2030 (in Quadrillion BTU*) | Per cent Increase |
|---|---|---|---|---|
| 1. | All | 472 | 678 | 44 |
| 2. | Liquids (including biofuels) | 160 | 210 | 31 |
| 3. | Coal | 120 | 160 | 33 |
| 4. | Natural Gas | 90 | 130 | 44 |
| 5. | Nuclear Energy | 20 | 27 | 35 |
| 6. | Renewables (excluding bio-fuels) | 30 | 50 | 67 |

*British Thermal Units

*Source*: Energy Information Administration, Department of Energy, Government of the United States of America (http://www.eia.doe.gov/oiaf/ieo/highlights.html)

**Table 12.3** Region-wise Per Capita Energy Consumption in the World from 2006 to 2016 [In Million Tonnes of Oil Equivalent (MTOE) Per Person]

| S. No. | Region | 2006 | 2010 | 2016 |
|---|---|---|---|---|
| 1. | North America | 2,824.1 | 2,777.8 | 2,788.9 |
| 2. | South & Central America | 567.8 | 641.7 | 705.3 |
| 3. | Europe & Eurasia | 3,023.5 | 2,952.8 | 2867.1 |
| 4. | Middle East | 592.2 | 734.2 | 895.1 |
| 5. | Africa | 334.8 | 388.9 | 440.1 |
| 6. | Asia Pacific | 3,924.3 | 4,674.7 | 5,579.7 |
| | Total World | 11,266.7 | 12,170.0 | 13,276.3 |

*Source*: BP Statistical Review of World Energy, June 2017, www.bp.com; retrieved on 7 January 2018.

It is evident from the data presented in Table 12.2 that marketed energy consumption in the world will grow significantly by the year 2030, with more than 30 per cent rise in almost all energy resources. This growth in energy consumption will escalate the demand for energy, as well as competition among states to procure more and more energy. The twists and turns in international relations in the coming decades would be determined by the politics and economics of energy resources. The largest consumers in energy resources will have advantages in industry and commerce, but will also face condemnation for polluting the environment and abetting global warming. In this context, it would be appropriate to look at the per capita consumption of energy, both region-wise and nation-wise, in the world. Table 12.3 highlights region-wise per capita energy consumption in the world from 2006 to 2016.

It could be observed from Table 12.3 that developed industrialized regions of the world consume more energy than the less developed regions. North America, a highly industrialized region, consumed 2,788.9 MTOE energy per person in 2016. For the same year, Europe and Eurasia, a developed region in terms of industrial and technological progress, consumed 2,867.1 MTOE energy. But in these two regions, energy consumption decreased in comparison to the year 2006. However, in the Asia Pacific region (which includes Australia and New Zealand), energy consumption per person increased from 3,924.3 MTOE in 2006 to 5,579.7 MTOE in 2016. The rise of Chinese and Indian economies could provide an explanation for this rise in per capita energy consumption. Conversely, in Africa per capita energy consumption remained lower than other regions during the period under consideration. Per capita energy consumption was also on the lower range in South and Central America, a less developed region in the world. In this context, it would be interesting to look at country-wise per capita energy consumption in the year 2016.

Table 12.4 illustrates per capita energy consumption in select countries of the world in 2016. It lists countries with highest per capita consumption of energy in 2016, as well as countries with lowest per capita energy consumption in the world in 2016. It could be observed from this table that industrialized nations with big population consumed more energy than countries with less industrialization and less population. Table 12.4 reveals that countries such as China, United States, India and Russia consumed more per capita energy than countries such as New Zealand, Norway, Portugal and Chile. One word of caution here: global consumption of energy must be matched or surpassed by production of energy in the world; otherwise, the world will face shortage of energy in the near future, and this may lead to chances of escalation of conflicts among nations.

**Table 12.4** Per Capita Energy Consumption of Select Countries in 2016 [In Million Tonnes of Oil Equivalent (MTOE) Per Person]

| S. No. | Name of the Country | Consumption in 2016 (in MTOE) |
|---|---|---|
| 1. | China | 3,123 |
| 2. | United States | 2,204 |
| 3. | India | 884 |
| 4. | Russia | 692 |
| 5. | Japan | 437 |
| 6. | Germany | 311 |
| 7. | Brazil | 289 |
| 8. | South Korea | 288 |
| 9. | Canada | 273 |
| 10. | Iran | 248 |
| 11. | France | 243 |
| 12. | Saudi Arabia | 223 |
| 13. | Belgium | 56 |
| 14. | Algeria | 55 |
| 15. | Sweden | 50 |
| 16. | Uzbekistan | 44 |
| 17. | Czech Republic | 40 |
| 18. | Chile | 38 |
| 19. | Kuwait | 37 |
| 20. | Columbia | 33 |
| 21. | Romania | 33 |
| 22. | Norway | 30 |
| 23. | Portugal | 22 |
| 24. | New Zealand | 21 |

*Source*: Global Energy Statistical Yearbook 2017, www.enernet.in; retrieved on 7 January 2018.

## Energy and International Relations Today

Energy resources play a crucial role in international politics and economy. Trade in energy resources constitutes the backbone of many national economies, and also a major part of world trade today. For instance, the economy of OPEC countries like Saudi Arabia, Kuwait, Iraq, Iran, Venezuela, Algeria and Nigeria are heavily dependent on oil exports. India has been earning substantial foreign exchange by exporting coal to different parts of the world. The industrialized North America and West Europe import most of the energy resources from other parts of the world to sustain their industries and 'developed' standards of living of the people. These regions of the world consume large energy products and their economy is also dependent on the import of energy resources. Trade in energy has become very lucrative nowadays, and countries and regional organizations are trying to reap benefits from energy trade. For instance, the Russian Federation has emerged as one of the largest exporters of oil and natural gas to Europe and other parts of the world, and this trade in energy is considered vital for the revival of Russian economy. The World Bank has advised South Asian countries to augment cooperation in energy trade, and the SAARC is trying to move ahead to achieve such cooperation.

Issues related to energy had always played a significant part in international politics. From the sixteenth to twentieth centuries, the European powers colonized countries of the Middle East, Latin America, Africa and Asia for energy resources like oil, coal and natural gas. Some Arab countries stopped supply of oil to the United States for the latter's support to Israel in the 1973 Arab–Israel war. The American economy was hit hard as oil prices soared in the American market. One of the largest importers of petroleum products, the United States faced acute shortage of oil and gasoline. This 'oil diplomacy' by the Arab countries in effect put the OPEC into limelight, and enhanced its manoeuvring power in world politics. Throughout the 1970s and 1980s, the OPEC remained at the centre of world politics as it controlled the price and market of oil. However, since the 1990s, its dominance in international politics has been decreasing due to the emergence of several non-OPEC oil and natural gas producing countries like Russia, Ukraine, Kazakhstan, Uzbekistan, Azerbaijan, Turkmenistan, Kirghizstan, Norway and Denmark. But it should be noted here that the OPEC still wields considerable clout in international politics.

Energy resources may lead to conflicts among states. One of the primary reasons for Iraqi attack on Kuwait in 1991 was to secure rights over the Kuwaiti oil fields. But when this aim could not be fulfilled, Iraqi forces burned the Kuwaiti oil reserves. Further, conflicting claims over energy resources in the Caspian Sea had soured the international relations between Russia and Iran, as also among countries surrounding the Caspian Sea. The possibility of generating hydro-electricity from rivers meandering through international political borders has generated conflict-situations among states. The Jordan river is a source of discontent among Israel, Syria, Lebanon and Jordan. The Nile flows through Egypt, Kenya, Sudan, Burundi, Uganda, Tanzania, Rwanda and Zaire. Several 'Nile-river states' have a cold relation among themselves, and the source of such unfriendly relations is the issue of the share of the water of the Nile for irrigation and hydro-electricity. The Farakka Barrage set up by India on the River Ganges created animosity with Bangladesh, which accused India of masterminding a plan to dry out Bangladesh. River water disputes are plenty in international politics, and several of these relate to generation of hydro-electric power from river water. Oil and gas pipelines, either proposed ones or those actually running through several states, also lead to conflict-situations. Chechen rebels damaged oil pipelines running from Azerbaijan to the Black Sea through Chechnya in southern Russia. The proposed natural gas pipeline from Iran to India via Afghanistan and Pakistan had been postponed due to objections from Pakistan. Energy and related issues thus often determine the turns and tides of international relations.

# Terrorism

## Definition and Short History

Terrorism is motivated violence aimed at destabilizing civil order and creating panic among people and governments. It is an act of violence that is usually politically motivated, with the ultimate design to threaten the targeted population or government. Individuals or groups resorting to such motivated violence are known as terrorists, although this fixed definition carries the risk of being motivated itself because an individual who is considered a terrorist by X, may be a freedom fighter to Y. Similarly, acts of terrorism may be treated by some as freedom struggles or fights for justice. Therefore, ubiquitous definitions of terrorism or terrorists are almost impossible. However, when organized violence is carried out with the particular motive of threatening the existing social and political order, when innocent lives are taken away for securing a particular goal, such violence may be treated as terrorism; and individuals or groups responsible for this violence may be called terrorists.

Terrorism, in the sense of motivated organized violence, is nothing new. The earliest examples of terrorism could be found in the first century AD, when Jewish groups like the Sicari and the Zealots killed Roman government officials with the ultimate motive to bring an end to Roman occupation in Palestine. Followers of other religions also resorted to methods of terrorism. In the eleventh century, 'Assassins', an offshoot of a Shia Muslim sect known as the Ismailis, killed their targets, usually politicians and government officials, who refused to convert to the assassins' version of Islam. Sacrifice was another cause behind terrorist acts carried out by the 'Thugees', a Hindu religious cult who strangled their victims, normally travellers, for offerings to the Hindu goddess 'Kali'. Thugees were very active from the seventh to the mid-nineteenth centuries, and allegedly killed nearly a million people. They, along with the assassins, were the early examples of religious terrorism, which resurfaced in the late twentieth century.

Terrorism in the modern sense originated in France in the late eighteenth century. In 1793–94, a new French Revolutionary Republic, led by Maximilien Robespierre, used terrorism to deal with 'subversive forces'. The first example of modern state terrorism, Robespierre considered the method of terrorism as a positive weapon to crush 'anti-revolutionary' elements. His government used the 'guillotine' to behead individuals who were suspected opponents of his regime. Nearly fifty thousand people were guillotined by the Revolutionary Republic before a popular uprising sent Robespierre and his trusted men to the guillotine. Later, in the 1930s, Hitler's Nazi Government resorted to horrific state terrorism when thousands of Jews were brutally assassinated.

## Types of Terrorism

This brief historical study of terrorism leads us to analyse different types of terrorism prevalent in the world today. Terrorism can be broadly classified into five types: political, ethnic, religious, state and international terrorism. But it must be noted here that there are thin lines of demarcation among different types of terrorism. For instance, ethnic, religious or international terrorism may be carried out to gain political objectives. In that sense, every type of terrorism may have ulterior political motives. Further, political terrorism may have ethnic or religious issues involved. This classification of terrorism is thus not an absolute one; it rather helps a comprehensive understanding of the issue of terrorism.A discussion of each type of terrorism follows.

### Political Terrorism

When a group or a political party resorts to organized violence for destabilizing the existing political order, with the motive to establish a new one, such violence may be termed as political terrorism. But terrorism here is a relative term again; those favouring the new political order may view this act of violence as a fight for justice and right to self-determination. In this sense of terrorism, the activities of the Irish Republican Army (IRA) or the Palestine Liberation Organization (PLO) were treated as political terrorism by the British or the Israelis. The activities of the Kurdish groups in Turkey or the 'Basque Fatherland' in Spain are also examples of political terrorism, because they also want to change the existing political orders.

## Ethnic Terrorism

Organized violence perpetuated for establishing ethnic dominance or to secure ethnic demands may be termed as ethnic terrorism. The LTTE's (Liberation Tigers of Tamil Elam) demand for a separate Tamil state, and its attack on civilian targets in Sri Lanka that killed thousands of ordinary Sinhalese people, could be cited as an example. In the 1990s, ethnic trouble in Bosnia took the shape of ethnic terrorism where the Serbs tried to wipe off the Muslim Albanians and other non-Serb communities like the Croatians. The desire to establish Serb domination over the region (known as former Yugoslavia) by the Serb leaders led to such ethnic terrorism. Hitler's repression over the Jews in Europe in the 1930s was another example of ethnic terrorism. In all these instances, ethnic terrorism had definite political motivations that led to large-scale organized violence.

## Religious Terrorism

When organized motivated violence is carried out in the name of preserving the 'dignity' of a religion and its followers, such activities may be termed as religious terrorism. The Al Qaeda, Talibans, Lebanese Hizbollah, Abu Nidal, Lashkar-e-Toiba and many such groups resort to terrorism to uphold the 'dignity' of their religion. The Al Qaeda, led by the Saudi oil baron Osama Bin Laden, vowed several times to punish those individuals and states that undermined Islam. It carried terrorist attacks on American embassies in different parts of the world before crashing two passenger planes into the World Trade Center (WTC) in New York on 11 September 2001. Nearly ten thousand people died in this ghastly terrorist strike, the biggest in American history since the Second World War. The Talibans assassinated people at will in Afghanistan for not following the 'practices' of Islam. The Lashkar-e-Toiba and similar other terrorist organizations are active in the Kashmir valley of India in order to 'liberate' Kashmir, a Muslim-majority province, from India. These organizations frequently target the Indian army and ordinary civilians to create panic as well as to draw attention of the media, people, the Indian government and the international community. Political motives also act as major forces behind religious terrorism.

## State Terrorism

When the government of a state resorts to organized violence to eliminate the 'opponents' with a view to establish its control, such acts of violence are known as state terrorism. It has been observed earlier that rulers like Robespierre and Hitler resorted to state terrorism to finish off their targeted opponents. In recent times, rulers like Pol Pot of Cambodia and Idi Amin of Uganda resorted to terrorist tactics to frighten people to follow their governments' dictates. In the mid-1970s, the Pol Pot regime forced city dwellers in Cambodia to go to the countryside to work in collective farms and forced labour projects. Malnutrition, slavery, forced labour and wanton execution in the countryside—later called the 'killing fields'—resulted in the death of 2.5 million people, approximately 21 per cent of the then population in Cambodia. Idi Amin, a military dictator and President of Uganda from 1971 to 1979, resorted to severe repression, especially against the Asians who lived in Uganda. Idi Amin's government was engaged in mass execution of 'opposing forces', severe human rights abuses, and torture that resulted in the death of nearly five hundred thousand people. Today, democratically elected governments are sometimes accused of pursuing state terrorism when they trample on human rights and engage in political killing of their opponents. Human rights organizations have levelled charges against several democratic governments in different parts of the world for the violation of basic human rights and fundamental freedoms of the people. A state may indirectly, or directly, help terrorist groups foment trouble in another country, mainly its adversary. Such acts also fall in the category of state terrorism.

### International Terrorism

Terrorist activities involving citizens of more than one country, and having transnational impacts, constitute international terrorism. It is also referred to as 'cross border terrorism'. If any Indian national or Indian group is involved in terrorist activites in India, that would be an instance of domestic terrorism; but if people from other states join hands with the Indians in carrying out terrorist activities in India, that would amount to international terrorism. We are more concerned with international terrorism in the study of international relations, due to its impact on world politics. The 9/11 terrorist attacks on the United States was certainly aided and masterminded by people across territories, but it had a profound impact on US security and foreign policies, as also on international politics. India frequently experiences cross border terrorism when different terrorist groups from neighbouring countries and adjacent regions target its military, government officials and ordinary citizens. Mumbai witnessed a recent spate of international terrorism on 26 November 2008 (26/11) when terrorist groups from a neighbouring state attacked and killed policemen and ordinary citizens at railway stations, in restaurants, hotels and roads. Sometimes several terrorist groups working in different parts of the world join hands to carry out international terrorism. The Al Qaeda was aided by splinter terrorist groups in Europe and America, and also by the Talibans, in its 9/11 attacks on the United States.

## The Changing Nature of Contemporary Terrorism

Psychological, socio-economic and ideological factors have been identified as major causes that push individuals towards terrorist activities. Researchers have proved that chemical imbalances in the brain may lead to mental conditions where rage, hatred and tendencies to defy authority could be noticed in some individuals. These persons are prone to violence, and may take resort to terrorism. Among the socio-economic factors, a traumatic and abused childhood or early life, uncaring families and extreme poverty may lead an individual to terrorist activities. Political ideologies that call for equality in the society, abolition of rich–poor divide, questioning the authority and mastering one's own destiny, always attracted people's attention and fomented radicalism. Individuals, under the magic spell of such political ideologies, may resort to the unconventional path of terrorism. Since ages, these psychological, socio-economic and ideological factors have led to the emergence and growth of terrorism all over the world. But as far as methods of terrorism are concerned, plenty of changes have taken place in recent times. Contemporary (post–Second World War) terrorism is vastly different from conventional (pre–Second World War) terrorism in its methods and techniques.

Although some scholars[4] opine that there is little difference in techniques between conventional and contemporary terrorism, as bombings, fire bombings, armed attacks, arsons and kidnappings are used by both, the arguments put forward by this book would be different. To begin with, can conventional terrorism think of using passenger planes and crashing them into high rise towers like the WTC? Can it think of using satellite phones and computer technology for terrorist activities? Answers to these questions would be negative. The techniques of the two differ simply because more and more sophisticated technologies and weapons are available to the contemporary terrorist. For instance, in Tokyo, Japan's capital, the doomsday cult Aum Shinrikyo released Sarin Nerve Gas on 20 March 1995 in the subway metro system, killing twelve people and injuring nearly four thousand. This use of chemical weapons by a group of religious fanatics brought huge changes to the techniques used by contemporary terrorists. At present, speculations are rife in international politics about the chances of terrorist groups getting hold of the weapons of mass destruction (WMDs). The face of contemporary terrorism would certainly undergo drastic changes if such a situation arises. Today, terrorist groups have their own web sites to propagate their ideas, something that was unheard of earlier. They also rely more on media, especially the electronic ones, to make public their views and to spread threats. The Al Qaeda and many other terrorist groups use these methods with remarkable regularity. The contemporary terrorist is sometimes backed by a very large network spreading across continents. The 9/11 terrorist attack on the United States is a case in point. This network involves personnel, satellite communications and computer technology. The terrorist attacks on Mumbai on 26 November 2008 were also carried out by one such large network. The conventional terrorist lacked such a sophisticated network.

## Terrorism and International Relations Today

The impact of terrorism on international relations today is quite profound. The issue of terrorism may contribute towards strengthening or deteriorating relations among states. It may also bring about changes in security and foreign policies of states. Further, it could propel adjustments and shifts in policies and programmes of regional and international organizations. Terrorism, to begin with, can make or break relations between states. The issue of terrorism continues to exert negative influence on the relation between India and Pakistan or Israel and the Arab states. Both India and Pakistan have been accusing each other of sponsoring terrorism in their lands. Both have urged the international community to declare the other state a 'state sponsoring terrorism'. On several occasions, the issue of terrorism deteriorated relations between the two neighbours. For instance, India cancelled all diplomatic talks for some time as a mark of protest against Pakistan's alleged involvement in the 26/11 terrorist attacks in Mumbai. Similarly, relations between Israel and some Arab states suffered due to terrorist activities by extremist Arab and Israeli groups. Several such examples could be drawn from different parts of the world where terrorism has directly or indirectly influenced deterioration of relations among states. Conversely, relations among states may be strengthened due to the menace of terrorism. Two or more states may come close to one another to combat terrorism. After the 9/11 attack, the United States sought help from many states, especially states of the South Asian region, to counter terrorist organizations like the Al Qaeda, Talibans, Lashkar-e-Toiba and others. The United States is working in close cooperation with the governments of Afghanistan, Pakistan and India for counter-terrorism purposes. It has been viewing India as a close strategic partner, mainly after the 9/11 incident. This American perception helped to give a tremendous boost to bilateral relations.

States alter their security and foreign policies due to the menace of terrorism. The American policy of 'war against terrorism' emerged after the 9/11 terrorist attacks. The Bush (Jr) government also announced the 'National Security Strategy' (NSS) in 2002, and the 'National Security and Strategic Policy' (NSSP) in 2004, two significant security policies after the terrorist attacks. India and Israel, who did not have diplomatic relations for a long time, are now engaged in security cooperation to counter the problem of terrorism. India's nuclear doctrine had to be reshaped to augment its security in the face of growing security and terrorist threats coming from different states and organizations. In fact, every state, from England to Nigeria, from Japan to Canada, from Australia to Bangladesh, is on a high security alert now due to the growing threats of international terrorism; and every state is revamping its security and foreign policies to counter the increasing challenge from global terrorism.

Regional organizations like the EU, ASEAN, SAARC, AU and others are today very much concerned about terrorism. In a 'Factsheet' entitled *The European Union and the Fight against Terrorism*, published on 9 March 2007, the EU observed:

> Terrorism poses a significant threat to the security of Europe, to the values of our democratic societies and to the rights and freedoms of European citizens. Acts of terrorism are criminal and unjustifiable under any circumstances. Terrorism must be countered both at national and international level. Action by the European Union has intensified since 9/11, and in particular since the horrendous attacks in Madrid (2004) and London (2005). . . . The EU's Counter-Terrorism Strategy covers four strands of work: Prevention, Protection, Pursuit and Response.[5]

Similarly, other regional organizations have also adopted newer policies to counter terrorism. For instance, the SAARC Summit held in Colombo in August 2008 declared:

> The Heads of State or Government strongly condemned all forms of terrorist violence and expressed deep concern over the serious threat posed by terrorism to the peace, stability and security of the region. They further recognized the growing linkages between the phenomenon of terrorism, illegal trafficking in narcotic and psychotropic substances, illegal trafficking of persons and firearms and underscored the need to address the problem in a comprehensive manner. They reiterated their commitment to strengthen the legal regime against terrorism by undertaking to implement all international conventions relating to combating terrorism to which Member States are parties, as well as the SAARC Regional Convention on Suppression of Terrorism and the Additional Protocol to the SAARC Regional Convention on the Suppression of Terrorism.[6]

These policy documents reveal the fact that terrorism has indeed propelled all regional organizations to think afresh about the security of the region and member-states.

Terrorism threatens international peace and security, as well as human rights. The United Nations (UN) was very much concerned about terrorism and searched for appropriate ways to combat it. It adopted sixteen universal instruments (thirteen instruments and three amendments) against international terrorism. Through the General Assembly, member-states of the UN have been coordinating counter-terrorism activities and continuing legal work to fight terrorism. The Security Council has also been active in countering terrorism through proper resolutions and by establishing several subsidiary bodies. At the same time, a number of UN programmes, offices and agencies remained engaged in specific activities against terrorism. A recent significant UN instrument against terrorism has been The United Nations Global Counter-Terrorism Strategy, adopted by the General Assembly on 8 September 2006.

> It is a unique global instrument that will enhance national, regional and international efforts to counter terrorism. This is the first time that all Member States have agreed to a common strategic approach to fight terrorism, not only sending a clear message that terrorism is unacceptable in all its forms and manifestation but also resolving to take practical steps individually and collectively to prevent and combat it. Those practical steps include a wide array of measures ranging from strengthening state capacity to counter terrorist threats to better coordinating United Nations system's counter-terrorism activities.[7]

The UN Global Counter Terrorism Strategy is reviewed by the UN General Assembly (UNGA) every two years, making it a living document designed to suit requirements of member states. The Fifth Review of the Strategy took place in June 2014, and the Sixth Review is scheduled to take place in 2018. The Global Counter-Terrorism Strategy in the form of a UNGA Resolution and an annexed Plan of Action has four pillars as listed here:

i. address the conditions conducive to the spread of terrorism;
ii. take measures to prevent and combat terrorism;
iii. act to build states' capacity to prevent and combat terrorism and to strengthen the role of the UN system in that regard; and
iv. take actions to ensure respect for human rights for all and the rule of law as the fundamental basis for the fight against terrorism.

Clearly, the largest international organization responsible for maintaining international peace and security views terrorism as the biggest threat to mankind, that may upset the maintenance of international peace in our times. Terrorism also poses a challenge to safeguarding of human rights and fundamental freedoms throughout the world. This growing menace has created ripples in world politics, and added an altogether new dimension in the study of international relations.

## QUESTIONS

1. How would you define globalization? Analyse different views on globalization.
2. Is the notion of sovereignty of the state in danger due to globalization? Argue your case.
3. Bring out the impact of environmental issues on international politics.
4. Write a note on the significance of energy in international relations today.
5. How would you define terrorism? What are the different types of terrorism?
6. Examine the impact of terrorism on international relations today.

## ENDNOTES

1. N. R. Narayana Murthy, 'The Impact of Economic Reforms on Industry in India: A Case Study of the Software Industry,' in K. Basu (ed.), *India's Emerging Economy: Performance and Prospects in the 1990s and Beyond* (New Delhi: Oxford University Press, 2004), 217.
2. Joseph Stiglitz, *Globalization and Its Discontent* (New York: W. W. Norton and Company, 2002), 247.
3. See, for instance, Kingsbury Benedict and Andrew Hurrell (eds), *The International Politics of the Environment* (New York: Oxford University Press, 1992). Also, D. H. Meadows, D. L. Meadows and J. Randers, Beyond the Limits: Confronting Global Collapse, Envisioning a Sustainable Future (Post Mills, VT: Chelsea Green Publishing, 1992).
4. See in this context, P. R. Viotti and M. V. Kauppi, *International Relations and World Politics: Security, Economy, Identity* (New Delhi: Pearson Education, 2007), 283.
5. The EU Council Secretariat, Brussels, 9 March 2007.
6. The SAARC Secretariat, *Fifteenth SAARC Summit: Declaration*; retrieved from http://www.saarc-sec.org/data/summit15/summit15declaration.htm/ on 13 August 2009.
7. As posted on the UN web site, http://www.un.org/terrorism/strategy-counter-terrorism.shtml/. Retrieved on 13 August 2009.

# Bibliography


Athwal, A. 2009. *China–India Relations: Contemporay Dynamics*. London: Routledge.

Bacevich, A. J. 2008. *The Limits of Power: The End of American Exceptionalism*. New York: Black Inc.

Bailey, K. C. (ed.). 1994. *Weapons of Mass Destruction: Costs Versus Benefits*. New Delhi: Manohar.

Bajpai, K., H. Jing and K. Mahbubani (eds.). 2015. *China-India Cooperation: Relations Between The Giants Of Asia*, New York: Routledge.

Bajpai, U. S. (ed.). 1983. *Non-Alignment: Perspectives and Prospects*. New Delhi: Lancers Publishers.

Bertallanfy, L. V. 1968. *General Systems Theory: Foundations, Development, Applications*. New York: George Braziller.

Boulding, K. 1962. *Conflict and Defence*. New York: Harper Collins.

Buira, A. (ed.). 2005. *The IMF and the World Bank at Sixty*. London: Anthem Press.

Bull, H. 1966. 'Society and Anarchy in International Relations', in Butterfield, H. and Wight, M. (eds.) (1966), *Diplomatic Investigations: Essays in the Theory of International Politics*, London: Allen and Unwin, pp. 35–50.

________. 1966a. 'The Grotian Conception of International Society', in Butterfield and Wight (eds.) (1966), *Diplomatic Investigations: Essays in the Theory of International Politics*, London: Allen and Unwin, (1966), pp. 51–73.

________. 1977. The Anarchical Society: A Study of Order in World Politics. London: Macmillan.

________. 2000. 'International Relations as an Academic Pursuit', in Alderson, Kai and Andrew Hurrell, *Hedley Bull on International Society,* Houndmills: Macmillan.

________. 2000a, 'Justice in International Relations'. In Alderson and Hurrell (2000), *Hedley Bull on International Society,* Houndmills: Macmillan.

Burchill, S., R. Devetak, A. Linklater, M. Paterson, C. Reus-Smit and J. True. 2001. *Theories of International Relations*. New York: Palgrave.

Buzan, B. 2001. 'The English School: An Underexpolited Resource in IR', *Review of International Studies*, 27(3), 471–88.

________. 2004. *From International to World Society? English School Theory and the Social Structure of Globalization*, Cambridge: Cambridge University Press 2004, 64.

Buzan, B. and R. Little. 2000. *International Systems in World History: Remaking the Study of International Relations*. Oxford: Oxford University Press.

Calvocoressi, P. 2001. *World Politics: 1954–2000*. New Delhi: Pearson Education.

Carr, E. H. 1939. *The Twenty Years' Crisis*. New York: Palgrave Macmillan.

Chatterjee, A. 2005. 'Human Rights and India–U.S. Relations during the Rao Premiership', *Jadavpur Journal of International Relations*, 9 (1).

________. 2008. 'Beyond Expectations: Remarkable Development in India–U.S. Relations during the Gujral Premiership', *Jadavpur Journal of International Relations*, 12 (1).

________. 2009. 'The UN at Sixty Three: Problems and Prospects of Reforming a Veteran', *Journal of Management and Social Sciences*, 5(1).

________. 2011. 'India-U.S. Relations: Expectations, Reality and the Future', *Journal of South Asian and Middle Eastern Studies*, 34(3).

________. 2012. 'India-Pakistan Relations: A Framework for Peace in Future', in Riaz Shaikh (ed.), *Back From the Brink: India-Pakistan Ties Revisited,* Karachi: Ushba Publishing International.

________. 2015. 'Will Democracy Survive? Afghanistan and the International Community Post 2014', *Journal of South Asian and Middle Eastern Studies*, 38(4).

________. 2017. *Neighbours, Major Powers and Indian Foreign Policy*, New Delhi: Orient BlackSwan.

Chin, C. B. 1998. *In Service and Servitude: Foreign Female Domestic Workers and the Malaysian Modernity Project.* New York. Columbia University Press.

Chopra, V. D. 2003. *New Trends in Indo-Russian Relations*. New Delhi: Kalpaz Publications.

Cirincione, J. et al. 2005. *Deadly Arsenals: Tracking Weapons of Mass Destruction*. Washington DC: Carnegie Endowment for International Peace.

Cohen, S. P. 1994. *Nuclear Proliferation in South Asia: The Prospects for Arms Control*. New Delhi: Lancer.

________. 2001. *India: Emerging Power*. New Delhi: Oxford University Press.

Cooper, A. F., J. English and R. Thakur. 2002. *Enhancing Global Governance: Towards a New Diplomacy?* New York: United Nations University Press.

Cortright, D., L. Gerber and G. A. Lopez. 2002. *Sanctions and the Search for Security: Challenges to UN Action*. Boulder: Lynne Rienner.

Derrida, J. 1974. *Of Grammatology*. Baltimore: Johns Hopkins University Press.

Deutsch, K. 1963. *The Nerves of Government: Models of Political Communication and Control*. New York: Free Press.

Devetak, Richard. 2001. 'Critical Theory', in Scott Burchill et al. (eds.), *Theories of International Relations*. New York: Palgrave.

Dharamdasani, M. D. (ed.). 2004. *Indo-Japan Relations: Challenges and Opportunities*. New Delhi: Kanishka.

Dickie, J. 2007. *The New Mandarins: How British Foreign Policy Works*. London: I. B. Tauris & Co. Ltd.

Dinan, D. 2004. *Europe Recast: A History of European Union*. London: Palgrave Macmillan.

Dutt, V. P. 1999. *India's Foreign Policy in a Changing World*. New Delhi: Vikas Publishing House.

Eccleston, B., M. Dawson and D. J. McNamara. 1998. *The Asia-Pacific Profile*. London: Routledge.

Enloe, C. 1989. *Bananas, Beaches, and Bases: Making Feminist Sense of International Politics*. Berkeley: University of California Press.

________. 1994. *The Morning After: Sexual Politics at the End of the Cold War*. Berkeley: University of California Press.

________. 1997. 'Margins, Silences, and Bottom-rungs: How to Overcome the Underestimation of Power in the Study of International Relations', in S. Smith, K. Booth and M. Zalewski (eds), *International Theory: Positivism and Beyond*. Cambridge: Cambridge University Press.

________. 2000. *Maneuvers: The International Politics of Militarizing Women's Lives*. Berkeley: University of California Press.

Ferguson, C. D. and W. C. Potter, with A. Sands, L. S. Spector and F. L. Wehling. 2005. *The Four Faces of Nuclear Terrorism*. New York: Routledge.

Foucault, M. 1977. *Discipline and Punish*. Harmondsworth: Gallimard.

Frankel, J. 1977. *International Relations in a Changing World*. London: Oxford University Press.

Ganguly, Sumit. 2016. *Engaging the World: Indian Foreign Policy Since 1947*, New Delhi: OUP.

Gates, C. L. and M. Than. 2001. *ASEAN Enlargement: Impacts and Implications*. Singapore: Institute of Southeast Asian Studies.

Gheciu, A. 2005. *NATO in the New Europe*. Stanford: Stanford University Press.

Gjelstad, J. 1996. *Nuclear Rivalry and International Order*. New Delhi: Sage.

Glassner, M. I. 1998. *The United Nations at Work*. Westport, CT: Praeger.

Goldstein, J. S. 2003. *International Relations* (5th Ed.). New Delhi: Pearson Education.

Gramsci, A. 1971. *Selections from the Prison Notebooks*, New York: International Publishers.

Guelke, A. 1995. *The Age of Terrorism and the International Political System*. New York: St. Martin's.

Guha-Khasnobis, B. 2004. *The WTO, Developing Countries and the Doha Development Agenda: Prospects and Challenges for Trade-led Growth*. Hampshire: Palgrave Macmillan.

Habermas, J. 1971. *Knowledge and Human Interests*, translated by Jeremy J. Shapiro. Boston: Beacon Press.

________. 1981. *The Theory of Communicative Action*. vol. 1, Boston: Beacon Press.

________. 1987. *The Philosophical Discourse of Modernity: Twelve Lectures,* translated by Frederick G. Lawrence. Cambridge, Mass.: MIT Press.

________. 1998. *The Inclusion of the Other: Studies in Political Theory*, Edited by Ciaran Cronin and Pablo De Greiff. Cambridge: MIT Press.

Hampson, F. O. and D. M. Malone. 2002. *From Reaction to Conflict Prevention: Opportunities for the UN System*. Boulder: Lynne Rienner.

Held, D. and D. Mepham. 2007. *Progressive Foreign Policy: New Directions for the UK*. Cambridge: Polity Press.

Henning, M. 2002. *The New African Initiative and the African Union: A Preliminary Assessment and Documentation*. Stockholm: Nordiska Afrikainstitutet.

Herz, J. 1958. *International Politics in the Atomic Age*. New York: Columbia University Press.

Hix, S. 2005. *The Political System of the European Union*. London: Palgrave MacMillan.

Hobson, J. A. 1902. *Imperialism: A Study*. London: Chatham.

Hoffman, M. 1987. 'Critical Theory and the Inter-paradigm Debate', *Millennium-Journal of International Studics,* 16, pp. 231 250.

Horkheimer, M. 1972. *Critical Theory: Selected Essays*. New York: Herder & Herder.

________. 1996. *Eclipse of Reason*. New York: Continuum.

Horkheimer, M., Adorno Th. (1997), *Dialectic of Enlightenment*. translated by John Cumming, New York: Continuum.

Hufbauer, G. C. and J. J. Schott. 2005. *NAFTA Revisited*. Washington DC: Institute for International Economics.

Hull, H. 1969. 'International Theory: The Case for a Classical Approach', in K. Knorr and J. N. Rosenau (eds), *Contending Approaches to International Relations*, Princeton: CQ Press.

Hurrell, A. and N. Woods (eds). 1999. *Inequality, Globalization, and World Politics*. New York: Oxford University Press.

Inoguchi, T. and P. Jain (eds). 2000. *Japanese Foreign Policy Today*. New York: Palgrave Macmillan.

Jackson, R. and G. Sorensen. 2003. *Introduction to International Relations: Theories and Approaches*. Oxford: Oxford University Press.

Jackson, R. 1996. 'Is there a Classical International Theory?', *International Theory: Positivism and Beyond*, Cambridge: Cambridge University Press.

Jentleson, B. W. 2000. *American Foreign Policy: The Dynamics of Choice in the 21st Century*. New York: W. W. Norton.

Kahol, Y. 2002. *SAARC Through the New Millennium*. New Delhi: Anmol Publishers.

Kaplan, L. S. 1999. *The Long Entanglement: NATO's First Fifty Years*. New York: Praeger.

Kaplan, M. A. 1957. *System and Process of International Politics*. New York: John Wiley and Sons.

Kapur, A., Y. K. Malik, H. A. Gould and A. G. Rubinoff (eds). 2002. *India and the United States in a Changing World*. New Delhi: Sage.

Kapur, H. 1994. *India's Foreign Policy: 1947–1992: Shadows and Substance*. New Delhi: Sage.

Kawashima, Y. 2005. *Japanese Foreign Policy at Crossroads*. Washington DC: Brookings Institution Press.

Kellner, Douglas. 1989. *Critical Theory, Marxism and Modernity*, Oxford: Polity Press

Keohane, R. O. 1984. *After Hegemony: Cooperation and Discord in the World Political Economy*. Princeton: Princeton University Press.

Keohane, R. O. and J. Nye (eds). 1972. *Transitionalism and World Politics*. Cambridge: Cambridge University Press.

Knight, A. W. 2000. *A Changing United Nations: Multilateral Evolution and the Quest for Global Governance*. New York: St. Martin's Press.

Krasner, S. D. 1999. *Sovereignty: Organized Hypocrisy*. Princeton: Princeton University Press.

Laqueur, W. 2001. *A History of Terrorism*. New Jersey: Transaction.

Lawson, S. 2004. *International Relations*. London: Polity.

Lederman, D., W. Maloney and L. Servén. 2005. *Lessons from NAFTA for Latin America and the Caribbean.* Palo Alto, USA: Stanford University Press.

Linklater, A. 1990. *Beyond Marxism and Realism: Critical Theory and International Relations*. London: Macmillan.

________. 1992. 'The Question of the Next Stage in International Relations Theory: A Critical Theoretical Point of View', *Millennium*, 21(1).

________. 1992. 'What is a Good International Citizen?', in P. Keal (ed.) *Ethics and Foreign Policy*, Sydney: Allen and Unwin.

________. 2007. *Critical Theory and World: Politics Citizenship, Sovereignty and Humanity*, New York: Routledge.

________. 2007. 'Critical Theory', in M. Griffiths (Ed.), *International Relations for the Twenty First Century: An Introduction*, London: Routledge

Linklater, A. and Hidemi Suganami. 2006. *The English School of International Relations: A Contemporary Reassessment*, Cambridge: Cambridge University Press.

Luterbacher, U. and D. F. Sprinz. 2001. *International Relations and Global Climate Change*. Boston: MIT.

Malone, D. M. 2012. *Does the Elephant Dance? Contemporary Indian Foreign Policy*, New Delhi: Oxford University Press, 2012.

Mandelbaum, M (ed.). 1998. *The New Russian Foreign Policy*. New York: Council on Foreign Relations Press.

Mankoff, J. 2009. *Russian Foreign Policy: The Return of Great Power Politics*. New York: Rowman & Littlefield.

McIntyre, W. D. 2001. *A Guide to the Contemporary Commonwealth*. London: Palgrave.

Menon, R. 2004. *Weapons of Mass Destruction*. New Delhi: OUP.

Misra, K. P. and K. R. Narayanan (eds). 1999. *Non-Alignment in Contemporary International Relations*. New Delhi: Vikas Publishing House.

Mistry, D. 2005. *Containing Strategic Missile Proliferation*. Seattle: University of Washington Press.

Morgenthau, H. J. 1972. *Politics Among Nations: The Struggle for Power and Peace* (5th Indian Edition). Calcutta: Scientific Book Agency.

Murphy, C. N. 2001. 'Critical Theory and the Democratic Impulse: Understanding a Century old Tradition', in R. W. Jones (ed.), *Critical Theory and World Politics*. London: Lynne Rienner Publishers.

Nahar, E. 1991. *SAARC: Problems and Prospects*. New Delhi: Sehgal Publishers.

Nas, J. and M. Fernandez-Kelly (eds). 1983. *Women, Men, and the International Division of Labour*. New York: State University of New York Press.

Neack, L. 2003. *The New Foreign Policy: U.S. and Comparative Foreign Policy in the 21st Century*. New York: Rowman & Littlefield.

Neumann, J. V. and O. Morgenstern. 1944. *Theory of Games and Economic Behaviour*. Princeton: Princeton Univeristy Press.

Nicholas, H. G. 1975. *The United Nations as a Political Institution*. London: Oxford University Press.

Nicholson, M. 2002. *International Relations: A Concise Introduction*. New York, Palgrave.

Ogden, Chris. 2014. *Indian Foreign Policy*, Cambridge: Polity Press.

Oman, C. 1994. *Globalization and Regionalization: The Challenge for Developing Countries*. Paris: OECD Development Centre.

Onuf, N. 1989. *World of Our Making: Rules and Rule in Social Theory and International Relations*. Columbia: University of South Carolina Press.

Palmer, N. D. and H. C. Perkins. 1953. *International Relations*. Boston: Houghton Mifflin.

Pande, S. 1994. *CTBT: India and the Nuclear Test Ban Treaty*. New Delhi: Cosmo.

________. 1995. *Future of NPT*. New Delhi: Lancer.

Pant, H. (ed.). 2009. *Indian Foreign Policy in a Unipolar World*. London: Routledge.

Partridge, J. A. 2008. *The Policy of England in Relation to India and the East; or, Alexandria*. London: Bibliolife.

Paterson, M. 1996. *Global Warming and Global Politics*. New York: Routledge.

Patrascu, E. and Z. A. Wani. 2015. *Discourse of Critical Theory in the Context of International Relations*, paper presented at RCIC '15.

Peterson, J. and M. Shackleton (eds). 2006. *The Institutions of the European Union*. London: Oxford University Press.

Peterson, V. S. and A. S. Runyan. 1993. *Global Gender Issues*. Boulder: West View Press.

Petro, N. N. 1997. *Russian Foreign Policy: From Empire to Nation-State*. London: Longman.

Pettman, J. J. 1996. *Working Women: A Feminist International Politics*. New York: Routledge.

Raja Mohan, C. 2015. *Modi's World: Expanding India's Sphere of Influence*, New Delhi: Harper Collins India.

Roberson, B.A. 2000. 'Probing the Idea and Prospects for International Society', *International Society and the Development of International Relations Theory*, London: Continuum.

Rosenau, J. N. 1961. *International Politics and Foreign Policy: A Reader in Research and Theory*. New York: Free Press.

________. 1992. *The United Nations in a Turbulent World*. Boulder: Lynne Rienner.

Runyan A. S. and V. S. Peterson. 1991. 'The Radical Future of Realism: Feminist Subversions of IR Theory', *Alternatives*, 16, Toronto.

Sarin, V. 2016. *India – ASEAN Trade and Economic Relations*, New Delhi: New Century Publications.

Sassen, S. 1991. *The Global City: New York, London, Tokyo*. Princeton: Princeton University Press.

Schott, J. J. (ed.). 2000. *The WTO After Seattle*, Washington DC: Institute for International Economics.

Schuman, W. and R. L. Stevens (ed.). 2007. *Economic Pressures and the Future*. New York: Free Press.

Shapiro, M. J. 1988. *The Politics of Representation*. London: Routledge.

Shearman, P. (ed). 1995. *Russian Foreign Policy since 1990*. Boulder: West View Press.

Shubik, M. 1954. *Readings in Games Theory and Political Theory*. Princeton: Princeton University Press.

Sikkink, K. and M. Keck. 1998. *Activists Beyond Borders: Advocacy Networks in International Politics*. Ithaca: Cornell University Press.

Sikri, R. 2009. *Challenge and Strategy: Rethinking India's Foreign Policy*. New Delhi: Sage.

Singham, A. W. 1986. *Non-Alignment in an Age of Alignment*. New York: Lawrence Hill and Co.

Smith, J. (ed.). 1990. *The Origins of NATO*. London: Exeter Press.

Smith, J. E. and S. L. Canby. 1987. *The Evolution of NATO with Four Plausible Threat Scenarios*. Ottawa: Canada Department of Defense.

Snyder, R., H. W. Bruck and B. Sapin. 1954. *Decision-Making as an Approach to the Study of International Politics*. Princeton: Princeton University Press.

Standing, G. 1992. 'Global Feminization Through Flexible Labor', in C. K. Wilber and K. P. Jameson (eds), *The Political Economy of Development and Underdevelopment*. New York: McGraw-Hill College.

Stasiulis, D. and A. B. Bakan. 1997. 'Negotiating Citizenship: The Case of Foreign Domestic Workers in Canada', *Feminist Review*, No. 57.

Steans, J. 1998. *Gender and International Relations: An Introduction*. New Brunswick: Own.

Stiglitz, J. 2002. *Globalization and Its Discontent*. New York: W. W. Norton and Company.

Stohl, M. and G. A. Lopez (ed.). 1988. *Terrible Beyond Endurance? The Foreign Policy of State Terrorism*. Westport: Greenwood.

Subrahmanium, K. 1986. *Nuclear Proliferation and International Security*. New Delhi: Lancer.

Suganami, H. 2010. 'The English School in a Nutshell', *Ritsumeikan Annual Review of International Studies,* Vol. 9, pp. 15–28.

Sutter, R. G. 2007. *Chinese Foreign Relations: Power and Policy Since the Cold War*. New York: Rowman & Littlefield.

Swanson, T. M. (ed.). 1998. *The Economics and Ecology of Biodiversity Decline: The Forces Driving Global Change*. New York: Cambridge University Press.

Sylvester, C. 1992. 'Feminist Theory and Gender Studies in International Relations', *International Studies Notes*, 16(1).

________. 1994. *Feminist Theory and International Relations in a Postmodern Era*. Cambridge: Cambridge University Press.

Teslik, L. H. 2008. *NAFTA's Economic Impact*. New York: Council of Foreign Relations.

Tessler, M. and I. Warriner. 1997. 'Gender, Feminism and Attitudes Toward International Conflict: Exploring Relationships with Survey Data from the Middle East', *World Politics*, No. 49.

Therborn, G. 1970. 'The Frankfurt School', *New Left Review*, 63.

The SAARC Secretariat. *From SARC to SAARC: Milestones in the Evolution of Regional Cooperation*, 1–7.

Tickner, J. A. 1992. *Gender in International Relations: Feminist Perspectives on Achieving Global Security*. New York: Columbia University Press.

Tickner, J. A. 1997. 'You Just Don't Understand: Troubled Engagements Between Feminists and IR Theorists', *International Studies Quarterly*, 41(4).

Upreti, R. C. (ed.). 2000. *SAARC: Dynamics of Regional Cooperation in South Asia*. New Delhi: Kalinga.

US Department of Commerce, International Trade Administration. 2008. *Top US Export Markets: Free Trade Area and Country Fact Sheet*. Washington DC: US Government Printing Press.

Walker, R. B. J. 1992. *Inside/Outside: International Relations as Political Theory*. Cambridge: Cambridge University Press.

________. 1993. *Inside/Outside*: *International Relations as Political Theory*, Cambridge: Cambridge University Press.

________. 1995. 'International Relations and the Concept of the Political', in K. Booth and S. Smith (eds), *International Relations Theory Today*. Pennsylvania: Pennsylvania State University Press.

Waltz, K. 1959. *Man, the State, and War: A Theoretical Analysis*. New York: Columbia University Press.

________. 1979. *Theory of International Politics*. New York: McGraw-Hill.

Weber, C. 1995. *Simulating Sovereignty: Intervention, the State and Symbolic Exchange*, Cambridge: Cambridge University Press.

Weintraub, S. 2004. *NAFTA's Impact on North America: The First Decade*. Washington DC: CSIS Press.

Wendt, A. 1992. 'Anarchy is What States Make of It: The Social Construction of Power Politics', *International Organisation*, 6(2).

________. 1995. 'Constructing International Politics', *International Security*, Vol. 20, No. 1. Washington DC.

________. 1999. *Social Theory of International Relations*. Cambridge: Cambridge University Press.

Wheare, K. C. 1960. *The Constitutional Structure of the Commonwealth*. New York: Clarendon Press.

Whittaker, D. J. 1997. *United Nations in the Contemporary World*. London: Routledge.

Wight, Gabriele and Brian Porter. (eds). 2005. *Four Seminal Thinkers in International Theory: Machiavelli, Grotius, Kant, and Mazzini*, London: Oxford University Press.

Woods, N. 1996. *Explaining International Relations Since 1945*. New York: Oxford University Press.

________. 2006. *The Globalizers: IMF, The World Bank and Their Borrowers*. Cornell: Cornell University Press.

Yalvac, F. 2015. 'Critical Theory: International Relations' Engagement with the Frankfurt School and Marxism', *International Studies*, December.

Ying, M., M. Kau and S. H. Marsh. (eds). 1993. *China in the Era of Deng Xiao Ping*. New York: M. E. Sharpe.

# Web Sites

Commonwealth of Nations: http://www.thecommonwealth.org/.
NATO: http://www.nato.int/.
UNO: http://www.un.org/.
On NPT from the UN web site: http://www.un.org/events/npt2005/.
CTBT: http://www.ctbt.org/.
FMCT: http://www.fmct.org/.
MTCR: http://www.mtcr.info/english/index/html/.
PBBW: http://www.pbbw.org/.
OPCW: http://www.opcw.org/.
SAARC Secretariat: http://www.saarc.sec.org/.
ASEAN Secretariat: http://www.aseansec.org/.
EU Secretariat: http://www.europa.eu/.
AU Secretariat: http://www.africa-union.org/.
NAFTA Secretariat: http://www.nafta-sec-alena.org/.
WTO. http://www.wto.org/.
IMF: http:// www.imf.org/.
World Bank: http://www. worldbank.org/.

# Index

## Q



## R



## S



## T